CLEARING THE PATH

[ COLLECTED WRITINGS OF ÑĀṆAVĪRA THERA ]

**Clearing the Path**
*(1960-1965)*

**Seeking the Path**
*Early Writings (1954-1960) & Marginalia*

Ñāṇavīra Thera

# Clearing the Path

(1960-1965)

Path Press Publications

First edition: 1987
Second revised and enlarged edition: 2010
ISBN 978 94 6090 004 4

Path Press Publications
*www.pathpresspublications.com*

# Contents

## A. NOTES ON DHAMMA (1960-1965)

## B. LETTERS (1960-1965)



## C. WRITINGS

# Editors' foreword

*Clearing the Path* is a work book. Its purpose is to help the user to acquire a point of view that is different from his customary frame of reference, and also more satisfactory. Necessarily, an early step in accomplishing this change is the abandonment of specific mistaken notions about the Buddha's Teaching and about the nature of experience. More fundamentally, however, this initial change in specific views may lead to a change in point-of-view, whereby one comes to understand experience from a perspective different from what one has been accustomed to—a perspective in which *intention, responsibility, context, conditionality, hunger*, and related terms will describe the fundamental categories of one's perception and thinking—and which can lead, eventually, to a fundamental insight about the nature of personal existence.

Such a change of attitude seldom occurs without considerable prior development, and this book is intended to serve as a tool in fostering that development. As such it is meant to be lived with rather than read and set aside. These notions are developed more fully throughout *Clearing the Path* but it is as well that they be stated concisely at the outset so that there need be no mistaking who this book is for: those who find their present mode of existence unsatisfactory and who sense, however vaguely, the need to make a fundamental change not in the world but in themselves.

*Clearing the Path* has its genesis in *Notes on Dhamma (1960-1963)*, printed privately by the Honourable Lionel Samaratunga (Dewalepola, Ceylon, 1963—see L. 63). Following production of that volume the author amended and added to the text, leaving at his death an expanded typescript, indicated by the titular expansion of its dates, *(1960-1965)*. Together with the Ven. Ñāṇavīra Thera's typescript was a cover letter:

> To the Prospective Publisher:
> The author wishes to make it clear that *Notes on Dhamma* is not a work of scholarship: an Orientalist (*in casu* a Pali scholar), if he is no more than that, is unlikely to make very much of the book, whose

> general tone, besides, he may not altogether approve. Though it does not set out to be learned in a scholarly sense, the book is very far from being a popular exposition of Buddhism. It is perhaps best regarded as a philosophical commentary on the essential teachings of the Pali Suttas, and presenting fairly considerable difficulties, particularly to 'objective' or positivist thinkers, who will not easily see what the book is driving at. From a publisher's point of view this is no doubt unfortunate; but the fact is that the teaching contained in the Pali Suttas is (to say the least) a great deal more difficult—even if also a great deal more rewarding—than is commonly supposed; and the author is not of the opinion that *Notes on Dhamma* makes the subject more difficult than it actually is.

The difficulties referred to in this cover letter gave rise to extensive correspondence between the Ven. Ñāṇavīra and various laypeople who sought clarification and expansion of both specific points and general attitudes and methods of inquiry. The author devoted considerable energy to this correspondence: some letters run to five thousand words, and three drafts was not uncommon. From one point of view the Ven. Ñāṇavīra's letters may be seen as belonging to the epistolary tradition, a tradition refined in an earlier era when much serious philosophical and literary discussion was conducted on a personal basis within a small circle of thinkers. On another view many of the letters can be regarded as thinly disguised essays in a wholly modern tradition. Indeed, one of these letters (L. 2) was published some years ago (in the 'Bodhi Leaf' series of the Buddhist Publication Society), stripped of its salutation and a few personal remarks, as just such an essay. The author himself offers a third view of the letters in remarking that at least those letters which contain direct discussion of Dhamma points 'are, in a sense, something of a commentary on the *Notes*' (L. 60). In this perspective the letters can be seen as both expansions and clarifications of the more formal discussions in the *Notes*. Those who find the mode of thought of the *Notes* initially forbidding might profitably regard the letters as a useful channel of entry.

Sāmaṇera Bodhesako

## NOTE TO THE SECOND EDITION

The influence of Ven. Ñāṇavīra Thera's writings on Buddhist thinkers still continues to increase, more than a quarter of a century after its publication. The first edition was prepared, edited and carefully presented by Ven. S. Bodhesako with Prof. Forrest Williams and published in 1987, just a few months before Ven. Bodhesako's untimely passing. The book has been out of print for quite a while and since then there have been many enquiries regarding the book. To respond to enquiries, the www.nanavira.org website was prepared with the texts of the whole book in html and PDF format; however, interest in having the book reprinted continued to be expressed, and a kind offer to prepare and print an updated version of *Clearing the Path* made this possible.

This second edition of *Clearing the Path* (2010) incorporates a number of spelling corrections and minor layout changes. It also includes some additions and alterations:

The first part of the book, 'Notes on Dhamma', is taken from an edition which was published by Path Press Publications in its entirely original format, in commemoration of the 50th anniversary of the late Ven. Ñāṇavīra Thera's *sotāpatti* (27th July 2009). Most of his editorial work in the section 'Notes on Dhamma' remains intact; in a few places, however, some necessary modifications have been made. The edition of *Notes on Dhamma* as the first part of *Clearing the Path* (1987) followed the text of the final manuscript as closely as possible, but due to the inherent limitations of software (Wordstar 3.31) and printer (NEC ELF spinwriter) the editor was unable to realise all the graphic details of the manuscript and some of Ven. Ñāṇavīra's detailed and careful instructions to the printer. This edition of 'Notes on Dhamma' reflects the original manuscript as close as possible. In this new edition the English translations of all Pali passages have returned to the original separate section, after the Glossary, entitled 'Translations (with Additional Texts)', and are not incorporated into the main body of the text alongside their respective Pali passages. However, the previous editors pointed out that:

a) in the note on BALA a more likely reading for the Aṅguttara passage quoted therein would be: *Tatra bhikkhave yaṃ idaṃ bhāvanābalaṃ sekham etaṃ balaṃ. Sekham hi so bhikkhave balaṃ āgamma rāgaṃ pajahati …*

b) Additional text 94 (Majjhima xiv,8) is quoted by the author as it is printed in the Burmese, Sinhalese, and Thai recensions as well as the P.T.S. edition; nevertheless the texts would seem to contain a corruption common to all of them (and therefore probably ancient) involving the word *anupādā* in both the first and the penultimate sentences quoted. No doubt these should read *upādā* (and the word 'not' would therefore be deleted from the translation of those lines). *Anupādā* in Sutta usage refers, apparently, only to the *arahat*'s lack of *upādāna*. A *puthujjana* failing in his attempt at holding any thing would be described in different terms in Pali—perhaps as *upādāniyaṃ alabhamāno*, 'not getting what can be held', or some similar construction. A parallel to the Majjhima passage is to be found at Khandha Saṃyutta 7: iii,16-18, where the reading is *upādā*, not *anupādā*.

Although it is our place to note such points, it is not our place to alter them, and in this matter the Ven. Ñāṇavīra's text has been allowed to stand unchanged.

In the editing of the 'Letters' (which were collected by Ven. Ñāṇasumana and Ven. Bodhesako during the first years after the author's death)[1] no constraints such as those pertaining to *Notes on Dhamma* apply. As it is noted in the first edition the considerable material regarded as superfluous had been pared away. In comparing the edition with its manuscript (named as *Collected Letters*) I decided to include in this edition almost all passages which were originally intended but not published in the book. However, the original letters are unfortunately not available and therefore the letters published here are in their most complete form.

In this edition we also included six letters written to his *dāyakas*; chief supporters, Mr. and Mrs. Perera (L. 3-L. 8) which were originally planned to be published in *Seeking the Path* (early writings of Ven. Ñāṇavīra till 1960). Even though they are not regarded as commentarial to 'Notes on Dhamma' we decided to include them here, since they were written after his *sotāpatti*. Also included here is the last letter to Sister Vajirā (L. 160), which was found in her former *kuṭi* and which concludes their correspondence. The letters which were previously published under 'Editorial Notes' (letters to Colombo Thera and Mr. G.) are transferred to the second part, among various other letters. Because of additions and relocations, the letters have been renumbered, and at the end of the book we have included a table with the corresponding numbers of the letters found in both editions of *Clearing the Path*.

1. Since 1965 numerous personal copies of the material contained in this volume have been made by interested individuals. In addition, in 1974-75, the Council on Research and Creative Work of the University of Colorado provided a grant-in-aid for the typing and reproduction (by photocopy) of thirty-five copies of an edition containing *Notes on Dhamma* and a less-complete version of the Letters than is contained herein. In 1987 the Buddhist Publication Society published a booklet (*The Tragic, the Comic and The Personal: Selected Letters of Ñāṇavīra Thera, Wheel* 339/341) containing excerpts from thirty letters.

There has also been a certain amount of standardization quietly attended to; principally, citation of quoted material and Sutta references. In keeping with the less formal structure of the letters, Sutta references are cited in a less formal (but self-explanatory) manner than that used in the 'Notes'. Books frequently quoted from are cited in abbreviated form. A key to those abbreviations is to be found at 'Suttas referents' and 'Abbreviations'. Also disclosed in this edition are the identities of the 'Colombo Thera', 'Venerable Thera', 'Mr. G.' and 'Mr. M.' They are Ven. Kheminda Thera, Ven. Siridhamma Thera, Mr. Bandy and Mr. Van Zeyst, respectively. The 'Editorial notes' have also been updated.

Where translations of French writings exist we have in most cases quoted the published version. (French passages were quoted in the original in letters to Mr. Brady, but herein English translations have been substituted.) However, the translations provided by the author in *Notes on Dhamma* have been retained.

In the third part of the book are two writings: a previously unpublished 'Suttas and Sartre'; and 'The Foundation of Ethics' both of which were discovered after their author's death.

With the additional texts the book has increased by more than 10,700 words in the 'Letters' section, and around 9,500 words in 'Writings'.

The footnotes are structured as follows: those indicated by a *letter* (a, b, c...) are the Ven. Ñāṇavīra Thera's footnotes; all those indicated by a *numeral* (1, 2, 3...) are editorial additions.

A table on p. 589 relates letter numbers in this volume to those in the original Path Press edition of 1987.

For any errors that remain, I take full responsibility.

* * *

Publication of *Clearing the Path* has been made possible through the contributions of various individuals who have themselves benefited from these writings and who wish to share them with a wider audience than has previously been possible. We are, indeed, grateful for their generosity.

Bhikkhu H. Ñāṇasuci
December 2010

## ABBREVIATIONS FOR PALI TEXTS

D. Dīghanikāya
M. Majjhimanikāya
S. Saṃyuttanikāya
A. Aṅguttaranikāya
Dhp. Dhammapada
Ud. Udāna
It. Itivuttaka
Sn. Suttanipāta
Thag. Theragāthā
Thig. Therīgāthā

## SUTTAS REFERENTS

Dīghanikāya (D.) and Majjhimanikāya (M.):
By Sutta number (in Arabic numerals), followed (/) by volume (in Roman numerals in lower cases) and page number (in Arabic numerals) of the Pali Text Society (P.T.S.) edition of the Pali text. Example: D.16/ii,118

Saṃyuttanikāya (S.):
By *saṃyutta* (in Roman numerals in lower cases) and Sutta number (in Arabic numerals), followed (/) by volume (in Roman numerals in lower cases) and page number (in Arabic numerals) of the P.T.S. edition of the Pali text. Sometime there will be also included a name of *saṃyutta* before of the referent. Example: Khandha Saṃy.—S.xxii.60/iii,69

Aṅguttaranikāya (A.):
By chapter (in Roman numerals in higher cases) and Sutta number (in Arabic numerals), followed (/) by volume (in Roman numerals in lower cases) and page number (in Arabic numerals) of the P.T.S. edition of the Pali text. Example: A.III.100/i,254-5

Dhammapada (Dhp.), Udāna (Ud.), Itivuttaka (It.), Suttanipāta (Sn.), Theragāthā (Thag.), Therīgāthā (Thig):
By chapter (in Roman numerals) and verse or Sutta number (in Arabic numerals), followed (/) by page number (in Arabic numerals) of the P.T.S. edition of the Pali text. Example: Dhp.xv.7/57

## ACKNOWLEDGEMENTS

Books frequently cited or quoted in the Letters are indicated therein in abbreviated form. Abbreviations used are as follows:

*6ET* = Blackham, *Six Existentialist Thinkers*
*PL* = Bradley, *Principles of Logic*
*Myth* = Camus, *The Myth of Sisyphus*
*PQM* = Dirac, *Principles of Quantum Mechanics*
*B&T* = Heidegger, *Being and Time*
*CUP* = Kierkegaard, *Concluding Unscientific Postscript*
*StP* = Ñāṇavīra Thera, *Seeking the Path*
*M&L* = Russell, *Mysticism and Logic*
*B&N* = Sartre, *Being and Nothingness*
*EN* = Sartre, *L'Être et le Néant*
*MIL* = Stebbing, *A Modern Introduction to Logic.*

We thank the many publishers who gave permission to use copyrighted material in this book. Publication data on material quoted or discussed in *Clearing the Path*:

Balfour, Gerald William, Earl of. *A Study of the Psychological Aspects of Mrs Willett's Mediumship, and of the Statement of the Communicators Concerning Process.* London: Society for Psychical Research, *Proceedings*, Vol. XLIII (May, 1935).
Blackham, H.J. *Six Existentialist Thinkers.* London: Routledge & Kegan Paul, 1951; New York: Macmillan, 1952; Harper Torchbooks, 1959.
Bradley, F.H. *Appearance and Reality.* London: Oxford University Press, (1893) 1962.
—. *Principles of Logic.* London: Oxford University Press, (1881) 1958.
Camus, Albert. *Exile and the Kingdom*, translated by Justin O'Brien. London: Hamish Hamilton, 1958; Penguin, 1962; New York; Random House, 1965; Vintage Books, 1965.
—. *The Fall*, translated by Justin O'Brien. New York: Knopf, 1964; London: Penguin, 1984.
—. *Le Mythe de Sisyphe.* Paris: Gallimard, 1942.
—. *The Myth of Sisyphus*, translated by Justin O'Brien. New York: Vintage, 1955.
—. *Noces.* Paris: Gallimard, 1959.

—. *The Rebel*, translated by Anthony Bower. London: Hamish Hamilton, 1953; Penguin, 1962.

—. *Selected Essays and Notebooks*, edited and translated by Philip Thody. London: Hamish Hamilton, 1970; Penguin, 1970; New York: Knopf, 1970.

Carroll, Lewis. *Alice's Adventures in Wonderland and Through the Looking Glass*. Spark Educational Publishing, 2003.

Connolly, Cyril: see Palinurus (pen name)

Dirac, P.A.M. *The Principles of Quantum Mechanics.* London: Oxford University Press, (1930) 4th edition, 1958.

Dostoievsky, Fyodor. *The Possessed.* The Ven. Ñāṇavīra seems to have had an Italian translation of *The Possessed*, from which he rendered passages into English.

Eddington, A.S. *New Pathways in Science*. London: Cambridge University Press, 1935.

Eddington, A.S. *The Philosophy of Physical Science.* London: Cambridge University Press, 1939.

Einstein, Albert. *The World As I See It*, translated by Alan Harris. London: John Lane The Bodley Head, 1935; New York: Citadel, 1979.

Eliot, T.S. *Poems [1901-1962].* London: Faber & Faber, 1974; New York: Harcourt Brace Jovanovich, 1963.

Ferm, Vergilius, editor. *An Encyclopedia of Religion.* New York: Philosophical Library, 1945.

Gallie, W.B. *Peirce and Pragmatism.* London: Pelican, 1952.

Graves, Robert. *The White Goddess.* London: Faber & Faber, 1948; New York: Farrar, Straus & Giroux, 1960 (rev. & enlgd.).

Grenier, Jean. *Absolu et Choix.* Paris: Presses Universitaires de France, 1961.

Grimsley, R. *Existentialist Thought.* Cardiff: University of Wales Press, 1955.

Heidegger, Martin. *Being and Time*, translated by J. Macquarrie and E.S. Robinson. London: SCM Press, 1962; New York: Harper & Row, 1962.

—. *What is Philosophy?*, translated by William Kluback and Jean T. Wilde. London: Vision Press, 1956; New York: New College University Press, 1956.

Housman, A.E. *Collected Poems.* London: Jonathan Cape Ltd., (1939) 1960; The Society of Authors as the literary representative of the Estate of A.E. Housman.

Husserl, Edmund. 'Phenomenology' in *Encyclopædia Britannica*, 14th edition (1955), 17:669-702.

Huxley, Aldous. *Doors of Perception and Heaven and Hell.* London: Chatto & Windus, 1968; New York: Harper & Row, 1970.

—. *Proper Studies.* London: Chatto & Windus, (1927) 1949.

Jaspers, Karl. *Philosophie.* Berlin: Springer, 1932.
Jefferson, Prof. Sir Geoffrey, F.R.S. 'Anatomy of Consciousness' in *Triangle, the Sandoz Journal of Medical Science*, Vol. 5, No. 2, 1961, pp. 96-100. Basle: Sandoz.
Kafka, Franz. *The Castle*, translated by Willa and Edwin Muir. London: Secker & Warburg, 1930; Penguin, 1957; New York: Knopf, 1968.
—. *The Trial*, translated by Willa and Edwin Muir. London: Victor Gollancz, 1935; Penguin, 1953; New York: Knopf, 1968.
Kierkegaard, Søren. *Concluding Unscientific Postscript*, translated by David F. Swenson. Princeton: Princeton University Press, 1941; London: Oxford University Press, 1945.
—. *Either/Or*, translated by David F. and Lillian M. Swenson and Walter Lowrie. London: Oxford University Press, 1941.
—. *Journals*, translated by Alexander Dru. London: Oxford University Press, 1939.
—. *Philosophical Fragments*, translated by David F. Swenson. Princeton: Princeton University Press, 1936, 1962.
Maugham, Robin. 'I Solve the Strange Riddle of the Buddhist Monk from Aldershot' in *The People*. London: 26 September 1965.
McTaggart, John M.E. *The Nature of Existence.* London: Cambridge University Press, 1921-27.
Ñāṇamoli Thera. *The Path of Purification.* Colombo: A. Semage, 1956.
Ñāṇavīra Thera. *Notes on Dhamma.* Path Press Publications, 2009.
—. *Seeking the Path.* Path Press Publications, 2010.
—. *The Letters of Sister Vajirā.* Path Press Publications, 2010.
Nietzsche, Friedrich. *The Genealogy of Morals*, translated by Horace B. Samuel. Edinburgh: J.N. Foulis, 1910.
—. *Beyond Good and Evil*, translated by Walter Kaufman. New York: Vintage, 1966.
Oppenheimer, Robert. *Science and the Common Understanding.* London: Oxford University Press, 1954.
Palinurus. *The Unquiet Grave.* London: Hamish Hamilton, 1945.
Russell, Bertrand. *An Inquiry into Meaning and Truth.* London: Allen & Unwin, 1940; Pelican, 1962.
—. *Mysticism and Logic.* London: Pelican, (1918) 1953.
—. *Nightmares of Eminent Persons, and Other Stories.* London: Bodley Head, 1954.
Sartre, Jean-Paul. *Being and Nothingness*, translated by Hazel E. Barnes. London: Methuen, 1957, 1969; New York: Philosophical Library, 1957; London and New York: Routledge, 2003.

—. *L'Être et le Néant.* Paris: Gallimard, 1943.

—. *Esquisse d'une Théorie des Émotions.* Paris: Hermann, 1939.

—. *L'Imagination.* Paris: Alcan, 1936.

—. *Imagination: A Psychological Critique*, translated by Forrest Williams. Ann Arbor: University of Michigan Press, 1962.

—. *Troubled Sleep*, translated (from *La Mort dans l'âme*) by Gerard Hopkins. New York: Bantam Books, 1961.

Schopenhauer, Arthur. *The Wisdom of Life: Being the First Part of Aphorismen Zur Lebensweisheit*, translated by T. Bailey Saunders. London: Allen & Unwin, 1890.

Stcherbatsky, T. *The Conception of Buddhist Nirvāna.* Leningrad, 1927.

Stebbing, L. Susan. *A Modern Introduction to Logic.* London: Methuen, (1930) 5th edition, 1946.

Tennent, Sir James Emerson. *Christianity in Ceylon.* London: John Murray, 1850.

Uexküll, Prof. Dr. Thure von. 'Fear and Hope in Our Time' in *The Medical Mirror. A Journal for the Medical Profession*, No. 6/1963. Darmstadt: E. Merck AG.

Warren, Henry Clarke. *Buddhism in Translations.* Cambridge: Harvard University Press, 1896; New York, Athaneum, 1963.

Wettimuny, R.G. de S. *Buddhism and Its Relation to Religion and Science.* Colombo: Gunasena, 1962.

—. *The Buddha's Teaching—Its Essential Meaning.* Colombo: Gunasena, 1969.

—. *The Buddha's Teaching and the Ambiguity of Existence.* Colombo: Gunasena, 1978.

Wittgenstein, Ludwig. *Tractatus Logico-Philosophicus*, translated by D.F. Pears and B.F. McGuinness. London: Routledge & Kegan Paul: 1961; New York: Humanities Press, 1961.

Wyschogrod, M. in *Kierkegaard and Heidegger*. London: Routledge & Kegan Paul, 1954.

Zaehner, R.C. *Mysticism: Sacred and Profane.* London: Oxford University Press, 1957.

# A

# NOTES ON DHAMMA

(1960-1965)

To the memory of my Upajjhāya,
the late Venerable Pälēnē Siri Vajirañāṇa Mahā Nāyaka Thera
of Vajirārāma, Colombo, Ceylon.

*Dve'me bhikkhave paccayā micchādiṭṭhiyā uppādāya. Katame dve. Parato ca ghoso ayoniso ca manasikāro. Ime kho bhikkhave dve paccayā micchādiṭṭhiyā uppādāyā ti.*

*Dve'me bhikkhave paccayā sammādiṭṭhiyā uppādāyā. Katame dve. Parato ca ghoso yoniso ca manasikāro. Ime kho bhikkhave dve paccayā sammādiṭṭhiyā uppādāyā ti.*[1]

*Aṅguttara* II, xi, 8 & 9 (A.I, 87)

# Preface

The principal aim of these *Notes on Dhamma* is to point out certain current misinterpretations, mostly traditional, of the Pali Suttas, and to offer in their place something certainly less easy but perhaps also less inadequate. These *Notes* assume, therefore, that the reader is (or is prepared to become) familiar with the original texts, and in Pali (for even the most competent translations sacrifice some essential accuracy to style, and the rest are seriously misleading).[a] They assume, also, that the reader's sole interest in the Pali Suttas is a concern for his own welfare. The reader is presumed to be subjectively engaged with an anxious problem, the problem of his existence, which is also the problem of his suffering. There is therefore nothing in these pages to interest the professional scholar, for whom the question of personal existence does not arise; for the scholar's whole concern is to eliminate or ignore the individual point of view in an effort to establish the objective truth—a would-be impersonal synthesis of public facts. The scholar's essentially horizontal view of things, seeking connexions in space and time, and his historical approach to the texts,[b] disqualify him from any possibility of understanding a Dhamma that the Buddha himself has called *akālika*, 'timeless'.[c] Only in a vertical view, straight down into the abyss of his own

---

**a.** These books of the Pali Canon correctly represent the Buddha's Teaching, and can be regarded as trustworthy throughout. (*Vinayapiṭaka*:) *Suttavibhaṅga*, *Mahāvagga*, *Cūḷavagga*; (*Suttapiṭaka*:) *Dīghanikāya*, *Majjhimanikāya*, *Saṃyuttanikāya*, *Aṅguttaranikāya*, *Suttanipāta*, *Dhammapada*, *Udāna*, *Itivuttaka*, *Theratherīgāthā*. (The *Jātaka* verses may be authentic, but they do not come within the scope of these *Notes*.) No other Pali books whatsoever should be taken as authoritative; and ignorance of them (and particularly of the traditional Commentaries) may be counted a positive advantage, as leaving less to be unlearned.

**b.** The P.T.S. (London Pali Text Society) Dictionary, for example, supposes that the word *attā* in the Suttas refers either to a phenomenon of purely historical interest (of the Seventh and Sixth Centuries B.C.) known as a 'soul', or else to the reflexive 'self', apparently of purely grammatical interest. All suggestion that there might be some connexion (of purely vital interest) between 'soul' and 'self' is prudently avoided.

**c.** The scholar's sterile situation has been admirably summed up by Kierkegaard.

personal existence, is a man capable of apprehending the perilous insecurity of his situation; and only a man who does apprehend this is prepared to listen to the Buddha's Teaching. But human kind, it seems, cannot bear very much reality: men, for the most part, draw back in alarm and dismay from this vertiginous direct view of being and seek refuge in distractions.

There have always been a few, however, who have not drawn back, and some of them have described what they saw. Amongst these, today, are the people known as existentialist philosophers, and an acquaintance with their mode of thinking, far from being a disadvantage, may well serve to restore the individual point of view, without which nothing can be understood. Here is a passage from an expositor of their philosophies.

> The main jet of Marcel's thinking, like all existentialism, is forced from the conclusion that the type of thought which dominates or encloses or sees through its object is necessarily inapplicable to the total situation in which the thinker himself as existing individual is enclosed,

---

'Let the enquiring scholar labour with incessant zeal, even to the extent of shortening his life in the enthusiastic service of science; let the speculative philosopher be sparing neither of time nor of diligence; they are none the less not interested infinitely, personally, and passionately, nor could they wish to be. On the contrary, they will seek to cultivate an attitude of objectivity and disinterestedness. And as for the relationship of the subject to the truth when he comes to know it, the assumption is that if only the truth is brought to light, its appropriation is a relatively unimportant matter, something that follows as a matter of course. And in any case, what happens to the individual is in the last analysis a matter of indifference. Herein lies the lofty equanimity of the scholar and the comic thoughtlessness of his parrot-like echo.'—S. Kierkegaard, *Concluding Unscientific Postscript*, tr. D.F. Swenson, Princeton 1941 & Oxford 1945, pp. 23-24. And here is Nietzsche. 'The diligence of our best scholars, their senseless industry, their burning the candle of their brain at both ends—their very mastery of their handiwork—how often is the real meaning of all that to prevent themselves continuing to see a certain thing? Science as self-anæsthetic: do you know that?'—F. Nietzsche, *The Genealogy of Morals*, Third Essay. And so, in the scholarly article on *Tāvatiṃsa* in the P.T.S. Dictionary, we are informed that 'Good Buddhists, after death in this world, are reborn in heaven'—but we are not told where good scholars are reborn.

We do not, naturally, forget what we owe to scholars—careful and accurate editions, grammars, dictionaries, concordances, all things that wonderfully lighten the task of reading the texts—and we are duly grateful; but all the science of the scholar does not lead to a comprehension of the texts—witness Stcherbatsky's lament: 'Although a hundred years have elapsed since the scientific study of Buddhism has been initiated in Europe, we are nevertheless still in the dark about the fundamental teachings of this religion and its philosophy. Certainly no other religion has proved so refractory to clear formulation.'—T. Stcherbatsky, *The Conception of Buddhist Nirvāṇa*, Leningrad 1927, p. 1.

> and therefore every system (since in principle a system of thought is outside the thinker and transparent to him) is a mere invention and the most misleading of false analogies. The thinker is concerned with the interior of the situation in which he is enclosed: with his own internal reality, rather than with the collection of qualities by which he is defined or the external relations by which his position is plotted; and with his own participation in the situation, rather than with the inaccessible view of its externality. His thought refers to a self which can only be pre-supposed and not thought and to a situation in which he is involved and which he therefore cannot fully envisage; so that in the nature of the case philosophic thought cannot have the complete clarity and mastery of scientific thought which deals with an object in general for a subject in general. To look for this type of thinking in philosophy is to overlook the necessary conditions of human thinking on ultimate questions; for philosophers to produce it at this time of day is sheer paralysis induced by superstitious regard for the prestige of contemporary science or of the classical philosophies.[d]

'The essence of man is to be in a situation' say these philosophers, and this is their common starting-point, whatever various conclusions—or lack of conclusions—they may eventually arrive at. Every man, at every moment of his life, is engaged in a perfectly definite concrete situation in a world that he normally takes for granted. But it occasionally happens that he starts to think. He becomes aware, obscurely, that he is in perpetual contradiction with himself and with the world in which he exists. 'I am, am I not?—but what am I? What is this elusive self that is always elsewhere whenever I try to grasp it? And this familiar world—why is it silent when I ask the reason for my presence here?' These insidious doubts about the assurance of his personal identity and the purpose of his existence in a world that has suddenly become indifferent to him begin to undermine his simple faith in the established order of things (whatever it may happen to be), whose function it is to relieve him of anxiety. And the great service performed by the existential philosophies is to prevent a return to complacency.

> The peculiarity of existentialism, then, is that it deals with the separation of man from himself and from the world, which raises the ques-

**d.** H.J. Blackham, *Six Existentialist Thinkers*, Routledge & Kegan Paul, London 1952, p. 83. This is a useful summary. (See also, for greater detail and further references, R. Grimsley, *Existentialist Thought*, University of Wales Press, Cardiff 1955).

> tions of philosophy, not by attempting to establish some universal form of justification which will enable man to readjust himself but by permanently enlarging and lining the separation itself as primordial and constitutive for personal existence. The main business of this philosophy therefore is not to answer the questions which are raised but to drive home the questions themselves until they engage the whole man and are made personal, urgent, and anguished. Such questions cannot be merely the traditional questions of the schools nor merely disinterested questions of curiosity concerning the conditions of knowledge or of moral or æsthetic judgements, for what is put in question by the separation of man from himself and from the world is his own being and the being of the objective world. ... These questions are not theoretical but existential, the scission which makes the existing individual aware of himself and of the world in which he is makes him a question to himself and life a question to him. ... Existential philosophies insist that any plain and positive answer is false, because the truth is in the insurmountable ambiguity which is at the heart of man and of the world.[e]

Existential philosophies, then, insist upon asking questions about self and the world, taking care at the same time to insist that they are unanswerable.[f] Beyond this point of frustration these philosophies cannot go. The Buddha, too, insists that questions about self and the world are unanswerable, either by refusing to answer them[g] or by indicating that no statement about self and the world can be justified.[h] But—and here is the vital difference—the

---

**e.** H.J. Blackham, *op. cit.*, pp. 151-3.

**f.** The scholar or scientist, with his objective method, cannot even ask such questions, since on principle he knows and wishes to know nothing of self, and nothing, therefore, of its inseparable correlative, the world. (The world, we must understand, is determined as such only with reference to self; for it is essentially 'what belongs to self', being that in which self is situated and implicated. My world, as Heidegger notes, is the world of my preoccupations and concerns, that is to say *an organized perspective of things all significant to me and signifying me*. The collection of independent public facts produced by the scientific method is inherently incapable of constituting a world, since it altogether lacks any unifying personal determinant—which, indeed, it is the business of science to eliminate. Things, not facts, *pace* Wittgenstein, make up my world.)

**g.** *Ekam antaṃ nisinno kho Vacchagotto paribbājako Bhagavantaṃ etad avoca. Kin nu kho bho Gotama, atth'attā ti. Evaṃ vutte Bhagavā tuṇhī ahosi. Kim pana bho Gotama, n'atth'attā ti. Dutiyam pi kho Bhagavā tuṇhī ahosi. Atha kho Vacchagotto paribbājako uṭṭhāyāsanā pakkāmi. Avyākata Saṃy.* 10 (S.iv,400)[2]

**h.** *Tatra bhikkhave ye te samaṇabrāhmaṇā evaṃvādino evaṃdiṭṭhino, Sassato attā*

Buddha can and does go beyond this point: not, to be sure, by answering the unanswerable, but by showing the way leading to the final cessation of all questions about self and the world.[i] [j] Let there be no mistake in the matter: the existential philosophies are not a substitute for the Buddha's Teaching—for which, indeed, there can be no substitute.[k] The questions that they persist in asking are the questions of a *puthujjana*, of a 'commoner',[l] and though they see that they are unanswerable they have no alternative but to go on asking them; for the tacit assumption upon which all these philosophies rest is that the questions are valid. They are faced with an ambiguity that they cannot resolve.[m] The Buddha, on the other hand, sees that the questions

---

*ca loko ca* (*Asassato attā ca loko ca* (and so on)), *idam eva saccaṃ mogham aññan ti, tesaṃ vata aññatr'eva saddhāya aññatra ruciyā aññatra anussavā aññatra ākāraparivitakkā aññatra diṭṭhinijjhānakkhantiyā paccattaṃ yeva ñāṇaṃ bhavissati parisuddhaṃ pariyodātan ti n'etaṃ ṭhānaṃ vijjati. Majjhima* xi,2 (M.ii,234)[3]

**i.** *Tayidaṃ saṅkhataṃ oḷārikaṃ, atthi kho pana saṅkhārānaṃ nirodho, Atth'etan ti. Iti viditvā tassa nissaraṇadassāvī Tathāgato tad upātivatto.*[4] *Ibid.* It is for this reason that the Ariya Dhamma is called *lokuttara*, 'beyond the world'.

**j.** It is all the fashion nowadays to hail modern science as the vindication of the Buddha's *anattā* doctrine. Here is an example from a recent book: 'This voidness of selfhood, which forms the distinguishing feature of the Buddhist analysis of being, is a view that is fully in accord with the conclusions drawn by modern scientific thinkers who have arrived at it independently.'[k] The supposition is that the Buddha solved the question of self and the world simply by anticipating and adopting the impersonal attitude of scientific objectivity. The seasoned thinker is not likely to be delayed by this sort of thing, but the beginner is easily misled.

**k.** To arrive at the Buddha's Teaching independently is to become a Buddha oneself. *N'atthi kho ito bahiddhā añño samaṇo vā brāhmaṇo vā yo evaṃ bhūtaṃ tacchaṃ tathaṃ dhammaṃ deseti yathā Bhagavā.*[5] *Indriya Saṃy.* vi,3 (S.v,230) See also the *Cūḷasīhanādasutta*, *Majjhima* ii,1 (M.i,63).

**l.** See, for example, the *Sabbāsavasutta*, *Majjhima* i,2 (M.i,8): *Ahan nu kho'smi, no nu kho'smi, kin nu kho'smi, kathan nu kho'smi*,[6] and so on.

**m.** Several of these philosophies, in their conclusions, point to a mystical solution of the existential ambiguity, seeking to justify it in some form of Transcendental Being. But they do not *deny* the ambiguity. Practising mystics, however, who have seen the Beatific Vision, who have realized union with the Divine Ground, are fully satisfied, so it seems, that during their mystical experience the ambiguity no longer exists. But they are agreed, one and all, that the nature of the Divine Ground (or Ultimate Reality, or whatever else they may call it) is inexpressible. In other words, they succeed, momentarily at least, in eliminating the mystery of the individual by raising it to a Higher Power: they envelop the mystery within the Mystery, so that it is no longer visible. ('By not thinking on self transcend self'—Augustine.) But a paradox is not resolved by wrapping it up inside a bigger one; on the contrary, the task is to unwrap it. Mahāyāna and Zen Buddhism have a strong mystical flavouring, but there is nothing of this in the Pali Suttas. Mystically inclined readers of these *Notes* will find them little to their taste.

are *not* valid and that to ask them is to make the mistake of assuming that they are. One who has understood the Buddha's Teaching no longer asks these questions; he is *ariya*, 'noble', and no more a *puthujjana*, and he is beyond the range of the existential philosophies; but he would never have reached the point of listening to the Buddha's Teaching had he not first been disquieted by existential questions about himself and the world. There is no suggestion, of course, that it is necessary to become an existentialist philosopher before one can understand the Buddha: every intelligent man questions himself quite naturally about the nature and significance of his own existence, and provided he refuses to be satisfied with the first ready-made answer that he is offered he is as well placed as anyone to grasp the Buddha's Teaching when he hears it. None the less many people, on first coming across the Suttas, are puzzled to know what their relevance is in the elaborate context of modern thought; and for them an indication that the existential philosophies (in their general methods, that is to say, rather than their individual conclusions) afford a way of approach to the Suttas may be helpful.

The Note on Fundamental Structure perhaps needs a remark. It is offered as an instrument of thought[n] to those who are looking for something on these lines, and such people will probably find it self-explanatory. The fact that it is unfinished is of no great consequence, since anyone who succeeds in following what there is of it will be able to continue it for himself as far as he pleases. Those who are unable to understand what it is all about would be best advised to ignore it altogether: not everybody needs this kind of apparatus in order to think effectively. The Figure in §I/13 was first suggested

---

**n.** It is for *negative* thinking. 'Precisely because the negative is present in existence, and present everywhere (for existence is a constant process of becoming), it is necessary to become aware of its presence continuously, as the only safeguard against it.'—S. Kierkegaard, *op. cit.*, p. 75. Positive or abstract thinking abstracts from existence and is thus incapable of thinking it continuously. The difficulty that arises for the positive thinker is expressed by Kierkegaard in these terms. 'To think existence *sub specie æterni* and in abstract terms is essentially to abrogate it... It is impossible to conceive existence without movement, and movement cannot be conceived *sub specie æterni*. To leave movement out is not precisely a distinguished achievement... But inasmuch as all thought is eternal, there is here created a difficulty for the existing individual. Existence, like movement, is a difficult category to deal with; for if I think it, I abrogate it, and then I do not think it. It might therefore seem to be the proper thing to say that there is something that cannot be thought, namely, existence. But the difficulty persists, in that existence itself combines thinking with existing, in so far as the thinker exists.' *Op. cit.*, pp. 273-4.

(though not in that form) by a chapter of Eddington's,[o] but neither its application nor the manner of arriving at it, as described in this Note, seems to have anything very much in common with Eddington's conception.[p]

A Pali-English Glossary together with English Translations of all quoted Pali passages will be found at the end of the book. These are provided in order to make the book more accessible to those who do not know Pali, in the hope that they will think it worth their while to acquire this not very difficult language. Some additional texts, referred to in the *Notes* but not quoted there, are also provided.

All textual references are given (i) by *Vagga* and *Sutta* number, and in the case of *Saṃyutta* and *Aṅguttara* references also by the title of the *Saṃyutta* and the number of the *Nipāta* respectively, and (ii) by Volume and Page of the P.T.S. editions. The P.T.S. reference is given within brackets after the *Vagga* and *Sutta* reference.

The views expressed in this book will perhaps be regarded in one quarter or another either as doubtful or as definitely wrong. To prevent misunderstandings, therefore, I should make it clear that I alone, as the author, am responsible for these views, and that they are not put forward as representing the opinion of any other person or of any body of people.

Ñāṇavīra

Būndala,
Ceylon.
14th September 1964

---

**o.** A.S. Eddington, *New Pathways in Science*, Cambridge 1935, Ch. XII.

**p.** A.S. Eddington, *The Philosophy of Physical Science*, Cambridge 1939, Ch. IX & X. The equivocal posture of the quantum physicist, who adopts simultaneously the reflexive attitude of phenomenology (which requires the observer) and the objective attitude of science (which eliminates the observer), expressing his results in equations whose terms depend on the principle that black is white, makes him singularly unfitted to produce intelligible philosophy. (Camus, in *L'Homme Révolté* (Gallimard, Paris 1951, p. 126), remarks on Breton's surrealist thought as offering the curious spectacle of a Western mode of thinking where the principle of analogy is persistently favoured to the detriment of the principles of identity and contradiction. And yet, in *The Principles of Quantum Mechanics* (Oxford (1930) 1958), Dirac introduces us, without turning a hair, to certain abstract quantities, fundamental to the theory, that (p. 53) can be replaced by 'sets of numbers with analogous mathematical properties'. These abstract quantities, as one reads the early chapters, do indeed have a surrealist air about them.)

## ABBREVIATIONS

| | |
|---|---|
| *NP* | A NOTE ON PAṬICCASAMUPPĀDA |
| *PS* | PARAMATTHA SACCA |
| *SN* | SHORTER NOTES |
| *FS* | FUNDAMENTAL STRUCTURE |

# I. A NOTE ON PAṬICCASAMUPPĀDA

*Api c'Udāyi tiṭṭhatu pubbanto tiṭṭhatu aparanto, dhammaṃ te desessāmi: Imasmiṃ sati idaṃ hoti, imass'uppādā idaṃ uppajjati; imasmiṃ asati idaṃ na hoti, imassa nirodhā idaṃ nirujjhatī ti.*[7]

*Majjhima* viii,9 (M.ii,32)

*Imasmiṃ sati idaṃ hoti, imass'uppādā idaṃ uppajjati; yadidaṃ avijjāpaccayā saṅkhārā, saṅkhārapaccayā viññāṇaṃ, viññāṇapaccayā nāmarūpaṃ, nāmarūpapaccayā saḷāyatanaṃ, saḷāyatanapaccayā phasso, phassapaccayā vedanā, vedanāpaccayā taṇhā, taṇhāpaccayā upādānaṃ, upādānapaccayā bhavo, bhavapaccayā jāti, jātipaccayā jarāmaraṇaṃ sokaparidevadukkhadomanass' upāyāsā sambhavanti; evam etassa kevalassa dukkhakkhandhassa samudayo hoti.*

*Imasmiṃ asati idaṃ na hoti, imassa nirodhā idaṃ nirujjhati; yadidaṃ avijjānirodhā saṅkhāranirodho, saṅkhāranirodhā viññāṇanirodho, viññāṇanirodhā nāmarūpanirodho, nāmarūpanirodhā saḷāyatananirodho, saḷāyatananirodhā phassanirodho, phassanirodhā vedanānirodho, vedanānirodhā taṇhānirodho, taṇhānirodhā upādānanirodho, upādānanirodhā bhavanirodho, bhavanirodhā jātinirodho, jātinirodhā jarāmaraṇaṃ sokaparidevadukkhadomanass' upāyāsā nirujjhanti; evam etassa kevalassa dukkhakkhandhassa nirodho hoti.*[8]

*Majjhima* iv,8 (M.i,262-3 & 264)

1. The traditional interpretation of *paṭiccasamuppāda* (of its usual twelve-factored formulation, that is to say) apparently has its roots in the *Paṭisambhidāmagga* (i,52), or perhaps in the *Abhidhammapiṭaka*. This interpretation is fully expounded in the *Visuddhimagga* (Ch. XVII). It can be briefly summarized thus: *avijjā* and *saṅkhārā* are *kamma* in the *previous* existence, and their *vipāka* is *viññāṇa*, *nāmarūpa*, *saḷāyatana*, *phassa*, and *vedanā*, in the present existence; *taṇhā*, *upādāna*, and *bhava*, are *kamma* in the *present* existence, and their *vipāka* is *jāti* and *jarāmaraṇa* in the *subsequent* existence.

2. This Note will take for granted first, that the reader is acquainted with this traditional interpretation, and secondly, that he is dissatisfied with it. It is not therefore proposed to enter into a detailed discussion of this interpretation, but rather to indicate briefly that dissatisfaction with it is not unjustified, and then to outline what may perhaps be found to be a more satisfactory approach.

3. As the traditional interpretation has it, *vedanā* is *kammavipāka*. Reference to *Vedanā Saṃy.* iii,2 (S.iv,230) will show that as far as concerns bodily feeling (with which the Sutta is evidently dealing) there are seven reasons for it that are specifically not *kammavipāka*. Only in the eighth place do we find *kammavipākajā vedanā*. This would at once limit the application of *paṭiccasamuppāda* to certain bodily feelings only and would exclude others, if the traditional interpretation is right. Some of these bodily feelings would be *paṭiccasamuppannā*, but not all; and this would hardly accord with, for example, the passage: *Paṭiccasamuppannaṃ kho āvuso sukhadukkhaṃ vuttaṃ Bhagavatā*[9] (*Nidāna/Abhisamaya Saṃy.* iii,5 (S.ii,38)).

4. There is, however, a more serious difficulty regarding feeling. In *Aṅguttara* III,vii,1 (A.i,176) it is clear that *somanassa*, *domanassa*, and *upekkhā*, are included in *vedanā*, in the specific context of the *paṭiccasamuppāda* formula-

tion. But these three feelings are mental, and arise (as the Sutta tells us) when the mind dwells upon (*upavicarati*) some object; thus they involve *cetanā*, 'intention', in their very structure. And the Commentary to the Sutta would seem to allow this, but in doing so must either exclude these mental feelings from *vedanā* in the *paṭiccasamuppāda* formulation or else assert that they are *vipāka*. In either case the Commentary would go against the Sutta we are considering. This Sutta (which should be studied at first hand) not only treats these mental feelings as included in *vedanā* but also specifically states that to hold the view that whatever a man experiences, pleasant, unpleasant, or neutral, is due to past acts, is to adopt a form of determinism making present action futile—one is a killer on account of past acts, a thief on account of past acts, and so on. To take these mental feelings as *vipāka* would be to fall into precisely this wrong view; and, in fact, the traditional interpretation, rather than that, prefers to exclude them from *paṭiccasamuppāda*, at least as *vedanā* (see *Visuddhimagga*, *loc. cit.*). Unfortunately for the traditional interpretation there are Suttas (e.g. *Majjhima* i,9 (M.i,53)[78]) that define the *paṭiccasamuppāda* item *nāmarūpa*—also traditionally taken as *vipāka*—in terms of (amongst other things) not only *vedanā* but also *cetanā*, and our Commentary is obliged to speak of a *vipakācetanā*. But the Buddha has said (*Aṅguttara* VI,vi,9 (A.iii,415)[79]) that *kamma* is *cetanā* (action is intention), and the notion of *vipakācetanā*, consequently, is a plain self-contradiction. (It needs, after all, only a moment's reflection to see that if, for example, the pleasant feeling that I experience when I indulge in lustful thoughts is the *vipāka* of some past *kamma*, then I have no present responsibility in the matter and can now do nothing about it. But I know from my own experience that this is not so; if I choose to enjoy pleasure by thinking lustful thoughts I can do so, and I can also choose (if I see good reason) to refrain from thinking such thoughts.)[a]

---

**a.** A present intention (or action) is certainly *determined*, but it is determined by a superior (or more reflexive) intention that *also* is present: it is, therefore, not *pre*-determined. (To be future is essentially to be under-determined. See *FS*.) Every voluntary (or reflexive) intention (i.e. every volition or act of will) is perpetually revocable, and every involuntary (or immediate) intention (i.e. every inclination or tendency) is voluntarily modifiable. (There is a mistaken idea, common (and convenient) enough, that our inclinations are in the nature of impulsions to which we can only submit, rather as a stone passively suffers the pressure that moves it. But, far from being an imposition that must be passively suffered, an inclination is an active seeking of a still only *possible* state of affairs. Cf. *'D'ailleurs, si l'acte n'est pas pur* mouvement, *il doit se définir par une* intention. *De quelque manière que l'on considère cette intention, elle ne peut être qu'un dépassement du donné vers un résultat à obtenir. ... Lorsque les psychologues, par*

5. Let us now consider *saṅkhārā*, which we shall make no attempt to translate for the moment so as not to beg the question. We may turn to *Nidāna/Abhisamaya Saṃy.* i,2 (S.ii,4) for a definition of *saṅkhārā* in the context of the *paṭiccasamuppāda* formulation. *Katame ca bhikkhave saṅkhārā. Tayo'me bhikkhave saṅkhārā, kāyasaṅkhāro vacīsaṅkhāro cittasaṅkhāro. Ime vuccanti bhikkhave saṅkhārā.*[10] But what are *kāya-saṅkhāra*, *vacīsaṅkhāra*, and *cittasaṅkhāra*? The *Cūḷavedallasutta* (*Majjhima* v,4 (M.i,301) & cf. *Citta Saṃy.* 6 (S.iv,293)) will tell us. *Kati pan'ayye saṅkhārā ti. Tayo'me āvuso Visākha saṅkhārā, kāyasaṅkhāro vacīsaṅkhāro cittasaṅkhāro ti. Katamo pan'ayye kāyasaṅkhāro, katamo vacīsaṅkhāro, katamo cittasaṅkhāro ti. Assāsapassāsā kho āvuso Visākha kāyasaṅkhāro, vitakkavicārā vacīsaṅkhāro, saññā ca vedanā ca cittasaṅkhāro ti. Kasmā pan'ayye assāsapassāsā kāyasaṅkhāro, kasmā vitakkavicārā vacīsaṅkhāro, kasmā saññā ca vedanā ca cittasaṅkhāro ti. Assāsapassāsā kho āvuso Visākha kāyikā, ete dhammā kāyapaṭibaddhā, tasmā assāsapassāsā kāyasaṅkhāro. Pubbe kho āvuso Visākha vitakketvā vicāretvā pacchā vācaṃ bhindati, tasmā vitakkavicārā vacīsaṅkhāro. Saññā ca vedanā ca cetasikā, ete dhammā cittapaṭibaddhā, tasmā saññā ca vedanā ca cittasaṅkhāro ti.*[11] Now the traditional interpretation says that *saṅkhārā* in the *paṭiccasamuppāda* context are *kamma*, being *cetanā*. Are we therefore obliged to understand in-&-out-breaths, thinking-&-pondering, and perception and feeling, respectively, as bodily, verbal, and mental *kamma* (or *cetanā*)? Is my present existence the result of my breathing in the preceding existence? Is thinking-&-pondering *verbal* action? Must we regard perception and feeling as intention, when the Suttas distinguish between them (*Phuṭṭho bhikkhave vedeti, phuṭṭho ceteti, phuṭṭho sañjānāti ...*[12] (*Saḷāyatana Saṃy.* iv,10 (S.iv,68)))? Certainly, *saṅkhārā* may, upon occasion, be *cetanā* (e.g. *Khandha Saṃy.* vi,4 (S.iii,60)[80]); but this is by no means always so. The *Cūḷavedallasutta* tells us clearly in what sense in-&-out-breaths, thinking-&-pondering, and perception and feeling, are *saṅkhārā* (i.e. in that body, speech, and mind (*citta*), are intimately connected with them, and do not occur without them); and it would do violence to the Sutta to interpret *saṅkhārā* here as *cetanā*.

---

*exemple, font de la tendance un état de fait, ils ne voient pas qu'ils lui ôtent tout caractère* d'appétit (ad-petitio).'—J.-P. Sartre, *L'Être et le Néant*, Gallimard, Paris 1943, p. 556. ('Besides, if the act is not pure *movement*, it must be defined by an *intention*. In whatever way we may consider this intention, it can only be a passing beyond the given towards a result to be obtained. ... When the psychologists, for example, turn tendency into a state of fact, they fail to see that they are taking away from it all character of *appetite* (*ad-petitio*).')) Cf. *SN*, CETANĀ (e).

**6.** Nevertheless, it would be a mistake to suppose from the foregoing that *saṅkhārā* in the *paṭiccasamuppāda* context *cannot* mean *cetanā*. One Sutta (*Nidāna/Abhisamaya Saṃy.* vi,1 (S.ii,82)) gives *saṅkhārā* in this context as *puññābhisaṅkhāra*, *apuññābhisaṅkhāra*, and *āneñjābhisaṅkhāra*, and it is clear enough that we *must* understand *saṅkhārā* here as some kind of *cetanā*. Indeed, it is upon this very Sutta that the traditional interpretation relies to justify its conception of *saṅkhārā* in the context of the *paṭiccasamuppāda* formulation. It might be wondered how the traditional interpretation gets round the difficulty of explaining *assāsapassāsā*, *vitakkavicārā*, and *saññā* and *vedanā*, as *cetanā*, in defiance of the *Cūḷavedallasutta* passage. The answer is simple: the traditional interpretation, choosing to identify *cittasaṅkhāra* with *manosaṅkhāra*, roundly asserts (in the *Visuddhimagga*) that *kāyasaṅkhāra*, *vacīsaṅkhāra*, and *cittasaṅkhāra*, are *kāyasañcetanā*, *vacīsañcetanā*, and *manosañcetanā*,—see §16—, and altogether ignores the *Cūḷavedallasutta*. The difficulty is thus, discreetly, not permitted to arise.

**7.** No doubt more such specific inadequacies and inconsistencies in the traditional interpretation of *paṭiccasamuppāda* could be found, but since this is not a polemic we are not concerned to seek them out. There remains, however, a reason for dissatisfaction with the general manner of this interpretation. The Buddha has said (*Majjhima* iii,8 (M.i,191)) that he who sees the Dhamma sees *paṭiccasamuppāda*; and he has also said that the Dhamma is *sandiṭṭhika* and *akālika*, that it is immediately visible and without involving time (see in particular *Majjhima* iv,8 (M.i,265)). Now it is evident that the twelve items, *avijjā* to *jarāmaraṇa*, cannot, if the traditional interpretation is correct, all be seen at once; for they are spread over three successive existences. I may, for example, see present *viññāṇa* to *vedanā*, but I cannot *now* see the *kamma* of the *past* existence—*avijjā* and *saṅkhārā*—that (according to the traditional interpretation) was the cause of these present things. Or I may see *taṇhā* and so on, but I cannot *now* see the *jāti* and *jarāmaraṇa* that will result from these things in the *next* existence. And the situation is no better if it is argued that since all twelve items are present in each existence it is possible to see them all at once. It is, no doubt, true that all these things can be seen at once, but the *avijjā* and *saṅkhārā* that I *now* see are the cause (says the traditional interpretation) of *viññāṇa* to *vedanā* in the *next* existence, and have no causal connexion with the *viññāṇa* to *vedanā* that I *now* see. In other words, the relation *saṅkhārapaccayā viññāṇaṃ* cannot be seen in either case. The consequence of this is that the *paṭiccasamuppāda* formulation (if the traditional interpretation is correct) is something that, in part at least, must be taken on trust. And even if there is memory of the past existence the situation is still unsatisfactory, since memory is not on the same level of certainty as present reflexive experience. Instead of *imass'uppādā idaṃ uppajjati, imassa nirodhā idaṃ nirujjhati* (see index 7), the traditional interpretation says, in effect, *imassa nirodhā idaṃ uppajjati*, 'with cessation of this, this arises'. It is needless to press this point further: either the reader will already have recognized that this is, for him, a valid objection to the traditional interpretation, or he will not. And if he has not already seen this as an objection, no amount of argument will open his eyes. It is a matter of one's fundamental attitude to one's own existence—is there, or is there not, a *present* problem or, rather, *anxiety* that can only be resolved *in the present*?

**8.** If *paṭiccasamuppāda* is *sandiṭṭhika* and *akālika* then it is clear that it can have nothing to do with *kamma* and *kammavipāka*—at least in their usual sense of ethical action and its eventual retribution (see *SN*, KAMMA)—; for the ripening of *kamma* as *vipāka* takes *time*—*vipāka* always follows *kamma* after an interval and is never simultaneous with it. It will at once be evident that if an interpretation of the *paṭiccasamuppāda* formulation can be found that does not involve *kamma* and *vipāka* the difficulties raised in §§3&4 will vanish; for we shall no longer be called upon to decide whether *vedanā* is, or is not, *kamma* or *vipāka*, and there will be no need for such contradictions as *vipākacetanā*. Irrespective of whether or not it is either *kamma* or *vipāka*, *vedanā* will be *paṭiccasamuppannā*. We shall also find that the apparent conflict of §§5&6 disappears; for when *saṅkhārā*, as the second item of the *paṭiccasamuppāda* formulation, is no longer necessarily to be regarded as *kamma*, we shall be free to look for a meaning of the word *saṅkhāra* that can comfortably accomodate the *kāya-*, *vacī-*, and *citta-saṅkhārā* of the *Cūḷavedallasutta*, as well as the *puñña-*, *apuñña-*, and *āneñja-abhisaṅkhārā* of *Nidāna/Abhisamaya Saṃy.* vi,1. (We may note in passing that though *kamma* is *cetanā*—action is intention—we are in no way obliged, when we deal with *cetanā*, to think in terms of *kamma* and its eventual *vipāka*. Present *cetanā* is structurally inseparable from present *saññā* and present *vedanā*; and thoughts about the future are quite irrelevant to the *present* problem of suffering—*Yaṃ kiñci vedayitaṃ taṃ dukkhasmin ti*[13] (*Nidāna/Abhisamaya Saṃy.* iv,2 (S.ii,53)).[b])

---

**b.** The anguish of the moment when a man apprehends that he is going to die is evidence of this perpetually present *saṅkhāradukkha* (see *Vedanā Saṃy.* ii,1, quoted in *SN*, NIBBĀNA), and has to do with the changing joys and miseries of this life only in so far as they are, in fact, *changing*. (cf. index **94**) It is this anguish that makes deliberate

**9.** It will be convenient to start at the end of the *paṭiccasamuppāda* formulation and to discuss *jāti* and *jarāmaraṇa* first. To begin with, *jāti* is 'birth' and not 're-birth'. 'Re-birth' is *punabbhavābhinibbatti*, as in *Majjhima* v,3 (M.i,294) where it is said that future 'birth into renewed existence' comes of *avijjā* and *taṇhā*; and it is clear that, here, two successive existences are involved. It is, no doubt, possible for a Buddha to see the re-birth that is *at each moment* awaiting a living individual who still has *taṇhā*—the re-birth, that is to say, that is *now* awaiting the individual who *now* has *taṇhā*. If this is so, then for a Buddha the dependence of re-birth upon *taṇhā* is a matter of direct seeing, not involving time. But this is by no means always possible (if, indeed, at all) for an *ariyasāvaka*, who, though he sees *paṭiccasamuppāda* for himself, and with certainty (it is *aparapaccayā ñāṇaṃ*), may still need to accept re-birth on the Buddha's authority.[c] In other words, an *ariyasāvaka* sees *birth* with immediate vision (since *jāti* is part of the *paṭiccasamuppāda* formulation), but does not necessarily see *re*-birth with immediate vision. It is obvious, however, that *jāti* does not refer straightforwardly to the *ariyasāvaka*'s own physical birth into his present existence; for that at best could only be a memory, and it is probably not remembered at all. How, then, is *jāti* to be understood?

**10.** *Upādānapaccayā bhavo; bhavapaccayā jāti; jātipaccayā jarāmaraṇaṃ* ... (see index **8**) The fundamental *upādāna* or 'holding' is *attavāda* (see *Majjhima* ii,1 (M.i,67)), which is holding a belief in 'self'. The *puthujjana* takes what appears to be his 'self' at its face value; and so long as this goes on he continues to *be* a 'self', at least in his own eyes (and in those of others like him). This is *bhava* or 'being'. The *puthujjana* knows that people are born and die; and since he thinks 'my self exists' so he also thinks 'my self

---

suicide, even if it is to be painless, such a difficult enterprise. Only the *arahat* has *no* anguish in the face of death:

*Nābhinandāmi maraṇaṃ nābhinandāmi jīvitaṃ,*
*Kālañ ca paṭikaṅkhāmi nibbisaṃ bhatako yathā;*
*Nābhinandāmi maraṇaṃ nābhinandāmi jīvitaṃ,*
*Kālañ ca paṭikaṅkhāmi sampajāno patissato.*[14]
*Theragāthā* vv. 606 & 607.

**c.** This, naturally, is not to be taken as denying the possibility of evidence for re-birth quite independent of what is said in the Suttas. (A curious view, that the Buddha was an agnostic on the question of re-birth and refused to pronounce on it, seems to be gaining currency. Even a very slight acquaintance with the Suttas will correct this idea. See e.g. *Majjhima* ii,2 (M.i,73-7).)

was born' and 'my self will die'. The *puthujjana* sees a 'self' to whom the words *birth* and *death* apply.[d] In contrast to the *puthujjana*, the *arahat* has altogether got rid of *asmimāna* (not to speak of *attavāda*—see *SN*, MAMA), and does not even think 'I am'. This is *bhavanirodha*, cessation of being. And since he does not think 'I am' he also does not think 'I was born' or 'I shall die'. In other words, he sees no 'self' or even 'I' for the words *birth* and *death* to apply to. This is *jātinirodha* and *jarāmaraṇanirodha*. (See, in *Kosala Saṃy.* i,3 (S.i,71), how the words *birth* and *death* are avoided when the *arahat* is spoken of. *Atthi nu kho bhante jātassa aññatra jarāmaraṇā ti. N'atthi kho mahārāja jātassa aññatra jarāmaraṇā. Ye pi te mahārāja khattiyamahāsālā... brāhmaṇamahāsālā... gahapatimahāsālā..., tesam pi jātānaṃ n'atthi aññatra jarāmaraṇā. Ye pi te mahārāja bhikkhū arahanto khīṇāsavā..., tesam pāyaṃ kāyo bhedanadhammo nikkhepanadhammo ti.*[15]) The *puthujjana*, taking his apparent 'self' at face value, does not see that he is a victim of *upādāna*; he does not see that 'being a self' depends upon 'holding a belief in self' (*upādānapaccayā bhavo*); and he does not see that birth and death depend upon his 'being a self' (*bhavapaccayā jāti*, and so on). The *ariyasāvaka*, on the other hand, does see these things, and he sees also their cessation (even though he may not yet have fully realized it); and his seeing of these things is direct. Quite clearly, the idea of *re*-birth is totally irrelevant here.

11. Let us now turn to the beginning of the *paṭiccasamuppāda* formulation and consider the word *saṅkhāra*. The passage from the *Cūḷavedallasutta* quoted in §5 evidently uses *saṅkhāra* to mean a thing from which some other thing is inseparable—in other words, *a necessary condition*. This definition is perfectly simple and quite general, and we shall find that it is all that we need. (If a *saṅkhāra* is something upon which something else depends, we can say that the 'something else' is *determined* by the first thing, i.e. by the *saṅkhāra*, which is therefore a 'determination' or a 'determinant'. It will be convenient to use the word *determination* when we need to translate *saṅkhāra*.)

---

**d.** While maintaining the necessary reservations (see Preface) about his views, we may observe that Heidegger, in his *Sein und Zeit* (Halle 1927, p. 374), subordinates the ideas of *birth* and *death* to that of *being*, within the unity of our existential structure. I exist, I *am*, as born; and, *as* born, I *am* as liable at every moment to die. (This book, in English translation (by J. Macquarrie & E. S. Robinson, *Being and Time*, SCM Press, London 1962), has only lately (1965) become available to me: I find that, where they disagree, Heidegger, as against Sartre, is generally in the right.)

12. Some discussion will be necessary if we are to see that *saṅkhāra*, whenever it occurs, always has this meaning in one form or another. We may start with the fundamental triad: *Sabbe saṅkhārā aniccā; Sabbe saṅkhārā dukkhā; Sabbe dhammā anattā.*[16] (*Dhammapada* xx,5-7 (Dh. 277-9)) A *puthujjana* accepts what appears to be his 'self' at face value. When he asks himself 'What is my self?' he seeks to identify it in some way with one thing or another, and specifically with the *pañc'upādānakkhandhā* or one of them (see *Khandha Saṃy.* v,5 (S.iii,46)[81]). Whatever thing (*dhamma*) he identifies as 'self', that thing he takes as being permanent; for if he saw it as impermanent he would not identify it as 'self' (see *SN*, DHAMMA). Since, however, he *does* see it as permanent—more permanent, indeed, than anything else—he will think '*Other* things may be impermanent, but not *this* thing, which is *myself*'. In order, then, that he *shall* see it as impermanent, indirect methods are necessary: he must first see that *this* thing is dependent upon, or determined by, some *other* thing, and he must then see that this *other* thing, this determination or *saṅkhāra*, is impermanent. When he sees that the *other* thing, the *saṅkhāra* on which *this* thing depends, is impermanent, he sees that *this* thing, too, must be impermanent, and he no longer regards it as 'self'. (See *SN*, SAṄKHĀRA.) Thus, when *sabbe saṅkhārā aniccā* is seen, *sabbe dhammā anattā* is seen. And similarly with *sabbe saṅkhārā dukkhā*. We may therefore understand *sabbe saṅkhārā aniccā as* 'All things upon which other things (*dhammā*) depend—i.e. all determinations (*saṅkhārā*)—are impermanent' with a tacit corollary 'All things dependent upon other things (*saṅkhārā*)—i.e. all determined things (*saṅkhatā dhammā*)—are impermanent'. After this, *sabbe dhammā anattā*, 'All things are not-self', follows as a matter of course.[e]

---

e. It may seem, upon occasion, that *saṅkhāra* and *dhamma* coincide. Thus the *pañc'upādānakkhandhā* are what *attavād'upādāna* depends on, and they are therefore *saṅkhārā*. But also it is with them that *attā* is identified, and they are thus *dhammā*. This situation, however, is telescoped; for in *attavād'upādāna*, which is a complex affair, what is *primarily* (though implicitly) identified as *attā* is *upādāna*, and the *pañc'upādānakkhandhā* are involved only in the second place. See *PS* §§3&4. (This, of course, is not the only way in which they are *saṅkhārā*, though §3 might give that impression. The reciprocal dependence of *viññāṇa* and *nāmarūpa*—with or without *upādāna*—is another. And see also what follows.) The word *upādāna* (lit. 'taking up') has a certain ambiguity about it. As well as 'holding' (seizing, grasping), which is eminently a characteristic of fire no less than of passion (the *upādāna* of *pañc'upādānakkhandhā* is *chandarāga*, 'desire-&-lust'), the word can also mean the *fuel* of a fire (*Majjhima* viii,2 (M.i,487); *Avyākata Saṃy.* 9 (S.iv,399-400)). The burning fuel, being held by the 'holding' fire, is itself the fire's 'holding'. The fire is burning, the fuel is burning: two aspects of the same thing.

13. Every thing (*dhamma*) must, of necessity, be (or be somehow included within) one or more of the *pañc('upādān)akkhandhā*, either generally—e.g. feeling in general, feeling as opposed to what is not feeling—or particularly—e.g. this present painful feeling as opposed to the previous pleasant feeling (present *as* a past feeling). In the same way, every determination (*saṅkhāra*) must also be one or more of the *pañc('upādān)akkhandhā*. Thus the *pañc('upādān)akkhandhā* can be regarded either as *saṅkhārā* or as *dhammā* according as they are seen as 'things-that-other-things-depend-on' or simply as 'things themselves'. See *Majjhima* iv,5 (M.i,228).[82]

14. *Saṅkhārā* are one of the *pañc'upādānakkhandhā* (or, in the case of the *arahat*, one of the *pañcakkhandhā*—see *Khandha Saṃy.* v,6 (S.iii,47)). The Sutta mentioned in §5 (*Khandha Saṃy.* vi,4)[80] says explicitly, in this context, that *saṅkhārā* are *cetanā*. If this is so, *cetanā* must be something that other things depend on. What are these things? The answer is given at once by the *Khajjanīyasutta* (*Khandha Saṃy.* viii,7 (S.iii,87)[83]): they are the *pañc('upādān)akkhandhā* themselves.[f]

---

f. This Sutta shows that *saṅkhārā*—here *cetanā*—determine not only *rūpa*, *vedanā*, *saññā*, and *viññāṇa*, but also *saṅkhārā*: *Saṅkhāre saṅkhārattāya saṅkhataṃ abhisaṅkharonti.... Saṅkhataṃ abhisaṅkharontī ti kho bhikkhave tasmā Saṅkhārā ti vuccanti.*[83] The question might arise whether these determinations that are determined by determinations do themselves determine (other) things or not. Are there determinations that do not, in fact, determine anything? The answer is that there cannot be. A determination is essentially *negative*—'*Omnis determinatio est negatio*' said Spinoza—, and a negative, a negation, only exists as a denial of something positive. The positive thing's *existence* is asserted by the negative in the very act of denying it (just as atheism, which exists as a denial of theism, is evidence that theism exists); and its *essence* (or nature) is defined by the negative in stating what it is *not* (if we know what atheism is we shall know at once what theism is). A *negative* thus determines both the existence and the essence of a *positive*.

In what way is *cetanā* negative? A sheet of paper lying on a table is determined *as a sheet of paper* by its potentialities or possibilities—i.e. by what it is *for*. It can be used for writing on, for drawing on, for wrapping up something, for wiping up a mess, for covering another sheet, for burning, and so on. But though it *can* be used for these things, it is *not actually* being used for *any* of them. Thus these potentialities *deny* the object lying on the table as it actually is (which is why they are potentialities and not actualities); nevertheless if it were not for the fact that *these particular* potentialities are associated with the object on the table we should not see the object as a 'sheet of paper'. These potentialities, which are *not* the object, determine it for what it is. We know what a thing is when we know what it is for. Thus these potentialities can also be understood as the *significance* or *purpose* of the object, and therefore as its *intention(s)*. (This account is necessarily restricted to the crudely utilitarian level, but will serve to give an

15. This leads us to the *puññābhisaṅkhāra*, *apuññābhisaṅkhāra*, and *āneñjābhisaṅkhāra*, of §6. These determinations are clearly *cetanā* of some kind—indeed the Sutta itself (*Nidāna/Abhisamaya Saṃy.* vi,1) associates the words *abhisaṅkharoti* and *abhisañcetayati*. A brief discussion is needed. The Sutta says: *Avijjāgato'yaṃ bhikkhave purisapuggalo puññañ ce saṅkhāraṃ abhisaṅkharoti, puññūpagaṃ hoti viññāṇaṃ.*[17] The word *puñña* is commonly associated with *kamma*, and the traditional interpretation supposes that *puññūpaga viññāṇa* is *puññakammavipāka* in the following existence. *Puñña* is certainly *kamma*, but nothing in the Sutta suggests that *puññūpaga viññāṇa* is anything other than the meritorious consciousness of one who is determining or intending merit. (When merit is intended by an individual he is conscious of his world as 'world-for-doing-merit-in', and consciousness has thus 'arrived at merit'.) In §14 we saw that *cetanā* (or intentions) of all kinds are *saṅkhārā*, and these are no exception. As we see from the Sutta, however, they are of a particular kind; for they are not found in the *arahat*. They are intentions in which belief in 'self' is implicitly involved. We saw in §10 that belief in 'self' is the condition for birth, and that when all trace of such belief is eradicated the word *birth* no longer applies. Belief in 'self', in exactly the same way, is the condition for consciousness, and when it altogether ceases the word *consciousness* no longer applies. Thus, with cessation of these particular intentions there is cessation of consciousness. The *arahat*, however, still lives, and he has both intentions (or, more generally, determinations) and consciousness; but this consciousness is *niruddha*, and the intentions (or determinations) must similarly be accounted as 'ceased'. (This matter is further discussed in §22. See also *SN*, VIÑÑĀṆA.) *Saṅkhārapaccayā viññāṇaṃ*, which means 'so long as there are determinations there is consciousness', is therefore also to be understood as meaning 'so long as there are *puthujjana*'s determinations there is *puthujjana*'s consciousness'. Even though the *Khajjanīyasutta* (§14) tells us that determinations are so called since 'they determine the

---

indication.) One of these intentions, though of a special kind (present only when there is *avijjā*), is that the object is *for me*—it is *mine*, *etaṃ mama*. And all these intentions are nothing more nor less than *cetanā*. (See also *SN*, CETANĀ & ATTĀ.) Determinations generally, whether they are *cetanā* or not, have two essential characteristics: (i) they are bound up with what they determine and (ii) they are *not* what they determine (or not wholly). And, of course, determinations in their turn require other determinations to determine them; which is why *saṅkhārā* are themselves *saṅkhatā*. Thus, a sheet of paper is *for* wiping up a mess, which is *for* having my room clean, which is *for* my personal comfort, which is *for* attending to my concerns, which is *for* my future comfort. Cf. Heidegger, *op. cit.*, p. 63 *et seq.*

determined' (which includes consciousness), we must not conclude that the determinations in 'determinations are a condition for consciousness' (*saṅkhārapaccayā viññāṇaṃ*) are determinations *because* they are a condition for consciousness: on the contrary, they are a condition for consciousness *because* they are determinations. Thus, *vitakkavicārā* determine *vacī*, which is why they are called *vacīsaṅkhāra*; and it is as a *saṅkhāra* that they are a condition for *viññāṇa*. In particular, *puññābhisaṅkhāra*, *apuññābhisaṅkhāra*, and *āneñjābhisaṅkhāra*, are *cetanā* that determine *viññāṇa* as *puññūpaga*, *apuññūpaga*, and *āneñjūpaga*, respectively. They are certain *intentions* determining certain consciousnesses. Since they *determine* something (no matter what), these intentions are *determinations* (as stated in the *Khajjanīyasutta*). *As* determinations they are a condition for *consciousness*. And as *puthujjana*'s determinations they are a condition for *puthujjana*'s consciousness (which is always *puññūpaga*, *apuññūpaga*, or *āneñjūpaga*). Exactly *why* determinations are a condition for consciousness will be discussed later.

**16.** There is nothing to add to what was said about *kāyasaṅkhāra*, *vacīsaṅkhāra*, and *cittasaṅkhāra*, in §5, except to note that we occasionally encounter in the Suttas the terms *kāyasaṅkhāra*, *vacīsaṅkhāra*, and *manosaṅkhāra* (not *cittasaṅkhāra*). These are to be understood (see *Nidāna/Abhisamaya Saṃy.* iii,5 (S.ii,40)) as *kāyasañcetanā*, *vacīsañcetanā*, and *manosañcetanā*, and should not be confused with the former triad.[g] Other varieties of *saṅkhārā* met with in the Suttas (e.g. *āyusaṅkhārā*, 'what life

g. So far are the expressions *cittasaṅkhāra* and *manosaṅkhāra* from being interchangeable that their respective definitions actually seem to be mutually exclusive. *Cittasaṅkhāra* is *saññā ca vedanā ca*; *manosaṅkhāra* is *manosañcetanā*; and the passage from the *Saḷāyatana Saṃyutta* (ix,10) quoted in §5 makes an explicit distinction between *vedanā*, *cetanā*, and *saññā*. But the two expressions are really quite different in kind, and are not to be directly opposed to each other at all. (i) The *citta* of *cittasaṅkhāra* is not synonymous with the *mano* of *manosaṅkhāra*: *citta*, here, means (conscious) experience generally, whereas *mano* distinguishes *thought* from *word* and *deed*. (ii) The word *saṅkhāra* has a different sense in the two cases: in the first it means 'determination' in a quite general sense (§11); in the second it is a particular *kind* of determination, *viz* intention or volition. (iii) The two compounds are grammatically different: *cittasaṅkhāra* is a *dutiya* (accusative) *tappurisa*, *cittaṃ* + *saṅkhāro*, 'that which determines mind (*citta*)'; *manosaṅkhāra* is a *tatiya* (instrumentive) *tappurisa*, *manasā* + *saṅkhāro*, 'determination (intention or volition) by mind (*mano*)', i.e. mental action (as opposed to verbal and bodily action)—cf. *Majjhima* vi,7 (M.i,389). Clearly enough (ii) and (iii) will apply *mutatis mutandis* to the two senses of the expressions *kāyasaṅkhāra* and *vacīsaṅkhāra*.

depends on', in *Majjhima* v,3 (M.i,295)), do not raise any particular difficulty. We shall henceforth take it for granted that the essential meaning of *saṅkhāra* is as defined in §11.

17. Consider now this phrase: *Tisso imā bhikkhave vedanā aniccā saṅkhatā paṭiccasamuppannā...*[18] (*Vedanā Saṃy.* i,9 (S.iv,214)). We see in the first place that what is *saṅkhata* is *anicca*; this we already know from the discussion in §12. In the second place we see that to be *saṅkhata* and to be *paṭiccasamuppanna* are the same thing. This at once tells us the purpose of *paṭiccasamuppāda* formulations, namely to show, by the indirect method of §12, that all the items mentioned therein are impermanent, since each depends upon the preceding item. The question may now arise, 'What about the first item—since there is no item preceding it, is it therefore permanent?'. In several Suttas (*Dīgha* ii,1 (D.ii,32); *Nidāna/Abhisamaya Saṃy.* vii,5 (S.ii,104); *ibid.* vii,7 (S.ii,112-5)) the series runs back to *nāmarūpapaccayā saḷāyatanaṃ, viññāṇapaccayā nāmarūpaṃ*, and then forward again with *nāmarūpapaccayā viññāṇaṃ*[19]. This is remarked upon by the Buddha (*Dīgha* ii,1 & *Nidāna/Abhisamaya Saṃy.* vii,5) as follows: *Paccudāvattati kho idaṃ viññāṇaṃ nāmarūpamhā nāparaṃ gacchati; ettāvatā jāyetha vā jīyetha vā mīyetha vā cavetha vā uppajjetha vā yadidaṃ nāmarūpapaccayā viññāṇaṃ, viññāṇapaccayā nāmarūpaṃ, nāmarūpapaccayā saḷāyatanaṃ,*[20] and so on. In this formulation it is clear that there is no 'first item with no item preceding it'—*nāmarūpa* depends upon *viññāṇa*, and *viññāṇa* depends upon *nāmarūpa*, each being determined by the other. If the *puthujjana* decides upon *viññāṇa* as 'self', he finds its permanence undermined by the impermanence of *nāmarūpa*; and if he decides upon *nāmarūpa* as 'self', its permanence is undermined by the impermanence of *viññāṇa*. (We may note in passing that the traditional interpretation of *nāmarūpa* as 'mind-&-matter'—see *Visuddhimagga* Ch. XVIII—is quite mistaken. *Rūpa* is certainly 'matter' (or perhaps 'substance'), but *nāma* is *not* 'mind'. Further discussion is out of place here, but see *SN*, NĀMA. We may, provisionally, translate as 'name-&-matter'.)

18. Since to be *saṅkhata* and to be *paṭiccasamuppanna* are one and the same thing, we see that each item in the series of §17 is preceded by a *saṅkhāra* upon which it depends, and that therefore the total collection of items in the series depends upon the total collection of their respective *saṅkhārā*. In this sense we might say that the total collection of items is *saṅkhārapaccayā*. But since this statement means only that each and every particular item of the series depends upon a particular *saṅkhāra*, it does

not say anything fresh. *Saṅkhārapaccayā*, however, can be understood in a different way: instead of 'dependent upon a collection of particular *saṅkhārā*', we can take it as meaning 'dependent upon the fact that there *are* such things as *saṅkhārā*'. In the first sense *saṅkhārapaccayā* is the equivalent of *paṭiccasamuppanna* ('dependently arisen'), and applies to a given series *as a collection of particular items*; in the second sense *saṅkhārapaccayā* is the equivalent of *paṭiccasamuppāda* ('dependent arising'), and applies to a given series *as the exemplification of a structural principle*. In the second sense it is true quite generally of *all* formulations of *paṭiccasamuppāda*, and not merely of *this* formulation (since any other formulation will consist of some other set of particular items). *Paṭiccasamuppāda* is, in fact, a structural principle (formally stated in the first Sutta passage[7] at the head of this Note), and not one or another specific chain of *saṅkhārā*. It is thus an over-simplification to regard any one given formulation in particular terms as *paṭiccasamuppāda*. Every such formulation *exemplifies* the principle: none states it. Any *paṭiccasamuppāda* series, purely in virtue of its being an exemplification of *paṭiccasamuppāda*, depends upon the fact that there *are* such things as *saṅkhārā*; and *a fortiori* the series of §17 depends upon the fact of the existence of *saṅkhārā*: if there were no such things as *saṅkhārā* there would be no such thing as *paṭiccasamuppāda* at all, and therefore no such thing as this individual formulation of it.

**19.** But though it is an over-simplification to regard any one series as *paṭiccasamuppāda*, it is not entirely wrong. For we find a certain definite set of items (*viññāṇa*, *nāmarūpa*, *saḷāyatana*, *phassa*, and so on) recurring, with little variation (*Dīgha* ii,2 (D.ii,56),[86] for example, omits *saḷāyatana*), in almost every formulation of *paṭiccasamuppāda* in particular terms. The reason for this recurrence is that, though *paṭiccasamuppāda* is a structural principle, the Buddha's Teaching is concerned with a particular problem, and therefore with a particular application of this principle. The problem is suffering and its cessation; the sphere in which this problem arises is the sphere of experience, of sentient existence or being; and the particular items, *viññāṇa*, *nāmarūpa*, and the rest, are the fundamental categories of this sphere. In consequence of this, the series, *nāmarūpapaccayā viññāṇaṃ*, *viññāṇapaccayā nāmarūpaṃ*, *nāmarūpapaccayā saḷāyatanaṃ*, *saḷāyatanapaccayā phasso*, and so forth, is the fundamental exemplification of *paṭiccasamuppāda* in the Buddha's Teaching, and the particular items are the basic *saṅkhārā*. (See *SN*, KAMMA for a Sutta passage where the *paṭiccasamuppāda* is exemplified on an entirely different level. Failure to understand that *paṭiccasamuppāda* is essentially a structural principle with widely different applications leads to confusion.) These particular items, then, being the fundamental categories in terms of which experience is described, are present in all experience; and this basic formulation of *paṭiccasamuppāda* tells us that they are all dependent, ultimately, upon *viññāṇa* (this is obviously so, since without consciousness there is no experience).[h] But since all these items, including *viññāṇa*, are dependent upon *saṅkhārā*, the series as a whole is *saṅkhārapaccayā*. (Though this is true in both the senses discussed in §18, the first sense yields us merely a tautology, and it is only the second sense of *saṅkhārapaccayā* that interests us.) If, therefore, we wish to express this fact, all we have to say is *saṅkhārapaccayā viññāṇaṃ*. Since *saṅkhārapaccayā* (in the sense that interests us) is the equivalent of *paṭiccasamuppāda*, *saṅkhārapaccayā viññāṇaṃ* presumably means '*viññāṇa* is *paṭiccasamuppāda*'. Let us try to expand this phrase.

20. Any given experience involves *paṭiccasamuppāda*, but it may do so in a number of different ways at once, each of which cuts across the others. Thus (experience of) the body is inseparable from (experience of) breathing, and (experience of) speaking is inseparable from (experience of) thinking; and both (experience of) breathing and (experience of) thinking are therefore *saṅkhārā*. But in all experience, as its fundamental categories and basic *saṅkhārā*, there are *viññāṇa*, *nāmarūpa*, and so on. Thus whenever there is breathing (*kāyasaṅkhāra*), or thinking (*vacīsaṅkhāra*), or, of course, perception and feeling (*cittasaṅkhāra*), there are *viññāṇa*, *nāmarūpa*, and so on, which also are *saṅkhārā*. Similarly, all experience is *intentional*: it is inseparable (except for the *arahat*) from *puññābhisaṅkhāra*, *apuññābhisaṅkhāra*, and *āneñjābhisaṅkhāra*. But in all experience, once again, there are *viññāṇa*, *nāmarūpa*, and so on, its fundamental categories and basic *saṅkhārā*.[i] In other words, *any* exempli-

---

**h.** *Viññāṇa*, being the *presence* of the phenomenon, of what is present, is negative as regards essence. Other things can be described directly by way of their positive essence as this or that, but not consciousness. Consciousness, however, is necessary before any other thing can be described; for if something is to be described it must first be present in experience (real or imaginary), and its presence is consciousness. Since consciousness can be described only as that upon which other things depend, it is the *existential determination* and nothing else. This will explain also what follows. (Note that the word *existential* is used here in the simple sense of a thing's existence as opposed to its essence, and not in the pregnant sense of *bhava*. See *SN*, VIÑÑĀṆA.)

**i.** See also the heterogeneous series of items (*pariyesanā*, *lābha*, and so on) appearing in the middle of the *paṭiccasamuppāda* formulation of *Dīgha* ii,2 (D.ii,58).

fication of *paṭiccasamuppāda* in the sphere of experience can be re-stated in the form of the *fundamental* exemplification of *paṭiccasamuppāda* in the sphere of experience, which is, as it must be, that beginning with *viññāṇa*. Thus *viññāṇa* and *paṭiccasamuppāda* are one. This, then, is the meaning of *saṅkhārapaccayā viññāṇaṃ*; this is why 'with determinations as condition there is consciousness'.

**21.** This discussion may perhaps have made it clear why *saṅkhārā* in the usual twelve-factored *paṭiccasamuppāda* series can include such a mixed collection of things as intentions of merit, demerit, and imperturbability, in-&-out-breaths, thinking-&-pondering, and perception and feeling. These things, one and all, are things that other things depend on, and as such are *saṅkhārā* of one kind or another; and so long as there are *saṅkhārā* of any kind at all there is *viññāṇa* and everything dependent upon *viññāṇa*, in other words there is *paṭiccasamuppāda*. (We may ignore the irrelevant exception of *āyusaṅkhāra* and *saññāvedayitanirodha*, lying outside the sphere of experience. See *Majjhima* v,3 (M.i,295).) Conversely, *viññāṇa* (and therefore *paṭiccasamuppāda*) ceases to exist when *saṅkhārā* of all kinds have ceased. (It might be asked why *kāyasaṅkhāra* and the other two are singled out for special mention as *saṅkhārā*. The answer seems to be that it is in order to show progressive cessation of *saṅkhārā* in the attainment of *saññāvedayitanirodha*—see *Majjhima* v,4 (M.i,301) and *Vedanā Saṃy.* ii,1 (S.iv,216)—or, more simply, to show that so long as there is *paṭiccasamuppāda* there is body, speech, or (at least) mind.)

**22.** It should be borne in mind that *paṭiccasamuppāda anulomaṃ* ('with the grain'—the *samudaya sacca*) always refers to the *puthujjana*, and *paṭilomaṃ* ('against the grain'—the *nirodha sacca*) to the *arahat*. *Avijjāpaccayā saṅkhārā* is true of the *puthujjana*, and *avijjānirodhā saṅkhāranirodho* is true of the *arahat*. This might provoke the objection that so long as the *arahat* is living he breathes, thinks-&-ponders, and perceives and feels; and consequently that cessation of *avijjā* does not bring about general cessation of *saṅkhārā*. It is right to say that with a living *arahat* there is still consciousness, name-&-matter, six bases, contact, and feeling, but only in a certain sense. Actually and in truth (*saccato thetato*, which incidentally has nothing to do with *paramattha sacca*, 'truth in the highest (or absolute) sense', a fallacious notion much used in the traditional exegesis—see *PS*) there is, even in this very life, no *arahat* to be found (e.g. *Avyākata Saṃy.* 2 (S.iv,384)—see *PS* §4 (a)); and though there is certainly consciousness and so on, there is no apparent 'self' *for whom* there is consciousness. *Yena viññāṇena Tathāgataṃ paññāpayamāno paññāpeyya, taṃ viññāṇaṃ Tathāgatassa pahīnaṃ ucchinnamūlaṃ tālāvatthukataṃ anabhāvakataṃ āyatiṃ anuppādadhammaṃ; viññāṇasankhāya vimutto kho mahārāja Tathāgato...*[21] (*Avyākata Saṃy.* 1 (S.iv,379)). There is no longer any consciousness pointing (with feeling and the rest) to an existing 'self' and with which that 'self' might be identified. And in the *Kevaddhasutta* (*Dīgha* i,11 (D.i,223)), *viññāṇaṃ anidassanaṃ*,[j] which is the *arahat*'s 'non-indicative consciousness', is also *viññāṇassa nirodho.* While the *arahat* yet lives, his consciousness is *niruddha*, or 'ceased', for the reason that it is *ananuruddha-appaṭiviruddha* (*Majjhima* ii,1 (M.i,65)). In the same way, when there is no longer any apparent 'self' to be contacted, contact (*phassa*) is said to have ceased: *Phusanti phassā upadhiṃ paṭicca / Nirūpadhiṃ kena phuseyyum phassā* [22] (*Udāna* ii,4 (Ud.12)). This matter has already been touched upon in §§10 & 15. (See also *SN*, VIÑÑĀṆA & PHASSA.)

**23.** *Saṅkhārapaccayā viññāṇaṃ*, as we now see, can be taken to mean that any specific series of *saṅkhāra-saṅkhatadhamma* pairs (one or more) of which the first contains *viññāṇa* is dependent upon the very fact that there are *saṅkhārā* at all. *Avijjāpaccayā saṅkhārā* will then mean that the very fact that there are *saṅkhārā* at all is dependent upon *avijjā*; and with cessation of *avijjā—avijjānirodhā*—all *saṅkhārā* whatsoever will cease—*saṅkhāranirodhā*. This is perhaps most simply stated in the lines from the *Vinaya Mahāvagga*: *Ye dhammā hetuppabhavā / Tesaṃ hetuṃ Tathāgato āha / Tesañ ca yo nirodho / Evaṃvādī mahāsamaṇo.*[24] Here, *Ye dhammā hetuppabhavā* are all things whatsoever that depend upon *hetū* ('conditions'—synonymous with *paccayā*). Since each of these things depends upon its respective *hetu* (as in any *paṭiccasamuppāda* formulation), it shares the same fate as its *hetu*—it is present when the *hetu* is present, and absent when the *hetu* is absent. Thus the *hetu* of them taken as a whole (*all* things that are *hetuppabhavā*) is no different from the *hetu* of their individual *hetū* taken as a whole. When there are *hetū* at all there are *hetuppabhavā dhammā*, when there are no *hetū* there are no *hetuppabhavā dhammā*; and *hetū*, being nothing else than *saṅkhārā*, have *avijjā* as condition. *Tesaṃ hetuṃ* ('their condition'), therefore, is

j. In the line *Viññāṇaṃ anidassanaṃ anantaṃ sabbatopahaṃ*[23], the compound *sabbatopahaṃ* (in *Majjhima* v,9 (M.i,329), *sabbatopabhaṃ*) is probably *sabbato* + *apahaṃ* (or *apabhaṃ*) from *apahoti*, *a* + *pahoti* (or *apabhavati* (*apabhoti*)). (Note that in the *Majjhima* passage preceding this line there is a Burmese v.l., *nāpahosi* for *nāhosi*.)

*avijjā*. To see the Dhamma is to see *paṭiccasamuppāda* (as noted in §7), and *avijjā* is therefore *non*-seeing of *paṭiccasamuppāda*. *Avijjāpaccayā saṅkhārā* will thus mean '*paṭiccasamuppāda* depends upon non-seeing of *paṭiccasamuppāda*'. Conversely, seeing of *paṭiccasamuppāda* is cessation of *avijjā*, and when *paṭiccasamuppāda* is seen it loses its condition ('non-seeing of *paṭiccasamuppāda*') and ceases. And this is cessation of all *hetuppabhavā dhammā*. Thus *tesaṃ yo nirodho* is cessation of *avijjā*.

24. We must now again ask the question of §17: 'What about the first item of the *paṭiccasamuppāda* formulation—since there is no item preceding it, is it therefore permanent?'. The first item is now *avijjā*, and the Buddha himself answers the question in a Sutta of the *Aṅguttara Nikāya* (X,vii,1 (A.v,113)). This answer is to the effect that *avijjā* depends upon not hearing and not practising the Dhamma. It is not, however, the only way of answering the question, as we may see from the *Sammādiṭṭhisutta* (*Majjhima* i,9 (M.i,54)). Here we find that *avijjā* depends upon *āsavā*, and *āsavā* depend upon *avijjā*. But one of the *āsavā* is, precisely, *avijj'āsava*, which seems to indicate that *avijjā* depends upon *avijjā*.[k] Let us see if this is so. We know that *saṅkhārā* depend upon *avijjā*—*avijjāpaccayā saṅkhārā*. But since something that something else depends upon is a *saṅkhāra*, it is evident that *avijjā* is a *saṅkhāra*. And, as before, *saṅkhārā* depend upon *avijjā*. Thus *avijjā* depends upon *avijjā*. Far from being a logical trick, this result reflects a structural feature of the first importance.[l] Before discussing it, however, we must note that this result leads us to expect that any condition upon which *avijjā* depends will itself involve *avijjā* implicitly or explicitly. (In terms of §23 the foregoing argument runs thus. *Avijjāpaccayā saṅkhārā* may be taken as 'with non-seeing of *paṭiccasamuppāda* as condition there is *paṭiccasamuppāda*'. But this itself is seen only when *paṭiccasamuppāda* is seen; for *paṭiccasamuppāda* cannot be seen as *paṭiccasamuppanna before paṭiccasamuppāda* is seen. To see *avijjā* or non-seeing, *avijjā* or non-seeing must cease. *Avijjā* therefore comes *first*; for, being its own condition, it can have no anterior term that does not itself involve *avijjā*.)

**k.** Cf. *Avijjā kho bhikkhu eko dhammo yassa pahānā bhikkhuno avijjā pahīyati vijjā uppajjatī ti.*[25] *Saḷāyatana Saṃy.* viii,7 (S.iv,50)

**l.** On the charge of 'circularity' that common sense may like to bring here, see Heidegger, *op. cit.*, pp. 314-6.

**25.** The faculty of *self-observation* or *reflexion* is inherent in the structure of our experience. Some degree of reflexion is almost never entirely absent in our waking life, and in the practice of mindfulness it is deliberately cultivated. To describe it simply, we may say that one part of our experience is immediately concerned with the world as its object, while at the same time another part of our experience is concerned with the immediate experience as its object. This second part we may call *reflexive* experience. (Reflexion is discussed in greater detail in *SN* & *FS*.) It will be clear that when there is *avijjā* there is *avijjā* in *both* parts of our experience, the immediate and the reflexive; for though, in reflexion, experience is divided within itself, it is still one single, even if complex, structure. The effect of this may be seen from the *Sabbāsavasutta* (*Majjhima* i,2 (M.i,8)) wherein certain wrong views are spoken of. Three of them are: *Attanā va attānaṃ sañjānāmī ti; Attanā va anattānaṃ sañjānāmī ti;* and *Anattanā va attānaṃ sañjānāmī ti*[26]. A man with *avijjā*, practising reflexion, may identify 'self' with both reflexive and immediate experience, or with reflexive experience alone, or with immediate experience alone. He does *not* conclude that *neither* is 'self', and the reason is clear: it is not possible to get outside *avijjā* by means of reflexion alone; for however much a man may 'step back' from himself to observe himself he cannot help taking *avijjā* with him. There is just as much *avijjā* in the self-observer as there is in the self-observed. (See *SN*, CETANĀ (b).) And this is the very reason why *avijjā* is so stable in spite of its being *saṅkhatā*.[m] Simply by reflexion the *puthujjana* can never observe *avijjā* and at the same time *recognize* it as *avijjā*; for in reflexion *avijjā* is the Judge as well as the Accused, and the verdict is always 'Not Guilty'. In order to put an end to *avijjā*, which is a matter of recognizing *avijjā* as *avijjā*, it is necessary to accept on trust from the Buddha a Teaching that contradicts the direct evidence of the *puthujjana*'s reflexion. This is why the Dhamma is *paṭisotagāmī* (*Majjhima* iii,6 (M.i,168)), or 'going *against* the stream'. The Dhamma gives the *puthujjana* the *outside* view of *avijjā*, which is inherently unobtainable for him by unaided reflexion (in the *ariyasāvaka* this view has, as it were, 'taken' like a graft, and is perpetually available). Thus it will be seen that *avijjā* in reflexive experience (actual or potential) is the condition for *avijjā* in immediate experience.

---

**m.** The *Aṅguttara* Sutta (X,vii,1) referred to in §24 begins thus: *Purimā bhikkhave koṭi na paññāyati avijjāya, Ito pubbe avijjā nāhosi, atha pacchā sambhavī ti. Evañ ce taṃ bhikkhave vuccati, atha ca pana paññāyati, Idapaccayā avijjā ti. Avijjaṃ p'ahaṃ bhikkhave sāhāraṃ vadāmi, no anāhāraṃ*[27]. (In the P.T.S. edition, for *c'etaṃ* read *ce taṃ* and adjust punctuation.)

It is possible, also, to take a second step back and reflect upon reflexion; but there is still *avijjā* in this self-observation of self-observation, and we have a third layer of *avijjā* protecting the first two. And there is no reason in theory why we should stop here; but however far we go we shall not get beyond *avijjā*. The hierarchy of *avijjā* can also be seen from the Suttas in the following way.

*Katamā pan'āvusoavijjā ...*
*Yaṃ kho āvuso dukkhe aññāṇaṃ,*
*dukkhasamudaye aññāṇaṃ,*
*dukkhanirodhe aññāṇaṃ,*
*dukkhanirodhagāminīpaṭipadāya aññāṇaṃ,*
*ayaṃ vuccat'āvuso avijjā.* (*Majjhima* i,9 (M.i,54))
*Katamañ ca bhikkhave dukkhaṃ ariyasaccaṃ ...*
*Katamañ ca bhikkhave dukkhasamudayaṃ ariyasaccaṃ ...*
*Katamañ ca bhikkhave dukkhanirodhaṃ ariyasaccaṃ ...*
*Katamañ ca bhikkhave dukkhanirodhagāminīpaṭipadā ariyasaccaṃ.*
*Ayam eva ariyo aṭṭhangiko maggo,*
*seyyathīdaṃ sammādiṭṭhi ...*
*Katamā ca bhikkhave sammādiṭṭhi ...*
*Yaṃ kho bhikkhave dukkhe ñāṇaṃ,*
*dukkhasamudaye ñāṇaṃ,*
*dukkhanirodhe ñāṇaṃ,*
*dukkhanirodhagāminīpaṭipadāya ñāṇaṃ,*
*ayaṃ vuccati bhikkhave sammādiṭṭhi.*[28]
(*Dīgha* ii,9 (D.ii,305-12))

*Avijjā* is non-knowledge of the four noble truths. *Sammādiṭṭhi* is knowledge of the four noble truths. But *sammādiṭṭhi* is part of the four noble truths. Thus *avijjā* is non-knowledge of *sammādiṭṭhi*; that is to say, non-knowledge of knowledge of the four noble truths. But since *sammādiṭṭhi*, which is knowledge of the four noble truths, is part of the four noble truths, so *avijjā* is non-knowledge of knowledge *of knowledge* of the four noble truths. And so we can go on indefinitely. But the point to be noted is that each of these successive stages represents an additional layer of (potentially) reflexive *avijjā*. Non-knowledge of knowledge of the four noble truths is non-knowledge of *vijjā*, and non-knowledge of *vijjā* is failure to recognize *avijjā* as *avijjā*. Conversely, it is evident that when *avijjā* is once recognized anywhere in this structure it must vanish everywhere; for knowledge of the four noble truths entails knowledge of knowledge of the four noble truths, and *vijjā* ('science') replaces *avijjā* ('nescience') throughout.[n]

**n.** Compare also the following:

*Rūpā (Saddā ... Dhammā) loke piyarūpaṃ sātarūpaṃ, etth'esā taṇhā uppajjamānā uppajjati ettha nivisamānā nivisati ... Rūpataṇhā (Saddataṇhā ... Dhammataṇhā) loke piyarūpaṃ sātarūpaṃ, etth'esā taṇhā uppajjamānā uppajjati ettha nivisamānā nivisati.*

And the converse:

*... etth'esā taṇhā pahīyamānā pahīyati ettha nirujjhamānā nirujjhati.*[29]

*Dīgha* ii,9 (D.ii,308-11)

Not only is there craving, but there is craving for craving as a condition for craving: indifference to craving destroys it. (*Taṇhā*, be it noted, is not the coarse hankering after what we do *not* have (which is *abhijjhā* or covetousness), but the subtle craving for *more* of what we have. In particular, I *am* because I *crave to be*, and with cessation of craving-for-being (*bhavataṇhā*, which is itself dependent on *avijjā* and, like it, without first beginning—*Aṅguttara* X,vii,2 (A.v,116)), 'I am' ceases. *Bhavataṇhā*, in fact, is the craving for more craving on which craving depends.)

# 2. PARAMATTHA SACCA

1. In *Bhikkhunī Saṃyutta* 10 (S.i,135) we find these verses.

*Māro pāpimā:*
*Kenāyaṃ pakato satto, kuvaṃ sattassa kārako,*
*Kuvaṃ satto samuppanno, kuvaṃ satto nirujjhatī ti.*
*Vajirā bhikkhunī:*
*Kin nu Sattoti paccesi, Māra, diṭṭhigataṃ nu te,*
*Suddhasaṅkhārapuñjo'yaṃ, nayidha sattūpalabbhati;*
*Yathā hi aṅgasambhārā hoti saddo Ratho iti,*
*Evaṃ khandhesu santesu hoti Satto ti sammuti.*
*Dukkham eva hi sambhoti, dukkhaṃ tiṭṭhati veti ca,*
*Nāññatra dukkhā sambhoti, nāññaṃ dukkhā nirujjhatī ti.*[30]

Let us consider them in some detail.

2. The speculative questions in the first two lines are of the same order as those of the *assutavā puthujjana* in the *Sabbāsavasutta* (*Majjhima* i,2 (M.i,8)) ending with: *Etarahi vā paccuppannam addhānaṃ ajjhattaṃ kathaṃkathī hoti, Ahan nu kho'smi, no nu kho'smi, kin nu kho'smi, kathan nu kho'smi, ayan nu kho satto kuto āgato, so kuhiṃgāmī bhavissatī ti*[31]. The word *satta* is found in both, and clearly with the same meaning. The *puthujjana* is speculating about himself, and *satta* in this context is himself considered, with a certain detachment, as a creature; it is a creature regarded, in one way or another, as a 'self'; for the *puthujjana* takes what appears to be his 'self' at face value—he regards himself as a 'self' (see *SN*, ATTĀ). It is the *puthujjana*'s concept of a creature. The third line (the first of the reply to Māra) confirms this; for Māra is asked, a little rhetorically perhaps, why he refers to 'the creature', why he has this involvement in (wrong) view. 'The creature' is an involvement in (wrong) view, *diṭṭhigata*, precisely when the creature is regarded in some way as 'self'; for this is *sakkāyadiṭṭhi* or 'personality-view', the view that *one is, in essence, somebody* (see *SN*, SAKKĀYA).

And the following passage: *Kim pana tvaṃ Poṭṭhapāda attānaṃ paccesī ti. Oḷārikaṃ kho aham bhante attānaṃ paccemi... Manomayaṃ kho aham bhante attānaṃ paccemi... Arūpiṃ kho aham bhante attānaṃ paccemi...*[32] (*Dīgha* i,9 (D.i,185)) allows us to understand *Satto ti paccesi*, reference to 'the creature', in exactly the same way, namely, the taking of the creature as 'self'.

3. *Suddhasaṅkhārapuñjo'yaṃ* follows at once; for if the regarding of the creature as 'self' is *sakkāyadiṭṭhi*, then the creature so regarded is *sakkāya*, which is the *pañc'upādānakkhandhā* (*Majjhima* v,4 (M.i,299)). And the *pañc'upādānakkhandhā* are *saṅkhārā* if they are what something else depends upon. What depends upon them? *Na kho āvuso Visākha taññeva upādānaṃ te pañc'upādānakkhandhā, na pi aññatra pañcah'upādānakkhandhehi upādānaṃ. Yo kho āvuso Visākha pañcas'upādānakkhandhesu chandarāgo taṃ tattha upādānan ti.*[33] (*Majjhima* v,4 (M.i,299)) *Upādāna*, therefore, depends upon the *pañc'upādānakkhandhā* (as we may also see from the usual *paṭiccasamuppāda* formulation). And the fundamental *upādāna* is *attavāda*, belief in 'self'. (See *NP* §§10, 12, & 13. Compare also *Khandha Saṃy.* ix,1 (S.iii,105): *Rūpaṃ upādāya Asmī ti hoti no anupādāya; vedanaṃ ... ; saññaṃ ... ; saṅkhāre ... ; viññāṇaṃ upādāya Asmī ti hoti no anupādāya*[34].)

4. *Nayidha sattūpalabbhati* now presents no difficulty. The *puthujjana* takes his apparent 'self' at face value and identifies it with the creature: the creature, for him, is 'self'—*Satto ti pacceti*. He does not see, however, that this identification is dependent upon his holding a belief in 'self', *attavād'upādāna*, and that this, too, is *anicca saṅkhata paṭiccasamuppanna*; for were he to see it, *upādāna* would vanish, and the deception would become clear—*Evam eva kho Māgandiya ahañ c'eva te dhammaṃ deseyyaṃ, Idan taṃ ārogyaṃ idan taṃ nibbānan ti, so tvaṃ ārogyaṃ jāneyyāsi nibbānaṃ passeyyāsi, tassa te saha cakkhuppādā yo pañcas'upādānakkhandhesu chandarāgo so pahīyetha; api ca te evam assa, Dīgharattaṃ vata bho ahaṃ iminā cittena nikato vañcito paladdho; ahaṃ hi rūpaṃ yeva upādiyamāno upādiyiṃ, vedanaṃ yeva ..., saññaṃ yeva ..., saṅkhāre yeva..., viññāṇaṃ yeva upādiyamāno upādiyim*[35] (*Majjhima* viii,5 (M.i,511)). With the vanishing of belief in 'self' the identification would cease. The *ariyasāvaka*, on the other hand, sees the creature as *pañc'upādānakkhandhā*; he sees that *upādāna* is dependent upon these *pañc'upādānakkhandhā*; and he sees that the *puthujjana* is a victim of *upādāna* and is making a mistaken identification. He sees that since the creature is *pañc'upādānakkhandhā* it cannot in any way be identified as 'self'; for if it could, 'self' would be impermanent, determined, dependently arisen; and the *ariyasāvaka* knows direct from his

own experience, as the *puthujjana* does not, that perception of selfhood, of an inherent *mastery* over things, and perception of impermanence are incompatible. Thus *nayidha sattūpalabbhati*, 'there is, here, no "creature" to be found', means simply 'there is, in this pile of pure determinations, no creature to be found such as conceived by the *puthujjana*, as a "self"'. The *Alagaddūpamasutta* (*Majjhima* iii,2 (M.i,138)) has *Attani ca bhikkhave attaniye ca saccato thetato anupalabbhamāne* ...[36], and the meaning is no different. The words *saccato thetato*, 'in truth, actually', mean 'in the (right) view of the *ariyasāvaka*, who sees *paṭiccasamuppāda* and its cessation'.[a]

5. The next two lines (5 & 6) contain the simile of the chariot. Just as the word 'chariot' is the name given to an assemblage of parts, so when the *khandhā* are present common usage speaks of a 'creature'. What is the purpose of this simile? In view of what has been said above the answer is not difficult. The *assutavā puthujjana* sees clearly enough that a chariot is an assemblage of parts: what he does *not* see is that the creature is an assemblage of *khandhā* (*suddhasaṅkhārapuñja*), and this for the reason that he regards it as 'self'. For the *puthujjana* the creature exists as a 'self' exists, that is to say, as an extra-temporal monolithic whole ('self' could never be either a thing of parts or part of a thing).[b] The simile shows him his mistake by pointing out that a creature exists as a chariot exists, that is to say, as a temporal complex of parts. When he sees this he no longer regards the creature as 'self', and, with the giving up of *sakkāyadiṭṭhi*, he ceases to be a *puthujjana*.

6. The final two lines (7 & 8) may be discussed briefly. It is in the nature of the *pañc'upādānakkhandhā* to press for recognition, in one way or another, as 'self'; but the *ariyasāvaka*, with his perception of impermanence, can no longer heed their persistent solicitation; for a mastery over things (which is what selfhood would claim to be; cf. *Majjhima* iv,5 (M.i,231-2)

---

**a.** The question discussed here, whether *saccato thetato* a 'self' is to be found, must be kept clearly distinct from another question, discussed in *NP* §22, *viz* whether *saccato thetato* the Tathāgata (or an *arahat*) is to be found (*diṭṭh'eva dhamme saccato thetato Tathāgate anupalabbhamāne* ...[37] *Avyākata Saṃy.* 2 (S.iv,384)). The reason why the Tathāgata is not to be found (even here and now) is that he is *rūpa-*, *vedanā-*, *saññā-*, *saṅkhāra-*, and *viññāṇa-saṅkhāya vimutto* (*ibid.* 1 (S.iv,378-9)), i.e. free from reckoning as matter, feeling, perception, determinations, or consciousness. This is precisely *not* the case with the *puthujjana*, who, *in this sense*, actually and in truth *is* to be found.

**b.** Cf. '*La nature même de notre être répugne à ce qui a des parties et des successions.*'—J. Grenier, *Absolu et Choix*, P.U.F., Paris 1961, p. 44. ('What has parts and successions is repugnant to the very nature of our being.')

& *Khandha Saṃy.* vi,7 (S.iii,66)[84])—a mastery over things that is seen to be undermined by impermanence is at once also seen to be no mastery at all, but a false security, for ever ending in betrayal. And this is *dukkha.* (See *SN*, DHAMMA.) Thus, when *attavād'upādāna* has been removed, there supervenes the right view that it is only *dukkha* that arises and *dukkha* that ceases. *Upāy'upādānābhinivesavinibaddho khvāyaṃ Kaccāyana loko yebhuyyena; tañ cāyaṃ upāy'upādānaṃ cetaso adhiṭṭhānābhinivesānusayaṃ na upeti na upādiyati nādhiṭṭhāti, Attā me ti. Dukkham eva uppajjamānaṃ uppajjati, dukkhaṃ nirujjhamānaṃ nirujjhatī ti na kaṅkhati na vicikicchati, aparapaccayā ñāṇam ev'assa ettha hoti. Ettāvatā kho Kaccāyana sammādiṭṭhi hoti.*[38] *Nidāna/Abhisamaya Saṃy.* ii,5 (S.ii,17)

7. The question now arises whether the word *satta*, which we have been translating as 'creature', can be used to denote an *arahat*. Once it is clear that, in a right view, nothing is to be found that can be identified as 'self', the application of the word *satta* becomes a question of usage. Is *satta* simply *pañc'upādānakkhandhā*—in which case it is equivalent to *sakkāya*—, or can it be applied also to *pañcakkhandhā*, as the sixth line might seem to suggest? If the latter, then (at least as applied to deities and human beings) it is equivalent to *puggala*, which is certainly used in the Suttas to refer to an *arahat* (who is the first of the *aṭṭhapurisapuggalā*),[c] and which can be understood in the obvious sense of one set of *pañcakkhandhā* as distinct from all other sets—an *arahat* is an 'individual' in the sense that one *arahat* can be distinguished from another. It is not a matter of great importance to settle this question (which is simply a matter of finding Sutta passages—e.g. *Khandha Saṃy.* iii,7 (S.iii,30); *Rādha Saṃy.* 2 (S.iii,190); *Aṅguttara* V,iv,2 (A.iii,35)—that illustrate and fix the actual usage of the word). It is of infinitely more importance to understand that the *puthujjana* will misapprehend *any* word of this nature that is used (*attā*, 'self'; *bhūta*, 'being'; *pāṇa*, 'animal'; *sakkāya*, 'person, somebody'; *purisa*, 'man'; *manussa*, 'human being'; and so on), and that the *ariyasāvaka* will not.

* * *

**8.** It is quite possible that the notion of *paramattha sacca*, 'truth in the highest, or ultimate, or absolute, sense' was in existence before the time of the *Milindapañha*; but its use there (Pt. II, Ch. 1) is so clear and unambiguous

c. The *diṭṭhisampanna* (or *sotāpanna*) is the *sattama puggala* or 'seventh individual'. *Aṅguttara* VI,v,12 (A.iii,373)

that that book is the obvious point of departure for any discussion about it. The passage quotes the two lines (5 & 6) containing the simile of the chariot. They are used to justify the following argument. The word 'chariot' is the conventional name given to an assemblage of parts; but if each part is examined individually it cannot be said of any one of them that it is the chariot, nor do we find any chariot in the parts collectively, nor do we find any chariot outside the parts. Therefore, 'in the highest sense', *there exists no chariot*. Similarly, an 'individual' (the word *puggala* is used) is merely a conventional name given to an assemblage of parts (parts of the body, as well as *khandhā*), and, 'in the highest sense', *there exists no individual*. That is all.

**9**. Let us first consider the validity of the argument. If a chariot is taken to pieces, and a man is then shown the pieces one by one, each time with the question 'Is this a chariot?', it is obvious that he will always say no. And if these pieces are gathered together in a heap, and he is shown the heap, then also he will say that there is no chariot. If, finally, he is asked whether apart from these pieces he sees any chariot, he will still say no. But suppose now that he is shown these pieces assembled together in such a way that the assemblage can be used for conveying a man from place to place; when he is asked he will undoubtedly assert that there *is* a chariot, that the chariot *exists*. According to the argument, the man was speaking in the *conventional* sense when he asserted the existence of the chariot, and in the *highest* sense when he denied it. But, clearly enough, the man (who has had no training in such subtleties) is using ordinary conventional language throughout; and the reason for the difference between his two statements is to be found in the fact that on one occasion he was shown a chariot and on the others he was not. If a chariot is taken to pieces (even in imagination) it ceases to be a chariot; for a chariot is, precisely, a vehicle, and a heap of components is *not* a vehicle—it is a heap of components. (If the man is shown the heap of components and asked 'Is this a heap of components?', he will say yes.) In other words, a chariot is most certainly an assemblage of parts, but it is an assemblage of parts *in a particular functional arrangement*, and to alter this arrangement is to destroy the chariot. It is no great wonder that a chariot cannot be found if we have taken the precaution of destroying it before starting to look for it. If a man sees a chariot in working order and says 'In the highest sense there is no chariot; for it is a mere assemblage of parts', all he is saying is 'It is possible to take this chariot to pieces and to gather them in a heap; and when this is done there will no longer be a chariot'. The argument, then, does not show the non-existence of the chariot; at best it merely asserts that an existing chariot can be destroyed. And when it is applied to an individual (i.e. a set of *pañcakkhandhā*) it is even less valid; for not only does it *not* show the non-existence of the individual, but since the functional arrangement of the *pañcakkhandhā* cannot be altered, even in imagination, it asserts an impossibility, that an existing individual can be destroyed. As applied to an individual (or a creature) the argument runs into contradiction; and to say of an individual 'In the highest sense there is no individual; for it is a mere asemblage of *khandhā*' is to be unintelligible.

10. What, now, is the reason for this argument? Why has this notion of 'truth in the highest sense' been invented? We find the clue in the *Visuddhimagga*. This work (Ch. XVIII) quotes the last four lines (5, 6, 7, & 8) and then repeats in essence the argument of the *Milindapañha*, using the word *satta* as well as *puggala*. It goes on, however, to make clear what was only implicit in the *Milindapañha*, namely that the purpose of the argument is to remove the conceit '(I) am' (*asmimāna*): if it is seen that 'in the highest sense', *paramatthato*, no creature exists, there will be no ground for conceiving that *I* exist. This allows us to understand why the argument was felt to be necessary. The *assutavā puthujjana* identifies himself with the individual or the creature, which he proceeds to regard as 'self'. He learns, however, that the Buddha has said that 'actually and in truth neither self nor what belongs to self are to be found' (see the second Sutta passage in §4). Since he cannot conceive of the individual except in terms of 'self', he finds that in order to abolish 'self' he must abolish the individual; and he does it by this device. But the device, as we have seen, abolishes nothing. It is noteworthy that the passage in the *Milindapañha* makes no mention at all of 'self': the identification of 'self' with the individual is so much taken for granted that once it is established that 'in the highest sense there is no individual' no further discussion is thought to be necessary. Not the least of the dangers of the facile and fallacious notion 'truth in the highest sense' is its power to lull the unreflecting mind into a false sense of security. The unwary thinker comes to believe that he understands what, in fact, he does not understand, and thereby effectively blocks his own progress.

# 3. SHORTER NOTES

## *ATAKKĀVACARA*

Sometimes translated as 'unattainable by reasoning' or 'not accessible to doubt'. But the Cartesian *cogito ergo sum* is also, in a sense, inaccessible to doubt; for I cannot doubt my existence without tacitly assuming it. This merely shows, however, that one cannot get beyond the *cogito* by doubting it. And the Dhamma *is* beyond the *cogito*. The *cogito*, then, can be reached by doubt—one doubts and doubts until one finds what one cannot doubt, what is inaccessible to doubt, namely the *cogito*. But the Dhamma cannot be reached in this way. Thus the Dhamma, though certainly inaccessible to doubt, is more than that; it is altogether beyond the sphere of doubt. The rationalist, however, does not even reach the inadequate *cogito*, or if he does reach it[a] he overshoots the mark (*atidhāvati—Itivuttaka* II,ii,12 (Iti. 43)); for he starts from the axiom that everything can be doubted (including, of course, the *cogito*). Cf. also *Majjhima* xi,2 (M.ii,232-3) & i,2 (M.i,8). See NIBBĀNA.

---

**a.** When he is being professional, the rationalist will not allow that what is inaccessible to doubt is even intelligible, and he does not permit himself to consider the *cogito*; but in his unprofessional moments, when the personal problem becomes insistent, he exorcizes the *cogito* by supposing that it is a rational proposition, which enables him to doubt it, and then to deny it. '*Les positivistes ne font qu'exorciser le spectre de l'Absolu, qui reparaît cependant toujours et vient les troubler dans leur repos.*'—J. Grenier, *op. cit.*, p. 44. ('The positivists do nothing but exorcize the spectre of the Absolute, which however always reappears and comes to trouble them in their sleep.') For Grenier, the Absolute is not (as with Bradley) the totality of experiences, but is to be reached at the very heart of personality by a thought transcending the relativity of all things, perceiving therein a void (pp. 100-1). Precisely—and what, ultimately, is this Absolute but *avijjā*, self-dependent and without first beginning? And what, therefore, does the Buddha teach but that this Absolute is *not* absolute, that it can be brought to an end? See *NP* §§24 & 25.

## *ATTĀ*

In the *arahat*'s reflexion what appears reflexively is only *pañcakkhandhā*, which he calls 'myself' simply for want of any other term. But in the *puthujjana*'s reflexion what appears reflexively is *pañc'upādānakkhandhā*, or *sakkāya*; and *sakkāya* (q.v.), when it appears reflexively, appears (in one way or another) as being and belonging to an extra-temporal changeless 'self' (i.e. a soul). The *puthujjana* confuses (as the *arahat* does not) the *self*-identity of simple reflexion—as with a mirror, where the *same* thing is seen from two points of view at once ('the thing itself', 'the selfsame thing')—with the 'self' as the *subject* that appears in reflexion—'my self' (i.e. 'I itself', i.e. 'the *I* that appears when *I* reflect'). For the *puthujjana* the word *self* is necessarily ambiguous, since he cannot conceive of any reflexion not involving reflexive experience of the subject—i.e. not involving manifestation of a soul. Since the *self* of self-identity is involved in the structure of the subject appearing in reflexion ('my self' = 'I itself'), it is sometimes taken (when recourse is not had to a supposed Transcendental Being) as the basic principle of all subjectivity. The subject is then conceived as a hypostasized play of reflexions of one kind or another, the hypostasis itself somehow deriving from (or being motivated by) the play of reflexions. The *puthujjana*, however, does not see that attainment of *arahattā* removes all trace of the desire or conceit '(I) am', leaving the entire reflexive structure intact—in other words, that subjectivity is a parasite on experience. Indeed, it is by his very failure to see this that he remains a *puthujjana*.

The question of *self-identity* arises *either* when a thing is seen from two points of view at once (as in reflexion,[a] for example; or when it is at the same time the object of two different senses—I am now both looking at my pen and touching it with my fingers, and I might wonder if it is the *same* pen in the two simultaneous experiences (see RŪPA)), *or* when a thing is seen to *endure* in time, when the question may be asked if it continues to be the *same* thing (the answer being, that a thing at any one given level of generality is the *invariant of a transformation*—see ANICCA (a) & *FS*—, and

**a.** In immediate experience the thing is present; in reflexive experience the thing is again present, but as implicit in a more general thing. Thus in reflexion the thing is *twice* present, once immediately and once reflexively. This is true of reflexion both in the loose sense (as reflection or discursive thinking) and *a fortiori* in the stricter sense (for the reason that reflection involves reflexion, though not *vice versa*). See MANO and also VIÑÑĀṆA (d).

that 'to remain the same' *means* just this).[b] With the question of a thing's self-identity (which presents no particular difficulty) the Buddha's Teaching of *anattā* has nothing whatsoever to do: *anattā* is purely concerned with 'self' as *subject*. (See PAṬICCASAMUPPĀDA (c).)

'Self' as *subject* can be briefly discussed as follows. As pointed out in PHASSA (b), the *puthujjana* thinks 'things are *mine* (i.e. are my concern) because I am, because I exist'. He takes the subject ('I') for granted; and if things are appropriated, that is because *he*, the subject, exists. The *diṭṭhisampanna* (or *sotāpanna*) sees, however, that this is the wrong way round. He sees that the notion 'I am' arises *because* things (so long as there is any trace of *avijjā*) present themselves as 'mine'. This significance (or intention, or determination), 'mine' or 'for me'—see *NP* (e)—, is, in a sense, a *void*, a *negative* aspect of the present thing (or existing phenomenon), since it simply *points to a subject*; and the *puthujjana*, not seeing impermanence (or more specifically, not seeing the impermanence of this ubiquitous determination), deceives himself into supposing that there actually exists a subject—'self'—independent of the object (which latter, as the *diṭṭhisampanna* well understands, is merely the *positive* aspect of the phenomenon—that which is 'for me'). In this way it may be seen that the *puthujjana*'s experience, *pañc'upādānakkhandhā*, has a *negative* aspect (the subject) and a *positive* aspect (the object). But care is needed; for, in fact, the division subject/object is not a simple negative/positive division. If it were, only the positive would be present (as an existing phenomenon) and the negative (the subject) would not be present *at all*—it would simply not exist. But the subject is, in a sense, phenomenal: it (or he) is an existing phenomenal negative, a *negative that appears*; for the *puthujjana* asserts the present reality of his 'self' ('the irreplaceable being that I am'). The fact is, that the intention or determination 'mine', pointing to a subject, is a complex structure involving *avijjā*. The subject is not simply a negative in relation to the positive object: it (or he) is *master* over the object, and is thus a kind of positive negative, a master who does not appear explicitly but who, somehow or other, nevertheless *exists*.[c] It is

**b.** 'It takes two to make the same, and the least we can have is some change of event in a self-same thing, or the return to that thing from some suggested difference.'—F.H. Bradley, *The Principles of Logic*, Oxford (1883) 1958, I,v,§1.

**c.** With the exception of consciousness (which cannot be directly qualified—see VIÑÑĀṆA (c)—every determination has a positive as well as a negative aspect: it is positive in so far as it *is* in itself something, and negative in so far as it is *not* what it determines. This is evident enough in the case of a thing's potentialities, which are given as images (or absents) together with the real (or present) thing. But the positive negativity of the subject, which is what concerns us here, is by no means such a simple affair: the

this master whom the *puthujjana*, when he engages in reflexion, is seeking to identify—in vain![d] This delusive mastery of subject over object must be rigorously distinguished from the *reflexive* power of control or choice that is exercised in voluntary action by *puthujjana* and *arahat* alike.

For a discussion of *sabbe dhammā anattā* see DHAMMA.

---

subject presents itself (or himself), at the same time, as certainly more elusive, and yet as no less *real*, than the object.

Images are present as absent (or negative) reality, but *as images* (or images of images) they are present, or real. Also, being plural, they are more elusive, individually, than reality, which is singular (see NĀMA). The imaginary, therefore, in any given part of it, combines reality with elusiveness; and it is thus easily supposed that what is imaginary is subjective and what is real is objective. But imagination survives the disappearance of subjectivity (*asmimāna, asmī ti chanda*): *Saṃvijjati kho āvuso Bhagavato mano, vijānāti Bhagavā manasā dhammaṃ, chandarāgo Bhagavato n'atthi, suvimuttacitto Bhagavā*[39]. *Saḷāyatana Saṃy.* xviii,5 (S.iv.164) The elusiveness of images is not at all the same as the elusiveness of the subject. (It is in this sense that science, in claiming to deal only with reality, calls itself objective.)

**d.** 'I urge the following dilemma. If your Ego has no content, it is nothing, and it therefore is not experienced; but if on the other hand it is anything, it is a phenomenon in time.'—F.H. Bradley, *Appearance and Reality*, Oxford (1893) 1962, Ch. XXIII.

# *ANICCA*

*Aniccatā* or 'impermanence', in the Buddha's Teaching, is sometimes taken as a 'doctrine of universal flux', or continuous change of condition. This is a disastrous over-simplification—see PAṬICCASAMUPPĀDA (c).

In the *Khandha Saṃyutta* (iv,6 (S.iii,38)) it is said of *rūpa, vedanā, saññā, saṅkhārā,* and *viññāṇa*: *uppādo paññāyati; vayo paññāyati; ṭhitassa aññathattaṃ paññāyati*[40].[a] These three *saṅkhatassa saṅkhatalakkhaṇāni* (*Aṅguttara* III,v,7 (A.i,152)), or characteristics whereby what is determined (i.e. a *saṅkhata dhamma*) may be known as such (i.e. as *saṅkhata*), concisely indicate the fundamental structure in virtue of which things are *things*—in virtue of which, that is to say, things are distinct, one from another. It is also in virtue of this structure that all experience, including the *arahat*'s, is intentional (see CETANĀ) or teleological (i.e. that things are *significant*, that they point to other, possible, things—e.g. a *hammer* is a thing for hammering, and what it is for hammering is *nails*; or, more subtly, a particular shade

---

**a.** Cf. *'La "chose" existe d'un seul jet, comme "forme" [Gestalt], c'est-à-dire comme un tout qui n'est affecté par aucune des variations superficielles et parasitaires que nous pouvons y voir. Chaque* ceci *se dévoile avec une loi d'être qui détermine son* seuil, *c'est-à-dire le niveau de changement où il cessera d'être ce qu'il est pour n'être plus, simplement.'*—J.-P. Sartre, *op. cit.*, pp. 256-7. ('The "thing" exists all at once, as a "configuration", that is to say as a whole that is unaffected by any of the superficial and parasitic variations that we may see there. Each *this* is revealed with a law of being that determines its *threshold*, that is to say the level of change where it will cease to be what it is, in order, simply, to be no more.' (The occurrence of the word *parasitic* both here and in *(c)* below is coincidental: two different things are referred to. Should we not, in any case, prefer the single word *subordinate* to *superficial and parasitic*?))

The third characteristic, *ṭhitassa aññathattaṃ*, occurs as 'Invariance under Transformation' (or similar expressions, e.g. 'Unity in Diversity' or 'Identity in Difference') in idealist logic (Bradley) and in relativity and quantum theories. The branch of mathematics that deals with it is the theory of groups.

This third characteristic answers the question *What?*—i.e. 'Is this the same thing that was, or is it another?' (see ATTĀ)—: it does *not*, as the argument *Na ca so na ca añño* in the *Milindapañha* mistakenly implies, answer the question *Who*? If the answer were quite as simple as that, it would not take a Buddha to discover it—a Bradley would almost do. In other words, the question of impermanence is not *simply* that of establishing these three characteristics. See NA CA SO for a discussion of the illegitimacy of the question *Who*? (It is perhaps being over-charitable to the *Milinda* to associate its argument with the three *saṅkhatalakkhaṇāni*: the *Milinda* is probably thinking in terms of flux or continuous change. Bradley, while accepting the principle of identity on the *ideal* level, does not reject a *real* continuous change: we may possibly not be wrong in attributing some such view to the *Milinda* in its interpretation of the Dhamma. See PAṬICCASAMUPPĀDA (C).)

of a particular colour is just *that* shade by pointing to all the other distinct shades that it *might* be, while yet remaining the same colour, but actually is *not* (cf. Spinoza's dictum '*Omnis determinatio est negatio*')).[b] The *arahat*'s experience, as stated above, is teleological, as is the *puthujjana*'s; but with the *arahat* things no longer have the particular significance of being 'mine'. This special significance, dependent upon *avijjā*, is not of the same kind as a thing's simple intentional or teleological significances, but is, as it were, a parasite upon them. Detailed consideration of this structure and its implications seems to lead to the solution of a great many philosophical problems, but these are no more than indirectly relevant to the understanding of the Buddha's Teaching.[c] Some people, however, may find that a description of this structure provides a useful instrument for thinking with. (See *FS*.)

For a discussion of *sabbe saṅkhārā aniccā* see DHAMMA.

---

**b.** McTaggart, in *The Nature of Existence* (Cambridge 1921-7, §§149-54), remarks that philosophers have usually taken the expressions 'organic unity' and 'inner teleology' as synonymous (the aspect of *unity* becoming the *end* in the terminology of the latter conception), and that they distinguish 'inner teleology' from 'external teleology', which is what we normally call volition. Without discussing McTaggart's views, we may note that the distinction between 'inner' and 'external' teleology is simply the distinction between immediate and reflexive intention. *Every* situation is an organic unity, whether it is a cube or bankruptcy we are faced with.

**c.** Some description of the complex parasitic structure of appropriatedness, of being mastered or in subjection ('mine'—see PHASSA), seems not impossible; but it is evidently of much less practical consequence to make such a description—supposing, that is to say, that it could actually be done—than to see how it *might* be made. For if one sees this (it would appear to be a matter of describing the peculiar weightage—see CETANĀ—of the special unitary intention 'mine', *superposed* on all other weightage, immediate or reflexive), then one *already* has seen that appropriatedness is in fact a parasite.

## *KAMMA*

Verses 651, 652, and 653, of the *Suttanipāta* are as follows:

651 *Kassako kammanā hoti, sippiko hoti kammanā,*
*vāṇijo kammanā hoti, pessiko hoti kammanā.*
652 *Coro pi kammanā hoti, yodhājīvo pi kammanā,*
*yājako kammanā hoti, rājā pi hoti kammanā.*
653 *Evam etaṃ yathābhūtaṃ kammaṃ passanti paṇḍitā*
*paṭiccasamuppādadasā kammavipākakovidā.*[41]

Verse 653 is sometimes isolated from its context and used to justify the 'three-life' interpretation of the twelve-factored formulation of *paṭiccasamuppāda* as *kamma/kammavipāka-kamma/kammavipāka*, an interpretation that is wholly inadmissible (see PAṬICCASAMUPPĀDA and *NP*). When the verse is restored to its context the meaning is clear: *kammaṃ paṭicca kassako hoti, sippiko hoti*, and so on; in other words, what one is *depends* on what one does. And the *result* (*vipāka*) of *acting* in a certain way is that one is known accordingly. For *vipāka* used in this sense see *Aṅguttara* VI,vi,9 (A. iii,413): *Vohāravepakkāhaṃ bhikkhave saññā vadāmi; yathā yathā naṃ sañjānāti tathā tathā voharati, Evaṃ saññī ahosin ti. Ayaṃ vuccati bhikkhave saññānaṃ vipāko*[42]. (For the usual meaning of *kammavipāka* as the more or less delayed retribution for ethically significant actions, see e.g. *Aṅguttara* III,iv,4 (A.i,134-6) [The P.T.S. numbering has gone astray here].)

The question of *kamma* or 'action'—'What should I do?'—is the *ethical* question; for all personal action—all action done by *me*—is either *akusala* or *kusala*, unskilful or skilful. Unskilful action is rooted in *lobha* (*rāga*), *dosa*, *moha*, or lust, hate, and delusion, and (apart from resulting in future *dukkha* or unpleasure) leads to arising of action, not to cessation of action—*taṃ kammaṃ kammasamudayāya saṃvattati na taṃ kammaṃ kammanirodhāya saṃvattati*[43]. Skilful action is rooted in non-lust, non-hate, and non-delusion, and leads to cessation of action, not to arising of action. (*Aṅguttara* III,xi,7&8 (A.i,263)) The *puthujjana* does not understand this, since he sees neither arising nor cessation of action;[a] the *diṭṭhisampanna*

a. A *puthujjana* may adopt a set of moral values for any of a number of different reasons—faith in a teacher, acceptance of traditional or established values, personal philosophical views, and so on—, but in the last analysis the necessity of moral values, however much he may feel their need, is not for him a matter of self-evidence. At the end of his book (*op. cit.*, p. 111) Jean Grenier writes: '*En fait toutes les attitudes que*

does understand this, since he sees both arising and cessation of action—*Yato kho āvuso ariyasāvako akusalañ ca pajānāti akusalamūlañ ca pajānāti, kusalañ ca pajānāti kusalamūlañ ca pajānāti, ettāvatā pi kho āvuso ariyasāvako sammādiṭṭhi hoti ujugatā'ssa diṭṭhi, dhamme aveccappasādena samannāgato, āgato imaṃ saddhammaṃ*[44] (*Majjhima* i,9 (M.i,46))—; the *arahat* not only understands this, but also has reached cessation of action, since for him the question 'What should *I* do?' no more arises. To the extent that there is still intention in the case of the *arahat*—see CETANĀ (f)—there is still conscious action, but since it is neither unskilful nor skilful it is no longer action in the ethical sense. Extinction, *nibbāna*, is cessation of ethics—*Kullūpamaṃ vo bhikkhave ājānantehi dhammā pi vo pahātabbā pageva adhammā*[45] (*Majjhima* iii,2 (M.i,135)).[b] See MAMA (a).

For a brief account of action see NĀMA; for a definition see RŪPA (b).

---

*nous avons passées en revue au sujet du choix ne se résignent à l'absence de vérité que par désespoir de l'atteindre et par suite des nécessités de l'action. Elles n'aboutissent toutes qu'à des morales provisoires. Un choix, au sens plein du mot, un "vrai" choix n'est possible que s'il y a ouverture de l'homme à la vérité; sinon il n'y a que des compromis de toutes sortes: les plus nobles sont aussi les plus modestes.'* ('In fact all the attitudes we have passed in review on the subject of choice are resigned to the absence of truth only out of despair of attaining it and as a consequence of the necessities of action. They end up, all of them, only at provisional moralities. A choice, in the full sense of the word, a "real" choice is possible only if man has access to the truth; if not there are only compromises of all kinds: the noblest are also the most modest.') And Sartre, more bleakly, concludes (*op. cit.*, p. 76) that man is bound by his nature to adopt values of one sort or another, and that, although he cannot escape this task of choosing, he himself is totally responsible for his choice (for there is no Divine Dictator of values), and there is absolutely nothing in his nature that can justify him in adopting this particular value or set of values rather than that. The *puthujjana* sees neither a task to be performed that can justify his existence—not even, in the last analysis, that of perpetual reflexion (Heidegger's *Entschlossenheit* or 'resoluteness', acceptance of the guilt of existing; which does no more than make the best of a bad job)—nor a way to bring his unjustifiable existence to an end. The *ariyasāvaka*, on the other hand, does see the way to bring his existence to an end, and he sees that it is this very task that justifies his existence. *Ariyaṃ kho ahaṃ brāhmaṇa lokuttaraṃ dhammaṃ purisassa sandhanaṃ paññāpemi.*[46] *Majjhima* x,6 (M.ii,181)

**b.** Hegel, it seems, in his *Phänomenologie des Geistes*, has said that there can only be an ethical consciousness in so far as there is disagreement between nature and ethics: if ethical behaviour became natural, conscience would disappear. And from this it follows that if ethical action is the absolute aim, the absolute aim must also be the absence of ethical action. This is quite right; but *is* ethical action the absolute aim? The difficulty is, precisely, to *see* the action that puts an end to action in the ethical sense. Whereas unskilful action is absolutely blameworthy as leading only to future unpleasure and to the arising of action, there is action, leading to a bright future, that yet does not lead to

# *CITTA*

*Cittavīthi*, 'mental process, cognitive series'. *Visuddhimagga*, Ch. XIV etc. It is, perhaps, not superfluous to remark that this doctrine, of which so much use is made in the *Visuddhimagga* (and see also the *Abhidhammatthasaṅgaha*), is a pure scholastic invention and has nothing at all to do with the Buddha's Teaching (or, indeed, with anything else). It is, moreover, a vicious doctrine, totally at variance with *paṭiccasamuppāda*, setting forth the arising of experience as a succession of items each coming to an end before the next appears (*imassa nirodhā idaṃ uppajjati*—cf. *NP* §7). The decay first seems to set in with the *Vibhaṅga* and *Paṭṭhāna* of the *Abhidhamma Piṭaka*. (See SAÑÑĀ, and refer to '*The Path of Purification*' (*Visuddhimagga* translation by the Ven. Ñāṇamoli Bhikkhu), Semage, Colombo 1956, Ch. IV, note 13.)

Connected with this doctrine is the erroneous notion of *anuloma-gotrabhu-magga-phala*, supposed to be the successive moments in the attainment of *sotāpatti*. It is sometimes thought that the word *akālika* as applied to the Dhamma means that attainment of *magga* is followed 'without interval of time' by attainment of *phala*; but this is quite mistaken.[a] *Akālika dhamma* has an entirely different meaning (for which see PAṬICCASAMUPPĀDA). Then, in the *Okkantika Saṃyutta* (S.iii, 225) it is stated only that the

---

the ending of action. See *Majjhima* vi,7 (M.i,387-92). The generous man, the virtuous man, the man even who purifies his mind in *samādhi*, without right view remains a *puthujjana*, and so does not escape reproach: *Yo kho Sāriputta imañ ca kāyaṃ nikkhipati aññañ ca kāyaṃ upādiyati tam ahaṃ Sa-upavajjo ti vadāmi*[47]. *Majjhima* xv,2 (M.iii,266)

**a.** The notion of two successive 'moments', A and B, as *akālika* or non-temporal is a confusion. Either A and B are *simultaneous* (as e.g. *viññāṇa* and *nāmarūpa*), in which case they are indeed *akālika*; or B follows A and they are *successive* (as e.g. the in-&-out-breaths), in which case they are *kālika*. Even if there is no interval of time between the ending of A and the beginning of B, it remains true that B comes *after* A, and *time* is still involved. The source of the confusion is in the contradictory idea of a moment as the smallest possible interval of time—i.e. as *absolute* shortness of time—, and therefore as *no* time. Two *successive* moments are, thus, also *no* time: 0 + 0 = 0. This is nothing but a mystification: it is like the notion of 'absolute smallness of size' in quantum theory (Dirac, *op. cit.*, pp. 3-4), introduced to compensate for other philosophically unjustifiable assumptions made elsewhere. (Quantum theory, of course, being an elaborate and ingenious rule of thumb, does not require philosophical justification; but *ipso facto* it provides no foundation for philosophy.) To the idea of a 'moment' as the shortest *empirically* observable interval of time there is no objection; but this merely marks the threshold below which changes are too small and rapid to be clearly apprehended as discontinuous and are grasped irrationally and ambiguously as a *flux*. What it does *not* mark is the boundary between *kālika* and *akālika*. See PAṬICCASAMUPPĀDA (c). A different approach to this whole question is outlined in *FS*.

*dhammānusārī* and the *saddhānusārī* (who have reached the *magga* leading to *sotāpatti*) are bound to attain *sotāpattiphala* before their death; and other Suttas—e.g. *Majjhima* vii,5&10 (M.i,439&479)—show clearly that one is *dhammānusārī* or *saddhānusārī* for more than 'one moment'. For *gotrabhu* see *Majjhima* xiv,12 (M.iii,256), where it says that he may be *dussīla pāpadhamma*. In Sutta usage it probably means no more than 'a member of the *bhikkhusaṅgha*'. For *anuloma* see SAKKĀYA (b).

See NĀMA (c) and the Glossary for meanings of *citta*. For *cittasaṅkhāra* as opposed to *manosaṅkhāra* see *NP* §§5 & 16.

# *CETANĀ*

See first, ANICCA, NĀMA, & *NP* (f). *Cetanā*, properly speaking, is 'intentional intention'—i.e. 'will' or 'volition'—, but the word *intention*, in its normal looser meaning, will include these, and is the best translation for *cetanā*. The following passage from Husserl's article 'Phenomenology' in the *Encyclopædia Britannica* may throw some light on a stricter or more philosophical sense of the word.

> But before determining the question of an unlimited psychology, we must be sure of the characteristics of psychological experience and the psychical data it provides. We turn naturally to our immediate experiences. But we cannot discover the psychical in any experience, except by a 'reflexion,' or perversion of the ordinary attitude. We are accustomed to concentrate upon the matters, thoughts, and values of the moment, and not upon the psychical 'act of experience' in which these are apprehended. This 'act' is revealed by a 'reflexion'; and a reflexion can be practised on every experience.[a] Instead of the matters themselves, the values, goals, utilities, etc., we regard the subjective[b] experiences in which these 'appear'. These 'appearances' are phenomena, whose nature is to be a 'consciousness-of' their ob-

---

**a.** Cf. 'Now by phenomenology Peirce means a method of examining any experience you please with a view to abstracting from it its most general and, as he claims, its absolutely necessary characteristics.'—W. B. Gallie, *Peirce and Pragmatism*, Penguin (Pelican) Books, London. The word 'abstracting' is unfortunate—see MANO (b). For more on 'reflexion' see DHAMMA (b) & ATTĀ (a).

**b.** Later in the same article Husserl speaks of the 'bare subjectivity of consciousness', thereby indicating that he identifies consciousness, in one way or another, with 'self'. He evidently accepts the *subject* revealed in reflexion (see ATTĀ) at face value, and regards it as consciousness (though for other *puthujjanā* it may be, instead, matter (substance) or feeling or perception or determinations or, in some way, all five—see *Khandha Saṃy.* v,5 (S.iii,46)). See VIÑÑĀṆA. This extract has to be taken with considerable reserve: Husserl's doctrine is not acceptable in detail.

Husserl goes on to make the following remarks. 'The "I" and "we," which we apprehend presuppose a hidden "I" and "we" to whom they are "present". ...But though the transcendental "I" (i.e. the reflexive "I" to whom the immediate "I" is revealed) is not my psychological "I," (i.e. the immediate "I" apprehended in reflexion) it must not be considered as if it were a second "I," for it is no more separated from my psychological "I" in the conventional sense of separation, than it is joined to it in the conventional sense of being joined.' Husserl seems to be aware that, taken in isolation, no single one of the trio of wrong views of the *Sabbāsavasutta* on the nature of reflexion—see *NP* §25—is adequate; but, also, he is unable to escape from them. So, by means of this

ject, real or unreal as it be. Common language catches this sense of 'relativity,' saying, I was thinking *of* something, I was frightened *of* something, etc. Phenomenological psychology takes its name from the 'phenomena' with the psychological aspect of which it is concerned: and the word 'intentional' has been borrowed from the scholastic to denote the essential 'reference' character of the phenomena. All consciousness is 'intentional'.

In unreflexive consciousness we are 'directed' upon objects, we 'intend' them; and reflexion reveals this to be an immanent process characteristic of all experience, though infinitely varied in form. To be conscious of something is no empty having of that something in consciousness. Each phenomenon has its own intentional structure, which analysis shows to be an ever-widening system of individually intentional and intentionally related components. The perception of a cube, for example, reveals a multiple and synthesized intention:[c] a continuous variety in the 'appearance' of the cube, according to the differences in the points of view from which it is seen, and corresponding differences in 'perspective', and all the differences between the 'front side' actually seen at the moment and the 'back side' which is not seen, and which remains, therefore, relatively 'indeterminate,' and yet is supposed equally to be existent. Observation of this 'stream' of 'appearance-aspects' [Sartre suggests 'profiles'] and of the manner of their synthesis, shows that every phase and interval is already in itself a 'consciousness-of' something, yet in such a way that with the constant entry of new phases the total consciousness, at any moment, lacks not synthetic unity, and is, in fact, a consciousness of one and the same object. The intentional structure of the train of a perception must conform to a certain type, if any physical object is to be perceived as There! And if the same object be intuited in other modes, if it be imagined, or remembered, or copied, all its intentional forms recur, though modified in character from what they were in the perception

---

ingenious verbal device, he attempts to combine them—and succeeds in falling, very elegantly, between three stools.

**c.** Bertrand Russell seems to say ('*Mysticism and Logic*', Penguin (Pelican) Books, London, VIIIth Essay) that a cube (or whatever it may be) is an *inference*, that all possible appearances of a cube are *inferred* from any single appearance. But this supposes that inference, which is a matter of logic or thinking (*takka*, *vitakka*), is fundamental and irreducible. Husserl, however, says that a cube is an *intention*. Note that *vitakka* does not go beyond first *jhāna*, whereas *cetanā* is present up to *ākiñcaññāyatana* (*Majjhima* xii,1 (M.iii, 25-9)).

> to correspond to their new modes. The same is true of every kind of psychical experience. Judgement, valuation, pursuit,—these also are no empty experiences, having in consciousness of judgements, values, goals and means, but are likewise experiences compounded of an intentional stream, each conforming to its own fast type.

Intentions may be regarded basically as the relation between the *actual* and the *possible*. A thing always presents itself from a particular point of view; there is an actual aspect together with a number of possible aspects.[d] The set of relations between the actual aspect and all the alternative aspects is the same, no matter which one of the various aspects should happen to be actual. It is in virtue of this that a thing remains the same, as the point of view changes. Intentions are the *significance of the actual aspect*; they are *every possible aspect*, and therefore the thing-as-a-whole. In intentional intention the possible aspects show themselves as possible, and the actual aspect, consequently, appears as *optional*. There is now exercise of *preference* (with the pleasant preferred to the unpleasant),[e] and this is volition in its simplest form. There is no limit, however, to the degree of reflexive complexity that may be involved—every reflexive attitude is itself optional. It will be seen that intentions by themselves are a purely structural affair, a

**d.** It seems that, at the first level of complexity, the actual aspect is *necessarily* accompanied by precisely *three* possible aspects (like a tetrahedron presenting any given face). For details see *FS* I. Cf. Bradley's acute observation (*op. cit.* (Logic), I,iv,§§13 & 14) that, in disjunctive judgement, where it is given that A is *b* or *c* (not both), though we can say with the certainty of knowledge that if A is *b* it is not *c*, we can say that if A is not *c* then it is *b* only if we make the assumption that, because we do not find a predicate of A that excludes *b* or *c* (i.e. *b*-or-*c*), therefore there is none. It now turns out that we do find such predicates and that the disjunction must be fourfold: if A is *b* or *c* it must be *b* or *c* or *d* or *e*. No doubt the only evident example is the three-dimensional nature of geometrical space, which can be represented by four points (the vertices of a tetrahedron), any one of which can be taken as the point of origin to the exclusion of the other three (which remain *possible*). (These mathematical illustrations are treacherous; they make things appear simpler than they are, and contain self-contradictions—'points', for example—; and the picture must be abandoned before it is allowed to mislead.)

**e.** This does not mean that what is preferred will necessarily be obtained; for each aspect, actual or possible, is presented with its own arbitrary inertia at the most immediate level of experience. Reflexive intention can only *modify* the *given* state of affairs. (Strictly, [there is] an arbitrary 'weightage' *prior* to (i.e. below) immediate intention; this is 'discovered' in a perspective by consciousness and immediate (involuntary) intention is a modification of it (and of that perspective); then reflexive intention is a modification of all this.) But, other things being equal, the pleasant dominates the unpleasant ('pleasant' and 'unpleasant' being understood here in their widest possible sense).

matter of negatives; and when the question is asked, 'What are the intentions *upon this occasion*?' the answer will be in the positive terms of *nāmarūpa* and *viññāṇa*.[f] We must also consider the matter of the difference of emphasis or 'weight' possessed by the various possible aspects: though each alternative to the actual aspect is *possible*, they are not all equally *probable* (or *potential*), and some stand out more prominently than others. The emphasized aspect may, of course, be the actual aspect as the negative of all the possible aspects; and this will tend to preserve the actual state of affairs. This is 'attention' (*manasikāra*) in its simplest terms: it may be described as 'direction of emphasis'. Clearly, there will be no intentional intention that does not involve attention. (A thing—a lump of iron, say—has many possible purposes; and these determine it for what it is; they are its intentions. But when the lump is to be used, one among these purposes must be attended to at the expense of the others—it cannot be used both for driving a nail into the wall and as a paper-weight at the same time.) And, naturally, where there is attention there is intentional intention (i.e. *cetanā*); and there is no consciousness without at least incipient attention. (I have taken attention as essentially reflexive, but it might be argued that there is already immediate attention as the perspective of immediate intention.)

**f.** Though there is intention (*cetanā*), both simple and reflexive (i.e. volition), in the *arahat*'s experience (*pañcakkhandhā*), there is no craving (*taṇhā*). In other words, there is, and there is not, intention with the *arahat*, just as there is, and there is not, consciousness (*viññāṇa*—q.v.). There is no consciousness without intention. Craving, however, is a gratuitous (though beginningless) parasite on the intentional structure described here, and its necessity is not to be deduced from the necessity of intention in all experience. Intention does *not* imply craving—a hard thing to understand! But if intention did imply craving, *arahattā* would be out of the question, and there would be no escape.

## *DHAMMA*

The word *dhamma*, in its most general sense, is equivalent to 'thing'—i.e. whatever is distinct from anything else (see ANICCA). More precisely it is *what* a thing is in itself, as opposed to *how* it is;[a] it is the *essence* or *nature* of a thing—that is, a thing *as* a particular essence or nature distinct from all other essences or natures. Thus, if a thing is a *solid pleasant shady tree for lying under that I now see*, its nature is, precisely, that it is *solid*, that it is *pleasant*, that it is *shady*, that it is a tree *for lying under*, and that it is *visible to me*. The solid pleasant shady tree for lying under that I see *is* a thing, a nature, a *dhamma*. Furthermore, each item severally—the solidity, the pleasantness, the shadiness, and so on—is a thing, a nature, a *dhamma*, in that each is distinct from the others, even though here they may not be independent of one another. These *dhammā*, in the immediate experience, are all *particular*. When, however, the *reflexive*[b] attitude is adopted (as it is in *satisampajañña*, the normal state of one practising the Dhamma), the particular nature—the solid pleasant shady tree for lying under that I see—is, as it were, 'put in brackets' (Husserl's expression, though not quite his meaning of it), and we arrive at the *nature* of the particular nature. Instead of *solid*, *pleasant*, *shady*, *tree for lying under*, *visible to me*, and so on, we have *matter* (or *substance*), *feeling*, *perception*, *determinations*, *consciousness*, and

---

**a.** *How* a thing is, is a matter of structure, that is to say, of intentions (*cetanā*) or determinations (*saṅkhārā*). See CETANĀ. These are essentially negative, whereas *dhamma* is positive.

**b.** This word is neither quite right nor quite wrong, but it is as good as any. See CETANĀ, MANO, and ATTĀ, and also *FS* (where, in Part I, the possibility of reflexion is shown to be structurally justified). The possibility of reflexion depends upon the fact that all experience (the five *khandhā* or aggregates) is hierarchically ordered in different levels of generality (or particularity), going to infinity in both directions. This supports another hierarchy, as it were 'at right angles' to the original hierarchy. In *immediacy*, attention rests on the world. This requires no effort. In *reflexion*, attention moves back one step from the world in this second hierarchy. It does not, however, move back spontaneously: it requires to be pulled back by an intention that embraces both the ground level and the first step. This pulling back of attention *is* reflexive intention. A *deliberate* entering upon reflexion requires a further reflexive intention; for deliberate intention is intention to intend (or volition). *Double* attention is involved. But though, in immediacy, attention rests at ground level, the entire reflexive hierarchy remains 'potential' (it is *there*, but not *attended to*), and immediacy is always under *potential reflexive observation* (i.e. it is *seen* but not *noticed*). Another way of saying this is that the 'potential' reflexive hierarchy—which we might call *pre-reflexive*—is a hierarchy of *consciousness* (*viññāṇa*), not of *awareness* (*sampajañña*). For awareness, reflexive intention is necessary.

all the various 'things' that the Suttas speak of. These things are of *universal* application—i.e. common to *all* particular natures (e.g. *eye-consciousness* is common to all things that have ever been, or are, or will be, *visible to me*)—and are the *dhammā* that make up the Dhamma. The Dhamma is thus the Nature of Things. And since this is what the Buddha teaches, it comes to mean also the Teaching, and *dhammā* are particular teachings. The word *matter*—'I will bear this matter in mind'—sometimes expresses the meaning of *dhamma* (though it will not do as a normal rendering).

*Sabbe saṅkhārā aniccā; Sabbe saṅkhārā dukkhā; Sabbe dhammā anattā.*[16] *Attā*, 'self', is fundamentally a notion of *mastery over things* (cf. *Majjhima* iv,5 (M.i,231-2) & *Khandha Saṃy.* vi,7 (S.iii,66)[84]). But this notion is entertained only if it is pleasurable,[c] and it is only pleasurable provided the mastery is assumed to be permanent; for a mastery—which is essentially a kind of absolute timelessness, an *unmoved* moving of things—that is undermined by impermanence is no mastery at all, but a mockery. Thus the regarding of a thing, a *dhamma*, as *attā* or 'self' can survive for only so long as the notion gives pleasure, and it only gives pleasure for so long as that *dhamma* can be considered as permanent (for the regarding of a thing as 'self' endows it with the illusion of a kind of super-stability in time). In itself, *as a* dhamma *regarded as* attā, its impermanence is not manifest (for it is pleasant to consider it as permanent); but when it is seen to be dependent upon *other dhammā* not considered to be permanent, its impermanence does then become manifest. To see impermanence in what is regarded as *attā*, one must emerge from the confines of the individual *dhamma* itself and see that *it depends on what is impermanent*. Thus *sabbe saṅkhārā* (not *dhammā*) *aniccā* is said, meaning 'All things that things (*dhammā*) depend

---

c. This notion is pleasurable only if it is itself taken as permanent (it is *my* notion); thus it does not escape *saṅkhāradukkha*. But unless this notion is brought to an end there is no escape from *saṅkhāradukkha*. The linchpin is carried by the wheel as it turns; but so long as it carries the linchpin the wheel will turn. (That 'self' is spoken of here as a *notion* should not mislead the reader into supposing that a purely abstract idea, based upon faulty reasoning, is what is referred to. The *puthujjana* does not by any means experience his 'self' as an abstraction, and this because it is not *rationally* that notions of subjectivity are bound up with nescience (*avijjā*), but *affectively*. Reason comes in (when it comes in at all) only in the second place, to make what it can of a *fait accompli*. *Avijjāsamphassajena bhikhave vedayitena phuṭṭhassa assutavato puthujjanassa, Asmī ti pi'ssa hoti, Ayaṃ ahaṃ asmī ti pi'ssa hoti, Bhavissan ti pi'ssa hoti,...*[48] *Khandha Saṃy.* v,5 (S.iii,46). And in *Dīgha* ii,2 (D.ii,66-8) it is in relation to feeling that the possible ways of regarding 'self' are discussed: *Vedanā me attā ti; Na h'eva kho me vedanā attā, appaṭisaṃvedano me attā ti; Na h'eva kho me vedanā attā, no pi appaṭisaṃvedano me attā, attā me vediyati vedanādhammo hi me attā ti.*[49])

on are impermanent'. A given *dhamma*, *as a* dhamma *regarded as* attā, is, on account of being so regarded, considered to be pleasant; but when it is seen to be dependent upon some other *dhamma* that, not being regarded as *attā*, is manifestly unpleasurable (owing to the invariable false perception of permanence, of super-stability, in one not free from *asmimāna*), then its own unpleasurableness becomes manifest. Thus *sabbe saṅkhārā* (not *dhammā*) *dukkhā* is said. When this is seen—i.e. when perception of permanence and pleasure is understood to be false—, the notion 'This *dhamma* is my *attā*' comes to an end, and is replaced by *sabbe dhammā anattā*. Note that it is the *sotāpanna* who, knowing and seeing that his perception of permanence and pleasure is false, is free from this notion of 'self', though not from the more subtle conceit '(I) am' (*asmimāna*);[d] but it is only the *arahat* who is entirely free from the (false) perception of permanence and pleasure, and 'for him' perception of impermanence is no longer unpleasurable. (See also *NP* §12 & *PS*.)

---

**d.** *Manifest* impermanence and unpleasurableness at a coarse level does not exclude (false) perception of permanence and pleasure at a fine level (indeed, manifest unpleasurableness *requires* false perception of permanence, as remarked above (this refers, of course, only to *saṅkhāradukkha*)). But the coarse notion of 'self' must be removed before the subtle conceit '(I) am' can go. What is not regarded as 'self' is more manifestly impermanent and unpleasurable (and, of course, not-'self') than what is so regarded. Therefore the indirect approach to *dhammā* by way of *saṅkhārā*. *Avijjā* cannot be pulled out like a nail: it must be unscrewed. See MAMA & SAṄKHĀRA.

## *NA CA SO*

*Na ca so na ca añño*, 'Neither he nor another'. This often-quoted dictum occurs in the *Milindapañha* somewhere, as the answer to the question 'When a man dies, who is reborn—he or another?'. This question is quite illegitimate, and any attempt to answer it cannot be less so. The question, in asking *who* is reborn, falls into *sakkāyadiṭṭhi*. It takes for granted the validity of the person as 'self'; for it is only about 'self' that this question—'Eternal (*so*) or perishable (*añño*)?'—can be asked (cf. PAṬICCASAMUPPĀDA, ANICCA (a), & SAKKĀYA). The answer also takes this 'self' for granted, since it allows that the question can be asked. It merely denies that this 'self' (which must be either eternal or perishable) is either eternal or perishable, thus making confusion worse confounded. *The proper way is to reject the question in the first place.* Compare *Aṅguttara* VI,ix,10 (A.iii,440), where it is said that the *diṭṭhisampanna* not only can *not* hold that the author of pleasure and pain was *somebody* (either himself or another) but also can *not* hold that the author was *not somebody* (neither himself nor another). The *diṭṭhisampanna* sees the *present* person (*sakkāya*) as arisen dependent upon *present* conditions and as ceasing with the cessation of these *present* conditions. And, seeing this, he does not regard the *present* person as *present* 'self'. Consequently, he does not ask the question *Who?* about the present. By inference—*atītānāgate nayaṃ netvā*[50] (cf. *Gāmaṇi Saṃy.* 11 (S.iv,328))[a]—he does not regard the *past* or *future* person as *past* or *future* 'self', and does not ask the question *Who?* about the past or the future. (Cf. Māra's question in line 2 of *PS* §1.)

(The *Milindapañha* is a particularly misleading book. See also ANICCA (a), PAṬICCASAMUPPĀDA (c), RŪPA (e), & *PS* §§8-10.)

**a.** *Dhamm'anvaye ñāṇaṃ* is knowledge dependent upon the inferability of the Dhamma—i.e. knowledge that the fundamental Nature of Things is invariable in time and can be inferred *with certainty* (unlike rational inference) from present to past or future. See *Nidāna/Abhisamaya Saṃy.* iv,3 (S.ii,58). In other words, generalization without abstraction—see MANO (b).

## *NĀMA*

In any experience (leaving out of account *arūpa*) there is a *phenomenon* that is *present* (i.e. that is cognized). The presence, or cognition, or consciousness, of the phenomenon is *viññāṇa* (q.v.). The phenomenon has two characteristics, *inertia* and *designation* (*paṭigha* and *adhivacana*). The *inertia* of a phenomenon is *rūpa* ('matter' or 'substance'), which may be seen also as its *behaviour*; and this *presents itself only in the passage of time (however short)*. (These four *mahābhūtā* are the general modes of behaviour or matter: *earthy*, or persistent and resistant, or solid; *watery*, or cohesive; *fiery*, or ripening, or maturing; *airy*, or tense, or distended, or moving. See RŪPA.) The *designation* of a phenomenon is *nāma* ('name'), which may be seen also as its *appearance* (the form or guise adopted by the behaviour, as distinct from the behaviour itself).[a] *Nāma* consists of the following (*Majjhima* i,9 (M.i,53)[78]): whether (the experience is) pleasant, unpleasant, or neutral (*vedanā* or 'feeling'); shape, colour, smell, and so on (*saññā* (q.v.) or 'perception (percepts)'); significance or purpose (*cetanā* (q.v.) or 'intention(s)'); engagement in experience (*phassa* (q.v.) or 'contact'); and (intentional) direction of emphasis (*manasikāra* or 'attention'). *Phassa* is included in *nāma* since *nāma*, in specifying *saññā*, necessarily specifies the pair of *āyatanāni* ('bases') and kind of *viññāṇa* involved (e.g. perception of sourness specifies tongue, tastes, and tongue-consciousness), whereas *rūpa* does not (inertia or behaviour does not specify its mode of appearance, visual, auditory, and so on): *nāma*, in other words, entails (but does not include) *viññāṇa*, whereas *rūpa* is simply 'discovered' by *viññāṇa* (see RŪPA). *Manasikāra* is included in *nāma* since, whereas *rūpa precedes manasikāra* (logically, not temporally: behaviour takes place whether it is attended to or not—the clock, for example, does not stop when I leave the

---

**a.** Inertia or behaviour, as just noted, is what we call 'matter' or 'substance', *rūpa*—and *nāma* is the appearance of *rūpa*—its 'name'. The appearance of *rūpa* is 'what it looks like', its description (though not the description of how [it] behaves). Conversely, *rūpa* is the behaviour of *nāma*—its 'matter'. So we get *nāmarūpa*, 'name-&-matter'. (N.B. Neither the use here of the word 'appearance' (= *manifestation*, as opposed to *substance*) nor our normal use of the word 'reality' (see (b) next page) has anything to do with the celebrated (and fictitious) distinctions between Appearance and Reality of Bradley and others. The idea that there is a so-called 'reality' behind or beyond phenomena ('mere appearance') is a mistake ('the illusion of hinder-worlds' in Nietzsche's phrase). Phenomena present themselves for what they are, and can be studied and described simply as they appear. But this is not to say that they are simple. Cf. Sartre, *op. cit.*, pp. 11-14.)

room), *nāma involves manasikāra*: experience is always particular or selective, one thing to the fore at once and the rest receding in the background. *Rūpa*, in other words, in order to appear—i.e. in order to be phenomenal as *nāmarūpa*—, must be *oriented*: a phenomenon cannot present all aspects at once with equal emphasis, but only in a perspective involving *manasikāra*. (*Manasikāra* is involved as an intentional modification of the perspective or direction of emphasis that is *given* at the most immediate level. Cf. CETANĀ (e) & Bradley, *op. cit.* (*Logic*), III/I, vi, §13.)

To be *present* is to be here-and-now; to be *absent* is to be here-and-then (then = *not* now; at some other time) or there-and-now (there = *not* here; at some other place) or there-and-then. *Attention* is (intentional) difference between presence and absence, i.e. between varying degrees of presence, of consciousness ('Let this be present, let that be absent!'). *Consciousness* is the difference between presence (in *any* degree) and utter non-presence (i.e. non-existence). (An image may be present or absent, but even if present it is always *absent reality*. Mind-consciousness, *manoviññāṇa*, is the presence of an image or, since an image can be absent, of an image of an image.)[b] *Intention* is the absent in relation to the present. Every present is necessarily accompanied by a number of absents—the present is singular, the absent is plural. Each absent is a *possibility* of the present, and the ordered total

---

**b.**

$$\text{Real} = \left\{\begin{array}{l}\text{Present}\\ \text{Central}\\ \text{Actual}\end{array}\right. \qquad \text{Imaginary} = \left\{\begin{array}{l}\text{Absent}\\ \text{Peripheral}\\ \text{Possible}\end{array}\right.$$

(The disjunctions 'central/peripheral' and 'actual/possible' (or 'certain/possible') represent two slightly different aspects of the more general 'present/absent': the former is as it is in strict reflexion, the latter is as it is in abstract judgement or discursive reflection—see MANO (b).) Although, relative to the *imaginary* of mental experience, five-base experience is *real*, yet, relative to what is *central* in a given field of five-base experience, whatever is *peripheral* in that field is already beginning to partake of the nature of the imaginary. In general, the further removed a thing is from the centre of consciousness the less real it is, and therefore the more imaginary. In mental experience proper, however, where there is more or less explicit withdrawal of attention from reality (see MANO), what is central in the field is, precisely, an image (which may be plural), with more imaginary images in the periphery. (There is no doubt that images are frequently made up of elements of past real (five-base) experience; and in simple cases, where the images are coherent and familiar, we speak of *memories*. But there are also images that are telepathic, clairvoyant, retrocognitive, and precognitive; and these do not conform to such a convenient scheme. The presence of an image, of an *absent* reality, is in no way dependent upon its ever previously (or even subsequently) being present as a *present* reality (though considerations of *probability* cannot be ignored). On the other hand, no image ever appears or is created *ex nihilo*. See *FS* (c) & (l).)

of the present's absents is the *significance* of the present (i.e. what it points to, or indicates, beyond itself), which is also its intention. (In general, no two absents—even of the same order—are of exactly the same 'weight'.) *Volition* (which is what is more commonly understood by 'intention') is really a double intention (in the sense used here), i.e. it is *intentional intention*. This simply means that certain of the absents (or possibles) are *intentionally emphasized* at the expense of the others. When, in the course of time, one absent comes wholly to predominate over the others (often, but not necessarily, the one preferred), the present suddenly vanishes, and the absent takes its place as the new present. (The vanished present—see ANICCA (a)—is now to be found among the absents.) This is a description of *action* (*kamma*) in its essential form, but leaving out of account the question of *kammavipāka*, which is *acinteyya* (*Aṅguttara* IV,viii,7 (A.ii,80)[85]), and therefore rather beyond the scope of these *Notes*. See also a definition of action in RŪPA (b), and an ethical account in KAMMA.

The passage at *Dīgha* ii,2 (D.ii,62-3)[86] is essential for an understanding of *nāmarūpa*, and it rules out the facile and slipshod interpretation of *nāmarūpa* as 'mind-&-matter'—*rūpa* is certainly 'matter' (or 'substance'), but *nāma* is not 'mind'.[c] The passage at *Majjhima* iii,8 (M.i,190-1)[87] makes it

---

c. When *nāma* is understood as 'mind' or 'mentality' it will inevitably include *viññāṇa* or consciousness—as, for example, in the *Visuddhimagga* (Ch. XVIII *passim*). This is entirely without justification in the Suttas; and it is clear enough that any mode of thinking that proposes to make a fundamental division between 'mind' and 'matter' will soon find itself among insuperable difficulties. 'Mind' (i.e. *mano* (q.v.) in one of its senses) *already* means 'imagination' as opposed to 'reality', and it cannot *also* be opposed to 'matter'. 'Reality' and 'matter' are not by any means the same thing—is real pain (as opposed to imaginary pain) also material pain? There are, to be sure, various distinctions between body and mind (in different senses); and we may speak of bodily (*kāyika*) pain as opposed to mental or volitional (*cetasika*) pain—see *Majjhima* v,4 (M.i,302); *Vedanā Saṃy.* iii,2 (S.iv,231)—, but these are distinctions of quite a different kind. Bodily pain may be real or imaginary, and so may volitional pain (grief), but *material* pain—painful feeling composed of matter—is a contradiction in terms. (Observe that there are two discrepant senses of the word *cetasikā* on two successive pages of the same Sutta (*Majjhima* v,4): (i) on one page (M.i,301) we find that *saññā* and *vedanā* are *cittasaṅkhāra* because they are *cetasikā* (see *NP* §5) and (ii) on the next (302) we find that *vedanā* may be either *kāyikā* or *cetasikā* (see above). *Citta* and *cetasika* are not fixed terms in the Suttas, and, as well as different shades, have two principal (and incompatible) meanings according to context, like their nearest English equivalent, 'mind, mental' (which, however, has to do duty also for *mano*—see Glossary). In (i), evidently, *cetasika* is 'mental' as opposed to 'material' (see also *NP* (g)), and in (ii) it is 'mental' as opposed to 'sensual'. In the Suttas the contexts are distinct, and confusion between these two senses does not arise; but a passage from Russell will provide a striking example of failure to distinguish between

clear that all five *upādānakkhandhā*, and therefore *viññāṇa* with *nāmarūpa*, are present both in five-base experience and in mental experience. Thus, a *visible* (real) stone persists (or keeps its shape and its colour—i.e. is earthy) *visibly* (or in reality); an *imagined* stone persists *in imagination*. Both the actual (real) taste of castor oil and the thought of tasting it (i.e. the imaginary taste) are unpleasant. Both matter and feeling (as also perception and the rest) are both real and imaginary.[d] See PHASSA (a). *Nāmarūpa* at *Dīgha* ii,2 (D.ii,63,§21)[86] may firstly be taken as one's own *cognized* body. Cf. *Nidāna/Abhisamaya Saṃy.* ii,9 (S.ii,24): *Avijjānīvaraṇassa bhikkhave bālassa/paṇḍitassa taṇhāya sampayuttassa evam ayaṃ kāyo samudāgato. Iti ayaṃ c'eva kāyo bahiddhā ca nāmarūpaṃ, itth'etaṃ dvayaṃ.*[51] This passage distinguishes between *nāmarūpa* that is external and one's own body. Together, these make up the totality of *nāmarūpa* at any time. The body, as *rūpa*, is independent of its appearance; but *together with its appearance*, which is how we normally take it, it is *nāmarūpa*. *Nāmarūpa* that is external is all cognized phenomena apart from one's own body. Cf. *Majjhima* xi,9 (M.iii,19):

---

them: 'I do not know how to give a sharp definition of the word "mental", but something may be done by enumerating occurrences which are indubitably mental: believing, doubting, wishing, willing, being pleased or pained, are certainly mental occurrences; so are what we may call experiences, seeing, hearing, smelling, perceiving generally.' (*Op. cit.*, VIIth Essay.) 'Mind', whether in English or Pali (*mano*, *citta*), represents an intersection of mutually incompatible concepts. Confusion is often worse confounded by the misunderstanding discussed in PHASSA (e), where matter is conceded only an inferred existence in a supposed 'external world' beyond my experience.)

**d.** A distinction approximating to that between *nāma* and *rūpa*, under the names '*forme*' and '*matière*', is made by Gaston Bachelard in his book *L'Eau et les Rêves, Essai sur l'imagination de la matière* (José Corti, Paris 1942). Bachelard regards matter as the four primary elements, Earth, Water, Fire, and Air, and emphasizes the *resistant* nature of matter (which would correspond to *paṭigha*). This book (there are also companion volumes on the other elements) is written from a literary rather than a philosophical point of view, but its interest lies in the fact that Bachelard makes these fundamental distinctions quite independently of the Buddha's Teaching, of which he apparently knows nothing. He is concerned, in particular, with the various '*valorisations*' of the four elements as they occur in literature, that is to say with the various *significances* that they may possess. These are examples of *saṅkhārā* (as *cetanā*): *rūpaṃ rūpattāya saṅkhataṃ abhisaṅkharonti*[53] (cf. *NP* (f)). The philosophical distinction between primary and secondary qualities also seems to approximate to that between *rūpa* and at least certain aspects of *nāma*. (Here is Bradley (*op. cit.* (*A.&R.*), Ch. I): 'The primary qualities are those aspects of what we perceive or feel, which, in a word, are spatial; and the residue is secondary.' But see RŪPA (e).) These indications may serve to assure the apprehensive newcomer that the technical terms of the Suttas do not represent totally strange and inaccessible categories. But it is one thing to make these distinctions (approximately, at least), and another thing to understand the Buddha's Teaching.

... *imasmiñ ca saviññāṇake kāye bahiddhā ca sabbanimittesu* ...[52] Though, as said above, we may *firstly* understand *nāmarūpa* in the *Dīgha* passage as one's own cognized body, properly speaking we must take *nāmarūpa* as the total cognized phenomena (which may not be explicitly formulated), thus: (i) 'I-[am]-lying-in-the-mother's-womb'; (ii) 'I-[am]-being-born-into-the-world'; (iii) 'I-[am]-a-young-man-about-town'. In other words, I am ultimately concerned not with this or that particular phenomenon in my experience but with myself as determined by my whole situation.

## *NIBBĀNA*

See *Itivuttaka* II,ii,7 (Iti.38).[89]

The opinion has been expressed (in the P.T.S. Dictionary) that *nibbāna* is not transcendental. If by 'transcendental' is meant 'mystical', either in the sense of having to do with a (supposed) Divine Ground or simply of being by nature a mystery, then *nibbāna* (or 'extinction') is not transcendental: indeed, it is anti-transcendental; for mystification is the state, not of the *arahat* (who *has* realized *nibbāna*), but of the *puthujjana* (who has *not*).[a]

---

**a.** Cf. *'De qui et de quoi en effet puis-je dire: "Je connais cela!" Ce coeur en moi, je puis l'éprouver et je juge qu'il existe. Ce monde, je puis le toucher et je juge encore qu'il existe. Là s'arrête toute ma science et le reste est construction. Car si j'essaie de saisir ce moi dont je m'assure, si j'essaie de le définir et de le résumer, il n'est plus qu'une eau qui coule entre mes doigts. Je puis dessiner un à un tous les visages qu'il sait prendre, tous ceux aussi qu'on lui a donnés, cette éducation, cette origine, cette ardeur ou ces silences, cette grandeur ou cette bassesse. Mais on n'additionne pas des visages. Ce coeur même qui est le mien me restera à jamais indéfinissable. Entre la certitude que j'ai de mon existence et le contenu que j'essaie de donner à cette assurance, le fossé ne sera jamais comblé. Pour toujours je serai étranger à moi-même. ... Voici encore des arbres et je connais leur rugueux, de l'eau et j'éprouve sa saveur. Ces parfums d'herbe et d'étoiles, la nuit, certains soirs où le coeur se détend, comment nierai-je ce monde dont j'éprouve la puissance et les forces? Pourtant toute la science de cette terre ne me donnera rien qui puisse m'assurer que ce monde est à moi.'*—A. Camus, *Le Mythe de Sisyphe*, Gallimard, Paris 1942, pp. 34-5. ('Of whom and of what in fact can I say "I know about that!" This heart in me, I can experience it and I conclude that it exists. This world, I can touch it and I conclude again that it exists. All my knowledge stops there, and the rest is construction. For if I try to grasp this self of which I am assured, if I try to define it and to sum it up, it is no more than a liquid that flows between my fingers. I can depict one by one all the faces that it can assume; all those given it, too, by this education, this origin, this boldness or these silences, this grandeur or this vileness. But one cannot add up faces. This same heart which is mine will ever remain for me undefinable. Between the certainty that I have of my existence and the content that I strive to give to this assurance, the gap will never be filled. Always shall I be a stranger to myself. ... Here, again, are trees and I know their roughness, water and I experience its savour. This scent of grass and of stars, night, certain evenings when the heart relaxes,—how shall I deny this world whose power and forces I experience? Yet all the science of this earth will give me nothing that can assure me that this world is mine.') A more lucid account by a *puthujjana* of his own predicament could scarcely be desired. This situation cannot be transcended so long as what appears to be one's 'self' is accepted at its face value: 'this self *of which I am assured*', 'this same heart *which is mine*'. The paradox (Marcel would speak of a *mystery*: a problem that encroaches on its own data)—the paradox, *attā hi attano n'atthi*[60] (*Dhammapada* v,3 (Dh.62)), must be resolved. This necessarily rather chromatic passage, which does not lend itself kindly to translation (though one is provided), makes the overtone of despair clearly audible. Needless perhaps to

For the *arahat*, all sense of personality or selfhood has subsided, and with it has gone all possibility of numinous experience; and *a fortiori* the mystical intuition of a trans-personal Spirit or Absolute Self—of a Purpose or an Essence or a Oneness or what have you—can no longer arise. Cf. Preface (m). Nor, for one who sees, is the nature of *nibbāna* a mystery at all. When a fire becomes extinguished (*nibbuta*) we do not suppose that it enters a mysterious 'transcendental state': neither are we to suppose such a thing of the person that attains *nibbāna*. See *Majjhima* viii,2 & *PS* (a).

But if 'transcendental' means 'outside the range of investigation of the disinterested scholar or scientist', then *nibbāna is* transcendental (but so are other things). And if 'transcendental' means 'outside the range of understanding of the *puthujjana*'—though the dictionary hardly intends this[b]—, then again it is transcendental. Only this last meaning corresponds to *lokuttara*. (i) Existence or being (*bhava*) transcends reason (*takka*, which is the range of the scholar or scientist), and (ii) extinction (*nibbāna*) transcends existence (which is the range of the *puthujjana*):

(i) There is no *reason* why I am, why I exist. My existence cannot be demonstrated by reasoning since it is not *necessary*, and any attempt to do so simply begs the question. The Cartesian *cogito ergo sum* is not a logical proposition—logically speaking it is a mere tautology. My existence is *beyond* reason.

(ii) I can assert my existence or I can deny it, but in order to do either I must exist; for it is I myself who assert it or deny it. Any attempt I may make to abolish my existence tacitly confirms it; for it is *my* existence that I am seeking to abolish. *Ye kho te bhonto samaṇabrāhmaṇā sato sattassa ucchedaṃ vināsaṃ vibhavaṃ paññāpenti te sakkāyabhayā sakkāyapari-*

---

say, this despair marks the extreme limit of the *puthujjana*'s thought, where it recoils impotently upon itself—and not by any means his normal attitude towards the routine business of living from day to day.

**b.** The dictionary merely says that *nibbāna* is not transcendental since it is purely and solely an *ethical* state to be reached in this birth. But this is altogether too simple a view. As pointed out in KAMMA, an understanding of the foundation of ethical practice is already beyond the range of the *puthujjana*, and ultimately, by means of ethical practice, the *arahat* completely and finally transcends it. *Nibbāna* is an ethical state inasmuch as it is reached by ethical practice, but inasmuch as that state is cessation of ethics *nibbāna* is transcendental. (It must be emphasized, lest anyone mistake this for a kind of antinomianism, that the *arahat* is in no way exempted from observance of the disciplinary rules of the Vinaya. How far he is capable of breaking them is another question. See *Aṅguttara* III,ix,5-7 (A.i,231-4) & IX,i,7&8 (iv,369-72).)

*jegucchā sakkāyaṃ yeva anuparidhāvanti anuparivattanti. Seyyathāpi nāma sā gaddūlabaddho daḷhe thambhe vā khīle vā upanibaddho tam eva thambhaṃ vā khīlaṃ vā anuparidhāvati anuparivattati, evam ev'ime bhonto samaṇabrāhmaṇā sakkāyabhayā sakkāyaparijegucchā sakkāyaṃ yeva anuparidhāvanti anuparivattanti.*[54] (*Majjhima* xi,2 (M.ii,232)) Cessation of 'my existence' (which is extinction—*bhavanirodho nibbānaṃ*[55] (*Aṅguttara* X,i,7 (A.v,9))) is *beyond* my existence. See ATAKKĀVACARA.

The idea of *nibbāna* as the ultimate goal of human endeavour will no doubt strike the common man, innocently enjoying the pleasures of his senses, as a singularly discouraging notion if he is told that it is no more than 'cessation of being'. Without actually going so far (overtly, at least) as to hope for Bradley's Absolute ('It would be experience entire, containing all elements in harmony. Thought would be present as a higher intuition; will would be there where the ideal had become reality; and beauty and pleasure and feeling would live on in this total fulfilment. Every flame of passion, chaste or carnal, would still burn in the Absolute unquenched and unabridged, a note absorbed in the harmony of its higher bliss.' (*Op. cit.* (*A.&R.*), Ch. XV)),—without perhaps going quite so far as this, even a thoughtful man may like to expect something a little more positive than 'mere extinction' as the *summum bonum*. We shrink before the idea that our existence, with its anguishes and its extasies, is *wholly* gratuitous, and we are repelled by the suggestion that we should be better off without it; and it is only natural that the *puthujjana* should look for a formula to save something from (as he imagines) the shipwreck.[c]

In the *Udāna* (viii,3 (Ud.80)) *nibbāna* is spoken of by the Buddha in these terms: *Atthi bhikkhave ajātaṃ abhūtaṃ akataṃ asaṅkhataṃ, no ce taṃ bhikkhave abhavissa ajātaṃ abhūtaṃ akataṃ asaṅkhataṃ na yidha jātassa bhūtassa katassa saṅkhatassa nissaraṇaṃ paññāyetha*[56]. 'Such a positive assertion of the existence of the Unconditioned' it is sometimes urged 'must surely imply that *nibbāna* is not simply annihilation.' *Nibbāna*, certainly, is not 'simply annihilation'—or rather, it is not annihilation at all: extinction, cessation of being, is by no means the same thing as the (supposed)

---

**c.** Jaspers, with the final and inevitable ruin of all his hopes, still reads his temptation to despair in a positive sense—we are able, he concludes, 'in shipwreck to experience Being' ('... *im Scheitern das Sein zu erfahren.*'—K. Jaspers, *Philosophie*, Springer, Berlin 1932, Vol. III, p. 237). But the Suttas are less accommodating. See *Majjhima* iii,2 (M.i,136-7) for an account of the eternalist's unrelieved angst in the face of subjective non-being (*ajjhattaṃ asati paritassanā*) upon hearing the Buddha's Teaching of extinction. He apprehends annihilation, despairs, and falls, beating his breast, into confusion. But not so the *ariyasāvaka*.

annihilation of an eternal 'self' or soul. (See the Sutta passage on p. 68.) And the assertion of the existence of *nibbāna* is positive enough—but what, precisely, is asserted? In the *Asaṅkhata Saṃyutta* (i,1 & ii,23 (S.iv,359&371)) we read *Yo bhikkhave rāgakkhayo dosakkhayo mohakkhayo, idaṃ vuccati bhikkhave asaṅkhataṃ/nibbānaṃ*[57]; and we see that, if we do not go beyond the Suttas, we cannot derive more than the positive assertion of the existence here of the destruction of lust, hate, and delusion. And this is simply a statement that to get rid, in this very life, of lust, hate, and delusion, *is* possible (if it were not, there would be no escape from them, and therefore—*Aṅguttara* X,viii,6 (A.v,144)—no escape from birth, ageing, and death). And the *arahat* has, in fact, done so. But if, in our stewing minds, we still cannot help feeling that *nibbāna* really ought, somehow, to be an eternity of positive enjoyment, or at least of experience, we may ponder these two Sutta passages:

*Tisso imā bhikkhu vedanā vuttā mayā, sukhā vedanā dukkhā vedanā adukkhamasukhā vedanā, imā tisso vedanā vuttā mayā. Vuttaṃ kho pan' etaṃ bhikkhu mayā, Yaṃ kiñci vedayitaṃ taṃ dukkhasmin ti. Taṃ kho pan'etaṃ bhikkhu mayā saṅkhārānaṃ yeva aniccataṃ sandhāya bhāsitaṃ...*[58] *Vedanā Saṃy.* ii,1 (S.iv,216)

*Āyasmā Sāriputto etad avoca. Sukhaṃ idaṃ āvuso nibbānaṃ, sukhaṃ idaṃ āvuso nibbānan ti. Evaṃ vutte āyasmā Udāyi āyasmantaṃ Sāriputtaṃ etad avoca. Kim pan'ettha āvuso Sāriputta sukhaṃ, yad ettha n'atthi vedayitan ti. Etad eva khv ettha āvuso sukhaṃ, yad ettha n'atthi vedayitaṃ.*[59] *Aṅguttara* IX,iv,3 (A.iv,414)

## *PAṬICCASAMUPPĀDA*

For a fuller discussion of some of this, see *NP*.

In spite of the venerable tradition, starting with the *Paṭisambhidāmagga* (or perhaps the *Abhidhamma Piṭaka*) and continued in all the Commentaries (see *Aṅguttara* V,viii,9 (A.iii,107,§4)), *paṭiccasamuppāda* has nothing to do with temporal succession (cause-and-effect). Precedence in *paṭiccasamuppāda* is structural, not temporal: *paṭiccasamuppāda* is not the description of a *process*. For as long as *paṭiccasamuppāda* is thought to involve temporal succession (as it is, notably, in the traditional 'three-life' interpretation), so long is it liable to be regarded as some kind of hypothesis (that there is re-birth and that it is *caused* by *avijjā*) to be verified (or not) in the course of time (like any hypothesis of the natural sciences), and so long are people liable to think that the necessary and sufficient criterion of a 'Buddhist'[a] is the acceptance of this hypothesis on trust (for no hypothesis can be known to be certainly true, since upon the next occasion it may fail to verify itself). But the Buddha tells us (*Majjhima* iv,8 (M.i,265)) that *paṭiccasamuppāda* is *sandiṭṭhiko akāliko ehipassiko opanayiko paccattaṃ veditabbo viññūhi*[61]. What temporal succession is *akālika*? (See CITTA (a).) For an *ariyasāvaka*, *paṭiccasamuppāda* is a matter of direct reflexive certainty: the *ariyasāvaka* has direct, certain, reflexive knowledge of the condition upon which *birth* depends. He has no such knowledge about *re*-birth, which is quite a different matter. He knows for himself that *avijjā* is the condition for birth; but he does not know for himself that when there is *avijjā* there is re-birth. (That there *is* re-birth, i.e. *saṃsāra*, may remain, even for the *ariyasāvaka*, a matter of trust in the Buddha.) The *ariyasāvaka* knows for himself that even in this very life the *arahat* is, actually, not to be found (cf. *Khandha Saṃy.* ix,3 (S.iii,109-15) and see *PS* (a)), and that it is wrong to say that the *arahat* 'was born' or 'will die'. With

**a.** To be a follower of the Buddha it is certainly *necessary* to accept on trust that for one who is not rid of *avijjā* at his death there is re-birth, but it is by no means *sufficient*. What *is* sufficient is to see *paṭiccasamuppāda*—*Yo paṭiccasamuppādaṃ passati so dhammaṃ passati*[62] (*Majjhima* iii,8 (M.i,191)). For those who cannot *now* see the re-birth that is at every moment awaiting beings with *avijjā*, the dependence of re-birth on *avijjā* must be accepted on trust. They cannot get beyond temporal succession in this matter and must take it on trust that it *is* a question of dependence (and not of cause-and-effect)—i.e. that it is *not* a hypothesis at all, but (for the Buddha) a matter of certainty. But accepting this on trust is not the same as seeing *paṭiccasamuppāda*. (*Past* and *future* only make their appearance with *anvaye ñāṇaṃ* (see NA CA SO (a)), not with *dhamme ñāṇaṃ*. 'As it is, so it was, so it will be.' *Paṭiccasamuppāda* is just 'As it is'—i.e. the *present* structure of dependence.)

*sakkāyanirodha* there is no longer any 'somebody' (or a person—*sakkāya*, q.v.) to whom the words *birth* and *death* can apply. They apply, however, to the *puthujjana*, who still 'is somebody'.[b] But to endow his birth with a condition in the past—i.e. a *cause*—is to accept this 'somebody' at its face value as a permanent 'self'; for cessation of birth requires cessation of its condition, which, being safely *past* (in the preceding life), cannot *now* be brought to an end; and this 'somebody' cannot therefore *now* cease. Introduction of this idea into *paṭiccasamuppāda* infects the *samudayasacca* with *sassatadiṭṭhi* and the *nirodhasacca* with *ucchedadiṭṭhi*. Not surprisingly, the result is hardly coherent. And to make matters worse, most of the terms—and notably *saṅkhāra* (q.v.)—have been misconceived by the *Visuddhimagga*.

It is sometimes thought possible to modify this interpretation of *paṭiccasamuppāda*, confining its application to the present life. Instead of *temporal succession* we have *continuous becoming*, conceived as a *flux*, where the effect cannot be clearly distinguished from the cause—the cause *becomes* the effect. But this does not get rid of the temporal element, and the concept of a flux raises its own difficulties.[c]

The problem lies in the *present*, which is always with us; and any attempt to consider past or future without first settling the present problem can only beg the question—'self' is either asserted or denied, or both, or both assertion and denial are denied, all of which take it for granted (see NA CA SO). *Any* interpretation of *paṭiccasamuppāda* that involves time is an attempt to resolve the present problem by referring to past or future, and is therefore *necessarily* mistaken. The argument that both past and future exist in the present (which, in a certain sense, is correct) does not lead to the resolution of the problem.

---

**b.** So long as there are the thoughts '*I* was born', '*I* shall die', there is birth and death: so long as the five *khandhā* are *sa-upādānā*, 'somebody' becomes manifest and breaks up.

**c.** The notion of *flux* can be expressed thus: A = B, B = C, A ≠ C, where A, B, and C, are consecutive (Poincaré's definition of continuity). This contradiction can only be concealed by verbal legerdemain. (The origin of this misleading notion, as of so many others in the traditional interpretation, seems to be the *Milindapañha*, which, to judge by its simile of the flame, intends its formula *na ca so na ca añño* to be understood as describing continuous change.) The misunderstanding arises from failure to see that change at any given level of generality *must* be discontinuous and absolute, and that there *must* be different levels of generality. When these are taken together, any desired approximation to 'continuous change' can be obtained without contradiction. But change, as marking 'the passage of time', is no more than change of aspect or orientation: change of substance is not *necessary*, nor is movement. (See ANICCA (a), CITTA (a), & *FS*.) Kierkegaard (*op. cit.*, p. 277) points out that Heraclitus, who summed up his doctrine of universal flux in the celebrated dictum that one cannot pass through the same river twice, had a disciple who remarked that one cannot pass through the same river even once. If everything is changing, there is no change at all.

The assumption of a single absolute time, conceived as a uniform continuity (or flux) of instants, leads at once to a very common misconception of the Dhamma:

A. Even if I *now* perceive things as self-identically persisting in time, my present perception is only one out of a flux or continuous succession of perceptions, and there is no guarantee that I continue to perceive the *same* self-identities for two successive instants. All I am therefore entitled to say is that there *appear* to be self-identities persisting in time; but whether it is so or not *in reality*, I am quite unable to discover.

B. The Buddha's teachings of impermanence and not-self answer this question in the negative: In reality no things exist, and if they appear to do so that is because of my ignorance of these teachings (which is *avijjā*).

But we may remark: (i) That A is the result of taking presumptively the rational view of time, and using it to question the validity of direct reflexive experience. But the rational view of time is itself derived, ultimately, from direct reflexive experience—how can we know about time at all, if not from experience?—, and it is quite illegitimate to use it to dig away its own foundations. The fault is in the act of rationalization, in the attempt to see time from a point outside it; and the result—a *continuous* succession of *isolated* instants each of no duration and without past or future (from a timeless point of view they are *all* present)—is a monster. The distinction in A (as everywhere else) between 'appearance' and 'reality' is wholly spurious. (ii) That since our knowledge of time comes only from perception of change, the nature of change must be determined before we can know the structure of time. We have, therefore, no antecedent reason—if we do not actually encounter the thing itself—for entertaining the self-contradictory idea (see Poincaré above) of continuous change. (iii) That, whether or not we do actually perceive continuous change, we certainly perceive discontinuous changes (so much is admitted by A), and there is thus a *prima-facie* case at least in favour of the latter. (iv) That the experiments of the Gestalt psychologists indicate that, in fact, we perceive only discontinuous changes, not continuous change (cf. Sartre, *op. cit.*, p. 190). (v) That if, nevertheless, we say that we do at times and in the normal way have intuitive experience, distinct and unambiguous, of continuous change, and if we also say that continuous change, in accordance with B, is what is meant by the teaching of impermanence, then it will follow that at such times we must enjoy a direct view of 'reality' and be free from *avijjā*. Why, then, should we need a Buddha to tell us these things? But if we reject the first premiss we shall have no longer any grounds for having to assert a uniformly continuous time, and if we reject the second we shall have no longer any grounds for wishing to assert it. (On the question of self-identity, see ATTĀ.)

Our undeniable experience of movement and similar things (e.g. the fading of lights) will no doubt be adduced as evidence of continuous change—indeed, it will be said that they *are* continuous change. That movement is evidence of what it is, is quite certain; but it is not so certain that it is evidence of continuous change. We may understand movement as, at each level of generality, a succession of contiguous fixed finite *trajectories* (to borrow Sartre's expression), and each such trajectory, at the next lower level, as a relatively faster succession of lesser trajectories, and so on indefinitely. But, as discussed

## *PHASSA*

*Phassa*, 'contact', is defined (*Saḷāyatana Saṃy.* iv,10 (S.iv,67-9)) as the coming together of the eye, forms, and eye-consciousness (and so with the ear and the rest). But it is probably wrong to suppose that we must therefore understand the word *phassa*, primarily at least, as *contact between these three things*.[a] So long as there is *avijjā*, all things (*dhammā*) are fundamentally as described in the earlier part of the *Mūlapariyāyasutta* (*Majjhima* i,1 (M.i,1)); that is to say, they are inherently *in subjection*, they are *appropriated*, they are *mine* (See ANICCA, MAMA, & *NP* (f)). This is the foundation of the notion that *I am* and that *things are in contact with me*. This contact between me and things is *phassa*. The *diṭṭhisampanna* sees the deception, but the *puthujjana* accepts it at its face value and elaborates it into a relationship between *himself* and the *world* (*attā ca loko ca*—which relationship is then capable of further elaboration into a variety of views (*Majjhima* xi,2 (M.ii,233))).[b] But though

---

in *FS* (h), our ability to perceive distinctions is limited, and this hierarchy of trajectories is anomalously apprehended as a series of discrete continuities of displacement—which is, precisely, what we are accustomed to call *movement*. In other words, it is only where our power of discrimination leaves off that we start talking about 'continuous change'. (Consideration of the mechanism of the cinematograph—see the foregoing reference—is enough to show that continuous change cannot safely be inferred from the experience of movement; but it must not be supposed that the structure of movement can be reduced simply to the structure of the cinematograph film. See also *FS* (m).)

**a.** This interpretation of *phassa* is not invited by the *Mahānidānasuttanta* (*Dīgha* ii,2 (D.ii,62)[86]), where *nāmarūpapaccayā phasso* is discussed without reference to *saḷāyatana*, and in terms of *adhivacanasamphassa* and *paṭighasamphassa*. These terms are more easily comprehensible when *phassa* is understood as 'contact between subject and object'. (It is an elementary mistake to equate *paṭighasamphassa* ('resistance-contact') with five-base-contact (*cakkhusamphassa* &c.) and *adhivacanasamphassa* ('designation-contact') with mind-contact (*manosamphassa*). *Adhivacana* and *paṭigha* correspond to *nāma* and *rūpa* respectively, and it is clear from *Majjhima* iii,8 (M.i,190-1)[87] that both *nāma and rūpa* are conditions for each of the six kinds of contact. See NĀMA.)

**b.** The *puthujjana* takes for granted that 'I am' is the fundamental fact, and supposes that 'things are mine (*or* concern me) *because* I am'. The *diṭṭhisampanna* sees that this is the wrong way round. He sees that there is the conceit (concept) '(I) am' *because* 'things are mine'. With perception of impermanence, the inherent appropriation subsides; 'things are mine' gives place to just 'things are' (which things are still *significant*—they point to or indicate other things—, but no longer point to a 'subject'); and 'I am' vanishes. With the coming to an end of the *arahat*'s life there is the ending of 'things are'. While the *arahat* still lives, then, there continue to be 'objects' in the sense of 'things'; but if 'objects' are understood as necessarily correlative to a 'subject', then 'things' can no longer be called 'objects'. See ATTĀ. Similarly with the 'world' as the correlative of 'self': so long as the *arahat* lives, there is still an organized perspective

the *diṭṭhisampanna* is not deceived, yet until he becomes *arahat* the aroma of subjectivity (*asmī ti*, '(I) am') hangs about all his experience. All normal experience is dual (*dvayaṃ*—see NĀMA, final paragraph): there are present (i) one's conscious six-based body (*saviññāṇaka saḷāyatanika kāya*), and (ii) other phenomena (namely, whatever is *not* one's body); and reflexion will show that, though both are objective in the experience, the aroma of subjectivity that attaches to the experience will naturally tend to be attributed to the body.[c] In this way, *phassa* comes to be seen as contact between the conscious eye and forms—but mark that this is *because* contact is *primarily* between subject and object, and not between eye, forms, and eye-consciousness. This approach makes it possible to see in what sense, with the entire cessation of all illusion of 'I' and 'mine', there is *phassanirodha* in the *arahat* (where, though there are still, so long as he continues to live, both the conscious body and the other phenomena, there is no longer any appropriation). But when (as commonly) *phassa* is interpreted as 'contact between sense-organ and sense-object, resulting in consciousness'—and its translation as '(sense-)impression' implies this interpretation—then we are at once cut off from all possibility of understanding *phassanirodha* in the *arahat*;[d] for the question whether or not the eye is the subject is not

---

of significant things; but they are no longer significant 'to him', nor do they 'signify him'. See Preface (f).

**c.** If experience were confined to the use of a single eye, the eye and forms would not be distinguishable, they would not appear as separate things; there would be just the experience describable in terms of *pañc'upādānakkhandhā*. But normal experience is always multiple, and other faculties (touch and so on) are engaged at the same time, and the eye and forms as separate things are manifest to them (in the duality of experience already referred to). The original experience is thus found to be a *relationship*: but the fleshly eye is observed (by the other faculties, notably touch, and by the eyes themselves seeing their own reflexion) to be invariable (it is always 'here', *idha*), whereas forms are observed to be variable (they are plural and 'yonder', *huraṃ*). Visual experience, however, also is variable, and its entire content is thus naturally attributed to forms and none of it to the eye. In visual experience, then, *forms are seen*, *the eye is unseen*, yet (as our other faculties or a looking-glass informs us) *there is the eye*. Also in visual experience, *but in quite a different way* (indicated earlier), *objects are seen*, *the subject is unseen* (explicitly, at least; otherwise it (or he) would be an object), yet *there is the subject* ('*I am*'). On account of their structural similarity these two independent patterns appear one superimposed on the other; and when there is failure to distinguish between these patterns, *the subject comes to be identified with the eye* (and *mutatis mutandis* for the other *āyatanāni*). See VIÑÑĀṆA for an account of how, in a similar way, consciousness comes to be superimposed on the eye (and the six-based body generally).

**d.** *Phusanti phassā upadhiṃ paṭicca*
*Nirūpadhiṃ kena phuseyyuṃ phassā.*[22] *Udāna* ii,4 (Ud.12)

even raised—we are concerned only with the eye as a sense-organ, and it is a sense-organ in *puthujjana* and *arahat* alike. Understanding of *phassa* now consists in accounting for consciousness starting from physiological (or neurological) descriptions of the sense-organs and their functioning. Consciousness, however, is not physiologically observable, and the entire project rests upon unjustifiable assumptions from the start.[e] This episte-

It must, of course, be remembered that *phassanirodha* in the *arahat* does not mean that experience as such (*pañcakkhandhā*) is at an end. But, also, there is no experience without *phassa*. In other words, to the extent that we can still speak of an eye, of forms, and of eye-consciousness (seeing)—e.g. *Saṃvijjati kho āvuso Bhagavato cakkhu, passati Bhagavā cakkhunā rūpaṃ, chandarāgo Bhagavato n'atthi, suvimuttacitto Bhagavā*[63] (*Saḷāyatana Saṃy.* xviii,5 (S.iv,164))—to that extent we can still speak of *phassa*. But it must no longer be regarded as contact with *me* (or with *him*, or with *somebody*). There is, and there is not, contact in the case of the *arahat*, just as there is, and there is not, consciousness. See CETANĀ (f).

**e.** The reader may note that the word 'sensation' is claimed by physiology: a sensation is what is carried by, or travels over, the nervous system. One respectable authority speaks 'in physiological terms alone' of 'the classical pathways by which sensation reaches the thalamus and finally the cerebral cortex'. Presumably, therefore, a sensation is an electro-chemical impulse in a nerve. But the word properly belongs to psychology: Sensation, according to the *Pocket Oxford Dictionary*, is 'Consciousness of perceiving or seeming to perceive some state or affection of one's body or its parts or senses or of one's mind or its emotions'. What, then, is sensation—is it nervous impulse? or is it consciousness? Or is it not, rather, a convenient verbal device for persuading ourselves that consciousness *is* nervous impulse, and therefore physiologically observable? 'Consciousness' affirms our authority 'is the sum of the activities of the whole nervous system', and this appears to be the current official doctrine.

The notion of *sensation*, however, as we see from the dictionary's definition, is an abomination from the start—how can one 'perceive the state of one's senses' when it is precisely *by means* of one's senses that one perceives? (See MANO.) Another individual's perception (with *his* eye) of the state of my eye may well have, in certain respects, a one-one correspondence with my perception (with *my* eye) of, say, a tree (or, for that matter, a ghost, or, since the eye as visual organ extends into the brain, a migraine); but it is mere lazy thinking to presume from this that when I perceive a tree I am *really* perceiving the state of my eye—and then, to account for my sensation, *inferring* the existence of a tree in a supposed 'external' world beyond my experience. The reader is referred to Sartre's excellent discussion of this equivocal concept (*op. cit.*, pp. 372-8), of which we can give here only the peroration. *'La sensation, notion hybride entre le subjectif et l'objectif, conçue à partir de l'objet, et appliquée ensuite au sujet, existence bâtarde dont on ne saurait dire si elle est de fait ou de droit, la sensation est une pure rêverie de psychologue, il faut la rejeter délibérément de toute théorie sérieuse sur les rapports de la conscience et du monde.'* ('Sensation, hybrid notion between the subjective and the objective, conceived starting from the object, and then applied to the subject, bastard entity of which one cannot say whether it is *de facto* or *de jure*,—

mological interpretation of *phassa* misconceives the Dhamma as a kind of natural-science-cum-psychology that provides an *explanation* of things in terms of cause-and-effect.

sensation is a pure psychologist's day-dream: it must be deliberately rejected from every serious theory on the relations of consciousness [which, for Sartre, is subjectivity] and the world.') Descartes, it seems, with his 'representative ideas', is the modern philosopher primarily responsible for the present tangle—see Heidegger, *op. cit.*, p. 200 *et seq.* (Heidegger quotes Kant as saying that it is 'a scandal of philosophy and of human reason in general' that there is still no cogent proof for the 'being-there of things outside us' that will do away with all scepticism. Then he remarks 'The "scandal of philosophy" is not that this proof is yet to be given, but that *such proofs are expected and attempted again and again*'.) Removal of the pseudo-problem of the 'external' world removes materialism, but does not remove matter (for which see NĀMA & RŪPA).

## *BALA*

The distinction between *indriya* and *bala* seems to be that *indriya*, 'faculty', means a qualitative range of capacity or extent of dominion in a given province, whereas *bala*, 'power', implies rather a quantitative superiority of endowment. As *faculties* the five items, *saddhā*, *viriya*, *sati*, *samādhi*, and *paññā*, are, in the *ariyasāvaka*, either effective or latent all at once (see *Indriya Saṃy.* vi,2 (S.v,228)) and are totally absent from the *puthujjana* (*ibid.* ii,8 (S.v,202)[88]). As *powers* they are the strength of the *ariyasāvaka*, who has equipment for practice of the Dhamma that is lacking in the *puthujjana*. *Katamañ ca bhikkhave bhāvanābalaṃ. Tatra bhikkhave yaṃ idaṃ bhāvanābalaṃ sekhānaṃ etaṃ balaṃ sekhamhi.*[64] (*Aṅguttara* II,ii,1 (A.i,52)) It is sometimes supposed that a *puthujjana* possesses these faculties and powers, at least in embryo, and that his task is to develop them. This is a misunderstanding. It is the *puthujjana*'s task to *acquire* them. It is for the *sekha*, who has acquired them, to develop them.

## *MANO*

Much mental activity (imagination) is to some extent reflexive (in a loose sense);[a] and reflexion brings to light not merely *things* (as does the unreflexive attitude) but also the *nature* of things (see DHAMMA). Thus *dhammā*, as the external counterpart of *mano*, can often be understood as 'universals'.[b]

---

**a.** For reflexion in the stricter sense see DHAMMA (b). Something of the distinction between these two senses of reflexion can be seen in the following two Sutta definitions of *sati* or 'mindfulness':

(i) *Ariyasāvako satimā hoti paramena satinepakkena samannāgato cirakatam pi cirabhāsitam pi saritā anussaritā.*[66] E.g. *Indriya Saṃy.* v,10 (S.v,225). This is more 'reflection' than 'reflexion'. *Sati*, here, is mindfulness (calling to mind) of the past, and therefore memory or recollection.

(ii) *Idha bhikkhave bhikkhu kāye kāyānupassī ... vedanāsu vedanānupassī ... citte cittānupassī ... dhammesu dhammānupassī viharati ātāpī sampajāno satimā vineyya loke abhijjhādomanassaṃ. Evaṃ kho bhikkhave bhikkhu sato hoti.*[67] *Vedanā Saṃy.* i,7 (S.iv,211) In this context, *sati* is mindfulness of the *present*. Here we might be said to have both the present and its image together.

**b.** A universal becomes an *abstraction* only in so far as an attempt is made to think it in isolation from all particular or concrete content—divorced, that is to say, from existence. The stricter the reflexion the less the abstraction.

A distinction must be made between 'relative universals', where the *content* of a given experience is generalized ('this horse', 'this brown', appear as examples or instances of 'horse' and 'brown', i.e. as one of 'all possible horses', of 'all possible browns'), and 'absolute universals', where the *characteristics* of a given experience *as such* are generalized ('this matter', 'this feeling', &c., appear as examples of 'matter', 'feeling', &c., i.e. as one of the *rūpakkhandhā*, of the *vedanākkhandhā*, and so on: see *Majjhima* xi,9 (M.iii,16-7))—cf. CETANĀ (a). The former is partly a discursive withdrawal from the real into the imaginary (or from the imaginary into the imaginary imaginary, as when a particular *imagined* horse is generalized); the latter, more radical, is an intuitive withdrawal from the immediate (both real and imaginary) into the reflexive, in the stricter sense of note (a (ii)) above. Cf. Bradley, *op. cit.* (*Logic*), I,ii,§§24-27. Note: (i) That 'this horse' is 'one of all possible appearances or aspects of this horse' before it is 'one of all possible horses', and unique particulars (e.g. 'Socrates') will not reach the second stage. (ii) That the appearance of universals (of any kind) is due to *reflexion* and not to *abstraction*; and *reflection* is a combination of both: thus 'relative universals' do not cease to be universals as reflexion becomes stricter; they simply tend to be disregarded (or 'put in brackets'). (iii) That *abstractions* and *ideas* are the same thing; and, though they do not exist *apart* from images, they are not anchored to any one particular image; but, in the sense that they necessarily have one or another concrete (even if multiple) imaginary content, the abstraction is illusory: abstraction is a discursive escape from the *singularity* of the real to the *plurality* of the imaginary—it is *not* an escape from the concrete. (This shows the reason for Kierkegaard's paradox—see Preface (n).) (iv) That it is a function of the practice of *samādhi* to reduce discursive thinking: mindfulness of

This does not mean, of course, that the mind will necessarily choose to attend to these universal things that appear; it may prefer to enjoy the images as the eye enjoys visible forms; nevertheless, it is reflexively withdrawn from the immediate world. See NĀMA (b).

Note that just as the eye, as *cakkhāyatana* or *cakkhudhātu*, is that *yena lokasmiṃ lokasaññī hoti lokamānī*[65] (*Saḷāyatana Saṃy.* xii,3 (S.iv,95)), i.e. that *thing in the world* dependent upon which there is *perceiving and conceiving of the world*, namely a spherical lump of flesh set in my face; so the mind, as *manāyatana* or *manodhātu*, also is that *yena lokasmiṃ lokasaññī hoti lokamānī*, i.e. that *thing in the world* dependent upon which there is *perceiving and conceiving of the world*, namely various ill-defined parts of my body, but principally a mass of grey matter contained in my head (physiological and neurological descriptions are strictly out of place—see PHASSA).[c] This is in agreement with the fact that all five *khandhā* arise in connexion with *each* of the six *āyatanāni*—see NĀMA & PHASSA (a). For 'perceiving and conceiving' see MAMA (a).

More loosely, in other contexts, the mind (*mano*) is simply 'imagination' or 'reflexion', which, strictly, in the context of the foregoing paragraph, is *manoviññāṇa*, i.e. the *presence* of images. See NĀMA (c). The *Vibhaṅga* (of the *Abhidhamma Piṭaka*) introduces chaos by supposing that *manodhātu* and *manoviññāṇadhātu* are successive stages of awareness, differing only in intensity (and perhaps *also*, somehow, in kind). See CITTA.

---

breathing is particularly recommended—*ānāpānasati bhāvetabbā vitakk'upacchedāya*[68] (*Udāna* iv,1 (Ud.37)). (The fact that almost nothing is said in these *Notes* about *samādhi* is due simply to their exclusive concern with right and wrong *diṭṭhi*, and is absolutely not to be taken as implying that the task of developing *samādhi* can be dispensed with.)

**c.** This account of mind (as *manāyatana*) is not entirely satisfactory. We should probably do better to envisage mind in this context as five imaginary *ajjhattāyatanāni* related to the five real *ajjhattāyatanāni* (eye, ear, and so on) as imaginary sights and sounds (and so on) are related to real sights and sounds. (See NĀMA (b).) The *world*, of course, includes both the real (or present) and the imaginary (or absent); and just as, to see real things, there must be a real eye (incarnating a real point of view) 'in the world', so, to see imaginary things, there must be an imaginary eye (incarnating an imaginary point of view) also 'in the world'. Cf. *Majjhima* v,3 (M.i,295).

*MAMA*

> *Cakkhuṃ, Etaṃ mama, eso'ham asmi, eso me attā ti samanupassati. Cakkhuṃ, N'etaṃ mama, n'eso'ham asmi, n'eso me attā ti samanupassati.* (*Majjhima* xv,6 (M.iii,284))

> 'This is mine; this am I; this is my self'—so he regards the eye. 'Not, this is mine; not, this am I; not, this is my self'—so he regards the eye.

If *N'etaṃ mama* is translated 'This is not mine' the implication is that *something other than this is mine*, which must be avoided. These three views (of which the *sotāpanna* is free) correspond to three degrees or levels of appropriation. *Etaṃ mama* is the most fundamental, a rationalization (or at least a conceptual elaboration) of the situation described in the *Mūlapariyāyasutta* (*Majjhima* i,1 (M.i,1-6)) and in the *Saḷāyatana Saṃyutta* iii,8 (S.iv,22-3). *Eso'ham asmi* is a rationalization of *asmimāna*. *Eso me attā* is a rationalization of *attavāda*—it is full-blown *sakkāyadiṭṭhi*. Though the *sotāpanna* is free of these views, he is not yet free of the *maññanā* of the *Mūlapariyāyasutta* (which is fundamental in all *bhava*) or of *asmimāna*, but he cannot be said to have *attavāda*.[a] See DHAMMA (d) & PHASSA. The

a. The *Mūlapariyāyasutta* is as follows. (i) The *puthujjana* 'perceives X as X; perceiving X as X, he conceives X, he conceives In X, he conceives From X, he conceives "X is mine"; he delights in X ...'. (ii) The *sekha* 'recognizes X as X; recognizing X as X, he should not conceive X, he should not conceive In X, he should not conceive From X, he should not conceive "X is mine"; he should not delight in X ...'. (iii) The *arahat* 'recognizes X as X; recognizing X as X, he does not conceive X, he does not conceive In X, he does not conceive From X, he does not conceive "X is mine"; he does not delight in X ...'. This tetrad of *maññanā*, of 'conceivings', represents four progressive levels of explicitness in the basic structure of appropriation. The first, 'he conceives X', is so subtle that the appropriation is simply implicit in the verb. Taking advantage of an extension of meaning (not, however, found in the Pali *maññati*), we can re-state 'he conceives X' as 'X conceives', and then understand this as 'X is pregnant'—pregnant, that is to say, with *subjectivity*. And, just as when a woman first conceives she has nothing to show for it, so at this most implicit level we can still only say 'X'; but as the pregnancy advances, and it begins to be noticeable, we are obliged to say 'In X'; then the third stage of the pregnancy, when we begin to suspect that a separation is eventually going to take place, can be described as 'From X'; and the fourth stage, when the infant's head makes a public appearance and the separation is on the point of becoming definite, is the explicit 'X is mine (*me*, not *mama*)'. This separation is first actually realized in *asmimāna*, where I, as subject, am opposed to X, as object; and when the subject eventually grows up he becomes the 'self' of *attavāda*, face to face with the 'world' in which he exists. (In spite of the simile, what is described here is a single graded structure all implicated in

*sotāpanna* (and the other two *sekhā*), in whom *asmimāna* is still present, know and see for themselves that notions of 'I' and 'mine' are deceptions. So they say *N'etaṃ mama, n'eso'ham asmi, n'eso me attā ti.* The *arahat* is quite free from *asmimāna*, and, not having any trace of 'I' and 'mine', does not *even* say *N'etaṃ mama, n'eso'ham asmi, n'eso me attā ti.*

---

the present, and not a development taking place in time. When there is *attavāda*, the rest of this edifice lies beneath it: thus *attavāda* requires *asmimāna* (and the rest), but there can be *asmimāna* without *attavāda*.) Note that it is only the *sekha* who has the ethical imperative 'should not': the *puthujjana*, not 'recognizing X as X' (he perceives X as X, but not as impermanent), does not see for himself that he should not conceive X; while the *arahat*, though 'recognizing X as X', no longer conceives X. See KAMMA.

## *RŪPA*

In the *Kevaddhasutta* (*Dīgha* i,11 (D.i,223)), it is said that the question 'Where do the four *mahābhūtā* finally cease?' is wrongly asked, and that the question should be 'Where do [the four *mahābhūtā*] get no footing? Where do *nāma* and *rūpa* finally cease?' Matter or substance (*rūpa*) is essentially *inertia* or *resistance* (see *Dīgha* ii,2 (D.ii,62)[86]), or as the four *mahābhūtā* it can be regarded as four kinds of *behaviour* (i.e. the four primary patterns of inertia—see NĀMA). Behaviour (or inertia) is independent of the particular sense-experience that happens to be exhibiting it: a message in the Morse code (which would be a certain complex mode of behaviour) could be received in *any* sense-experience (though seeing and hearing are the most usual). In any one kind of sense-experience there is revealed a vast set of various behaviours, of various patterns of inertia; and in any other contemporary sense-experience there is revealed a set that, to a great extent, corresponds to this first set.[a] (One particular group of behaviours common to all my sense-experiences is of especial significance—it is 'this body', *ayaṃ kāyo rūpī catummahābhūtiko*[69] (*Majjhima* viii,5 (M.i,500)).) Thus, when I *see* a bird opening its beak at intervals I can often at the same time *hear* a corresponding sound, and I say that it is the (visible) bird that is (audibly) singing. The fact that there seems to be one single (though elaborate) set of behaviours common to all my sense-experiences at any one time, and not an entirely different set for each sense, gives rise to the notion of one single material world revealed indifferently by any one of my senses. Furthermore, the material world of one individual largely corresponds to that of another (particularly if allowance is made for difference in point of view), and we arrive at the wider notion of one general material world common to all individuals.[b] The fact that a given mode of behav-

---

**a.** Mind-experience is not considered in this Note to avoid complication. It is not, however, essentially different. See MANO (c).

**b.** Natural science, in taking this concept as its starting-point and polishing it a little to remove irregularities, has no place for the individual and his sense-experience (let alone mind-experience or imagination); for the material world of science is *by definition* utterly without point of view (in relativity theory *every* point is a point of view, which comes to the same thing), it is uniformly and quite indifferently *communal*—it is essentially *public*). Consciousness, intention, perception, and feeling, not being public, are not a part of the universe of science. Science is *inherently* incapable of understanding the nature of material change due to conscious action—which is, concisely, reflexive exercise of preference for one available mode of behaviour (or set of them) at the expense of the others. (Quantum physics, in hoping to reinstate the 'observer'—even if only

iour can be common to sense-experiences of two or more different kinds shows that it is independent of any one particular kind of consciousness (unlike a given perception—blue, for example, which is dependent upon eye-consciousness and not upon ear-consciousness or the others); and being independent of any one particular kind of consciousness it is independent of *all* consciousness *except for its presence or existence*. One mode of behaviour can be distinguished from another, and in order that this can be done they must *exist*—they must be present either in reality or in imagination, they must be *cognized*. But since it makes no difference in what form they are present—whether as sights or sounds (and even with one as visible and one as audible, and one real and one imaginary)—, the difference between them is not a matter of consciousness.[c] Behaviour, then, *in itself* does not involve consciousness (as perception does), and the *rūpakkhandha* is not *phassapaccayā* (as the *saññākkhandha* is)—see *Majjhima* xi,9 (M.iii,17). In itself, purely as inertia or behaviour, matter cannot be said to *exist*. (Cf. Heidegger, *op. cit.*, p. 212.) And if it cannot be said to *exist* it cannot be said

---

as a point of view—, is merely locking the stable door after the horse has been stolen.)

**c.** A visual and an auditive experience differ in consciousness (whether or not they differ in matter); but between two different visual (or auditive) experiences the difference is in matter (or substance, or inertia) and not in consciousness. (At this point the question might be asked, 'What is the *material* difference between the simple experiences of, for example, a blue thing and a red thing (ignoring spatial extension)?' The immediate answer is that they are simply *different* things, i.e. *different inertias*. But if it is insisted that one inertia can only differ from another in *behaviour* (i.e. in *pattern* of inertia)—in other words, that no inertia is absolutely simple—, we shall perhaps find the answer in the idea of a difference in *frequency*. But this would involve us in discussion of an order of structure underlying the four *mahābhūtā*. See *FS* (j).) Thus it will be observed that all difference in appearance (*nāma*) is difference in either consciousness (*viññāṇa*) or matter (*rūpa*). Why is this? Neither consciousness nor matter, by itself, can *appear* (or be manifest); for consciousness by itself lacks substance or specification—it is pure presence or existence without any *thing* that is present (or exists)—, and matter by itself lacks presence or existence—it is pure substance or specification, of which one cannot say 'it *is*' (i.e. 'it is *present* (or *absent*)'). Appearance or manifestation must necessarily partake of both consciousness and matter, but as an *overlapping* (———=———) and not simply an addition (for the simple superposition of two things each itself incapable of appearing would not produce appearance). Appearance is existence *as* substance, or substance *as* existence, and there must be *also* simple existence (or consciousness) and simple substance (or matter) to support this imbrication. Appearance, in a manner of speaking, is *sandwiched* between consciousness and matter: there must be *rūpa*, and *nāma*, and *viññāṇa* ($\underline{\;r\;}\;\underline{\underline{\;n\;}}\;\underline{\;v\;}$). (There is more to be said about this, but not briefly.) It is because of this structure that all differences in appearance can be resolved into differences either of consciousness or of matter (or both).

to *cease*. Thus the question 'Where do the four *mahābhūtā* finally cease?' is improper. (The question will have been asked with the notion in mind of an *existing* general material world common to all. Such a general world could only exist—and cease—if there were a general consciousness common to all. But this is a contradiction, since consciousness and individuality (see SAKKĀYA) are one.) But behaviour can get a footing in existence by being *present in some form*. As *rūpa* in *nāmarūpa*, the four *mahābhūtā* get a borrowed existence as the *behaviour* of *appearance* (just as feeling, perception, and intentions, get a borrowed substance as the *appearance* of *behaviour*). And *nāmarūpa* is the condition for *viññāṇa* as *viññāṇa* is for *nāmarūpa*. When *viññāṇa* (q.v.) is *anidassana* it is said to have ceased (since *avijjā* has ceased). Thus, with cessation of *viññāṇa* there is cessation of *nāmarūpa*, and the four *mahābhūtā* no longer get a footing in existence. (The passage at *Saḷāyatana Saṃyutta* xix,8 (S.iv,192), ... *bhikkhu catunnaṃ mahābhūtānaṃ samudayañ ca atthagamañ ca yathābhūtaṃ pajānāti*[70], is to be understood in this sense.)

From the foregoing discussion it can be seen that in order to distinguish *rūpa* from *nāma* it is only necessary to separate what is (or could be) common to two or more kinds of consciousness from what is not. But care is needed. It might seem that *shape* is *rūpa* and not *nāma* since it is present in both eye-consciousness and body-consciousness (e.g. touching with the fingers). This, however, is a mistake. Vision is a *double* faculty: it cognizes both colour and shape (see *FS* §§I/4 & II/8). The eye *touches* what it *sees* (it is only necessary to run the eye first across and then down some vertical lines or bars to discover this), and the result is *coloured shapes*. The eye is capable of intentional movement more delicate even than the fingers, and the corresponding perception of shapes is even more subtle.[d] Similar considerations apply, though in a much lesser degree, to hearing (and even to taste and to smell) where perception of shape, when present (however vaguely), corresponds to movement, real or imaginary (which will include the directional effect of two ears), of the head or of the entire body.[e] But

**d.** Strictly, the shapes are there before the eyeball is moved, just as the hand perceives the shape of an object merely by resting on it; *movement* of the eyeball, as of the fingers, only confirms the perception and makes it explicit. This does not matter: we are concerned only to point out the similarity of the eye and the hand as both yielding perceptions of shape, not to give an account of such perceptions.

**e.** This discussion, it will be seen, makes *space* a secondary and not a primary quality (see NĀMA (d)): space is essentially *tactile* (in a wide sense), and is related to the body (as organ of touch) as colours and sounds (and so on) are related to the eye and the ear—indeed, we should do better to think of 'spaces' rather than of any absolute

provided different kinds of consciousness are adequately distinguished, this method gives a definite criterion for telling what is matter from what is not. It is consequently not necessary to look for strict analysis of the four *mahābhūtā*: provided only that our idea of them conforms to this criterion, and that they cover all the primary modes of matter, this is all that is needed. Thus it is not necessary to look beyond the passage at *Majjhima* xiv,10 (M.iii,240) for a definition of them. (It is easy, but fatal, to assume that the Buddha's Teaching is concerned with analysis for its own sake, and then to complain that the analysis is not pushed far enough.) A human body in action, clearly enough, will present a behaviour that is a highly complex combination of these primary modes: it is behaviour of behaviour, but it still does not get beyond behaviour. (It is important to note that the laws of science—of biochemistry and physics in particular—do *not* cover behaviour (i.e. matter) associated with conscious (intentional) action.)[f]

---

'space'. Space, in fact, has no right to its privileged position opposite time as one of the joint basic determinants of matter: we are no more entitled to speak of 'space-(&-)time' than we are of 'smell-(&-)time'. Time itself is not absolute (see PAṬICCASAMUPPĀDA (c) & *FS* §II/5), and material things, as they exist, are not 'in' time (like floatage on a river), but rather have time as their characteristic; space, however, besides not being absolute, is not, strictly, even a characteristic of matter. On the other hand, our first four sense-organs are each a part of the body, which is the fifth, and space *does* hold a privileged position relative to colour, sound, smell, and taste. Thus we sometimes find in the Suttas (e.g. *Majjhima* vii,2 (M.i,423)) an *ākāsadhātu* alongside the four *mahābhūtā*; and for practical purposes—which is ultimately all we are concerned with—space can be regarded as a quasi-material element. But the *Milindapañha* has no business whatever to put *ākāsa* together with *nibbāna* as *asaṅkhata*.

**f.** *Pace* Russell: 'Physical things are those series of appearances whose matter obeys the laws of physics'. *Op. cit.*, VIIIth Essay, §xi.

## *VIÑÑĀṆA*

Consciousness (*viññāṇa*) can be thought of as the *presence* of a phenomenon, which consists of *nāma* and *rūpa*. *Nāmarūpa* and *viññāṇa* together constitute the phenomenon 'in person'—i.e. an *experience* (in German: *Erlebnis*). The phenomenon is the *support* (*ārammaṇa*—see first reference in (c) p. 87) of consciousness, and all consciousness is consciousness *of* something (*viz*, of a phenomenon). Just as there cannot be *presence* without *something* that is present, so there cannot *be* something without its being to that extent *present*—thus *viññāṇa* and *nāmarūpa* depend on each other (see *NP* §17). 'To be' and 'to be present' are the same thing.[a] But note that 'being' as *bhava*, involves the existence of the (illusory) *subject*, and with cessation of the conceit (concept) '(I) am', *asmimāna*, there is cessation of being, *bhavanirodha*. With the *arahat*, there is just *presence of the phenomenon* ('This is present'), instead of the presence (or existence) of an apparent 'subject' *to whom* there is present an 'object' ('I am, and this is present to (*or* for) me', i.e. (what appears to be) the subject is present ('I am'), the object is present ('this is'), and the object concerns or 'belongs to' the subject (the object is 'for me' or 'mine')—see PHASSA & ATTĀ); and consciousness is then said to be *anidassana*, 'non-indicative' (i.e. not pointing to the presence of a 'subject'), or *niruddha*, 'ceased' (see *NP* §22). *Viññāṇanirodha* refers indifferently to *anidassana viññāṇa* (*saupādisesa nibbānadhātu*, which refers to the living *arahat*: *Itivuttaka* II,ii,7 (Iti.38)[89]) and to cessation, at the *arahat*'s death, of all consciousness whatsoever (*anupādisesa nibbānadhātu*).[b]

---

**a.** A distinction must be made. 'To be' and 'being' are (in English) ambiguous. On the one hand they may refer to the *existence* of a phenomenon as opposed to *what it is* that exists (namely, the phenomenon). This is *viññāṇa* (though it does not follow that *viññāṇa* should be translated as 'being' or 'existence'). On the other hand they may refer to the *existing thing*, the *phenomenon as existing*; in other words, to the *entity*. But a further distinction must be made. The entity that the Buddha's Teaching is concerned with is not the *thing* but the *person*—but not the person *as opposed* to the thing, as subject in distinction from object. Personal existence is a synthetic relationship, dependent upon *upādāna*, and consisting of a subject and his objects. Being or existence in this pregnant sense is *bhava*, at least as it occurs in the *paṭiccasamuppāda* context, and the 'entity' in question is *sakkāya* (q.v.) or *pañc'upādānakkhandhā*. (It must be noted that the 'existence' of the living *arahat* is, properly speaking, not *bhava* but *bhavanirodha*, since the conceit '(I) am' has ceased. Strictly, there is no *arahat* to be found. See (b).) *Bhava* is to be translated as 'being' (or 'existence').

**b.** Strictly, we cannot speak of the 'living *arahat*' or of the '*arahat*'s death'—see *NP* §§10 & 22. The terms *saupādisesa* and *anupādisesa nibbānadhātu*, which sometimes give trouble, may be rendered 'extinction-element with/without residue'. *Saupādisesa*

*Viññāṇanirodha*, strictly speaking, is cessation of *viññāṇ'upādānakkhandha* as *bhavanirodha* is cessation of *pañc'upādānakkhandhā* (i.e. *sakkāyanirodha*), but it is extended to cover the final cessation of *viññāṇakkhandha* (and therefore of *pañcakkhandhā*) at the breaking up of the *arahat*'s body.

Consciousness, it must be noted, is emphatically no more 'subjective' than are the other four *upādānakkhandhā* (i.e. than *nāmarūpa*). (This should be clear from what has gone before; but it is a commonly held view that consciousness is essentially subjective, and a slight discussion will be in place.) It is quite wrong to regard *viññāṇa* as the subject to whom the phenomenon (*nāmarūpa*), now regarded as object, is present (in which case we should have to say, with Sartre, that consciousness as subjectivity is *presence to* the object). *Viññāṇa* is negative as regards essence (or 'what-ness'): it is not *part* of the phenomenon, of what is present, but is simply the presence of the phenomenon.[c] Consequently, in visual experience (for example), *phenomena are seen, eye-consciousness is not seen* (being negative as regards essence), yet *there is eye-consciousness* (eye-consciousness is present *reflexively*).[d]

---

and *anupādisesa* occur at *Majjhima* xi,5 (M.ii,257&259), where they can hardly mean more than 'with/without something (stuff, material) left'. At *Majjhima* i,10 (M.i,62) the presence of *upādisesa* is what distinguishes the *anāgāmī* from the *arahat*, which is clearly not the same thing as what distinguishes the two extinction-elements. *Upādisesa* must therefore be *unspecified* residue.

**c.** See *Khandha Saṃy.* vi,2 (S.iii,54). *Viññāṇa* is *positively* differentiated only by what it arises in dependence upon. E.g., that dependent upon eye and visible forms is eye-consciousness, and so with the rest. Cf. *Majjhima* iv,8 (M.i,259). That none of the five *upādānakkhandhā* is to be regarded as 'subjective' can be seen from the following passage: *So yad eva tattha hoti rūpagataṃ vedanāgataṃ saññāgataṃ saṅkhāragataṃ viññāṇagataṃ te dhamme aniccato dukkhato rogato gaṇḍato sallato aghato ābādhato parato palokato suññato anattato samanupassati*[71] (*Majjhima* vii,4 (M.i,435)). (This formula, which is applied in turn to each of the ascending *jhāna* attainments, should be enough to dispel any idea that *jhāna* is a mystical experience, in the sense—see Preface (m)—of being intuition of, or union with, some Transcendental Being or Absolute Principle.)

**d.** In reflexion, different *degrees* of consciousness, of presence, will be apparent. Distinction should be made between immediate presence and reflexive presence:

Immediate presence: 'a pain is', or 'consciousness of a pain'.

Reflexive presence: 'there is an existing pain', or 'there is consciousness of a pain'.

We can say 'there is consciousness', which means 'there is immediate presence' ('of a pain', of course, being understood or 'in brackets'), and this is reflexive evidence. But we cannot say 'consciousness is', or 'consciousness of consciousness' (i.e. immediate presence of immediate presence), since presence cannot be immediately present as a pain can. In French, the verbal distinction is more marked: *être/y avoir* (*'ceci est'/'il y a ceci'*). In Pali, the distinction is: *ruppati/atthi rūpaṃ*; *vediyati/atthi vedanā*; *sañjānāti/atthi saññā*; *abhisaṅkharonti/atthi saṅkhārā*; *vijānāti/atthi viññāṇaṃ*. (The reflexive reduplication

In this way consciousness comes to be associated with the body (*saviññāṇaka kāya*), and is frequently identified as the subject, or at least as subjectivity (e.g. by Husserl (see CETANĀ (b)) and Sartre (*op. cit.*, p. 27)). (To follow this discussion reference should be made to PHASSA, particularly (c), where it is shown that there is a natural tendency for subjectivity to be associated with the body. Three distinct pairs of complementaries are thus seen to be superimposed: eye & forms (or, generally: six-based body & externals); consciousness & phenomena; subject & objects. To identify consciousness and the subject is only too easy. With attainment of *arahattā* all trace of the subject-&-objects duality vanishes. Cf. also ATTĀ (c).)

---

of experience is, of course, reduplication of all five *khandhā*, not of *viññāṇa* alone.)

## *SAKKĀYA*

*Sakkāya* is *pañc'upādānakkhandhā* (*Majjhima* v,4 (M.i,299)), and may conveniently be translated as 'somebody' or 'person' or, abstractly, 'personality'. See *PS*, also for what follows.

An *arahat* (while alive—that is, if we can speak of a 'living *arahat*') continues to be *individual* in the sense that 'he' is a sequence of states (*Theragāthā* v. 716)[90] distinguishable from other *arahanto* (and *a fortiori* from individuals other than *arahanto*). Every set of *pañcakkhandhā*[a]—not *pañc'upādānakkhandhā* in the *arahat*'s case—is unique, and individuality in this sense ceases only with the final cessation of the *pañcakkhandhā* at the breaking up of the *arahat*'s body. But a living *arahat* is no longer *somebody* or a *person*, since the notion or conceit '(I) am' has already ceased. *Individuality* must therefore be carefully distinguished from *personality*,[b] which is: being a person, being somebody, being a subject (to whom objects are present), selfhood, the mirage 'I am', and so on. The *puthujjana* is not able to distinguish them—for him individuality is not conceivable apart from personality, which he takes as selfhood. The *sotāpanna* is able to distinguish them—he sees that personality or 'selfhood' is a deception dependent upon *avijjā*, a deception dependent upon not seeing the deception, which is not the case with individuality—, though he is not yet free from an aroma of subjectivity, *asmimāna*. The *arahat* not only distinguishes them but also has entirely got rid of all taint of subjectivity—'he' is individual but in no way personal. For lack of suitable expressions (which in any case would puzzle the *puthujjana*) 'he' is obliged to go on saying 'I' and 'me' and 'mine' (cf. *Dīgha* i,9 (D.i,202); *Devatā Saṃy.* iii,5 (S.i,14)[91]). Individuality where the *arahat* is concerned still involves the perspective or orientation that things

**a.** Past, future, and present, 'five aggregates': matter (or substance), feeling, perception, determinations, and consciousness.

**b.** Taken in conjunction with what follows it, this evidently means 'A *puthujjana* must take good care to become a *sotāpanna*'. In other words, a purely intellectual distinction (i.e. without direct experience) is not possible. (This statement perhaps requires some modification to allow for the *anulomikāya khantiyā samannāgato*. One who is *anulomikāya khantiyā samannāgato*, though a *puthujjana*, is not at that time *assutavā* (through hearing the Dhamma he has some understanding, but he can still lose this and return to his former state). But to be *anulomikāya khantiyā samannāgato* it is by no manner of means enough to have studied the Suttas and to profess oneself a follower of the Buddha. See *Aṅguttara* VI,x,3-6 (A.iii,441-3) & CITTA. *Anulomikāya khantiyā samannāgato* may be translated 'endowed with acquiescence in conformity (*scil.* with the Dhamma)'; such an individual is not of contrary view to the Teaching, but does not actually see it for himself.)

necessarily adopt when they *exist*, or are *present*, or are *cognized*; and for each individual the perspective is different. Loss of *upādāna* is not loss of point of view. See RŪPA and remarks on *manasikāra* in NĀMA.

*Sakkāyadiṭṭhi* (*Majjhima* v,4 (M.i,300)) is sometimes explained as the view or belief (often attributed to a purely verbal misunderstanding)[c] that in one or other of the *khandhā* there is a permanent entity, a 'self'. These rationalized accounts entirely miss the point, which is the distinction (*Khandha Saṃy.* v,6 (S.iii,47)) between *pañc'upādānakkhandhā* (which is *sakkāya*) and *pañcakkhandhā* (which is *sakkāyanirodha*). To have *diṭṭhi* about *sakkāya* is not an optional matter (as if one could regard *sakkāya* from the outside and form *diṭṭhi* about it or not, as one pleased): *sakkāya contains sakkāyadiṭṭhi* (in a latent form at least) as a necessary part of its structure.[d] If there is *sakkāya* there is *sakkāyadiṭṭhi*, and with the giving up of *sakkāyadiṭṭhi* there comes to be cessation of *sakkāya*. To give up *sakkāyadiṭṭhi*, *sakkāya* must be *seen* (i.e. as *pañc'upādānakkhandhā*), and this means that the *puthujjana does not see pañc'upādānakkhandhā as such* (i.e. he does not *recognize* them—see MAMA (a) and cf. *Majjhima* viii,5 (M.i,511)). A *puthujjana* (especially one who puts his trust in the Commentaries) sometimes comes to believe that he *does* see *pañc'upādānakkhandhā* as such, thereby blocking his own progress and meeting with frustration: he cannot see what further task is to be done, and yet remains a *puthujjana*.

---

**c.** If *avijjā* were simply a matter of verbal misunderstanding, a maggot would be an *arahat*.

**d.** The reader is referred to the passage (d) in the Preface, quoted from Blackham. It is not possible to lay too much stress on this point. See also DHAMMA (c), NIBBĀNA (a), & *NP* §§24 & 25.

## *SAṄKHĀRA*

A full discussion of this key word is given in *NP*. It is there maintained that the word *saṅkhāra*, in *all* contexts, means 'something that something else depends on', that is to say a *determination* (determinant). It might be thought that this introduces an unnecessary complication into such passages as *Vayadhammā saṅkhārā appamādena sampādetha*[72] and *Aniccā vata saṅkhārā*[73] (*Dīgha* ii,3 (D.ii,156&7)). Why, instead of telling us that *things* (*dhammā*) are impermanent and bound to disappear, should the Buddha take us out of our way to let us know that *things that things depend on* are impermanent and bound to disappear? The answer is that the Dhamma does not set out to *explain*, but to *lead*—it is *opanayika*. This means that the Dhamma is not seeking disinterested intellectual approval, but to provoke an effort of comprehension or insight leading to the abandonment of *attavāda* and eventually of *asmimāna*. Its method is therefore necessarily indirect: we can only stop regarding *this* as 'self' if we see that what *this* depends on is impermanent (see DHAMMA for more detail). Consider, for example, the *Mahāsudassanasuttanta* (*Dīgha* ii,4 (D.ii,169-99)), where the Buddha describes in detail the rich endowments and possessions of King Mahāsudassana, and then finishes: *Pass'Ānanda sabbe te saṅkhārā atītā niruddhā vipariṇatā. Evaṃ aniccā kho Ānanda saṅkhārā, evaṃ addhuvā kho Ānanda saṅkhārā, yāvañ c'idaṃ Ānanda alam eva sabbasaṅkhāresu nibbindituṃ, alaṃ virajjituṃ, alaṃ vimuccituṃ*[74]. This is not a simple statement that all those things, being impermanent by nature, are now no more; it is a lever to prize the notion of 'selfhood' out of its firm socket. Those things were *saṅkhārā*: they were things on which King Mahāsudassana depended for his very identity; they determined his person as 'King Mahāsudassana', and with their cessation the thought 'I am King Mahāsudassana' came to an end. More formally, those *saṅkhārā* were *nāmarūpa*, the condition for *phassa* (*Dīgha* ii,2 (D.ii,62)[86]), upon which *sakkāyadiṭṭhi* depends (cf. *Dīgha* i,1 (D.i,42-3) together with *Citta Saṃy.* 3 (S.iv,287)).

## *SAÑÑĀ*

*Saññā* and *viññāṇa* (perception and consciousness) may be differentiated as follows. *Saññā* (defined in *Aṅguttara* VI,vi,9 (A.iii,413)) is the quality or percept itself (e.g. blue), whereas *viññāṇa* (q.v.) is the presence or consciousness of the quality or percept—or, more strictly, of the thing exhibiting the quality or percept (i.e. of *nāmarūpa*). (A quality, it may be noted, is unchanged whether it is present or absent—blue is blue whether seen or imagined—, and the word *saññā* is used both of five-base experience and of mental experience.)

It would be as wrong to say 'a feeling is perceived' as it would 'a percept is felt' (which mix up *saññā* and *vedanā*); but it is quite in order to say 'a feeling, a percept, (that is, a felt thing, a perceived thing) is cognized', which simply means that a feeling or a percept is present (as, indeed, they both are in all experience—see *Majjhima* v,3 (M.i,293)[92]). Strictly speaking, then, what is *cognized* is *nāmarūpa*, whereas what is *perceived* (or *felt*) is *saññā* (or *vedanā*), i.e. only *nāma*. This distinction can be shown grammatically. *Vijānāti*, to cognize, is active voice in sense (taking an objective accusative): consciousness *cognizes a phenomenon* (*nāmarūpa*); consciousness is always consciousness *of* something. *Sañjānāti*, to perceive, (or *vediyati*, to feel) is middle voice in sense (taking a cognate accusative): perception *perceives* [a percept] (or feeling feels [a feeling]). Thus we *should* say 'a blue thing (= a blueness), a painful thing (= a pain), is cognized', but 'blue is perceived' and 'pain is felt'. (In the Suttas generally, due allowance is to be made for the elasticity in the common usage of words. But in certain passages, and also in one's finer thinking, stricter definition may be required.)

At *Dīgha* i,9 (D.i,185), Poṭṭhapāda asks the Buddha whether perception arises before knowledge, or knowledge before perception, or both together. The Buddha gives the following answer: *Saññā kho Poṭṭhapāda pathamaṃ uppajjati, pacchā ñāṇaṃ; saññ'uppādā ca pana ñāṇ'uppādo hoti. So evaṃ pajānāti, Idapaccayā kira me ñāṇaṃ udapādī ti.*[75] *Saññā* thus precedes *ñāṇa*, not only temporally but also structurally (or logically). That is to say, *perception is structurally simpler than knowledge*; and though perception comes first in time, it does not cease (see CITTA) in order that knowledge can arise.[a] However many stories there are to a house, the ground floor is

---

a. Cf. Bradley on judgement (*op. cit.* (*Logic*), T.E. II): 'I have taken judgement as the more or less conscious enlargement of an object, not in fact but as truth. The object is thus not altered in existence, but qualified in idea. ... For the object, merely as perceived, is not, as such, qualified as true.' And on *inference* (T.E. I): 'And our inference, to retain

built first; but it is not then removed to make way for the rest. (The case of *vitakkavicārā* and *vācā*—*NP* §5—is parallel.)

The temptation must be resisted (into which, however, the *Visuddhimagga* (Ch. XIV) falls) to understand *viññāṇa*, in the primitive context of the *khandhā*, as a more elaborate version of *saññā*, thus approximating it to *ñāṇa*. But, whereas there is always consciousness when there is perception (see above), there is not always knowledge (which is *preceded* by perception). The difference between *viññāṇa* and *saññā* is in *kind*, not in *degree*. (In looser contexts, however,—e.g. *Majjhima* v,7 (M.i,317)—*viññāṇa* does tend to mean 'knowing', but not in opposition to *saññā*. In *Majjhima* xv,1 (M.iii,259-60)[93] & xiv,8 (227-8)[94] *viññāṇa* occurs in both senses, where the second is the complex consciousness of reflexion, i.e. the presence of a *known* phenomenon—of an *example of a universal*, that is to say.)

---

its unity and so in short be an inference, must ... remain throughout within the limits of its special object.' 'Every inference, we saw, both starts with and is confined to a special object.' 'If, on the one hand, the object does not advance beyond its beginning, there clearly is no inference. But, on the other hand, if the object passes beyond what is itself, the inference is destroyed.' For Bradley, all inference is an ideal self-development of a real object, and judgement is an implicit inference. (For 'real' and 'ideal' *we* shall prefer 'immediate' and 'reflexive', at least in the first place.)

This will scarcely be intelligible to the rationalist, who does not admit any experience more simple, structurally speaking, than knowledge. For the rationalist, moreover, all knowledge is explicitly inferential, whereas, as Sartre has pointed out (*op. cit.*, p. 220), there is no knowledge, properly speaking, other than intuitive. Inference is merely instrumental in leading to intuition, and is then discarded; or, if intuition is not reached, it remains as a signpost. Rational knowledge is thus at two removes from perception (which, of course, is intuitive); and similarly with descriptive knowledge. Intuition is immediate contact between subject and object (see PHASSA); with the reflexive reduplication of intuitive knowledge (see ATTĀ (a) & MANO (b)), this becomes immediate contact between knowing (reflecting) subject and known (reflected) object; which, in the case of the *arahat*, is simply (presence of) the known thing. Cf. also Heidegger, *op. cit.*, pp. 59-62 & 212-30.

# 4. FUNDAMENTAL STRUCTURE

Showing 'Invariance under Transformation'

*Tīṇ'imāni bhikkhave saṅkhatassa saṅkhatalakkhaṇāni. Katamāni tīṇi. Uppādo paññāyati, vayo paññāyati, ṭhitassa aññathattaṃ paññāyati. Imāni kho bhikkhave tīṇi saṅkhatassa saṅkhatalakkhaṇānī ti.*[76]

*Aṅguttara* III,v,7 (A.i,152)

*Tayo'me bhikkhave addhā. Katame tayo. Atīto addhā, anāgato addhā, paccuppanno addhā. Ime kho bhikkhave tayo addhā ti.*[77]

*Itivuttaka* III,ii,4 (Iti.53)

# I. STATIC ASPECT

1. Let o represent a thing.[a]

2. If we wish to represent another thing, not o, we must represent it by another symbol; for we cannot distinguish between o and o except by the fact of their being spatially separated, left and right, on this page; and since this is a representation, not of a structure *in* space (i.e. of a spatial object), but of the structure *of* space (amongst other things), which structure is not itself spatial, such spatial distinctions in the representation must not be taken into account.[b] Thus, whether we write o once or a hundred times still only one thing is represented.

3. Let us, then, represent a thing other than o by x. (We are concerned to represent only the *framework* within which things exist, that is to say the *possibility* of the existence of things; consequently it does not matter whether there *are* in fact things—it is enough that there *could* be. But the actual existence of things is indispensable evidence that they *can* exist; and when there actually is a given thing o, there actually are, also, *other* things.)[c] We now have *two* things, o and x.

---

a. An *existing* thing is an *experience* (in German: *Erlebnis*), either present or (in some degree) absent (i.e. either immediately or more or less remotely present). See *SN*, NĀMA & RŪPA.

b. See *SN*, RŪPA (e), where it is shown that space is a secondary, not a primary, quality.

c. All this, of course, is tautologous; for 'to be a thing' means 'to be able to be or exist', and there is no *thing* that *cannot* exist. And if anything exists, everything else does (see (a) above). Compare this utterance of Parmenides: 'It needs must be that what can be thought of and spoken of is; for it is possible for it to be, and it is not possible for what is no thing to be'. (Parmenides seems to have drawn excessive conclusions from this principle through ignoring the fact that a thought is an imaginary, and therefore *absent*, experience—or rather, a complex of absent experiences—; but the principle itself is sound. The images involved in thinking must, individually at least (though not necessarily in association), already in some sense be *given*—i.e. as what is *elsewhere*,

4. We are, however, still unable to distinguish them; for, since spatial distinctions are to be disregarded, we cannot tell which is the original thing, o or x. Experience shows us that when we are conscious of one thing we are not also equally conscious of another thing; or, better, it can always be observed (by reflexion) that two (different) experiences are not both the centre of consciousness at the same time. The difference between two things is, ultimately, their order of priority—one is 'this' and the other is 'that'—, and this difference we represent by a difference in shape; for if two things are identical in all qualitative respects, have *all* their properties in common (including position if they are tactile things—and it must be remembered that the eye, since it is muscular, is also an organ of touch, giving perceptions of space and shape as well as of colour and light),[d] no priority is evident, and there are not *two* things, but only one; and thus difference in priority can be represented by difference of qualitative property. But difference in shape alone only tells us that if one of them is 'this' the other is 'that'—it does not tell us *which* is 'this'.[e]

5. We have, then, to distinguish between *first* and *second*, or *one* and *two*. At first sight this seems easy—*one* is obviously o and *two* is o x. But since it makes no difference *where* we write these symbols (spatial distinctions being of no account), we cannot be sure that they will not group themselves o o and x. Since o and o are only one thing, namely o, we are back where we started.

6. To say that o and o are only one thing is to say that there is *no* difference between them; and to say that o and x are two things is to say that there *is* a difference between them (no matter which precedes). In other words,

---

or *at some other time*, or both—at the immediate level, before they can be thought. Perhaps the method of this Note will suggest a reconciliation between the Parmenidean absolute denial of the existence of no thing, with its corollary, the absolute existence of whatever does exist, and the merely *relative* existence of every thing as implied by the undeniable fact of change.)

**d.** Strictly, we should not go *from* muscles *to* spatial perceptions. Spatial perceptions come first; then we observe that whenever there are spatial perceptions a muscular organ can be found; finally we conclude that a muscular organ is *very probably* a condition for spatial perceptions. See *SN*, PHASSA & RŪPA.

**e.** McTaggart, I discover, (*op. cit.* §45) bases his version of fundamental structure on a twofold direct appeal to experience: first, that something exists, and secondly, that more than one thing exists. But this is not enough: it is essential also to see that, of two things, in so far as they are *two*, one is 'this' and one is 'that'.

*two* things define a thing, namely the difference between them. And the difference between them, clearly, is what has to be done to pass from one to the other, or the *operation of transforming* one into the other (that is, of interchanging them). A little thought will show that this operation is *invariant* during the transformation (a 'journey from A to B'—to give a rough illustration—remains unchanged as a 'journey from A to B' at all stages of the journey), and also that the operation is a thing of a higher or more general order than either of the two things that define it (a 'journey from A to B' is more general than either 'being in A' or 'being in B' since it embraces both: a 'journey from A to B' may be *defined* as the operation of transforming 'being in A' into 'being in B' and 'not being in B' into 'not being in A'). Each of these two things, furthermore, is itself an operation of the same nature, but of a lower or more particular order (a 'journey from one part of A (or B) to another' is 'being in A (or B)', just as a 'journey from A to B' is 'being in Z', where A and B are adjacent towns and Z is the province containing them). But we must get back to our noughts and crosses.

7. Since o o is *one*, and o x is *two* (though the order of precedence between o and x is not determined), it is evident that we can use these two pairs to distinguish between *first* and *second*. In *whatever* way the four symbols, o, o, o, and x, may pair off, the result is the same (and it makes no difference whether o o is regarded as one thing and o x as two things, or, as in the last paragraph, o o is regarded as no operation and o x as one operation—*nought* precedes *one* as *one* precedes *two*). We have only to write down these four symbols (in any pattern we please) to represent 'two things, o and x, o preceding x'.

8. As these four symbols pair off, we get two distinguishable things, o o and o x (which are 'o first' and 'x second'). These two things themselves define an operation—that of transforming o o into o x and o x into o o. This operation is itself a thing, which we may write, purely for the sake of convenience, thus: $\begin{smallmatrix} o & o \\ o & x \end{smallmatrix}$.

9. It will readily be seen that if $\begin{smallmatrix} o & o \\ o & x \end{smallmatrix}$ is a thing, then another thing, not $\begin{smallmatrix} o & o \\ o & x \end{smallmatrix}$, will be represented by $\begin{smallmatrix} x & x \\ x & o \end{smallmatrix}$; for if we take $\begin{smallmatrix} o & o \\ o & x \end{smallmatrix}$ as 'o precedes x', then we must take $\begin{smallmatrix} x & x \\ x & o \end{smallmatrix}$ as 'x precedes o'. But we do not know which comes first, $\begin{smallmatrix} o & o \\ o & x \end{smallmatrix}$ or $\begin{smallmatrix} x & x \\ x & o \end{smallmatrix}$. By repetition of the earlier discussion, we see that we must take three of one and one of the other to indicate precedence; and in this way we arrive at a fresh thing (of greater complexity) represented

by $\begin{array}{cc|cc} o & o & o & o \\ o & x & o & x \\ \hline o & o & x & x \\ o & x & x & o \end{array}$. Here it is clear that though in the fourth quarter, $\begin{smallmatrix} x & x \\ x & o \end{smallmatrix}$, x precedes o, yet the first quarter, $\begin{smallmatrix} o & o \\ o & x \end{smallmatrix}$, precedes the fourth quarter. So in the whole we must say 'o precedes x *first*, and then x precedes o'.

10. Obviously we can represent the negative of this fresh thing by $\begin{array}{cc|cc} x & x & x & x \\ x & o & x & o \\ \hline x & x & o & o \\ x & o & o & x \end{array}$, and repeat the whole procedure to arrive at a thing of still greater complexity; and there is no limit to the number of times that we can do this.

11. In §7 we said that in whatever way the four symbols, o, o, o, and x, may pair off, the result is the same. In how many ways can they pair off? To find out we must number them. But a difficulty arises. So long as we had the four symbols written down *anywhere*, the objection that we were using spatial distinctions to distinguish one o from another did not arise (and in §8 we noted that we chose to write them $\begin{smallmatrix} o & o \\ o & x \end{smallmatrix}$ purely for convenience' sake). Once we number them (1, 2, 3, 4), however, the objection becomes valid; for the only distinction between o(1) and o(2) and o(3)—apart from the numbers attached to them—is their relative spatial positioning on this page. But at least we know this, that $\begin{smallmatrix} o & o \\ o & x \end{smallmatrix}$ represents 'o precedes x'; and so it follows that, even if we cannot distinguish between the first three, x comes fourth. In any way, then, in which we *happen* to write down these four symbols, *x marks the fourth place*. (If, for example, we had written them o x o o, the symbol x would still mark the fourth place.) And if x comes in the fourth place in the first place, it will come in the first place in the fourth place. This means that we can choose the first place at our convenience (only the fourth place being already fixed) and mark it with 'x in the fourth place', i.e. $\begin{smallmatrix} o & o \\ o & x \end{smallmatrix}$. With the fourth place determined, we are left with a choice of three possible arrangements: $\begin{array}{cc|cc} o & o & & \\ o^{1} & x & & \\ \hline & & x & o \\ & & o^{4} & o \end{array}$, $\begin{array}{cc|cc} & & o & o \\ & & o^{1} & x \\ \hline & & o & x \\ & & o^{4} & o \end{array}$, $\begin{array}{cc|cc} & & & \\ & & & \\ \hline o & o & o & o \\ o^{1} & x & x^{4} & o \end{array}$. Note that we must adjust the position of x in the *fourth* tetrad to come in whichever place we choose as the *first*. Let us (again purely for convenience' sake) choose the first of these three possibilities. It is clear that if x comes in the fourth place in the first place and in the first place in the fourth place, it will come in the third place in the second place and in the second place in the third place. So now we can complete the scheme thus: $\begin{array}{cc|cc} o & o & o & o \\ o^{1} & x & x & o \\ \hline o & x & x & o \\ o & o & o^{4} & o \end{array}$. But although we can now distinguish between the second place and the third place, we

cannot tell which of the two, $\begin{smallmatrix} o & o \\ x & o \end{smallmatrix}$ or $\begin{smallmatrix} o & x \\ o & o \end{smallmatrix}$, is the second and which the third: all we can say is that if one of them is the second the other is the third. This, as we shall see, is all that is necessary. Let us refer to them,

for convenience, as 2/3 and 3/2, so: $\begin{smallmatrix} o & o & o & o \\ o_{1} & x & x & o_{2/3} \\ o_{3/2} & x & x & o_{4} \\ o & o & o & o \end{smallmatrix}$ . Replacing symbols by

numbers, we finally have this:

$$\begin{matrix} \text{I} & 2/3 & 2/3 & \text{I} \\ \text{I} & & 2/3 \\ 3/2 & 4 & 4 & 3/2 \\ 3/2 & 4 & 4 & 3/2 \\ 3/2 & & 4 \\ \text{I} & 2/3 & 2/3 & \text{I} \end{matrix}$$ (the figure is enlarged to

accommodate the numerals).

**12.** In this way the four symbols, o, o, o, and x, when written $\begin{smallmatrix} o & o \\ o & x \end{smallmatrix}$, can

be numbered $\begin{matrix} \text{I} & 2/3 \\ 3/2 & 4 \end{matrix}$ ; and we see that pairing off can be done in three

ways: (I - 2/3) (3/2 - 4), (I - 3/2) (2/3 - 4), and (I - 4) (2/3 - 3/2). These may be understood as the operations, respectively, (i) of interchanging

column $\begin{matrix} \text{I} \\ 3/2 \end{matrix}$ with column $\begin{matrix} 2/3 \\ 4 \end{matrix}$, (ii) of interchanging row $\text{I} \quad 2/3$ with row

$3/2 \quad 4$ , and (iii) of doing both (i) and (ii) in *either* order and therefore both together (this really means that the three operations are mutually independent, do not obstruct one another, and can all proceed at once).[f]

And these, when set out in full—first the original arrangement $\begin{matrix} \text{I} & 2/3 \\ 3/2 & 4 \end{matrix}$

(which may be taken as the zero operation of no interchange), and then

the results of the other three operations, $\begin{matrix} 2/3 & \text{I} \\ 4 & 3/2 \end{matrix}$, $\begin{matrix} 3/2 & 4 \\ \text{I} & 2/3 \end{matrix}$, and $\begin{matrix} 4 & 3/2 \\ 2/3 & \text{I} \end{matrix}$ —,

make up the figure at the end of the last paragraph. It is easily seen that no question of priority between 2/3 and 3/2 arises.

---

f. If we describe the three operations as 'horizontal interchange', 'vertical inter-change', and 'diagonal interchange', it will readily be seen that *any* one of the three is equivalent to the other two done together. And since each is *both* the other two, it is *not either* of them.

13. We have found that a thing can be represented, in increasing complexity of structure, as follows: o, $\begin{smallmatrix} o & o \\ o & x \end{smallmatrix}$ , $\begin{smallmatrix} o & o & o & o \\ o & x & o & x \\ o & o & x & x \\ o & x & x & o \end{smallmatrix}$ , and so on, indefinitely. The first of these, o, clearly does not allow of further discussion; but the second, $\begin{smallmatrix} o & o \\ o & x \end{smallmatrix}$ , as will be seen from what has gone before, can be regarded as a combination, or rather *superposition*, of *four operations*: no interchange, interchange of columns $\left(\begin{smallmatrix} o & o \\ o & x \end{smallmatrix} - \begin{smallmatrix} o & o \\ x & o \end{smallmatrix}\right)$, interchange of rows $\left(\begin{smallmatrix} o & o \\ o & x \end{smallmatrix} - \begin{smallmatrix} o & x \\ o & o \end{smallmatrix}\right)$, and interchange of columns and rows together $\left(\begin{smallmatrix} o & o \\ o & x \end{smallmatrix} - \begin{smallmatrix} x & o \\ o & o \end{smallmatrix}\right)$; the whole being represented so: $\begin{smallmatrix} o & o & o & o \\ o & x & x & o \\ o & x & x & o \\ o & o & o & o \end{smallmatrix}$ . A thing represented by $\begin{smallmatrix} o & o \\ o & x \end{smallmatrix}$ , that is to say, consists of four members, one of which corresponds to each of the four operations. As we go to greater complexity and consider a thing represented by $\begin{smallmatrix} o & o & o & o \\ o & x & o & x \\ o & o & x & x \\ o & x & x & o \end{smallmatrix}$, we find that the following operations are superposed: no interchange; interchange of column 1 with column 2 and of column 3 with column 4; similar interchange of rows; interchange of column 1-&-2 with column 3-&-4; similar interchange of rows; and any or all of these together. The total is sixteen; and the whole representation is given below (the numbers are not necessary but are given for clarity's sake, with 2/3 just as 2 and 3/2 as 3 and corresponding simplifications in the other numbers).

| | | | | | | | | | | | | | | | |
|---|---|---|---|---|---|---|---|---|---|---|---|---|---|---|---|
| o | o | o | o | o | o | o | o | o | o | o | o | o | o | o | o |
| o | x | o | x | x | o | x | o | o | x | o | x | x | o | x | o |
| 1 | | | | 2 | | | | 5 | | | | 6 | | | |
| o | o | x | x | o | o | x | x | x | x | o | o | x | x | o | o |
| o | x | x | o | x | o | o | x | x | o | o | x | o | x | x | o |
| o | x | o | x | x | o | x | o | o | x | o | x | x | o | x | o |
| o | o | o | o | o | o | o | o | o | o | o | o | o | o | o | o |
| 3 | | | | 4 | | | | 7 | | | | 8 | | | |
| o | x | x | o | x | o | o | x | x | o | o | x | o | x | x | o |
| o | o | x | x | o | o | x | x | x | x | o | o | x | x | o | o |
| o | o | x | x | o | o | x | x | x | x | o | o | x | x | o | o |
| o | x | x | o | x | o | o | x | x | o | o | x | o | x | x | o |
| 9 | | | | 10 | | | | 13 | | | | 14 | | | |
| o | o | o | o | o | o | o | o | o | o | o | o | o | o | o | o |
| o | x | o | x | x | o | x | o | o | x | o | x | x | o | x | o |
| o | x | x | o | x | o | o | x | x | o | o | x | o | x | x | o |
| o | o | x | x | o | o | x | x | x | x | o | o | x | x | o | o |
| 11 | | | | 12 | | | | 15 | | | | 16 | | | |
| o | x | o | x | x | o | x | o | o | x | o | x | x | o | x | o |
| o | o | o | o | o | o | o | o | o | o | o | o | o | o | o | o |

Here we have sixteen members, one corresponding to each operation (as before). If we go to still more complex representations of a thing (as indicated in §10) we shall get 64 members, and then 256 members, and so on, indefinitely. Note that any of these representations can—more strictly, though less conveniently—be written in one line, in which case there are no columns-and-rows; and we are then concerned throughout only with interchanges of symbols—singly and in pairs, in pairs of pairs and in pairs of pairs of pairs, and so on. (This, incidentally, throws light on the structure of a line; for we are taking advantage of the structure of a line to represent structure in general. The structure of the line—or, more exactly, of *length*—is seen when we superpose all the members of the representation.)

14. It is a characteristic of all these representations that the operation of transforming any given member into any other member of the set transforms *every* member of the set into another member of the same set. The whole, then, is *invariant under transformation*. Attention, in other words, can shift from one aspect of a thing to another while the thing as a whole remains *absolutely* unchanged. (This universal property of a thing is so much taken for granted that a structural reason for it—or rather, the possibility of representing it symbolically—is rarely suspected.) See *SN*, CETANĀ (Husserl's cube).

15. Representations of a thing in greater complexity than the 4-member figure show the structure of successive *orders of reflexion* (or, more strictly, of *pre-reflexion*—see *SN*, DHAMMA (b)). Thus, with 16 members we represent the fundamental structure of the fundamental structure of a thing, in other words the structure of first-order reflexion; whereas with four members we have simply first-order reflexion or the structure of the immediate thing. (In first-order reflexion, the immediate thing is merely an *example* of a thing: it is, as it were, 'in brackets'. In second-order reflexion—the 16-member figure—, first-order reflexion is 'in brackets' as an *example* of fundamental structure.) In the 16-member representation, *any* two of the other 15 members of the set together with a given member uniquely define a tetrad with the structure of the 4-member representation; and *any* such tetrad uniquely defines three other tetrads such that the four tetrads together form a tetrad of tetrads, and this again with the same structure. From this it can be seen that the structure of the structure of a thing is the same as the structure of a thing, or more generally that the structure of structure has the structure

of structure.[g] The 16-member representation gives the fundamental structure of first-order reflexion, just as 4 members represent the fundamental structure of immediacy, and the single member (o) represents simply immediacy, the thing.

**16.** The same structure, naturally, is repeated at each level of generality, as will be evident from the numbers in the figure at the end of §11. The whole (either at the immediate or at any reflexive level) forms a hierarchy infinite in both directions[h] (thus disposing, incidentally, of the current assumptions of *absolute smallness*—the electron—in quantum physics, and *absolute largeness*—the universe—in astronomical physics).[i] It will also be

---

**g.** There is an old axiom: *Quidquid cognoscitur, per modum cognoscentis cognoscitur*—Whatever is known, is known in the mode of the knower. This would imply that, if the mode (or structure) of immediate experience were different from that of reflexive experience, it would be systematically falsified in the very act of being known. A further act of reflexion would then be necessary to reveal the falsification. And this, in turn, would involve a further falsification, requiring yet a further act of reflexion. And so on indefinitely, with no end to the falsification; and fundamental structure (if any) would never be knowable. But we now see that the modes of immediate and of reflexive experience are the same, and consequently that any further act of reflexion can only confirm the original reflexive evidence, which is therefore apodictic. Fundamental structure guarantees reflexive knowledge of it.

**h.** The structure of the immediate hierarchy, based on

| | |
|---|---|
| o | o |
| o | x |

, comes into view when the operations of interchange of §12 are themselves subjected to these operations. The original operations are given by

| | | | |
|---|---|---|---|
| o | o | o | o |
| o | x | x | o |
| o | x | x | o |
| o | o | o | o |

, and we operate on this to get

| | | | | | | | |
|---|---|---|---|---|---|---|---|
| o | o | o | o | o | o | o | o |
| o | x | x | o | x | o | o | x |
| o | x | x | o | x | o | o | x |
| o | o | o | o | o | o | o | o |
| o | x | x | o | x | o | o | x |
| o | o | o | o | o | o | o | o |
| o | o | o | o | o | o | o | o |
| o | x | x | o | x | o | o | x |

; and, clearly, we can continue indefinitely. Similarly for the hierarchies of each level of reflexive experience.

**i.** It is evident, in practice, that limits are encountered. There is, for example, a limit to the degree of smallness that can be distinguished. The reason for this is to be looked for on the volitional level. In order for a thing to be distinguished (or isolated) it must be observable *at leisure*, and this is a voluntary reflexive capacity. Beyond a certain degree of smallness this capacity fails. The smallest thing that can be distinguished has a certain appreciable size, but the visual (tactile) oscillations can no longer be controlled reflexively so that one part may be distinguishable from another part. And conversely, evident that successive *orders* of reflexion generate a hierarchy that is infinite, though in one direction only (perpendicular, as it were, to the doubly infinite particular-and-general hierarchy).

17. The foregoing discussion attempts to indicate in the barest possible outline the nature of fundamental structure in its static aspect. Discussion of the dynamic aspect must deal with the structure of *duration*, and will go on to distinguish *past*, *present*, and *future*, at any time, as over-determined, determined, and under-determined, respectively. The way will then be open for discussion of *intention*, *action*, and *choice*, and the teleological nature of experience generally.

---

above a certain degree of largeness it is not possible to pass from one part to another at will, so as to appreciate the whole. Similar considerations will apply to perceptions other than size. The range of voluntary reflexion is not dictated by fundamental structure and varies (we may presume) from individual to individual, and particularly from individuals of one species to those of another. The ranges of an elephant and of an ant, at least as regards spatial perceptions, will scarcely overlap at all.

The existence of such limits can easily be demonstrated by an artificial device. If a cinematograph film is projected slowly enough, we perceive a series of stills, each of which we can examine individually. When the projection is speeded up, this examination becomes more difficult, and the series of stills is seen as a flicker. Then, at a certain point, the flickering ceases and we see simply a single (moving) picture. If, on the other hand, the projection is slowed down instead of speeded up, there comes a point past which the individual stills are no longer grasped as forming part of a series, and the unity of the film as a whole is lost.

# II. DYNAMIC ASPECT

1. Between its appearance and its disappearance a thing *endures*.

2. To fix the idea of duration we might imagine some rigid object—a lamp, say—together with the ticking of a clock. Both are necessary; for if either is missing the image fails. The image is no doubt rather crude, but will perhaps serve to make it clear that duration—what we sometimes call 'the passage of time'—is a combination of unchange and change. *Duration* and *Invariance under Transformation* are one and the same.

3. We saw, in Part I, that a thing can be represented by the four symbols, o, o, o, and x, which pair off to define the operation of interchanging o o and o x. This, we found, can be done in three ways, $\begin{array}{cc:cc} \mathrm{o} & \mathrm{o} & \mathrm{o} & \mathrm{o} \\ \mathrm{o} & \mathrm{x} & \mathrm{x} & \mathrm{o} \end{array}$, $\begin{array}{cc} \mathrm{o} & \mathrm{o} \\ \mathrm{o} & \mathrm{x} \\ \hdashline \mathrm{o} & \mathrm{x} \\ \mathrm{o} & \mathrm{o} \end{array}$, and $\begin{array}{cc:cc} \mathrm{o} & \mathrm{o} & & \\ \mathrm{o} & \mathrm{x} & & \\ \hdashline & & \mathrm{x} & \mathrm{o} \\ & & \mathrm{o} & \mathrm{o} \end{array}$, or by interchange of columns, of rows, and of both together. We do not need, at present, to distinguish them, and we can take interchange of columns, $\begin{array}{cc:cc} \mathrm{o} & \mathrm{o} & \mathrm{o} & \mathrm{o} \\ \mathrm{o} & \mathrm{x} & \mathrm{x} & \mathrm{o} \end{array}$, as representative of the whole. When o o is transformed into o x and *vice versa*, the thing or operation (o, o, o, x) is invariant—all that has happened is that the symbols have rearranged themselves: $\begin{array}{cc} \mathrm{o} & \mathrm{o} \\ \mathrm{o} & \mathrm{x} \end{array}$ has become $\begin{array}{cc} \mathrm{o} & \mathrm{o} \\ \mathrm{x} & \mathrm{o} \end{array}$. This is one unit of duration—one *moment*. Clearly enough we can repeat the operation, so: $\begin{array}{cc:cc} \mathrm{o} & \mathrm{o} & \mathrm{o} & \mathrm{o} \\ \mathrm{x} & \mathrm{o} & \mathrm{o} & \mathrm{x} \end{array}$. It is still the *same* operation, namely interchange of columns. (The operation of transforming o o into o x automatically transforms o x into o o—when the old 'o first' becomes the new 'x second', the old 'x second' becomes the new 'o first', as with our journey of §I/6 from A to B—, and each time we are ready to start afresh.) This gives us a second moment; and by continued repetition we can get as many moments as we please, with the thing as a whole remaining unchanged.

4. We know, however, that the structure is hierarchical; and 'a time must come' when the thing as a whole changes—just as $\begin{smallmatrix} o & o \\ o & x \end{smallmatrix}$ becomes $\begin{smallmatrix} o & o \\ x & o \end{smallmatrix}$, so $\begin{matrix} O & O \\ O & X \end{matrix}$ must become $\begin{matrix} O & O \\ X & O \end{matrix}$. How many times must the transformation be repeated before the transformation is itself transformed? For how many moments does a thing endure? Let us suppose that it endures for a certain finite number of moments, say a hundred. Then, after a hundred moments the thing changes, and after another hundred moments it changes again, and after yet another hundred moments it changes yet again, and so on. It will be seen that we do not, in fact, have a combination of unchange and change, but two different *rates* of change, one slow and one fast, just like two interlocking cog-wheels of which one revolves once as the other revolves a hundred times. And we see that this fails to give the idea of duration; for if we make the large cog-wheel really unchanging by holding it fast, the small cog-wheel also is obliged to stop. Similarly, we do not say 'a minute *endures* for sixty seconds' but 'a minute *is* sixty seconds'—it would never occur to us to *time* a minute with a stop-watch. To get duration, the difference between the unchanging and the changing must be absolute: the unchanging must be unchanging *however* much the changing changes.[j] If a thing *endures*, it endures for ever. A thing is eternal.

---

j. This will clearly permit different *relative* rates of change, or frequencies, at the same level. The ratios between such frequencies would seem to be arbitrary, but it is clear that they can change only discontinuously. In other words, the *substance* of my world (real and imaginary) at any time is not dictated by fundamental structure, and vanishes abruptly. (See *SN*, RŪPA (c).) The only change considered by the main body of this Note, in its present incomplete form, is change of orientation or perspective. Duration does not require change of substance, though the converse is not true. (Might it not be that with every change of orientation in the world of one sense there is a corresponding change of substance in the world of each of the others? This is partly observable at least in the case of intentional bodily action; which, indeed, seems to change the substance also of its own world—as when the left hand alters the world of the right. But this supposition is not without its difficulties.)

The 'unchange' that is here in question is on no account to be confused with what is described in *SN*, ATTĀ as an 'extra-temporal changeless "self"'. Experience of the supposed subject or 'self' (a would-be extra-temporal personal *nunc stans*) is a gratuitous (though beginningless) imposition or parasite upon the structure we are now discussing. See *SN*, CETANĀ (f). (Cf. in this connexion the equivocal existentialist positions discussed by M. Wyschogrod in *Kierkegaard and Heidegger: The Ontology of Existence*, Routledge & Kegan Paul, London 1954.)

5. A thing changes, then, after an *infinity* of moments. And since the structure is hierarchical, each moment must itself endure for an infinity of moments of lesser order before it can give place to the next moment. And, naturally, the same applies to each of these lesser moments. It might perhaps seem that with such a congestion of eternities no change can ever take place at any level. But we must be careful not to introduce preconceived notions of time: just as the structure is not *in* space but *of* space (amongst other things)—see §I/2—, so the structure is not *in* time but *of* time. Thus we are not at all obliged to regard each moment as lasting the same length of *absolute* time as its predecessor; for we have not encountered 'absolute time'. Naturally, if we regard a given thing as *eternal*, then each of the infinite moments for which it endures will be of the same duration—one unit. But if this eternal thing is to change (or transform), then clearly the infinite series of moments must *accelerate*. If each successive moment is a definite fraction (less than unity) of its predecessor, then the whole infinite series will come to an end sooner or later.

6. Now we see that *three* levels of the hierarchy are involved: on top, at the most general level of the three, we have a thing enduring eternally unchanged; below this, we have a thing changing at regular intervals of one unit of duration, one moment; and below this again, in *each* of these regular intervals, in *each* of these moments, we have an infinite series of moments of lesser order accelerating and coming to an end. We have only to take into account an *eternal* thing of still higher order of generality to see that our former eternal thing will now be changing at regular intervals, that the thing formerly changing at regular intervals will be accelerating its changes (and the series of changes repeatedly coming to an end at regular intervals), and that the formerly accelerating series will be a doubly accelerating series of series. There is no difficulty in extending the scheme infinitely in both directions of the hierarchy; and when we have done so we see that there is no place for anything absolutely enduring for ever, and that there is no place for anything absolutely without duration.[k]

**k.** It would be a mistake to attempt to take up a position outside the whole system in order to visualize it as passing from the future into the past through a 'present moment' in a kind of universal time. At any given level of generality, the 'present moment' lasts for one whole eternity relative to the next lower level, and there is thus no such thing as a 'present moment' for the system as a whole; nor has the system any outside (even imaginary) from which it may be viewed 'as a whole'.

7. We can represent a thing by O. This, however, is eternal. To see the structure of change we must go to the 4-symbol representation $\begin{smallmatrix} o & o \\ o & x \end{smallmatrix}$, where o and x are things of the next lower order of generality. From §3 it will be seen that O is the *invariant* operation of interchange of columns: $\begin{smallmatrix} o & o \\ o & x \end{smallmatrix}$ becomes $\begin{smallmatrix} o & o \\ x & o \end{smallmatrix}$, and then $\begin{smallmatrix} o & o \\ x & o \end{smallmatrix}$ becomes $\begin{smallmatrix} o & o \\ o & x \end{smallmatrix}$, and so on, to infinity. But now that we have found that moments (or things) *come to an end*, some modification in this account is needed. In $\begin{smallmatrix} o & o \\ o & x \end{smallmatrix}$, o is 'this' and x is 'that' (i.e. 'not-this'), as we saw in Part I. When the moment marked by one interchange of columns comes to an end, 'this' vanishes entirely, and we are left just with 'that', which, clearly, is the new 'this'. The o's disappear, in other words. Thus when $\begin{smallmatrix} o & o \\ o & x \end{smallmatrix}$ has become $\begin{smallmatrix} o & o \\ x & o \end{smallmatrix}$ we shall not, contrary to what we have just said, have the same operation simply in the opposite sense, i.e. $\begin{smallmatrix} o & o & \vdots & o & o \\ x & o & \vdots & o & x \end{smallmatrix}$, since all that remains is $x \vdots x$. In the repetition of the operation, then, x will occupy the same position as o in the original, and O (i.e. 'interchange of columns') will now be represented by $\begin{smallmatrix} x & x \\ x & o \end{smallmatrix}$. The second interchange of columns will thus be $\begin{smallmatrix} x & x & \vdots & x & x \\ x & o & \vdots & o & x \end{smallmatrix}$, the third interchange will be $\begin{smallmatrix} o & o & \vdots & o & o \\ o & x & \vdots & x & o \end{smallmatrix}$, and the fourth $\begin{smallmatrix} x & x & \vdots & x & x \\ x & o & \vdots & o & x \end{smallmatrix}$, and so on. It will be evident that, while O is invariant (eternally), the symbols at the next lower level of generality will be alternating between o and x. (For convenience we may start off the whole system with the symbol o at each level, though in different sizes, to represent 'this'; and we may then allow these to change to x as the system is set in motion. But we can only do this *below a given level*, since if only we go up far enough we shall always find that the system has *already* started. We cannot, therefore, start the system at any absolute first point—we can only 'come in in the middle'. It will be seen, also, that the system is not reversible: future is future and past is past. But this will become clearer as we proceed.)

8. Disregarding other things, consciousness of a thing while it endures is constant: and this may be counted as unity. We can regard consciousness of a thing as the thing's *intensity* or *weight*—quite simply, the degree to which it *is*. In §I/12 (f) we noted that *any* interchange is equivalent to the other two done together. Thus, to pass from 1 to 4 it is necessary to go by way of both 2/3 and 3/2, so: $\begin{smallmatrix} o & \rightarrow & o \\ \downarrow & & \downarrow \\ o & \rightarrow & x \end{smallmatrix}$. The intensity or weight must therefore be distributed among the four symbols in the following way:

$$\begin{matrix} & o \rightarrow o \\ o & \downarrow \\ \downarrow & x \\ o \rightarrow x & \end{matrix}, \text{ or } \begin{matrix} 2 & 1 \\ 1 & 2 \end{matrix}$$

. This will mean that the intensity of o is two-thirds of the whole, and of x, one-third. (A moment's reflexion will verify that 'this' is necessarily more intense than 'that'. Visual reflexion will do here; but it must be remembered that visual experience, which is easy to refer to, is structurally very complex—see §I/4—, and visual evidence normally requires further breakdown before revealing aspects of fundamental structure. It is usually less misleading to think in terms of sound or of extension than of vision, and it is advisable in any case to check the evidence of one sense with that of another.) When $\begin{smallmatrix}o&o\\o&\end{smallmatrix}$ vanishes we shall be left with x, whose intensity is only one-third of the whole. But just as $\begin{smallmatrix}o&o\\o&\end{smallmatrix}$ stands to x in the proportion of intensity of 2:1, so $\begin{smallmatrix}x&x\\x&\end{smallmatrix}$ of a lesser order stands to o of the same lesser order in the same proportion, and so on indefinitely. Thus we obtain a hierarchy of intensity, $\frac{1}{2}, \frac{1}{4}, \frac{1}{8}, \frac{1}{16}, \frac{1}{32}, \ldots$ to infinity, the sum of which is unity. The total intensity at any time must be unity, as we noted above; and when the first term of this hierarchy, $\begin{smallmatrix}o&o\\o&\end{smallmatrix}$, which is $\frac{1}{2}$ the total intensity, vanishes, it is necessary to increase the intensity of the rest to compensate for this loss; and to do this we must make x, when it becomes $\begin{smallmatrix}x&x\\x&\end{smallmatrix}$, *be* (or *exist*) correspondingly *faster*. This is achieved, clearly enough, by *doubling* the rate of existence (i.e. *halving* the relative length) of each successive moment. (When the first term of $\frac{1}{2} + \frac{1}{4} + \frac{1}{8} + \frac{1}{16} + \ldots$ vanishes, it is only necessary to double the remainder, $\frac{1}{4} + \frac{1}{8} + \frac{1}{16} + \frac{1}{32} + \ldots$, to restore the *status quo*.)

**9.** If we go to the 16-member representation it will be clearer what is happening. This representation, $\begin{array}{cc|cc} o&o&o&o\\ o&x&o&x\\ \hline o&o&x&x\\ o&x&x&o \end{array}$, combines two adjacent levels of generality: it is a combination of $\begin{matrix}O&O\\O&X\end{matrix}$ and $\begin{smallmatrix}o&o\\o&x\end{smallmatrix}$. But this combination, we see, can be made in two ways: $\begin{array}{c|c} \begin{smallmatrix}o&o\\o&x\end{smallmatrix} & \\ \hline & \end{array}$ $\begin{array}{c|c} & \begin{smallmatrix}o&o\\o&x\end{smallmatrix} \\ \hline & \end{array}$ $\begin{array}{c|c} & \\ \hline \begin{smallmatrix}o&o\\o&x\end{smallmatrix} & \end{array}$ $\begin{array}{c|c} & \\ \hline & \begin{smallmatrix}x&x\\x&o\end{smallmatrix} \end{array}$ and $\begin{array}{c|c} o & o \\ \hline o & x \end{array}$ $\begin{array}{c|c} o & o \\ \hline o & x \end{array}$ $\begin{array}{c|c} o & o \\ \hline o & x \end{array}$ $\begin{array}{c|c} x & x \\ \hline x & o \end{array}$. Alternatively, however, we can regard the combination of $\begin{matrix}O&O\\O&X\end{matrix}$ and $\begin{smallmatrix}o&o\\o&x\end{smallmatrix}$ not as that of two adjacent levels of generality, but as that of the *present* and the *future* on the same level of generality; and, clearly, this too can be made in these two ways. If, furthermore, we regard the *first* of these two ways in which the combination of $\begin{matrix}O&O\\O&X\end{matrix}$ and $\begin{smallmatrix}o&o\\o&x\end{smallmatrix}$ can be made as the combination of two adjacent, equally present, levels of generality, we must regard the *second* way as the combination of the present and the future, both of the same level of generality; and, of course, *vice versa*. This means that, from the point of view of $\begin{matrix}O&O\\O&X\end{matrix}$,

$\begin{smallmatrix} \text{o} & \text{o} \\ \text{o} & \text{x} \end{smallmatrix}$ can be regarded either as *present but of lower order* or as *of the same order but future*. (And, of course, from the point of view of $\begin{smallmatrix} \text{o} & \text{o} \\ \text{o} & \text{x} \end{smallmatrix}$, $\begin{matrix} \text{O} & \text{O} \\ \text{O} & \text{X} \end{matrix}$ can be regarded either as *present but of higher order* or as *of the same order but past*.) In other words, the general/particular hierarchy can equally well be regarded—or rather, *must at the same time be regarded*—as the past, present, and future, at any one level of generality. (A simple illustration can be given. Consider this figure:

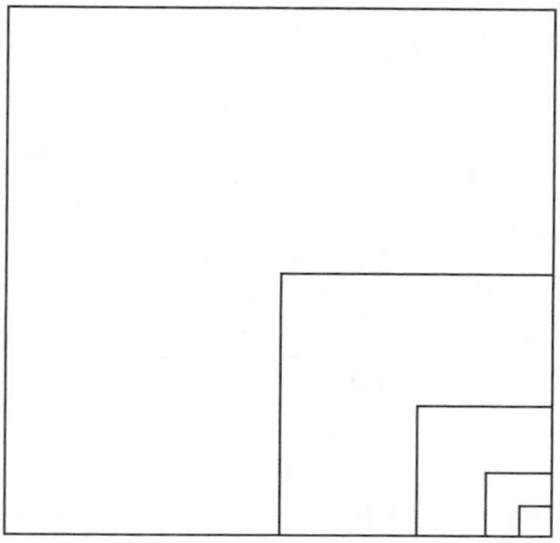

It presents itself *either* as a large square enclosing a number of progressively smaller squares all within one plane at the same distance from the observer, *or* as a number of squares of equal size but in separate planes at progressively greater distances from the observer, giving the appearance of a corridor. A slight change of attention is all that is needed to switch from one aspect to the other. In fundamental structure, however, *both* aspects are equally in evidence.) This allows us to dispose of the tiresome paradox (noted, but not resolved, by Augustine) that, (i) since the past is over and done with and the future has not yet arrived, we cannot possibly know anything about them in the present; and (ii) there is, nevertheless, present perception and knowledge of the past and of the future (memory is familiar to everyone,[1] and retrocognition and precognition are well-known occurrences; though it is clear that awareness of movement or of change of substance provides

1. All memory involves perception of the past, but perception of the past is not in itself memory. The question of memory, however, does not otherwise concern us in these *Notes*. (The attention we give to whatever happens to be present will, no doubt, permanently increase its weightage relative to all that does not come to be present.)

more immediate evidence[m])—the very words *past* and *future* would not exist if experience of what they stand for were inherently impossible.[n]

10. *Past* and *future* (as well as *present*) exist in the present; but they exist *as* past and *as* future (though what exactly the pastness of the past—'this is over and done with'—and the futurity of the future—'this has not yet arrived'—consist of will only become apparent at a later stage when we discuss the nature of intention). And since each 'present' is a self-sufficient totality, complete with the entire past and the entire future, it is meaningless to ask whether the past and the future that exist at present are the same as the *real* past or future, that is to say as the present that *was existing* in the past and the present that *will be existing* in the future: 'the present that existed in the past' is simply another way of saying 'the past that exists in the present'.[o] From this it will be understood that whenever we discuss past, present, and future, we are discussing the present hierarchy, and whenever we discuss the present hierarchy we are discussing past, present, and future. The two aspects are rigorously interchangeable:

---

**m.** Neither movement nor change of substance is fundamental: fundamental structure is *necessary* for them to be *possible*, and this is true also of their respective *times* (see §4 (j)). In other words, the time (past, present, future) that is manifest in movement and in change of substance is dependent upon, but does not share the structure of, the time that is discussed in these pages. Thus, in movement, the time is simply that of the hierarchy of trajectories (see *SN*, PAṬICCASAMUPPĀDA (c)), and its structure is therefore that of the straight line (see §I/13): the time of movement, in other words, is perfectly homogeneous and infinitely subdivisible. In itself, therefore, this time makes no distinction between *past*, *present*, and *future*, and must necessarily rest upon a substructure that does give a meaning to these words. In fundamental time, each unit—each moment—is absolutely indivisible, since adjacent levels are heterogeneous.

**n.** McTaggart has argued (*op. cit.*, §§325 *et seq.*) that the ideas of past, present, and future, which are essential characteristics of change and time, involve a contradiction that can only be resolved in an infinite regress. This regress, he maintained, is vicious, and change and time are therefore 'unreal'. It is clear enough that perception of movement, and therefore of time, does involve an infinite reflexive (or rather, pre-reflexive) regress. We perceive uniform motion; we perceive accelerated motion, and recognize it as such; we can perhaps also recognize doubly accelerated motion; and the idea of still higher orders of acceleration is perfectly acceptable to us, without any definite limit: all this would be out of the question unless time had an indefinitely regressive hierarchical structure. If this regress is vicious, then so much the worse for virtue. But see §I/15 (g), which indicates that it is not in fact vicious.

**o.** These remarks do not imply that the present that *will be existing* in the future is *now* determined; on the contrary (as we shall see) it is *under*-determined—which is what makes it *future*. Similarly, the past is *now* what is over-determined.

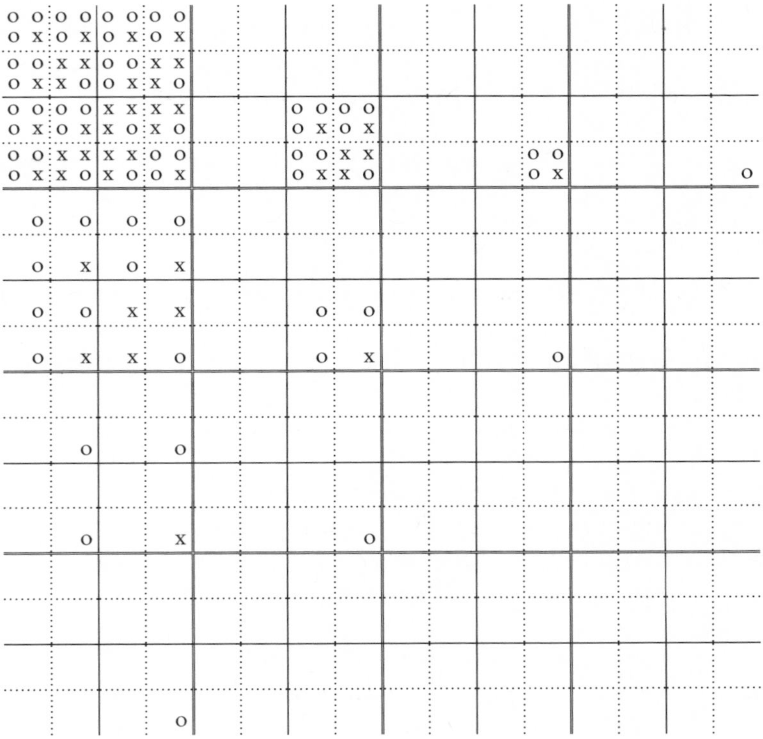


11. In §3 we took the interchange of columns as representative of all three possible interchanges: (i) of columns, (ii) of rows, and (iii) of both together. We must now discriminate between them. Neglecting the zero operation of no interchange, we may regard a thing as a superposition of these three interchanges (§I/13). We saw in §8 that $\begin{smallmatrix}\text{o} & \text{o}\\ \text{o} & \end{smallmatrix}$ ('this') has twice the intensity or weight of $\begin{smallmatrix}\text{x} & \text{x}\\ \text{x} & \end{smallmatrix}$ ('that'), and this is obviously true of each of the three possible interchanges. But this imposes no restriction whatsoever on the intensities of the three interchanges *relative one to another*: what these relative intensities shall be is a matter of complete indifference to fundamental structure. Let us, therefore, choose convenient numbers; let us suppose that the weight of interchange of columns, $\begin{smallmatrix}\text{o} & \text{o} & \vdots & \text{o} & \text{o}\\ \text{o} & \text{x} & \vdots & \text{x} & \text{o}\end{smallmatrix}$, is one-half of the total, of interchange of rows, $\begin{smallmatrix}\text{o} & \text{o}\\ \text{o} & \text{x}\\ \cdots & \cdots\\ \text{o} & \text{x}\\ \text{o} & \text{o}\end{smallmatrix}$, one-third, and of interchange of both, $\begin{smallmatrix}\text{o} & \text{o} & \vdots & & \\ \text{o} & \text{x} & \vdots & & \\ \cdots & \cdots & \vdots & \cdots & \cdots\\ & & \vdots & \text{x} & \text{o}\\ & & \vdots & \text{o} & \text{o}\end{smallmatrix}$, one-sixth, the total being unity. Then, in interchange of columns, 'this' $\left(\begin{smallmatrix}\text{o} & \text{o}\\ \text{o} & \text{x}\end{smallmatrix}\right)$ will have the value $\frac{6}{18}$, and

'that' $\begin{pmatrix} o & o \\ x & o \end{pmatrix}$ the value $\frac{3}{18}$ ; in interchange of rows, 'this' $\begin{pmatrix} o & o \\ o & x \end{pmatrix}$ will have the value $\frac{4}{18}$ , and 'that' $\begin{pmatrix} o & x \\ o & o \end{pmatrix}$ the value $\frac{2}{18}$ ; and in interchange of both, 'this' $\begin{pmatrix} o & o \\ o & x \end{pmatrix}$ will have the value $\frac{2}{18}$ , and 'that' $\begin{pmatrix} x & o \\ o & o \end{pmatrix}$ the value $\frac{1}{18}$ . It will be observed that the three 'this' $\begin{pmatrix} o & o \\ o & x \end{pmatrix}$ are indistinguishable, whereas the three 'that', $\left(\begin{matrix} o & o \\ x & o \end{matrix},\ \begin{matrix} o & x \\ o & o \end{matrix} \text{ and } \begin{matrix} x & o \\ o & o \end{matrix}\right)$ are not; and that consequently we simply have one single 'this', of value $\frac{12}{18}$ or $\frac{2}{3}$ , and three separate 'that', of respective values, $\frac{3}{18}$ , $\frac{2}{18}$ and $\frac{1}{18}$, totalling $\frac{1}{3}$ . *No matter what the relative weights of the three interchanges may be, the weight of 'this' is always twice the combined weights of the three 'that'*. This means, in effect, that however much the relative weights of the three 'that' may vary among themselves, the weight of 'this' remains constant.

**12.** The question now arises, *which* of these three possible interchanges is the one that will take place when the time comes for 'this' to vanish and 'that' to become 'this'. We said, in §7, that a thing, O, is the *invariant* operation of interchange of columns to infinity. This, however, is equally true of interchange of rows and of both columns and rows. In other words, O is simply the invariant operation of interchange, no matter whether of columns, of rows, or of both. Any or all of these interchanges are O. It will be seen, then, that the invariance of O is unaffected by the distribution of weight among the three possible interchanges that can take place. A simplified illustration may make this clearer. Suppose my room contains a chair, a table, a bed, and a wardrobe. If there is no other article of furniture in the room, the chair is *determined* as the chair by its *not* being the table, the bed, or the wardrobe. In other words, the piece of furniture in my room that is not-the-table, not-the-bed, and not-the-wardrobe, is the chair. But so long as all these determinations are to *some* extent present it matters not at all where the emphasis is placed. The question of *degree*, that is to say, does not arise. If, when I am about to sit down and start writing, I pay attention to the chair, it will present itself strongly to me as being not-the-table, but perhaps only faintly as not-the-wardrobe, and hardly at all as not-the-bed; but if I pay attention to it when I am feeling sleepy, it will be most strongly present as not-the-bed, and much less as not-the-table and not-the-wardrobe. In either case the chair keeps its identity unaltered as 'the piece of furniture that is neither table, bed, nor wardrobe'.

**13.** Let us consider two adjacent levels of generality, O and o, where O endures for one moment while o undergoes an infinity of transformations in an accelerating series. But the symbols O and o simply give the immediate thing (§I/15), and we need to see the *structure* of the thing. We must therefore write each thing in the form $\begin{smallmatrix} O & O \\ o & x \end{smallmatrix}$ and expand accordingly. We also need to see the structure of the two adjacent levels at the

same time. This will give us the figure of §I/16 (h), *viz:*

$$
\begin{array}{cc|cc|cc|cc}
o & o & o & o & o & o & o & o \\
o^a x & x^b o & x & o & o & x \\
\hline
o & x & x & o & x & o & o & x \\
o^c o & o^d o & o & o & o & o \\
\hline
o & x & x & o & x & o & o & x \\
o & o & o & o & o & o & o & o \\
\hline
o & o & o & o & o & o & o & o \\
o & x & x & o & x & o & o & x
\end{array}
$$

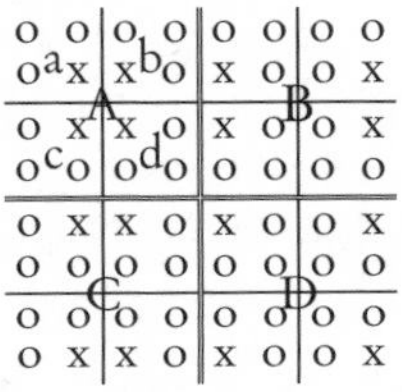

(This figure is out of scale: it should be one-quarter the size.) We see that O is represented by $\begin{smallmatrix} A & B \\ C & D \end{smallmatrix}$ and o by $\begin{smallmatrix} a & b \\ c & d \end{smallmatrix}$. (Note that D, for example, is simply $\begin{smallmatrix} a & b \\ c & d \end{smallmatrix}$ with interchange of both columns and rows, i.e. $\begin{smallmatrix} d & c \\ b & a \end{smallmatrix}$, and similarly with B and C.) Let us suppose that, at the lower level, repeated interchange of columns (a-b, c-d) is taking place. This, naturally, will be taking place in all four quarters, A, B, C, and D. Let us also suppose that, to begin with, the relative weights of the three possible interchanges of O are 1(A-B) : 2(A-D) : 3(A-C). We have seen in §7 that whenever an interchange, $\begin{smallmatrix} o & o \\ o & x \end{smallmatrix} \begin{smallmatrix} o \\ x \end{smallmatrix} \begin{smallmatrix} o \\ o \end{smallmatrix}$ say, takes place, it is actually not simply an interchange, but a disappearance of $\begin{smallmatrix} o & o \\ o \end{smallmatrix}$ leaving just x. This x is then the fresh $\begin{smallmatrix} x & x \\ x & o \end{smallmatrix}$, which in its turn becomes o, and so on. In other words, each time what we have represented as an interchange takes place, *things lose a dimension*. This statement can be inverted, and we can say that the present, each time it advances into the future, *gains* a dimension, with the consequence that immediately future things, when they become present, will necessarily appear with one dimension less. Though, from one point of view, O remains invariant throughout the series of interchanges (it *is* the series of interchanges, of any or all of the three possible kinds), from another point of view, each time an interchange takes place O vanishes and is replaced by *another* O differing from the earlier O only in that having been *future* to it (or of *lower order*—see §9) it has, relative to it, a second dimension. We must at once qualify this statement. The loss of a dimension takes place at the level, not of O, but of o, which is at a lower level of generality; and properly speaking we should say that O loses an *infinitesimal part* of its one dimension each time there is the loss of a dimension at the level of o. Similarly, O's successor is only *infinitesimally* future or of lower order. In other words, O's dimension is of a higher order than that of o. But consideration of O's possible interchanges takes place at the level of o, as we may gather from the necessity, noted above, of writing O in the reflexive form $\begin{smallmatrix} o & o \\ o & x \end{smallmatrix}$. It must therefore be understood that when we say that each future O has one more dimension than the present O, the dimension in question is a dimension of o, not of O. The original O, then, while present, has one dimension: its successor, so long as it is future, has two dimensions: and when this becomes present it appears as having one dimension, just as its predecessor did when present. But the original O now has no dimension; for it has vanished. (That is to say, o has vanished: O is actually no more than infinitesimally closer to the point of vanishing—which means that it remains absolutely the same, in the ordinary meaning of that word. But we have to remember that changes in a thing's internal distribution of weight—the weight, that is, of its determinations—do not affect it.) Relatively speaking, then, each next future O has one more dimension, at the level of o, than the present O, even though it has but one dimension when it is itself present. If, therefore, the relative weights of the possible interchanges of the original O are in the proportions 3:2:1, the relative weights of the succeeding O, when it becomes present, will be in the proportion 9:4:1, that is, with each number squared. Following that, the next O will have relative weights 81:16:1, and so on. It is obvious, first, that the most heavily weighted of the possible interchanges will tend more and more to dominate the others and, in a manner of speaking, to draw all the weight to itself; and secondly, that it can only draw the *entire* weight to itself after an infinity of squarings, that is, of interchanges at the level of o. As soon as one of the three possible interchanges has drawn the entire weight to itself and altogether eliminated its rivals, that interchange takes place (at the level of O).[p] In the case we are considering there will be interchange of rows, i.e. of A and C, and of B and D. Notice that this interchange is quite independent of the kind of interchange that is taking place at the next lower level: interchange of rows at the level of O does not in the least require that the interchange at the level of o should also have been of rows.

(UNFINISHED)

---

**p.** §I/4 (d) would seem to imply that three different frequencies are involved, all converging to infinity together. This will complicate the arithmetic, but can scarcely prevent the eventual emergence of one dominating interchange. (If they are not all to be squared together, the relative weights a : b : c must be made absolute before each squaring: $\frac{a}{a+b+c}$, $\frac{b}{a+b+c}$, $\frac{c}{a+b+c}$.)

# GLOSSARY

# &

# TRANSLATIONS
(with additional texts)

# Glossary

This Pali-English Glossary contains all the Pali terms used in this book together with their English equivalents (sometimes only approximate). Only the separate elements of some compound words are given. Words occurring in quoted Pali passages and whose meaning may be discovered from the English renderings of such passages (given after this Glossary) are not always listed separately.

*Akālika* – timeless, intemporal.
*akusala* – unskilful.
*acinteyya* – not to be speculated about, unthinkable.
*ajjhatta* – inside, internal, subjective. (Opp. *bahiddhā.*)
*añña* – other, another. (Opp. *sa.*)
*aṭṭhapurisapuggalā* – (the) eight individual men.
*atakkāvacara* – not in the sphere of reason or logic.
*atidhāvati* – (to) overrun, overshoot.
*attavāda* – belief in self.
*attā* – self.
*atthi* – there is.
*adhivacana* – designation.
*anattā* – not-self.
*anāgāmī* – non-returner.
*anicca* – impermanent.
*aniccatā* – impermanence.
*anidassana* – non-indication, non-indicative.
*anupādisesa* – without residue.
*anuruddha-paṭiviruddha* – approving-&-disapproving, accepting-&-rejecting, attracting-&-repelling.
*anuloma* – with the grain, in conformity. (Opp. *paṭiloma.*)
*anulomikāya khantiyā samannāgato* – one endowed with acquiescence in conformity.
*anvaya* – inference, inferability.
*aparapaccayā* – not dependent on others.
*apuñña* – demerit.
*abhijjhā* – covetousness.
*abhisaṅkharoti* – (to) determine.
*abhisaṅkhāra* = *saṅkhāra.*
*abhisañcetayati* – (to) intend, will.
*arahat* – one who is worthy. (Usually untranslated.)
*arahattā* – state of the *arahat.*
*ariya* – noble. (Opp. *puthujjana.*)
*ariyasāvaka* – noble disciple.
*arūpa* – immaterial.
*avijjā* – nescience. (Opp. *vijjā.*)
*asaṅkhata* – non-determined.
*asmimāna* – conceit '(I) am. ('Conceit', *māna*, is to be understood as a cross between 'concept' and 'pride' – almost the French '*orgueil*' suitably attenuated. *Asmi* is 'I am' without the pronoun, like the Latin '*sum*'; but plain 'am' is too weak to render *asmi*, and *ahaṃ asmi* ('*ego sum*') is too emphatic to

be adequately rendered 'I am'.)
*asmī ti chanda* – desire '(I) am'. (See *asmimāna*.)
*assāsapassāsā* – in-&-out-breaths.
*assutavā* – uninstructed.

*Ākāsa* – space.
*ākiñcaññāyatana* – nothingness-base.
*āneñja* – immobility, unshakability, imperturbability.
*āyatana* – base.
*āyusaṅkhāra* – life-determination.
*āsava* – canker, intoxication.

*Idha* – here.
*indriya* – faculty.

*Ucchedadiṭṭhi* – annihilationist-view. (Opp. *sassatadiṭṭhi*.)
*upavicarati* – (to) dwell upon, ponder.
*upādāna* – holding.
*upekkhā* – indifference.

*Etaṃ* – this, that.

*Opanayika* – leading.

*Kamma* – action.
*kāya* – body.
*kāyika* – bodily.
*kālika* – temporal, involving time.
*kusala* – skilful.
*khandha* – aggregate, mass, totality.

*Gotrabhu* – become of the clan or lineage. (Sometimes translated as 'one who destroys the lineage'; the etymologists seem to be in doubt.)

*Cakkhu* – eye.
*citta* – mind, consciousness, cognition, spirit, heart, purpose, (conscious) experience, &c. (*Citta* is sometimes synonymous with *mano*, and sometimes not; it is occasionally equivalent to *viññāṇa* in certain senses. Related to *cetanā*, but more general. Its precise meaning must be determined afresh in each new context.)
*cittavīthi* – mental process, cognitive series.
*cetanā* – intention, volition, will.
*cetasika* – mental. (See *citta*.)

*Jarā* – ageing, decay.
*jāti* – birth.
*jhāna* – meditation.

*Ñāṇa* – knowledge.

*Takka* – reasoning, logic.
*taṇhā* – craving.
*Tathāgata* – (usually untranslated epithet of) the Buddha, (and, by transference, of) an *arahat*.
*Tāvatiṃsa* – 'Heaven of the Thirty-Three'.
*theta* – reliable, actual.

*Diṭṭhi* – view. (Usually, wrong view.)
*diṭṭhigata* – going to, involved with, consisting of, (wrong) view.
*diṭṭhisampanna* – (one) attained to (right) view. (= *sotāpanna*.)
*dukkha* – unpleasure (opp. *sukha*), pain, suffering.
*dutiya*, *tatiya tappurisa* – accusative, instrumentive dependent determinative compound. (Grammatical terms.)
*dussīla* – immoral, unvirtuous.
*domanassa* – grief.
*dosa* – hate.
*dvayaṃ* – dyad, duality.
*dhamma* – thing, image, idea, essence, universal, teaching, Teaching, nature, natural law, ethic, ethical law, &c. (cf. the Heraclitan 'logos').
*dhamm'anvaya* – inferability of the

*dhamma* (to past and future).
*dhammānusārī* – teaching-follower. (Opp. *saddhānusārī*.)
*dhātu* – element.

*Nāma* – name.
*nāmarūpa* – name-&-matter.
*nidassana* – indication, indicative.
*nibbāna* – extinction.
*nibbuta* – extinguished.
*niruddha* – ceased.
*nirodha* – ceasing, cessation.

*Paccaya* – condition.
*pañcakkhandhā* – five aggregates.
*pañc'upādānakkhandhā* – five holding aggregates. (This needs expansion to be intelligible.)
*paññā* – understanding.
*paṭigha* – resistance.
*paṭiccasamuppanna* – dependently arisen.
*paṭiccasamuppāda* – dependent arising.
*paṭiloma* – against the grain. (Opp. *anuloma*.)
*paṭisotagāmī* – going against the stream.
*paramattha sacca* – truth in the highest, or ultimate, or absolute, sense.
*paritassanā* – anxiety, anguish, *angst*.
*pariyesanā* – seeking.
*pahoti* – (to) originate.
*pāṇa* – animal, living being.
*pāpadhamma* – evil-natured.
*pāpima* – evil one.
*puggala* – individual.
*puñña* – merit.
*puthujjana* – commoner. (Opp. *ariya*.)
*punabbhavābhinibbatti* – coming into renewed being, re-birth.
*purisa* – man, male.
*phala* – fruit, fruition.
*phassa* – contact.

*Bala* – power, strength.
*bahiddhā* – outside, external, objective. (Opp. *ajjhatta*.)
*bhava* – being, existence.
*bhikkhu* – monk, almsman.
*bhikkhunī* – nun, almswoman.
*bhūta* – being.

*Magga* – path.
*maññati* – (to) conceive. (See *asmimāna*.)
*maññanā* – conceiving. (See *asmimāna*.)
*manasikāra* – attention.
*manussa* – human (being).
*mano* – mind. (See *citta*.)
*mama* – mine, of me.
*maraṇa* – death.
*mahābhūta* – great entity.
*micchādiṭṭhi* – wrong view. (Opp. *sammādiṭṭhi*.)
*me* – mine. (Weaker than *mama*.)
*moha* – delusion.

*Rāga* = *lobha*.
*ruppati* – (to) 'matter', be broken. (Untranslatable verb from *rūpa*.)
*rūpa* – matter, substance, (visible) form.

*Lakkhaṇa* – mark, characteristic.
*lābha* – gain.
*loka* – world.
*lokuttara* – beyond the world, world-transcending.
*lobha* – lust.

*Vacī* – speech.
*vicāra* – pondering.
*vijānāti* – (to) cognize, be conscious (of).
*vijjā* – science. (Opp. *avijjā*.)
*viññāṇa* – consciousness, knowing.
*vitakka* – thinking, thought.
*vipāka* – ripening, result, consequence.
*viriya* – energy, exertion.

*vedanā* – feeling.
*vediyati* – (to) feel.

*Sa* – that, the same. (Opp. *añña*.)
*sa-* – with. (Prefix.)
*saupādisesa* – with residue.
*sakkāya* – person, somebody, personality.
*sakkāyadiṭṭhi* – personality-view.
*saṅkhata* – determined.
*saṅkhāra* – determination, determinant.
*saṅgha* – Community, Order.
*sacca* – truth.
*sañcetanā* = *cetanā*.
*sañjānāti* – (to) perceive.
*saññā* – perception, percept.
*saññāvedayitanirodha* – cessation of perception and feeling.
*sati* – mindfulness, recollection, memory.
*satta* – creature, sentient being.
*sattama puggala* – seventh individual.
*saddhā* – faith, confidence, trust.
*saddhānusārī* – faith-follower. (Opp. *dhammānusārī*.)
*sandiṭṭhika* – evident, immediately visible.
*samādhi* – concentration.
*samudaya* – appearing, arising, coming into being.
*sampajañña* – awareness.
*samphassa* = *phassa*.
*sammādiṭṭhi* – right view. (Opp. *micchādiṭṭhi*.)
*sassatadiṭṭhi* – eternalist-view. (Opp. *ucchedadiṭṭhi*.)
*saḷāyatana* – six bases.
*saṃsāra* – running on (from existence to existence).
*sukha* – pleasure. (Opp. *dukkha*.)
*sutavā* – instructed.
*sekha* – one in training, (self-)trainer.
*so* (see *sa*).
*sotāpatti* – attaining of the stream.
*sotāpanna* – stream-attainer.
*somanassa* – joy.

*Huraṃ* – yonder.
*hetu* – condition (= *paccaya*).

# Translations

(with additional texts)

These renderings of quoted Pali passages are as nearly literal and consistent as English will allow; but, even so, they must be accepted with reserve.

1. *Aṅguttara* II, xi, 8 & 9

There are, monks, these two conditions for the arising of wrong view. Which are the two? Another's utterance and improper attention. These, monks, are the two conditions for the arising of wrong view.

(Repeat, substituting 'right view' for 'wrong view' and 'proper attention' for 'improper attention'.)

2. *Avyākata Saṃy.* 10

Being seated at one side, the wanderer Vacchagotta said to the Auspicious One,

—How is it, master Gotama, does self exist?

When this was said the Auspicious One was silent.

—How then, master Gotama, does self not exist?

A second time, too, the Auspicious One was silent.

Then the wanderer Vacchagotta got up from his seat and went away.

3. *Majjhima* xi,2

Therein, monks, those recluses and divines whose belief and view is thus, 'Self and the world are eternal [Self and the world are non-eternal (and so on)], just this is truth and all else foolishness',—that other merely than faith, other than preference, other than tradition, other than excogitation, other than acquiescent meditation of a (wrong) view, they should have private knowledge, purified and cleansed, such a thing is not possible.

4. *Ibidem*

This is determined and coarse; but there is such a thing as cessation of determinations—that there is. Knowing thus, and seeing the escape, the Tathāgata passes beyond.

**5.** *Indriya Saṃy.* vi,3
Outside here there is no other recluse or divine who sets forth as the Auspicious One does so real and factual and justified a Teaching.

**6.** *Majjhima* i,2
Am I? Am I not? What am I? How am I? (See **31**.)

**7.** *Majjhima* viii,9
But, Udāyi, let be the past, let be the future, I shall set you forth the Teaching: When there is this this is, with arising of this this arises; when there is not this this is not, with cessation of this this ceases.

**8.** *Majjhima* iv,8
When there is this this is, with arising of this this arises; that is to say, with nescience as condition, determinations; with determinations as condition, consciousness; with consciousness as condition, name-&-matter; with name-&-matter as condition, six bases; with six bases as condition, contact; with contact as condition, feeling; with feeling as condition, craving; with craving as condition, holding; with holding as condition, being; with being as condition, birth; with birth as condition, ageing-&-death, sorrow, lamentation, pain, grief, and despair, come into being; thus is the arising of this whole mass of unpleasure (suffering).

When there is not this this is not, with cessation of this this ceases; that is to say, with cessation of nescience, ceasing of determinations; with cessation of determinations, ceasing of consciousness; with cessation of consciousness, ceasing of name-&-matter; with cessation of name-&-matter, ceasing of six bases; with cessation of six bases, ceasing of contact; with cessation of contact, ceasing of feeling; with cessation of feeling, ceasing of craving; with cessation of craving, ceasing of holding; with cessation of holding, ceasing of being; with cessation of being, ceasing of birth; with cessation of birth, ageing-&-death, sorrow, lamentation, pain, grief, and despair, cease; thus is the ceasing of this whole mass of unpleasure (suffering).

**9.** *Nidāna/Abhisamaya Saṃy.* iii,5
The Auspicious One, friend, has said that pleasure and unpleasure are dependently arisen.

**10.** *Nidāna/Abhisamaya Saṃy.* i,2
And which, monks, are determinations? There are, monks, these three determinations: body-determination, speech-determination, mind-determination. These, monks, are called determinations.

**11.** *Majjhima* v,4
—But, lady, how many determinations are there?
—There are, friend Visākha, these three determinations: body-determination, speech-determination, mind-determination.
—But which, lady, is body-determination, which is speech-determination, which is mind-determination?
—The in-&-out-breaths, friend Visākha, are body-determination, thinking-&-pondering are speech-determination, perception and feeling are mind-determination.
—But why, lady, are the in-&-out-breaths body-determination, why are thinking-&-pondering speech-determination, why are perception and feeling mind-determination?
—The in-&-out-breaths, friend Visākha, are bodily, these things are bound up with the body; that is why the in-&-out-breaths are body-determination. First, friend Visākha, having thought and pondered, afterwards one breaks into speech; that is why thinking-&-pondering are speech-determination. Perception and feeling are mental, these things are bound up with the mind; that is why perception and feeling are mind-determination.

**12.** *Saḷāyatana Saṃy.* iv,10
Contacted, monks, one feels; contacted, one intends; contacted, one perceives;...

**13.** *Nidāna/Abhisamaya Saṃy.* iv,2
Whatever is felt counts as unpleasure (suffering). (See **58**.)

**14.** *Theragāthā* 606, 607
606 I delight not in death, I delight not in life,
I await my time like a hireling his wage;
607 I delight not in death, I delight not in life,
I await my time composed and aware.

**15.** *Kosala Saṃy.* i,3
—For one who is born, lord, is there anything other than ageing-&-death?
—For one who is born, great king, there is nothing other than ageing-&-death. Those, great king, who are wealthy warriors... wealthy divines... wealthy householders...,—for them, too, being born, there is nothing other than ageing-&-death. Those monks, great king, who are worthy ones, destroyers of the cankers...,—for them, too, it is the nature of this body to break up, to be laid down.

**16.** *Dhammapada* xx,5-7
All determinations are impermanent;
All determinations are unpleasurable (suffering);
All things are not-self.

**17.** *Nidāna/Abhisamaya Saṃy.* vi,1
If, monks, this individual man, who is involved in nescience, is determining a meritorious determination, consciousness has arrived at merit.

**18.** *Vedanā Saṃy.* i,9
There are, monks, these three feelings, which are impermanent, determined, dependently arisen…

**19.** *Dīgha* ii,1
with name-&-matter as condition, six bases;
with consciousness as condition, name-&-matter;
with name-&-matter as condition, consciousness.

**20.** *Ibidem*
This consciousness turns back from name-&-matter, it does not go further; thus far may one be born or age or die or fall or arise; that is to say, with name-&-matter as condition, consciousness; with consciousness as condition, name-&-matter; with name-&-matter as condition, six bases;…

**21.** *Avyākata Saṃy.* 1
That consciousness by which the Tathāgata might be manifested has been eliminated by the Tathāgata, cut off at the root, dug up, made non-existent, it is incapable of future arising; the Tathāgata, great king, is free from reckoning as consciousness…

**22.** *Udāna* ii,4
Contacts contact dependent on ground—
How should contacts contact a groundless one?

**23.** *Dīgha* i,11
Non-indicative consciousness, limitless, wholly non-originating.

**24.** *Vinaya Mahāvagga*
Of things originating with conditions,
The Tathāgata has told the condition,
And what their cessation is.
The Great Recluse speaks thus.

**25.** *Saḷāyatana Saṃy.* viii,7
Nescience, monk, is the one thing with a monk's elimination of which nescience is eliminated and science arises.

**26.** *Majjhima* i,2
With self I perceive self; With self I perceive not-self; With not-self I perceive self.

**27.** *Aṅguttara* X,vii,1
An earliest point of nescience, monks, is not manifest: 'Before this, nescience was not; then afterwards it came into being'. Even if that is said thus, monks, nevertheless it is manifest: 'With this as condition, nescience'. I say, monks, that nescience, too, is with sustenance, not without sustenance.

**28.** *Majjhima* i,9 & *Dīgha* ii,9

which, friends, is nescience?...
That which is non-knowledge of suffering,
non-knowledge of arising of suffering,
non-knowledge of ceasing of suffering,
non-knowledge of the way that leads to ceasing of suffering,
this, friends, is called nescience.
And which, monks, is the noble truth of suffering...
And which, monks, is the noble truth of arising of suffering...
And which, monks, is the noble truth of ceasing of suffering...
And which, monks, is the noble truth of the way that leads to ceasing of suffering?
Just this noble eight-factored path,
that is to say: right view...
And which, monks, is right view?...
That which is knowledge of suffering,
knowledge of arising of suffering,
knowledge of ceasing of suffering,
knowledge of the way that leads to
ceasing of suffering,
this, monks, is called right view.

**29.** *Dīgha* ii,9
Visible forms [Sounds ... Images (Ideas)] are dear and agreeable in the world; herein this craving arises, herein it adheres ...
Craving-for-visible-forms [Craving-for-sounds ... Craving-for-images (-ideas)] is dear and agreeable in the world; herein this craving arises, herein it adheres ...
... herein this craving is eliminated, herein it ceases.

30. *Bhikkhunī Saṃy.* 10
Māra the Evil One:
By whom is this creature formed? Who is the creature's maker? 1
Who is the arisen creature? Who is the creature that ceases? 2
Vajirā the nun:
Why do you refer to 'the creature', Māra, are you involved in
(wrong) view? 3
This is a pile of pure determinations; there is, here, no creature
to be found. 4
Just as for an assemblage of parts there is the term 'a chariot', 5
So, when there are the aggregates, convention says 'a creature'. 6
It is merely suffering that comes into being, suffering that
stands and disappears, 7
Nothing apart from suffering comes into being, nothing other
than suffering ceases. 8

31. *Majjhima* i,2
Or he is a self-questioner about the present period: 'Am I? Am I not? What am I? How am I? This creature—whence has it come? Whither is it bound?'

32. *Dīgha* i,9
—But to what self, Poṭṭhapāda, do you refer?
—To a coarse self, lord, I refer ... To a made-of-mind self, lord, I refer ... To an immaterial self, lord, I refer ...

33. *Majjhima* v,4
The five holding aggregates, friend Visākha, are not just holding; but neither is there holding apart from the five holding aggregates. That, friend Visākha, in the five holding aggregates which is desire-&-lust, that therein is holding.

34. *Khandha Saṃy.* ix,1
Holding matter there is '(I) am', not not holding; holding feeling ... ; holding perception ... ; holding determinations ... ; holding consciousness there is '(I) am', not not holding.

35. *Majjhima* viii,5
Just so, Māgandiya, if I were to set you forth the Teaching, 'This is that good health, this is that extinction', you might know good health, you might see extinction; with the arising of the eye, that in the five holding aggregates which is desire-&-lust would be eliminated for you; moreover it would occur to you, 'For a long time, indeed, have I been cheated and deceived and defrauded by this mind (or heart—*citta*): I

was holding just matter, holding just feeling, holding just perception, holding just determinations, holding just consciousness'.

**36.** *Majjhima* iii,2
Since both self, monks, and what belongs to self actually and in truth are not to be found ...

**37.** *Avyākata Saṃy.* 2
since here and now the Tathāgata actually and in truth is not to be found ...

**38.** *Nidāna/Abhisamaya Saṃy.* ii,5
This world for the most part, Kaccāyana, is bound by engaging, holding, and adherence; and this one [i.e. this individual] does not engage or hold or resolve that engaging or holding, that mental resolving adherence and tendency: 'My self'. 'It is just suffering that arises, suffering that ceases'—about this he does not hesitate or doubt, his knowledge herein is independent of others. So far, Kaccāyana, is there right view.

**39.** *Saḷāyatana Saṃy.* xviii,5
The Auspicious One, friend, possesses a mind (*mano*); the Auspicious One cognizes images (ideas) with the mind; desire-&-lust for the Auspicious One there is not; the Auspicious One is wholly freed in heart (*citta*). (Cf. **63**)

**40.** *Khandha Saṃy.* iv,6
Arising (appearance) is manifest; disappearance is manifest; change while standing is manifest. (Cf. **76**)

**41.** *Suttanipāta* 651, 652, 653
651 By action is one a farmer, by action a craftsman,
By action is one a merchant, by action a servant,
652 By action is one a thief, by action a soldier,
By action is one a priest, by action a king.
653 In this way the wise see action as it really is,
Seeing dependent arising, understanding result of action.

**42.** *Aṅguttara* VI,vi,9
Perceptions, monks, I say result in description; according as one perceives such-and-such, so one describes: 'I was perceptive thus'. This, monks, is called the result of perceptions.

**43.** *Aṅguttara* III,xi,7
That action leads to arising of action, that action does not lead to ceasing of action.

**44.** *Majjhima* i,9
In so far, friends, as a noble disciple understands unskill and understands the root of unskill, understands skill and understands the root of skill, so far too, friends, the noble disciple has right view, his view is correct, he is endowed with tried confidence in the Teaching, he has arrived at this Good Teaching.

**45.** *Majjhima* iii,2
Comprehending the parable of the raft, monks, you have to eliminate ethical things too, let alone unethical things.

**46.** *Majjhima* x,6
I, divine, make known the noble world-transcending Teaching as the business of man.

**47.** *Majjhima* xv,2
One who lays down this body, Sāriputta, and takes hold of another body, he I say is blameworthy.

**48.** *Khandha Saṃy.* v,5
To the uninstructed commoner, monks, contacted by feeling born of nescience-contact, it occurs '(I) am', it occurs 'It is this that I am', it occurs 'I shall be', …

**49.** *Dīgha* ii,2
My self is feeling; My self is not in fact feeling, my self is devoid of feeling; My self is not in fact feeling, but neither is my self devoid of feeling, my self feels, to feel is the nature of my self.

**50.** *Gāmaṇi Saṃy.* 11
having induced the principle to past and future

**51.** *Nidāna/Abhisamaya Saṃy.* ii,9
A stupid/intelligent man, monks, constrained by nescience and attached by craving, has thus acquired this body. So there is just this body and name-&-matter externally: in that way there is a dyad.

**52.** *Majjhima* xi,9
... in this conscious body and externally in all objects ...

**53.** *Khandha Saṃy.* viii,7
Matter as matter is the determined that they determine. (See **83**.)

**54.** *Majjhima* xi,2
Those recluses and divines who make known the annihilation, perishing, and unbeing, of the existing creature,—they, through fear of personality, through loathing of personality, are simply running and circling around personality. Just, indeed, as a dog, tied with a leash to a firm post or stake, runs and circles around that same post or stake, so these recluses and divines, through fear of personality, through loathing of personality, are simply running and circling around personality.

**55.** *Aṅguttara* X,i,7
Extinction is cessation of being.

**56.** *Udāna* viii,3
There is, monks, (a) non-born, non-become, non-made, non-determined; for if, monks, there were not that non-born, non-become, non-made, non-determined, an escape here from (the) born, become, made, determined, would not be manifest.

**57.** *Asaṅkhata Saṃy.* i,1 & ii,23
The destruction, monks, of lust, of hate, of delusion,—this, monks, is called (the) non-determined/extinction.

**58.** *Vedanā Saṃy.* ii,1
There are, monk, these three feelings stated by me: pleasant feeling, unpleasant feeling, neither-unpleasant-nor-pleasant feeling—these three feelings have been stated by me. But this, monk, has been stated by me: 'Whatever is felt counts as unpleasure (suffering)'. That, however, monk, was said by me concerning the impermanence of determinations... (See **18**.)

**59.** *Aṅguttara* IX,vi,3
The venerable Sāriputta said this:
—It is extinction, friends, that is pleasant! It is extinction, friends, that is pleasant!
When this was said, the venerable Udāyi said to the venerable Sāriputta,
—But what herein is pleasant, friend Sāriputta, since herein there is nothing felt?
—Just this is pleasant, friend, that herein there is nothing felt.

**60.** *Dhammapada* v,3
(His) very self is not (his) self's. (More freely: He himself is not his own.)

**61.** *Majjhima* iv,8
immediate, timeless, evident, leading, to be known privately by the wise.

**62.** *Majjhima* iii,8
He who sees dependent arising sees the Teaching.

**63.** *Saḷāyatana Saṃy.* xviii,5
The Auspicious One, friend, possesses an eye; the Auspicious One sees visible forms with the eye; desire-&-lust for the Auspicious One there is not; the Auspicious One is wholly freed in heart (*citta*). (Cf. **39**.)

**64.** *Aṅguttara* II,ii,1
And which, monks, is the development-power? Herein, monks, as to the development-power, this is the trainers' power, in trainers.

**65.** *Saḷāyatana Saṃy.* xii,3
[that] by which, in the world, one is a perceiver and conceiver of the world

**66.** *Indriya Saṃy.* v,10
The noble disciple is mindful, he is endowed with the highest mindfulness and discretion, he remembers and recalls what was done and what was said long ago.

**67.** *Vedanā Saṃy.* i,7
Here, monks, a monk dwells contemplating the body in the body ... feelings in feelings ... mind in the mind ... ideas in ideas, ardent, aware, mindful, having put away worldly covetousness and grief. Thus, monks, is a monk mindful.

**68.** *Udāna* iv,1
Mindfulness of breathing should be developed for the cutting-off of thoughts.

**69.** *Majjhima* viii,5
this body composed of matter, of the four great entities

70. *Saḷāyatana Saṃy.* xix,8
... a monk understands as they really are the arising and ceasing of the four great entities.

71. *Majjhima* vii,4
Whatever herein there is of matter, of feeling, of perception, of determinations, of consciousness, these things he regards as impermanent, as suffering, as sickness, as a boil, as a dart, as a calamity, as an affliction, as alien, as wasting, as void, as not-self.

72. *Dīgha* ii,3
To disappear is the nature of determinations; strive unremittingly.

73. *Dīgha* ii,3
Impermanent indeed are determinations; to arise (appear) and disappear is their nature.

74. *Dīgha* ii,4
See, Ānanda, how all those determinations have passed, have ceased, have altered. So impermanent, Ānanda, are determinations, so unlasting, Ānanda, are determinations, that this, Ānanda, is enough for weariness of all determinations, enough for dispassion, enough for release.

75. *Dīgha* i,9
Perception, Poṭṭhapāda, arises first, knowledge afterwards; but with arising of perception there is arising of knowledge. One understands thus: 'With this as condition, indeed, knowledge arose in me.'

76. *Aṅguttara* III,v,7
There are, monks, these three determined-characteristics of what is determined. Which are the three? Arising (appearance) is manifest; disappearance is manifest; change while standing is manifest. These, monks, are the three determined-characteristics of what is determined.

77. *Itivuttaka* III,ii,4
There are, monks, these three periods. Which are the three? The past period, the future period, the present period. These, monks, are the three periods.

* * *

Some of the more important Sutta passages referred to in the *Notes*, but not quoted, are given here (with translation) for the reader's convenience.

**78.** *Majjhima* i,9
*Vedanā saññā cetanā phasso manasikāro, idaṃ vuccat'āvuso nāmaṃ; cattāri ca mahābhūtāni catunnañ ca mahābhūtānaṃ upādāya rūpaṃ, idaṃ vuccat'āvuso rūpaṃ; iti idañ ca nāmaṃ idañ ca rūpaṃ, idaṃ vuccat'āvuso nāmarūpaṃ.*

Feeling, perception, intention, contact, attention,—this, friends, is called name; the four great entities and matter held (i.e. taken up by craving) from the four great entities,—this, friends, is called matter; thus, this name and this matter,—this, friends, is called name-&-matter.

**79.** *Aṅguttara* VI,vi,9
*Cetanāhaṃ bhikkhave kammaṃ vadāmi; cetayitvā kammaṃ karoti kāyena vācāya manasā.*

Action, monks, I say is intention; intending, one does action by body, by speech, by mind.

**80.** *Khandha Saṃy.* vi,4
*Katamañ ca bhikkhave rūpaṃ...*
*Katamā ca bhikkhave vedanā...*
*Katamā ca bhikkhave saññā...*
*Katame ca bhikkhave saṅkhārā. Chayime bhikkhave cetanākāyā, rūpasañcetanā saddasañcetanā gandhasañcetanā rasasañcetanā phoṭṭhabbasañcetanā dhammasañcetanā. Ime vuccanti bhikkhave saṅkhārā...*
*Katamañ ca bhikkhave viññāṇaṃ...*

And which, monks, is matter?...
And which, monks, is feeling?...
And which, monks, is perception?...
And which, monks, are determinations? There are, monks, these six bodies of intention: intention of visible forms, intention of sounds, intention of smells, intention of tastes, intention of touches, intention of images/ideas. These, monks, are called determinations...
And which, monks, is consciousness?...

**81.** *Khandha Saṃy.* v,5
*Ye hi keci bhikkhave samaṇā vā brāmaṇā vā anekavihitaṃ attānaṃ samanupassamānā samanupassanti, sabbe te pañc'upādānakkhandhe samanupassanti etesaṃ vā aññataraṃ.*

Whatever recluses or divines there may be, monks, who in various ways regard self, they are all regarding the five holding aggregates or a certain one of them.

**82.** *Majjhima* iv,5
*Rūpaṃ bhikkhave aniccaṃ, vedanā aniccā, saññā aniccā, saṅkhārā aniccā, viññāṇaṃ aniccāṃ; rūpaṃ bhikkhave anattā, vedanā anattā, saññā anattā, saṅkhārā anattā, viññāṇaṃ anattā; sabbe saṅkhārā aniccā, sabbe dhammā anattā.*

Matter, monks, is impermanent, feeling is impermanent, perception is impermanent, determinations are impermanent, consciousness is impermanent; matter, monks, is not-self, feeling is not-self, perception is not-self, determinations are not-self, consciousness is not-self; all determinations are impermanent, all things are not-self.

**83.** *Khandha Saṃy.* viii,7
*Kiñ ca bhikkhave rūpaṃ vadetha...*
*Kiñ ca bhikkhave vedanaṃ vadetha...*
*Kiñ ca bhikkhave saññaṃ vadetha...*
*Kiñ ca bhikkhave saṅkhāre vadetha. Saṅkhataṃ abhisaṅkharontī ti bhikkhave tasmā Saṅkhārā ti vuccanti. Kiñ ca saṅkhataṃ abhisaṅkharonti.*
*Rūpaṃ rūpattāya saṅkhataṃ abhisaṅkharonti,*
*Vedanaṃ vedanattāya saṅkhataṃ abhisaṅkharonti,*
*Saññāṃ saññattāya saṅkhataṃ abhisaṅkharonti,*
*Saṅkhāre saṅkhārattāya saṅkhataṃ abhisaṅkharonti,*
*Viññāṇaṃ viññāṇattāya saṅkhataṃ abhisaṅkharonti.*
*Saṅkhataṃ abhisaṅkharontī ti kho bhikkhave tasmā Saṅkhārā ti vuccanti.*
*Kiñ ca bhikkhave viññāṇaṃ vadetha...*

And what, monks, do you say is matter?...
And what, monks, do you say is feeling?...
And what, monks, do you say is perception?...
And what, monks, do you say are determinations? 'They determine the determined': that, monks, is why they are called 'determinations'.
And what is the determined that they determine?
Matter as matter is the determined that they determine,
Feeling as feeling is the determined that they determine,
Perception as perception is the determined that they determine,
Determinations as determinations are the determined that they determine,
Consciousness as consciousness is the determined that they determine.
'They determine the determined': that indeed, monks, is why they are called 'determinations'.
And what, monks, do you say is consciousness?...

**84.** *Khandha Saṃy.* vi,7
*Rūpaṃ [Vedanā... Saññā... Saṅkhārā... Viññāṇaṃ...] bhikkhave anattā. Rūpañ ca h'idaṃ bhikkhave attā abhavissa nayidaṃ rūpaṃ ābādhāya saṃvatteyya, labbhetha ca rūpe, Evaṃ me rūpaṃ hotu, evaṃ me rūpaṃ mā ahosī ti. Yasmā ca kho bhikkhave rūpaṃ anattā tasmā rūpaṃ ābādhāya saṃvattati, na ca labbhati rūpe, Evaṃ me rūpaṃ hotu, evaṃ me rūpaṃ mā ahosī ti.*

Matter [Feeling... Perception... Determinations... Consciousness...], monks, is not-self. For if, monks, matter were self, then matter would not lead to affliction, and one would obtain of matter 'Let my matter be thus, let my matter not be thus'. As indeed, monks, matter is not-self, so matter leads to affliction, and it is not obtained of matter 'Let my matter be thus, let my matter not be thus'.

**85.** *Aṅguttara* IV,viii,7
*Kammavipāko bhikkhave acinteyyo na cintetabbo, yaṃ cintento ummādassa vighātassa bhāgī assa.*

The ripening of action, monks, is unthinkable, should not be thought [i.e. should not be speculated about]; for one thinking (it) would come to madness and distraction.

**86.** *Dīgha* ii,2
*Nāmarūpapaccayā phasso ti iti kho pan'etaṃ vuttaṃ; tad Ānanda iminā p'etaṃ pariyāyena veditabbaṃ yathā nāmarūpapaccayā phasso. Yehi Ānanda ākārehi yehi liṅgehi yehi nimittehi yehi uddesehi nāmakāyassa paññatti hoti, tesu ākāresu tesu liṅgesu tesu nimittesu tesu uddesesu asati, api nu kho rūpakāye adhivacanasamphasso paññāyethā ti.*

*No h'etaṃ bhante.*

*Yehi Ānanda ākārehi yehi liṅgehi yehi nimittehi yehi uddesehi rūpakāyassa paññatti hoti, tesu ākāresu tesu liṅgesu tesu nimittesu tesu uddesesu asati, api nu kho nāmakāye paṭighasamphasso paññāyethā ti.*

*No h'etaṃ bhante.*

*Yehi Ānanda ākārehi yehi liṅgehi yehi nimittehi yehi uddesehi nāmakāyassa ca rūpakāyassa ca paññatti hoti, tesu ākāresu tesu liṅgesu tesu nimittesu tesu uddesesu asati, api nu kho adhivacanasamphasso vā paṭighasamphasso vā paññāyethā ti.*

*No h'etaṃ bhante.*

*Yehi Ānanda ākārehi yehi liṅgehi yehi nimittehi yehi uddesehi nāmarūpassa paññatti hoti, tesu ākāresu tesu liṅgesu tesu nimittesu tesu uddesesu asati, api nu kho phasso paññāyethā ti.*

*No h'etaṃ bhante.*

*Tasmātih'Ānanda es'eva hetu etaṃ nidānaṃ esa samudayo esa paccayo phassassa yadidaṃ nāmarūpaṃ.*

*Viññāṇapaccayā nāmarūpan ti iti kho pan'etaṃ vuttaṃ; tad Ānanda iminā p'etaṃ pariyāyena veditabbaṃ yathā viññāṇapaccayā nāmarūpaṃ. Viññāṇaṃ va hi*

*Ānanda mātu kucchiṃ na okkamissatha, api nu kho nāmarūpaṃ mātu kucchismiṃ samucchissathā ti.*

*No h'etaṃ bhante.*

*Viññāṇaṃ va hi Ānanda mātu kucchiṃ okkamimitvā vokkamissatha, api nu kho nāmarūpaṃ itthattāya abhinibbattissathā ti.*

*No h'etaṃ bhante.*

*Viññāṇaṃ va hi Ānanda daharass'eva sato vocchijjissatha kumārassa vā kumārikāya vā, api nu kho nāmarūpaṃ vuddhiṃ virūlhiṃ vepullaṃ āpajjissathā ti.*

*No h'etaṃ bhante.*

*Tasmātih'Ānanda es'eva hetu etaṃ nidānaṃ esa samudayo esa paccayo nāmarūpassa yadidaṃ viññāṇaṃ.*

*Nāmarūpapaccayā viññāṇan ti iti kho pan'etaṃ vuttaṃ; tad Ānanda iminā p'etaṃ pariyāyena veditabbaṃ yathā nāmarūpapaccayā viññāṇaṃ. Viññāṇaṃ va hi Ānanda nāmarūpa patiṭṭhaṃ nālabhissatha, api nu kho āyati jātijaramaraṇadukkhasamudayasambhavo paññāyethā ti.*

*No h'etaṃ bhante.*

*Tasmātih'Ānanda es'eva hetu etaṃ nidānaṃ esa samudayo esa paccayo viññāṇassa yadidaṃ nāmarūpaṃ.*

*Ettāvatā kho Ānanda jāyetha vā jīyetha vā mīyetha vā cavetha vā uppajjetha vā, ettāvatā adhivacanapatho, ettāvatā niruttipatho, ettāvatā paññattipatho, ettāvatā paññavacaraṃ, ettāvatā vaṭṭaṃ vaṭṭati itthataṃ paññāpanāya, yadidaṃ nāmarūpaṃ saha viññāṇena.*

—'With name-&-matter as condition, contact', so it was said: how it is, Ānanda, that with name-&-matter as condition there is contact should be seen in this manner. Those tokens, Ānanda, those marks, those signs, those indications by which the name-body is described,—they being absent, would designation-contact be manifest in the matter-body?

—No indeed, lord.

—Those tokens, Ānanda, those marks, those signs, those indications by which the matter-body is described,—they being absent, would resistance-contact be manifest in the name-body?

—No indeed, lord.

—Those tokens, Ānanda, those marks, those signs, those indications by which the name-body and the matter-body are described,—they being absent, would either designation-contact or resistance-contact be manifest?

—No indeed, lord.

—Those tokens, Ānanda, those marks, those signs, those indications by which name-&-matter is described,—they being absent, would contact be manifest?

—No indeed, lord.

—Therefore, Ānanda, just this is the reason, this is the occasion, this is the arising, this is the condition of contact, that is to say name-&-matter.

'With consciousness as condition, name-&-matter', so it was said: how it is, Ānanda, that with consciousness as condition there is name-&-matter should be seen in this manner. If, Ānanda, consciousness were not to descend into the mother's womb, would name-&-matter be consolidated in the mother's womb?

—No indeed, lord.
—If, Ānanda, having desceended into the mother's womb, consciousness were to turn aside, would name-&-matter be delivered into this situation?
—No indeed, lord.
—If, Ānanda, consciousnesss were cut off from one still young, from a boy or a girl, would name-&-matter come to increase, growth, and fullness?
—No indeed, lord.
—Therefore, Ānanda, just this is the reason, this is the occasion, this is the arising, this is the condition of name-&-matter, that is to say consciousness.

'With name-&-matter as condition, consciousness', so it was said: how it is, Ānanda, that with name-&-matter as condition there is consciousness should be seen in this manner. If, Ānanda, consciousness were not to obtain a stay in name-&-matter, would future arising and coming-into-being of birth, ageing, death, and unpleasure (suffering), be manifest?
—No indeed, lord.
—Therefore, Ānanda, just this is the reason, this is the occasion, this is the arising, this is the condition of consciousness, that is to say name-&-matter.

Thus far, Ānanda, may one be born or age or die or fall or arise, thus far is there a way of designation, thus far is there a way of language, thus far is there a way of description, thus far is there a sphere of understanding, thus far the round proceeds as manifestation in a situation,—so far, that is to say, as there is name-&-matter together with consciousness.

**87.** *Majjhima* iii,8
*Yato ca kho āvuso ajjhattikañ c'eva cakkhuṃ [sotaṃ, ghānaṃ, jivhā, kāyo, mano] aparibhinnaṃ hoti, bāhirā ca rūpā [saddā, gandhā, rasā, phoṭṭhabbā, dhammā] āpāthaṃ āgacchanti, tajjo ca samannāhāro hoti, evaṃ tajjassa viññāṇabhāgassa pātubhāvo hoti. Yaṃ tathābhūtassa rūpaṃ taṃ rūp'upādānakkhandhe saṅgahaṃ gacchati; ...vedanā...; ...saññā...; ...saṅkhārā...; yaṃ tathābhūtassa viññāṇaṃ taṃ viññāṇ'upādānakkhandhe saṅgahaṃ gacchati.*

It is when, friends, the internal eye (ear, nose, tongue, body, mind) is unbroken, and external visible forms (sounds, smells, tastes, touches, images/ideas) come in the way, and there is the appropriate connexion,—it is then that there is the appearance of the appropriate kind of consciousness. Of what thus comes into existence, the matter goes for inclusion in the holding aggregate of matter; ...the feeling...; ... the perception...; ...the determinations...; of what thus comes into existence, the consciousness goes for inclusion in the holding aggregate of consciousness.

**88.** *Indriya Saṃy.* ii,8
*Yassa kho bhikkhave imāni pañc'indriyāni sabbena sabbaṃ sabbathā sabbaṃ n'atthi, tam ahaṃ Bāhiro puthujjanapakkhe ṭhito ti vadāmi.*

In whom, monks, altogether and in every way there are not these five faculties, of him I say 'An outsider, one who stands on the commoner's side'.

**89.** *Itivuttaka* II,ii,7

*Dve'mā bhikkhave nibbānadhātuyo. Katamā dve. Saupādisesā ca nibbānadhātu anupādisesā ca nibbānadhātu.*

*Katamā ca bhikkhave saupādisesā nibbānadhātu. Idha bhikkhave bhikkhu arahaṃ hoti khīṇāsavo vusitavā katakaraṇīyo ohitabhāro anuppattasadattho parikkhīṇabhavasaṃyojano sammadaññāvimutto. Tassa tiṭṭhant'eva pañc'indriyāni, yesaṃ avighātattā manāpāmanāpaṃ paccanubhoti sukhadukkhaṃ paṭisaṃvediyati. Tassa yo rāgakkhayo dosakkhayo mohakkhayo, ayaṃ vuccati bhikkhave saupādisesā nibbānadhātu.*

*Katamā ca bhikkhave anupādisesā nibbānadhātu. Idha bhikkhave bhikkhu arahaṃ hoti khīṇāsavo vusitavā katakaraṇīyo ohitabhāro anuppattasadattho parikkhīṇabhavasaṃyojano sammadaññāvimutto. Tassa idh'eva bhikkhave sabbavedayitāni anabhinanditāni sītibhavissanti, ayaṃ vuccati bhikkhave anupādisesā nibbānadhātu.*

*Imā kho bhikkhave dve nibbānadhātuyo.*

There are, monks, these two extinction-elements. Which are the two? The extinction-element with residue and the extinction-element without residue.

And which, monks, is the extinction-element with residue? Here, monks, a monk is a worthy one, a destroyer of the cankers, one who has reached completion, done what was to be done, laid down the burden, achieved his own welfare, destroyed attachment to being, one who is released through comprehending rightly. His five faculties (seeing, hearing, smelling, tasting, touching) still remain: owing to their being intact he experiences what is agreeable and disagreeable, he feels what is pleasant and unpleasant. It is his destruction of lust, hate, and delusion, monks, that is called the extinction-element with residue.

And which, monks, is the extinction-element without residue? Here, monks, a monk is a worthy one, a destroyer of the cankers, one who has reached completion, done what was to be done, laid down the burden, achieved his own welfare, destroyed attachment to being, one who is released through comprehending rightly. All his feelings, monks, not being delighted in, will become cold in this very place: it is this, monks, that is called the extinction-element without residue.

These, monks, are the two extinction-elements.

**90.** *Theragāthā* 715, 716

715 *Na me hoti Ahosin ti, Bhavissan ti na hoti me;*
*Saṅkhārā vibhavissanti: tattha kā paridevanā.*
716 *Suddhaṃ dhammasamuppādaṃ suddhaṃ saṅkhārasantatiṃ*
*Passantassa yathābhūtaṃ na bhayaṃ hoti gāmaṇi.*

715 'I was' is not for me, not for me is 'I shall be';
Determinations will un-be: therein what place for sighs?
716 Pure arising of things, pure series of determinants—
For one who sees this as it is, chieftain, there is no fear.

**91.** *Devatā Saṃy.* iii,5

*Yo hoti bhikkhu arahaṃ katāvī*
*Khīṇāsavo antimadehadhārī,*
*Mānaṃ nu kho so upāgamma bhikkhu*
*Ahaṃ vadāmī ti pi so vadeyya*
*Mamaṃ vadantī ti pi so vadeyyā ti.*
*Pahīnamānassa na santi ganthā,*
*Vidhūpitā mānaganthassa sabbe;*
*Sa vītivatto yamataṃ sumedho*
*Ahaṃ vadāmī ti pi so vadeyya*
*Mamaṃ vadantī ti pi so vadeyya;*
*Loke samaññaṃ kusalo viditvā*
*Vohāramattena so vohareyyā ti.*

—A monk who is a worthy one, his task done,
His cankers destroyed, wearing his last body,—
Is it because this monk has arrived at conceit
That he might say '*I* say',
And that he might say 'They say *to me*'?
—For one who is rid of conceit there are no ties,
All his ties of conceit (*mānaganthā'ssa*) are dissolved;
This wise man, having got beyond conceiving (*yaṃ mataṃ*),
Might say '*I* say',
And he might say 'They say *to me*':
Skilled in worldly expressions, knowing about them,
He might use them within the limits of usage.

**92.** *Majjhima* v,3

*Yā c'āvuso vedanā yā ca saññā yañ ca viññāṇaṃ, ime dhammā saṃsaṭṭhā no visaṃsaṭṭhā, na ca labbhā imesaṃ dhammānaṃ vinibbhujitvā vinibbhujitvā nānākaraṇaṃ paññāpetuṃ. Yaṃ h'āvuso vedeti taṃ sañjānāti, yaṃ sañjānāti taṃ vijānāti, tasmā ime dhammā saṃsaṭṭhā no visaṃsaṭṭhā, na ca labbhā imesaṃ dhammānaṃ vinibbhujitvā vinibbhujitvā nānākaraṇaṃ paññāpetuṃ.*

That, friend, which is feeling, that which is perception, that which is consciousness,—these things are associated, not dissociated, and it is not possible to show the distinction between these things having separated them one from another. For what, friend, one feels that one perceives, what one perceives that one cognizes,—that is why these things are associated, not dissociated, and it is not possible to show the distinction between these things having separated them one from another.

93. *Majjhima* xv,1
*Tasmātiha te gahapati evaṃ sikkhitabbaṃ. Na rūpaṃ upādiyissāmi, na ca me rūpanissitaṃ viññāṇaṃ bhavissatī ti. Na vedanaṃ ... Na saññaṃ ... Na saṅkhāre ... Na viññāṇaṃ upādiyissāmi, na ca me viññāṇanissitaṃ viññāṇaṃ bhavissatī ti. Evaṃ hi te gahapati sikkhitabbaṃ.*

Therefore, householder, you should train yourself thus. 'I shall not hold matter, nor shall my consciousness be hanging to matter.' 'I shall not hold feeling...' 'I shall not hold perception...' 'I shall not hold determinations...' 'I shall not hold consciousness, nor shall my consciousness be hanging to consciousness.' For thus, householder, should you train yourself.

94. *Majjhima* xiv,8
*Kathañ c'āvuso anupādā paritassanā hoti. Idh'āvuso assutavā puthujjano ariyānaṃ adassāvī ariyadhammassa akovido ariyadhamme avinīto sappurisānaṃ adassāvī sappurisadhammassa akovido sappurisadhamme avinīto rūpaṃ [vedanaṃ, saññaṃ, saṅkhāre, viññāṇaṃ] attato samanupassati rūpavantaṃ [... viññāṇavantaṃ] vā attānaṃ attani vā rūpaṃ [... viññāṇaṃ] rūpasmiṃ [... viññāṇasmiṃ] vā attānaṃ. Tassa taṃ rūpaṃ [... viññāṇaṃ] vipariṇamati aññathā hoti, tassa rūpa [... viññāṇa] vipariṇām'aññathābhāvā rūpa [... viññāṇa] vipariṇāmānuparivatti viññāṇaṃ hoti, tassa rūpa [... viññāṇa] vipariṇāmānuparivattajā paritassanā dhammasamuppādā cittaṃ pariyādāya tiṭṭhanti, cetaso pariyādānā uttāsavā ca hoti vighātavā ca apekhavā ca anupādāya ca paritassati. Evaṃ kho āvuso anupādā paritassanā hoti.*

And how, friends, is there anxiety at not holding? Here, friends, an uninstructed commoner, unseeing of the nobles, ignorant of the noble Teaching, undisciplined in the noble Teaching, unseeing of the good men, ignorant of the good men's Teaching, undisciplined in the good men's Teaching, regards matter [feeling, perception, determinations, consciousness] as self, or self as endowed with matter [... consciousness], or matter [... consciousness] as belonging to self, or self as in matter [... consciousness]. That matter [... consciousness] of his changes and becomes otherwise; as that matter [... consciousness] changes and becomes otherwise so his consciousness follows around (keeps track of) that change of matter [... consciousness]; anxious ideas that arise born of following around that change of matter [... consciousness] seize upon his mind and become established; with that mental seizure, he is perturbed and disquieted and concerned, and from not holding he is anxious. Thus, friends, is there anxiety at not holding.

# B

# LETTERS (1960-1965)

I

# 'To be opened in the event of my death'

[L. 1][1]

NAMO TASSA BHAGAVATO ARAHATO SAMMĀSAMBUDDHASSA

*—Ekaṃ samayaṃ Ñāṇavīro bhikkhu Būndalagāme viharati araññakuṭikāyaṃ. Tena kho pana samayena Ñāṇavīro bhikkhu rattiyā paṭhamaṃ yāmaṃ caṅkamena āvaraṇīyehi dhammehi cittaṃ parisodheti, yathāsutaṃ yathāpariyattaṃ dhammaṃ cetasā anuvitakketi anuvicāreti manasānupekkhati. Atha kho Ñāṇavīrassa bhikkhuno evaṃ yathāsutaṃ yathāpariyattaṃ dhammaṃ cetasā anuvitakkayato anuvicārayato manasānupekkhato virajaṃ vītamalaṃ dhammacakkhuṃ udapādi, Yam kiñci samudayadhammaṃ sabbaṃ taṃ nirodhadhammanti.*

*So dhammānusārī māsaṃ hutvā diṭṭhipatto hoti.*

(27.6.1959)

*'Atthi Kassapa maggo atthi paṭipadā yathā paṭipanno sāmaṃ yeva ñassati sāmaṃ dakkhīti, Samaṇo va Gotamo kālavādī bhūtavādī atthavādī dhammavādī vinayavādīti.'*

*'Diṭṭhivisūkāni upātivatto,*
*Patto niyāmaṃ paṭiladdhamaggo,*
*Uppannañāṇo 'mhi anaññaneyyo*
*Eko care khaggavisāṇakappo'*

These books contain the Buddha's Teaching; they can be trusted absolutely from beginning to end:
(Vinaya Piṭaka:) Suttavibhaṅga, Mahāvagga, Cūḷavagga; (Sutta Piṭaka:) Dīghanikāya, Majjhimanikāya, Saṃyuttanikāya, Aṅguttaranikāya, Suttanipāta, Dhammapada, Udāna, Itivuttaka, Theratherīgāthā.
No other books whatsoever can be trusted. Leaving aside Vinaya seek the meaning of these books in your own experience. Do not seek their meaning in any other books: if you do you will be misled.

Ñāṇavīra

## 2

# Letter to Mr. N.Q. Dias

**[L. 2]** **27 March 1962**

Dear Mr. Dias,

The Pali for 'awareness' (as you are no doubt aware) is *sampajañña*. In the Suttas it is frequently linked with 'mindfulness' or *sati*, in the compound *sati-sampajañña*, 'mindfulness-and-awareness'. In the Satipaṭṭhāna Sutta awareness (of bodily actions) is included in the section on mindfulness of the body, so we can perhaps conclude that, while it is not different from mindfulness, awareness is rather more specialized in meaning. Mindfulness is general recollectedness, not being scatter-brained; whereas awareness is more precisely *keeping oneself under constant observation*, not letting one's actions (or thoughts, or feelings, etc.) pass unnoticed.

Here, to begin with, are three Sutta passages to indicate the scope of the practice of awareness in the Buddha's Teaching.

> (a) And how, monks, is a monk aware? Here, monks, in walking to and fro a monk practises awareness; in looking ahead and looking aside he practises awareness; in bending and stretching...; in using robes and bowl...; in eating, drinking, chewing, and tasting...; in excreting and urinating...; in walking, standing, sitting, sleeping, waking, speaking, and being silent, he practises awareness. (Vedanā Saṃyutta—S.xxxvi.7/iv,211)

> (b) And which, monks, is the development of concentration that, when developed and made much of, leads to mindfulness-and-awareness? Here, monks, feelings are known as they arise, feelings are known as they endure, feelings are known as they vanish; perceptions are known as they arise, perceptions are known as they endure, perceptions are known as they vanish; thoughts are known as they arise, thoughts are known as they endure, thoughts are known as they vanish. (A.IV,41/ii,45)

> (c) Here, Ānanda, a monk is mindful as he walks to, he is mindful as he walks fro, he is mindful as he stands, he is mindful as he sits, he is mindful as he lies down, he is mindful as he sets to work. This, Ānanda, is a mode of recollection that, when developed and made much of in this way, leads to mindfulness-and-awareness. (A.VI,29/iii,325)

The next thing is to sort out a verbal confusion. When our actions become habitual we tend to do them without thinking about them—they become 'automatic' or 'instinctive' (scratching one's head, for example, or blinking one's eyes). We commonly call these 'unconscious actions', and this usage is followed by psychology and science generally. But this is a misunderstanding. There is, strictly speaking, no such thing as an '*unconscious* action'. The Buddha defines 'action' (*kamma*) as 'intention' (*cetanā*), and there is no intention without consciousness (*viññāṇa*). An *unconscious* action is no action at all, it is purely and simply *movement* as when, for example, a tree sways in the wind, or a rock is dislodged by the rain and rolls down a mountainside and derails a train (in this latter case it is quaintly called, in legal circles,[1] 'an Act of God' but if there is no God there is no Act, only the movement of the rock).

In the Buddha's Teaching, all consciousness is action (by mind, voice or body) and every action is conscious. But this does not mean that every action is done in awareness—indeed, what is commonly called an 'unconscious action' is merely a (conscious) action that is done *not deliberately*, that is done *unawares*. What we commonly call a '*conscious* action' is, strictly speaking, a *deliberate* action, an action that requires some thought to perform (as, for example, when we try to do something that we have not done before, or only infrequently). When we do such actions, we have to consider what we are doing (or else we shall make a mistake); and it is this *considering what we are doing* that constitutes 'awareness'. An action that we do without considering what we are doing is an action that is done without 'awareness'.

So long as we are awake, obviously enough, there is always some degree of awareness present, since new problems, large or small, are always presenting themselves, and we are obliged to *consider* them (even if only for a moment or two) in order to deal with them. (When we *dream*, on the other hand, awareness is in abeyance; and it is this very fact that *we are unable to look at our dream problems objectively* that distinguishes dreams from waking experience. When we are awake we are always aware 'I am awake', but when we dream we are *not* aware 'I am dreaming'; and, in fact, when we have a nightmare and struggle to wake up, all we are doing is *trying to remem-*

*ber [or become aware] that we are dreaming*, and if we succeed we wake up.) But though, unlike in sleep, there is always some degree of awareness present in our waking life, it is normally only enough to enable us to deal with unexpected circumstances as they occur; for the rest we are *absorbed* in what we are doing—whether it is the daily task of earning a livelihood, or our personal affairs with our emotional attitudes towards other people (affection, dislike, fury, lust, boredom, and so on), it makes no difference. To maintain a detached attitude is difficult when there is much routine work to be done in a hurry, and it robs our personal relationships with others of all emotional satisfaction. We prefer to get through our work as quickly and with as little effort as possible, and then to wallow in our emotions like a buffalo in a mud-hole. Awareness of what we are doing, which is always an effort, we like to keep to the absolute minimum. But we cannot avoid awareness altogether, since, as I remarked earlier, it is necessary in order to deal with unexpected problems, however insignificant, as they arise.

But this awareness is practised merely for the purpose of overcoming the obstacles that lie in the path of our daily life—it is practised simply in order to get through the business of living as expeditiously and as efficiently as possible.

Awareness in the Buddha's Teaching, however, has a different purpose: it is practised for the purpose of attaining release from living. These two different purposes, while not directly opposed, do not in fact co-operate—they are, as it were, at right angles to each other; and since the amount of awareness that can be practised at any one time is limited, there is competition between these purposes for whatever awareness is available. Thus it happens that in activities requiring much awareness simply for their successful performance (such as writing this letter) there is not much scope for the practice of awareness leading to release (though no doubt if I got into the unlikely habit of writing this same letter twice a day over a number of years I should be able to devote more of the latter to it).

The Buddha tells us (in the It.III,30/71-2) that three things harm the progress of the *sekha bhikkhu* (one who has reached the Path but who has not arrived at *arahat*ship): fondness for work (i.e. building, sewing robes, doing odd jobs, and so on), fondness for talk, and fondness for sleep. In the first two, as we can see, much awareness must be devoted to successful performance of the task in hand (making things, expounding the Dhamma), and in the third no awareness is possible. From the passages I quoted earlier it is clear that awareness for the purpose of release is best practised on those actions that are habitual and do not require much thought to perform—walking, standing, sitting, lying down, attending to bodily needs of various kinds, and so on. (The reference to 'sleeping' in passage (a) means that one should go to sleep with awareness, bearing in mind the time to awaken again; it does not mean that we should practise awareness while we are actually asleep.) Naturally a *bhikkhu* cannot altogether avoid doing jobs of work or occasionally talking, but these, too, should be done mindfully and with awareness as far as possible: 'he is mindful as he sets to work', 'in speaking and being silent he practises awareness'. The normal person, as I remarked above, does not practise awareness where he does not find it necessary, that is to say, in his habitual actions; but the *bhikkhu* is instructed not only to do these habitual actions with awareness but also, as far as possible, to confine himself to these actions. Drive and initiative in new ventures, so highly prized in the world of business and practical affairs, are impediments for one who is seeking release.

And how does one practise this awareness for the purpose of release? It is really very simple. Since (as I have said) all action is conscious, we do not have to undertake any elaborate investigation (such as asking other people) to find out what it is that we are doing so that we can become aware of it. All that is necessary is a slight change of attitude, a slight effort of attention. Instead of being fully absorbed by, or identified with, our action, we must continue, without ceasing to act, to *observe* ourselves in action. This is done quite simply by asking ourselves the question 'What am I doing?' It will be found that, since the action was always conscious anyway, we *already*, in a certain sense, *know* the answer without having to think about it; and simply by asking ourselves the question we become *aware* of the answer, i.e. of what we are doing. Thus, if I now ask myself 'What am I doing?' I can immediately answer that I am 'writing to Mr. Dias', that I am 'sitting in my bed', that I am 'scratching my leg', that I am 'wondering whether I shall have a motion', that I am 'living in Būndala', and so on almost endlessly.

If I wish to practise awareness I must go on asking myself this question and answering it, until such time as I find that I am automatically (or habitually) *answering the question without having to ask it.* When this happens, the practice of awareness is being successful, and it only remains to develop this state and not to fall away from it through neglect. (Similar considerations will of course apply to awareness of feelings, perceptions, and thoughts—see passage (b). Here I have to ask myself 'What am I feeling, or perceiving, or thinking?', and the answer, once again, will immediately present itself.)

The objection is sometimes raised that it is not possible to do two things at once, and that it is therefore not possible both to act and to be aware of the action at one and the same time. But this opinion is a pure prejudice, based upon a certain false notion of the nature of consciousness (or of experience). It is perfectly possible to be doing a number of things at the same time (for example, I am breathing as I write this letter, and I do not interrupt the one in order to do the other); it is not possible to devote *equal attention* to all of them at the same time, but this is another matter. And this is true also of acting and being aware of the action. This can be verified very simply; all that is necessary is to start walking and, while still walking, to ask oneself the question 'What am I doing?'; it will be found that one can give oneself the answer 'I am walking' without ceasing to walk (i.e. it is not necessary to come to a halt, or break into a run, or fall down, in order to answer the question).

Why should one practise awareness? I can think of three good reasons immediately, and there are doubtless others besides.

In the first place, a person who is constantly aware of what he is doing will find it easier to keep his *sīla*. A man who, when chasing his neighbour's wife, knows 'I am chasing my neighbour's wife', will not be able to conceal from himself the fact that he is on the point of breaking the third precept,[2] and will correct himself sooner than the man who chases his neighbour's wife without considering what he is doing. In brief, awareness leads to self-criticism and thence to self-correction.

In the second place, awareness is cooling and is directly opposed to the passions (either lust or hate), which are heating (this has no connexion with the mysterious qualities that are inherent in Oriental food, but missing from food in the West). This means that the man who constantly practises awareness has a powerful control over his passions; indeed, the constant practice of awareness actually inhibits the passions, and they arise less and less frequently.

In the third place, the practice of awareness is an absolute pre-requisite for the understanding of the essence of the Buddha's Teaching. The reason for this is that the Dhamma is concerned not with any one single experience (consciousness, feeling, etc.) as such, but with experience (consciousness, feeling, etc.) in general. We do not need the Buddha to tell us how to escape from any particular experience (whether it is a simple headache or an incurable cancer), but we do need the Buddha to tell us how to escape from all experience whatsoever. Now, in the normal state of being absorbed by what we are doing (that is, of non-awareness) we are concerned only with this or that particular experience or state of affair ('she loves me; she loves me not...'), and we are in no way concerned with experience in general ('what is the nature of the emotion of love?'). But when we become aware of what we are doing (or feeling, etc.), the case is different. Though we are still doing (or feeling), we are also observing that doing or feeling with a certain degree of detachment, and at that time the *general nature* of 'doing' and 'feeling' comes into view (the particular doing and feeling that happen to be present now merely appear as *examples* of 'doing' and 'feeling' in general); and it is when this general nature of things comes into view that we are able, with the Buddha's guidance, to grasp the universal characteristics of *anicca*, *dukkha*, and *anattā*. But here we are getting into deep waters, and I do not wish to add difficulties to a subject that is already not very easy.

P.S. Note that the three advantages of practising awareness mentioned in the last paragraph correspond to *sīla*, *samādhi*, and *paññā*, respectively.

# 3

# Letters to Mr. and Mrs. Perera

**[L. 3]** **16 October 1960**

Dear Mr. Perera,

I am sorry you find that you are losing your temper easily, for the Buddha has said that anger is very much more to be blamed than lust. I suggest that you might try to act in this way: whenever you feel you are losing your temper and are about to say some angry words, stop whatever you are doing and count up to ten slowly before you say anything. It is possible that this will give you time to cool off a little and you may not say your angry words at all. But you must practise this sometimes when you are not angry so that you can still be able to do it when you do get angry.

You can also repeat these words to yourself every evening before going to sleep, and in the morning when you wake up:

'When I get angry this is pleasing to my enemies in seven ways.

1. When I get angry I am ugly to look at, and this is pleasing to my enemies.
2. When I get angry I do not rest or sleep in comfort, and this is pleasing to my enemies.
3. When I get angry I have ill-fortune, I have bad luck, and this is pleasing to my enemies.
4. When I get angry I lose my wealth, and this is pleasing to my enemies.
5. When I get angry I lose my good reputation, and this is pleasing to my enemies.
6. When I get angry I lose my friends, and this is pleasing to my enemies.
7. When I get angry I do wrong actions by mind, word, and deed, and when I die I shall go to a bad destiny, a place of misery and unhappiness, and this is pleasing to my enemies.'[1]

You can also think this: 'When I lose my temper and throw angry words at other people I am like a man who picks up a lump of excrement in his hand to throw at other people. When he throws it he may hit other people or he may miss them, but in any case he makes himself stink first.'

**[L. 4]** **12 March 1961**

Dear Mrs. Perera,
When a person feels that he may be at fault, it is right and proper for him to speak about it and not conceal it. The Buddha has said that this is the way to progress. When people tell me of their success or failure I give what advice I can; but these things do not concern me personally, since I have my own work to attend to.

Life is not easy for anybody. It is not easy for you; it is not easy for your husband; and, also, it is not easy for me. But at the present time we have the immense good fortune to know what the Buddha teaches, and know what we must do *now* to make things easier for ourselves *in the future*. When two people live together they sometimes make each other happy and they sometimes make each other miserable. So long as there is craving and attachment this will happen, and if a person wishes to avoid it he must live alone. But that is not possible for everybody. What matters is not what others do but what we ourselves do—it is our own actions, our own *kamma*, whose fruit we experience, not other people's. So a person ought to be a good husband or good wife (as the case may be) even if the other person has faults. It is hard to be perfect, but at the time of death one should be able to say to oneself, 'I have done my best, I have done nothing that I regret.' Remember that it is more important to follow the Buddha's Teaching than it is to be happy in this life; but this is not an easy thing to understand.

**[L. 5]** **2 August 1961**

Dear Mr. Perera,
It is very difficult for you (or for anybody else) to hurt my feelings, and I much prefer people to talk bluntly to me rather than to wrap up their meaning in a lot of fine words. You can always remember this: that amongst the laymen and *dāyakas* who have helped me in this life, I do not know of any single one to whom I am more grateful than yourself.

**[L. 6]** **26 October 1961**

Dear Mrs. Perera,
The Sutta in question is the Jīvaka Sutta (of Majjhimanikāya).[1] This Sutta does not prohibit people from eating meat, but says that *bhikkhus* may not eat meat that they have seen, heard, or suspected as having been killed on their account. Perhaps the Ven. Mahāthera might try to talk to the two spirits in a friendly manner, and perhaps ask them what they want and if they need some help.

**[L. 7]** **19 July 1962**

Dear Mr. Perera,
Dealing in opium and ganja is the same as dealing in intoxicants, and is therefore one of the ways of livelihood that the Buddha has said to be unsuitable for a Buddhist layman. As for prostitution, I am not aware that the Buddha has said it is wrong for a woman to gain her livelihood in this way; but it is obvious enough that a woman should not choose this profession unless she is quite unable to make her living in any better way. It must be remembered that, generally speaking, a woman is dependent upon a man for her living, and that a man will usually only undertake to support a woman if she is pleasing to him; and the principal way in which a woman pleases a man is by her bodily attractions. Although the Buddha nowhere praises sensual pleasures, he does not altogether condemn them in people who live as laymen and laywomen. He has not said that men and women should never come together, and we know that even those who are *sotāpanna* or *sakadāgāmī* still enjoy sensual pleasures (if they are not monks or nuns). Although, clearly enough, it is better for a woman to use her attractions to get a husband who will support her and to whom she can remain faithful, this may not always be possible for her (for example, her husband might die and leave her a penniless widow, or he might abandon her), and she may find that she must make her own living. But if a woman decides to become a prostitute she should take good care to keep the five precepts. In the first place she should not become a prostitute if there is anyone (a man or a relative, or even a society) who is already giving her a livelihood. If there is not, and she is quite independent, then she must always honour the arrangements that she makes with her clients. If, as a prostitute, she accepts, or agrees to accept, payment from a man, then she must regard herself as that man's wife until the engagement or contract has come to an end. If

she fails to do this and goes with another man (either with payment or for nothing) before discharging her obligation to the first man, then she breaks the third precept and becomes *kāmesu micchācārinī*. There is a Jātaka story (I forget which) that describes how a prostitute who was tempted by Sakka managed to keep her precepts even though she was thereby reduced to the verge of starvation. Thus it is possible (though perhaps not very easy) for a woman to live as a prostitute and at the same time to keep the precepts. But it is not a profession that is to be recommended, and a woman should only adopt it as a last resort.

An old man can pull a rickshaw for a living if he wishes—that is a matter of his own choice, and he does no harm to other people and can perfectly well keep the precepts. No doubt he will soon ruin his health and perhaps kill himself if he continues to do so, but this is not against the Buddha's Teaching. On the other hand, if a person engages this old man's rickshaw, he should have compassion on the old man and not make him over-exert himself, and he should pay him generously.

As for using animals for work, to plough, or to draw a cart, and so on, there is no harm in this, but the animal should be cared for, well fed, and not overworked. And when the animal gets too old for work it should be allowed to live out the remainder of its life in peace and comfort.

**[L. 8]** **23 January 1965**

Dear Mrs. Perera,

The root of the whole trouble, as the Buddha has pointed out, is desire or affection. A husband has affection for his wife and his wife has affection for him; and this is very pleasant for both of them while it lasts. But, as the Buddha has said, all things that are dear to one change and become different in the course of time—it is a universal law. So it may happen, perhaps, that the husband gets affection also for some other person and offends against the wife. And his wife, because of her affection for her husband, now feels grief and becomes angry, and perhaps speaks bad words and offends against her husband. In this way, because of affection, people offend against each other, and suffer accordingly.

To the *arahats*, who have got rid of all affection, who have nothing dear to them in the entire world, this cannot happen. They do not give offence, and they do not feel offended when other people do them wrong; and for them it is no longer possible to live at home with a family. They are happy when they are alone. But it is not possible for anybody to become *arahat* just by wishing it, and most people have to live with their affections and make the best of a bad job. How is this to be done? Best of all is to control the mind, to guard one's thoughts and not to allow oneself to enjoy thoughts that are wrong. But this is very difficult, and it needs a great deal of practice to be successful. The next best thing is to control one's speech and one's actions—never to allow an evil thought that has arisen to be expressed as evil words or evil deeds. And though this, too, is difficult, it is possible for those who live in a family at home to achieve success in this. But this, too, needs practice. Each time one fails one should confess one's failure, and then determine to do better next time. But success may not come all at once. Just as a young child when it is learning to walk falls down not once, but many times, and yet eventually, by repeated effort, manages to walk without falling—just so, one who is trying to keep the five *sīlas*, and to restrain words and deeds, may fall down many times before he is strong enough to achieve success. One should not think, 'I am now not able to control myself, therefore I shall never be able to control myself,' but 'I am now not able to control myself, therefore let me make an effort so that I shall be able to control myself in the future.' In this way, success is possible. This is true both for the husband if he cannot restrain his actions, and for the wife if she cannot restrain her speech.

And remember, always, that the wise person is quickly offended by his own faults and feels sharp disgust; but he is not offended by other people's faults, even if they are against him. Thus he corrects himself, and does not feel anger towards others.

# 4
# Letters to Mrs. Irene Quittner

**[L. 9]** **11 January 1964**

Dear Mrs. Quittner,[1]
As far as I can gather from what you say, it may be such that you are one of the (regrettably) few people to whom the *Notes* are really addressed. So I think that I ought to give you the opportunity—if you want it—of writing direct to me about things in the *Notes* that are not clear to you. Many things, certainly, are difficult in themselves, and more words about them will probably not help much; but there may be other things about which the *Notes* are unnecessarily obscure, and perhaps also things left out without any apparent reason; and here some further discussion might be useful. (In this connexion, your lament that the notes on *nāmarūpa* are inadequate may be justified. In the first place, however, a certain amount of amplification will be found in other notes[a] and in the second place, I am not at all sure that a detailed study of the intricacies of *nāmarūpa*—particularly *à la Ñāṇavīra*—may not easily become a misdirection of effort: the very fact that the *Notes* say considerably more on this question than is to be found in the Suttas is already a doubtful recommendation. See *Notes*, RŪPA, last paragraph, third sentence from the end. But in these days of printed books a greater detail is demanded, and is perhaps not entirely objectionable. In any case, to say more I should have to say a lot more; and though the flesh is willing, the spirit is weak.)

I am by no means vexed that, as well as commendable, you should have found the book 'arrogant, scathing, and condescending,' since the fact that it seems so is not altogether unintentional—though, also, it is not wholly a contrived effect. The individual notes were, for the most part, originally inscribed in the margins of my P.T.S. dictionary,[2] without any immediate thought of publication. And yet, they were written in exactly the same tone

**a.** In general, as you get more familiar with the book you may find that difficulties raised in one part are answered—or partly—in another.

as what you find in the present book.[b] In transcribing the notes for publication it was not through negligence that no attempt was made to alter the style: I preserved it knowing quite well that it would keep the reader at a distance—which was what I wanted. Certainly, it is galling for the European (and perhaps not galling enough for the Oriental) to be treated as if he had no opinion worth consulting: the European reader expects his author to submit his reasons for what he says, so as to enable the reader to judge for himself; the author is required to take the reader into his confidence, and if he does not it is resented. In dealing with rational matters this is quite in order; both parties are assumed to have the same objective point of view (the same *absence* of point of view, in other words), and the reader follows the author's arguments in order to decide whether he agrees or disagrees; and having done so, he shuts the book and passes on to the next. But if the question at issue is not within the sphere of reason, all this is a misunderstanding. If the book is an invitation, or perhaps a challenge, to the reader to come and share the author's point of view (which may require him first to adopt *some* point of view instead of remaining objectively without any at all), it obviously defeats its own purpose if it starts out by allowing the reader to assume that he already does so. (At this point, I would refer you to three Suttas of the Aṅguttara: V,xvi,1-3/iii,174-6, i.e. Book of the Fives, Suttas 151-153, or the first three of the Saddhamma Vagga.)[3] In a live discussion, or in a correspondence, the appropriate relationship can perhaps be established gradually and painlessly; but in a book, impersonally addressed to unknown readers, the situation is less accommodating, and some outrage to the reader's self-respect (especially if it is what Camus calls '*l'orgueil européen*')[4] must be expected. Without presuming to say whether the *Notes* are adequate in this respect, I shall try to show what I mean by referring to a point that you yourself have raised.

In your letter you have remarked—presumably with reference to note (a) of the Preface—that the author, with a few strokes of the pen, has re-

---

**b.** A man, cast up alone on a desert island, might, after a time, and seeing no other people, give up wearing clothes without feeling immodest. Some strangers, landing on his island many years later and seeing him, might tell him about his immodesty in emphatic terms. But by that time he would quite likely have forgotten what the word means. So it is with one's thoughts. After a certain time in solitude they forget their modesty and go about naked. If one then shows them to a stranger without clothing them decently, he may well find them arrogant. But the word is no longer familiar. (I am, in any case, something of a solitary by nature, sadly lacking in warmth of feeling either for or against other people. This, really, is the unpardonable offence, and all the rest follows from it.)

duced the three baskets to two,[5] and that without giving any reasons. It is now 2500 years after the *parinibbāna*,[6] and we find ourselves faced with a large accumulation of texts (to speak only of the Pali), some certainly reporting what the Buddha actually said, and others, no less certainly, the work of commentators, scholiasts, and so on; but one and all claiming to represent—or rather, claimed by Tradition as representing—the Buddha's true and original Teaching. The first difficulty, today, is to get started: it is obvious enough that we cannot accept all these texts, but where are we to draw the line? All we can do is to make a preliminary critical survey, and then, with an intelligent guess, divide the texts into those we will accept and those we will not. Having made the division we lay aside the critical attitude and set to work to grasp the Teaching. It would not be unduly difficult in the *Notes* to muster an array of critical arguments leading to the rejection of the Abhidhamma Piṭaka. But at once the reader would have something positive and objective to seize hold of, and a learned controversy would start up moving more and more passionately away from the point at issue. 'In general,' says Kierkegaard,

> all that is needed to make the question simple and easy is the exercise of a certain dietetic circumspection, the renunciation of every learned interpolation or subordinate consideration, which in a trice might degenerate into a century-long parenthesis. (*CUP*, pp. 29-30)

So, in the *Notes*, there is nothing of this (though see the last sentence, first paragraph, of CITTA). The reader is unceremoniously (condescendingly?) informed, at the start of the book, which texts the author regards as authentic and which not. Without so much as 'by your leave' the author decides for the reader where the line shall be drawn. The reader either throws the book away, or else swallows what seems to be an insult to his critical intelligence and accepts the book on the author's terms. If the book is all that it sets out to be (though the author must not on any account suggest to the reader that it might not be), it is possible that the reader may eventually come to share the author's point of view. If this should happen, the author's reasons for rejection of texts (here the Abhidhamma Piṭaka) will at once become perfectly evident—indeed, they will become the reader's own reasons. All is then forgiven and forgotten.

Do not forget that the book is written in Ceylon and not in England. With you there is no sacrosanct Buddhist tradition, and people will listen to new ideas proclaimed even in a normal tone of voice: here it is quite otherwise. People will listen, but only if the unfamiliar is uttered loudly and firmly enough to inspire them with courage to think against tradition. Once the ice is broken they may take the plunge; and one or two already—laymen—seem to have embarked on a serious study of the *Notes*. The few English-speaking monks who have seen the book mostly don't like it, but traditional orthodoxy does not have the same official backing here as it does in hard-headed Burma. We have thought it prudent not to send copies to the two *pirivena* universities here, which are strongholds of Sinhalese Nationalism; but we have received a polite letter from the Librarian of the Maha-Chulalongkorn University in Bangkok saying that the book will be 'a useful work of reference' for the many monks of various nationalities who come to study there. There is a certain ambiguity about the Siamese that I have not yet fathomed.

**[L. 10]** **12 April 1964**

Many thanks for your letter of the 4th. I am glad to know that mine arrived safely, though it does seem to have taken a long time getting to you. In any case I hardly expected an immediate reply—if, indeed, any reply at all (I have a bad habit of writing unceremonious letters to complete strangers, and, naturally enough, they tend not to be answered).

If you feel like it, and if I am still about the place, by all means come and see me when you next visit Ceylon. I shall be only too happy to discuss things with you; but, at the same time, I rather fancy that I am less proficient at talking than at writing. Although earlier I did discourage both visitors and correspondents, the situation has since changed. My chronic digestive disorder has worsened and has now been joined by a nervous complaint (caused, ironically enough, by a drug prescribed to cure the amœbiasis), and the combination drastically reduces the time I can devote to practice: in consequence of this I have to get through my day as best I can with thinking, reading, and writing (it is only on this account that the *Notes* have made their appearance). So outside disturbances are now sometimes positively welcome.

Possibly the Ven. Siridhamma Thera,[1] in saying that *paṭiccasamuppāda* is taught in the present by Burmese and Siamese meditation masters, was referring to the Vibhaṅga or Paṭisambhidā interpretations mentioned at the foot of p. 676 (Ch. XVII, n. 48) of the Ven. Ñāṇamoli Thera's *Path of Purification* (Visuddhimagga translation).[2] I admit that I have not investigated these, but from all accounts they are unsatisfactory. In any case, the *paṭiccasamuppāda* formulation (as I see it) does not admit of alternative interpretations—there is one and one only. I do not see that anyone offering a number of different interpretations as equally valid can possibly be right in any of them. (It is quite possible that someone actually reaching *sotāpatti*, and therefore seeing *paṭiccasamuppāda* for himself, might still hesitate before deciding on the meaning of the expanded—twelve term—formulation, since what he sees for himself is *Imasmiṃ sati idaṃ hoti*,[3] etc., and not its expansion in terms—*avijjā*, *saṅkhārā*, and so on—whose meaning he may not know. But one thing is certain: *whatever* interpretation he gives will be in conformity with his private knowledge, *Imasmiṃ sati...*, and since he has *already* grasped the essence of the matter he will not look around for alternative interpretations.) But the Ven. Thera may have had something else in mind when he spoke.

There are several new references to, and quotations from, Bradley. I had already referred to him in ANICCA (a) without having read him, and merely on the strength of what others have said about him. But now I am actually in the course of reading his *Principles of Logic*, and I find that the reference was fully justified. It is satisfactory (and satisfying) to find someone else who has had the same thoughts (within limits, naturally) as oneself, particularly after the singularly depressing experience of reading some of the more recent English philosophers (Bertrand Russell & Co.). Bradley's idealism won't do, of course; but it is incomparably better than the current realism.

I am always pleased when I find a connexion between the Suttas and outside philosophies: it is not, to be sure, that the former can be reduced to the latter—the Dhamma is not just *one* way of thinking amongst others—, but rather that the Buddha has seen all that these philosophers have seen, and he has *also* seen what they could not see; and to discover this is extraordinarily exhilarating. Nobody can say to the Buddha, 'There is this or that that you have not taken into account'[4]: it is all taken into account, and still more. The Suttas give not the slightest pretext for the famous Sacrifice of the Intellect—Ignatius Loyola and Bodhidharma are strange bedfellows,[5] indeed. Certainly there is more to the Dhamma than intellect (and this is sometimes hard for Europeans to understand), but there is nothing to justify the wilful abandonment of the Principle of Identity.

People, mostly, seem to be finding it difficult to make very much of the *Notes* (I, too, find it difficult sometimes, so I cannot say that I am astonished). The university professors who have had copies are silent except one from America who (very politely) attributes their unintelligibility to his ignorance of Pali, but whether this excuses me or him is not quite clear. Few *bhikkhus* have had copies, but one has remarked that 'they contain a lot of mistakes'—which, from the traditional point of view, is quite true. This would probably be the opinion of the great majority, who, however, would perhaps add that, in a foreigner, it is excusable. Laymen here are sometimes interested, and at all events not hostile (except for one, who has been provoked to a fit of indiscriminate xenophobic fury, embracing Dahlke and the Ven. Ñāṇatiloka Mahāthera[6] as well as myself—also strange bedfellows!). Expressions of approval have come from Germany and 'Les Amis du Bouddhisme' of Paris, I am pleased to learn, are enthusiastic. About thirty copies went to England, but (apart from a bare acknowledgement from Nottingham, and a brief note from a personal acquaintance) yours has been the only comment we have received. Of course, it is not easy to know to whom to send, and the choice of addresses is largely a matter of chance. From Columbia University Buddhist Study Group (Washington) we have this cryptic utterance. 'This material will be used to augment our collections in the most useful way with the understanding that your gift has been made without limiting condition.'

About the second paragraph of CETANĀ (b) of the *Notes*, this is a question that has, quite rightly, troubled G.W. Balfour (*Psychological Aspects of Mrs Willett's Mediumship, and of the Statement of the Communicators Concerning Process*). When the personality is split, asks Balfour, which is the 'true self'. (This is a fascinating book, but for us a digression.)

And about Preface (n) of the *Notes*, I find that this question is touched upon slightly by Prof. E.A. Burtt in the third essay (p. 54) of 'Knowledge and Conduct' (BPS *Wheel* 50).[7] He does not seem to have read Kierkegaard. His essay is reprinted from the *Maha Bodhi* of December 1956.

## [L. 11] 14 July 1964

The Principle (or Law) of Identity is usually stated as 'A is A', which can be understood as 'Everything is what it is'. Bradley (*PL*, Ch. V, p. 141) remarks that, in this form, it is a tautology and says nothing at all.

> It does not even assert identity. For identity without difference is nothing at all. It takes two to make the same, and the least we can have is some change of event in a self-same thing, or the return to that thing from some suggested difference. For, otherwise, to say "it is the same as itself" would be quite unmeaning.

Stebbing (*MIL*, p. 470) says

> The traditional interpretation of the law is metaphysical. If "A" be regarded as symbolizing a subject of attributes, then the formula may be interpreted as expressing the permanence of substance, or the persisting of something through change.

The second paragraph of ATTĀ says, in effect, that the Principle of Identity—taken, that is, with Bradley's qualification that there must be 'some change of event' to make it meaningful—is no less valid in the Dhamma than it is everywhere else. Acceptance of this Principle (as you will see also from the Stebbing quotation and from my further treatment in ANICCA, PAṬICCASAMUPPĀDA (c), & *FS*) means rejection of the popular notion that 'impermanence' in the Dhamma means 'universal flux'. With the rejection of this notion we come to see that the question of *anattā* can deal, not with the self-identity of things, but only with 'self' as the subject ('I', 'myself' etc.). But if one starts off sacrificing the intellect by assuming that the *anattā* teaching is denial of the Principle of Identity, then at once there is chaos.

In referring to Loyola and Bodhidharma in my last letter, I had in mind two 'wilful abandonments of the Principle of Identity.' (i) Loyola: 'In order never to go astray, we must always be ready to believe that what I, personally, see as *white* is *black*, if the hierarchical Church defines it so.' (ii) Bodhidharma (or, rather, a modern disciple of his, in an article—'Mysticism & Zen', I think—in *The Middle Way*[1]): 'The basic principle of Zen is "A is not A".' (Note, in parenthesis, that once people start denying the Principle of Identity the question may arise whether the bare statement 'A is A' is quite as meaningless as Bradley supposes. A lot has been made in modern French writing, philosophical as well as literary, of Audiberti's imaginative phrase *la noirceur secrète du lait*;[2] and this suggests that it may not be altogether meaningless to assert the contrary, 'white is white'. This might perhaps seem trivial, except that a great deal of modern thinking—including mathematics—is based on a deliberate rejection of one or another of the Laws of Thought, of which Identity is the first. This may be all very well in poetry or physics, but it won't do in philosophy—I mean as a fundamental principle. Every ambiguity, for a philosopher, should be a sign that he has further to go.)

Thank you kindly for your offer to send any drug that I might need, but the trouble is that nobody quite seems to know what has gone wrong. I have just spent a month in Colombo[3] in the hands of various doctors, but nothing has come of it and I am back where I was. It is not a matter of any very great consequence.

# 5
# Letters to Mr. Wijerama

**[L. 12]** **4 March 1964**

Dear Mr. Wijerama,

Many thanks for your admirably detailed letter. The attitude you speak of, that of cursing the world and oneself, is, in a sense, the beginning of wisdom. Revolt is the first reaction of an intelligent man when he begins to understand the desperate nature of his situation in the world; and it is probably true to say that nothing great has ever been achieved except by a man in revolt against his situation. But revolt alone is not enough—it eventually contradicts itself. A man in blind revolt is like someone in a railway compartment trying to stop the train by pushing against the opposite seat with his feet: he may be strong enough to damage the compartment, but the damaged compartment will nevertheless continue to move with the train. Except for the *arahat*, we are all in this train of *saṃsāra*, and the problem is to stop the train whilst still travelling in it. Direct action, direct revolt, won't do; but something, certainly, must be done. That it *is*, in fact, possible to stop the train from within we know from the Buddha, who has himself done it:

> I, *bhikkhus, being myself subject to birth, decay, and death*, having seen the misery of subjection to birth, decay, and death, went in search of the unborn, undecaying, undying, uttermost quietus of extinction (*nibbāna*), and *I reached the unborn, undecaying, undying, uttermost quietus of extinction.* (M.26/i,167)

Revolt by all means, but let the weapons be intelligence and patience, not disorder and violence; and the first thing to do is to find out exactly what it is that you are revolting against. Perhaps you will come to see that what you are revolting against is *avijjā*.

Now for flux. I see that you make a certain distinction between physical objects and mental states: let us therefore consider first physical objects.

You say 'The idea of continuous change or that everything is continuously changing seems to me to be correct. But the difficulty arises when the idea is extended and it is stated that this object is not the same object. The chair that is in front of me being of matter is undergoing change. In that sense it will not be the same chair. But in another sense but much more real is the idea that the chair is there and till it breaks down it will be so. This is still valid in spite of the changes that are taking place which may or may not be perceptible so long as the chair could be used as a chair.'

The distinction that you make here between 'the idea of continuous change' and 'the idea that the chair is there' is of the greatest importance, since it marks the distinction between the scientific view and the existential (or phenomenological) view. The question arises: Are these two views compatible, or if not, which is correct?

In spite of the fact that you say 'The idea of continuous change is a matter of observation and it accords with the scientific view that matter is subject to continuous change,' I wish to suggest that the idea of continuous change is *not* a matter of observation (I shall discuss this later), but is purely and simply a theoretical consequence of the scientific claim to achieve complete objectivity. (Science aims at completely eliminating the observer—or individual point of view—from its results, thereby attaining complete generality. As soon as the observer is reinstated, as in quantum theory, change once again becomes discontinuous. The existential view, on the other hand, is that for an existing individual the world *necessarily* presents itself in one perspective or another. No individual can possibly see the world as science claims to see it, from all points of view at once. See Preface (f).)

You say 'The chair that is in front of me *being of matter* is undergoing change.' This sounds as if you are *deducing* continuous change from the fact that the chair is of matter, and I suggest that what you are doing is to apply an abstract notion *that you have learnt about theoretically* to your concrete experience (i.e. to the '*much more real* idea that the chair is there'). The fact that you speak of 'changes that are taking place which...may not be perceptible' also gives the impression that you are making theoretical assumptions about the nature of change—how do you know anything about changes *that you cannot perceive*? (Here is Sartre speaking about material objects that are there in front of him:

> Of course someone will object that I merely fail to see changes ... But this is to introduce very inappropriately a scientific point of view. Such a point of view, which nothing justifies, is contradicted by our very perception ... [*B&N*, p. 205])

You say 'the difficulty arises when...it is stated that the object is not the same object.' Quite true; but you yourself show the way out of the difficulty when you say 'When it is said that the infant is not the same as the grown up man ... it is correct. When it is said that it is the same infant who has grown up it is also correct....' When an infant grows up into a man, we perceive that the infant has changed, and we express this by saying that the infant both is and is not the same as the man (we are taking the infant and the man only as physical objects, not as 'selves', which is a different question). Clearly, then, in order for us to be able to say 'this has changed' two things are necessary: (i) sameness, and (ii) not-sameness, or difference. Unless there is something that remains the same, we cannot say 'this'; and unless there is something that is different, we cannot say 'changed'.

Take your mango tree. Ten years ago it was a small plant, now it is a big fruit-bearing tree, and in virtue of this *difference* you say it has *changed*; but both the small plant and the big tree are mango, and both are in the same place (the small mango plant has not grown up into a jak tree, nor is it now in another part of your garden), and in virtue of this *sameness* you say that it is *not another* tree. Or consider a leaf that changes colour—first it is green, then when it dies it becomes brown, but it is still the same leaf. What remains the same is the *shape*, and what is different is the *colour*, and so we say '*this* leaf has *changed*.' This is quite simple owing to the fact that vision is a *double* sense, giving us perceptions both of shape and of colour, and it often happens that one remains constant while the other varies.

But let us take a more difficult case, and consider a change of colour alone. Suppose I have some blue curtains, and after a time I notice that 'the blue has faded'—how are we to understand this? Obviously, if I look at the curtains one day and find that they are crimson I shall not say 'the blue has faded' for the good reason that crimson is not blue at all—it is a different colour altogether. So I shall say simply 'the curtains have changed their colour' (just like the leaf). But if I say 'the blue has faded' I am saying that the curtains are still blue, but a slightly different blue, a lighter blue. What remains the same here is the *general* determination 'blue', and what is different is the particular *shade* of blue.

Take another case. I am looking at a spoon on the table in front of me. First I fix my attention on the bowl of the spoon and see the handle less distinctly out at one side; then I fix my attention on the handle and see the bowl less distinctly out at the other side. The spoon, as a whole, remains unchanged—in both cases it is exactly the same spoon. What is different is the particular *aspect* of the spoon within the general experience called 'seeing a spoon'. (Cf. CETANĀ.) Two points arise here.

1. Leaving aside the cases where one sensible quality varies while another remains constant (the leaf, for example) and considering only the more fundamental cases where the change takes place within one and the same sensible quality or characteristic, we notice that it is always the more *general* feature that remains invariable while the subordinate or more *particular* feature varies. This suggests that there may be a certain *structure of change* that must be taken into account whenever we consider the question of change; and if this is so, it will mean that the statement 'everything is changing' needs strict qualification. (In the last part of the *Notes* I have tried to give a formal account of this fundamental structure within which change takes place, but I expect that you have perhaps not been able to make very much of it. No matter.)

2. If it is possible, in any given change, to make a clear-cut distinction between those features that do not vary and those that do, it will follow that the distinction between *sameness* and *difference* is absolute: in other words, that we cannot say '*approximately* the same' or '*approximately* different'. (So long as we use the word 'approximate' at all that will be an indication that we have failed to make the distinction properly clear-cut, since 'approximately the same' means 'the same but with a difference' and 'approximately different'—i.e. 'somewhat different' or 'rather different'—means 'different but partly the same'.) If this is so, it will follow that all change takes place discontinuously; for if 'same' means 'absolutely the same' and 'different' means 'absolutely different', there can be no intermediate category between sameness and difference.

Perhaps you will object that it is ridiculous to speak of one's curtains 'fading discontinuously', and from the common-sense point of view I would agree with you. But the fact remains that we do not 'see our curtains fading'; what happens is that one day we 'notice' that the curtains 'have faded'; and this is a sudden perception. No doubt, after a few more weeks, we shall notice that the curtains have faded still more, and we shall *infer* that all this time the curtains have been *gradually* fading 'without our noticing it'. 'But' you may say 'do we not sometimes actually *see* things in process of changing—as when, for example, the lights are quickly lowered at the cinema and fade in five or ten seconds?' We do: but observe that, in the first place, the change is from 'steady light' to 'fading light' and then from 'fading light' to 'darkness'. In other words, 'fading light' is perceived as a *thing* distinct from both 'steady light' and 'darkness', and the change from one to another of these things is discontinuous. In the second place, there are reasons for supposing that what we actually perceive when we see a 'fading light'—which has the same essential structure as a 'flying arrow'—cannot be properly described as 'continuous change'.

A. The 'Gestalt' school of psychology has specialized in experimental investigation of perception of change, and has reported that every change that we perceive takes place suddenly and absolutely. (See the passage from Sartre translated in ANICCA (a).) Whenever a perceived change is described as 'taking place continuously' it is to be presumed either that the necessary analysis of a complex experience is beyond the power of the perceiver, or else that, unwittingly, rationalization has taken place. (That we do, in fact, have experience of movement and other such changes is, of course, not to be denied; but these experiences are notoriously difficult to describe, and the problem of motion has puzzled philosophers from time immemorial.)

B. It can be shown by argument that the notion of continuous change is self-contradictory (in other words, that it contains a short circuit somewhere). There are two ways of doing this.

(i) The first is to show that all experiences that we might be tempted to describe as 'continuous change' (motion of material objects, fading [or brightening] of lights and colours, decay of matter, and so on) can be adequately and completely described in terms of discontinuous changes at different levels of generality. I am satisfied that the dialectic outlined in *FS* is capable of doing this (which is one reason why I have included it in the *Notes*), but unless you have understood this note I cannot hope to make myself intelligible to you here. I have summed up this argument against the idea of flux in PAṬICCASAMUPPĀDA:

> The misunderstanding [involved in the definition of flux or continuous change] arises from failure to see that change at any given level of generality *must* be discontinuous and absolute, and that there *must* be different levels of generality. When these are taken together, any desired approximation to 'continuous change' can be obtained without contradiction. [p. 71]

(The starting-point of any discussion of motion must always be Zeno's Eleatic arrow. Some account of this celebrated paradox is given by Bertrand Russell—*M&L*, pp. 79-83—but the problem is not so easily solved as Russell likes to think.)[a]

(ii) The second way of dealing with the notion of flux is to discuss it

a. The solution described by Russell solves the problem by leaving it out. The problem is: What is time?

directly, and to show that it cannot be defined without encountering a self-contradiction. This, in fact, is what I have tried to do in the briefest possible way in PAṬICCASAMUPPĀDA (c), with the definition borrowed from Poincaré: A = B, B = C, A ≠ C. Let us, however, consider the notion of flux in more detail. The word itself means a *flowing*, and the idea it conveys is that of *smooth transition*, that is, *continuous change*. This is evidently opposed to discontinuous change, but without implying no-change or fixity.

My dictionary defines it as 'a continuous succession of changes,' which we can use as a starting point. A *succession* of changes clearly means *one change after another*, and a *continuous* succession of changes will mean that there is no interval of time between these changes. But how much time does a single change take? *Either* it takes some time, in which case we are obliged to say that each individual change is a continuous change, and therefore itself a flux; *or* it takes no time and is instantaneous, in which case we have to conclude that a flux is itself instantaneous, since the individual changes take no time, and there is no time *between* the changes. The second alternative at once raises the objection that you cannot have a *succession* of changes—one change *after* another—if *no* time is involved. The first alternative—that every individual change is a flux—makes the definition circular: 'a flux is a continuous succession of fluxes,' and we still do not know what a flux is.

Perhaps, then, we are wrong in thinking that 'a continuous succession of changes' is the same as 'continuous change'. If these two are not the same, and 'continuous change' is the truth, then we must deny the existence of separate individual changes: there will be *change*, but not *changes* or *a change*. In other words we must renounce all attempts at defining flux in terms of individual changes, and must seek, rather, to take a *sample* of flux, of continuous change, and describe it. Here, then, is a flux—continuous change. Let us take a slice of this flux and divide it into three consecutive sections, calling them A, B, and C (note that we cannot take three consecutive *instants* in the flux without falling into contradiction, since instants, which are of *no* time, cannot be *consecutive*, i.e. *both* contiguous *and* successive—if two instants are contiguous both are of *no* time and have *no* time between them, and there is still *no* time and therefore no *succession*; if they are successive both are of *no* time and have *some* time *between* them, therefore they are not *contiguous*).

We have to ignore for the moment the fact that each of these three sections itself consists of continuous change, and we regard each section as a whole, without inquiring what is going on inside. We are expressly forbidden to introduce the idea of an individual change, and so we must say that 'A is the same as B' (A = B) and that 'B is the same as C' (B = C); for if we postulate that A and B (or B and C) are *both* contiguous *and* different we thereby automatically define a discrete individual change—there is '*a* change' at the junction of A and B, where A changes to B. So far so good. But a flux is, in fact, *change*; and so we must introduce the idea of *difference* into our description. Let us therefore say that 'A is different from C' ($A \neq C$). Since A and C are not contiguous we have not defined any discontinuous change between them, and all is well—between A and C there is *change* but not *a change*. So our description—$A = B$, $B = C$, $A \neq C$—does, in fact, agree with the notion of flux as continuous change. And we can take each individual section (A, B, and C) in turn and divide it into three lesser sections (a, b, and c) and describe it in the same way ($a = b$, $b = c$, $a \neq c$). In this way our description can be seen to apply to any sample of the flux that we like to take. But, alas! our description contains a self-contradiction: $B = C$ (or $C = B$) and $A \neq C$; therefore $A \neq B$; but also $A = B$; therefore both $A = B$ and $A \neq B$; and this outrages the Law of Contradiction, 'A is not both B and not-B'.

Regarding states of mind, which you differentiate (quite rightly) from physical objects in that they do not come within the sphere of science (though I cannot agree that they are 'not objects': they are *mental* objects),—you seem to think, and again you are right, that the notion of flux or continuous change does not apply to them. I have a slight impression that one reason why you do not apply the notion of flux to mental states is, precisely, that they are not in the sphere of science; and this, in its turn, suggests to me that you *do* apply the notion of flux to physical objects because they *are* in the sphere of science—in other words, out of 'superstitious regard for the prestige of contemporary science' (see Preface to *Notes*). It is quite possible that I am doing you an injustice here, but this is a matter that you must decide for yourself—in any case, I am only recording the impression that I get from your letter.[b] But though I say that you are right in thinking that the notion of flux cannot be applied to states of mind, you will have gathered from what has gone before that I maintain that the notion of flux *also* cannot be applied to physical objects. Once the notion of flux is ruled out entirely, it becomes clear that the structure of change of mental states (or mental objects) has much more in common with that of physical

**b.** It is perhaps worth noting in passing that the current 'orthodox' interpretation regards mental states as no less of a flux than physical objects. Here is an example: 'The stream of self-awareness that the uninstructed conceive to be a soul is made up of point-moments of consciousness, each of which has no more than a momentary duration.' This is pure speculation, with no relation at all to actual experience.

objects than might appear at first sight. (You say that mental states such as pleasure and grief 'appear, vanish, and reappear'—but is this not true also of physical objects? Do we not have *familiar* sights, sounds, smells, tastes, and bodily contacts?) It is necessary to remember that the three characteristics (*Notes*, ANICCA), namely *arising*, *disappearance*, and *change while persisting*, apply to *all* experience, whether of physical objects or of states of mind. (The last characteristic, *ṭhitassa aññathattaṃ*, I understand as expressing the combination of absolute sameness and absolute difference that I suggested earlier in this letter was the essential structure of all change.)

As I understand your last paragraph, I gather that you consider that all mental states cease when one becomes *arahat*. This is not so (except in the particular sense of 'cease' of *NP* §22 & VIÑÑĀṆA). There are still mental states for the *arahat* so long as he continues to live, but these states are now wholly free of lust, hate, and delusion. In other words, there is still consciousness for the *arahat* until his body breaks up in death. See also PHASSA (b).

Perhaps you will be wondering why it is that I am so anxious to destroy the notion of flux—or at least to eliminate it from the context of the Dhamma (I have nothing to say against its use in the context of science, nor have I anything to say against science itself in its proper place; but its proper place is not the Dhamma: scientific thinking and Dhamma thinking belong to two quite different orders, as I hope to have made plain in the Preface to the *Notes*). The reason is to be found in your letter itself. You say 'The word flux means continuous change. If this idea is applied to everything it would be correct to say that what I see now, e.g. a tree, is not the same as I continue to watch it as it is subject to continuous change' and also 'I have heard as an extension of the same idea, Buddhist monks saying, pointing to an object, that the object is not there.' This doctrine is a complete misunderstanding and is wholly misleading. And, as you quite rightly point out, it is based on the notion of universal flux. In order, therefore, to undermine this false doctrine, it is necessary to point out that the notion of flux, at least as applied to experience, is a self-contradiction.

But why, if it is false, is this doctrine taught? The answer is, because it provides a conveniently simple interpretation of the Suttas, easily learned and easily preached. The Buddha has said that 'What is impermanent, that is suffering; what is suffering, that is not-self.' This is understood (or rather, misunderstood) in the following way.

Impermanence is taken to mean continuous change (flux), and (as you have said) if this notion is correct, the idea of a thing's continuing self-identity cannot be maintained—what *appears* to be the self-same tree persisting in time is not *really* the same since it is continuously changing. In consequence of this, the idea of *self* is an illusion; and it only persists on account of our *avijjā*, or ignorance of the truth of universal flux. If we remove this ignorance, we shall see that what we formerly took to be a lasting (or existing) selfsame tree ('A = A', the Principle of Self-identity) really has no abiding self at all—it does not *really* exist. And this explains why 'what is impermanent, that is not-self.' And what is wrong with this? What is wrong with it is—as perhaps you have noticed—that it does *not* explain why what is impermanent is *suffering*, and what is *suffering* is not self.

Suffering (*dukkha*) is the key to the whole of the Buddha's Teaching,[c] and any interpretation that leaves suffering out of account (or adds it, perhaps, only as an afterthought) is at once suspect. The point is, that suffering has nothing to do with a tree's self-identity (or supposed lack of self-identity): what it *does* have to do with is *my* 'self' as subject (I, ego), which is quite another matter (see *PS* §6). As I point out (ATTĀ), 'With the question of a thing's self-identity (which presents no difficulty) the Buddha's Teaching of *anattā* has nothing whatsoever to do: *anattā* is purely concerned with "self" as *subject*.' But this is very much more difficult to grasp than the misinterpretation based on the notion of flux, so flux inevitably gets the popular vote (like the doctrine of *paramattha sacca*, of which it is really a part). The misinterpretation is actually of Mahāyānist origin; and in one of their texts (Prajñāpāramitā) it is specifically stated that it is only on account of *avijjā* that things appear to exist, whereas *in reality* nothing exists. But the fact is that, even when one becomes *arahat*, a tree continues to have a self-identity; that is to say, it continues to exist as the *same* tree (though undergoing subordinate changes on more particular levels—falling of leaves, growth of flowers and fruit, etc.) until it dies or is cut down. But for the *arahat* the tree is no longer '*my* tree' since all notions of 'I' and 'mine' have ceased.

I don't know whether all this discussion will make my criticism of the notion of flux any clearer to you, but it may at least make you aware that there are serious objections to the introducing of this notion from scientific contexts into Dhamma contexts. If this letter raises any fresh difficulties, please let me know.

P.S. If you do not want to keep this letter when you have finished with it, I would suggest that, rather than destroy it, you might give it to Mr. Samaratunga to put in his file.

---

c. 'Both formerly, monks, and now, it is just suffering that I make known and the cessation of suffering.' (M.22/i,140)

**[L. 13]** **20 March 1964**

I am reading Bradley's *Logic*, a book to which I refer in ANICCA (a) and SAÑÑĀ (a). This deals with the question of change and non-change, and particularly with the question how I can have knowledge of past and future if my perception is confined to the present.[a] Bradley's solution (which is inadequate, though extremely interesting) is by way of inference—we have immediate appearance, and from this we *infer* reality, though we can never be quite certain of it. But, as you will have seen, it is possible, if one has *assumed* the Idealist position (which is a mistake,[b] though a full elucidation would take us into fundamental structure), to find another solution by *mis*-applying the Sutta teachings of *anicca*/(*dukkha*)/*anattā*. Bradley's work has enabled me to see the situation in greater detail, though it still remains the same in essentials—'Buddhist monks saying, pointing to an object, that the object is not there.'

**[L. 14]** **2 May 1964**

Thank you for your letter. May I say that I again appreciate the fact that you have stated your questions in a clear and coherent way that makes the (rather difficult) task of answering them convincingly really quite a pleasure. And a well-put question sometimes almost answers itself.

You ask for Sutta references of passages where the Buddha has 'explained in specific terms the structure of change.' Beyond the two *uppāda*/*vaya*/*ṭhitassa aññathattaṃ* references (both given in ANICCA), I do not know of any at all. Perhaps this will astonish you; but the fact that the Buddha does not seem to have discussed the structure of change beyond this is, I think, not hard to understand. The point is this: provided a person does not have any preconceived ideas about the structure of change, an understanding of this structure is not necessary for the attainment of *nibbāna*.

An intelligent person observes that there is such a thing as change, that the things in his world do change from time to time; and the Buddha informs him that nothing that exists is exempt from change, that all existing things do come to an end sooner or later. And when that person considers this fact and applies it in the proper way (with *yoniso manasikāra*) to his own existence, it is enough (given certain other conditions) to lead him to

a. This brings about the view that I have given briefly in PAṬICCASAMUPPĀDA (c).

b. There is no opposition between 'appearance' and 'reality'.

enlightenment. (You may refer to SAṄKHĀRA for an elaboration of this statement).

In general, it seems that the Buddha did not encourage philosophical or metaphysical investigation of matters that do not lead to *nibbāna*, for the good reason that a man might spend a lifetime in fruitless investigation and discussion of such matters, and die still unsatisfied, whereas he might quite quickly attain the goal by attending to the right things. (You may profitably read the Cūḷamāluṅkya Sutta—M.63/i,431—on this question.)[1] And it must be admitted that the whole question of the structure of change is one of the most difficult in philosophy.

Why then (you might ask) have I raised the question, when the Buddha did not? The reason is this: that today we do *not* approach the Dhamma without preconceived notions about change. In the prevailing scientific atmosphere we are all taught at school, particularly in the study of mathematics and science, that change is a continuous flux (we do not necessarily learn it *explicitly*, but it is implicit in these studies); and so, when we leave school, we *know already* that change is a flux, without even looking to see if it is so. And the consequence of this is that erroneous interpretations of the Dhamma (as I have already pointed out to you) have become firmly established.

Now, even supposing that my own speculations on the structure of change are somewhere near the mark (which, of course, remains an open question), I quite see that other people whose talents lie in other directions, might well scratch their heads over *FS* for years without making anything of it at all; and it is for this reason that I have given warnings that it is only for those who find it useful. Nevertheless, I have decided to include it, as well as some other philosophical discussion of change, in order at least to show that there is an alternative to the idea of flux. Once somebody is prepared to abandon the idea of flux as an article of faith that he has learnt (almost) on his mother's knee, he *may* come to see that these current interpretations of the Dhamma must not be accepted without question. And once he does this, then it is probably not necessary for him to inquire any further into the structure of change.[a]

---

**a.** These ideas of 'Identity in Difference' and 'Invariance under Transformation' are not really new. F. H. Bradley wrote his *Logic*, which I am just finishing, in 1883, and he got the idea from earlier writers. But it went out of fashion with the logical positivists—Russell & Co. who, I must warn you, are *most* misleading, particularly Russell himself—, and has more recently started to return to favour in quantum theory. Here is a sentence from P.A.M. Dirac's *Principles of Quantum Mechanics* (1930): 'The important

Let us now consider the principle that 'when change takes place within one and the same sensible quality or characteristic it is always the more general feature that remains invariable while the subordinate or more particular feature varies.' A little consideration, I think, will show you that this is really a tautology, and cannot therefore be denied. What I mean to say is this. If I am asked what I understand by the words 'particular' and 'general', I shall reply that what is *general* embraces two (or more) *particulars*, in such a way that each particular thing is an example or instance of the more general thing. (A number of leaves from different kinds of trees will each be a particular shade of green, and therefore all different one from another; but each and every one of these leaves is an instance of green in general.) And from this definition of 'particular' and 'general' it follows that any two particulars can be interchanged without affecting the general. (I can pick one leaf, and say 'this is green', and then I can throw it away and pick another leaf from a different tree, and say 'this, too, is green'. There is a *change* in the particular green that is in my hand, and unchange of *sameness* in the general green.) And it also follows that the converse is not true: there cannot be change of the *general* leaving any *particular* unchanged. (If the general colour of all the leaves changes from green to brown, every single leaf will be an instance or example of brown, and I shall be unable to find any leaf that is any shade of green at all.)

It should be clear that the principle enunciated above is implied in the very meaning of the words 'particular' and 'general'. But the question now is: Are we in fact entitled to make this distinction between 'particular' and 'general'? Do we in fact perceive a general green as well as a particular green? This is really a matter for each person to decide for himself, and instead of arguing the point I shall suggest a method of approach to individual cases.

*Assuming* that we are entitled to make this distinction, we see that in order to discover the general it is only necessary to put two particulars together, and what they have *in common* will be the general. This, I think, is clear. But also we can put it in a different way: we can say that whenever two particulars are found together, they *ipso facto* reveal the general. This means that whenever we perceive a *togetherness* of particulars, we do so *because* we perceive what they have in common (though it may be difficult to say precisely what it is). Whenever we see *two* (or more) *different* things that nevertheless *seem to belong to each other*, we are at once entitled to

---

things in the world appear as the invariants ... of ... transformations.' (p. vii) And, of course, as soon as you say 'invariant', you rule out 'flux'.

turn the situation the other way round and say that we see *one and the same* more general thing *presenting two different aspects.*[b]

If you have grasped this idea, you will see that it can be applied to perception of change. In perception of change, we have first A, and then B; but we must *also* have the 'belonging-togetherness' of A and B, otherwise we fail to connect A's disappearance and B's appearance and do not say that 'A has changed into B' or that 'A has become B'.

If I see a jug on the table, and then I go out of the room and come back a short while later and see a glass on the table instead of the jug, I do not say 'the jug has become the glass' because I do not perceive them as belonging together. But if (by some miracle) the jug vanishes while I am actually looking at it and is immediately replaced by a glass, I shall rub my eyes and say 'How extraordinary! The jug seems to have become a glass'; and I say this because the disappearance of the jug and the appearance of the glass are perceived as *connected* (owing to contiguity in space and time).

Consider, now, the block of ice that melts and is immediately replaced by a pool of water. As you say, if we know beforehand that it is the nature of ice to melt and be replaced by water, there is no difficulty in seeing that a general feature has not changed; so we must suppose that we have never seen ice before, and also (by a stretch of the imagination) that we have never seen water before, either. So, then, a block of ice is brought in and placed on the floor in front of us; it melts, and there is a pool of water in its place. As in the case of the jug and the glass, we connect the first thing (the disappearance of the ice) with the second thing (the appearance of the pool of water) because they are spatially and temporally contiguous, and we say 'How remarkable—the thing called "ice" has changed into the thing called "water"!'. But what, here, are the particulars, and what the general?

The *particulars* are (i) the perceived spatio-temporal existence of the ice, and (ii) the perceived spatio-temporal existence of the water, and these are *different* (a) spatially, because the ice and the water do not have the same

**b.** If we see a cow and a horse and a tree, we at once perceive—without *thinking* about it at all, and without any previous knowledge—that the cow and the horse 'belong together' and that the cow (or the horse) and the tree do not. Turning this round, we say that the cow and the horse are different aspects of one single more general thing, namely 'four-legged bestiality', and that the tree is not. It might be objected that 'four-legged bestiality' is merely an abstract idea that we do not 'perceive' at all; but this is not so. We *at once* perceive the 'togetherness' of the cow and the horse, and it is merely in order to give it a name and express it in words that we have to start thinking: the *thing* is perceived directly, but it may quite well happen that the thing does not have a familiar *name*.

shape (the ice stands up, the water lies flat) and (b) temporally, because the ice is followed by the water. The *general* is the perceived spatio-temporal existence of the whole ice/water transformation, and this is *one and the same* (a) spatially, because both ice and water were in the same part of the room, and (b) temporally, because both were in the same part of the afternoon.

But suppose the disappearance of the ice in front of us was immediately followed by the appearance of a pool of water in the next room; or that it was followed, not immediately, but two days later by a pool of water in front of us. Here, first the spatial, and secondly the temporal, contiguity is missing, and we fail to perceive 'togetherness' and so we do not say that the ice has changed into the water. If the ice and the water are in different rooms or on different days, then *both* the general *and* the particular have varied and we do not perceive the *change* of ice into water.

This, of course, is not the only way that we perceive the change of the block of ice into the pool of water; but it is perhaps the most fundamental. There is also the question of the substance. Even without previous acquaintance with ice or water, we may perceive that though the particular reflections and transparencies are different before and after, yet the general characteristic of 'transparency' has remained invariant, and we are inclined to say that it is the 'same stuff' in two different forms. But, in English, there is no single *word* to cover both ice and water (unless we say $H_2O$), and it might seem that we do not *perceive* both as different aspects of one more general thing. But, as explained above, with the cow and horse, this is a mistake. (In Sinhalese, for example, although we can speak of *wandura* and *rilawa*, we cannot—as far as my slight knowledge goes—refer to both by one single word, as we can in English with the word 'monkey'.[2] But this does not mean that the perceptions of an Englishman and a Sinhala are different.)

The case of the butterfly is much more complex. In the first place, we have not *two*, but *four* particulars: egg/caterpillar/chrysalis/butterfly. And the change from the egg to the butterfly may be a matter of months, not of a few minutes like the ice to water. We may, of course, actually observe any one of these three transformations (egg/caterpillar, caterpillar/chrysalis, chrysalis/butterfly), and then, as in the case of the ice/water, we sensually (visually) perceive the 'togetherness' as well as the difference, and we speak of 'seeing a change'.[c] But we never actually see (at least on one occasion) all

c. Note here—a further complication!—that, in a sense, we do actually perceive the past (and the future) as well as the present; and this is explained in *FS* §II/10. But you had better, for the time being at least, simply think that we 'perceive the past with our memory'.

the three changes from egg to butterfly; and what actually happens is that, from different observations of these various changes at different times, we build up an *imaginary picture* of the whole affair, by means of which we can, if we wish, perceive *in imagination* all the three changes in the course of a few seconds. And it is to this imaginary experience that we refer when we speak of the 'change from egg to butterfly'. But this imaginary experience follows the same principles as the real experience, and we can only speak of the (imaginary) change, egg/caterpillar/chrysalis/butterfly, if we perceive (in imagination) the 'togetherness' of these four particulars. As to the *name* of this togetherness, we meet with the same difficulty as before—there is no single word. The best we can do (after some thought) is 'a living insect of the *lepidoptera* family'.

And when we come to the case of the man (the infant who grows up), the situation is impossibly complex. We have first to separate the man *as he sees himself* (that is, principally, his store of memories) from the man *as he is seen by others* (his body, his behaviour, his habits, his gestures, his temperament, his wife, his family, his occupation, his social position, his nationality, his health, his wealth, his police record, and so on). Then we take any one of these aspects we please, and consider, in the way I have indicated above, how Citizen Perera is perceived (or perceives himself) as a 'togetherness' of different particulars. His bank manager (if he is so fortunate as to have one) will perceive him as 'a bank account by the name of Perera', and this bank account will be a 'togetherness' of varying particular balances at six-monthly intervals. His mother will perceive him quite differently—as a body that has issued from hers and has gradually grown up, a 'togetherness' (which she might describe as 'flesh of my flesh'), of such successive particulars as pregnancy, birth, suckling, weaning, nursing in sickness, having a son at school, in a government office as a clerk, having a married son, having a son to support her in her old age, to give her a good funeral, and so on. His wife will perceive him as...well, there are many different ways in which wives perceive their husbands—and some wives have much the same sort of view as the bank manager. But no doubt you will be able to fill in details.

As to states of mind, the principle certainly applies in the same way. Whenever we speak of a 'change of mind' (which we often do), we do so because we perceive (by introspection or reflexion) a 'togetherness' of different particulars. When I say 'I changed my mind about going to Colombo,' that means that I perceived a 'togetherness', describable as 'possibility of a journey to Colombo', that presented itself successively in two different particular aspects, 'about to go to Colombo' and '*not* about to go to Colombo'. With change of moods, description is more difficult; but we sometimes find we have certain definite sets of emotions governed by a more general state of mind. When we are in love, for example, we experience sudden changes from exaltation to depression, from joy to misery, which we do not have at other times. (Consider the state of mind of a lover waiting for his loved one, who is five minutes late.) And the 'togetherness' of these different emotions is the more general thing that we call 'being in love'.

I think, perhaps, that this will be enough for you to be getting on with. It is hardly possible to do more than give an indication, and then to let people try and see the thing for themselves. But in all cases where an 'objective scientific point of view' is adopted, there will necessarily be complete failure to understand the principle that we are discussing; and for this reason I would suggest that you read Russell (if you *must* read him) with a certain amount of circumspection—Russell's logic is *not* the same as Bradley's logic.

On the question of flux (or continuous change), I should like to suggest a certain reflection. If one were asked what the immediate evidence was for the existence of flux, the answer would almost certainly be, It is our experience of motion, the fact that we perceive movement. But, now, when we go to the cinema we sit in front of a screen, and we spend two or three hours 'perceiving moving pictures'—we are perfectly satisfied that we *do* perceive movement at the cinema, and the only difference from the live theatre is the flatness of the screen and the black-and-white colouring. We are just as much excited or emotionally disturbed by a cinema show as we are by a theatre performance. But when we pause to consider the mechanism of the cinema, we come to understand that (looking at the matter from a slightly different point of view) all we really perceive is a succession of perfectly still pictures (Russell mentions this, but we are not here concerned with the conclusions he draws). And this being so, we are obliged to admit that perception of movement *need not be evidence of flux*: we *cannot safely infer* 'continuous change' from 'perception of movement'. I say this, not to *prove* that there is *not* 'continuous change', but to introduce a doubt into the unquestioning belief that there *is* 'continuous change'. If I can introduce a doubt, that may be enough. (I do not, however, want to suggest that the structure of change or movement is simply that of the cinema film.) These remarks are rather concentrated philosophy, and you may not make very much of them at present, but they might be of use a little later on.

# 6

# Letters to Dr. M.R. de Silva

**[L. 15]** **5 September 1961**

Dear Dr. de Silva,

You told me that you had read Francis Story's *The Case for Rebirth* (BPS, Wheel 12/13) and found that it helped you to accept rebirth as a fact. I have now just read this booklet myself, and perhaps a few observations might not be out of place.

To begin with, the examples of (what appear to be) rebirth are good, and there is no reason at all not to take them at their face value. Such cases, while not amounting to *logical demonstration* of the necessity of rebirth (which is not possible anyway, since, let alone *re*-birth, logic cannot even demonstrate the necessity of *birth*—is there any *logical* reason why you, Dr. de Silva, should have been born?), cannot easily be dismissed on some other hypothesis.[a]

The remainder of Mr. Story's booklet, however, sets out to *explain* rebirth, either in terms taken from the Suttas ('Dependent Origination,' *paṭiccasamuppāda*) or the exegetical literature ('Cognitive Series,' *cittavīthi*), or else in scientific or pseudo-scientific terms. This part of the booklet is worthless (or worse), and any acceptance of rebirth based on it is built on quicksand; for not only are the explanations bogus,[b] but they should never have been attempted in the first place. The Buddha does not explain *how* rebirth takes place; he states simply that, unless craving has ceased, rebirth *does* take place. It may be that a more detailed description of the phenomenon of rebirth than is found in the Suttas could be made, but

---

**a.** I would strongly recommend G.N.M. Tyrrell's *The Personality of Man* (Pelican Books A165, published by Penguin Books). It gives an intelligent summary of various supernormal phenomena, and includes some solid evidence for rebirth.

**b.** (i) 'Dependent Origination' has—in spite of a venerable tradition—nothing whatsoever to do with 'Kamma and Re-birth', (ii) the 'Cognitive Series' is rubbish anyway, and (iii) Science, since it excludes the scientist, has nothing to say about the scientist's—or anyone else's—rebirth.

(a) it would be irrelevant and unnecessary (because it is quite enough just to accept rebirth), and (b) it would not be in terms of 'cause and effect' (i.e. it would be strictly a description and not an explanation).

This distinction between description and explanation is of vital importance, and is really what I was talking about when I said that the Buddha's Teaching cannot be understood by one who (however unwittingly) adopts the scientific attitude (which is also the scholar's attitude). I suggested that a more fruitful approach to the Dhamma, at least for one accustomed to Western ideas, might be made by way of the existential or phenomenological philosophers, who have developed a more direct and fundamental approach to things than that of empirical science with its inductive and statistical methods. These methods give, at best, only *probable* results; whereas the phenomenologist, not going beyond description of *present* phenomena, enjoys *certainty*.

Unfortunately, as I told you, few of the more important writings of this school of thinkers are available in English; so I thought it might be of use to translate one or two passages and send them (prefaced by three quotations from a typical modern logician) for you to read at your leisure. You may, perhaps, find them rather heavy going until you get more familiar with an unaccustomed manner of thinking. The long passage, which consists of most of the introduction to Sartre's short treatise on emotion, may also serve as an introduction to phenomenology in general. It must be emphasized that this is not in any way a substitute for the Buddha's Teaching—all these thinkers are still enmeshed in *avijjā*. We are not, in fact, interested in this or that particular result of the phenomenological method, but rather with the method itself—direct reflexion. And even when we succeed in adopting the attitude of direct reflexion (in place of the scientific attitude, which consists, precisely, in assuming that there is no such thing as an attitude at all), we still have to understand the Dhamma.

I have inserted a few notes where they seemed called for; I hope you will not find them distracting.[1]

From L. Susan Stebbing, *MIL*:

1. The problem of the logical justification of induction is not one that need concern the scientist. (p. 495)

This advice to the scientist to shut his eyes may perhaps be to the advantage of science: it is certainly to the disadvantage of the scientist, who will plunge deeper and deeper in ignorance.

2. To justify scientific method it is necessary that we should be able to justify the assumption of the inductive hypothesis, which can alone permit us to conclude that the laws of nature are simple enough for us to discover them, so that we may regard nature as ultimately intelligible. Meanwhile the scientist continues to assume that the laws of nature are ultimately simple. (pp. 418-19)

3. Every modern logician recognizes that the foundation of the theory of induction is to be found in the theory of probability. (p. 496)

From J.-P. Sartre, *L'Imagination*:

4. Perhaps, however, error does not creep into the reflective act itself. Perhaps error appears at the inductive level, when, on the basis of facts, one establishes laws. If so, would it be possible to create a psychology which would remain a psychology of experience, yet would not be an inductive science? Is there a kind of privileged experience which would put us directly in contact with the law? A great contemporary philosopher[c] thought so, and we shall now ask him to guide our first steps in this difficult science. (p. 126)

5. ... but reflection must not be confused with introspection, which is a special mode of reflection aimed at grasping and establishing empirical facts. To convert the results of introspection into scientific laws there must ensue an inductive transition to generality. There is another type of reflection, utilized by the phenomenologist, which aims at the discovery of essences. That is to say, it begins by taking its stand from the outset on the terrain of the universal. Though proceeding in terms of examples, little importance is attached to whether the individual fact which serves as underpinning for the essence is real or imaginary. Should the 'exemplifying' datum be pure fiction, the very fact that it was imaginable means that it embodied the sought-for essence that is sought, for the essence is the very condition of its possibility. (p. 128)

(i) This last sentence means that the experience of reality and the experience of images are *in essence* the same, i.e. that the characteristics of all experi-

c. This refers to Husserl.

ence *as experience* are invariable, whether its object is real or imaginary. (ii) Naturally, an image *as image* has its own particular essence or nature or character that distinguishes it from the real *as real*.
(iii) The word 'essence' as used in this and other passages is the key to most of the important shades of meaning of the word '*dhamma*' in the Suttas. A thing's essence or nature or *dhamma* is what differentiates it from some *other* thing. Indeed, *dhamma* sometimes simply means 'thing'. A table *as table* has a different essence from a chair *as chair*, though both *as things* have the same essence (or *dhamma*) of impermanence. Thus *dhamma* may also mean 'universal law'. And in some contexts *dhamma* means 'image' or 'idea', i.e. something imagined or thought.

From an article on Husserl's philosophy in Kern, *Dictionary of Religions: Philosophy*:

6. Our task is not that of deducing the rational but of describing the conceivable, or that which comes with *Evidenz* as incontrovertibly given. (p. 580)

(i) The 'conceivable' is, of course, anything that can be imagined (not excluding the real). See the preceding passage.
(ii) The 'evidence' of our senses (or of our imagination) is incontrovertible: when, for example, I feel a sharp pain in my finger there is absolutely no doubt about it, even if my sense of vision tells me (no less incontrovertibly) that my finger has been amputated. We are not concerned to reconcile or *explain* this disagreement—*that* task we leave to those who 'deduce the rational', in this case the neurologists.

From J.-P. Sartre, *Esquisse d'une Théorie des Émotions*:

7. a. [On 'the associationists':] Sartre deals with them with excessive severity in *L'Imagination*.

b. [On 'Dasein':]
(i) The word *Dasein*, as used by Heidegger, means the mode of existence of the human being. This human mode of existence is Being-in-the-world; the human being is a self in the midst of a world of things and other beings, and is inseparably related to this world. (ii) The phrase *attā ca loko ca*, 'the

self and the world', is quite often found in the Suttas, always in connexion with some wrong view—'the self and the world are eternal', 'the self and the world are not eternal', and so on—; and it is obvious that we shall not be able to discover why these views are wrong until we know what this phrase means. Clearly enough we shall do better to ask Heidegger, Sartre, *et al.* than the positive psychologists.

c. [On Sartre's criticism of psychologists who believe that the facts of mental life somehow group themselves:] Cf. Thomas Huxley: 'Sit down before fact as a little child, be prepared to give up every preconceived notion, follow humbly wherever...nature leads.' Sartre would retort that, if you do this, nature won't lead anywhere at all—you will simply remain sitting down before fact, as a little child.

d. [On Husserl's uses of 'transcendental and constitutive consciousness' and 'putting the world in brackets', alluded to by Sartre:]
(i) The word 'transcendental' as used by Husserl has no connexion with the Sutta word *lokuttara*, which is sometimes so translated. Transcendental consciousness is consciousness that goes beyond or *transcends* normal immediate consciousness: this is a kind of non-deliberate *reflexive* consciousness (of which more below). This consciousness is *constitutive* since it presides over immediate consciousness, which is concerned only with the particular, and gives it general teleological significance: without it there can be no experience.
(ii) 'Putting the world in brackets'. In our normal everyday activities we are totally absorbed in our experiences, in the world. It is possible, however, with practice, to take a step back (as it were) and, without ceasing to have experiences, to *observe* these experiences *as they take place*. In order to adopt this attitude of self-observation or deliberate reflexion we simply withdraw attention from the (variable) *content* of our experiences (which is 'the world') and direct it to the (invariable) *structure* of these same experiences: thus 'the world', though not altogether ceasing to exist, is 'put in brackets'.

e. [On Sartre's discussion of Husserl's 'absolute proximity of consciousness with respect to itself' and the self-awareness of consciousness as existing:]
(i) The phrase 'the absolute proximity of consciousness with respect to itself' refers to two adjacent *layers* of consciousness within one single complex experience. (This is probably a misinterpretation of Sartre's statement, but it is what he *ought* to have meant by it.) The bottom layer is *immediate* consciousness, and the layer above is *reflexive* consciousness. Since one can

also reflect on reflexion, there is no limit to the number of layers that can be so employed. It is important to understand that these layers of consciousness are all contemporary with each other, though they all depend upon the lowest layer, consciousness of the world.
(ii) 'All consciousness exists in the exact measure that it is consciousness of existing.' *If* this means whenever there is consciousness (*of* an object) there is *at the same time* the consciousness 'I am', then this statement is absolutely correct (Sartre would no doubt agree with this interpretation of his statement; but he would certainly disagree about how this interpretation should itself be interpreted)—with the vital qualification that it does not apply to the *arahat*. Sartre has within limits succeeded in describing his own state, which is that of a *puthujjana*, an ordinary person. But since he has not understood the Buddha's Teaching he cannot see any escape or way beyond his own state. The *arahat*, however, is rid of *asmimāna*, the notion 'I am'; but until the breaking up of his body there is still consciousness of objects and also reflexive consciousness. The *arahat* sees the *puthujjana*'s state (and the *arahat*'s state) with an *arahat*'s eyes, Sartre sees the *puthujjana*'s state with a *puthujjana*'s eyes (and does not see the *arahat*'s state at all): the view is not the same. This instance admirably illustrates both the importance and the limitations of Sartre's philosophy.

f. [On Heidegger's notion that, as his own possibility, an existent can *lose* himself precisely by choosing to *be* himself and thus gain himself:] This awkward sentence probably means that a man can gain individual existence by choosing to be personally responsible for every decision he makes, or he can lose his individuality by regarding himself as one of a crowd and declining responsibility by doing as others do.

g. [On the notion of Heidegger that in the being of the existent, the existent refers himself to his being:] See passage no. 11 below, where this same thing is said in different words by someone else.

h. [On Heidegger's notion of the 'inauthentic' man:] The word 'inauthentic' is used by Heidegger to describe the ostrich-like attitude of the man who seeks to escape from his inescapable self-responsibility by becoming an anonymous member of a crowd. This is the normal attitude of nearly everybody. To be 'authentic' a man must be constantly and deliberately aware of his total responsibility for what he is. For example, a judge may disclaim personal responsibility for sentencing people to punishment. He will say that as a judge it is his duty to punish. In other words it is as an *anonymous representative of the Judiciary* that he punishes, and it is the Judiciary that must take the responsibility. This man is *inauthentic.* If he wishes to be *authentic* he must think to himself, whenever he sits on the Bench or draws his salary, 'Why do I punish? Because, as a judge, it is my duty to punish. Why am I a judge? Is it perhaps my duty to be a judge? No. I am a judge because I myself *choose* to be a judge. I *choose* to be one who punishes in the name of the Law. Can I, if I *really* wish, choose *not* to be a judge? Yes, I am absolutely free at any moment to stop being a judge, if I so choose. If this is so, when a guilty man comes up before me for sentence, do I have any alternative but to punish him? Yes, I can get up, walk out of the courtroom, and resign my job. Then if, instead, I punish him, am I responsible? I am totally responsible.'

i. [On the absoluteness, according to both Heidegger and Husserl, of appearance of the phenomenon:] Appearance is the absolute because there is no reality concealed behind it. This is a matter of cardinal importance. Freud's celebrated 'unconscious' withers and dies before the blast of Sartre's criticism in *L'Être et le Néant*. Sartre gives us instead the notion of 'bad faith' or tacit self-deception, a far more delicate instrument. But the important point is this, that nothing of what I am at present can hide from reflexion; and I am thus *totally* open to self-criticism. Were this not so, meditation would be no more effective against our mental defilements than skin lotion is against smallpox.

Here, to conclude, are some extracts from *CUP*, written in 1846 by Kierkegaard, the first of the modern Existentialist thinkers:

8. Let the enquiring scholar...his parrot-like echo. (pp. 23-4)[2]

9. Precisely because the negative is present in existence, and present everywhere (for existence is a constant process of becoming), it is necessary to become aware of its presence continuously, as the only safeguard against it. In relying upon a positive security the subject is merely deceived. (p. 75)

The *Postscript* was written in 1846. Kierkegaard is the first of the modern existentialist thinkers.

10. *When the question of truth is raised in an objective manner, reflection is directed objectively to the truth, as an object to which the knower is related. Reflection is not focussed upon the relationship, however, but upon the question of whether it is the truth to which the knower is related. If only the object to which he is related is the truth, the subject is accounted to be in the truth. When the question of truth is raised subjectively, reflection is directed subjectively to the nature of the individual's relationship; if only the mode of this relationship is in the truth,*[d] *the individual is in the truth even if he should happen to be thus related to what is not true.* (p. 178)

11. Existence constitutes the highest interest of the existing individual, and his interest in his existence constitutes his reality. (p. 279)

12. It is forbidden to an existing individual to forget that he exists. (p. 271)[3]

**[L. 16]** **10 December 1961**

Regarding the passages I sent you earlier, and also our talk at the Hermitage,[1] I do not want to give the impression that it is necessary to study and master these things. All that I am concerned to do is to make you aware of the existence of an order of things *underlying* the scientific order of things. The general assumption today is that the *only* order is the scientific order, and once one leaves that one enters the chaotic and mystical realms of emotion, religion, art, 'subjectivity', and so on. This assumption is quite stultifying and fatal to any wholesome and profitable attitude to life. If, in your reading and in your life, you can make yourself aware that there is a fundamental order in all things that is not confined to the field and attitudes of science, then you can safely read books about matters that science is unable to take into account (paranormal phenomena, telepathy, precognition, and so on, as well as evidence for rebirth), without fear of bewilderment and disorientation. You will be able to understand that these apparently impossible and contradictory happenings ('they *cannot* be true, because if they were they would upset all our ideas about the world') are, in fact, perfectly possible, and within the natural order of things. But you need not *study* it—only be *aware* of it. It is only when the peculiar limitations of one's thinking that are characteristic of this scientific 'age of reason' in which we live are removed

**d.** Heidegger would say '... is authentic'.

that it becomes possible to read and listen to the Dhamma with any degree of sympathetic understanding.

It is a misfortune of mine that I am not able to put things in a simple way; I am too fond of getting into detail and taking my listeners in amongst the trees where they can no longer see the wood as a whole. So please do not feel intimidated or discouraged by my perhaps rather complicated way of putting things—it is not at all necessary to follow everything I say.

**[L. 17]** **13 January 1962**

Yes, you are quite right. It only leads to frustration to attempt to explain E.S.P. phenomena[1] on a scientific basis. Dr. Grey Walter, a pioneer of electroencephalography, who seems quite well disposed towards E.S.P. workers, has remarked that the electrical brain impulses with which he is dealing cannot possibly have any connexion (as some people have hoped) with E.S.P. phenomena.[2] The relevant passages can be found in his book *The Living Brain*. And attempts to explain the Dhamma on a rational scientific basis only result in such wholly misleading effusions as Francis Story's 'The Four Noble Truths' (BPS *Wheel* 34/35), which was published recently. The Ven. Siridhamma Thera has reported unfavourably on *The Mind Unshaken*, and I have no great desire to read it. Thank you all the same.

**[L. 18]** **26 March 1962**

A short while ago you were good enough to send me a copy of *Triangle* with an article 'Anatomy of Consciousness' by the late Prof. Sir Geoffrey Jefferson F.R.S.[1] I sent you my comment upon it in a couple of lines in a postcard; this, of course, was totally inadequate, but I did not at that time find it convenient to say more. I know that I shall now again risk being incomprehensible to you, but I regard the current orthodox attitude of science to the question of consciousness as being such an obstacle (particularly for medical men) to the understanding of the Buddha's Teaching (and even to a no more than ordinarily intelligent and wholesome understanding of life) that it is a risk I am cheerfully prepared to take. (And, after all, nothing obliges you to read what I have to say if you don't wish to.) It is a matter of regret to me that, though I have been so well treated by so many doctors in Ceylon, and have found them, as people, so friendly and easy to talk to, I am yet quite unable to get beyond a certain point with them and discuss things that really matter. Always there arises a barrier of incomprehension, and I perceive that, even though I am still being listened to, communication is no longer taking place. No doubt the question is not easy, but it must be faced; and this article 'Anatomy of Consciousness' seems to offer a convenient point of departure for a discussion.

Prof. Jefferson, in his article, tells us that 'consciousness depends upon (or "is the sum of")[a] the activities of the whole intact nervous system, central and peripheral'; and the article clearly takes it for granted that an elucidation of the nervous system and its workings, if it were complete, is all that would be required for a total understanding of consciousness. 'We shall agree in the belief' says Prof. J. 'that whatever mental qualities human beings display during consciousness are derived in the end from the millions of cells in the cortex and from infinitely elaborate internuncial connections with subcortical structures.' This is certainly the generally accepted view in scientific circles.

Two assumptions are implicit in this attitude. The first is that between each possible state of the nervous system and each possible state of consciousness there exists a one-to-one correspondence. With this assumption we shall not quarrel (though a practical demonstration of its validity obviously offers certain difficulties). The second assumption is that the working of the nervous system strictly obeys the established laws of science, and in particular those of physics and bio-chemistry.

A physiologist (or neurologist), clearly enough, is bound to make this second assumption: it is the assumption of every man of science that the results of his investigations can be arranged in an ordered pattern exemplifying regular laws of behaviour, and furthermore that these laws of behaviour hold not only in the restricted field of his own investigations but universally in all branches of science to which they may be applicable. Thus, for example, the biologist accepts without question the laws established by the experimental chemist as well as those established by people who have investigated the behaviour of electricity; and the theoretical physicist assumes that, ultimately, the behaviour of all things whatsoever can be accounted for in terms of certain fundamental laws that are his special field of study. Failure to make this assumption, it might seem, must obviously lead to chaos—what hope of understanding the order of the universe and man's place in it unless we assume that the universe *is* ordered (i.e. that the same experiment repeated at different times and in different places will always give the same result)?

---

**a.** 'To depend upon' and 'to be the sum of' are not the same thing, but Prof. J. does not notice this inconsistency. We shall refer to it again later.

What hope for suffering humanity if vaccination (for example) had purely random effects, producing immunity from smallpox in one, precipitating the measles in another, and simply giving a slight squint to a third? Medicine would be impossible unless cures could be predicted with some confidence. Besides, in view of the astonishing successes of modern science (and medical science in particular), what sane person could possibly be tempted to doubt this assumption—does not the success of the scientific method abundantly justify the assumptions it makes?

To begin with, doubting of this scientific assumption (supposing that it is necessary to doubt it) does not necessarily land us in chaos. To deny the universality of the order discovered by science and embodied in its laws is not by any means to deny that science discovers any order at all. Nor is it to deny that there is any universal order. If, as may be thought, there is a universal order of more fundamental nature than that revealed by science (though quantum theory, in a muddled way, is partly aware of it),[b] we can quite well allow the scientific order a limited validity within this universal order. (Logicians, whose task it is to investigate such matters, are well aware that the laws of science are only *probably*, not *certainly*, true.) 'Things' we may say 'obey the laws of science...except when they don't.' Or, to be more precise, 'the laws of science are less uniformly valid in one region than in another.' Details are not necessary here; what is important is the general idea.

But is it necessary to doubt the scientific assumption? Are we obliged to reject the simple and convenient view of the universal validity of science for the undeniably more complicated and tiresome view suggested above? Imagine that, by accident, you rest your bare arm on a hot stove. You will undoubtedly lift your arm in a hurry. Why? Because contact with the hot stove is painful, you may say. But this won't do at all. What we want is an account of the changes that took place in your nervous system from the time your arm was rested on the stove to the time it was raised; and this account must be in strictly scientific terms. Pain, however, is *not* a scientific term. We can speak of an electrical or chemical impulse travelling along a nerve up your arm to your brain; for these are all things that can be publicly observed (in theory at least) by each one of a team of physiologists who are experimenting on you. But the pain you feel is strictly private: not even in

**b.** 'With the recognition that there is no logical reason why Newtonian and other classical principles should be valid outside the domains in which they have been experimentally verified has come the realization that departures from these principles are indeed necessary.' (*PQM*, p. 230)

theory can the team of physiologists observe it.[c] (You can *tell* them that you feel pain, of course, but this does not make the pain public: what is public here is the sound of your voice, and the meaning of the words you utter is quite irrelevant—to allow that your words are meaningful is to beg the whole question.) A physiologist can observe an *impulse* moving up your arm, but he cannot observe a *pain* moving up your arm; only you can do that (if, for example, a red-hot needle is moved on your skin from the elbow to the shoulder; but not, of course, if your nerve is stimulated at a stationary point, when all you will feel is a stationary pain). This means (and I shall emphasize it by underlining it) that a physiologist must make no reference whatsoever to feeling (pleasure, pain, indifference) in his account of human behaviour. If he fails to abstain he abandons scientific method.

A physiologist is bound to maintain that the pain you felt when your arm was against the stove had nothing at all to do with the immediately subsequent removal of the arm from the stove (nor with your remarks about it); he *must* maintain this because he is obliged to claim, if he is to be consistent, that he can fully account for the movement of your arm (and the sound of your voice) in terms of neural mechanisms alone and without any reference to the pain. And if feeling plays no part in our actions we must count it a fortunate coincidence that the state of the nervous system to which the painful feeling of a burning arm corresponds *happens* to be one that brings about removal of the arm from the hot surface: if the converse were true, and the nervous system pressed the arm down still harder on the hot surface, we should have a pretty miserable time of it. Imagine it: each time we felt pain we should find the neural mechanism making the body do the very thing that aggravated the pain; and perhaps we should find ourselves recoiling from pleasure 'as if we had been burned'. But no; our bodies, by

c. No two people can observe the same pain. If a nerve, visible to a number of observers, is stimulated, only one (at most) of the observers (namely, the one who happens to own the nerve) will experience the pain; and his report of the experiment ('stimulation of nerve causes pain') will contradict the report of the other observers ('stimulation of nerve does not cause pain'). *Either*, then, the same cause—the observed stimulation of the nerve—can produce two different effects for two different observers (which undermines the scientific hypothesis of the invariability of cause-and-effect for all observers at all times and in all places), *or* pain (and feeling in general) is outside the scope of science. (Imagine the consternation and dismay in a physical laboratory amongst a group of observers gathered round a piece of electrical apparatus, if, whenever one particular switch was turned, one of the observers reported that a certain bulb glowed brightly, while the other observers all reported that the bulb remained dead. Might they not send the freak observer to the pathological laboratory for observation?)

some happy chance, do just what we should wish them to do—when there is pleasure the body acts in such a way as to prolong it, and when there is pain the body takes action to bring it to an end. Or can it possibly be that feeling does, after all, dictate—to some extent at least—what our bodies shall do? Were we perhaps wrong in so categorically rejecting your original explanation that you raised your arm because contact with the hot stove was painful?

Or consider the case of a man who takes alcohol. Are the motions of buying the bottle, opening it, pouring the contents into a glass, and finally swallowing, wholly to be accounted for without any reference to the fact that he finds it *pleasant* to be intoxicated? Certainly, there is good experimental evidence that our behaviour will accommodate itself, after a short period, to a change of environment in such a way as to give us the least possible discomfort in the altered circumstances.[d] This is the principle upon which the conditioning of reflexes depends—a rat is repeatedly made uncomfortable by an electric shock if he behaves in a certain way, and, in consequence, 'learns' to behave in a different way.

But if we are to allow, as clearly enough we must, that feeling is capable of affecting the state of the nervous system (either by determining a specific action, such as raising the arm off a hot stove, or by conditioning a fairly lasting change in behaviour), then we shall find ourselves obliged to abandon the postulate of the universal validity of the laws of science. So long as feeling depended upon the state of the nervous system and the state of the nervous system upon scientific determinism, all was well; but if, in addition, the state of the nervous system must be admitted to depend upon feeling, then (at least in the eyes of science) we enter the realms of chaos; for feeling, not being publicly observable, is not a scientific entity, and cannot therefore be governed by any laws of science, and the behaviour of the nervous system, accordingly, ceases to be wholly rational. In short, the living body, and the nervous system in particular, are regions where the laws of science are manifestly less uniformly valid than elsewhere.

In your recent letter you said that you see that there is not much use in your studying paranormal phenomena because you find yourself trying to explain and understand them on a scientific, rational, basis; and you don't think this can really be done. You are quite right, of course, in thinking that

---

**d.** Observe that scientifically speaking, this sentence and the next beg the question. We have argued that feeling is outside the domain of science, and we cannot now introduce *scientific* evidence that feeling affects behaviour. This 'experimental evidence' is private to each individual who experiments upon himself.

these phenomena cannot be explained on a scientific basis; but this is the very reason why they should be studied. Certainly, they cannot be explained or understood in a hurry, but this is no great matter; the important thing is that they afford striking and varied evidence (both spontaneous and experimental) that the laws of rational science are not universally valid. And it is failure or refusal to accept this fact that so effectively blocks the way to progress in clear thinking of a fundamental nature.

The achievements of the rational methods of science have been so striking, and the methods themselves are so beautifully simple and tidy, that there is a natural tendency on the part of rationalists to make the wholly irrational assumption that reason (or science) is capable of accounting for everything. Indeed, this assumption is so very nearly an axiom (except in isolated pockets—see footnote *b*) that the strongest emotional resistances are encountered by anyone who ventures to question it. Yet there is a failure of rational science that is still more striking than the most striking of its successes; and that is...to account for itself.

Without the scientist there is no science; but science cannot, without inconsistency, admit the existence of the scientist; for the scientist is a man, and a man is not to be explained if feeling is ignored; and feeling is outside the domain of science. Science, however, in its claim to universal validity, is unwilling to recognize this; and a bastard entity has been brought into existence to make this claim seem valid. This bastard entity is *sensation*. Prof. Jefferson says 'When we analyze in physiological terms alone...' and then proceeds to speak of '...the classical pathways by which sensation reaches the thalamus and finally the cerebral cortex.' *Sensation*, in Prof. J.'s view, is a purely physiological term. This means that it is nothing more nor less than an electrical or chemical impulse (I believe there is still some uncertainty in this matter) travelling along a nerve. Under no circumstances, then, can the word 'sensation' be taken to mean 'feeling'. But obviously this is just what it *does* mean in ordinary usage. A painful sensation is a painful feeling, or more simply, a pain. And this being so, the word 'sensation' cannot possibly be a physiological term. But the physiologist, by using it *as if* it were a physiological term, manages to fuse two strictly incompatible meanings into a single word, and this gives the illusion that the two meanings are the same. We saw (para. 1) that Prof. J. uses the two expressions 'to depend upon' and 'to be the sum of' as if they meant the same thing, and this is nothing else than the very ambiguity we have been discussing, but in another form. To be just, I don't suppose that the Professor is aware of the duplicity; he is deceiving himself in good faith, in company, no doubt, with almost all his colleagues; for the ambiguity is so convenient and so unobtrusive (to a non-philosophical eye, at least) that it would be regarded as ridiculous, if not positively heretical, even to point it out, let alone to object to it. Nevertheless, it is with the help of this piece of verbal legerdemain that the pleasing illusion of the universal validity of rational science is maintained.[e]

It must now be remarked that the current scientific interpretation of the word 'consciousness' is itself inadequate (quite apart from the fact that consciousness is just as much beyond the domain of science as feeling). From Prof. J.'s article (as well as from other sources) it is evident that 'consciousness', for the scientist, means 'rational thought' or 'awareness of what one is doing or thinking'. The Professor seems to exclude 'automatic or conditioned behaviour' from conscious activity, and this is in accordance with current scientific opinion. But conditioned behaviour, as we noted before, involves feeling (pleasure or pain); and to exclude this feeling from consciousness is to invite confusion. (Does an unconscious pain hurt? If you say 'yes,' I ask 'how do you know, seeing that you are not conscious of it?' If you say 'no,' I ask 'then how can you tell it is a pain and not a pleasant feeling?, how do you know there is any feeling at all?') This restriction of consciousness to rational thought is simply a prejudice of rationalism; and in the Buddha's Teaching it is specifically stated that consciousness (*viññāṇa*), feeling (*vedanā*) and perception (*saññā*) are inseparable[2]—whenever there is any one of them there are all three. But to understand this a more subtle and intelligent approach to consciousness (or, more generally, to experience) is necessary.

The mistake is to approach consciousness by way of the body. But rational science, being essentially the study of what is public, namely *matter*, has no alternative. The laws of science are the laws of matter, and if these laws are universal then consciousness (whatever it may be) must necessarily be subordinate to matter. What science overlooks, and cannot help overlooking, is the fact that in order to know the body it is *first* necessary to be conscious of it—the body is an *object* (amongst other objects) *of consciousness*, and to seek to investigate consciousness by way of the body, instead of the other way round, is to put the cart before the horse. Consciousness comes first, and if it is to be known it must be studied directly (that is to say, by immediate reflexion). This matter has been stated clearly by J.-P. Sartre, who, in his principal work dealing with consciousness, writes more than 250 pages out of a total of 700 before mentioning the body at all. This is what he says.

---

**e.** I do not wish to suggest that this is all that is necessary to maintain the illusion. Denial of the two-way interaction of matter and feeling is not the only weak point of the rationalist position; but it is the only one that interests us here.

> Perhaps some may be surprised that we have treated the problem of knowing without raising the question of the body and of the senses and even once referring to it. It is not my purpose to misunderstand or to ignore the role of the body. But what is important above all else, in ontology as elsewhere, is to observe strict order in discussion. Now the body, whatever may be its function, appears first as the *known*. We cannot therefore refer knowledge back to it, or discuss it before we have defined knowing, nor can we derive knowing in its fundamental structure from the body in any way or manner whatsoever. (*EN*, pp. 270-1; *B&N*, p. 218)

And Sartre goes on to point out that whatever knowledge we have about our own body is derived in the first place from seeing other people's bodies. As a doctor this will be evident to you—you know about the structure of your own heart not from having dissected it but from having dissected other people's bodies in your student days. Knowledge of our own body is thus very indirect, and this is particularly true of the nervous system.

The foregoing remarks are generally applicable to all those medical men—perhaps the majority?—who have allowed their scientific attitude towards medicine (which is admirable in its proper place) to affect and infect their general outlook on life, so that they now quite fail to understand what it is to be an existing individual. But more especially these remarks apply to those among them who think of investigating the Buddha's Teaching. It might well happen that a doctor, reading the Suttas for the first time, and coming across such a passage as this:

> There are in this body head-hairs, body-hairs, nails, teeth, skin, flesh, sinews, bones, bone-marrow, kidneys, heart, liver, midriff, spleen, lights, bowels, entrails, gorge, dung, bile, phlegm, pus, blood, sweat, fat, tears, grease, spittle, snot, oil-of-the-joints, urine (S.xxxv.127/iv,111, etc.)

would think to himself, 'As anatomy, this is hopelessly inadequate; any first-year student knows a hundred times as much; and besides, there is no sort of order about it'; and he would congratulate himself that medical science has made such enormous progress since the Buddha's day. His first reaction would thus be to dismiss these primitive notions as trivial and obsolete. Then, turning the page, he might encounter this passage:

> He regards matter—or feeling, or perception, or determinations, or consciousness—as self. That is a determination.... In an uninformed commoner contacted by feeling born of nescience-contact, monks, there is craving arisen; thence is born that determination. Thus, monks, that determination is impermanent, determined, dependently arisen; and that craving too is impermanent, determined, dependently arisen; and that feeling too is impermanent, determined, dependently arisen; and that contact too is impermanent, determined, dependently arisen; and that nescience too is impermanent, determined, dependently arisen. (S.xxii.81/iii,96-7)

Our doctor finds this altogether incomprehensible—there is nothing about it in the textbooks, not even in those on the shelves of the psychiatry department—, and concludes that, presuming it does actually mean something, it is quite beyond his powers of understanding. Thus his second reaction is baffled humiliation. In this way he oscillates between the opposite poles of superiority and inferiority to the texts, and is unable to find anything on the same level as his own understanding—it is all either beneath him or above him. The trouble is, as no doubt you will have gathered, that our doctor has got things the wrong way round. He is accustomed, on the one hand, to elaborate and intricate descriptions of the body and its workings (whole textbooks—whole libraries, no doubt—are devoted to the heart and the kidneys), and on the other hand he has never been required to digest anything more than the most artless pronouncements about consciousness. And this is because medical science puts the body first and consciousness (if considered at all) afterwards.

But the Suttas put consciousness first and the body a bad second, for reasons that I hope to have made clear; and it is to be expected that statements about consciousness will be complex and those about the body simple. If our doctor can manage to reverse the order of his thinking (which needs practice), he may stand some chance of finding the Buddha's Teaching at least partly intelligible instead of wholly baffling and frustrating. The first passage quoted above is, of course, not a primitive attempt at anatomical description, but is designed to lead a person to disgust with the body; and exact physiology is obviously out of place. The second passage is, admittedly, of extreme difficulty; but the Dhamma, I am afraid, *is* difficult, and it serves no useful purpose to pretend that it is not. (Those booklets that presume to explain the Dhamma on a scientific basis do the greatest possible dis-service to seriously interested enquirers. It is far better for a man to understand that he does *not* understand the Dhamma, than it is for him to believe falsely that he does understand it. The former attitude may encourage progress; the latter can only obstruct it.) It is in the hope of clearing away at least some of the preliminary obstacles to a right approach to the Buddha's Teaching that I have written this to you.

**[L. 19]** **25 May 1962**

I have finished the Beverley Nichols.[1] I think that one question is raised that calls for a detailed reply. B.N. describes how a certain morphia addict became 'changed'—i.e., found faith in God—and, as a result, lost all interest in the drug; and he points out that to give up a drug-addiction is one of the hardest things in the world (with which we may agree). The question, then, is this: What has the Buddha's Teaching to offer a drug-addict that Christianity has not? Indeed, might it not be true to say that, in comparison with the complete and spectacular cure of Christianity where all that is required is an act of self-surrender, the subtle and abstruse Teaching of the Buddha, hard to understand even for the abstinent man, has nothing to offer? And this is the answer. Christianity does not cure the addict at all; it merely substitutes faith for morphia, it replaces one drug with another. The Buddha's Teaching offers not merely cure but total immunity for all time. Let us, however, look more closely.

Not myself being a religious person I have no first-hand knowledge of the 'faith in God' that is able to take the place of morphia, and I am therefore unable to describe it as a personal experience. But something can be said about the pharmacology of this potent drug. God—the Christian God, at least—is an impossible compound of the temporal and the eternal. He is temporal because he understands man, knows what is best for him, is pleased when man is good and angry when man is naughty (which is usually the case, and so 'God is angry every day' as it is said), will listen to man's prayers, and will help him—in short, God is man's Heavenly Father. All this is only possible for a being who, though no doubt a glorified edition, is essentially no different from man. God can only comprehend man if he himself has some acquaintance with man's weaknesses, he can only have compassion on the drug-addict if he himself knows what it is to be a drug-addict. (B.N. suggests that Christ, who was God, was subject to sexual desire.) God, therefore, like man, must *exist* (i.e. must be contingent in time). But, also, God is omniscient, omnipotent, and changeless—in a word, eternal—otherwise he would not be *God*. It is these attributes that distinguish him from man. Obviously enough, these two aspects are absolutely irreconcilable, a fact that Kierkegaard, the most intelligent of Christian philosophers, has been at pains to emphasize.

According to Kierkegaard, God does not exist—he is eternal.[a] Nevertheless, God existed as a man, as Jesus of Nazareth. This is absolutely impossible, it is a contradiction in terms; to assert that the eternal became temporal, that God became man, is scandalous and outrageous—in a word, *absurd*. '*Therefore*' says Kierkegaard 'I believe it.' Kierkegaard describes the Christian as 'crucified upon a paradox'—accepting as a matter of faith what he *knows* to be ridiculous. To be a Christian—to have faith, even, in an eternal *and* benevolent God who is not specifically Christian—is to assert, against one's better judgement, that black is white.[b] But few Christians have Kierkegaard's better judgement against which they must assert that black is white. The vast majority are quite unaware that they are crucified upon a paradox, and are only too happy to nail their colours (black-and-white, presumably) to the mainmast in an emotional orgy of faith. And why should this drug be so extraordinarily intoxicating? The contradictory assumption that God is at once eternal and temporal enables Christians to indulge in the peculiar luxury of having their God and eating him (which they do literally, as they believe). A Christian is encouraged to believe that his own personal welfare is the particular province and special care of the Omniscient, Omnipotent, and Eternal Spirit of the Universe, who is infinitely and passionately interested in the smallest and most insignificant of his doings. Might this not, conceivably, upon occasion, and for certain people, be a far more potent drug even than morphia? But (it might be asked) is not this addiction to faith in God in any case less harmful

---

**a.** Observe a more subtle contradiction here, overlooked by Kierkegaard. To say *anything* about God, even that he is *eternal*, is tacitly to assume that he exists (i.e. is *temporal*). To say that something is eternal is to assume that there *is* something to which the attribute 'eternal' applies. If God is eternal, we may be sure of one thing, namely, that God *is* (whether he is eternal or anything else). In brief, an *eternal* God is a self-contradictory notion.

**b.** This 'sacrifice of the intellect,' which Saint Ignatius Loyola says is 'so pleasing unto God,' is required also, incidentally, of the quantum physicist: he has to subscribe to the proposition that *there are numbers that are not quantities*. It is not, however, required of the follower of the Buddha, whose *saddhā*—trust or confidence—is something like that of the patient in his doctor. The patient accepts on trust that the doctor knows more about his complaint than he himself does, and he submits himself to the doctor's treatment. So far, indeed, from saying to his disciples 'You must accept on trust from me that black is white,' the Buddha actually says, in effect, 'What you must accept on trust from me is that you yourselves are unwittingly assuming that black is white, and that this is the reason for your suffering.'[2]

than addiction to morphia—indeed, positively beneficial? What does the Buddha say?

> 'I do not, monks, see any other single thing that so leads to the arising of bad (*akusala*) things that have not arisen, or to the growth and development of bad things that have arisen, as wrong view.' 'I do not, monks, see any other single thing that so leads to the non-arising of good (*kusala*) things that have not arisen, or to the decline of good things that have arisen, as wrong view.' 'I do not, monks, see any other single thing that so leads beings, upon the breaking up of their bodies, upon their death, to arising in the evil destiny, in the waste, in hell, as wrong view.' (A.I,ii,8/i,30-31)

Better, then, in the long run, to be a morphia addict with right view (as far as this is possible), than an abstainer with wrong view (which is very possible).[c]

What, now, has the Buddha to offer the drug-addict? In the first place the Buddha requires intelligence of a man, else nothing can be done. In the second place the Buddha tells us that the taking of intoxicants (which of course will include morphia and so on) leads to the decline of intelligence. Putting two and two together, we find that to give up drugs a man must understand that unless he gives them up he will not be able to give them up, or in other words, *to give up drugs one must understand the way to give up drugs, which is to give them up*. At first glance this does not seem to be very helpful—'A glimpse of the obvious' perhaps you will say, 'of *course* the addict understands that the way to give up drugs is to give them up: the whole trouble is that he *can't* give them up.' But is this just a glimpse of the obvious?

Let me recall my own experience when I gave up cigarettes. I had been smoking forty or more a day for several years when I decided to give them up. Not being able to do things in half-measures I stopped smoking all at once. I remember walking in the park not long after I had finished my last cigarette, and feeling pleased with myself that I had actually taken the decision. (I also felt rather light-headed, which was no doubt a deprivation symptom—this continued for some days.) But the principal thought that

---

**c.** I do not wish to suggest that all Christians go to hell. There are many different kinds of wrong view (even within Christianity) and some are worse than others. And one can hold one's views tenaciously or weakly. A Christian, strong in good works, and little interested in Christian dogma, might well have a good destiny.

assailed me was this: though I had no doubt that I could stick to my resolution, there was one thing that I *really* needed to confirm it and to fortify me in my determination not to have another cigarette, and that one thing was...a cigarette. Far from its being obvious to me that in order to give up cigarettes I should give up cigarettes, I had the greatest of trouble to resist the pressing suggestion that in order to give up cigarettes I should *take* a cigarette.

Let me also tell you of the researches of Dr. Klar[3] when he was in Persia shortly after the war. Dr. Klar, besides being a physician, is also interested in psychology; and he had with him in Persia an ingenious device for reading a person's character and state of mind. (This consists of a number of cards each with about eight pairs of coloured squares pasted on them. The subject is simply required to indicate which colour in each pair he prefers. He 'read' us all at the Hermitage, with devastatingly accurate results that did not really please all of us. But this is a digression.)[4] He told us that eighty percent of all Persians over the age of thirty-five (I think he said) take opium (and also that all Persians tell lies on principle—but this is another digression), and with such a wealth of material to hand[d] he was able to do some research. He would give each addict two readings, one before taking opium and one after. The readings all said the same thing: *before* the opium the mental state of the addict was abnormal and disorganized; *after* the opium the mental state was normal and organized. The effect of the opium on the addict was not, as one might think, to disintegrate the personality; on the contrary, the effect was to integrate a disintegrated personality. The opium was necessary to restore the addict to normal. (I have heard similar observations from another doctor who was for many years a medical missionary in China: if you want to do business with an opium addict, drive your bargain when the effect of his last dose is wearing off.)

What can we conclude from all this? We conclude that, unlike a 'normal' person who may take a drug once in a way for the novelty or pleasure of the effect, and who at that time becomes 'abnormal', the confirmed addict is 'normal' only when he has taken the drug, and becomes 'abnormal' when he is deprived of it. The addict reverses the usual situation and is dependent upon the drug to keep him in his normal integrated state. (This does not mean, of course, that the addict derives *pleasure* from occasional deprivation as the abstainer does from occasional intoxication; quite the contrary: in both cases the drugged state is more pleasant, but for the one it is normal and for the other it is abnormal.) The addict can only do his work efficiently and

---

**d.** In Persia, evidently, opium is the religion of the masses.

perform his normal functions if he takes the drug, and it is in this condition that he will make plans for the future. (If he cannot take the drug the only plan he makes is to obtain another dose as quickly as possible.) If he decides that he must give up his addiction to the drug (it is too expensive; it is ruining his reputation or his career; it is undermining his health; and so on) he will make the decision only when he is in a fit state to consider the matter, that is to say *when he is drugged*; and it is from this (for him, *normal*) point of view that he will envisage the future. (Thus, it was *as a smoker* that I decided to give up smoking.) But as soon as the addict puts his decisions into effect and stops taking the drug he ceases to be normal, and decisions taken when he was normal now appear in quite a different light—and this will include his decision to stop taking the drug. *Either*, then, he abandons the decision as invalid ('How could I possibly have decided to do such a thing? I must have been off my head') and returns to his drug-taking, *or* (though he approves the decision) he feels it urgently necessary to return to the state in which he originally took the decision (which was when he was drugged) *in order to make the decision seem valid again*. (And so it was that I felt the urgent need of a cigarette to confirm my decision to give them up.) In both cases the result is the same—a return to the drug. And so long as the addict takes his 'normal' drugged state for granted at its face value—i.e. *as* normal—, the same thing will happen whenever he tries to give up his addiction.

Not only is the drug addict in a vicious circle—the more he takes the more he wants, the more he wants the more he takes—, but until he learns to take an *outside* view of his situation, and is able to see the *nature* of drug-addiction, he will find that all his attempts to force a way out of the vicious circle simply lead him back in again. (A vicious circle is thus a closed system in stable equilibrium.) It is only when the addict *understands* addiction, and holds fast to the right view that—in spite of all appearances, in spite of all temptations to think otherwise—his 'normal' drugged state is *not* normal, that he will be able to put up with the temporary discomfort of deprivation and eventually get free from his addiction. In brief, then, an addict decides to give up drugs, and he supposes that in order to do so all that is necessary is to give them up (which would certainly be a glimpse of the obvious were it not that he is profoundly deceiving himself, as he very soon finds out). No sooner does he start giving them up than he discovers (if he is very unintelligent) that he is mistaken and has made the wrong decision, or (if he is less unintelligent) that though the decision is right he is wrong about the method, and that *in order to give up drugs it is necessary to take them*. It is only the intelligent man who understands (against all appearances) that both the decision and the method are right; and it is only he that succeeds. For the intelligent man, then, the instruction 'to give up drugs it is necessary to give them up,' far from being a glimpse of the obvious, is a profound truth revealing the nature of addiction and leading to escape from it.

I would ask you to pause before dismissing this account as fanciful; this same theme—the vicious circle and the escape from it by way of understanding and in spite of appearances—is the very essence of the Buddha's Teaching. The example discussed above—drug-addiction—is on a coarse level, but you will find the theme repeated again and again right down to the finest level, that of the four noble truths. It will, I think, be worthwhile to illustrate this from the Suttas.

In the 75th Sutta of the Majjhimanikāya (M.i,506-8) the Buddha shows the vicious circle of sensual desire and its gratification in the simile of a man with a skin disease (*kuṭṭhi*—a leper?). Imagine a man with a fiercely itching skin disease who, to relieve the itching, scratches himself with his nails and roasts himself near a brazier. The more he does this the worse becomes his condition, but this scratching and roasting give him a certain satisfaction. In the same way, a man with finely itching sensual desire seeks relief from it in sensual gratification. The more he gratifies it the stronger becomes his desire, but in the gratification of his desire he finds a certain pleasure. Suppose, now, that the skin disease were cured; would that man continue to find satisfaction in scratching and roasting himself? By no means. So, too, a man who is cured of sensual desire (an *arahat*) will find no more pleasure in sensual gratification.

Let us extend the simile a little. You, as a doctor, know very well that to cure an itching skin disease the first thing to do is to prevent the patient from scratching and making it worse. Unless this can be done there is no hope of successfully treating the condition. But the patient will not forego the satisfaction of scratching unless he is made to understand that scratching aggravates the condition, and that there can be no cure unless he voluntarily restrains his desire to scratch, and puts up with the temporarily increased discomfort of unrelieved itching. And similarly, a person who desires a permanent cure from the torment of sensual desire must first be made to understand that he must put up with the temporarily increased discomfort of celibacy (as a *bhikkhu*) if the Buddha's treatment is to be successful. Here, again, the way out of the vicious circle is through an understanding of it and through disregard of the apparent worsening of the condition consequent upon self-restraint.

Consider, now, the four noble truths. The fourth of these truths is, 'This is the way leading to the cessation of suffering, that is to say, the noble eight-factored path'; and the first factor of this path is 'right view', which is defined as knowledge of the four noble truths. But, as before, the fourth truth is the way leading to cessation of suffering. So we come to the proposition, 'The way leading to cessation of suffering is knowledge of the way leading to the cessation of suffering,' or 'To put an end to suffering one must understand the way to put an end to suffering.' And what is this but a repetition, at the most fundamental level, of our original theme, 'To give up drugs one must understand the way to give up drugs'?[e]

Not everybody is addicted to morphia, but most people are addicted to sensual gratification, and all except the *ariyasāvakas* are addicted to their own personality (*sakkāyadiṭṭhi*),[f] and even the *ariyasāvakas*, with the exception of the *arahat*, still have a subtle addiction, the conceit 'I am' (*asmimāna*). The *arahat* has put an end to all addiction whatsoever. There is thus no form of addiction that the Buddha's Teaching will not cure, provided the addict is intelligent and willing to make the necessary effort.

P.S. I don't know what you will make of this (I mean the latter part). In a way it is infinitely more difficult than either of the other things that I sent you, but that is because it is quite different. *They* were concerned only with method, and if either of them was found difficult that was mainly owing to lack of philosophical background. *This* deals directly with the Buddha's Teaching, and is difficult because no amount of philosophical background will help. *Their* principal aim (as we see in retrospect) was the purely negative one of preventing you from attempting to translate *this* into terms of psychology (the earlier one) or of physiology (all knowledge, for example, of the physiological changes produced by opium is totally irrelevant). You may perhaps find (whether you follow it or not) that this is of more vital interest than the other two.

---

**e.** The rationalist, who would not for a moment dream of practising the Buddha's Teaching, can never understand that this is anything else than a glimpse of the obvious. Arthur Koestler, on first meeting the Buddha's Teaching, exclaimed 'But it's all tautologous, for Heaven's sake!'

**f.** Below this point, though the essential structure of addiction remains the same, it is no longer possible to get an outside view of it by voluntary effort. In other words, one cannot give up *sakkāyadiṭṭhi* (and become *sotāpanna*) as simply as one can give up tobacco, merely by deciding to do so and sticking to the decision. Indeed, it is so difficult that it takes a Buddha to find out about it and tell others.

**[L. 20]** **6 June 1962**

About three months ago I had a fresh attack of amœbiasis.[1] The manifestations were as follows: increased abdominal discomfort, 'hungry' feeling in the afternoon (except after thick curd), specific tenderness about the region of the left end of the transverse colon, abdominal distension, increased quantity of mucus (I normally have little), thick opaque mucus with traces of blood (not thought to be due to piles), slightly increased constipation. During the last few days these manifestations have recurred, and this morning I noticed a trace of blood in the thick mucus. On the principle of Occam's Razor, which says that entities should not be multiplied unnecessarily (a thing the amœba have yet to learn), I presume this recurrence is due to inadequate treatment two months ago (though, just as I have regular *dāna dāyakas*, it is possible also that I have amongst them a regular amœba *dāyaka* who re-infects me from time to time). I wonder, therefore, if you would give me some indication of the best course to follow, both to eradicate the present infection and prevent recurrence and also to guard against fresh infection (which I seem to get rather easily in these parts).

Stomach trouble is really the principal occupational hazard of the *bhikkhu* (who has no control over the preparation of the food he gets), and we must expect to have to put up with a certain amount of it. But amœbiasis is very damaging to the practice of concentration (though perhaps in other respects it may not be very serious—'Just a little scarring of the intestine' as one doctor told me, rather leaving me wondering whether he would describe a bullet through one's brains as 'Just a little perforation of the head'), and it seems worthwhile taking precaution against it if that is at all possible.

Beverley Nichols tells us that one of the principles of the Oxford Group is 'Absolute Unselfishness', which is perhaps worth discussing briefly. Some casual English visitors (two 'grisly English faces'—Cyril Connolly's phrase—hitchhiking around the world) came the other day and asked me whether it wasn't rather selfish to sit here alone seeking my own welfare. The idea was, no doubt, that I should busy myself with helping others, like Albert Schweitzer,[2] who is generally regarded these days as the model of unselfish devotion to the service of others. Another Albert—Einstein—has something to say about this:

> Everything that the human race has done and thought is concerned with the satisfaction of felt needs and assuagement of pain. One has to keep this constantly in mind if one wishes to understand spiritual movements and their development. Feeling and desire are the

> motive forces behind all human endeavour and human creation, in however exalted a guise the latter may present itself to us. ('Religion and Science' in *The World As I See It*, p. 23)

Why, then, does Albert Schweitzer devote his life to the care and cure of lepers in Africa? Because, says Albert Einstein, he *feels the need* to do so; because in doing so he *satisfies his desire*. And what does the Buddha say? 'Both formerly, monks, and now, it is just suffering that I make known, and the ending of suffering.' (M.22/i,140) Einstein has, to some extent, understood that suffering is the fundamental fact and the basis of all action. The Buddha has completely understood this; for he knows also the way of escape, which Einstein does not. When, therefore, the question 'What should I do?' arises,[a] the choice is not between *being selfish* and *being unselfish*; for *whatever* I do I cannot *avoid* being selfish—*all* action is selfish. The choice is between being selfish in Schweitzer's way—by unselfish devotion to the welfare of others—and being selfish in the Buddha's way—

> The welfare of oneself should not be neglected for the welfare of others, however great; recognizing the welfare of oneself, one should be devoted to one's own welfare. (Dhp.166)

How are we to choose between these two ways of being selfish? The answer is: 'choose the way of being selfish that leads to the *ending* of being selfish; which is the Buddha's way, not Schweitzer's.' There are many earnest Buddhists in Ceylon who are scandalized by the Buddha's words quoted above; but naturally enough they will not admit such a thing, even to themselves; either they skip that verse when they read the Dhammapada or else they add a footnote explaining that the Buddha really meant something quite different. Here is the actual note made by a very well known Ceylon Thera: 'One must not misunderstand this verse to mean that one should not selflessly work for the weal of others. Selfless service is highly commended by the Buddha.'[3] But this itself is a complete misunderstanding of the Buddha's Teaching. Time and again the Buddha points out that it is only those who have successfully devoted themselves to their own welfare and made sure of it (by reaching *sotāpatti*) that are *in a position* to help others—one himself sinking in a quicksand cannot help others to get out, and if he wishes to help

---

**a.** For most people, of course, the question does *not* arise—they are already fully devoted to seeking the means for gratification of their sensual desires and fulfillment of their worldly ambitions.

them he must *first* get himself out (and if he *does* get himself out, he may come to see that the task of helping others to get out is not so easy as he formerly might have supposed). The notion of 'Absolute Unselfishness' is less straightforward than people like to think: it applies, if properly understood (but nobody less than *sotāpanna* does properly understand it), to the Buddha and to the other *arahats* (which does not mean to say that they will necessarily devote themselves to 'selfless service'), but not to anyone else.

**[L. 21]** **19 June 1962**

I enclose a cutting[1] from a piece of the Daily Telegraph in which some *dāna* was wrapped (these scraps of newspaper provide me with a window through which I can see what is going on in the outside world—a strange landscape, with English football and the Belgian Stock Exchange occupying the foreground). The cutting provides a fair example of the muddled thinking about which I wrote to you earlier. You will see from it that, whereas you and I (and presumably Mr. Coghlan too, who wrote the letter) seek food when we feel hungry, a cat seeks food when its stomach is empty: it does not *feel* anything at all. All its actions—such, for example, as screeching and bolting when boiling water is poured on it—take place simply as a result of a stimulus to its cybernetic brain. It would, it seems, be a great mistake to suppose that a scalded cat suffers pain. The cat is perfectly indifferent to what is going on since it feels nothing—indeed this statement is excessive, since the cat does not even feel indifferent.

Actually, the 'cybernetic brain' is a considerable advance on Professor Jefferson, and is the subject of Dr. Ross Ashby's book *Design for a Brain*. The principles of cybernetics, of teleological or end-seeking or purposive behaviour (which can be expressed mathematically) are very instructive *provided* the proper order is observed—consciousness or experience first, and the body, if at all, a bad second. But Ross Ashby and his disciple Coghlan follow the prevailing fashion of 'scientific common sense', and put the body first. The argument runs something like this. Our own experience, and the observed behaviour of others, is teleological (which is perfectly true); and since our experience or behaviour is entirely dependent upon the state of our nervous system (which is exactly half the truth, and therefore false), our nervous system (or brain) must *therefore* be a cybernetic machine. It is then the simplest thing in the world to assert that our experience or behaviour is teleological *because* our brain is a cybernetic machine (explicable, of course, in 'purely physiological terms' as Professor Jefferson would say)—an assertion for which there is no independent evidence whatsoever. Confusion is then worse confounded by the unexplained addition of 'conscious intelligence and will', whose connexion with the cybernetic mechanism of the nervous system is left completely in the dark. However, enough of this.

I notice that at the top of the hospital notepaper there is the motto '*Ārogya paramā lābhā.*' Everybody naturally takes this to mean that *bodily health is the highest gain*, and it might seem to be a most appropriate motto for a hospital. But perhaps you would be interested to know what the Buddha has to say about it. The following passage is from Majjhimanikāya, M.75/i,508-10 (in which the simile of the leper who scratches and roasts himself also appears). The Buddha is talking to Māgandiya, a Wanderer (*paribbājaka*—follower of a certain traditional school of teaching):

> Then the Auspicious One (*Bhagavā*) uttered these lines:
> —Good health is the highest gain,
> *nibbāna* is the highest pleasure,
> and the eight-factored path is the one
> that is peaceful and leads to the deathless.
> *(Ārogya paramā lābhā nibbānaṃ paramaṃ sukhaṃ,*
> *Aṭṭhaṅgiko ca maggānaṃ khemaṃ amatagāminan ti.)*
>
> When this was said, the Wanderer Māgandiya said to the Auspicious One:—It is wonderful, Master Gotama, it is marvellous, Master Gotama, how well said it is by Master Gotama 'Good health is the highest gain, *nibbāna* is the highest pleasure.' I, too, Master Gotama, have heard this saying handed down from teacher to pupil by Wanderers of old 'Good health is the highest gain, *nibbāna* is the highest pleasure.' And Master Gotama agrees with this.
>
> —But in this saying that you have heard, Māgandiya, handed down from teacher to pupil by Wanderers of old 'Good health is the highest gain, *nibbāna* is the highest pleasure,' what is that good health, what is that *nibbāna*?
>
> When this was said, the Wanderer Māgandiya stroked his own limbs with his hand.—This, Master Gotama, is that good health, this is that *nibbāna*. At present, Master Gotama, I am in good health and have pleasure; there is nothing that afflicts me.
>
> —Suppose, Māgandiya, there was a man blind from birth, who could see no forms either dark or light, no blue forms, no yellow forms, no red forms, no crimson forms, who could see neither even nor uneven, who could see no stars, who could see neither sun nor

moon. And suppose he were to hear a man who could see, saying 'What a fine thing is a white cloth that is beautiful to look at, clean and spotless!', and were then to go in search of such cloth. And suppose some man were to deceive him with a coarse cloth stained with grease and soot, saying 'Here good man is a white cloth for you that is beautiful to look at, clean and spotless.' And suppose he were to accept it and put it on, and being pleased were to utter words of pleasure 'What a fine thing is a white cloth that is beautiful to look at, clean and spotless!'—What do you think, Māgandiya, would that man blind from birth have accepted that coarse cloth stained with grease and soot and have put it on, and being pleased would he have uttered words of pleasure 'What a fine thing is a white cloth that is beautiful to look at, clean and spotless!' because he himself knew and saw this, or out of trust in the words of the man who could see?

—Certainly, Master Gotama, that man blind from birth would have accepted that coarse cloth stained with grease and soot and put it on, and being pleased would have uttered words of pleasure 'What a fine thing is a white cloth that is beautiful to look at, clean and spotless!' without himself knowing and seeing this, but out of trust in the words of the man who could see.

—Just so, Māgandiya, sectarian Wanderers are blind and sightless, and without knowing good health, without seeing *nibbāna*, they still speak the line 'Good health is the highest gain, *nibbāna* is the highest pleasure.' These lines, Māgandiya, 'Good health is the highest gain, *nibbāna* is the highest pleasure, and the eight-factored path is the one that is peaceful and leads to the deathless' were spoken by Arahat Fully Awakened Ones (*sammāsambuddhā*) of old; but now in the course of time they have been adopted by commoners (*puthujjanā*). This body, Māgandiya, is diseased, ulcered, wounded, painful, sick. And you say of this body that is diseased, ulcered, wounded, painful, sick, 'This, Master Gotama, is that good health, this is that *nibbāna*.' You, Māgandiya, do not have that noble eye (*ariyacakkhu*) with which to know good health and to see *nibbāna*.

(The Buddha then goes on to indicate to Māgandiya what is really meant by 'good health' and '*nibbāna*'.)

P.S. If you have any reason at all for keeping them there is absolutely no need to return my letters to me. I only suggested it in case you were thinking of destroying them. In any case I don't want this one back.

**[L. 22, postcard]** **20 June 1962**

In my letter to you containing the extract from Majjhimanikāya, Sutta 75, I translated one passage near the end as follows: 'This body, Māgandiya, is diseased, ulcered, wounded, painful, sick…' On second thought, I see that this is not quite what is meant. Please substitute the following:

> This body, Māgandiya, is a disease, an ulcer, a wound, a sore, an affliction. It is of this body, which is a disease, an ulcer, a wound, a sore, an affliction, that you say 'This, Master Gotama, is that good health, this is that *nibbāna*'…

**[L. 23]** **6 July 1962**

In my letter telling you of the unfortunate effects of the 'Entamide'[1] (effects for which I am no doubt partly to blame—no smoke without fire) I said that I had returned to normal after stopping the drug. After a few days, however, there was a relapse, and though the situation remains under control there is really not very much improvement, and I do not get very much sleep. I have the impression[2] that there is a continuous, though variable, specific stimulation, which, though no doubt neutral in itself (it is, indeed, disagreeable when observed dispassionately), is a pressing invitation to sensual thoughts. I have never experienced anything like this before.

I wonder, therefore, if you would be good enough to send me a sedative to enable me to sleep at night, and also anything else that you think might be helpful. Sedatives, in the last analysis, are not a final cure for this condition, but they may help to make things easier. The cure is essentially a matter of raising the mind above the waist and keeping it there, but this treatment takes time and is hard work (as you may gather from my letter on drug-addiction).

**[L. 24]** **Vassa 1962**

Many thanks for your letter. I am not certain that delay in replying to letters is necessarily a vice: it allows time for reflexion.

The colour of the 'Oblivion' is delicious—I am tempted to wonder whether the therapeutic effects of the appearance of drugs (as well as their taste) has been sufficiently studied. A placebo, I imagine, should always taste revolting.[1]

**[L. 25]** **12 July 1962**

Thank you for sending me the copy of *Panminerva Medica.*[1] The idea that diseases are useful as a means of adaptation to adverse circumstances, namely pathogenetic causes, would perhaps be valid if the only alternative, in such circumstances, to being sick (and surviving) were death—though even so, as you suggest, the incurable cancer patient might need some persuading before accepting this principle. But why does Prof. Vacira assume that without pathogenetic processes we should die? Or to put the matter another way, since Prof. V. is clearly a firm believer in cause-and-effect he will consider that pathogenetic causes and pathogenetic processes are indissolubly linked—where there is one there is the other. This being so, if he regards pathogenetic processes as 'indispensable' he must inevitably regard pathogenetic causes as equally necessary. Admitting that man will always encounter adverse circumstances, is it necessary to assume that they must be pathogenetic? There are pathogenetic causes *only* if they result in pathogenetic processes, and from this point of view pathogenetic processes serve no useful purpose whatsoever—we should be far better off without them.

The Buddha tells us (D.26/iii,75) that in periods when the life-span of man is immensely long he suffers from but three diseases: wants, hunger, and old age—none of which involves pathogenetic processes. Man falls from this state of grace when his behaviour deteriorates; until, gradually, he arrives at a state where his life-span is extremely short and he is afflicted by innumerable calamities. General improvement in behaviour reverses the process. It seems, then, that adverse circumstances become pathogenetic causes as a result of the immorality of mankind as a whole. But this connexion between the General Theory of Pathology and what we may call the General Theory of Morality remains hidden from the eyes of modern scientific philosophy.

**[L. 26]** **11 December 1962**

My present situation is this. As you will remember, I first got this affliction (satyriasis?) last June, and I fear that it is still with me. During the first two months, certainly, it became much less acute, and I had hopes that it would altogether disappear. But for the last three and a half months I have noticed no further improvement. With an effort I can ignore it for a few days at a time, but it remains always in the background, ready to come forward on the slightest encouragement.

I find that, under the pressure of this affliction, I am oscillating between two poles. On the one hand, if I indulge the sensual images that offer themselves, my thought turns towards the state of a layman; if, on the other hand, I resist them, my thought turns towards suicide. Wife or knife, as one might say. For the time being, each extreme tends to be checked by the other, but the situation is obviously in unstable equilibrium. (Mental concentration, which affords relief, is difficult for me on account of my chronic digestive disorders, as you already know; and I cannot rely on it for support.) I view both these alternatives with distaste (though for different reasons); and I am a faintly nauseated, but otherwise apathetic, spectator of my oscillations between them. Sooner or later, however, unless my condition much improves, I may find myself choosing one or the other of these unsatisfactory alternatives; and a fresh attack of amœbiasis, which is always possible, might well precipitate a decision.

**[L. 27]** **21 December 1962**

I expect that the medicines will provide relief, at least for the time being. The misery of existence is that things are only temporary. If only we could, say, take a single dose of a drug that would ensure us an unlimited and unfailing supply of libido (with, of course, appropriate means of gratifying it) for all eternity, we should be happy. (The Muslims, I believe, are told that in Paradise a single embrace lasts for a thousand years. This is clearly an improvement on our terrestrial arrangements, but it is not the answer. A thousand years, eventually, come to an end. And then what?) Or again, if by a single dose of some other drug we could be absolutely cured of libido for all eternity (which is, in fact, *nibbāna* or extinction), then too we should be happy. But no. We have libido when we cannot satisfy it (when, of course, we should be better off without it[a]), and when we want it, it fails.[b] Then comes death, painfully, and the comedy begins again.

I am sure that you are already well aware that the problems confronting me at the present time arise from my past amœbiasis and not from this more recent complaint of satyriasis (which has only aggravated the situation). The

---

**a.** But *na kho pan'etaṃ icchāya pattabbaṃ*—that is not obtained simply by wishing.[1] (D.22/ii,307; M.141/iii,250)

**b.** I never had it like this when I was a layman, when I could gladly have used it; and now, when I do have it, I have come to see that it is a treacherous and lethal possession, and that I use it at my peril.

ravages of amœbiasis play havoc with the practice of mental concentration, and if I cannot practise mental concentration I have no further use for this life. The idea of suicide first occurred to me nearly two years ago, and since then I have watched it becoming more definite and more frequent. Against this background it was more or less inevitable that my present complaint, when it appeared, should offer itself as a suitable occasion and excuse for putting the idea of suicide into practice. Although I wrote to you in my last letter that I was oscillating between the extremes of disrobing and suicide, there is no doubt at all (barring accidents) which I should choose. For me at least, the more intelligent of these two courses of action is suicide; a return to lay life would be pure weakness, and in any case I should be miserable. (How should I get my living? I should have to marry a rich and no doubt hideous widow in order to keep going. Quite unthinkable. Or perhaps I should take up with some lady of easy virtue who would earn enough to support us both. But I believe that this sort of arrangement is not considered very respectable.)[3]

But how is one to kill oneself? Early last month I did in fact attempt it, but failed through a miscalculation. I had read that two elderly ladies in England had succeeded in asphyxiating themselves, and I thought to myself that what two old ladies can do I can do. Rash assumption! These old ladies are much tougher than our masculine pride is willing to admit, and I have to give them full credit for accomplishing a very difficult feat. I found it quite impossible, when the lack of oxygen began to make itself felt, to resist the impulse to get fresh air. One lives and learns (a particularly suitable motto for the unsuccessful suicide, don't you think?). Perhaps it needs practice to reach the critical point—one more breath each day, until finally one is able to arrive at unconsciousness. In any case, I do not feel tempted to try this again.

What about the knife? In theory this seems quick and simple, provided one slices in the right place and does not try sawing through the windpipe. But in practice it is extremely difficult to cut one's throat in cold blood (even if there is hot blood to follow). It needs desperation, or at least a strong sense of urgency (or a course of reserpine perhaps?) to screw one up to the necessary pitch. The thought of living even one more day has to be intolerable. I tried this about ten days ago, but even if I had not been interrupted by a heavy thunderstorm, which flooded the place and brought me back to ground level, it is very doubtful whether I should have gone through with it. My attitude is far too reflexive, and the necessary sense of urgency and despair is lacking.[c]

---

c. During those attempts a disagreeable feeling in the belly (more exactly, the ac-

Poison? Expert knowledge is wanted here; otherwise one may easily make things very unpleasant for oneself without producing the desired effect. Hysterical women drink oxalic acid to revenge themselves on their callous lovers by the spectacle of their agony, but this is obviously not my cup of tea. Besides, how is a *bhikkhu* to obtain a suitable poison? Eyebrows may be raised if he asks a *dāyaka* for, say, a small bottle of iodine, twenty soda-mint tablets, and a quarter-ounce of potassium cyanide. And certain types of poison are unsuitable. It is best to die mindful and aware, and overdoses of opiates, hypnotics, or anaesthetics are therefore to be avoided.

Hanging seems to be unnecessarily painful unless done skilfully; and this district has no suitable precipices for throwing oneself over. A surprising number of *bhikkhus* seem to possess pistols these days, but I am not one of them, so shooting is out. I can swim, so drowning is difficult. To be decapitated by a train I should need to go to Matara; and pouring kerosene oil over one's clothes and setting oneself alight, though certainly spectacular (especially at night), must be a frightful experience (but I believe it is sometimes done).[4]

There remains a form of suicide that one hears surprisingly little about—starvation. Why is this? Is it not perhaps because, as Albert Camus remarks,[5] one rarely commits suicide as a result of reflexion? Most suicides mature unawares in the innermost recesses of a man's being, until one day the crisis is precipitated by some trivial occurrence and the man ends his life with a sudden gesture. He may shoot or plunge, but he will hardly think of starving to death.

Those, on the other hand, whose decision to kill themselves is not emotional but deliberate, those that is to say who wish to kill themselves (or at least give that impression) for some particular reason, nearly always favour starvation. Here you find, for example, the hunger-striker who aims at political or other ends, the 'faster unto death' who is protesting against some injury, real or imagined, personal or public. But these people are usually not called 'suicides', partly, perhaps, because they rarely go the whole way, but principally, I fancy, because the term 'suicide' has emotional overtones associated with the act of killing oneself for no better reason than that one has had enough of this life.

Such a gesture threatens to undermine the precarious security of Society, which is based on the convention that 'life is worth living'. Suicide puts

---

centuation of my normal discomfort) made itself felt, no doubt due to the nervous strain. Also, on one occasion, slight incontinence of urine, which I remember having had once before: at school, whilst waiting my turn to go on the stage and sing. School is hell.[2]

in question this unquestionable axiom, and Society inevitably regards it with fear and suspicion as an act of treachery.[d] If the victim should fail in his attempt, Society takes its revenge upon his temerity by putting him in prison (where, presumably, he is expected to learn that, actually, life really is worth living). Those, on the other hand, who can show good reason for ending their lives (the man, for example, with a political grievance) do not by their act put this convention in question, and they are therefore regarded as safe and perfectly respectable. Thus they escape the opprobrious name. Starvation and suicide, then, are rarely associated with each other.

From my point of view, however, I see that they might well be associated. I shall not stop here to discuss suicide in the light of the Dhamma, except to remark that though it is never encouraged it is not the heinous offence it is sometimes popularly thought to be, and that the consequences of the act will vary according to circumstances—for the *puthujjana* they can be disastrous, but for the *arahat* (the Venerable Channa Thera—S.xxxv.87/ iv,55-60—for example) they are nil. I want, rather, to consider the evident advantages that starvation can offer to someone who decides upon suicide as a result of reflexion.

(i) One's action is less likely to be misconstrued as the effect of a sudden mental aberration. Though this may be a matter of unimportance for oneself, it may not be so for other people. In certain cases it can be of importance to understand why a person chose to kill himself.

(ii) One has ample time (a fortnight? a month? or longer?) in which to reconsider one's decision and reverse it if necessary.

(iii) I have heard it said that in starvation the first thing to disappear is the sexual urge. If true, this has obvious advantages for me in my present condition, since a death accompanied by sensual desire is most unfortunate.

(iv) Since the principal obstacle, in my case, to mental concentration is the discomfort and malaise resulting from the ingestion of food, it seems possible that mental concentration might actually benefit from starvation.

(v) One has the opportunity for contemplating the approach of death at one's leisure, and for ridding oneself of any remaining worries or concerns connected with this life.

---

**d.** It is customary, in England at least, for Coroners' courts to give the verdict 'Suicide while the balance of his mind was disturbed.' This insult automatically puts the victim in the wrong and reassures Society that all is for the best in the best of all possible worlds. Have you ever noticed that Socialist governments have a particular horror of the individual's suicide? It is a direct criticism of their basic tenets.

(vi) One can watch the progressive emaciation of one's body. This is *asubhasaññā*, wherein the body appears as an object of disgust.

(vii) One can directly observe the dependence of the body on food. This is *idappaccayatā*, which leads to *aniccasaññā* or perception of impermanence.

(viii) It is said that in starvation the mind becomes progressively clearer (though more dissociated) as the body gets weaker.

(ix) Starvation seems to offer a good chance for a conscious and lucid death, which is most desirable.

(x) The discomforts of starvation, though no doubt unpleasant, are apparently quite endurable (that is, if one can judge from the astonishingly large number of people who undertake voluntary fasts for trivial reasons). I imagine it is more uncomfortable to starve slowly on inadequate food than to do without food altogether. Without food one might even forget about it, but not with regular small reminders of its existence.

(xi) I imagine that, as deaths go, death by starvation is not excessively painful. Presumably the body gets progressively feebler, but no one particular organ tends to give out before the others. I am not well informed on this matter, and should welcome enlightenment.

The great disadvantage of suicide by starvation is that it is not the sort of thing (unless one knows of a solitary cave with a good water supply) that one can do on the sly. Questions are bound to be asked. Public opinion will have to be flouted. Perhaps the best course is to announce one's intention beforehand and be prepared to put up with visits from kindly people, perhaps more well meaning than well informed, who come to save one from one's own rash folly. If they get too importunate one can always indulge the malicious pleasure of asking them if they are coming to the funeral.

And do I actually propose to do this? Nietzsche once said, 'The thought of suicide gets one through many a bad night.'[6] This is quite true; but one cannot think suicide in this way unless one regards it as a course of action that one might actually adopt. And when I consider my present situation I am forced to admit that I do intend to adopt it (though I cannot say when): my present horizon is bounded by this idea. Even if the sexual trouble settles (which it does not seem to be in any hurry about), there remains the digestive disorder (which, of course, won't improve). It is this latter complaint that raises the problem; the other only makes it more pressing.

I think I once told you that I had always been extraordinarily fortunate in my life with the things that had happened to me. Perhaps you might think that I now need to revise this view. But that is not so. Although, certainly, this recent complaint has no redeeming feature, and may perhaps push me to my death, it is actually an affair of relatively minor importance and inspires me more with disgust than with despair. And whether my life ends now or later is also, ultimately, a matter of indifference to me.

P.S. There is no need at all to answer this letter (unless you wish). Its purpose is already achieved. Writing of suicide has got me through several bad days.

**[L. 28]** **4 January 1963**

I am really most grateful to you for your sympathetic letter. Certainly, I should not have written as I did had I thought that you were one of those unintelligent people whose well-meant advice is more likely to drive one to suicide than to save one from it. Doctors, of course, cannot afford to be shocked professionally at the strange antics of their patients, but they can sometimes be remarkably bigoted in private. I know, however, that you yourself have your own difficulties to contend with, and are not likely to be in a hurry to sit in judgement on other people; and it is for this reason that I did not write to you solely in your capacity as a doctor. I am also grateful to you for not at once attributing my 'morbid fancies'—some of which, after all, were added as literary embellishment—to a convenient abstract clinical entity.

It is curious, is it not, that whereas, since Freud, the most extravagant fancies in the realm of love are considered to be perfectly normal (a person without them is regarded as a case for treatment), in the realm of death (the other great pole of human life) any strange fancies are still classed as 'morbid'. The Suttas reverse the situation: sensual thoughts are the thoughts of a sick man (sick with ignorance and craving), and the way to health is through thoughts of foulness and the diseases of the body, and of its death and decomposition. And not in an abstract scientific fashion either—one sees or imagines a rotting corpse, for example, and then pictures one's very own body in such a state.

Our contemporaries are more squeamish. A few years ago a practising Harley Street psychiatrist, who was dabbling in Buddhism, came to see me. I opened the conversation by saying 'At some time in his life, every intelligent man questions himself about the purpose of his existence.' Immediately, and with the most manifest disapproval, the psychiatrist replied 'Anybody who thinks such thoughts is mentally diseased.' Thus with a single gesture, he swept half-a-dozen major philosophers (some of whom have held chairs in universities—which guarantees their respectability if not their philosophy) into the lunatic asylum—the criminal lunatic asylum, to judge from his tone. I have never seen a man in such a funk. But this is a digression.

No, I have not discussed the matter with anyone else. As far as Dhamma goes, I am quite well aware of the situation: I know that to kill oneself is an act of weakness, but also that, for me, it is better than disrobing; and I know what I risk and what I do not risk by such an act. I do not know of anyone who can add anything to this. As regards discussing it with a friend, not only do I have nobody by whom I can possibly make myself understood (and misunderstanding, in a case like this, has the effect of isolating one still more completely)[a] but, precisely, I do not feel the need to make myself understood (I am one of those people who think of other people as 'they', not as 'we').[1]

If, in fact, I now appear to be trying to make myself understood, that is to be seen as a measure of self-defence rather than as an appeal for help (I do not speak, of course, of the medical aspect, where help is always welcome). To be more explicit: it is possible that you may understand this; and if so you may be able to translate it into terms that would be acceptable to other people who would certainly not understand me directly. (It is precisely the attempt to understand directly that creates the misunderstanding: you will have noticed that my last letter was not really a direct communication to you at all, but rather a discussion of my situation with myself, which I wrote down and posted to you. No wonder you found it difficult to reply!) You will see, then, that far from feeling the need to discuss the matter with somebody else (in a direct manner, in any case) I am actually seeking to put a buffer (in this case, your good self) between myself and other people, so that if it should come to the point I may in some measure be spared the exhausting task of explaining the unexplainable. (Naturally, I am not doing this as a matter of deliberate policy; but now that you have raised the question I see that it is so.) There are times when the idea of ceasing to take food from tomorrow onwards seems to be the most natural thing in the world (if food upsets one, why go on taking it?), and it is the thought that if I do I shall inevitably be asked to explain myself that makes me pause.

What, now, of the future? My present attitude is quite unchanged since my last letter, and I continue to live from day to day by force of habit, with Nietzsche's brinkmanship formula to help over the rough patches. How long this will go on I have no idea. I have long since abandoned all hope of an improvement in my amœbic condition; which means that I do not

---

**a.** It is extraordinarily depressing to be accredited with all sorts of motives—resentment, remorse, grief ('a secret sorrow'), despair, and so on—that are totally absent.

despair when it does not improve. But it also seems that I no longer have any very pressing reason for living. This makes the question of my death a matter of comparative indifference, and the prospect does not cause me great concern. I do not feel that discussion with other people will alter this.

But absence of a reason for living is not necessarily a reason for dying (though the visiting psychiatrist was assuming the contrary, hence his panic at the suggestion that the purpose of life might be questionable). Absence of a reason for living simply makes the decision to die easier. The reason for ending one's life is the discomfort and difficulty of one's situation, and this is why any medical help that can be given is welcome. It is perhaps possible that my secondary complaint might improve in the course of time, and the situation would then become easier. Well and good if it does. On the other hand, I might get re-infected with amœbiasis; and this possibility raises a question. If this should happen, would it be possible to treat the infection without again provoking the erotic stimulation? Can you answer this question for me? If the answer is negative, it at once becomes evident that I cannot afford to get the infection again; for I should have to choose between erotic stimulation and untreated amœbiasis, either of which would almost certainly upset the apple cart. And the question of avoiding re-infection raises further problems.

I am glad you have managed to find time to visit the Hermitage for a few days. You will be able to get instructions on how to develop *maraṇasati* or mindfulness of death (unscientifically, of course).

**[L. 29]** **15 January 1963**

Thank you very much indeed for your long letter. To judge from its fluency and vigour you must have benefited from your stay at the Hermitage. Letters from Colombo—*anybody's* letters—generally have a remarkable air of stuffiness about them. I have always found (and so did the Ven. Ñāṇamoli Thera)[1] that in Colombo one's head seems to be stuffed with cotton waste: thinking is an enormous effort, like one of those monstrous dreams where one's legs get heavier and heavier until one can hardly move at all. As soon as I return to the Hermitage (or better still here) my head clears and I become an intelligent human being again. Perhaps this is making too much of what may only be a personal impression; but, anyway, I found your letter refreshing.

Sydney Smith[2] on suicide sounds most educative—on the condition that he is approached not too hastily so as to avoid lack of reaction (objectivity) or inappropriate reaction (immediacy). One needs to be subjective enough to taste the horror of the human situation one's own situation—and reflexive enough to face it without panic.[a] And to think that human birth is accounted by the Buddha a good destiny, hard to come by!

You suggest that my amœbiasis may not be under control yet. Speaking as a patient, of course, I cannot be sure about this; but it seems to me that my symptoms are at present remaining more or less static, with neither improvement nor deterioration. Certainly they are appreciably worse than three years ago, but since then I have had three manifest re-infections (one perhaps a relapse) which might account for this. But I shall not say that you are wrong.

I should perhaps make it clear that the first idea (two years ago) of suicide as a tentative possibility was due quite as much to a decreased interest in living as it was to deterioration in my physical condition (the former factor,

---

**a.** The relationship between these four attitudes—objectivity, immediacy, subjectivity, and reflexion—is worth consideration. At first sight it might seem that there is no difference between immediacy and subjectivity, or between objectivity and reflexion. Subjectivity and objectivity, certainly, are opposed; and so are immediacy and reflexion. But immediacy (which is naive acceptance of whatever is presented) is compatible with objectivity, as we see from Thomas Huxley's advice to the scientist: 'Sit down before fact as a little child'—; and reflexion is compatible with subjectivity (for subjectivity is 'being oneself', and reflexion, being 'self awareness', is within subjectivity). Thus:[3]

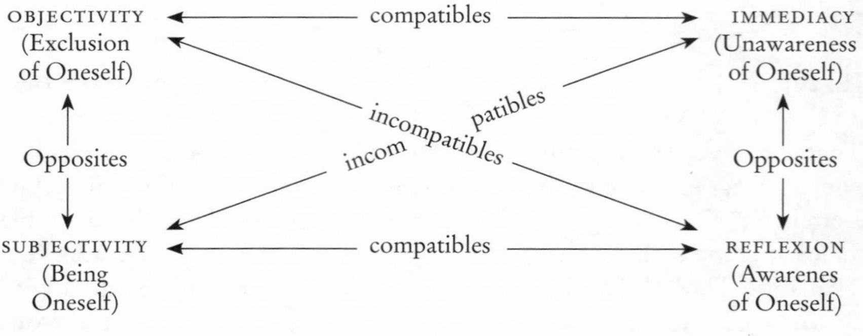


In emotional excitement objectivity and reflexion alike tend to vanish, and subjectivity then approximates to immediacy. It is this that gives subjectivity its bad name; for few people know of any subjectivity beyond emotional immediacy. Their escape from emotion is towards objectivity, in the form of distractions, rather than towards reflexion, which is the more difficult way of self control. Goethe once described the advice 'Know Thyself' (inscribed in the temple of Apollo at Delphi) as 'a singular requisition with which no man complies, or indeed ever will comply: man is by all his senses and efforts directed to externals—to the world about him.'

actually, was and is partly independent of the latter).[4] In other words, it would be a mistake to regard my change of attitude simply and solely as the cumulative effect of long-standing amœbiasis. Furthermore, I should not have attempted suicide, nor still be regarding it (intermittently) as an immediate possibility, were it not for the additional strain of the erotic stimulation. The amœbic condition alone (unless it deteriorates) is probably not enough (though I cannot be quite sure) to provoke decisive action, though it *does* remain the predisposing condition. It might be likened to a wooden beam, eaten by white ants, still strong enough to support the present weight, but liable to collapse if an additional burden is placed upon it.

About discussing my situation with other people, please do as you think fit. I am independent enough of other people's opinions not to be disturbed if they know about it, but at the same time I am not particularly anxious to become an object of public curiosity (and I should be grateful if you would not let __ get wind of it or he might want to come here to photograph me).

I have not hitherto raised the question with you of what I may be or represent for other people, but since you have made some encouraging remarks on the subject, something might be said. To oneself, reflexively, one never presents a clear-cut rounded-out picture. One can never, as a matter of structural principle, see oneself as one sees another person. When Robert Burns asked the Good Lord for the gift of seeing ourselves 'as ithers see us' he was asking for the impossible (and Chestov, the Russian philosopher, would say that he had made the application in the proper quarter: 'One only turns to God to obtain the impossible—for the possible, men are enough').[b] What I am in the eyes of another is a dimension of myself that is inherently hidden from me. When, therefore, people tell one what they think of one it always comes as something of a shock, pleasant or unpleasant as the case may be. To try to create an impression upon other people is extremely risky, since the effect of one's effort is absolutely beyond one's control; and if one bears this in mind one does not get unduly elated or depressed by what others say of one.

For my part, I have come to Ceylon and am doing what I am doing purely and simply for my own benefit, and for this reason my action appears to me as perfectly normal, neither a matter for approval nor for disapproval, the only possible point for criticism being whether or not my action will lead to the desired result. If, then, other people derive benefit from what I am

**b.** In Ceylon this distinction is not always observed. Candidates for examination not only obtain advance copies of the papers, but take the added precaution of applying to Kataragama[5] to get them through.

doing that is all to the good, and I am not displeased; but it must necessarily remain a secondary consideration—though not for that reason entirely without weight.

People do support me remarkably well and I am more grateful to them than I can easily say, and it is only proper to consider their point of view before making final decisions. Of course, one sometimes meets with ambiguities. I heard that a person of consequence who once visited me here remarked afterwards that I was 'setting a good example for the others,' but I notice that neither the person in question nor 'the others' show any signs of following my example. The Ven. Ñāṇamoli Thera was more direct—'You're a thorn in their side' he said. The situation, after all, is quite understandable. People born in Ceylon and other Buddhist countries have the Buddha's Teaching as their national heritage; they have been Buddhists since their birth, and no further action on their part is required. The idea that it is necessary to *become* a Buddhist is thus well-nigh incomprehensible—if you *are* a Buddhist already, what can it possibly mean to become one? The consequence of this situation is that when a non-Buddhist sets about becoming a Buddhist—by taking the Buddha at his word and actually trying to practise—the born-Buddhists are at a loss to understand quite what he can be doing, and they are uncertain whether to class him as a sage or simpleton.

You say that you are worried about 'the absolutely dispassionate and purely objective tone' in which I discuss my own probable suicide. I am glad that you are worried about this. In all my correspondence with you both now and earlier I have been hoping to be able to communicate the idea of what Heidegger calls 'authenticity'; and if you have felt a little uneasiness at a practical illustration of what I have been trying to convey that is not a bad sign. 'The very maximum of what one human being can do for another in relation to that wherein each man has to do solely with himself,' said Kierkegaard 'is to inspire him with concern and unrest.' (*CUP*, p. 346) And beyond preventing you from falling into complacency I do not think there is very much that anyone else can do for you in this particular department.

But the question of authenticity (which more or less corresponds to the subjectivity-reflexion pair of attitudes discussed earlier) is another matter. If this mode of thinking can be achieved, it is capable of making a great deal of difference to one's life. Once one recognizes that one is totally responsible for all one's decisions and actions, one can no longer hide behind convenient ready-made excuses; and this, though it makes life rather less comfortable by removing one's habitual blinkers, endows one with unexpected self-reliance and resilience in difficult situations.[c] And once it becomes habitual to think in this way the task of living is discovered to be a full-time job and not merely a drudge to be got through by killing time as best one can. In other words, it abolishes boredom.[d] Finally, as I think I mentioned some time ago, it is only in this authentic or responsible attitude that the Buddha's Teaching becomes intelligible.

---

**c.** Let us keep things in their proper proportion. I am not anything very much out of the ordinary in this respect. My eminence, whatever there may be of it, is due—as Karl Marx said of John Stuart Mill's—to the flatness of the surrounding countryside. I am better at theorizing—at talking—than at practice. I do not wish to give you the impression that the next time I come to hospital for operation the anaesthetic can be dispensed with.

**d.** The common view is that the remedy for boredom is variety or distraction, but this only aggravates the malady. The real remedy is repetition. Here is Kierkegaard again:

> Whoever fails to understand that life is repetition, and that this is its beauty, has passed judgement upon himself; he deserves no better fate than that which will befall him, namely to be lost. Hope is an alluring fruit which does not satisfy, memory is a miserable pittance that does not satisfy, but repetition is life's daily bread, which satisfies and blesses. When a man has circumnavigated the globe it will appear whether he has the courage to understand that life is repetition, and the enthusiasm to find therein his happiness.... In repetition inheres the earnestness and reality of life. Whoever wills repetition proves himself to be in possession of a pathos that is serious and mature.[6]

Nietzsche, in his turn, has his doctrine of Eternal Recurrence which expresses the crass senselessness of things, the eternal lack of purpose in the universe; so that to will the eternal cycle with enthusiasm and without hope is the ultimate attainment of affirmation. And here is a dialogue from Dostoievsky's *The Possessed*:

> —Old philosophical commonplaces, always the same from the beginning of time, murmured Stavrogin with an air of careless pity.
> —Always the same! Always the same from the beginning of time and nothing else! echoed Kirilov, his eyes shining, as if his victory was contained in this idea.

This passage underlines the futility of the historical method of dealing with religions and philosophies. The Buddha's Teaching is *not* simply a reaction to the earlier Hinduism, as our modern scholars inform us *ad nauseam*. If it is, the scholars will have to explain why I am a follower of the Buddha without being a disgruntled Hindu. Modern scholarship is inauthenticity in its most virulent form. (Talking of suicide, it is perhaps noteworthy that both of Dostoievsky's characters kill themselves: Stavrogin out of indifference and self disgust; Kirilov, after years of planning the gesture, in order to demonstrate to mankind that there is no God and that men are free to do as they please. My suicide will be less didactic.)

You say that I am one who thinks not only of other people but also of himself as 'they'. I see what you mean and I will not deny it, but it needs stating differently. Two paragraphs back I pointed out that it is inherently impossible to see oneself (unless one is simply thinking of one's body) as one sees another person (at least, not authentically), so I cannot be 'they' to myself as others are 'they' to me. People, for the most part, live in the objective-immediate mode (discussed earlier). This means that they are totally absorbed in and identified with positive worldly interests and projects, of which there is an unending variety. That is to say, although they differ from one another in their individual natures, the *contents* of their respective positivities, they are all alike in being *positive*. Thus, although the fundamental relation between positives is conflict (on account of their individual differences), they apprehend one another as all being in the same boat of positivity, and they think of men generally in terms of human solidarity, and say 'we'.

But the person who lives in the subjective-reflexive mode is absorbed in and identified with, not the positive world, but himself. The world, of course, remains 'there' but he regards it as accidental (Husserl says that he 'puts it in parentheses, between brackets'), and this means that he dismisses whatever positive identification he may have as irrelevant. He is no longer 'a politician' or 'a fisherman', but 'a self'. But what we call a 'self', unless it receives positive identification from outside, remains a void, in other words a *negative*. A 'self', however, is positive in this respect—it seeks identification. So a person who identifies himself with himself finds that his positivity consists in negativity—not the confident 'I am this' or 'I am that' of the positive, but a puzzled, perplexed, or even anguished, 'What am I?'. (This is where we meet the full force of Kierkegaard's 'concern and unrest'.) Eternal repetition of this eternally unanswerable question is the beginning of wisdom (it is the beginning of philosophy); but the temptation to provide oneself with a definite answer is usually too strong, and one falls into a wrong view of one kind or another. (It takes a Buddha to show the way out of this impossible situation. For the *sotāpanna*, who has understood the Buddha's essential Teaching, the question still arises, but he sees that it is unanswerable and is not worried; for the *arahat* the question no longer arises at all, and this is final peace.)

This person, then, who has his centre of gravity in himself instead of in the world (a situation that, though usually found as a congenital feature, can be acquired by practice), far from seeing himself with the clear solid objective definition with which other people can be seen, hardly sees himself as anything definite at all: for himself he is, at best, a 'What, if anything?'.

It is precisely this lack of assured self-identity that is the secret strength of his position—for him the question-mark is the essential and his positive identity in the world is accidental, and whatever happens to him in a positive sense the question-mark still remains, which is all he really cares about. He is distressed, certainly, when his familiar world begins to break up, as it inevitably does, but unlike the positive he is able to fall back on himself and avoid total despair. It is also this feature that worries the positives; for they naturally assume that everybody else is a positive and they are accustomed to grasp others by their positive content, and when they happen to meet a negative they find nothing to take hold of.

It quite often happens that a positive attributes to a negative various strange secret motives, supposing that he has failed to understand him (in a positive sense); but what he has failed to understand is that there is actually nothing there to be understood. But a negative, being (as you point out) a rare bird himself, is accustomed to positives, by whom he is surrounded, and he does not mistake them for fellow negatives. He understands (or at least senses) that the common factor of positivity that welds them together in the 'we' of human solidarity does not extend to him, and mankind for him is 'they'. When a negative meets another negative they tend to coalesce with a kind of easy mutual indifference. Unlike two positives, who have the differences in their respective positivities to keep them apart, two negatives have nothing to separate them, and one negative recognizes another by his peculiar transparency—whereas a positive is opaque.

Yes, I had my tongue in my cheek when I suggested mindfulness of death as a subject of meditation for you. But *also*, though you could hardly know this, I had a perfectly serious purpose at the back of my mind. It happens that, for Heidegger, contemplation of one's death throughout one's life is the key to authenticity. As Sartre has observed, Heidegger has not properly understood the nature of death, regarding it as *my* possibility, whereas in fact it is always accidental, even in suicide (I cannot kill myself directly, I can only cut my throat and *wait* for death to come). But death of one's body (which is always seen from outside, like other people's bodies) can be imagined and the implications envisaged. And this is really all that is necessary (though it must be added that there are other ways than contemplation of death of becoming authentic). Here, then, is a summary of Heidegger's views on this matter (from *6ET*, pp. 96-7):

> Death, then, is the clue to authentic living, the eventual and omnipresent possibility which binds together and stabilizes my existence. ... I anticipate death...by living in the presence of death as

> always immediately possible and as undermining everything. This full-blooded acceptance...of death, lived out, is authentic personal existence. Everything is taken as contingent. Everything is devalued. Personal existence and everything encountered in personal existence is accepted as nothing, as meaningless, fallen under the blow of its possible impossibility. I see all my possibilities as already annihilated in death, as they will be, like those of others in their turn. In face of this capital possibility which devours all the others, there are only two alternatives: acceptance or distraction. Even this choice is a rare privilege, since few are awakened by dread to the recognition of the choice, most remain lost in the illusions of everyday life. To choose acceptance of death as the supreme and normative possibility of my existence is not to reject the world and refuse participation in its daily preoccupations, it is to refuse to be deceived and to refuse to be identified with the preoccupations in which I engage: it is to take them for what they are worth—nothing. From this detachment springs the power, the dignity, the tolerance, of authentic personal existence.

If you found *mettā bhāvanā* relatively easy, it is quite possible that you were doing it wrong (*mettā bhāvanā* is notoriously easy to misconceive), in which case you were quite right to prefer *ānāpānasati*, which, if you found difficult, you may have been doing properly. It is difficult, at least to begin with. The two main faults are (i) a tendency to follow the breath inside the body, whereas attention should be kept about the region of the gate of the nose, and (ii) a tendency to squint at the nose, which induces headache, the cure for which is to practise *ānāpānasati* while walking up and down (which obliges one to look where one is walking instead of at the nose). I have, myself, never formally practised *mettā bhāvanā*, but the Ven. Kassapa Thera has made a success of it.

Thank you for the verses, expressing, perhaps, a layman's view of monks. Here are two in exchange, expressing a (Japanese) monk's view of laymen:

> She'd like to hear the sermon
> But she also wants
> To stay at home and bully her daughter-in-law.
> Their faces all look
> As if they thought
> They're going to live for ever.

An inauthentic lot, apparently.

Please excuse all these words, but, as you know, I find writing helpful, and besides, there is always the chance that you might find something here of use to you (though I know that some of it is not particularly easy stuff—even supposing that I am not talking nonsense).

**[L. 30]** **22 January 1963**

The present situation is only tolerable provided I can look forward to, at least, a very considerable improvement in the fairly near future. (Beside the fact that I cannot be doing myself very much good going on in this way, I am cut off from both the pleasures of the senses and the pleasures of renunciation—though, to be sure, I still have the joys of amœbiasis—; and it is distasteful for me to think of even a week more of this, and a year or over is out of the question.) But, in fact, the stimulation or sensitivity seems to be continuing unabated, and my hopes of an early improvement—and even of any improvement at all—are not very great. I feel it is better to let you know my view of the matter while my decision is still suspended.

As you know, the seat of the emotions is the bowels (not the heart, as is sometimes romantically supposed): all strong emotion can be felt as a physical affection of the bowels even after the emotion itself has subsided. (I have found that anger is constipating, lust sometimes loosening, and apprehension a diuretic; and strong fear, I believe, is a purgative.)

**[L. 31]** **28 January 1963**

During the last two or three days things seem to have improved a bit. With the help of the 'Reactivan' and of a spell of good weather, mental concentration has so much advanced that for the first time in seven months I have been more or less free of thoughts both of lust and of suicide. This is a considerable relief, even though it may only be temporary (mental concentration depends very largely on circumstances beyond one's control—health, weather, and so on).

For the time being, then, even though I have not yet resigned myself to the prospect of continuing to live, I find that I am relying a little less on Nietzsche and a little more on Mr. Micawber[1] (though both ended up badly—Nietzsche went mad and Mr. Micawber went to Australia).

**[L. 32]** **9 February 1963**

Many thanks for your kind letter heaving a sigh of relief at my recovery. The change, in fact, seems to be definitive, and came about almost as abruptly as the onset of the original condition. The stimulation, actually, remains; it seems to vary with the state of my guts and the time of day; but it no longer presents itself as specifically erotic—it is something like a desire to micturate. The recovery, that is to say, is mental rather than physical (though perhaps that will follow), and the severity and stability of the condition while it persisted was due in part to its being a vicious circle of addiction. Like all vicious circles it was not easy to break out of, and the best that I could do was temporary forcible suppression by opposing the thought of suicide. Only by a radical improvement in mental concentration which is indifferent alike to sensuality and suicide, was it possible to escape from it.

The improvement in mental concentration has not kept up (I cannot expect very much in my present condition), but I have not fallen back into the vicious circle. Of course, so long as the stimulation remains it is a danger to me, as a constant invitation to return; and there may arise fresh difficulties in the future with possible re-infections of amœbiasis; but at the moment all is well (though perhaps the handwriting is already showing a tendency to relapse).

Naturally, I am still not enamoured of life, and I continue to hope for a not-too-painful death in the not-too-distant future; but, with the exception of the prospect of a visit to the dentist in a few days' time, I no longer feel immediately suicidal.

**[L. 33]** **1 March 1963**

No, you are quite wrong. Far from being sick of doctors I am more and more grateful to them as time goes by; and as for their various treatments… well, I have to confess that I am rather fond of taking medicines, which, on the whole, have never done me very much harm. It is this sick body that I am sick of, not the doctors with their unfailing kindness to me.

I have been suffering from acute elephantiasis—infestation by elephants. They come at night and wander about trumpeting in the surrounding jungle. Once one gets used to it, it is really rather pleasant, since it means one will not be disturbed by unwelcome human visitors.

P.S. After taking 'Librium' for the first time today I have experienced an unusual freedom from intestinal discomfort (with corresponding benefit to concentration). If this is its normal effect it will be a pleasure to take.

**[L. 34]** **7 March 1963**

You said something in your last letter about the laughter that you find behind the harsher tones in what I write to you. This is not unconnected with what I was saying earlier about the difference between positive and negative thinkers. At the risk of being tiresome I shall quote Kierkegaard on this subject at some length. (Fortunately, you are not in the least obliged to read it, so it is really no imposition.)

> Negative thinkers therefore always have one advantage, in that they have something positive, being aware of the negative element in existence; the positive have nothing at all, since they are deceived. Precisely because the negative is present in existence, and present everywhere (for existence is a constant process of becoming), it is necessary to become aware of its presence continuously, as the only safeguard against it. In relying upon a positive security the subject is merely deceived. (*CUP*, p. 75)

> But the genuine subjective existing thinker is always as negative as he is positive, and *vice versa*. (*ibid*, p. 78)

> That the subjective existing thinker...is immature. (*ibid*, p. 81)[1]

> What lies at the root of both the comic and the tragic...is the discrepancy, the contradiction between the infinite and the finite, the eternal and that which becomes. A pathos which excludes the comic is therefore a misunderstanding, is not pathos at all. The subjective existing thinker is as bi-frontal as existence itself. When viewed from a direction looking toward the eternal[2] the apprehension of the discrepancy is pathos; when viewed with the eternal behind one the apprehension is comic. When the subjective existing thinker turns his face toward the eternal, his apprehension of the discrepancy is pathetic; when he turns his back to the eternal and lets this throw a light from behind over the same discrepancy, the apprehension is in terms of the comic. If I have not exhausted the comic to its entire

> depth, I do not have the pathos of the infinite; if I have the pathos of the infinite I have at once also the comic. (*ibid*, pp. 82-3)
>
> Existence itself...involves a self-contradiction. (*ibid*, p. 84)[1]

And where does the Buddha's Teaching come in? If we understand the 'eternal' (which for Kierkegaard is ultimately God—i.e. the soul that is part of God) as the 'subject' or 'self', and 'that which becomes' as the quite evidently impermanent 'objects' in the world (which is also Kierkegaard's meaning), the position becomes clear. What we call the 'self' is a certain characteristic of all experience, that seems to be eternal. It is quite obvious that for all men the reality and permanence of their selves, 'I', is taken absolutely for granted; and the discrepancy that Kierkegaard speaks of is simply that between my 'self' (which I automatically presume to be permanent) and the only too manifestly impermanent 'things' in the world that 'I' strive to possess. The eternal 'subject' strives to possess the temporal 'object', and the situation is at once both comic and tragic—comic, because something temporal cannot be possessed eternally, and tragic, because the eternal cannot desist from making the futile attempt to possess the temporal eternally. This tragi-comedy is suffering (*dukkha*) in its profoundest sense. And it is release from this that the Buddha teaches. How? By pointing out that, contrary to our natural assumption (which supposes that the *subject* 'I' would still continue to exist even if there were no *objects* at all), the existence of the subject depends upon the existence of the object; and since the object is manifestly impermanent, the subject must be no less so. And once the presumed-eternal subject is seen to be no less temporal than the object, the discrepancy between the eternal and the temporal disappears (in four stages—*sotāpatti*, *sakadāgāmitā*, *anāgāmitā*, and *arahatta*); and with the disappearance of the discrepancy the two categories of 'tragic' and 'comic' also disappear. The *arahat* neither laughs nor weeps; and that is the end of suffering (except, of course, for bodily pain, which only ceases when the body finally breaks up).

In this way you may see the progressive advance from the thoughtlessness of immediacy (either childish amusement, which refuses to take the tragic seriously, or pompous earnestness, which refuses to take the comic humorously) to the awareness of reflexion (where the tragic and the comic are seen to be reciprocal, and each is given its due), and from the awareness of reflexion (which is the limit of the *puthujjana*'s philosophy) to full realization of the *ariya dhamma* (where both tragic and comic finally vanish, never again to return).

**[L. 35]** **16 April 1963**

As regards possible help to other people, I have made notes on my understanding of the Buddha's Teaching, and there is the prospect that they will be printed. I should be glad to see them safely through the press myself personally (though they are, in fact, in good hands). This gives me at least a temporary reason for continuing to live, even though the survival of the notes affects other people more than myself. (A doubt remains, however, whether anybody will find the notes intelligible even if they do survive.)

In any case, whereas some days ago the heart was noticeably missing beats more or less continuously throughout the day (though with greater frequency at some times than at others), now the heart seems to have returned entirely to normal with the exception of the two short periods when I lie down after meals. So long, then, as this improvement is maintained (due, as I take it, to the calming effect of the concentration) I shall not start on the phenobarbitone:[1] in the first place because a hypnotic is damaging to concentration (and I value the concentration as much for its own sake as for its curative effect on the heart)—'Librium', incidentally, though it facilitates sleep, does not seem to be specifically hypnotic and does no harm to concentration—; and in the second place because this concentration cannot (on the law of averages) last very much longer, and then (if the heart has not wholly returned to normal) the phenobarbitone will be more urgently needed (without concentration, sex will probably raise its ugly head again).

Now for a fresh complication. Yesterday, I noticed that my heart was missing beats at a very variable rate. There is no pain or discomfort, but the missing beats are quite noticeable even without feeling the pulse—perhaps describable as a 'slight momentary breathlessness.' Not knowing anything about this condition or what it signifies I have ignored it and carried on as before. But perhaps you can tell me something about it. In particular, I should be glad to know if there is any likelihood of a complete heart failure without any warning (this is important, because one should, if possible, not be taken unawares by death). As I have told you, I shall not be heartbroken (or is that, medically speaking, exactly the wrong term?) if I died in the near future; but, like everybody else, I am anxious to avoid as much pain and discomfort as possible.

In general, I am not very anxious to come to Colombo and, in particular, if there is any probability of a sudden and unexpected death I shall stay here. If there is nothing urgent in the situation you can tell me about it at your leisure; but I should be glad of a postcard if there are no immediate consequences to be expected and nothing in particular to be done. In any case, there is no need for you or anyone else to make a journey here in order to examine me. I am not unduly concerned (after all, I am taking 'Librium', am I not? and this abolishes anxiety), and shall continue in the normal way.

**[L. 36] 22 April 1963**

There is nothing like the thought of the possibility of a sudden death, perhaps within a few hours, to keep one's attention securely fixed on the subject of meditation, and consequently concentration has very much improved during the past few days. Not only is no even remotely erotic thought allowed admittance, but also the Buddha himself has said that in one who consistently practises *ānāpānasati* there is agitation neither in mind nor in body[1] (and from what little that I have done of this, I know it to be true). And what better sedative could there be than that? Furthermore, if one succeeds in practising concentration up to the level of fourth *jhāna*, all breathing whatsoever ceases,[2] which means that the body must be very tranquil indeed. Of course, I know that if one takes enough barbiturates the same effect will ensue—the breathing will cease—; but if you stop the breathing with barbiturates there may be some difficulty in getting it started again, a difficulty that does not arise with fourth *jhāna*. ('Librium', incidentally, though it facilitates sleep, does not seem to be specifically hypnotic and does no harm to concentration.)

The question of coming to Colombo for a check-up has a certain comic aspect about it in the present circumstances. If I could be reasonably certain that after the check-up was ended I should be informed[a] 'Your condition is hopeless—we do not expect you to last another week,' I might work up some enthusiasm about it. But what I fear is that I shall be told 'Your condition is fine—absolutely nothing to worry about—carry on just as before.' What would Doctor think if, having told me this in a cheerful voice, I were to step outside his consulting room and there, on his front doorstep, in the middle of all his waiting patients, cut my throat—might he not wonder whether the check-up had really been worth while? It may be, later on, if anything comes of the proposal to print my *Notes*, that I shall have to visit Colombo in any case to see the printers; and if by then the idea of a check-up is no longer such a topsy-turvy (to find out if one's health is good enough to oblige one to kill oneself), why then perhaps we go ahead with it.

---

**a.** You yourself once said that you thought I had a fairly strong body.

**[L. 37]** **25 April 1963**

The weather, happily, continues to be bright and bone dry; my guts, by some miracle, are giving little trouble; and concentration has been steadily improving—indeed, it is better now than it has been at any time during the past couple of years or so. Apart from my usual 30mg of 'Librium' I have been taking 'Reactivan' and caffeine in the afternoon, supplemented by strong tea and coffee in the evening. These are perhaps not exactly the sedative prescribed by Dr. Wickramasuriya, but the effect is excellent—my heart has now not missed a beat for more than two days and seems to be quite normal again. The phenobarbitone I can keep in case the disorder returns under less favourable conditions for concentration, or I can give it to talkative visitors who come and disturb me.

If anyone is going to commit suicide—not that I advocate it for anyone—it is a great mistake to do it when one is feeling at one's most suicidal. The business should be carefully planned so that one is in the best possible frame of mind—calm, unmoved, serene—when one does it. Otherwise one may end up anywhere. The present time, therefore, would seem to be the best for me to kill myself, if that is my intention. All the melancholy farewell letters are written (they have to be amended and brought up to date from time to time, as the weeks pass and my throat is still uncut);[1] the note for the coroner is prepared (carefully refraining from any witty remarks that might spoil the solemn moment at the inquest when the note is read aloud); and the mind is peaceful and concentrated.

But it is precisely when all obstacles have been removed and everything is ready that one least feels like suicide. There is the temptation to hope that the good weather will last (which it won't), that one's guts are improving (which they aren't), and that *this* time at least one will make some real progress. So it is just possible (though I don't want to commit myself) that, weakly giving in to the temptation to survive, I shall once again let slip a golden opportunity of doing away with myself.

**[L. 38]** **9 June 1963**

I think that you have met Mr. Samaratunga. It is he who is busying himself with the publication of the *Notes on Dhamma* I have written, and it is on this account that I have thought it advisable to inform him of the nature of my present bodily disorders, of the fact that I have already attempted suicide, and that it remains a possibility that I shall make another attempt.[1]

That is to say, I did not wish him to embark on an undertaking that he might later regret, in the event of my suicide in the not-too-distant future. He seemed to be distressed at what I had to tell him, and has kindly offered his help; but he says that the situation is beyond his unaided powers, and has asked me if he can discuss the matter with you. I have told him that I have no objection. If, therefore, he does consult you, please consider yourself at liberty to talk to him freely about it; but I would prefer that you erred on the pessimistic side rather than the optimistic, for two reasons: (i) If things go wrong he will be less upset if he has not been led to expect too much, and (ii) I have not, in fact, asked for his help, and unless there is a very good chance of cure or at least substantial relief I am not at all inclined to start upon a course of treatment that will be burdensome for me and perhaps expensive for him. There is nothing more discouraging than to submit to a course of medical discipline and at the end of it to find oneself no better off than before.

The heart continues to miss beats each day from time to time—particularly (i) when I lie down after meals and in the evenings, and (ii) when I indulge in erotic thoughts. No doubt continuation of this condition will not do the heart any good (which in some respects would be an advantage, as an insurance against a ripe old age: many, many happy returns—of amœbiasis), but I do not see that anything more than a temporary cure can be achieved so long as the nervous disorder continues.

In my last letter I told you that the condition had been cured by good mental concentration. This (as expected) did not last—both the weather and the guts went wrong, and the heart again started missing beats. Humpty Dumpty in *Alice through the Looking Glass* seems to have had much the same sort of heart trouble brought on by excessive nervous agitation:

My heart went hop, my heart went thump;
I filled the kettle at the pump. (p. 223)

P.S. If you should meet Dr. Wickramasuriya and he asks after me, please assure him that I am taking honey daily for my heart. He insisted that honey is very good for strengthening the heart, adding that 'it contains all the unknown vitamins'—an irresistible recommendation! If we were offered the choice between a pill containing a generous quantity of all the vitamins hitherto discovered and one containing all those not yet discovered who would hesitate for a moment? The effect of the discovered vitamins is known and limited, but the undiscovered vitamins hold out boundless hopes of regeneration (especially if swallowed during a total eclipse of the sun).

Besides, the assertion about honey has the delightful property of being irrefutable except retrospectively—it is always unassailable at the time it is uttered. For suppose some new vitamin is discovered in (say) the skin of a certain plantain but is found not to be present in honey, then it is true that before the discovery of this vitamin the assertion about honey was mistaken, since this particular unknown vitamin was actually not contained in honey; but now that this vitamin has been discovered it is no longer amongst those that are 'unknown', and though we may have to confess that, yesterday, our assumption that honey contains all the unknown vitamins was perhaps a little premature, *today* we can be quite sure, without fear of contradiction, that it is absolutely true. The question arises, if a well-known doctor were to announce impressively, 'Gum Arabic contains all the unknown vitamins,' would he get people to swallow it?

**[L. 39]** **23 November 1963**

Kierkegaard's attitude towards his books was that nobody was competent to review them except himself—which, in fact, he proceeded to do, his later works containing a review of his earlier ones. I have much the same attitude towards the *Notes*.

The last section of the *Notes*—*FS*—is really a remarkably elegant piece of work, almost entirely original, and also quite possibly correct. I am obliged to say this myself, since it is highly improbable that anybody else will. It is most unlikely that anyone will make anything of it. The reason that I do not want to leave it out is principally that it provides a formal demonstration of certain structural features (intention and reflexion, for example) to which frequent appeal is made in the earlier part of the *Notes*, and so long as the demonstration is there, these features (whose existence it is fashionable, in certain circles, to ignore) cannot simply be dismissed as fictions. Besides, it always inspires confidence in an author if he has a few pages of incomprehensible calculations at the end of his book.

I thank you for hoping that I am in good condition; and, indeed, I should be only too delighted to be able to oblige. But the fact of the matter, alas! is that I am really very much as I was before. True, I have had no fresh attack of amœbiasis, but the old discomforts remain, and the troublesome erotic stimulation continues as before. Morale remains rather precarious. I have to recognize the ominous fact that I have now given up all hope of making any further progress for myself in this life.

This means, not only that for bodily comfort I am depending on drugs (stimulations, sedatives), but also that my reason for continuing to live is more or less dependent upon outside circumstances (at present, mostly upon business of one kind or another connected with the *Notes*, or upon an occasional windfall in the form of an interesting book). And all these external things are highly insecure. Once they go (as they may do at any time), I shall be left with no very good reason for continuing to live, and quite a good one for discontinuing. However, the situation does not cause me sleepless nights, and, really, nobody will be less distressed by my absence than I shall.

In any case, my present position has a great advantage: it gives me the freedom to say whatever I think needs saying without troubling whether I am making myself unpopular in the process. Unfortunately, however, reckless outspokenness on the subject of the Dhamma does not seem, in Ceylon, to produce unpopularity at all—rather the contrary. A certain Venerable Thera, on receiving a copy of the *Notes*—which condemns, point by point, almost everything in a published book of his—has written an amiably inconsistent eulogy of the *Notes*, commending Mr. Samaratunga's intentions to print it, and giving names of people to whom it might well be sent. (The point is, of course, that he wrote his book not out of any heartfelt conviction, but simply in accordance with the established tradition—and, I may say, did it very competently. And, being safe in the anonymity of the tradition, he does not feel that the *Notes* apply to him personally.)

## [L. 40] 13 February 1964

Many thanks for sending me *The Medical Mirror*.[1] I don't know how it is in England—philistinism is the usual order of the day—, but it seems that the German doctors are not insensitive to current trends of philosophical thought.

I was struck by the remarks of one doctor whose task it is to look after patients suffering from anxiety. Formerly, no doubt, anxiety in patients would have been attributed to nervous (and therefore physiological) disorders, and the remedy would have been treatment by drugs or perhaps surgery. (Even now in America, I believe, the opinion is that all mental disorder will eventually be amenable to treatment by new psychotropic drugs and neurosurgical techniques—but then the Americans are the least philosophical of mortals. One of Sartre's characters remarks somewhere that 'For an American, to think about something that worries him, that consists in doing all he can not to think about it.')[2] In other words, the whole matter of mental sickness would have been regarded as intelligible—in theory at least—in purely deterministic terms. But now this German doctor says

> As some people commit suicide in order to escape fear, the knowledge of death also cannot be the ultimate reason of fear. Fear rather seems to be directly related to freedom, to man, whose task as an intellectual being it is to fashion his life in freedom. His personality is the authority which permits this freedom. But his freedom, on the other hand, allows man to become aware of himself. This encounter with himself makes him fearful.

With this, compare the following summary of Heidegger's philosophical views.

> The only reality is 'care' at every level of existence. For the man who is lost in the world and its distractions this care is a fear that is short and fleeting. But let this fear once take cognizance of itself and it becomes anxiety, the perpetual climate of the lucid man 'in whom existence comes into its own'. (*Myth*, p. 18)

Man, in short, becomes anxious when he learns the nature of his existence; he becomes afraid when he finds he is free.

But if this is true, it is true always. Why, then, is anxiety so much more prevalent today, apparently, than it was formerly? The world is more comfortable than it was (and nobody has invented more unpleasant forms of death than have always existed), and yet mental homes are multiplying and full to overflowing. Why should it be so? This is where Nietzsche comes in—he is the diagnostician of our times. Nietzsche declared that 'God is dead,' and called himself the first accomplished nihilist of Europe. Not, indeed, that Nietzsche himself assassinated God; he found him already dead in the hearts of his contemporaries; and it was by fate, not choice, that he was a nihilist. He diagnosed in himself and in others the inability to believe and the disappearance of the primitive foundation of all faith, that is, belief in life. (I am quoting Camus.)[3]

Here, in a Buddhist tradition, it is not always realized how much in Europe the survival of death, and therefore of valid ethical values, is bound up with the idea of God. Once God is 'dead' (and he started dying, convulsively, with the French Revolution), life for the European loses its sense. '*Has existence then a significance at all?*—the question' (says Nietzsche) 'that will require a couple of centuries even to be completely heard in all its profundity.'[4] And so the task that Nietzsche set himself was to find out if it was possible to live without believing in anything at all: to be absolutely free, in other words.

Being a man of integrity (there are not so many after all) he used himself as a guinea-pig—and paid the price with madness. But he discovered in the process that complete liberty is an intolerable burden, and that it is only possible to live if one accepts duties of one sort or another. But what duties? The question, for the European, is still unanswered. ('No one would start to play a game without knowing the rules. Yet most of us play the interminable game of life without them, because we are unable to find out what they are.'—Cyril Connolly in 1944.)[5] In the old days, when God was still alive—when Christianity was still a living force in Europe—, people were faced, just as they are now, with the anxious question 'What should I do?';[6] but the answer then was ready to hand—'Obey God's commandments'—and the burden of anxiety was lifted from their shoulders. They feared God, no doubt, but they did not fear themselves. But now that God is dead, each man has to carry the burden for himself, and the burden—for those who do not shirk the issue and bury their ostrich heads in the sands of worldly distractions—is impossibly heavy. No, it is not death that these anxiety-ridden inmates of our asylums fear—it is life.

'And what is the answer?' perhaps you will ask. As I have tried to indicate (in KAMMA), the answer, for the ordinary person, is not self-evident. On the other hand, he may well feel that there *ought* to be some answer—as indeed Nietzsche himself did when he wrote

> It is easy to talk about all sorts of immoral acts; but would one have the strength to carry them through? For example, I could not bear to break my word or to kill; I should languish, and eventually I should die as a result—that would be my fate.[7]

And this feeling is not mistaken—except that one can never have certainty about it until one has actually seen the Buddha's Teaching for oneself. In the meantime, all one can do is take it on trust—even if for no other reason than to keep out of the mental home. But these days are so arsyvarsy that anyone who *does* succeed in seeing the Buddha's Teaching may well find himself lodged, willy-nilly, in an asylum.

I was fascinated by the account of 'a surgical super-operation reported recently from abroad [America?], where in nine hours of hard work a patient was operated for a malign tumour, an intervention which removed the entire pelvis including the legs and re-established new openings for urinary and intestinal tract.' Just imagine—no more itching piles, no more ingrowing toenails. But surely they could have removed a lot more? After all, one can still live without such useless impedimenta as arms, eyes, teeth, and tongue, and with only one lung and one kidney, and perhaps no more than half a liver. No wonder the writer comments that the surgeon should make inquiries about the patient's reserves of asceticism—just the right word!—before he starts on his labour of love!

**[L. 41]** **19 August 1964**

You are right; life is not so very simple for anyone. And once one has got fixed habits and is accustomed to one's little self-indulgences, and perhaps made a certain position for oneself in the world (professional seniority, the regard of one's colleagues, and so on), it is not so easy to make a drastic change and take a leap into what is really something of an unknown element.

As to Gibbon: he should be read slowly, not perhaps so much for what he says (though it is great fun sometimes) as for how he says it. I have read right through him three times, with great enjoyment. But it is rather a pity that you have the Everyman's edition, which has been modernized as regards spelling and punctuation. The earlier editions keep Gibbon's original spelling and his full complement of commas. I remember reading the first three chapters out loud to myself simply to enjoy the perfect balance of the sentences. And the footnotes! 'The inhabitants of Oxyrhincus, who worshipped a small fish in a magnificent temple.' Here you have the full weight of Gibbon's contempt for 'superstition' in all its forms, and expressed with the utmost economy of words. 'Grotius [a Dutch theologian],[1] who has so accurately defined the limits of omnipotence....' Poor Grotius! No, don't miss the footnotes, whatever you do. And doesn't he infuriate the Christians!

P.S. Thank you for the Jātaka reference. Any passage omitted in translation or left 'in the decent obscurity of a learned language' is an irresistible invitation—and very often an anti-climax. Gibbon quotes certain passages from (alas!) Greek authors, and leaves them untranslated. In particular, from Procopius (who wrote both a public and a private history—you may guess which is more interesting!) on the Empress Theodora (Justinian's wife), who did not exactly start life as a convent girl.[a] But Gibbon remarks that he

**a.** I find I have also made the following remark, which may help you in your

knew a bishop who was particularly fond of quoting one of these passages. Prof. Denis Brojan, an English resident in U.S.A., reported a few years ago that Americans have published a complete edition of *Sade*, but 'leaving the intolerably obscene passages in the decent obscurity of the French.'[b]

---

reading: 'Vitalian, Dietician, and Minimax, superfluous Roman Emperors.' (They may come useful if you run short.)

**b.** How long will it be, I wonder, before they can safely publish a Sinhalese translation of *Lady Chatterly's Lover* (or *Lady Lovely's Chatter*, as somebody put it), leaving the offensive passages 'in the decent obscurity of the English'?

# 7
# Letters to Mr. R.G. de S. Wettimuny

**[L. 42]** **12 May 1962**

Dear Mr. Wettimuny,
I was delighted to get your book[1] this afternoon, and perhaps even more with the graceful letter that accompanied it. Although we have, from time to time, discussed the Dhamma in the past, it was difficult from such fragmentary discussions to find out what exactly you understood by the Buddha's Teaching; but now that you have obliged yourself to set down your ideas all together in print, I hope to have a better chance. It is my own experience that there is nothing like sitting down and putting one's ideas on paper to clarify them, and, indeed, to find out what those ideas really are. I have a private dictum, 'Do not imagine that you understand something unless you can write it down'; and I have not hitherto found any exception to this principle. So, as you say, one writes by learning, and learns by writing.

What I *hope* to find, when I come to read the book, is that you have formed a single, articulated, consistent, whole; a whole such that no one part can be modified without affecting the rest. It is not so important that it should be correct[a]—that can only come later—, but unless one's thinking is all-of-a-piece there is, properly speaking, no *thinking* at all. A person who simply makes a collection—however vast—of ideas, and does not perceive that they are at variance with one another, has actually no ideas of his own; and if one attempts to instruct him (which is to say, to *alter* him) one merely finds that one is adding to the junk-heap of assorted notions without having any other effect whatsoever. As Kierkegaard has said, 'Only the truth that edifies is truth *for you*.' (*CUP*, p. 226) Nothing that one can say to these collectors of ideas is truth *for them*. What is wanted is a man who will argue a single point, and go on arguing it until the matter is clear

**a.** Nobody, after all, who has not reached the path can afford to assume that he is right about the Buddha's Teaching.

to him, *because he sees that everything else depends upon it*. With such a person communication (i.e., of truth that edifies) can take place.

**[L. 43]** **29 June 1962**

Thank you for your letter. Yes, I have finished the book, and, as I hoped, I have found that it gives me a fairly coherent idea of your view of the Dhamma and enables me to see in what respects it differs from mine. The most I can say in a letter, without writing at inordinate length, is to indicate a fundamental point of difference between our respective views, and then to consider very briefly what consequences are entailed.

On p. 302 you say, 'The Arahat Grasps only towards the end of all Grasping.' With this I do not agree. There is no grasping (*upādāna*) whatsoever in the *arahat*. The *puthujjana* is describable in terms of *pañc'upādānakkhandhā*, but the *arahat* (while he still lives) only in terms of *pañcakkhandhā*. *Upādāna* has already ceased.

There are four kinds of *upādāna—kāma, diṭṭhi, sīlabbata*, and *attavāda*—, and the *arahat* has none (see M.11/i,67). The expression in the Suttas for the attainment of *arahatship* is *anupādāya āsavehi cittaṃ vimucci.*[1] The term *sa-upādisesa-nibbānadhātu*, which applies to the living *arahat*, you take (p. 299) as '*Nibbāna* with the Grasping Groups remaining.' But this, in fact, has nothing to do with *upādāna*. *Upādisesa* means simply 'stuff remaining' or 'residue'. In M.10/i,62 the presence of *upādisesa* is what distinguishes the *anāgāmī* from the *arahat*, and this is clearly not the same precise thing as what distinguishes the living *arahat* (*sa-upādisesa-nibbānadhātu*) from the dead *arahat* (*an-upādisesa-nibbānadhātu*). *Upādisesa* is therefore *unspecified* residue, which with the living *arahat* is *pañcakkhandhā*. The *arahat* says *pañcakkhandhā pariññātā tiṭṭhanti chinnamūlakā* (Thag.120),[2] and the *mūla* (or root) that is *chinna* (or cut) is *upādāna*. This means that there can still be *rūpa, vedanā, saññā, saṅkhārā*, and *viññāṇa without upādāna*.[3]

This statement alone, if it is correct, is enough to invalidate the account on p. 149 (and elsewhere) of life as a *process* of grasping—i.e., a flux, a continuous *becoming*. For this reason I expect that you will be inclined to reject it as mistaken. Nevertheless, I must point out that the two doctrines upon which your account of grasping seems principally to rely—namely, the simile of the flame (p. 146) and the celebrated expression '*na ca so na ca añño*' (p. 149), both of which you attribute to the Buddha—are neither of them to be found in the Suttas. They occur for the first time in the

Milindapañha, and there is no evidence at all that they were ever taught by the Buddha.

You will see, of course, that if we reject your account of grasping as a *process*, we must return to the notion of *entities*, and with this to the notion of a thing's *self-identity* (i.e., for so long as an entity *endures* it continues to be 'the self-same thing'). And would this not be a return to *attavāda*? The answer is, No. With the question of a thing's *self-identity* (which presents no difficulty if carefully handled) the Buddha's Teaching of *anattā* has nothing whatsoever to do. *Anattā* is purely concerned with 'self' as *subject* ('I'). And this is a matter of considerably greater difficulty than is generally supposed.[4]

In brief, then, your book is dealing with a false problem; and the solution proposed, however ingenious, is actually beside the point—it is not an answer (either right or wrong) to the problem of *dukkha*, which is strictly a *subjective* problem.

Perhaps this response to your request for criticism may seem unexpectedly blunt; but where the Dhamma is concerned 'polite' replies designed only to avoid causing possible displeasure by avoiding the issue serve no useful purpose at all and make confusion worse confounded. Since I think you are a person who understands this, I have made no attempt to conceal my thought.

## [L. 44] 8 July 1962

Thank you for your letter. I am glad to find that you have not misunderstood mine, and that you apparently see that the principal point of disagreement between us is a matter of some consequence.

You say: 'But if the idea of Grasping is not applicable to the living Arahat when, for example, he is taking food,—then I am confronted with a genuine difficulty. In other words, if one cannot say that when the Arahat is taking food, he is (not) *taking hold* in some fashion or other, then I am faced with the difficulty of finding or comprehending what basically is the difference between *life*-action and other action, as of physical inanimate things.'

The first remark that must be made is that anyone who is a *puthujjana* *ought* to find himself confronted with a difficulty when he considers the Buddha's Teaching. The reason for this is quite simply that when a *puthujjana does* come to understand the Buddha's Teaching he thereby ceases to be a *puthujjana*. The second remark (which, however, will only displace your difficulty from one point to another, and not remove it) is that *all* conscious action is *intentional* (i.e., purposive, teleological). This is as true for the *arahat* as it is for the *puthujjana*. The *puthujjana* has *saṅkhār'upādānakkhandha* and the *arahat* has *saṅkhārakkhandha*. *Saṅkhāra*, in the context of the *pañcakkhandhā*, has been defined by the Buddha (in Khandha Saṃy.—S. xxii.56/iii,60) as *cetanā* or intention.

*Intentionality* as a necessary characteristic of all consciousness is well recognized by the phenomenological (or existential) school of philosophy (have a look at the article 'Phenomenology' in the *Encyclopædia Britannica*),[1] and though the subject is not particularly easy it presents no inherent difficulties. But in order to understand the nature of intention it is absolutely necessary to return to the notion of 'entities', and to consider the *structure of their temporary persistence*, which is 'Invariance under Transformation'. This principle occurs in quantum mechanics and in relativity theory, and in the Suttas it makes its appearance as *uppādo paññāyati; vayo paññāyati; ṭhitassa aññathattaṃ paññāyati*,[2] three characteristics that apply to all the *pañcakkhandhā* (see Khandha Saṃy.—S. xxii.37/iii,38). *Intentionality* is the essential difference between *life*-action and action of inanimate things.

But now this difficulty arises. What, precisely, is *upādāna* (*grasping*, or as I prefer, *holding*) if it is not synonymous with *cetanā* (intention)? *This*, and not any other, is the fundamental question raised by the Buddha's Teaching; and it is extremely difficult to *see* the answer (though it can be *stated* without difficulty). The answer is, essentially, that all notions of subjectivity, of the existence of a subject (to whom objects are present), all notions of 'I' and 'mine', are *upādāna*. Can there, then, be intentional conscious action—such as eating food—without the notion 'It is I who am acting, who am eating this food'? The answer is, Yes. The *arahat* intentionally eats food, but the eating is quite unaccompanied by any thought of a subject who is eating the food. For all non-*arahats* such thoughts (in varying degrees, of course) do arise. The *arahat* remains an *individual* (i.e. distinct from other individuals) but is no longer a *person* (i.e. a *somebody*, a *self*, a *subject*). This is not—as you might perhaps be tempted to think—a distinction without a difference. It is a genuine distinction, a very difficult distinction, but a distinction that *must* be made.[3]

On the question of *anicca/dukkha/anattā* it is necessary, I am afraid, to be dogmatic. The *aniccatā* or impermanence spoken of by the Buddha in the context of this triad is by no means simply the impermanence that everybody can see around him at any moment of his life; it is something very much more subtle. The *puthujjana*, it must be stated definitely, does *not* have *aniccasaññā*, does *not* have *dukkhasaññā*, does *not* have *anattasaññā*. These three things stand and fall together, and nobody who still has *attavādupādāna* (i.e. nobody short of the *sotāpanna*) perceives *aniccatā* in the essential sense of the term.

For this reason I consider that any 'appreciation of Buddhism by nuclear physicists' on the grounds of similarity of views about *aniccatā* to be a misconception. It is worth noting that Oppenheimer's dictum,[4] which threatens to become celebrated, is based on a misunderstanding. The impossibility of making a definite assertion about an electron has nothing to do with the impossibility of making a definite assertion about 'self'. The electron, in quantum theory, is defined in terms of *probabilities*, and a definite assertion about what is essentially indefinite (or rather, about an 'indefiniteness') cannot be made. But *attā* is not an *indefiniteness*; it is a *deception*, and a deception (a mirage, for example) can be as definite as you please—the only thing is, that it is *not* what one takes it for. To make any assertion, positive or negative, about *attā* is to accept the false coin at its face value. If you will re-read the Vacchagotta Sutta (Avyākata Saṃy.—S.xliv.8/iv,395-7), you will see that the Buddha refrains *both* from asserting *and* from denying the existence of *attā* for this very reason. (In this connection, your implication that the Buddha asserted that there is no self requires modification. What the Buddha said was '*sabbe dhammā anattā*'—no thing is self—, which is not quite the same. '*Sabbe dhammā anattā*' means 'if you look for a self you will not find one,' which means 'self is a mirage, a deception.' It does not mean that the mirage, as such, does not exist.)

I should perhaps say, in order to forestall possible misunderstandings, that I consider Dahlke's statement,

> 'Consciousness and its supporting points are not opposites, but transitions, one the form of development of the other, in which *saṅkhāras* represent that transition-moment in which thinking as *vedanā* and *saññā*, in the glow of friction, is on the point of breaking out into *viññāṇa*',

to be wholly mistaken. This is not '*paṭicca-saṃ*' at all. Perhaps you will have already gathered that I should disagree with this from my last letter.

**[L. 45]** **18 July 1962**

That the *puthujjana* does *not* see *aniccatā* is evident from the fact that the formula, 'Whatever has the nature of arising, all that has the nature of ceasing,' which is clearly enough the definition of *aniccatā*, is used only in connection with the *sotāpanna*'s attainment: *Tassa... vītamalaṃ dhammacakkhuṃ udapādi. Yaṃ kiñci samudayadhammaṃ, sabbaṃ taṃ nirodhadhamman ti.*[1] *Aniccatā* is seen with the *sotāpanna*'s *dhammacakkhu*, or eye of the *dhamma*. I am glad, nevertheless, that you are managing to turn your mind towards *aniccatā* at times, though of course you will not *really* see it until you know yourself to be a *sotāpanna*.

Your book as it stands has the merit of being to a great extent consistent (quite apart from whether or not it is correct). This is perhaps due in part to the fact that you are, in your own words, 'standing on Dahlke's shoulders'; and Dahlke, undeniably, is consistent (though I admit I have not read him for many years). Unfortunately, though he is consistent, I consider him to be mistaken; and, in particular, I do not see that my ideas on intentionality can in any way be reconciled with Dahlke's views.

What I feel, then, is this: that so long as you are concerned with making corrections and modifications to your book in preparation for a second edition it would be worse than useless for you to embark on a study of what I (or anyone else) have to say on the subject of intentionality. In the first place, intentionality cannot be introduced into your book without bringing with it profound inconsistencies (I have already said that the entity, and therefore the concept, must be reinstated before intentionality can be understood; and this would be in direct conflict with your Chapter II). In the second place, so long as you are occupied with your book you are committed to Dahlke's views (otherwise you would scrap it), and any attempt to reconcile intentionality with Dahlke in your own mind would result in confusion. For these reasons I think it would be better for you to finish revising your book and to have the second edition published (since this is your intention) *before* investigating intentionality. It would be then be best to come here, preferably for a couple of days (or at least one full day), so that you can look at what I have written and discuss it with me in person. As I said, my notes on intentionality are scattered, and it is not very convenient for me to part with them—particularly just at present, when I am still working on them. The subject, in any case, is not to be rushed.[2]

Many thanks for repeating your kindly request to be informed of anything you can do for me. At present there is nothing that I need, though I shall let you know if there comes to be in the future. My present indisposition is more a matter of waiting and hoping for improvement than actual treatment. Many thanks, also, for the stamps, which certainly will be useful.

Returning to the beginning of your letter. You say of the *arahat*, 'To him now everything is: "This is not mine, this is not I, this is not my self"' (p. 301). But this describes the *sekha* (*sotāpanna, sakadāgāmī, anāgāmī*), not the *asekha* (*arahat*). For the *sekha*, thoughts of 'I' and 'mine' still arise, but he *knows* and *sees* that they are mistaken, and therefore he is one who says, 'This is not mine, this is not I, this is not my self.' The *asekha* or *arahat*, on the other hand, does *not* have thoughts of 'I' and 'mine', and consequently he has already, while still living, come to an end of saying 'This is not mine, this is not I, this is not myself.' The *puthujjana* thinks: 'This is mine…'; the *sekha* thinks: 'This is not mine…'; and the *asekha* thinks neither.

# 8
# Letters to the Honourable Lionel Samaratunga

**[L. 46]** **3 March 1963**

Dear Mr. Samaratunga,[1]
Many thanks for your letter, which gives me the opportunity of clarifying certain things about *Notes on Dhamma*.

I quite see that the sentence referring to the Milindapañha as a misleading book is likely to provoke criticism. But you will find that I have made uncomplimentary remarks not only about the Milinda (see *PS*, final paragraphs, NA CA SO, ANICCA (c), and PAṬICCASAMUPPĀDA (c)) but also about the Paṭisambhidāmagga of the Sutta Piṭaka (see *NP* §§1&2 and PAṬICCASAMUPPĀDA), about the Vibhaṅga and Paṭṭhāna of the Abhidhamma Piṭaka (see CITTA), about the Visuddhimagga (see *NP* §§1&2, CITTA, and PAṬICCASAMUPPĀDA), about the Abhidhammatthasaṅgaha (see CITTA), and finally about all Pali books *en bloc* with the exception of the twelve or thirteen of the Vinaya and Sutta Piṭakas (see Preface (a)). Of these, the Paṭisambhidā, the Vibhaṅga, and the Paṭṭhāna, which belong to the Tipiṭaka (whereas the Milinda does not, except in Burma), are regarded with still greater veneration than the Milinda; and the Visuddhimagga, having been written in Ceylon, is very dear to nationalist sentiment (it is part of the cultural heritage of Ceylon). Furthermore, the views that I have set forth are, I think, without exception, contrary to the accepted traditional interpretation of the Dhamma.[2] It is precisely for this reason that I have thought it necessary to put them down in writing, and to indicate as misleading the exegetical books that are responsible for the current misinterpretations of the Suttas. Thus it is part and parcel of my purpose to denounce the Milinda, which in my view is a particularly guilty offender (because it is so popular). (Incidentally, it is not my purpose to *demonstrate* the unreliability of the Milinda as a whole by inference from one or two isolated instances, but to state categorically and on my own authority that it is *in fact* a generally misleading book. The same applies to my adverse remarks on other books.)

Perhaps I may have given you the impression that these various notes of mine were not originally intended for publication (on account of excessive difficulty). But this needs some qualification. I certainly wrote these notes with a view to their eventual publication, and in their present form (with the uncomplimentary remarks about the Milinda and all); but not necessarily in my lifetime. I wished to leave these views on record for the benefit of anyone who might later come across them. I was not so much concerned whether anyone would want to publish them after my death, as to leave them in the form in which I wanted them published (if they were to be published at all).[3]

When you first asked me if I was going to have the notes published, I hesitated for two reasons. First, as I told you, I was doubtful whether the average intelligent layman, who cannot devote much time to private thinking, would derive any benefit from them. Secondly, I was well aware that, if published, they might stir up a hornet's nest on account of their outspoken disagreement with traditional ideas, and this might have unpleasant consequences for the author or for the publisher. However, having read them, you told me that you did find them of interest and that you thought that others might too. So the first objection was removed. The second objection is more complex. Let us consider the kinds of people to whom these notes might give offence.

(i) The self-appointed guardians of Sinhala cultural traditions. Since these notes are in English and their author is a non-Sinhala (who cannot be expected to know any better) they can hardly be taken seriously; though the publisher might come in for some abuse.

(ii) The sincere traditionalists, who have spent all their lives studying and teaching the traditional commentarial interpretation. These will be mostly the elderly and learned Mahātheras who, for the most part, do not read English and who, in any case, are unlikely to pay much attention to what is written by a junior *bhikkhu*.

(iii) Those with vested interests in Buddhism. Writers of textbooks, school-teachers, self-appointed Buddhist leaders, and all those whose position requires them to be authorities on the Dhamma. Their interests will be best served by ignoring the *Notes* altogether, certainly not by drawing attention to them by criticizing them.

(iv) Professional scholars—university professors, etc. These are more likely to object to my criticisms of themselves as sterile scholars than to my adverse comments on the Milinda or on other books. If they write serious criticisms of the *Notes*, there is no difficulty in replying to them (and perhaps even with profit).

(v) Popular writers on Buddhism. These are the people who are likely to write irresponsible and emotionally charged criticisms in the various Buddhist journals. Such articles, however, are ephemeral, and satisfy only those who have no more intelligence than themselves. There is so much of this sort of thing already that a little more will not make much difference; and an intelligent person is quite likely to consider that adverse criticism by such writers is in fact a commendation. It is usually not necessary to reply to such criticisms.

(vi) Finally, it is quite possible that the appearance of the *Notes* in print will be greeted with complete indifference and absence of all criticism whatsoever.

As far as I am concerned, if my health were good enough to allow me to devote all my time to practice, I should find the business of preparing these *Notes* for publication and of answering possible criticisms of them an intolerable disturbance; as it is, however, my general condition seems to be deteriorating, and a certain amount of literary activity may actually be welcome to help me pass the time. That it is possible that I may make myself an unpopular figure by having these notes published is not a prospect that worries me in the least. Though, as I said earlier, the notes were primarily intended for posthumous publication, I see two possible advantages in having them published before my death. The first is that an authoritative unmutilated edition can be assured, and the second is that serious objections and criticisms can be answered and possible obscurities can be cleared up.

So much having been said, perhaps you will be in a better position to see how you stand in this matter. I can only agree to your publishing the *Notes* if you yourself consider that they should be published; that is to say, in spite of the facts that they go against the accepted traditional interpretation of the Dhamma, and that they may therefore possibly provoke adverse criticism.

Of course, if you do still decide to publish, much unnecessary criticism can be avoided by judicious distribution of the book. As far as I gathered, it was your idea to have the book distributed privately (and presumably free of charge) to suitable individuals and to selected libraries (and possibly societies), and not to have it exposed for public sale. My own view is that the book should be as widely dispersed as possible in places where it is likely to be preserved.

**[L. 47]** **8 March 1963**

I am glad to see that we are in complete agreement regarding the manner and purpose of publication of the book. I am particularly glad to know that you do not regard the Dhamma as something for sale—it is so utterly beyond price that it *can* only be communicated as a gift. Unfortunately, however, the world (particularly in these days) is so mercenary that anything given free is looked upon with suspicion; and for this reason I feel that we should take particular care to avoid all impression that we are distributing propaganda. A small, well-printed, and attractively presented 'private edition' is what we should aim at, rather than a perhaps larger number of 'booklets for free distribution'.

**[L. 48]** **9 March 1963**

Thank you for your letter asking whether you should prepare an index. I had already considered this matter and had decided that an index was not needed for the following reasons:

(i) The book is sufficiently short for anyone who is interested to learn his way about it fairly quickly. (And the last part, *FS*, has really nothing very much in it to be indexed except noughts and crosses.)

(ii) I have provided a considerable amount of cross-references in the text itself, so that a reader interested in one particular subject can without difficulty locate different passages dealing with that subject.

(iii) The third part itself, *SN*, is already arranged under subject headings in the Pali alphabetical order, and a glance at the Table of Contents is enough to locate the article that is sought.

(iv) I have something of a feeling that an index would not be entirely in keeping with the character of the book. What I mean is this: although the book is largely in the form of notes, and might therefore seem to be in the nature of a work of reference, it is actually intended to be read and digested as a single whole, with each separate note simply presenting a different facet of the same central theme. A person using the book as it is intended to be used would come, in the course of time, to regard it as an organic whole, with each part related to every other part, and would thus find an index an irrelevance. The presence of an index, on the other hand, might encourage a casual reader simply to refer to the word or subject of immediate interest to him and to neglect its essential relationship to every other part of the book. In a word, an index might make the book *too easy*.

To find the meaning of any one single word in the book it is necessary to read the whole book.

This is as I see the question; but if you have a strong view that an index would be an advantage, I am open to persuasion.

**[L. 49]** **22 March 1963**

There is a certain matter about which I am in doubt, and which you may be able to clarify. I have quoted various short passages from books that are copyrighted, and I do not know whether it is necessary to obtain permission if they are to be printed. I believe that a certain latitude in this matter is allowed (by the Berne Convention, is it not?), and that reasonably short quotations may be made under certain circumstances without infringing copyright; but I do not know whether the passages I have quoted go beyond this. It is perhaps unlikely that anyone would actually want to prosecute in this particular case (especially if the book is not to be sold), but I do not want to find myself in the position of having taken what I was not entitled to take. Would you be able to make sure that we are in order about this?

Perhaps you have seen the latest BPS publication, 'Knowledge and Conduct' (*Wheel* 50), by three university professors? In odd moments I have been browsing in Kierkegaard's *Concluding Unscientific Postscript*, which is a sustained polemic against objective speculative philosophy, and the three professors could hardly have chosen a more unfortunate time to arrive here in print. It is perhaps a little ironical that these three professors writing of Buddhism, of whom two at least[1] would, I presume, profess to call themselves Buddhists,[a] should compare so unfavourably with the Christian Kierkegaard. But Kierkegaard at least existed as an individual human being (even though his Christianity makes him a distorted figure), whereas these professors seem to be under the impression that such a thing is not really necessary, and this puts them in a slightly ridiculous light as individuals

---

**a.** The terms 'Buddhism' and 'Buddhist' have for me a slightly displeasing air about them—they are too much like labels that one sticks on the outside of packages regardless of what the packages happen to contain. I do not, for example, think of myself or yourself or anyone else to whom the Buddha's Teaching is a matter of personal concern as a 'Buddhist'; but I am quite content to allow the census authorities to speak of so many million 'Buddhists' in Ceylon, and to let disinterested ('unbiased') scholars take 'Buddhism' as their field of study. Prof. Malalasekera's *Encyclopaedia of Buddhism* does in fact deal with 'Buddhism'; but whether it has very much connexion with the Buddha's Teaching is another question.

and tends to stultify whatever there might be of value in their thinking and writing.

Prof. Wijesekera starts off by calling witnesses to testify to the Buddha's competence as an ethicist. This detestable practice (which nevertheless is remarkably common) of bringing forward unsolicited testimonials by distinguished personages to the Buddha's good character reveals not only a complete lack of sense of proportion, but also (as I suspect) something of an inferiority complex—rather as if one found it necessary to prove to the world at large that being a follower of the Buddha is not something to be ashamed of. But if one must do this sort of thing, it is as well not to mix up witnesses for the prosecution with those for the defence. Prof. Wijesekera quotes Albert Schweitzer in praise of the Buddha. But Schweitzer's philosophy is 'Reverence for Life', whereas the Buddha has said that just as even the smallest piece of excrement has a foul smell so even the smallest piece of existence is not to be commended. So if Schweitzer praises the Buddha he is labouring under a misapprehension. Schweitzer has certainly misunderstood the Buddha's Teaching, and possibly his own philosophy as well. (In the Buddha's day people thought twice before presuming to speak his praises, understanding very well that they lacked the qualifications to do so. See the opening to the Cūḷahatthipadopama Sutta—M.27/i,175-8.)[2]

Prof. Wijesekera then quotes Rhys Davids, who speaks of 'the historical perspective of ethical evolution' and declares that 'the only true method of ethical inquiry is surely the historical method.' What does Kierkegaard say?

> For study of the ethical, every man is assigned to himself. His own self is as material for this study more than sufficient; aye, this is the only place where *he* can study it with any assurance of certainty. Even another human being with whom he lives can reveal himself to his observation only through the external; and in so far the interpretation is necessarily affected with ambiguities. But the more complicated the externality in which the ethical inwardness is reflected, the more difficult becomes the problem of observation, until it finally loses its way in something quite different, namely, in the aesthetic. The apprehension of the historical process therefore readily becomes a half poetic contemplative astonishment, rather than a sober ethical perspicuity.... The more simplified the ethical, the more perspicuous does it become. It is therefore not the case, as men deceitfully try to delude themselves into believing, that the ethical is more clearly evident in human history, where millions are involved, than in one's

> own poor little life. On the contrary, precisely the reverse is true, and it is more clearly apparent in one's own life, precisely because one does not here so easily mistake the meaning of the material and quantitative embodiment. The ethical is the inwardness of the spirit, and hence the smaller the circumstances in which it is apprehended, provided it really is apprehended in its infinitude, the more clearly is it perceived; while whoever needs the world-historical accessories in order, as he thinks, the better to see it, proves thereby precisely that he is ethically immature. (*CUP*, pp. 127-8)

In other words, Kierkegaard understands very well that the ethical is the answer to the question 'What should I do?', and that the more one becomes involved with history the more one loses sight of the ethical. History is accidental to ethics.

Rhys Davids, however, is not content even to look for the ethical in history; he seeks to examine history in order to see there the perspective of ethical evolution. Naturally this assumes that a certain pattern of ethical change is historically visible. But history is the record (limited and somewhat arbitrary) of the deeds man has done and the thoughts he has expressed; and the pattern of ethical change recorded by history must therefore be either the pattern (in space and time) of man's actual behaviour or the pattern (in space and time) of his thoughts about how he should behave. What it *cannot* be is the pattern (in space and time) of how man should have behaved (unless, of course, this is identical either with how he has behaved or with how he has thought he should behave—which, however, cannot be decided by history). In other words, if history is made the basis for the study of ethics, the emphasis is shifted from the question 'What should I do?' to the question, either 'What does man do?' or 'What does man think he should do?'.

The view that ethics are identical with man's actual behaviour is self-destructive (for if a man cannot help doing what he should do, the word *ethics* loses its meaning altogether); but it is certainly true (as Prof. Wijesekera himself says) that the majority of scientific and materialistic thinkers hold the view that ethics are relative—i.e. are concerned with the question 'What does man think he should do?', which receives different answers in different times and places.

And what about Prof. Wijesekera himself—does he remain faithful to the authority he has quoted and follow the historical method, which must lead him to ethical relativity, or does he call to mind that he is an existing human being and a Buddhist to boot, and arrive at the conclusion that ethics are absolute and the same for all beings at all times and in all places? The answer seems to be that he starts out historically ('...it is essential to discuss as briefly as possible the development of the moral consciousness during the pre-Buddhist Upanishads', etc. etc.) and then changes horses in mid-stream; for when he comes to Buddhist ethics he quietly drops the idea of ethical evolution and arrives unhistorically, as a thinly disguised Buddhist, at the quite correct conclusion that the Buddha's ethics are universally valid.

Perhaps it is too much to say that he actually arrives at this conclusion, but at least he gets as far as advocating it as worthy of serious consideration by an 'unbiased student of Buddhism'. Prof. Wijesekera does not seem to be quite clear what ethics are or what he himself is (the two problems are intimately related); and to the extent that he professes to be a Buddhist while at the same time regarding Buddhism objectively he becomes for Kierkegaard a figure of comedy:

> If...he says that he bases his eternal happiness on his speculation, he contradicts himself and becomes comical, because philosophy in its objectivity is wholly indifferent to his and my and your eternal happiness. (*CUP*, p. 53)

Dr. Jayatilleke, in the second essay, represents logic. This is evident from the way he turns the Four Noble Truths into propositions, or statements of fact. That they are not *facts* but *things* (of a particular kind) can be seen from the Dhammacakkappavattana Sutta (Vinaya Mahāvagga I/Vin.i,10; Sacca Saṃy.—S.lvi.11/v,421-24), where *dukkha* is *pariññeyya*, 'to be known absolutely', *samudaya* is *pahātabba*, 'to be abandoned', *nirodha* is *sacchikātabba*, 'to be realized', and *magga*, the fourth Truth, is *bhāvetabba*, 'to be developed'. A fact, however, is just a fact, and one cannot do anything to it, since as such it has no significance beyond itself (it does not imply any other fact not contained in itself)—it just *is* (and even whether it *is* is doubtful).

But *things* are significant; that is to say, they are imperatives, they call for action (like the bottle in *Alice in Wonderland* labelled 'Drink Me!'). Heidegger, and Sartre after him, describe the world as a world of *tasks to be performed*, and say that a man at every moment of his life is engaged in performing tasks (whether he specifically pays attention to them or not). Seen in this light the Four Noble Truths are the ultimate tasks for a man's performance—Suffering commands 'Know me absolutely!', Arising commands 'Abandon me!', Cessation commands 'Realize me!', and the Path commands 'Develop me!'.

But by transforming things into facts (and the Four Noble Truths, which are descriptions of things, into propositions) I automatically transform myself into logic—that is to say, I destroy my situation as an existing individual engaged in performing tasks in the world, I cease to be *in concreto* (in Kierkegaard's terminology) and become *sub specie æterni.* (By regarding the Four Noble Truths as propositions, not as instructions, I automatically exempt myself from doing anything about them.) The world (if it can still be called a world) becomes a logician's world—quite static and totally uninhabited. (It is significant that Wittgenstein, in his celebrated *Tractatus Logico-Philosophicus*, which helped to establish modern logical positivism, starts off by declaring: '1. The world is everything that is the case. 1.1 The world is the totality of facts, not of things.' Compare, in this connexion, the note in the Preface to *Notes* where it is said 'Things, not facts, make up my world.')

Kierkegaard would be more severe on Dr. Jayatilleke than on Professor Wijesekera:

> It is not denied that objective thought has validity; but in connection with all thinking where subjectivity must be accentuated, it is a misunderstanding. If a man occupied himself, all his life through, solely with logic, he would nevertheless not become logic; he must therefore himself exist in different categories. Now if he finds that this is not worth thinking about, the choice must be his responsibility. But it will scarcely be pleasant for him to learn, that existence itself mocks everyone who is engaged in becoming purely objective. (*CUP*, pp. 85-6)

Lastly we come to Prof. Burtt. He says that he thinks that the Buddha considered that 'philosophy...must start from where we are rather than from somewhere else.' Very good! This is excellently well said, and is precisely the point that the Preface to the *Notes* was seeking to establish. And not only does he say this, but he also urges it as a matter that philosophers should consider with the utmost seriousness. And what about Prof. Burtt? Surely, after all this, he will set the example by starting himself to philosophize from where he is and not from somewhere else—will he not start by considering his situation as an existing individual human being who eats and sleeps and blows his nose and lectures on Philosophy at Cornell University and draws his salary once a quarter? Oh no, not a bit of it! In order to philosophize he finds it necessary to

> achieve a broad perspective on the history of thought, in the West and in the East, and...adequately assess the long-run significance of Buddhism with its various schools when viewed in such a perspective. (p. 42)

More historical perspectives!

This means that instead of starting from where he is, Prof. Burtt is proposing to become *sub specie æterni* and start from everywhere at once, or, since this is the same as becoming so totally objective that he vanishes from himself and becomes identified with speculative philosophy in the abstract, from nowhere at all. This itself is comic enough, since, as Kierkegaard points out, he is in the process of forgetting, in a sort of world-historical absentmindedness, what it means to be a human being. But he becomes doubly comic when, having performed this comical feat of forgetting that he is an existing individual, he solemnly issues a warning to philosophers against doing any such thing. For Prof. Burtt, Kierkegaard prescribes drastic treatment:

> In this connection it will perhaps again appear how necessary it is to take special precautions before entering into discussion with a philosophy of this sort: first to separate the philosopher from the philosophy, and then, as in cases of black magic, witchcraft, and possession by the devil, to use a powerful formula of incantation to get the bewitched philosopher transformed into a particular existing human being, and thus restored back to his true state. (*CUP*, p. 324)

Perhaps there is, in all this, a certain amount of over-emphasis and caricature; I have no doubt that the worthy professors in question (whom I have never met) are really charming and delightful people when one knows them personally. Nonetheless, the objectivizing tendency that they represent so hopelessly emasculates people's understanding of the Buddha's Teaching that it is almost a duty to put them in the pillory when they venture to make a public appearance in print.

Incidentally, this business of 'starting from where we are' is really the theme of *FS*, which you found puzzling. The point is that abstract or objective or scientific thought abolishes the distinction between 'here' and 'elsewhere', between 'this' and 'other things'—in short, the negative or the principle of contradiction—, and is consequently unable to start from anywhere in particular, and starts from everywhere (or, what is the same thing, from nowhere). But an existing individual is always somewhere in particular, here and not elsewhere; and what is needed is to show the structure of existence without losing sight of this fact—nay, understanding that the entire structure of existence rests upon this fact. Since nobody else, so far as I know, has undertaken this task, I have had to do it myself (in order to clarify my own thinking—to see how I can think existence without ceasing to exist,[b] i.e. to make plain the structure of *reflexive* thinking). But provided the principle of 'starting from where we are' presents no difficulty and is not forgotten, there is no need at all for anyone to attempt to follow the formal discussion of *FS*. And in any case, as I have remarked elsewhere, this is only indirectly connected with the Buddha's Teaching proper. (You are the only person who has seen it, and I was a little curious to know what you would make of it. But perhaps it will not be readily comprehensible to anyone who does not have Kierkegaard's difficulty—see note (b)—, or some allied problem, on his mind. It has been of the greatest value to me.)

With regard to any of my past writings that you may come across (I do not think there is very much), I would ask you to treat with great reserve anything dated before 1960, about which time certain of my views underwent a modification. If this is forgotten you may be puzzled by inconsistencies between earlier and later writings. If, on the other hand, you should encounter inconsistencies in what I have written since 1960, I should be very glad if you would point them out to me, as I am not aware that my views have undergone any further modification and such inconsistencies are probably attributable to carelessness of expression or hasty thinking.

## [L. 50] 1 April 1963

I should be glad if you will bear in mind that the publication of this book is not a matter of personal importance to me. It may perhaps be of importance to other people whether the book is published (though this can only be decided in retrospect), but for me it is a matter of only incidental concern. (I did not come to Ceylon in order to write about the Dhamma, and had

**b.** To think existence *sub specie æterni* and in abstract terms is essentially to abrogate it, and the merit of the proceeding is like the much trumpeted merit of abrogating the principle of contradiction. It is impossible to conceive existence without movement, and movement cannot be conceived *sub specie æterni*. To leave movement out is not precisely a distinguished achievement.... It might therefore seem to be the proper thing to say that there is something that cannot be thought, namely existence. But the difficulty persists, in that existence itself combines thinking and existence, in so far as the thinker exists. (*CUP*, pp. 273-4)

I kept in good health it is probable that I should have found neither the time nor the inclination to do so.) This means, then, that you should please yourself what steps you take to publish it, without feeling that I shall be much worried one way or the other.

By all means write to me about points that puzzle you either in Blackham's book (*6ET*) or in what I have written—if you think my brains are worth picking, then by all means pick them. You told me earlier that you had set out to ask me about certain points that puzzled you, but that, upon reading through what you had written, it seemed so foolish that you tore it up. This is a great mistake. It is absolutely essential in philosophical matters (however it may be in legal matters when one is sitting on the Bench representing the Majesty of the Law) not to be afraid of appearing ridiculous by a display of ignorance (it is only fools who will think one ridiculous if one does so). Cf. Camus: 'All of Dostoievsky's heroes question themselves as to the meaning of life. In this they are modern: they do not fear ridicule.' (*Myth*, p. 77)

Unless a person is prepared to reveal himself (as one takes off one's clothes and reveals one's body to the doctor), it is not possible for another person (even if he is competent to do so) to straighten out his tangled views and show him what line of thought he should follow. In this matter, I myself am quite well aware that every time I open my mouth or put pen to paper in order to express unconventional thoughts (which I do quite often) I risk being thought a complete fool by other people (or even by myself in retrospect): but being happily endowed with a faculty for ignoring what other people think of me, this does not give me sleepless nights.

## [L. 51] 11 April 1963

I am glad to say the unpolished specimens of your ignorance are satisfactorily un-ignorantly relevant to the matter in hand. The truly ignorant question is the irrelevant question.

To begin with, there is your 'overwhelming desire to know something of the Dhamma which gets precedence to Fundamental Structure.' Perhaps a simile will make the matter clear. No doubt you are acquainted with the game of chess, played on a board of 64 squares, with a number of pieces and pawns moving according to certain fixed rules. This I shall call 'dispassionate chess' in contrast to 'passionate chess', which I shall now describe.[1]

Imagine that, in order to add an (unwanted) interest to the game of dispassionate chess, some foolish person were to conceive the pieces as being subject to various passions having the effect of modifying their moves. The bishops, for example, being enamoured of the queen, would be diverted from their normal strict diagonal course when passing close to her, and would perhaps take corresponding steps to avoid the presence of the king out of fear of his jealousy. The knights would make their ordinary moves except that, being vain fellows, they would tend to move into a crowd of admiring pawns. The castles, owing to a mutual dislike, would always stay as far distant from each other as possible. Passionate chess would thus differ from dispassionate chess in that the moves of the pieces, though still normally governed by the rules of dispassionate chess, would be seriously complicated under the influence of passion; but both passionate and dispassionate chess would be played on the same chessboard of 64 squares.

We can take passionate chess as representing the behaviour of the *puthujjana*, which is complicated by craving, and dispassionate chess as the behaviour of the *arahat*, which is entirely free from irregularities due to craving. The chessboard, on which both kinds of chess alike are played, is Fundamental Structure.

Now the Buddha is concerned with transforming the *puthujjana* into an *arahat*, that is to say, with removing the undesirable complications of passionate chess in order to restore the parity of dispassionate chess; and for this purpose an examination of the structure of the chessboard is clearly an irrelevant matter, since it is exactly the same in both kinds of chess. In this way it may perhaps be seen that an understanding of the Dhamma does not depend on an understanding of Fundamental Structure, and takes precedence. A study of Fundamental Structure may, however, be found necessary (at least in times when the Dhamma is no longer properly understood, which rather seems to be the situation today) in order to re-establish this important fact (for, of course, an understanding of what is *not* the Dhamma may lead to an understanding of what *is* the Dhamma).

I am sorry about the repellent mathematical appearance of the note (I used to be a mathematician in a small way), but I can assure you that no knowledge of mathematics is required to follow it. You simply start from a positive ('this') and a negative ('not-this') and see where it leads you, following the one rule of avoiding self-contradiction.

The first result is that *three* negatives, not *one*, are absolutely required (which, incidentally, is why space is necessarily three-dimensional—i.e. *if* you can move from here to there, you must *also* be able to move in two other directions all mutually at right angles). This leads us at once to the next point—the negative.

The great advantage of your having so intelligently displayed your ignorance is that you have at once put your finger on the vital spot. You say 'The negative cannot appear in immediate experience. It is at most an inference and is therefore forbidden (?)' The bracketed query, which I take to mean that you are doubtful whether the negative as inference can be accepted as a basic irreducible concept, is fully justified. You cannot *start* with inference (which is a logical category) for the very good reason that in order to *infer* you must have something to infer *from*, and what you infer from is thus automatically more primitive than the inference. Furthermore, you cannot infer 'not-A' from 'A', since inference is of necessity from like to like. (In its simplest form, inductive inference is by 'simple enumeration'—'if A has occurred so many times it will probably occur again'. And it is well known that deductive inference does not add anything to what is already given in the premises.) From 'A' you can only infer 'more A', but the original 'A' from which you infer 'more A' is not itself an inference.

So, too, if you infer 'not-A' there must be an original 'not-A' that is not itself an inference. This means that your statement that the negative cannot appear in immediate experience is a fundamental mistake.[a] If the negative appears *at all* (which of course it does) it *must* appear *first* in immediate experience. From the fact that you are at A you cannot *infer* that movement from A—i.e. to not-A—is possible: movement is an immediate experience, revealing immediately the existence of the negative. (And, incidentally, the fact that space is three-dimensional—if movement in one dimension is possible, it is possible also in two other dimensions—is also a matter of immediate experience. This shows that the discussion in *FS* is not logical or inferential, but a pre-inferential description of the structure of experience. A logician will make neither head nor tail of it.)

Try a simple experiment. Fix your gaze on some given object, A, in your room. Then, *without shifting your gaze from A*, ask yourself if anything else in the room is at that time visible to you. You will find that you can also see a number of *other* objects surrounding A, but less distinctly. These other objects, though visible at the same time as A, form, as it were, the background to A, which occupies the foreground or centre of attention.

---

**a.** Compare Kierkegaard:

> Negative thinkers always have one advantage, in that they have something positive, being aware of the negative element in existence; the positive have nothing at all, since they are deceived. Precisely because the negative is present in existence, and present everywhere (for existence is a constant process of becoming) it is necessary to become aware of its presence continuously, as the only safeguard against it. In relying upon a positive security the subject is merely deceived. (*CUP*, p. 75)

These are objects that are *peripherally* visible, whereas A is *centrally* visible, or, if you prefer, A is *present* whereas the other objects are, in a manner of speaking, partly absent—i.e. *not* present. But all these other objects, though they are not-A, are given in the same immediate experience as A. I do not think, if you carry out the experiment carefully, that you will conclude that all these peripherally—non-centrally—visible objects, which are negatives of the centrally visible A, are simply *inferred from A*. How can you possibly *infer* the bookshelf in the corner of the room from the pen lying on your desk?

You say that you 'determine what is on the table as a sheet of paper because of its positive qualities.'[b] Let us take a perhaps more obvious example. You go into a room and you find there a chair. You proceed to enumerate its 'positive qualities'—its shape, size, colour, texture, rigidity, material, and so on. Then, on some later occasion, somebody asks you 'What is a chair?' Will you not reply quite simply and without hesitation 'A chair is something to sit on'? Or would you give a detailed positive description of a chair, but omitting to mention the fact that you can sit on it? But if you say it is something to sit on, can you explain how you derive (or infer) this surely not unimportant characteristic of a chair from the list of purely positive qualities that you have made (bearing in mind, of course, that this list cannot contain the slightest reference to the anatomy of the human body, which is certainly not amongst the positive qualities of a chair)?

Perhaps you might say that you *know* that a chair is something to sit on from past experiences with such things as you have positively described. In this case I shall not disagree with you, but shall ask you instead how '*past* experience' comes to be *present* (for, after all, it is in the present that you are describing a chair as something to sit on). Perhaps you might then explain that you *now remember* your past experience. I then ask 'What is memory?' If you are a neurologist you will perhaps give me a description of the nervous organization of the brain and of the traces or impressions left there by each experience, enabling it to be recalled on a future occasion. Perhaps I might then ask about people who remember their past existences

---

**b.** You speak of its potentialities (i.e. its negatives) for determining it as being as far-fetched as its not being on fire. But suppose I were to say that the sheet of paper is *combustible*—would you call that far-fetched? Or would you be satisfied that I had mentioned a positive quality of the paper? But what does 'combustible' mean? That the paper is actually burning? No. That it is not burning? Not exactly, since a glass of water also is not burning, but we do not call a glass of water 'combustible'. Does it not then simply mean that the paper *could* burn, that 'to be on fire' is one of its potentialities? It *is not* on fire, but it *might* be.

when they had quite a different brain. Or perhaps, since you are not, in fact, a neurologist with a convenient hypothesis handy, you might allow that just at the moment you are not in a position to give an entirely adequate account of the matter. This would then give me the opportunity of putting it to you that your 'past experience' of a present object A is simply the more or less elaborately organized collection of images that immediately present themselves whenever we are directly faced with the actual object A.

My past experiences of A are the (mental) associations that the sight of A now has for me. If I now see a chair I *automatically have at the same time* certain images, either implicit or explicit (in which latter case we call them 'memories'), of myself sitting on things like A or of seeing other people sitting on them. The actual sight of a chair, together with an accompanying image of sitting on one, enables me to say—without any hesitation at all, without any rational act of inference whatsoever—'This is for sitting on'. The (negative) image of sitting is given together with the (positive) sight of a chair, and determines the chair for what it is. An act of inference is only involved if the object with which we are faced is unfamiliar (i.e. we have no past experience of it, and present images arising in association with it are inadequate to determine it); and in this case we have to set in motion the complicated machinery of *thinking* about it, or perhaps we may even have to acquire the necessary 'past experiences' by experimenting with it. But even in such a case as this, the inadequacy of our images associated with the actual sight of the object is enough to determine it immediately as 'strange object, to be treated with caution'. In other words, even when we resort to inference to determine an object, it has *already* been determined (as 'requiring investigation') by negatives (i.e. images) *given in immediate experience together with the positive object.*

Perhaps we can now come to Sartre's waiter, who is no doubt waiting for us.[2] The point is, that a man is not a waiter as a stone is a stone. You can take a stone and enumerate all its qualities (actual and potential) and the stone *is* all those things (actually or potentially) *all the time*. But if we enumerate the qualities of a waiter we shall find that we have a list of various tasks or duties to be performed at different times of the day. To be a waiter is to get up at 5:30 a.m., to take the tram to the café where he works, to start up the coffee percolator, to sweep the floor, to polish the tables, to put them outside on the terrace, to attend to the customers, and so on and so forth. But a man cannot in the very nature of things do all these things at once; he can only do them one at a time. If he is sweeping the floor he cannot also be polishing the tables and attending to the customers. This means that he can never be completely a waiter in the sense that a stone is completely a stone; for he cannot fulfil all the requirements of 'being a waiter' at once. He may attempt to realize his 'state of being a waiter' by throwing himself heart and soul into his work and even by exaggerating the typical gestures associated with waiters; nevertheless he can never succeed in coinciding absolutely with his aim of 'being a waiter'.

The negative here is obvious—to be a stone is simply to be a thing, but to be a waiter is to perform a series of tasks one after another and *not* all at once. The waiter is determined as a waiter not so much by what he actually *is* doing, but by all the things that he is *not* doing but that he recognizes it is his duty to do. The waiter is determined by his negatives.

But the waiter is separated from (or trying to be) a waiter, not a journalist nor a diplomat. This simply means that at some point in his life he *chose* to be a waiter (i.e. to *aim* at being a waiter in the sense just described) and not to be a journalist or a diplomat. This means that his immediate world is so organized that 'being a waiter' is present, 'being a dishwasher' is absent (though perhaps not so far absent as he might wish), 'being a journalist' is far absent, and 'being a diplomat' is very remotely absent indeed.[c]

But all these absences (or negatives), by which his present ('being a waiter') is determined, normally remain on the level of immediate unreflexive experience (or consciousness—he is *conscious* of them, but not *aware* of them, which is a distinction to which I refer, if I remember rightly, in the letter to Mr. Dias on *satisampajañña*.)[3] If he is asked 'Are you a diplomat?' he will answer 'No, I am a waiter' without even having to think about it (just as you answered your enquirer 'A chair is something to sit on' without having to think about it). If these absences, these negatives, these determinations of what he is (a waiter), were present on the reflexive level instead of remaining on the level of immediacy, he would spend his day muttering to himself 'I am neither a journalist nor a diplomat, but a waiter; and if I do not behave myself I shall perhaps become a dishwasher'; but normally, unless he is a very neurotic waiter, this does not happen.

'Man is not a substance that thinks, but a separation from all substance.' (*6ET*, p. 113) If man were a substance (as a stone is a substance) he would entirely coincide with himself, and no thought (which is necessarily teleological) would be possible. The stone does not think because it is already fully and completely a stone, but the waiter (who is at best only teleologi-

c. Note that the relative distances of the absences, i.e. their perspective, is an important consideration. A waiter is only just 'not a dishwasher' but very thoroughly 'not a diplomat'. A journalist, on the other hand, would be more nearly equidistant from dishwashing and diplomacy.

cally aiming at being a waiter) is obliged to think about all the tasks he has to perform in order to be a waiter, an aim that is never fulfilled. Similarly with 'I am not, therefore I think.' (*6ET*, p. 113)

You say 'The Dhamma, I thought, was based on the higher levels of immediate experiences, as for instance the realization of the *pañc'upādānakkhandhā*.' This is not very clear. The practice of the Dhamma is carried out in a state of *satisampajañña* (as I remark in DHAMMA), and *satisampajañña* is reflexive experience and *not* immediate experience. Certainly there are different levels of *satisampajañña* (as when an attitude of *satisampajañña* is adopted towards *satisampajañña* on a lower level), but even the lowest level of *satisampajañña* is reflexive and not immediate.

I am not anxious to go into much detail here on *pañc'upādānakkhandhā*, partly because it would be largely a repetition of what I have already said in *Notes on Dhamma*, a detailed study of which you are postponing until they are printed. But a certain amount can be said. It is a mistake to say that *viññāṇa* is composed of *vedanā, saññā*, and *saṅkhārā*. The *five* items, *rūpa, vedanā, saññā, saṅkhārā*, and *viññāṇa*, can also be regarded as *three*: *viññāṇa* and *nāma-rūpa*, where *nāma* is *vedanā, saññā*, and *saṅkhārā*.[4] From VIÑÑĀṆA and from NĀMA (c) you will see that *viññāṇa* (or consciousness) is to be regarded as the *presence of nāma-rūpa* and is *not* to be included in *nāma*. It is absolutely necessary to start one's thinking from the *experience* (*nāmarūpaṃ saha viññāṇena*—D.15/ii,64)[5] as the basic unit. Each experience consists of these five items, and each fresh experience consists of a fresh set of these five items.

You quote the passage from DHAMMA about the shady tree and putting it in brackets reflexively; and then you say 'The *vedanā, saññā, saṅkhārā, viññāṇa* are in me—*rūpa* is in the tree. Or is the *rūpa* also in me?'[d] This is a confusion of thought that arises from not taking the experience as the basic unit. If there were no experience there would be no *tree* and no *me*; consequently the experience has priority over *tree* and *me*, in the sense that the *tree* and *me* depend upon the occurrence of the experience. It is therefore a confusion to reverse the situation and ask which part of the experience is 'in me' and which part 'in the tree'. All that can be said is that 'there is experience of a shady tree', and that this experience can be analysed into the *pañc'upādānakkhandhā*. One can say that *rūpa, vedanā, saññā, saṅkhārā*, and *viññāṇa* (and also the *tree* and *me*) are in the experience

**d.** What happens when my immediate experience of a tree is 'put in brackets' and seen reflexively is that the 'tree' becomes 'an example of *rūpa*' and 'I' become 'an example of *attavādupādāna*, of holding to the assertion of *self*'.

(more strictly they *constitute* the experience), but one cannot ask where the experience is.

You raise the question of other people: 'What happens when I meet person B?' The whole question of other people is extremely involved, and cannot be dealt with before one has settled the question of oneself. But I think Sartre's account (of which Blackham gives a *précis*) is correct in principle. I do not think the question can be profitably discussed here, partly on account of the complexity and partly because it is not really necessary for an understanding of the Dhamma. What can be said is this. The appearance of another person besides myself does not in any very simple way make two *pañc'upādānakkhandhā* instead of just one, for the reason that nobody can see them both in the same way at the same time (like two marbles) and then count 'one, two'. The appearance of somebody else is a certain *modification* of my experience that requires elaborate description.

With your paragraph 'The whole of the Dhamma applies to me...', I see no reason, in a general way, to disagree. The Dhamma concerns me and me alone, just as it concerns you and you alone, and everybody else in the same way.

I do not actually recall the details of our conversation about the resentment that arises when sentence is passed on one found guilty, but I offer this suggestion. In the first place it is necessary to be 'authentic' and not to deceive oneself. One says to oneself 'I am a Judge by my own free choice, and if I wished to stop being a Judge at any time there is nothing to prevent me. Therefore, whatever I do as a Judge is my own responsibility. Now, I choose to continue to be a Judge, and this means that I choose to perform all the functions expected of a Judge, amongst which is the passing of sentence on guilty prisoners.' One then goes on to say 'But although it is incumbent upon a Judge to pass the sentence prescribed by Law on guilty prisoners, it is by no means incumbent upon him to feel resentment when he does so. If, therefore, I feel resentment when I do pass sentence I am going beyond what is expected of me. This resentment does no good to the prisoner; it does no good to me; and it is not required by Law. Furthermore, I do not know this prisoner personally, and he has done no harm to me, and there is no conceivable reason why I should allow myself to become personally affected by his misdeeds or his fate. My duty, for which I accept responsibility, is to pass the prescribed sentence, nothing more. Let me therefore perform my duty and not concern myself further in the matter.'

**[L. 52]** **28 April 1963**

As you probably know, I have been suffering, for many years, from the effects of chronic amœbiasis. But what perhaps you do not know is that last June I developed a complication of a nervous nature. This nervous disorder is particularly disagreeable for a *bhikkhu*, and involves the practice of a restraint that is not required of laymen. These disorders not only make my life uncomfortable, but also (which is of far greater consequence) leave me with little hope of making any further progress in the Buddhasāsana in this life. This being the situation, I decided upon suicide; and I did in fact, several months ago, make an attempt (which failed only because the method chosen was inadequate). My doctor is fully informed both of my bodily disorders and of my intentions, and he has done and continues to do what he can to ease the situation. However, my condition does not improve, and I am still of the same mind.

As regards Vinaya and Dhamma I am well aware of the situation and do not need to seek the advice of others. Suicide, though a fault, is not (contrary to a widespread opinion) a grave offence in Vinaya (it is a *dukkaṭa*);[1] and as regards Dhamma I know better than anyone else how I am placed. Taking all these matters into consideration I do not find, at least as far as my own personal situation is concerned, any very strong reason (though I regret the *dukkaṭa*) to restrain me from taking my life (naturally, I am speaking only of my own case—for others there may be, and most probably are, very grave objections of one kind or another to suicide). My condition and my state of mind vary from time to time; and whereas on some days I may think weeks or possibly even months ahead, on others it is painful and distasteful to me to think even a few days ahead.

There remains, of course, the practical difficulty of actually killing oneself (having already tried once, I am aware that it is not very easy), but with sufficient determination it should not prove altogether impossible.

All this is purely for your information, and no action on your part is called for (except that I would ask you to treat the matter as confidential). But the reason that I am telling you this is that, as I gather from your letters, you seem to be of the opinion that I have managed to gain some understanding of the Buddha's Teaching, and that you wish to profit by it. Since this appears to be your view, I feel that I should warn you that time may be short. Although no fixed term to my life is decided upon, the situation remains precarious, and I cannot give any assurance that I shall not end my life without further warning. If, then, you have questions to ask, or any matters to discuss, I would advise you not to delay. Do not hesitate, thinking perhaps that you may be disturbing me. If I should find there is disturbance, nothing obliges me to reply to your letters, and I can easily ask you to stop writing.

I am quite well aware, of course, that in philosophical matters one's questions do not all arise at once, but that very often the settling of one question gives rise to another, and when that is settled still further questions may arise; and also, one's ideas take time to mature. But this cannot be helped—questions that have not yet arisen cannot, obviously, be asked. All that I wish to say is that when you do have questions that seem important it might be well not to postpone asking them.

Now that I have said so much, it is possible that you may appreciate something of the perverse complexities of the situation in which I find myself. Not the least of the peculiarities of my situation is the fact that, for one reason or another, there is nobody that I know of who is in a position to give me advice. This means that I have to rely entirely on my own judgement in whatever decisions I may take—whether it is a question, for example, of determining what I (or others) stand to lose by my killing myself, or a question, for another example, of the advisability of writing this letter to you.

In this last connection, something more should perhaps be said. On the one hand, I do not know you very well, and there is always a risk of misunderstanding in being too open with comparative strangers. On the other hand, it is absolutely necessary in the present circumstances that I find someone with more than average intelligence and *saddhā* with whom to entrust certain matters—specifically, the *Notes on Dhamma*. I do not know of anyone in Ceylon who, simply upon reading them, would see whether or not the *Notes* are correct (I am not speaking so much of the note on *FS*); nevertheless it seems to me that you are one of the possibly very few who might suspect that they are in fact correct (whether or not they are *adequate* is quite another matter). Since, then, I do not think that I should quickly find a more suitable (or more interested) person than yourself, I feel that it is advisable not to keep you in ignorance of the fact that I shall very possibly take my own life.

With reference to my last letter, there are one or two points that perhaps need further clarification. I think that I said that whenever I am faced with a real chair I am also presented simultaneously with various images, implicit or explicit, of myself or others sitting on such things as I now see. The *explicit* images, I said, are what we call 'memories', and I now wish to add that the *implicit* images are more or less what we call 'instincts'. Thus, if I am tired and I see a chair, I may not have a specific *memory* of sitting on one on previous occasions, but I shall simply have an *instinct* to go and sit on it. This, though it is *conscious* (in the sense referred to in the letter on *satisampajañña*) does not reach the level of *awareness*—I am conscious of my instincts but usually (unless I perform a deliberate act of *reflexion*, which is a practice to be encouraged) not aware of them (they are on the level of immediacy).

Possibly the word 'image' may not be clear to you. An image need not be *visual*—it might be *verbal* (as when some set of words, a formula for example, runs through our mind), or *tactile* (we can imagine the experience of stroking a cat without actually visualizing a cat), or *gustatory* (we can imagine the taste of castor oil, perhaps even to the point of actual nausea) and so on. A *thought* or an *idea* is an image (or a succession of them), and you can often use one of these words in place of 'image' if you prefer (though 'image' is really more satisfactory, since there are immediate images ['instincts', for example] that do not reach the reflexive status of thoughts or ideas).

In my opinion it is a matter of considerable importance to see the universal presence of the negative. It is not a very easy thing to do (since it requires one to break with habitual ways of thinking), but once it is done one has quite a different way of looking at things generally—at the world—to the slovenly positivistic view that most people normally have, and that modern scientific methods of education do so much to encourage. Without seeing the negative it is impossible to understand what is meant by 'The essence of man is to be in a situation' (see Preface and also Blackham, *passim*). And yet, even when this negative view has been achieved, there is still a start to be made on the Buddha's Teaching.

**[L. 53] 2 May 1963**

In the list of queries that you sent me about a month ago, there occurs the following passage: '... I try to get my existence by identifying myself with being a waiter. I fear to separate, or fear that I would get lost. The waiter gives me an identity, a position. So it helps me to exist. "No one wants to be an individual human being" through fear that he "would vanish tracelessly."'

I was puzzled by this passage, since I took the second part ('No one wants...') as a continuation of the first part, which is obviously dealing with Sartre's waiter (and which I hope to have explained—perhaps not adequately—in my long reply to you). But I did not recall that Sartre has said anywhere that nobody wants to be an individual human being through fear of vanishing tracelessly.

I now find, however, that it is a quotation from Kierkegaard.[1] What Kierkegaard is saying is that the spirit of the age (the Nineteenth Century) is such that men have become too cowardly to look facts in the face and to accept the burden and responsibility of living as individual human beings. (Like a judge who disowns all responsibility for passing sentence on a prisoner, saying that it is the Judiciary, not he, that is responsible.)[2] People (says Kierkegaard) are now afraid that if they let go of the collective or universal safeguards by which they are assured of an identity (membership of a professional association, of a political party, of the world-historical-process, etc.) they would altogether cease to exist. (Things, apparently, were bad enough in Kierkegaard's day, but the Twentieth Century is a thousand times worse. The most glaring example in modern times is the Communist Party; and in Communist countries if you do not have a Party Membership Card you are counted as nothing.)

This passage, then, about the fear of vanishing tracelessly, has no connexion with Sartre's waiter. A man can be a waiter and also an individual human being: what he can *not* be is a member of the Communist Party (or in Kierkegaard's day, a Hegelian philosopher—and it is well known how much Marx borrowed from Hegel) while still remaining an individual human being. In the first case there is no contradiction; in the second case there *is* a contradiction (a communist—like the judge who regards himself purely as an anonymous member of the Judiciary—is *inauthentic* [in Heidegger's terms] or *in bad faith* [in Sartre's terms]). The fact that Sartre himself became a member of the Communist Party for a certain time is one of the minor comedies of the last few years.

**[L. 54]** **4 May 1963**

Thank you for your three letters of 1st, 1st, and 2nd, respectively. There does not seem to be anything in the first two calling for immediate comment (unless my letter of 28th April ranks as one of Huxley's 'marsupials of the mind' or one of the Ven. Ñāṇamoli Thera's 'midnight horrors'). So I shall reply only to your last kindly and distressed letter (hoping that the initial shock has worn off and that you have recovered some of your normal composure).

What I told you in my letter of the 28th about my ill health and suicidal intentions was 'for information only'. If it were not for the fact that you are at present engaged in having the *Notes* printed I should have kept quiet. In other words, I thought I ought to give you the opportunity of changing your mind (if you wished to do so) before you were committed in an enterprise that you might later regret—that is, in the event of my suicide. I wish to emphasize this fact, and to assure you that the risk still remains unchanged.

About all the various points that you raise, you will perhaps excuse me for not replying in detail. During the past year, naturally enough, I have had time to consider the situation from many angles, and the points that you have brought to my attention have not escaped me. But my situation is considerably more complex (and also more simple) than I think you are aware of, and there are certain aspects of it that I am not in a position to discuss with you.[1] This means that if we do attempt to discuss the situation (apart from such things as the purely medical aspect) with one another, we are almost certain to be at cross purposes, and it is for this reason that I do not wish to say more than I have said above, and would ask you to consider this as being the only point at issue.

Regarding the question of a *bhikkhu*'s suicide, the view that it is better for him to disrobe rather than kill himself when he finds he can make no further progress is—if you will forgive me for saying so—a layman's view. There was at least one *bhikkhu* in the Buddha's day—the Ven. Channa Thera—who (in spite of what the Commentary says) killed himself as an *arahat* owing to incurable sickness; and there are many other examples in the Suttas of *bhikkhus* who—as *ariyapuggalas*—took their own life (and some became *arahat* in doing so—Ven. Godhika Thera, Ven. Vakkali Thera, for example).[2] One (who became *arahat*), the Ven. Sappadāsa Thera, could not get rid of lustful thoughts for twenty-five years, and took his razor to cut his throat, saying

> *satthaṃ vā āharissāmi, ko attho jīvitena me*
> *kathaṃ hi sikkhaṃ paccakkhaṃ kālaṃ kubbetha mādiso* (Thag. 407)
>
> I shall use the knife—what use is this life to me?
> How can one such as I meet his death having put aside the training (i.e. disrobed)?

And the Buddha himself warns (in the Mahāsuññata Sutta—M.122/iii,109-18) that one who becomes a layman after following a teacher may fall into the hells when he dies. There is no doubt at all that, whatever public opinion may think, a *bhikkhu* is probably worse advised to disrobe than to end his life—that is, of course, if he is genuinely practising the Buddha's Teaching. It is hard for laymen (and even, these days, for the majority of *bhikkhus*, I fear) to understand that when a *bhikkhu* devotes his entire life to one single aim, there may come a time when he can no longer turn back—lay life has become incomprehensible to him. If he cannot reach his goal there is only one thing for him to do—to die (perhaps you are not aware that the Buddha has said that 'death' for a *bhikkhu* means a return to lay life—Opamma Saṃy.—S.xx.10/ii,271).

There is in my present situation (since the nervous disorder that I have had for the past year consists of an abnormal, persistent, sometimes fairly acute, erotic stimulation) a particularly strong temptation to return to the state of a layman; and I have not the slightest intention of giving in to it. This erotic stimulation can be overcome by successful *samatha* practice (mental concentration), but my chronic amœbiasis makes this particularly difficult for me. So for me it is simply a question of how long I can stand the strain. (I do not think you would think the better of me for disrobing under these conditions.)

I must thank you most sincerely for the offers of material help—visits to specialists, change of environment, and so on—and these we can discuss later. But here again there are complexities. For example, I am best able to deal with the situation described above in a dry climate and living alone (and I have found no better place than Būndala); so a change of environment will almost certainly be a change for the worse. And Dr. de Silva has already consulted specialists on my behalf, and the drugs prescribed are of some help. I may say that, though I am usually uncomfortable, I am certainly not in any kind of pain, and I am not in the least worried about my situation—worry I leave to other people (my doctor, I think, was worried to begin with, but he seems to be getting over it quite nicely; and now perhaps you are worried).

Because Būndala suits me better than anywhere else I am not anxious to leave here even for a few days. If, however, you are going ahead with the *Notes* and they reach the proof stage, it may be advisable for me to come for two or three days to see the printer personally. In the meantime, since I have a certain interest in seeing that the printing is properly done, it is perhaps unlikely that I shall attempt to abolish myself. But please do not be too disappointed if you find that I meet your constructive suggestions for improving matters with evasive answers—after all, neither this letter nor that of the 28th is, properly speaking, an appeal for help (though I am nonetheless appreciative of the offers of help so readily made).

**[L. 55]** **15 May 1963**

About Huxley's strange creatures of the mind, and the late Ven. Ñāṇamoli Thera's mental monsters and hostile systems. Though few such experiences have come my way, I have no doubt at all that these curious (and perhaps terrifying) things are to be met with in certain mental circumstances. That weird and fantastic creatures do actually exist, though normally invisible to us, we may gather from the reports (in the Suttas, for example; see the Lakkhaṇa Saṃy.—S.xix./ii,254-62) of people who have practised meditation and developed the *dibbacakkhu* or 'divine eye' (I am occasionally asked by visitors whether in my meditations I have 'had any experiences'—quite an improper question to put to a *bhikkhu*—and by this they usually mean 'have I seen any *devā* or other unusual objects?' Fortunately I am able to assure them that I have not seen any at all, not a single one.)

But all these various creatures, whether they exist in their own right—i.e. are independently conscious—or not (and this distinction is not always easy to make simply by looking at them), are of interest only to the lover of variety, to the collector of strange objects. To suppose, as Huxley does (and it is this fidelity of his to the scientific method that condemns him never to be more than a second-rate thinker), that by collecting and examining the various objects of the mind one can learn something essential about the nature of mind is much the same as supposing that one can learn something about the structure of the telescope by making a list of the great variety of objects one can see through it. The phenomenological method (of existential thinkers) is not in the least concerned with the peculiarities (however peculiar they may be) of the individual specimen; what it is concerned with is the universal nature of experience as such.

Thus, if a phenomenologist sees a duck-billed platypus, he does *not* exclaim with rapture 'What a strange creature! What a magnificent addition to the sum of human knowledge (and also to my collection of stuffed curiosities)!'; he says, instead, 'This is an example of a living being,' thus putting the platypus with all its duck-billed peculiarities 'in brackets' and considering only the universal characteristics of his experience of the platypus. But a dog would have done just as well; for a dog, too, is 'an example of a living being'; and besides, there is no need to go all the way to Australia to see one. The phenomenologist does not seek *variety*, he seeks *repetition*—repetition, that is to say, of experience (what it is experience *of* does not interest him in the least), so that he may eventually come to understand the *nature* of experience (for experience and existence are one and the same). And this is just as true of imaginary (mental) experience as of real experience. The

Ven. Sāriputta Thera, for all his proficiency in the practice of *jhāna*, had not developed the *dibbacakkhu* (Thag. 996). And even so he was the leading disciple of the Buddha, and the foremost in *paññā*, or understanding. After the Buddha himself there was nobody who understood the Dhamma as well as he—and yet, on his own admission, he was unable to see 'even a goblin' (Ud. IV,4/40). Evidently, then, the seeing of strange creatures, in normal or abnormal states of mind, does not advance one in wisdom.

When one is dead one is at the mercy of one's publishers (a strong argument for staying alive!), and I do not know how many of the late Ven. Ñāṇamoli Thera's essays (in the BPS booklet)[1] he would have wanted to appear in print. Naturally, I was aware of many of his views, since we used to exchange lengthy letters; but that was at a time when my own views were still unsettled. On reading these essays now, I see much that is quite unacceptable—but alas! he is no longer here for me to dispute the matter with. He was, in my opinion (and perhaps also his own), a better poet than prose writer; nevertheless he manages to infuse a certain sympathetic personal (and somewhat ambiguous) atmosphere into many of his passages.[2] I would suggest a certain caution in reading these essays with too great a thirst for philosophical enlightenment—you might find yourself led into one of the blind alleys of thought from which the author himself is unable to show the way out (the last essay in particular is dangerous ground—so also pp. 27-30)—, though from other aspects, perhaps, you may well derive enjoyment.

**[L. 56]** **16 May 1963**

For several reasons I should prefer you not to discuss my situation with anyone else, at least for the present (though I shall not prohibit you).

In the first place, I do not think there is any great urgency in the matter. As I think I told you, it is improbable that I shall decide to kill myself (unless the situation takes an unexpected turn for the worse) so long as there is the business of shepherding the *Notes* through the press to be done. (This does not necessarily mean, of course, that I am determined to kill myself the moment that they are safely in print.) So you can probably count on a breathing-space in which nothing very much will happen. Incidentally, I very rarely act on impulse, and it is most unlikely that I shall end my life in a sudden fit of depression. If I should decide upon it (and it still remains only a *possibility*), it would be as the result of deliberation; and I should do it only after careful preparation. Also, though the Ven. Siridhamma Thera is fairly well informed about my situation, there are things that I have not told him (or anyone else), and I do not think he would be able to add very much to what you already know. (It would rather be a case of playing *Hamlet* without the Prince of Denmark.) Besides, I do not really feel the need to 'be discussed'—not, indeed, that I have any particular objection, but simply that I do not see that the situation requires it (though, admittedly, my view of the situation is quite different from yours).

In the second place, I hope to be seeing Dr. de Silva personally in the course of the next two or three months, and I had rather discuss the situation (from the medical point of view) fully with him before anything is decided.

Do not think that I regard suicide as praiseworthy—that there can easily be an element of weakness in it, I am the first to admit (though the Stoics regarded it as a courageous act)—, but I certainly regard it as preferable to a number of other possibilities. (I would a hundred times rather have it said of the *Notes* that the author killed himself as a *bhikkhu* than that he disrobed; for *bhikkhus* have become *arahats* in the act of suicide, but it is not recorded that anyone became *arahat* in the act of disrobing.)

By all means let the *devas* prevent it—let them bring about some improvement in my health, some easing of the situation, and all may be well; or let them send sudden death, an elephant, a *polonga* (there are plenty here), or simply a heart attack, and again the horrid deed of suicide is averted. But in the meantime the situation remains.

## [L. 57] 19 May 1963

Your question about *satisampajañña*.[1] *Observing* the particular 'doing' or 'feeling' is *reflexive* experience. The 'doing' or 'feeling' itself (whether it is *observed* or not) is *immediate* experience. But since one obviously cannot *observe* a 'doing' or a 'feeling' unless that 'doing' or 'feeling' *is at the same time present*, there is no reflexive experience (at least in the strict sense used here) that does not contain or involve immediate experience. Reflexive experience is a *complex structure* of which immediate experience is a *less complex part* (it is possible that I use the term 'reflexive consciousness' a little ambiguously—i.e. either to denote reflexive experience *as a whole* or to distinguish the purely reflexive part of reflexive experience from the immediate part).

*Yes*: observing the 'general nature' of an experience is reflexion (though there are also other kinds of reflexion). *No*: in reflexively observing the 'general nature' of an experience you have *not* 'left out the immediate experience'; you have merely 'put the immediate experience in brackets'—that is to say, by an effort of will you have *disregarded* the individual peculiarities of the experience and *paid attention* to the general characteristics (just as you might disregard a witness' stammer when he is giving evidence and pay attention to the words he is uttering). You simply consider the immediate experience as 'an example of experience in general'; but this does not in any way abolish the immediate experience (any more than your disregarding the stammer of the witness stops his stammering).

A *sekha* (*bhikkhu* or *layman*), as you rightly say, is a *sotāpanna*, a *sakadāgāmī*, or an *anāgāmī*, and the word '*sekha*' means 'one who is training (*scil.* to become *arahat*)'. If he is *sotāpanna* he has *at most* seven more human existences—he *cannot* take an eighth human birth.[2] But if (as a *bhikkhu* in good health) he exerts himself now in the practice of meditation he may become *sakadāgāmī, anāgāmī*, or even *arahat*, in this very life. In this case he either reduces or completely cancels the number of fresh existences (as man or *deva*) he will have to undergo. If, however, he spends his time doing jobs of work, talking, or sleeping, he may die still as a *sotāpanna* and have to endure up to seven more human existences (not to speak of heavenly existences). In this sense, therefore, these things are obstacles for the *sekha*: they prevent him from *hastening* his arrival at *arahattā*, but they *cannot* prevent his *ultimate* arrival (see 'The Mirror of the Dhamma', BPS *Wheel* 54, p. 39, verse 9).[3]

I am delighted to hear that you are shocked to learn from the Buddha that a *sekha bhikkhu* can be fond of work, talk, or sleep. (I make no apology for speaking bluntly since (i) if I do not do it nobody else will, and (ii) as I have already told you, time may be short.)

Quite in general, I find that the Buddhists of Ceylon are remarkably complacent at being the preservers and inheritors of the Buddha's Teaching, and remarkably ignorant of what the Buddha actually taught. Except by a few learned *theras* (who are dying out), the contents of the Suttas are practically unknown. This fact, combined with the great traditional reverence for the Dhamma as the National Heritage, has turned the Buddha's Teaching into an immensely valuable antique Object of Veneration, with a large placard in front, 'DO NOT TOUCH'. In other words, the Dhamma in Ceylon is now totally divorced from reality (if you want statistical evidence, tell me how many English-educated graduates of the University of Ceylon have thought it worthwhile to become *bhikkhus*).[4] It is simply taken for granted (by *bhikkhus* and laymen alike) that there are not, and cannot possibly be, any *sekha bhikkhus* (or laymen) actually walking about in Ceylon today. People can no longer imagine what kind of a creature a *sotapānna* might conceivably be, and in consequence superstitiously credit him with every kind of perfection—but deny him the possibility of existence.

I venture to think that if you actually read through the whole of the Vinaya and the Suttas you would be aghast at some of the things a real live *sotāpanna* is capable of. As a *bhikkhu* he is capable of suicide (but so also is an *arahat*—I have already quoted examples); he is capable of breaking all the lesser Vinaya rules (M.48/i,323-5; A.III,85/i,231-2); he is capable of disrobing on account of sensual desires (e.g. the Ven. Citta Hatthisāriputta—A.VI,60/iii,392-9); he is capable (to some degree) of anger, ill-will, jealousy, stinginess, deceit, craftiness, shamelessness, and brazenness (A.II,16/i,96). As a layman he is capable (contrary to popular belief) of breaking any or all of the five precepts (though as soon as he has done so he recognizes his fault and repairs the breach, unlike the *puthujjana* who is content to leave the precepts broken).

There are some things in the Suttas that have so much shocked the Commentator that he has been obliged to provide patently false explanations (I am thinking in particular of the *arahat*'s suicide in M.144/iii,266 and in the Saḷāyatana Saṃy.—S.xxxv.87/iv,55-60 and of a drunken *sotāpanna* in the Sotāpatti Saṃy.—S.lv.24/v,375-7). What the *sotāpanna* is absolutely incapable of doing is the following (M.115/iii,64-5):—

(i) To take any determination (*saṅkhāra*) as permanent,
(ii) To take any determination as pleasant,
(iii) To take any thing (*dhamma*) as self,
(iv) To kill his mother,
(v) To kill his father,
(vi) To kill an *arahat*,
(vii) Maliciously to shed a Buddha's blood,
(viii) To split the Saṅgha,
(ix) To follow any teacher other than the Buddha.

All these things a *puthujjana* can do.

Why am I glad that you are shocked to learn that a *sekha bhikkhu* can be fond of talk (and worse)? Because it gives me the opportunity of insisting that unless you bring the *sekha* down to earth the Buddha's Teaching can never be a reality for you. So long as you are content to put the *sotāpanna* on a pedestal well out of reach, it can never possibly occur to you that it is your duty to become *sotāpanna* yourself (or at least to make the attempt) here and now in this very life; for you will simply take it as axiomatic that you cannot succeed. As Kierkegaard puts it,

> Whatever is great in the sphere of the universally human must … not be communicated as a subject for admiration, but as an ethical *requirement*. (*CUP*, p. 320)

This means that you are not required to *admire* a *sotāpanna*, but to *become* one.

Let me illustrate the matter in a different way. It is possible that you were living as a young man in India in the Buddha's day, and that at the same time there was a young girl of a neighbouring family who had been with her parents to hear the Buddha teach. And she may have understood the Buddha's Teaching and become *sotāpanna*. And perhaps she might have been given to you in marriage. And you, being a *puthujjana*, would not know that she was a *sekha* (for remember, a *puthujjana cannot recognize an ariya*—an *ariya* can only be recognized by another *ariya*). But even though she was *sotāpanna* she might have loved you, and loved being loved by you, and loved bearing your children, and enjoyed dressing beautifully and entertaining guests and going to entertainments, and even been pleased at the admiration of other men. And she might have taken a pride in working to keep your house in order, and enjoyed talking to you and to your friends and relations. But every now and again, when she was alone, she would have called to mind her *sotāpanna*'s understanding of the true nature of things and been secretly ashamed and disgusted at still finding delight in all these satisfactions (which she would see as essentially *dukkha*). But, being busy with her duties and pleasures as your wife, she would not have had the time to do much practice, and would have had to be content with the thought that she had only seven more human births to endure at the most.

Now suppose that one day you had gone to see the Buddha, and he had told you that your wife was not a *puthujjana* like yourself, but an *ariya*, one of the Elect—would you have been content to put her out of reach on a pedestal (where she would, no doubt, have been very unhappy), saying to yourself 'Ah, that is too difficult an attainment for a humble person like me'? Or would not rather your masculine pride have been stung to the quick and be smarting at the thought that your devoted and submissive wife should be 'one advanced in the Dhamma', while you, the lord and master of the household, remained an ordinary person? I think, perhaps, that you would have made an effort at least to become the equal of your wife.

It is possible that you may have been disturbed by my recent letters in which I have informed you of my situation. I do not mean only by the content (i.e. that it is possible that I may take my life), but also by the style. You may have felt that I have stated the facts in a callous way, that I do not take the matter seriously enough, that I am indifferent to other people's feelings, and that perhaps even some of my remarks are almost offensive. Let me assure you that I have not the slightest desire to offend you or anyone else, and if I have seemed offensive that I am sorry for it. But also let me say that my style is deliberate and is not unconnected with the foregoing remarks about the present total divorce of the Dhamma from reality. The point is this: for me the Dhamma is real, and it is the only thing that I take seriously: if I cannot practise the Dhamma as I wish, I have no further desire to live. Though I say it myself, it seems to me that this attitude is a necessary corrective to the prevalent blindly complacent view of the Dhamma as something to be taken for granted—that is to say, as a dead letter—; and I regard it almost as a duty to reflect this attitude in my writing, even at the risk of giving offence. (For most Buddhists in Ceylon—I will not say for you—there are many things that they take far more seriously than the Dhamma, and when I show too plainly that I regard these as worthless trifles, offence is easily taken.)

I do not know how you will receive this letter. It is easy to make mistakes and to miscalculate the effect of what one says. In any case, please accept my assurances that it is written with the best of intentions and with the desire to communicate to you something that I regard as being of paramount importance.

**[L. 58]** **29 May 1963**

As regards my views on the Abhidhamma Piṭaka, for my general attitude see Preface (a). More particularly, I consider that none of the Abhidhamma is the Buddha's word, and furthermore, that it is a positively misleading compilation, often inconsistent with the Suttas. This does not mean, however, that I regard every single statement in it as false—the short work, the Puggala Paññatti, may well be trustworthy in parts. But I must confess that most of my acquaintance with the Abhidhamma is at second hand. I have never, myself, found anything in it of the slightest value to me, and I normally advise people to leave it entirely alone. If you press me, I might express myself more emphatically on the uselessness and misleadingness of the Abhidhamma, but since I do not think you are violently enamoured of it, perhaps I have said enough.

**[L. 59]** **11 June 1963**

Mr. Perera came this evening and showed me a money order that you had sent him asking him to buy me a knife to replace the missing one. If I had even remotely thought that you were going to do this, I should by no means have sent you the postcard.

What happened was this. When you and your party first arrived the knife was borrowed to cut up some oranges and was then returned to me. Then you all went down to your car, leaving me to take my *dāna*. Shortly afterwards, the boy from the village whom you brought with you came and asked me for the knife. Assuming that you had sent him in order to borrow it again, I gave it to him and thought no more about it. When I did not find it after your departure I thought that, inadvertently, you had probably taken it with you. Hence the postcard. But it may be that the boy wanted it for himself and took this opportunity of asking for it. My command of Sinhala, however, is by no means equal to the task of questioning him about it, even if I felt inclined to do so (which I don't). The village boys frequently ask me for things, and I can never make out whether they want them on loan or as a gift; but once I have given something, even on loan, I find it distasteful to press for its return. Indeed, I now feel rather ashamed at having sent you the postcard at all. In any case, very much merit to you.

When you were here, you remarked that I say much more about reflexion in the *Notes* than is to be found in the Suttas. This, I think, is rather deceptive. Certainly I discuss it more *explicitly* than the Suttas; but it has to be remembered that every time the Suttas mention *sati*, or mindfulness, they are speaking of reflexion; and out of the thirty-seven *bodhipakkhiyā dhammā*, no less than eight are *sati* (in one form or another—four *satipaṭṭhāna*, one *satindriya*, one *satibala*, one *satisambojjhaṅgha*, one *sammāsati* [*maggaṅga*]).

Most of the Suttas were addressed to monks, not laymen (see the Anāthapiṇḍikovāda Sutta, late in the Majjhima,[1] where Anāthapiṇḍika bursts into tears); and monks, in the Buddha's day, were familiar with reflexion through their practice of *samādhi*, or mental concentration (there is no concentration without mindfulness), and they did not need to have the matter explained to them (a swimming instructor can talk more about swimming than a fish, but there is no doubt that a fish can swim better).

But times have changed: people no longer practise mental concentration (not even *bhikkhus*); on the other hand they now read books, which they did not in the Buddha's day. Formerly, people accepted on trust that the practice of concentration and reflexion was possible and had beneficial results, and without more ado they set themselves to practise. Now, however, people want to understand all about things before they actually do them—a change of attitude for which the invention of printing is responsible. (This new attitude has its advantages and its disadvantages. On the one hand, there is now no Buddha to give infallible guidance, and it is necessary to use one's intelligence and think out matters for oneself if one is to discover the right path; but on the other hand, to think out matters for oneself takes time, and this means that one may easily put off starting the actual practice until it is too late in life to make the necessary progress.)

If people today (I am thinking more particularly of Europeans or those with a European education) are going to be got to practise reflexion (and thence concentration) they will ask for information about it first; and it is rather with this in mind that I have discussed the matter so explicitly in the *Notes*. (One of the principal reasons for including *FS*, which is not directly Dhamma, is the fact that it offers a formal justification for the assumption that reflexion is at least *possible*. Without such intellectual justification—which, incidentally, requires some actual experience of reflexion [not necessarily done in awareness of the fact][a] to grasp—many people will not even make the attempt to see if they can do it.)

I am quite prepared to admit that this explicit treatment may perhaps actually hold up certain people, who would get along faster without it—people, that is to say, with good *saddhā* in the Buddha, and who are prepared to sit down at once and practise. From this point of view it will be seen that, far from being an advance on the Suttas (as one might hastily think upon observing that the Suttas omit it), this explicit treatment is really a step backwards: a formal discussion of what the Suttas take for granted as already understood is a retreat to a more elementary stage (this should be clear from the fact that the existential philosophers understand and practise reflexion, but do *not* understand the essence of the Buddha's Teaching—the Four Noble Truths).

## [L. 60] 22 June 1963

I wish to repeat what I said earlier, namely, that I do not want you to think that you are under any obligation whatsoever to publish the *Notes* or to get them published. If you find it distasteful to enlist the aid of other people in

**a.** If this were not so, it would fail to be a justification, since the *form* of such a communication must exemplify the *content*, or *quidquid cognoscitur, per modum cognoscentis cognoscitur*. (See *FS* (g).)

this matter, I have no desire to press you to do so. In particular, please do not interpret my having told you of my possible suicidal intentions (which remain unchanged) as an attempt to force you to take action. What I am asking of you is not that you should publish the *Notes*—which is your affair—, but that you should undertake the responsibility of ensuring that *if* they are published at all they are published properly and without any alterations. No doubt you already understand all this, but there is no harm in my saying it again.

Compared with the *senāsana* or resting place of *bhikkhus* in former days, this *kuṭi* is a well-appointed and luxurious bungalow, and the conditions of life here easy and soft. As regards solitude, however, this place seems to accord with the Buddha's recommendations (A.X,11/v,15-16) that it should be neither too near nor too far from a village, that it should not be crowded by day and should be silent at night, that it should be easily approachable (though the road was, in fact, made after the *kuṭi* was built), and that it should be free from mosquitos and snakes and other such creatures. I do not think it would be easy to find a better place for practice of the *Buddhadhamma*—but for that, alas! it also needs good health. Though places like this are probably rare in Ceylon, I believe they are more frequently found in Burma, where meditation—I do not mean the officially sponsored belly-meditation—is perhaps more practised than it is here.

I have found that, living as a *bhikkhu* at the Island Hermitage, one's attitude towards snakes undergoes a gradual change. There are (or were before the mongoose came) plenty of snakes there, and they are never killed. The Ven. Ñāṇāloka Mahāthera[1] is an adept at catching them and putting them in glass jars for export to the mainland (he must have caught hundreds). After a while I myself managed to catch one or two small ones and found that they are much less ferocious than one thinks. (The late Ven. Ñāṇamoli Thera developed a sympathy for cobras and a corresponding antipathy for mongooses.) The Mahāthera, at one time, so I believe, used to catch *polongas* simply by grasping them suddenly by the neck and the tail; but he was eventually dissuaded by other *bhikkhus* from this rather cavalier method of dealing with them.

Here, I have had several encounters with *polongas*, and they have always behaved in exemplary fashion. Once I was about to tread on one coiled on the path in front of me, but before I put my foot down it quietly uncoiled, moved a couple of yards, and coiled up again behind a small bush. On another occasion I inadvertently touched one under some leaves, and it remained perfectly motionless. But usually they slither away when I get too close. I have always regretted pointing out a snake to laymen, or asking them to remove one, since they invariably kill it or throw stones at it or otherwise maltreat it. (At the Hermitage I was once bitten by a ratsnake that was chasing a rat. The rat got away, and the snake bit my big toe instead. I am told that, now that I have been bitten by such a low caste fellow as a ratsnake, no other snake will deign to touch me.)

You ask whether *aniccatā* (or impermanence) in the Dhamma does not refer to things regarded objectively rather than subjectively. Certainly, *aniccatā* does not not refer to things regarded objectively (note the double negative); and there are, no doubt, passages in the Suttas where this meaning is intended (or at least not excluded). It is clear enough that a person regarding any thing as objectively permanent (as the Christians, for example, regard God or heaven or hell) cannot even begin to understand the Buddha's Teaching. An aspiring Buddhist must first of all understand that there is no single thing (objectively speaking) that lasts for ever.

But if *aniccatā* means no more than this, we soon run into difficulties; for modern physical science, which is as objective as can be, says the same thing—indeed, it goes further and says that everything is constantly changing. And this is precisely the point of view of our modern commentators. The Buddha, as you may know, has said,

> *Yad aniccaṃ taṃ dukkhaṃ;*
> *yaṃ dukkhaṃ tad anattā*
>
> What is impermanent is suffering;
> what is suffering is not-self;

and I was told that one gentleman several years ago argued from this that since a stone is impermanent it must therefore experience suffering. And not only he, but also most of the Buddhist world agree that since a stone is impermanent—i.e. in perpetual flux (according to the scientific concept)—it has no lasting self-identity; that is to say, it is *anattā* or not-self. The notion that a stone feels pain will probably find few supporters outside Jain circles; but this objective interpretation of the Buddha's Teaching of *anattā* is firmly established.

'But what' perhaps you may ask 'is wrong with this?' In the first place, it implies that modern science has caught up with the Buddha's Teaching (which, presumably, we can now afford to throw overboard, since science is bound to make further progress)—see, in this connexion, note (j) in the Preface of *Notes*, beginning 'It is all the fashion …'. In the second place, it involves the self-contradictory notion of universal flux—remember the disciple of Heraclitus, who said that one cannot cross the same river even once (meaning that if everything is in movement there is no movement at all).[a] In the third place, if *aniccatā* refers only to things regarded objectively and not subjectively (as you suggest), the subject is *ipso facto* left out of account, and the only meaning that is left for *attā* or 'self' is the self-identity of the object. But—as I point out in the admittedly very difficult article ATTĀ—the Dhamma is concerned purely and simply with 'self' as subject ('I', 'mine'), which is the very thing that you propose to omit by being objective. The fact is, that the triad, *anicca/dukkha/anattā* has no intelligible application if applied *objectively* to things. The objective application of *aniccatā* is valid in the exact measure that objectivity is valid—that is to say, on a very coarse and limited level only. Objectivity is an abstraction or rationalization from subjectivity—even the scientist when he is engaged on his experiments is *at that time* subjective, but when he has finished his series of experiments he eliminates the subjectivity (himself) and is left with the objective result. This means that though there can be no objectivity without an underlying subjectivity, there can quite possibly be subjectivity without objectivity; and the objective *aniccatā* is only distantly related to the much finer and more subtle subjective *aniccatā*. It must be remembered that it is only the *ariya*, and not the *puthujjana*, who perceives pure subjective *aniccatā* (it is in seeing subjective *aniccatā* that the *puthujjana* becomes *ariya*; and at that time he is wholly subjective—the coarse objective perception of *aniccatā* has been left far behind)—see, in this connexion, *PS* §4 (I think). Objective *aniccatā* can be found outside the Buddha's Teaching, but not subjective *aniccatā*.[b]

---

**a.** I have made a point, in the *Notes*, of objecting to this notion; and one of the reasons why I am anxious that the note on fundamental structure should not be excluded is that it offers a quite different, and essentially subjective (or reflexive) approach to the philosophical problem of change and time. If, as you said, you have managed to gather something from the second part of *FS*, you will perhaps be aware that the objective notion of universal flux is hardly adequate—that the problem of impermanence cannot be dealt with objectively.

**b.** Two points. (i) The word 'subjective' has the same ambiguity as the word 'self': it is used both for the *reflexive attitude* (or, at the minimum, *assertion of the individual point of view*) and for the *subject* ('I', 'myself'). As pointed out in ATTĀ, the *puthujjana* is not able to dissociate these two things, but the *sekha* sees that in the *arahat* the latter (the conceit 'I am') has come to an end while the former (the individual point of view, with the possibility of reflexion) still remains. (Kierkegaard actually identifies reflexion with selfhood.)

(ii) The *Notes* are concerned only with the essential application of the Buddha's Teaching, and consequently there is no mention of objective *aniccatā* (or of other things

Let us, however, consider your particular example—a person of whom you are fond. Suppose it is your son; and suppose (as indeed we may hope) that he has a long life ahead of him and that he arrives at death (which he cannot avoid) as an old man, many years after your own death. *Subjectively* speaking from your point of view, he is impermanent on account of the fact that you yourself die before him and thereby your experience of him is cut off. More strictly speaking, he is impermanent for you on account of the fact that even in this life your experience of him is not continuous—you only see him from time to time. *Objectively* speaking, according to your suggestion, he is impermanent because he himself will die in due course, and you will not survive to witness his death. But if this is to be completely objective (as far as complete objectivity is possible) the last part of this statement is irrelevant. To be completely objective we must say:

All men are mortal.
Lionel Samaratunga's son is a man.
Therefore Lionel Samaratunga's son is mortal.

So stated, it is quite generally true, and is the concern of no-one in particular. It is so generally true that it would serve in a textbook of logic as an example of a syllogism in Barbara[2] (though usually, instead of Lionel Samaratunga's son, it is Socrates whose mortality is logically demonstrated).[c]

But how many students of logic are going to shed tears when they read that Lionel Samaratunga's son is destined to die? How many have so much as heard of Lionel Samaratunga, let alone of his son? (And anyway, how many students of logic shed a tear even over the death of Socrates, of whom they may perhaps have heard?) But if you were to come across this syllogism

---

on the same level). This is by design, not by accident. Most people, as soon as they arrive at the objective perception of *aniccatā*, are quite satisfied that they have now understood the Buddha's Teaching, and they do not see that there is anything further to be done. The *Notes* are *intended* to be difficult—to challenge the complacency of these people and make them really think for themselves (instead of simply agreeing with what they have read in some book or other and imagining that this constitutes thought). It is hardly to be expected at this rate that the *Notes* will ever be popular.

**c.** Actually, to have a syllogism in Barbara, we must be still more general and say: 'All men are mortal. All Lionel Samaratunga's sons are men. Therefore all Lionel Samaratunga's sons are mortal.' In this way it is not assumed that Lionel Samaratunga necessarily has any sons: all that is asserted is that *if* he has any sons, they are mortal. We could even go further and leave out all mention of Lionel Samaratunga, but the syllogism then becomes so general as to have very little content. Every increase in objectivity takes us further from reality.

unexpectedly, it is not impossible that you might feel emotionally moved (as perhaps at this very moment you may be feeling a little uncomfortable at my having chosen an example so near home). And why should this be so? Because you are fond of Lionel Samaratunga's son and cannot regard this syllogism in Barbara, which speaks of his mortality, quite so objectively as a student of logic. In other words, as soon as feeling comes in at the door objectivity flies out the window. Feeling, being private and not public, is subjective and not objective (see my letter to Dr. de Silva discussing Prof. Jefferson's article).[3] And the Buddha has said (A.III.61/i,176) that it is 'to one who feels'[4] that he teaches the Four Noble Truths. So, then, the Dhamma must *essentially* refer to a subjective *aniccatā*—i.e. one that entails *dukkha*—and not, in any *fundamental* sense, to an objective *aniccatā*, which we can leave to students of logic and their professors. (Feeling is not a logical category at all.)

'But how' you might be wondering 'can the death of my son be a subjective matter for me, supposing (as is likely) that I die first?' At this point I am glad to be able to quote the late Venerable Ñāṇamoli Thera (*Pathways*, p. 36):

> Consciousness without an object is impossible—not conceivable—and objects without consciousness, when talked about, are only a verbal abstraction; one cannot talk or think about objects that have no relation to consciousness. The two are inseparable and it is only a verbal abstraction to talk about them separately (legitimate of course in a limited sphere).

The very fact that you are able to *think* the death of your son makes it an object of consciousness (and therefore subjective)—it is an image or a series of images, and images are the objects of mind-consciousness (*manoviññāṇa*). So however objectively you think you are thinking your son's death, the whole thought is within subjectivity. Even though it may be highly improbable that you will *actually* be present at your son's death, you are nevertheless present *in imagination* whenever you think it—you imagine your son an old man lying sick on his deathbed, and you yourself are watching the scene (still in imagination) from some definite point of view (standing at the foot of the bed, for example). At once the perception of your son's impermanence is there (an imaginary perception, of course); but if your imagination is vivid, and you are strongly attached to your son, and you are perhaps fatigued after a trying day's work, this may be enough to bring real tears to your eyes, even though the entire scene is enacted in the realm of the imaginary. (I know, for my own part, that I am far more strongly moved by episodes in books than by those in real life, which usually leave me cold. This, of course, is what the author of the book is aiming at when he uses what Kierkegaard calls 'the foreshortened perspective of the aesthetic,' which leaves out unromantic details—the hero's interview with his bank manager about his overdraft; the heroine's visit to the dentist to have two decayed teeth stopped—in order to heighten the reader's emotional tension. My emotional reaction is entirely in the sphere of the imaginary; for what is the real in this case?—a number of marks in black printer's ink on a few white sheets of paper.)[d]

To sum up. The Dhamma does indeed permit you to regard the material object before you as something that will perish at some future time; but this is not so purely objective a matter as you might think (the purer the objectivity, the more meagre the real content; and, *vice versa*, the reality of the material object before you imposes a limit on the degree of objectivity with which you can regard it). The fact that the mere thought of somebody's or something's eventual decay (about which you will perhaps know nothing when it actually takes place) is capable of arousing feelings of one sort or another is evidence for this.[e] But in any case, as one progresses in meditation one advances from the coarser to the finer, and the objective (speculative or rational) *aniccatā* is the first thing to be eliminated. After that, one gradually reduces mixed subjective-and-objective thoughts or imaginings or memories about past and future *aniccatā*. And finally, one is wholly concentrated on perception of *aniccatā* in the *present* experience; and this is purely subjective. Only when this has been achieved is it possible to extend the same pure subjectivity to past and future (this is called *dhammanvaye ñāṇaṃ*, to which I make references in NA CA SO and PAṬICCASAMUPPĀDA (a); this,

---

**d.** Incidentally, when an apparently aesthetic writer does *not* use the foreshortened perspective he at once becomes an ethical or moral writer. James Joyce's *Ulysses* is an outstanding example. Though the book was once banned for obscenity, it is nevertheless profoundly moral. The Ven. Soma Thera, when he read it, was inspired with a strong disgust with life and desire for solitude. The book is about seven hundred pages, and takes about as long to read as the total period of time covered by the action of the book—eighteen hours.

**e.** Does a judge feel nothing at the thought of the impending dissolution (which he will not witness) of the material object before him, if that object happens to be a guilty murderer he has just sentenced to death? Justice Amory, I believe, used to treat himself to muffins for tea on such occasions. Did he eat them *objectively*, I wonder. (The fact that one can feel pleasure at the perception of the impermanence of something one dislikes shows that the Buddha's *yad aniccaṃ taṃ dukkhaṃ* is a very much more subtle affair.)

properly speaking, is beyond the range of the *puthujjana*.)

No, I had not heard about the Vietnamese monk who set himself alight. One can admire unreservedly the fortitude of such people, who allow themselves to be burned to death while maintaining a perfect calm. At once one thinks 'Should I be able to do the same?'. If it should happen to me accidentally now, the answer would certainly be no. I should certainly allow myself a grimace and a groan or two (to say the very least). But the comparison is not really just. This monk was evidently already fired internally with enthusiasm or resentment, and from there it may be no very great step to fire oneself externally with petrol and flames. But I feel neither enthusiasm nor resentment at the present time, and rarely even at other times. Besides, the monk evidently had a large and appreciative audience, and this must help a lot. Before an interested and, I think, slightly hostile crowd, one might put up quite a good performance. But these acts of heroism are not uncommon in the world's history. In the editor's notes to my Kierkegaard I find the following:

> Mucius Scaevola is said to have thrust his right hand into the fire and let it burn up before the Etruscan king, Porfinnas, without altering the expression on his face. (*CUP*, p. 568)

But perhaps the most celebrated of these auto-incendiaries is Kalanos. You will remember, no doubt, that Kalanos (the Greek version of the Sanskrit *Kalyāṇa*) was an Indian ascetic—though not a Buddhist—who accompanied Alexander's army on its withdrawal from India. At a certain moment he announced that his time had come to die, and arranged for a funeral pyre to be constructed. He mounted the pyre, had it set alight, and, sitting cross-legged, remained motionless until his body was consumed by the flames.

What an occasion! With the entire Greek army, and probably Alexander the Great himself, watching him; with each one of those hardened and undefeated veterans, themselves no stranger to pain and mutilations, wondering if he himself would be capable of such cold-blooded endurance: with the eyes of posterity upon him (his peculiar fame has come down for more than twenty centuries); and with the honour of Indian asceticism at stake (and Indian asceticism is India);—how could he fail? For a moment one could almost wish to have been Kalanos. And yet, from the point of view of Dhamma, all this is foolishness—a childish escapade. The Christian 'Witness for the Faith' is the martyr, singing hymns in the midst of the flames; the Buddhist 'Witness for the Faith' is the *ariya*, peaceably giving instruction in the Dhamma and leading others to his own attainment.[5]

A man may take his own life for many reasons, and it is impossible to make a general statement; but whenever suicide is a *gesture*—done, that is, to impress or influence or embarrass others—it is always, so it seems to me, a sign of immaturity and muddled thinking. However much we may admire the fortitude of this Vietnamese monk, the wisdom of his action remains very much in doubt. I do not know the details of the provocation offered by the Catholic Head of State, but the monk appears to have killed himself 'fighting for the cause of Buddhism.' Certainly this action is infinitely more honourable than the setting fire to churches and the crowning of statues that seem to be the favoured methods of giving battle in this country; but it does not follow that it is any the less misguided.

It might, perhaps, be as well if you did not destroy my letters to you—those, at least, containing discussion of Dhamma points—in the first place because I may wish to refer you to them, which is easier than writing them afresh each time; and in the second place because they are, in a sense, something of a commentary on the *Notes*, and may be found useful later on. Of course, they are not written with the same care as the *Notes*, and some looseness of thought or expression may be found in them. If you should feel the temptation to destroy them (it has happened before now, and my letters actually were once committed to the flames[6]), I would ask you to return them to me instead; but so long as you are not so tempted, please keep them—for, after all, they belong to you.

## [L. 61]

**27 June 1963**

I am of the opinion that no publisher will accept the *Notes*. They are far too difficult even for the averagely intelligent reader (they are more difficult than I think you suspect—as I expect you will find when you start going into them in detail), and they assume also that the reader is acquainted with the Pali Suttas.[1] This makes their appeal extremely limited, and no publisher can expect to cover his expenses if he publishes them. The sole reason for having them in print (or at least duplicated by cyclostyle) is to make them available for the chance reader (one in a million) who would benefit. I think, therefore, that it would be a waste of effort to approach any publisher with them.

On the other hand, the idea of cyclostyling them is probably good. I am prepared[a] to do the stencilling myself (I have done it before), and in my present condition it has the advantage of being a sedative form of occupation (if I can't do meditation, then stencilling the *Notes* is no worse than lying on my bed). Of course, if you should happen to be successful in getting the necessary support for printing the book in the immediate future, there will then be no need for me to do the stencilling.

If you have no objection, I should be interested to read what Huxley has to say about his chemically produced marsupials of the mind. It is not a matter of importance to me, but simply a curiosity; and on damp days I am sometimes glad of something to read.

**[L. 62]** **3 July 1963**

I have just glanced at the Huxley. I think it is of importance to emphasize that wherever he uses the word 'religion' this has absolutely no connexion (whatever *he* may think about it) with the essence of the Buddha's Teaching (*Dukkha, Samudaya, Nirodha, Magga*). I am aware that Huxley mentions Buddhism; but all his Buddhism (including that of his novels—*After Many A Summer* and so on) is Mahāyāna. And, in spite of all our religious demagogues have to say about it, Mahāyāna is *not* the Buddha's Teaching. People say that it is most desirable at the present time that Buddhists the world over should be united. Perhaps it is desirable, perhaps not; but in whatever way they do propose to unite, it must be done not on the pretext that Mahāyāna correctly interprets the basic Teaching. (Alas! Much that passes in Theravādin countries for the correct interpretation comes from Mahāyāna. The Milindapañha, I think, is largely responsible.)

**[L. 63]** **6 July 1963**

About the Vietnam affair. You speak of a monk who poured petrol over the intending suicide, and also of others who took part in the procession. A Theravādin *bhikkhu* doing these things might find himself in an equivocal position, since it is a *pārājika* offence ('defeat') to encourage a person to suicide, if as a result of that encouragement he actually kills himself. To pour petrol and (to a lesser extent) to follow in the procession might almost

**a.** Provided, of course, I can continue to persuade myself to stay alive (I say this in order not to commit myself absolutely—it is a safety valve).

be interpreted in this sense. But these monks were (I presume) Mahāyāna monks, and their ordination is not, strictly speaking, recognized by us as valid. For us, they are *upāsakas* and not bound by our Vinaya rules.

As for gruesome (*asubha*, 'foul') objects, these are specifically recommended in the Suttas as objects of meditation for getting rid of sensual desire. In Ceylon, unfortunately, rotting human corpses are hard things to find (the police and the health authorities disapprove of such things), but in India, so I am told, one may still come across them quite easily.

The difficulty of understanding *aniccatā* may be realized from the fact that it is seen, in the full sense of *ñāṇadassana*, 'knowledge and seeing', only by the *ariya* and not by the *puthujjana*. Similarly with *dukkha* and *anattā*. For this reason I can by no means agree with the following statement (from the late Ven. Ñāṇamoli Thera's 'Three Cardinal Discourses of the Buddha', BPS *Wheel* 17, p. 28): 'The two characteristics of Impermanence and Suffering in the world were well recognized in ancient Indian philosophies and have never been peculiar to Buddhism.'

Now for the Huxley. The preliminary indication that I gave in my last letter has been fully confirmed by a reading of the entire book.[1] The book demonstrates Huxley's prodigious wealth of culture, his great talent as a writer (the passage on draperies, for example, is delightful), and his hopelessly muddled thinking. He speaks (on p. 12) of 'such ancient, unsolved riddles as the place of mind in nature and the relationship between brain and consciousness,' but his book does not contribute anything towards their solution. And it has nothing, nothing whatsoever, to do with the Buddha's Teaching.

Actually, these 'ancient, unsolved riddles' have remained unsolved for the good reason that they are insoluble; and they are insoluble because they are illegitimate. The first one comes of making a gratuitous division of things into 'mind' and 'matter' (see NĀMA (b)), and the second comes of assuming that a study of the body will lead to an understanding of consciousness (see my letter to Dr. de Silva about Prof. Jefferson's article).[1] But Huxley's confused thinking seems to be incapable of making even the simplest of philosophical distinctions.

For example, on p. 37 he says 'Meanwhile I had turned...to what was going on, inside my head, when I shut my eyes'; and on the next page, 'What it [the mescaline] had allowed me to perceive, inside, was...my own mind.' For Huxley, then, one's mind is inside one's head. But what is inside one's head is one's brain. So, without any further qualification, we are led to suppose that 'mind' and 'brain' are the same thing. But (quite apart from considerations raised in the Jefferson letter) this needs a great deal of qualification, as you will see if you will read MANO, particularly (b). As it stands, in Huxley's context, it is patently false.

And again, Huxley speaks both of the 'subconscious' and of the 'unconscious'. But the 'subconscious' is Jung's notion, whereas the 'unconscious' is Freud's. Jung, at one time, was a disciple of Freud; but later he broke away and set up his own doctrine in opposition—partly, at least—to that of Freud. Are we to suppose, then, that Huxley has succeeded in harmonizing these two doctrines? Not in the least; the words are used without any attempt at definition. And, in any case, what is the relationship, if any, of either of these doctrines to the other concepts that he introduces? He does not tell us. But I do not propose to undertake an analysis of Huxley's inconsistencies—for a reason that I shall allow Kierkegaard to explain.

> Very often the care and trouble taken in such matters proves to have been wasted; for after taking great pains to set forth an objection sharply, one is apt to learn from a philosopher's reply that the misunderstanding was not rooted in any inability to understand the divine philosophy, but in having persuaded oneself to think that it really meant something—instead of merely being loose thinking concealed behind pretentious expressions. (*CUP*, p. 101)

For this reason, too, it is very difficult to underline passages—as you asked me to do—that are either 'right' or 'very wrong'.

The meditation that is spoken of by Huxley has no connexion at all with that taught by the Buddha. Huxley's meditation is essentially *visionary* or, at its limits, *mystical*: and the characteristic of all such meditation is that you have to wait for something to happen (for visions to appear, for revelations to be vouchsafed, and so on). What chemicals can do is to hasten this process, which formerly required fasting and self-mortification. And even when the visions do condescend to appear (or God condescends to reveal himself), the length of time they last is out of the meditator's control.

In the practices taught in the Suttas, on the other hand, this is by no means the case. In the first place, it is not a matter of visions or revelations, but of the *focusing of attention* (*citt'ekaggatā*, 'one-pointedness of mind'). [If you want to know what is present in *jhāna* see the Anupada Sutta, M.111/iii,25-7. No mention is made there of 'heroic figures' or 'Gothic palaces' or 'transparent clusters of gems'.] In the second place, once these attainments (I refer here particularly to the *jhānas*) have been thoroughly mastered, the meditator can enter upon them and leave them at will—just as one can switch on the electric light and then switch it off again as one pleases. And if he has several at his command, he can choose which one he will enter upon. He can even skip intermediate attainments if he so desires—he can leave first *jhāna*, skip second *jhāna*, and enter upon third *jhāna*. And he can stay in these attainments (if he is really well practised) for as much as a week at a time[2] without emerging at all. Furthermore, when he sees things in his meditations they are quite unlike the things that Huxley describes. To take a single example, on p. 98 we read

> The more than human personages of visionary experience never 'do anything'. (Similarly the blessed never 'do anything' in heaven.) They are content merely to exist ... But action, as we have seen, does not come naturally to the inhabitants of the mind's antipodes. To be busy is the law of *our* being. The law of *theirs* is to do nothing.

But the *devas*, from the Sutta accounts, are extremely busy (let me refer you, for example, to the Cūḷataṇhāsaṅkhaya Sutta, M.37/i,251-56, where Sakka, the king of the gods, actually *says* he is very busy); and the commentaries (for what they are worth) tell us that the *devas* spend much of their time in litigation—to decide which young nymph belongs to whom. (As a judge, you should find yourself very advantageously placed when you go to heaven, if this account can be relied on.)

Moreover, the revelations and insights of visionary and mystical experiences have nothing to do with the insight, the *ñāṇadassana*, of the *ariya*. All these things remain strictly within the kingdom of *avijjā*: these celebrated mystics that Huxley speaks of are just as much *puthujjanas* for all their mystical experiences, their 'Infused Contemplations'—perhaps even more so, indeed, since they become even more deeply embedded in *micchādiṭṭhi* ('wrong view'), which the Buddha speaks of (in A.I.ii.8/i,33) as being the most blameworthy of all blameworthy things. That this is so—i.e. that the mystical view is 'wrong view'—can be seen from the way Huxley himself firmly rejects the Teaching of the Pali Suttas and embraces Mahāyāna.

Mahāyāna is based (I am speaking only of the philosophical aspect) on two wrong views. (i) That all our normal experience is merely appearance, *behind* which there lurks Reality (which it is the business of the *yogin* to seek out), and (ii) that what the Buddha taught was that this Reality behind appearance is *the non-existence of things*. We can sum this up by saying that Mahāyānists (generally speaking—and also many Theravādins) hold that the Buddha taught that things do not *really* exist, but only appear to, that this apparent existence is due to *avijjā* or ignorance. Huxley is not concerned with the second of these two views (to which, perhaps, he might not subscribe), but only with the first, which is common to all mystics at all times and in all places. It is Huxley's theme that mescaline gives admittance, or partial admittance, for a limited period, to the Reality behind appearance.

Let us consider the question of *reality*. In my writings I use the word 'real' from time to time, and almost always in opposition to the word 'imaginary', and *not* in opposition to 'apparent'. Reference to NĀMA (b) will show you that, for me, 'real' = 'present' whereas 'imaginary' = 'absent'.

A simple illustration. When you are at Balapitiya, at that time and for you Balapitiya is 'real' since it is present, whereas Colombo is 'imaginary' since it is absent. At Balapitiya you can *see* Balapitiya but you can only *imagine* Colombo. When you go to Colombo the position is reversed: Colombo is then 'real' or 'present' and Balapitiya is 'imaginary' or 'absent'. In a similar way, when someone is seeing his ordinary work-a-day world, the objects in that world are 'real' or 'present', and the objects at the 'antipodes of his mind'—the begemmed Gothic palaces, and so on—are 'imaginary' or 'absent' (note that absence admits of degrees—things may be more absent or less absent). But if, by means of flagellation or mescaline, or in any other way, he visits the antipodes of his mind, the objects there become 'real' or 'present' and those in the ordinary world 'imaginary' or 'absent'.

But now, if such a person declares, whether in his normal state or not, that the objects at the antipodes of his mind are 'more real' than those in his ordinary world, then he is using the word 'real' in a different sense. What he *should* say, if he is to avoid ambiguity, is that these 'more real' objects are simply 'more vivid' or 'more significant' than the everyday objects. But the word 'real' has an emotive power that the other words lack, and he sticks to it. In this way, the more vivid, more significant, objects of his visionary experience become 'Reality' (with a capital 'R', naturally) and the objects of his ordinary life, merely 'appearance'. If he is a full-blooded mystic he will speak not merely of 'Reality', but of 'Ultimate Reality', which is equated with the 'Dharma-Body', the 'Godhead', the 'Void', the 'All', the 'One', the 'Order of Things', the 'Ground', and so on—such expressions are sprinkled liberally throughout Huxley's book.[a]

The fact is, however, that the notion of Reality concealed behind appearances is quite false. At different times there is consciousness either of *different* things or of the *same* thing seen differently—i.e. with different

---

**a.** I once read a statement by a distinguished Hindu that 'Siva is Ultimate Reality and Parvati is his wife'. It must come as a bit of a shock to a mystic when at last he reaches Ultimate Reality to find that it is married. Mr. and Mrs. Ultimate Reality. Mescalin does not seem to take one as far as this.

determinations or significances. And this is true even of the *arahat* (while still living) as compared with the *puthujjana*: he does not retreat 'from appearances into an entirely transcendental Nirvana' (Huxley, p. 36), he simply sees the same thing as the *puthujjana* but without the significance due to *rāga*, *dosa*, and *moha* ('lust', 'hate', and 'delusion').

I will not deny that the tendency to seek transcendental meaning (to 'invent God', in other words) is inherent in the *puthujjana*'s situation.[b] It is an attempt to find a solution to the existential ambiguity of which I speak (quoting Blackham) in the Preface to the *Notes*. On the philosophical level, it is perhaps most clearly evident in the case of Jaspers (see Blackham); but the merit of the existential philosophers is that they recognize the self-contradiction involved in their efforts to find God. (Some of them, of course, prefer to remain in the existential ambiguity—Nietzsche and Sartre, for example.) The mystics, on the other hand, entirely fail to recognize this inherent self-contradiction, and are quite convinced that they are achieving Union with the Divine, or the Beatific Vision (which for Huxley is Enlightenment—p. 60).

But, as I point out in the Preface, the Buddha transcends the existential ambiguity, not by answering the unanswerable (which is what the mystics seek to do—whence the name 'mystic', for an unanswerable question, clearly enough, can only receive a mysterious answer), but by discovering the source of the ambiguity and removing it. The *arahat* is *sītabhūta*, 'become cold',[3] and for him there is nothing to seek, since there is no longer any 'seeker'.

In brief, then, the answer to your implied question 'Can chemical devices such as mescaline, or electrical proddings of the brain, in any way replace or abbreviate the long and perhaps tedious journey on the path of meditation as taught in the Pali Suttas?',—the answer to this question is an unqualified NO. Visionary experiences are without significance in the Buddha's Teaching.

About the brain as a reducing valve. Huxley quotes (p. 21) Prof. C.D. Broad.

> We should do well to consider much more seriously than we have hitherto been inclined to do the type of theory which Bergson puts forward in connection with memory and sense perception. The suggestion is that the function of the brain and nervous system and sense

---

**b.** Kierkegaard: 'It is then not so much that God is a postulate, as that the existing individual's postulation of God is a necessity.' (*CUP*, p. 179) Dostoievsky: 'All that man has done is to invent God in order not to kill himself. This is the summary of universal history up to this moment.' (Kirilov, in *The Possessed*)

> organs is in the main *eliminative* and not productive. Each person is at each moment capable of remembering all that has ever happened to him and of perceiving everything that is happening everywhere in the universe. The function of the brain and nervous system is to protect us...by shutting out most of what we should otherwise perceive or remember at any moment ...

This passage may throw light for you on *FS*, particularly the first two footnotes, ending 'And if anything exists, everything else does.' But introduction of the *brain* and the *nervous system* and the *sense organs* to explain the selectiveness of our perception is both illegitimate (see once more the Jefferson letter) and unnecessary. In *FS* I have tried to indicate the inherent structure governing the selectivity of consciousness (i.e. the fact that not everything is equally present at once), and I have nowhere been obliged to mention the brain and so on. I would refer you also to RŪPA and to the remarks on *manasikāra* ('attention') in NĀMA. The notion of 'Mind at Large', though it contains some truth, is really not very different from 'a general consciousness common to all' (see RŪPA, about half way through), and does not correspond to anything that actually exists. And when the brain is introduced as a kind of mechanical valve—and a leaky valve to boot—we find ourselves in an impossible tangle.

**[L. 64]** **10 July 1963**

The doctor is quite right about amœbiasis—it affects brain-workers more than brawn-workers. Unless one learns to live with it—to accept that it is incurable (that is, the after-effects)—it is possible to develop an anxiety-complex about it. But I have had the disease for twelve years now, and am perfectly well accommodated to it. It causes me no anxiety, but merely a distaste for living. The nervous disorder (the erotic stimulation) however, is a different kettle of fish. This was not caused by amœbiasis, but, suddenly and acutely, by a drug taken to cure amœbiasis. This too causes me no anxiety, but it *does* give me an appetite for several young women daily. Satisfaction of this appetite being out of the question, my distaste for living is intensified. And the combination of the two reduces my capacity for meditation to a very low level. All this, however, is really neither here nor there—it is purely a personal problem, and not of much importance.

The writer's ideas, as you suggest, will not stand close analysis. It is just possible that by 'objective' he meant 'dispassionate', as opposed to 'subjective' understood as 'giving free rein to one's passions'—i.e. 'un-self-controlled'. In this case he might be justified. But if he was thinking of scientific objectivity as opposed to reflexive subjectivity, then, of course, he is not justified. But 'subjective' and 'objective' are used in different ways by different people, and should be avoided unless one is prepared to take the trouble to define what one means by them.

I feel that the doctor is perhaps over-estimating the danger of misuse of the *Notes*. After all, for the ordinary person they are practically unreadable, and they can by no stretch of the imagination be regarded as propaganda. (Nobody could describe them as 'inflammatory'.) The *Notes* are designed primarily for people with a European background. (I imagine, for example, that the *Notes* are absolutely untranslatable into Sinhala, and consequently a purely Sinhalese-educated person will make nothing of them.) Naturally, this is unavoidable, since I simply do not think as a Sinhala. I would suggest that a fairly liberal distribution should be made to university Buddhist societies. English-speaking university students who are beginning to think for themselves (are they?) might well be interested in a fresh approach to the Dhamma. Provisionally, then, in addition to the people and institutions you have in mind, I would say 250 copies (perhaps this is a shade on the generous side). But what are your views?[1]

**[L. 65]** **13 July 1963**

The idea of signing (rather than typing) my name after the Preface seems to have a double advantage: (i) It will authenticate the book ('None genuine without the signature "Ñāṇavīra" [Registered Trade Mark] on each package'), and (ii) it will emphasize the fact that I am personally responsible for the views expressed in the book. But how much demand will there be for the *Notes*? I have no idea at all. Spare copies should be available for intelligent casual inquirers and for people asking for copies. Even though the Preface says that book 'assumes that the reader is familiar with the Pali Suttas,' it is possible that someone reading the book might be stimulated to *become* familiar with the Pali Suttas. As I said in my last letter, I do not think we need be scared by the Catholic Action into excessive timidity regarding distribution—though perhaps it might be injudicious to send a copy to the Archbishop of Colombo.

P.S. Your Huxley has allowed me to add another footnote to the Preface, warning off the mystics.

**[L. 66]** **23 July 1963**

I have just taken more than a day to rewrite an inadequate passage in the *NP*. The rewritten passage is a particularly tough one, and will take you weeks to unravel; but I hope that, when you succeed in doing so, it will afford you some pleasure. The whole note, however, is difficult, and you might perhaps wonder if it is really necessary to get such an intellectual grasp of *paṭiccasamuppāda* in order to attain the path. The answer is, by no means. But what *is* necessary for a *puthujjana* in order to attain is that he should not imagine that he understands what in fact he does not understand. He should understand that he does *not* understand. If the *Notes*, by their difficulty, succeed in bringing about this negative understanding but nothing more, they will not have been in vain.

I am fortunately endowed with a considerable capacity for remembering the context of passages, even upon a single reading. This was of use to me during the war when, as an interrogator, I was obliged to have an up-to-date card-index memory for keeping my subjects on the straight and narrow path of truthfulness.[1] It is of infinitely more use to me now, since it enables me to turn up remote Sutta passages with a minimum of delay. I have occasionally found myself being used as an index to the Suttas by my fellow *bhikkhus*. On the other hand I find it very difficult to memorize a passage literally. I doubt whether I know more than three or four Suttas by heart. I simply cannot comprehend the Venerable Ānanda Thera, who memorized the whole of the Suttas and recited them at the First Council. I am essentially a man of libraries.

Kafka is an ethical, not an aesthetic, writer. There is no *conclusion* to his books. *The Castle* was actually unfinished, but what ending could there be to it? And there is some doubt about the proper order of the chapters in *The Trial*—it does not really seem to matter very much in which order you read them, since the book as a whole does not get you anywhere. (An uncharitable reader might disagree, and say that it throws fresh light on the Judiciary.) In this it is faithful to life as we actually experience it. There is no 'happy ending' or 'tragic ending' or 'comic ending' to life, only a 'dead ending'—and then we start again.

We suffer, because we refuse to be reconciled with this lamentable fact; and even though we may *say* that life is meaningless we continue to think and act as if it had a meaning. Kafka's heroes (or hero, 'K.'—himself and not himself) obstinately persist in making efforts that they understand perfectly well are quite pointless—and this with the most natural air in the world. And, after all, what else can one do? Notice, in *The Trial*, how the notion of *guilt* is taken for granted. K. does not question the fact that he is guilty, even though he does not know of *what* he is guilty—he makes no attempt to discover the charge against him, but only to arrange for his defence. For both Kierkegaard and Heidegger, guilt is fundamental in human existence. (And it is only the Buddha who tells us the charge against us—*avijjā*.) I should be glad to re-read *The Castle* when you have finished it (that is, if 'finished' is a word that can be used in connexion with Kafka).

You may have difficulty in getting a copy of *Ulysses* locally. The book is grossly obscene, and not in the least pornographic. Customs officials, however, confuse these two things, and *Ulysses* has suffered at their hands. Of one early edition of five hundred copies, 499 were burnt by the Customs at Folkestone.

As for suggesting further books for reading, all I can think of at the moment is a recent Penguin called *Exile and the Kingdom*. It is a translation of six short stories by Albert Camus. I don't know anything about the book, but I know quite a lot about the author (he is the Camus that I have quoted in the *Notes*). Nearly everything that he has written is stimulating, and it might be worth while getting this book. (Besides, I should like to read it myself.)

**[L. 67]** **2 August 1963**

In his book *Le Mythe de Sisyphe* (which I quote in the *Notes*), Camus includes an essay on Kafka. Later on, perhaps, I may translate this for you, since it will throw some light on both Camus and Kafka. But I do not promise.

You wonder how it is that learned men catch on to the significance of a book. I would suggest that it is not so much the 'learned' (if by that the academic university scholar is meant) as the 'intellectual' man who sees the significance of a book.

Two things seem to be necessary. First, a certain maturity of outlook on life, wherein the questions raised by life are clearly present (i.e. the man is looking, either for an answer to these questions, or, preferably, for a further clarification of the questions themselves). This man will read books not so much 'for the story' (though he *may* do that by way of relaxation) as for the fresh light that they may throw on his problems. In other words, he will be *looking* for the significance; and it is likely that he will find it if it is there. Secondly, a community of cultural background with the author of the book is necessary. In these days of widespread dissemination of books, any cultured European can be assumed to have the same general cultural background as any other cultured European. (The most intelligent of Chinamen, brought up solely on the Chinese Classics, would have difficulty in making anything of Kafka.)

It is worth noting that the East (by which I mean India and surrounding countries—the Far East is already West again) is not naturally intellectual. Practically all present-day intellectualism in Ceylon (for example) is imported (by way of books). In Europe, intellectualism takes precedence over tradition; in the East, it is the reverse. In Dhamma terms, the European has an excess of *paññā* over *saddhā*, and he tends to reject what he cannot understand, even if it is true; the Oriental has an excess of *saddhā* over *paññā*, which leads him to accept anything ancient, even if it is false. In Ceylon, therefore, an increase of intellectualism (again, I do not mean *scholarship*) will do no harm. A more intelligent approach to the mass of Pali books, to separate the right from the wrong, is essential if the *Sāsana* is to become alive again. (In this connexion, the *Notes* attempt to provide an intellectual basis for the understanding of the Suttas, without abandoning *saddhā*. It was, and is, my attitude towards the Suttas that, if I find anything in them that is against my own view, *they* are *right*, and *I* am *wrong*.[1] I have no reason to regret having adopted this attitude. Regarding the Commentaries, on the other hand, the boot is on the other leg—if this does not sound too incongruous.)

**[L. 68]** **20 August 1963**

This morning I finished reading through the carbon copy of the *Notes* and gave the final touches to the stencils. There is no doubt that the book has benefited from my having had to type it out again. I have been able to make additions (one long one) and check the entire text for possible inconsistencies. I am particularly pleased that I have not found it necessary to erase anything: I am satisfied that the book does in fact say what I have to say (indeed, I am almost sorry that someone else did not write the book so that I should have the pleasure of reading it for the first time: this is not vanity but an expression of satisfaction that I find myself in agreement with myself). And now you have what you wanted—all the *Notes* under one cover. I suggest that the outer cover should be *jet black*, which gives a very elegant appearance.

I am glad to hear that you are making something of the Kafka. It is really quite in order to interpret him as you feel inclined: there is probably no one single interpretation that is absolutely right to the exclusion of all others.

Camus loses much in translation, but he is still very readable. 'The Renegade' is a warning against trying to demonstrate by personal example that God is Good. The trouble is that it is just as possible to demonstrate by personal example that God is Evil. If God is almighty (and he would not be God if he were not almighty), and Evil exists (which it does), then God is responsible for it. God cannot be both almighty *and* good. This is perfectly well understood by Kafka, who knows that God is capable of making indecent proposals to virtuous young women: '...is it so monstrous that Sortini, who's so retiring, ...should condescend for once to write in his beautiful official hand a letter, however abominable?' (*The Castle*, p. 185) What a deliciously explosive sentence!

But what is a virtuous person, who trusts in God, to do when he gets a command from God to commit evil? Followers of the Buddha are spared these frightful decisions, but others are not. Arjuna had some compunctions about joining battle with his kith and kin, but Krishna, or God, in the person of his charioteer, told him to go ahead.[1] And in Christian Europe these dilemmas are the order of the day. European thought cannot be understood until it is realized that every European is asking himself, consciously or unconsciously, whether God exists. Everything hinges on the answer to this question; for the problem of good and evil, and of personal survival of death ('the immortality of the soul'), are one with the problem of God's existence. It is this fact that makes the Buddha's Teaching incomprehensible to the European—'How' he asks 'can there be Ethics and Survival of Death if there is no omnipotent God?' The European will passionately affirm God or passionately deny God, but he cannot ignore God. Sir Francis Younghusband, commenting on the fact that there is hardly any reference to an omnipotent God (*Issaranimmāna*, 'Creator God') in the Suttas, attributes the omission to the supposed fact that the Buddha had far too much reverence for God ever to presume to speak of him.[2] What other explanation could there be? The idea of a moral but Godless universe is quite foreign to European thought.

**[L. 69]** **25 August 1963**

You ask whether the cover should be glossy or dull. The answer is that it should be a *dull matt black*. A glossy cover has a meretricious look and leads the reader to expect that the book will be glossy all the way through, like the American magazines. When he opens the book and finds only dull cyclostyled philosophy instead of glossy blondes he is likely to be disappointed. Besides, a glossy black reminds one of the shiny seat of too-long-worn black serge trousers, an unsightly affliction, common enough in Europe, but in Ceylon confined, I suppose, to the members of the legal profession. The cover should be about as stiff as a playing card. If you are sending me samples, no doubt I shall find something suitable.

'The Adulterous Woman' repeats one of Camus's favourite themes: marriage with inanimate Nature, the sea, the sky, the earth. This theme is found in his earliest published essays, which, in fact, are called *Noces* (nuptials). But here, too, the title (*Exile and the Kingdom*) is significant. (You will have noticed this theme in the last of the stories, 'The Growing Stone'. D'Arrast, the Frenchman of noble ancestry, is an exile from modern bourgeois France where he has no place, and seeks citizenship in the sweaty kingdom of Iguape.) Camus's conception of man (shared by other existential writers) is that of an exile in search of the kingdom from which he has been expelled (like Adam and Eve from the Garden of Eden). But this kingdom does not exist and has never existed (for God does not exist). Man, therefore, ever hopeful, spends his time in a hopeless quest for peace of mind and security from *angoisse* or anxiety. (A. E. Housman speaks of man as 'alone and afraid in a world he never made.')[1] Nostalgia, then, is man's *natural* condition.

So I take this theme of union with Nature as a symbolical attempt at a solution of this insoluble situation. The adulterous woman herself says that 'She wanted to be liberated even if Marcel, even if the others, never were!' (p. 26). Union with Nature ('...the unchanging sky, where life stopped, where no one would ever age or die any more.' [p. 27]) offers itself as a possible solution, even though Camus is aware that it is *not* a solution ('She knew that this kingdom had been eternally promised her and yet that it would never be hers...' [p. 23]). But I have no doubt that his image had a great deal more significance for Camus, with his strong feeling for landscape, than I have suggested here: indeed, it seems likely that he actually had in his youth some emotional experience, some 'spiritual revelation', on these lines, and that this made a lasting impression on him. But he is too intelligent to be deceived.

His theme in *Le Mythe de Sisyphe* (quite his best book) is that there is *no* solution. Man's invincible nostalgia for clarity and reason is opposed by an irrational, unreasonable, world; and from the conjunction of these two the *Absurd* is born. The Absurd, of course, is simply another name for the essential ambiguity of man's situation in the world; and this ambiguity, this *hopeless* situation, is lucidly portrayed by Camus in the extract I have made in NIBBĀNA. But in view of the fact that there is *no* solution (I am not speaking of the Buddhadhamma, of course) what is one to do? 'Face the situation' says Camus 'and do not try to deceive yourself by inventing God—even an evil God.' You will see at once why Camus is interested in Kafka.

In *The Castle*, K. is engaged in the hopeless task of getting himself recognized as Land Surveyor by the Authorities in the Castle—that is, by God. K. is a stranger in the village (an *exile*), and he is seeking permission to live permanently in the village (which is, of course, the *kingdom*—of heaven, if you like). But so long as he is engaged in this *hopeless* task, he has *hope*; and Camus maintains (quite rightly, of course) that he is in contradiction with himself. If the situation is hopeless, one has no business to have hope. Camus points out that Amalia, the girl who indignantly rejected God's immoral proposal (the deceitful promise of eternal bliss in heaven, if you like to take it that way—but God, since he made man in his own image, is presumably capable of being immoral in as many ways as man), is the only character in *The Castle* who is entirely without hope (she has made herself eternally unworthy of God's grace by refusing to lose her honour—her intellectual integrity, if you like—for his sake); and that it is she that K. opposes with the greatest vehemence.

Camus accuses Kafka of deifying The Absurd (which, naturally, produces an Absurd God—but still God, for all that [or rather, *because* of that; for if God is comprehensible one can no longer *believe* in him, one *understands* him and that is an end of the matter]). *The Trial*, however, commends itself to Camus as a completely successful portrayal of The Absurd (with which, perhaps, to judge from your recent letters, you might agree). In *The Trial*, K. is not concerned with hope (he is not seeking anything): he lets his hopeful uncle (who is seeking to preserve the family honour) do the talking with the advocate while he himself goes off to amuse himself with the advocate's girls. In *The Castle*, on the other hand, K. makes love to the barmaid precisely because she is the mistress of one of the Castle officials and offers the hope of a channel of communication with the Castle. It is the Castle that K. wants, not the girl. In *The Trial*, K. is simply defending himself against the importunities of an irrational and capricious God, whereas in *The Castle* he is seeking them. In *The Trial* K. is defending himself against the charge of *existing* by disclaiming responsibility (but this is not enough to acquit him): in *The Castle*, K. is trying to convince the Authorities that he is *justified* in existing (but the Authorities are hard to convince). In the first, K. denies God; in the second, he affirms God. But in both, K. *exists*; and his existence is Absurd.

I have just been sent a book from England that might interest you. It is Lord Balfour's *A Study of the Psychological Aspects of Mrs Willett's Mediumship, and of the Statement of the Communicators Concerning Process.* I do not think that you have any doubts about rebirth, but this book seems to me to be quite exceptionally good evidence for it; and the various philosophical problems discussed (between the living and the dead) are themselves of no little interest. There is, in particular, a disagreement between Balfour (living) and Gurney (dead) about the possibility of there being a split within one and the same person. This disagreement can only be resolved when the distinction between the notion of a *person* (*sakkāya, attā*) and that of an *individual* (*puggala*) becomes clear. (This distinction, as you will remember, is discussed in the *Notes.*) Balfour denies that a person, a self, can be split without *ipso facto* becoming *two* persons, *two* selves (i.e. two quite different people): Gurney affirms it. Balfour is wrong for the right reason: Gurney is right for the wrong reason.[2]

If you can find no way of getting the *Notes* duplicated, why not try the Ministry of Cultural Affairs, who might be sympathetic (provided they do not actually read them)? I must, however, confess to a rooted dislike—perhaps you share it?—of seeking the help of Official (particularly Government) Bodies. Whenever anyone addresses me in his official capacity, I am at once filled with a desire to attack the Official Body he represents. I have every sympathy with the Irishman who, on being fined five shillings for Contempt of Court, asked the Magistrate to make it ten shillings; 'Five shillings' he explained 'do not adequately express the Contempt I have for this Court.' I am quite unable to identify myself with any organized body or cause (even if it is a body of opposition or a lost cause). I am a born blackleg. I thoroughly approve of E.M. Forster's declaration, 'If I had to choose between betraying my country and betraying my friend, I hope I should have the guts to betray my country.' For me, there is no doubt that the very small word in the centre of the blank canvas at the end of 'The Artist at Work' is *solitaire*, not *solidaire*.

**[L. 70]** **2 September 1963**

I think it is extremely clever of you to have made such satisfactory arrangements for the cyclostyling of the *Notes*. Saturday the 7th September sounds an auspicious date, and your presence in person will no doubt ensure that the circumstances are entirely favourable. I am sorry that I too cannot be there to see the birth of the book.

**[L. 71]** **7 September 1963**

Feelings of fear and helplessness at times of sickness or danger are very unpleasant, but they can also be very instructive. At such times one may get an almost pure view of *bhavataṇhā*, craving for existence. The fear is not fear of anything in particular (though there may *also* be that), but rather of *ceasing to exist*, and the helplessness is an *absolute* helplessness in the face of impending annihilation. I think that it is very probable that these feelings will put in an appearance at any time that one thinks one is going to die (whether one actually dies or not), and it is perhaps half the battle to be prepared for this sort of thing. Once one knows that such feelings are to be expected one can take the appropriate action quickly when they actually occur, instead of dying in a state of bewilderment and terror.

What is the appropriate action? The answer is, Mindfulness. One cannot *prevent* these feelings (except by becoming *arahat*), but one can look them in the face instead of fleeing in panic. Let them come, and try to *watch* them: once they know themselves to be observed they tend to wither and fade away, and can only reassert themselves when you become heedless and off your guard. But continued mindfulness is not easy, and that is why it is best to try and practise it as much as possible while one is still living. Experiences such as yours are valuable reminders of what one has to expect and of the necessity for *rehearsing* one's death before one is faced with it.

The passage from the Satipaṭṭhāna Sutta that you quote gives an *example* of the existentialist (i.e. reflexive or phenomenological) attitude, but I hesitate before saying how far it is an explicit reference to it. The trouble is that it is not a particularly easy passage to translate. The usual translation, which is different in important respects from the one you have sent me, runs something like this:

> 'There is the body', thus mindfulness is established in him, to the extent necessary for knowledge and (adequate) mindfulness. And he dwells unattached and clings to nothing in the world.[a]—M.10/i,57-8

But I must admit that, though I accept this translation for lack of a better, I am not altogether satisfied that it is correct. (I once had a quite different translation to either this one or the one you have sent me but I later aban-

**a.** The 'extent necessary' means the extent necessary to attain *arahatta*. There is no further necessity for the practice of mindfulness *after* one has attained this.

doned it.) On the other hand, I am even less satisfied that the Pali text as it stands will bear the translation of your letter. (Does *paṭissati* mean more than *sati*? I don't know.)

The whole question of relying on translations of the Suttas is a troublesome one. Some people may disagree with what I have to say about it at the beginning of the Preface to the *Notes*, and will consider that I am too severe; nevertheless, I stick to it—I am prepared to argue the point, me Lud. If there *have* to be translations let them at least be literal and let translators not add things of their own in the attempt to make things easier for the reader—it doesn't. But sometimes one is misled by the modern editor of texts themselves, when he too definitely fixes the punctuation or fails to give alternative readings. (There is a neat example of this, which you will find in a footnote towards the end of *NP*. It is a matter of deciding whether *cetaṃ* should be *c'etaṃ*, 'and this', or *ce taṃ*, 'if that'. If you choose the first you put a full stop in one place: if you choose the second you must put the full stop in another place. Although it makes no difference to the general meaning of the passage, the second alternative makes the passage read much more smoothly. But the editor has chosen *c'etaṃ* and has placed his full stop accordingly. If he had left *cetaṃ* and omitted the full stop altogether he would not have wasted so much of my time.) I sometimes feel that the original texts should be given without any punctuation at all, leaving it to the reader to decide. ('I said that the honourable member was a liar it is true and I am sorry for it.')

**[L. 72] 12 September 1963**

I am glad that the cyclostyling has been completed. I assume that the result is at least legible (though of course one cannot expect much more than that from cyclostyling). It is good that you have taken the trouble to compare the finished product with the carbon copy and to arrange for the re-doing of what was necessary: attention to such details is essential if the reader is not to have the impression that the book is simply being thrown at him; and a carefully prepared book is itself an invitation to be read.

(It is astonishing, in this respect, what a low standard of typography and book production the French will put up with. They seem almost incapable of producing—at least cheaply—a clear and tidy page such as one finds, for example, in the Penguin books.[1] On the other hand, the French language is itself such a clear and tidy instrument of expression that one tends to overlook the scruffiness of the printing.)

'*Aimer*', in French means 'to love'; but it is also used where we should use the weaker word 'to like'. '*Aimez-vous Brahms...?*' is 'Do you like Brahms...?' rather than 'Do you love Brahms...?' The question 'Do you like Brahms...?' is a polite way of opening a conversation at a tea or cocktail party if you can't think of anything else to say.[a]

I have never read any Sagan[2]; though I believe she is all the rage amongst French intellectuals.

**[L. 73]** **21 September 1963**

The Ven. Siridhamma Thera's trepidations about the hostile criticism that we may encounter are probably well founded (even with judicious distribution). Naturally, I have always taken this into account, and I should not have decided on having the *Notes* made public had I been at all unsure of my position. I am quite prepared to meet verbal attacks—indeed, they might be positively welcome as a distraction from my bodily woes. And if some misguided zealot were to go so far (an unlikely event, I fear) as to decide that my existence is no longer desirable, he would save me a lot of trouble. In any case, since I am not seeking to be a popular figure, the prospect of becoming an unpopular one does not worry me in the least.

**[L. 74]** **28 September 1963**

I think you told me that you had found the Bertrand Russell unreadable.[1] This is quite as it should be. You asked me some time ago to suggest books for reading; but since I am rather out of touch with the world of books as it is today, and also don't know what is available in Ceylon, I have not been able to give you many positive indications. But at least I can give you a negative indication—don't read Russell, not for his philosophy anyway. Russell's influence (in the English-speaking world, that is to say) is very great, and it is almost wholly pernicious. He accepts 'scientific common

**a.** I might add, in case you are curious to know, that I do *not* like Brahms—or perhaps I should say that I *did* not like Brahms, since it is now more than fifteen years since I heard any. On the other hand, I used to love—not just 'like'—Beethoven. I never had any time at all for popular music of any kind—perhaps if I had I should have been more 'human', as they say; but I should have been less likely to become a *bhikkhu*.

sense' as the basis for his thought, and this is precisely the thing I am at pains to combat in the *Notes*.[a] Russell's philosophy is rather like the gaudy cover to his book—patchy and specious. The best things about him are his repeated admissions of failure, often just at the point where he seems about to recant his former views and make a real advance. But his roots are too firmly embedded in 'scientific common sense'.

Consider his argument. On p. 13 he says

> Physics assures us that the occurrences which we call 'perceiving objects' are at the end of a long causal chain which starts from the objects, and are not likely to resemble the objects except, at best, in certain very abstract ways.

(With this you may compare PHASSA from the words 'But when (as commonly)...' to the end.) Then Russell says

> We all start from 'naive realism', i.e., the doctrine that things are what they seem. We think that grass is green, that stones are hard, and that snow is cold. But physics assures us that the greenness of grass, the hardness of stones, and the coldness of snow, are not the greenness, hardness, and coldness that we know in our own experience, but something very different. ...Naive realism leads to physics, and physics, if true, shows that naive realism is false. Therefore naive realism, if true, is false; therefore it is false... These considerations induce doubt...

Certainly they induce doubt; but Russell is either unable or unwilling to see that what is doubtful is the truth of physics. Why can he not see that, in the process of deriving physics from naive realism, something odd has happened—something unjustified put in, or something essential dropped out—that might account for the disagreement? (See RŪPA (b).) *Assuming* the truth of physics (in spite of the accumulated experimental evidence that phys-

---

**a.** In this connexion, though you may find the note on Fundamental Structure as unreadable as Russell, there will, perhaps, be those more professionally philosophical than yourself who do manage to read Russell but yet are dissatisfied with him and all that his thinking implies. Possibly they may find that the note on *FS* offers something quite, quite different, and certainly more satisfying aesthetically. (I rather flatter myself that the note on *FS* says a great deal in a few elegant pages. Not everybody will agree; but at least I do not think that anybody can accuse me of verbosity.)

ics is sometimes false[b]), he constructs a paradox, that 'naive realism, if true, is false,' and then proceeds to write three hundred pages of self-mystification.

On p. 303 he tells us 'I do not, it is true, regard *things* as the object of inquiry, since I hold them to be a metaphysical delusion.' A metaphysical delusion? Nonsense! *Things* are given in immediate experience, and as soon as we enter upon reflexion we are directly aware that 'There are things'. (As for not regarding them as the object of inquiry, you have only to look at the opening of the note on *FS* to see that there can be two opinions about that.) 'The net result' claims Russell 'is to substitute articulate hesitation for inarticulate certainty.' If he had claimed to replace articulate certainty by inarticulate hesitation, I should feel more inclined to agree with him.

*Crome Yellow*,[c] on the other hand, like all Huxley's early books, and also his later books when he is not being mystical or trying to reconstruct the world, is instructive in its destructiveness (even if I have long ago learned the lessons). Perhaps destructiveness (or at least this kind of destructiveness) is more necessary for the West than the East, since the West *thinks* more than the East—it is more literate, anyway, whereas the East *practises* more than the West—and consequently has a greater accumulation of wrong views (I am speaking of Ethics). In my own case, certainly, a great deal of rubbish had to be cleared away before I could begin to approach the Buddha's Teaching, and here I have much to thank Huxley for. But Huxley's later works have become more and more mystical and constructive, and then he writes nonsense. (It is astonishing the way good European writers and artists run to seed when they settle in America.) Practically everything, for example, that is said by Mr. Propter in *After Many A Summer* is misleading in one way or another (he *speaks* of the Pali texts, but he *preaches* Mahāyāna.) The Fifth Earl is much more instructive.

But in *After Many A Summer*, at least, Huxley does not speak in praise of sensuality (i.e. sex[d]); whereas in his most recent books it seems that the achievement of a satisfactory sexual relationship is exalted, along with chemical

---

**b.** Russell allows, elsewhere, that physics can never be more than *probably* true, which means to say that there is no *logical* reason why it should not sometimes be false. But 'scientific common sense' is an act of faith that *in fact* physics is always true, and experimental evidence to the contrary is not enough to shake this faith.

**c.** The house described in the book really exists: it is Beckley (Park), near Oxford. The late Ven. Ñāṇamoli Thera used to know the people who live there, and was an occasional visitor. (I met them once in London, and found them very much less interesting than Huxley's characters. We played bridge.)

**d.** Of course, listening to Beethoven *also* is sensuality, but when you have said 'sex' you have said all. A man who can give up sex can give up Beethoven.

mysticism, as among the highest aims to be striven for. This idea, of course, is not so uncommon: there seems to be a widespread view, not in Ceylon only, that if a man does not become a monk—Buddhist or other—it is his duty to marry. This is quite mistaken. The Buddha's Teaching is perfectly definite—a satisfactory sexual relationship within the limits of the third precept (which, however, allows rather more latitude than is commonly supposed), though allowable for an *upāsaka*, comes a bad third. If you can't be a *bhikkhu*, be a *brahmacārī upāsaka*; if you can't manage that, then keep the third precept (preferably limiting yourself to your wife or wives). The Buddha condemns the notion *N'atthi kāmesu doso*—There's no harm in sensuality—(A.III.111/i,266; Ud.VI,8/71)—as a wrong view that swells the charnel grounds, i.e. leads one to repeated births and deaths. To get out of *saṃsāra*, first this view must be given up, and then sensuality itself must be given up—an easy or difficult matter according to circumstances, but usually difficult.

Joyce's *Ulysses* is a destructive book, and so too is Gibbon's *History of the Decline and Fall of the Roman Empire*. Gibbon is a very entertaining writer, and I can recommend the *Decline and Fall* as profitable reading if ever you are feeling complacent about the wisdom and virtues of the human race. He is incapable of writing a dull page, whether he is discussing circumcision amongst the Ethiopians or the Pandects of Justinian. (I am, personally, very fond of Gibbon's account of a particularly unsavoury character called George of Cappadocia—better known as St. George of England. George of Cappadocia started his career as a successful army contractor, and eventually rose by extremely questionable methods to the episcopal throne of Egypt, where he spent his time liquidating his enemies. The celebrated 'dragon' slain by St. George was none other than St. Athanasias, his rival to the bishopric of Alexandria and a man of considerable importance in both ecclesiastical and secular history. The English pretend that nothing is known of the life of their patron saint, which I cannot but regard as wishful thinking.)

Since the book contains about three thousand pages and covers fourteen centuries (100-1500 A.D.—the Roman Empire had an incredibly long death-agony), you would not be able to read it in a week-end: a good occasion might be if ever you are confined to bed for a month or so. One must read Gibbon slowly in order to relish the full flavour of his irony and his perfectly balanced sentences;[e] and a small atlas is useful for reference. I have

**e.** Gibbon tells us that, apart from the first three chapters, which he wrote out three times before he was satisfied with the style, he wrote out the book once only, and it was printed direct from this first draft. Even in writing this letter to you I have had to make two drafts, and this fair copy contains erasures and corrections.

read the entire work three times since being in Ceylon (in the earlier days of my amœbiasis), and I am quite ready to start again.

The communicators in the *Willett* scripts were the people who, while living, founded the Society for Psychical Research.[f] This, no doubt, is the reason for their interest in experiment, rather than that scientific investigations are a normal part of existence as a discarnate spirit. Henry Sidgwick was the first President and Myers and William James (the American psychologist, brother of Henry James) were Presidents in 1900 and 1894-5 respectively. Gurney was an early member. An account of the founding of the Society is given in G.N.M. Tyrell's *The Personality of Man*. The Society is still active.[2]

The Ven. Siridhamma Thera mentioned the communications he had received from his brother, one of which seemed to be referring to myself—so no doubt I am 'under observation', as presumably we all are. About spirits in the East, one of the reasons for their being here may be that given in the Ratana Sutta, second verse (Sn. 223), where it is said that human beings bring them offerings (*baliṃ*) day and night. The Buddha, in certain Sutta passages, encourages laymen to make offerings to those spirits who are capable of receiving them. This, I think, is more than just the offering of merits. (I never advise anyone *not* to make material offerings to spirits, but to be quite clear in their mind what they are doing. Gifts given to anyone, human or not, bring merit, but do not lead to *nibbāna*. And spirits certainly do, upon occasion, give protection. I am not in agreement with the modern sceptical tendency.)

The reason for my (qualified) approval of self as 'me as I know myself' was rather to mark *dis*approval of Myers's notion of self as the 'subliminal', which *ex hypothesi* is beyond the range of what they rather unfortunately call 'conscious knowledge'—by which they mean reflexive awareness. I do not by any means wish to give the impression that Balfour has resolved the problem of 'self'—being a *puthujjana* he does not know what he is talking about when he speaks of 'self'—; but if I were asked 'What is the normal meaning of the word *attā* in the Suttas?' I would reply 'It means "me as I know myself in the act of reflection,"' though I would go on to say that this is not in the very least an answer to the question 'What is "self"?' (See ATTĀ, first paragraph.)

Yes, I have read one or two descriptions of death (autobiographical, of course), and they are much in agreement with your account of Stead's death. Did you, by any chance, read this account in a book called *Four from the*

f. I have just discovered, by chance, that both the Pali Text Society and the Society for Psychical Research were founded in 1882. Those enterprising Victorians!

*Dead*? It contains communications from four people who had died—one was Stead, and one was the medium's own husband (a doctor who had committed suicide by swallowing poison while walking along the road). I forget how the other three died, but I remember that the doctor said that after taking poison (cyanide, I believe—very quick) he suddenly found himself standing and looking down at his own dead body on the ground. As you quite rightly point out, the new surroundings may be warmer than what one has been accustomed to—that is, if one has not taken the precaution of becoming *sotāpanna*.

**[L. 75] 3 November 1963**

Though there is not very much to say, here are a few thoughts about Kafka's *Trial*. As I remarked on an earlier occasion, it seems to me that the crime with which K. is charged is that of *existing*, and that this is why the charge is never made explicit. Everybody *exists*, and it would be ridiculous to charge one man with this crime and not the next man as well. But not everybody feels *guilty* of existing; and even those who do are not always clear about *what* it is precisely that they feel guilty of, since they see that the rest of mankind, who *also* exist, go through life in a state of blissful innocence. The criminal charge of existing cannot be brought home to those who are satisfied of their innocence (since judicial censure is worse than futile unless the accused recognizes his guilt), and also it cannot be brought home to those who recognize their guilt but who are not satisfied that it is of *existing* that they are guilty (since judicial censure fails of its intended effect if the accused, though aware of guilt, believes that the charge against him has been wrongly framed). To secure a conviction, then, the charge must be one simply of guilt; and so, in fact, it is in *The Trial*.

'"Yes," said the Law-Court Attendant, "these are the accused men, all of them are accused of guilt." "Indeed!" said K. "Then they're colleagues of mine."' (pp. 73-4) And this charge of guilt, clearly enough, can only be brought against those who are guilty of guilt, and not against those who do *not* feel the guilt of existing. But who is it that feels the guilt of existing? Only he who, in an act of *reflexion*, begins to be *aware* of his existence and to see that it is inherently unjustifiable. He understands (obscurely, no doubt, at first) that, when he is challenged to give an account of himself, he is unable to do so. But who is it that challenges him to give an account of himself? In *The Trial* it is the mysterious and partly corrupt hierarchical Court; in reality it is he himself in his act of reflexion (which also is hierarchically ordered). *The Trial*, then, represents the criminal case that a man brings against himself when he asks himself 'Why do I exist?' But the common run of people do *not* ask themselves this question; they are quite content in their simple way to take things for granted and not to distress themselves with unanswerable questions—questions, indeed, that they are scarcely capable of asking. K.'s landlady, a simple woman, discussing K.'s arrest with him, says

> 'You are under arrest, certainly, but not as a thief is under arrest. If one's arrested as a thief, that's a bad business, but as for this arrest—It gives me the feeling of something very learned, forgive me if what I say is stupid, it gives me the feeling of something abstract which I don't understand, but which I don't need to understand either.' (p. 27)

So, then, K. is under arrest, *but he has arrested himself*. He has done this simply by adopting a reflexive attitude towards himself. He is perfectly free, if he so wishes, to set himself at liberty, merely by ceasing to reflect. 'The Court makes no claims upon you. It receives you when you come and it relinquishes you when you go.' (The priest on p. 244.) But is K. free to *wish* to set himself at liberty? Once a man has begun to reflect, to realize his guilt, is he still free to *choose* to return to his former state of grace? Once he has eaten the fruit of the tree of reflexive knowledge he has lost his innocence,[a] and he is expelled from the terrestrial paradise with its simple joys. Having tasted the guilty pleasures of knowledge can he ever want to return to innocence? Can he, in terms of *The Trial*, secure a 'definite acquittal' from guilt, or does his case have a fatal fascination for him?

> 'In definite acquittal the documents relating to the case are completely annulled, they simply vanish from sight, not only the charge but also the records of the case and even the acquittal are destroyed, everything is destroyed.' (pp. 175-6)

'Definite acquittal', in other words, is a total forgetting not merely of one's actual past reflexions but of the very fact that one ever reflected at all—it is a complete forgetting of one's guilt. So long as one remembers having reflected, one goes on reflecting, as with an addiction; and so long as one

---

**a.** Note the ambiguity, the ambivalence, of this word *innocence*, so close to *ignorance*, just as *guilt* and *knowledge* are sometimes almost synonymous. Adam and Eve, after eating the apple, *knew* that they were naked, and *they were ashamed*.[1]

continues to reflect, one holds one's guilt in view; for the Court—one's reflexive inquisitor—, 'once it has brought a charge against someone, is firmly convinced of the guilt of the accused,' and 'never in any case can the Court be dislodged from that conviction.' (p. 166) To reflect *at all* is to discover one's guilt. So, then, is it possible to get a 'definite acquittal', to choose to unlearn to *reflect*? 'I have listened to countless cases in their most crucial stages, and followed them as far as they could be followed, and yet—I must admit it—I have never encountered one case of definite acquittal.' (Titorelli, on p. 171.) No, whatever theory may say, *in practice* having once tasted guilt one cannot unlearn reflexion and return to the innocence of immediacy, the innocence of a child.

The best one can do to ward off the inexorable verdict—'Guilty, with no extenuating circumstances'—is to seek either 'ostensible acquittal' (p. 176), wherein awareness of one's essential guilt is temporarily subdued by makeshift arguments but flares up from time to time in crises of acute despair, or else 'indefinite postponement' (pp. 177-8), wherein one adopts an attitude of bad faith towards oneself, that is to say one regards one's guilt (of which one is perpetually aware) as being 'without significance', thereby refusing to accept responsibility for it.

K., however, is not disposed to try either of these devices, and seems, rather, to want to bring matters to a head. He dismisses his advocate as useless—perhaps the advocate in *The Trial* represents the world's professional philosophers—, and sets about organizing his own defence. For this purpose he recruits, in particular, women helpers, perhaps regarding them as the gateway to the Divine (if I remember rightly, this is one of Denis's earlier views—in *Crome Yellow*—that makes life so complicated for him). This view is clearly mystical, and is denounced in *The Trial*. '"You cast about too much for outside help," said the priest disapprovingly, "especially from women. Don't you see that it isn't the right kind of help?"' (p. 233)

In *The Castle*, on the other hand, K. uses women to get him entrance into the kingdom of heaven, and perhaps with some effect; but in *The Castle* guilt is evidence of the existence of God, and the guiltier one is the better chance one has of getting the favour of the Castle (thus Amalia indignantly rejects the immoral proposals of one of the gentlemen from the Castle and is promptly cut off from the Divine Grace, whereupon her sister Olga prostitutes herself with the meanest Castle servants in the hope of winning it back).

In *The Trial* the task is to come to terms with oneself without relying on other people; and although we may sympathize with K. and the other accused in their efforts to acquit themselves before the Court, actually the

Court is in the right and K. and the others in the wrong. There are three kinds of people in *The Trial*: (i) the innocent (i.e. ignorant) mass of humanity, unable to reflect and thus become aware of their guilt, (ii) the (self-)accused, who are guilty and obscurely aware of the fact but who refuse to admit it to themselves and who will go to any lengths to delay the inevitable verdict (the grovelling Herr Block of Chapter VIII, for example, has no less than six advocates, and has succeeded in protracting his case for five years), and (iii) the (self-)condemned man, who, like K. in the final chapter, faces up to the desolating truth and accepts the consequences.

> 'The only thing for me to go on doing is to keep my intelligence calm and discriminating to the end. I always wanted to snatch at the world with twenty hands, and not for a very laudable motive either. That was wrong, and am I to show now that not even a whole year's struggling with my case has taught me anything? Am I to leave this world as a man who shies away from all conclusions?' (p. 247)

For the reflexive man who retains his lucidity, there is only one verdict—'Guilty'—and only one sentence—death. K.'s death in *The Trial* is the death of worldly hope; it is the immediate consequence of the frank recognition that one's existence *is* guilty (that is to say, that it is unjustifiable); and this execution of the capital sentence upon hope is actually the inevitable conclusion to *The Trial.* I think you told me that you had found that K.'s death was an arbitrary and artificial ending to the book, which ought to have finished inconclusively. This would certainly have been true of Block, who clearly did not have the moral courage to face facts: Block would never have condemned himself to death (i.e. to a life without hope), and to have him executed by divine fiat would have been senseless. But with K. it was different: just as he had arrested himself by becoming reflexive, so he had to execute himself by admitting his guilt; and this is the furthest that anyone can go—in the direction of understanding, that is—without the Buddha's Teaching.

**[L. 76] 6 November 1963**

I am glad to hear that all the copies for the listed addresses have gone off. We can now sit back and wait to see what effect the book has. (I read in the papers[1] that there was an earth tremor felt in Ceylon during the past day or two, but perhaps we are not entitled to assume that we have been responsible for it.) In any case I do not suppose that the majority of the recipients will do more than acknowledge receipt without comment (and many, perhaps, will not even do that). But actually, I am more concerned that the copies should have been distributed than that they should be generally appreciated. If I have one reader only who benefits from it I shall be satisfied (but I do not think he will be found in the H.S.C. and Entrance Forms). I admit, however, that I am curious to know what the professor and others like him will make of it—I feel that their professional reputation requires them to make *something* of it, but *what*? In any case, the professor's prompt acknowledgement perhaps indicates interest as well as courtesy. Our Colombo friend may find some of the things in the *Notes* rather unpalatable—but then they were not written to pander to people's tastes.

I do not know the Venerable M.A. either, but I feel that if he is both 'Venerable' and 'Vice Principal' he is hardly likely to be the sort of person we are trying to reach.

What I said in my last letter about K.'s reason for recruiting, in particular, women to help his case—namely, that he perhaps regarded them as the 'Gateway to the Divine'—is excessive. It is true enough of *The Castle*, where K. is seeking God's grace; but in *The Trial* K. is simply attempting to justify his own existence, and his relations with women do not go beyond this. Here is an illuminating passage from Sartre:

> Whereas before being loved we were uneasy about that unjustified, unjustifiable protuberance which was our existence, whereas we felt ourselves "*de trop*," we now feel that our existence is taken up and willed even in its tiniest details by an absolute freedom [i.e. that of the one who loves us][a] which at the same time our existence conditions [since it is our existence that fascinates our lover][a] and which we ourselves will with our freedom. This is the basis for the joy of love when there is joy: we feel that our existence is justified. (*B&N*, p. 371)

In *The Trial*, then, K. is seeking to use women to influence the susceptible Court ('Let the Examining Magistrate see a woman in the distance and he almost knocks down his desk and the defendant in his eagerness to get at her.'—p. 233). In other words, K. is trying to silence his self-accusations of guilt by helping himself to women (which does indeed have the effect—

a. My brackets.

temporarily—of suppressing his guilt-feelings by making his existence seem justified). But K. is told—or rather, he tells himself—that this sort of defence is radically unsound (in Dr. Axel Munthe's opinion, a man's love comes to an end when he marries the girl). And, in fact, Sartre's detailed analysis of the love-relationship shows only too clearly its precarious and self-contradictory structure.

**[L. 77]** **14 November 1963**

I have now returned to Būndala armed with some heavy authorities with which to add weight to any replies I may be called upon to make to people's comments on the *Notes*. Learned objections usually call for learned replies, and a salvo of passages from about page 650 of some forbidding work can be quite effective. But learned objections to the *Notes* are actually a misunderstanding, since the *Notes* is not a learned book at all (though this is not to say that it is an easy book); and the more intelligent objections that may be raised cannot be answered simply by reference to authority. Learned objections must, no doubt, be answered; but it is the more urgent personal objection that it is worth taking trouble with. But will there be anything more than polite acknowledgments?

The Ven. Siridhamma Thera remarked that if the H.S.C. and Entrance Form students make use of the *Notes* when studying for their examinations they are certain to fail. This, of course, is perfectly true; and, indeed, I should be horrified to learn that the *Notes* had been approved as a textbook for school or university use. I have made the *Notes* as unattractive, academically speaking, as possible; and it is hardly conceivable that anyone could be so perverted as to set their pupils to learning them by rote. No—let them stick to the *citta-vīthi*, which, being totally meaningless, is eminently suited for an examination subject.

I have started making corrections and additions to the *Notes*, in the carbon copy. The corrections, fortunately, are very minor, and concern only such things as faults in style and grammatical slips; but the additions are more substantial and, I hope, make things clearer. No doubt I shall go on making them as they occur to me.

My general impression, so far, is that NA CA SO is attracting most attention.[1] This is perhaps understandable, since the natural question to ask, upon being told that the Buddha denies a 'self' (a misleading statement) but asserts rebirth, is 'Who, then, is reborn?'; and the answer comes out pat: *Na ca so, na ca añño*, 'Neither the same (person) nor another.' The consequence is, that everyone supposes that this celebrated (and facile) phrase is the key to the whole of the Buddha's Teaching. It must therefore come as rather a shock—almost as a scandal—to find it criticized by a *bhikkhu* whose sanity nobody had hitherto seen any reason to question. Certainly, there is hardly a single popular book on Buddhism that fails to quote this phrase—many of them seem to suppose that it is found in the Suttas (at least, they do not point out that it is *not* found in the Suttas).

**[L. 78] 18 November 1963**

Thank you for your letter of the 15th, enclosing a fresh set of acknowledgements.

I thought it would be tactful to send the local doctor a copy. He says, however, that he 'much treasures it', which is all very well; but does he propose to *read* it? No. 10 seems to be rather a scatterbrain—not only has he misunderstood the printed slip and seems not to know the meaning of the phrase, 'With the Compliments of the Publisher,' but apparently thinks that six or seven pages are missing from the *Notes* simply because they are not numbered. Is he, perhaps, unaccustomed to reading books? The fact that a copy of *Notes* should have been returned to you is really no reason for despair. Though in this particular case it seems to have been due simply to a misunderstanding, it is conceivable that someone might send back his copy as a gesture of strong disapproval with the contents. At least this would show that he had read the book, and also that he had understood enough of it to provoke a strong reaction: and this is really more than we can hope from the majority of the people we have sent it to. In fact, if the entire edition were returned with contumely, we should be able to congratulate ourselves on having produced a profound effect—and remember that hate and love are very close. As it is, however, I fear that the book will be 'much treasured', but not 'much read'. (After all, if people *do* start sending back their copies, we shall be able to send them out to an entirely fresh set of people—beginning with the Archbishop of Colombo, perhaps?)

I find it a little discouraging that, in no less than four replies, the title of the book is given as 'Notes on *the* Dhamma'. This carelessness in such an obvious matter makes one wonder if it really is worth the trouble of spending perhaps an entire morning working on a single sentence to get it exactly right, with the necessary and sufficient degree of qualification, not too much and not too little, to guard against all possible misinterpretation. If readers are going to add and subtract words to suit themselves, all this seems to be so much wasted effort (apart, of course, from the satisfaction one derives from actually getting a recalcitrant sentence to express one's meaning precisely—but then this is at least half the pleasure of writing).

I am not too anxious to have the *Notes* associated in any way with the BPS, if only because the *Notes* condemn most of the views that the BPS is concerned to propagate.[1]

Palinurus is Cyril Connolly, who edited the highbrow magazine *Horizon* throughout the last war. It maintained a persistently high standard, when standards everywhere else were deteriorating, but it ran at a loss and was kept in being by a wealthy and disinterested patron (I forget whom). Connolly is of interest as a particularly articulate and well-read example of the despairing modern European intellectual (Camus was another). He has lost all faith in religion (his ideas about the Dhamma, which he puts together with Christianity, are quite mistaken), and yet sees no hope outside religion. Connolly, who is quite as cultured as Huxley, lacks Huxley's missionary zeal for the salvation of mankind (on a modest scale) through mysticism for the few and mescalin for the masses, and consequently sees nothing for it but continuation of the 'book-bed-bath defence system'. And, after all, Europe actually has nothing better to offer than despair, together with a number of elaborate and fairly efficacious—but strictly temporary—devices for concealing despair. The only permanent defence against despair—*sīla-samādhi-paññā*—is quite unknown in the West (and, alas! it is becoming almost unknown in the East).

You will have noticed that my interpretation of *The Trial* as the account of a man who, at a certain point in his life, suddenly asks himself why he exists, and then considers various possible justifications for his existence until he is finally obliged to admit honestly to himself that there is *no* justification, corresponds to what I have said in the Preface to the *Notes*:

> Every man, at every moment of his life, is engaged in a perfectly definite concrete situation in a world that he normally takes for granted. But it occasionally happens that he starts to think. He becomes aware, obscurely, that he is in perpetual contradiction with himself and with the world in which he exists.

*The Trial* describes what happens to a man when he starts to think: sooner or later he condemns himself as unjustified, and then despair begins (K.'s execution, the execution of hope, is the beginning of despair—henceforth he is a dead man, like Connolly and Camus and so many other intelligent Europeans, and do what he may he can never quite forget it). It is only at this point that the Buddha's Teaching begins to be intelligible. But it must be remembered that for Connolly and the others, death at the end of this life is the final death, and the hell of despair in which they live will come to an end in a few years' time—why, then, should they give up their distractions, when, if things get too bad, a bullet through their brain is enough? It is only when one understands that death at the end of this life is *not* the final end, that to follow the Buddha's Teaching is seen to be not a mere matter of choice but a matter of necessity. Europe does not know what it *really* means to despair.

**[L. 79]** **24 November 1963**

I was particularly pleased to get your last letter since it seems to show that you are managing to make some sense out of the *Notes*—and this, in its turn, means that I have succeeded, to that extent, at least, in making the *Notes* intelligible. PHASSA, to which you make particular reference, is by no means the easiest in the book; and though you do not indicate how far the subordinate notes are comprehensible to you, it is already a considerable advance to have grasped that 'contact' is primarily 'an appropriation by a misconceived self' (to use your own words). By way of contrast, here is the Milindapañha's account of 'contact':

> "Bhante Nāgasena, what is contact?"
> "Your majesty, contact is the act of coming in contact."
> "Give an illustration."
> "It is as if, your majesty, two rams were to fight one another. The eye is comparable to one of these rams, form to the other, and contact to their collision with each other."
> "Give another illustration."
> "It is as if, your majesty, the two hands were to be clapped together. The eye is comparable to one hand, form to the other, and contact to their collision with each other."
> "Give another illustration."
> "It is as if, your majesty, two cymbals were to be clapped together. The eye is comparable to one cymbal, form to the other, and contact to their collision with each other."
> "You are an able man, bhante Nāgasena."
> (from Warren's *Buddhism in Translations*, pp. 186-87)

An admirable demonstration of how to explain a difficulty by leaving it out! Can you wonder that the Milinda is such a popular book? Everybody can understand it; and one begins to ask oneself, really, if it was altogether necessary to have made the Suttas quite so difficult. And now we have this interfering busybody come to tell us that 'The Milindapañha is a particularly misleading book'![a]

I quite agree that comments on the *Notes* are likely to be few and slow, and I also agree that it is a matter of very secondary importance. Constructive criticism will probably be negligible (though I might get some ideas for improvements and additions—particularly to meet unforeseen objections); and we are certainly not seeking anybody's *Imprimatur* to sanction our appearance in public. The principal reason, surely, for our saying that we should be glad to hear the comments that people may wish to make is to find out how much adverse or positively hostile reaction the *Notes*, with their rather anti-traditional tone, are likely to arouse—in other words, to find out to what extent (if at all) the Ven. Siridhamma Thera's apprehensions and, more particularly, the other doctor's alarmist forebodings are justified. In brief, to find out whether any precautions are necessary if and when the *Notes* are made generally available to the public at large. For the rest, so long as we know that a few people at least are likely to find them helpful, that is all that really matters. (Naturally, I am curious to know what people's first impression is, in order to satisfy my author's vanity; but this is quite beside the point.)

Is one always morally obliged to acknowledge the receipt of a gift that one has not asked for? One does, of course, if it is something pleasant, or if one wants to keep on good terms with the donor. But if a complete stranger sends me, say, a book of Christian or communist propaganda (perhaps even with a genuine desire to edify me), then, I have to admit, I feel no obligation at all to give any indication that I have received it. And if I am sent positively subversive literature, is it not perhaps my duty to get the police to arrest the donor? Each case, no doubt, we have to take on its merits—and, after all, can we be so sure that the people to whom we are so enthusiastically sending the *Notes* will be receiving them with an equal enthusiasm?

---

**a.** Kierkegaard once remarked that, since all his contemporaries were busily engaged in making everything (i.e. Christianity) easy, the only task left for him was to make it difficult again. And this he proceeded to do, not without effect. During the last months of his life he launched a bitter attack on the falsity and hypocrisy of the Established Church in Denmark with its state-salaried priests. He expected to suffer persecution for this attack; but, instead, became a popular figure.

**[L. 80]** **30 November 1963**

I have finished Russell's *Nightmares* and must confess that they did not come up to expectation. No doubt it was my fault for expecting too much, knowing how unsatisfactory I find his philosophical views; but I had hoped that, at least, when he was not writing normal philosophy, he would be entertaining. Alas! I found his wit insipid, and his serious passages almost intolerable—there was something of the embarrassment of meeting a Great Man for the first time, and finding him even more preoccupied with trivialities than oneself.

In his Introduction, Russell says 'Every isolated passion is, in isolation, insane; sanity may be defined as a synthesis of insanities,' and then he proceeds to give us examples of isolated insanities—the Queen of Sheba as Female Vanity, Bowdler as Prudery, the Psycho-Analyst as Social Conformity, and so on. Amongst these, as you noted, is the Existentialist as Ontological Scepticism. Here, Russell's satire is directed partly against what Sartre has called 'a literature of extreme situations'; and this, for an Englishman, is no doubt a legitimate target, since the English do not admit that there are such things—though, of course, this makes the English a target for the satire of the rest of Europe, particularly the French.

But what Russell is *not* entitled to do is to group the insanity of doubting one's existence along with the other insanities, and this for the simple reason that it *precedes* them. One may be vain or modest; one may be prudish or broad-minded; one may be a social conformist or an eccentric; but in order to be *any* of these things, one must at least *be*. The question of one's existence must be settled *first*—one cannot be insanely vain if one doubts whether one exists at all and, precisely, Russell's existentialist does not *even* succeed in suffering—except when his philosophy is impugned (but this merely indicates that he has failed to apply his philosophy to itself, and not, as Russell would have us believe, because he has failed to regard his philosophy in the light of his *other* insanities). The trouble really is, that Russell does not, or rather will not, admit that *existence* poses a problem at all; and, since he omits this category from all his thinking nothing he says concerns anybody in particular.

It is noteworthy that the one nightmare that did amuse me, that of the Metaphysician, does in fact represent Russell's own personal nightmare—a fear of discovering existence (for existence and the negative—'not'—go hand in hand). But Russell has long ago firmly repressed this fear by harsh logical measures, and it only shows its head when he is off his logical guard. Once upon a time, Russell said 'Whatever A may be, it certainly is'; but that was in 1903. Since then Russell has learned sanity (his own brand), and has declared (in 1919) 'It is of propositional functions that you can assert or deny existence.' In other words, Russell holds that you can assert 'lions exist', and that this *means* '"X is a lion" is sometimes true', but that if you say 'this lion exists' you have said something meaningless. From this it follows that Russell regards the assertion 'I exist' as a meaningless utterance, and this allows him to regard the existentialist as a lunatic.

It is no doubt true that the assertions, 'I exist', 'I do not exist', and so on, are meaningless, *but only in the eyes of one who is no longer a puthujjana.* And, even then, they are not meaningless *in Russell's sense*. According to one of the Commentaries, the Buddha once said that 'all *puthujjanas* are mad', and from this point of view the *puthujjana*'s doubts about his existence are insanity. But this is not Russell's point of view, since he is still a *puthujjana.*

Together with existence, Russell has removed the word 'not' from Logic (even if he does not go so far as his metaphysician Bumblowski, who has expelled it from his ordinary language). Russell came to the conclusion (I speak from memory) that to say 'A is not B', where A and B are individual things, is illegitimate; what one should say is '"A is B" is false'. Thus, instead of *exists* and *not*, Russell has *true* and *false*; but whereas the first pair applies to *things*, the second pair applies to *facts*—it is only of *propositions* that you can assert the truth or the falsity. (For the significance of this replacement of *things* by *facts*—it is the foundation of positivism—I would refer you to note (f) of the Preface to the *Notes*.) I may say that I enjoyed Russell's idea of a special department of Hell for those philosophers who have refuted Hume—this is one of the few points about which I agree with Russell (but does it not make nonsense of Russell's whole philosophy of the acceptance of 'scientific common sense'? Russell would be only too happy to be *able* to refute Hume).

I was interested by the 'Mathematician's Nightmare', but for quite a different reason. There, you will remember, Professor Squarepoint has a vision in which all the numbers come to life and dance a ballet. Amongst these numbers there is one that refuses to be disciplined, and insists on coming forward. It is 137,[1] and this number is the cosmic number that Sir Arthur Eddington found to be at the base of physics. Now it so happened that I used to be interested in Eddington's interest in this apparently rather undistinguished number, perhaps even *because* it is so undistinguished in every other respect. And it happened that my interest in this number enabled me, indirectly, to write *FS*. Although, now, I have entirely lost my interest in 137, and although it plays no part in my description of Fundamental Structure, yet it is not difficult to trace it in the *Notes*. In §I/9, I say that the structure of a thing of certain complexity is represented by $\begin{array}{cc:cc} o & o & o & o \\ o & x & o & x \\ \hdashline o & o & x & x \\ o & x & x & o \end{array}$. This is arrived at by purely phenomenological description (i.e. in the *reflexive* description of experience as such). Now, Eddington (I reproduce his arguments as far as I remember them) says that this figure represents the structure of a 'particle' (in nuclear physics).[a] Now, so long as Eddington sticks to the figure above as the structure of a 'particle' he remains (whether he knows it or not) within the field of phenomenology (which requires an 'observer' as well as an 'observed'—like the 'subject' and 'object' in *phassa*). But Eddington is a quantum physicist, and must treat his results with scientific objectivity (which eliminates the 'observer' or 'subject'—see the last footnote to the Preface), and so he must do away with himself. How does he do it? Answer: by putting another 'particle', similar to the first, to take his place. Eddington then quietly retires, leaving *a relationship between two identical 'particles'*. To find out the nature of this relationship we simply have to multiply the two 'particles' together. Since each 'particle' has 10 o's and 6 x's, simple arithmetic gives us 100 oo's, 36 xx's, and 120 xo's (or ox's). For some reason that I now forget, we ignore the unlike pairs (xo's and ox's), and consider only the oo's and xx's. Added together these come to 136. And this, so it seems, is *the number of degrees of freedom of the electron*. But there is a snag: since the two particles we multiplied together are absolutely indistinguishable in all respects, we can never know, in any calculation, whether we have got them the right way round or not. So one extra degree of freedom has to be added to compensate for our uncertainty. The total number is therefore 137. (I am afraid, perhaps, that these pages may be something of 'The District Judge's Nightmare'; but there's nothing in them of any importance whatsoever.)

In any case, thank you for sending the book, which both satisfied my curiosity and exercised my critical faculty.

---

**a.** I do not allow the validity of the arguments he uses to *derive* this figure; such, for example, as the postulate that a given particle A has an equal chance of existing or of *not* existing. This strange assumption, which has currency neither with Russell nor with me, has as its immediate consequence the remarkable conclusion that *exactly the same number of things exist as do not exist*. (Whatever one may think of this, it is apparently good currency in quantum theory, if we are to judge from the following utterance by Dirac: 'We may look upon these unoccupied states as holes among the occupied ones... The holes are just as much physical things as the original particles...' [*PQM*, p. 252] But it must be remembered that quantum theory is an *ad hoc* system made to account for the observed facts and produce results. So long as it does this [and it does it only rather imperfectly] nobody bothers about whether it is intelligible or not.)

**[L. 81]** **8 December 1963**

I had heard vaguely about President Kennedy's assassination from several people. It seems to have been rather a spectacular affair on the whole—first the actual assassination of the President at long range by a skilled marksman, and then the televised murder of the alleged assassin (even out of court, I see, you will only allow that the assassin was 'alleged') by the owner of a night-club. Splendid copy for the newspapers. Personally, I am inclined to feel that the fact of a murderer's victim being a politician should be taken as an extenuating circumstance when he comes to be tried. Politicians can be extremely provoking.

The news of Huxley's death,[1] on the other hand, makes me rather melancholy. I had hoped vaguely (probably without good reason) that he might have found something in the *Notes* of use to him, in payment of the debt that I owe him for the instruction that I derived from his books in my earlier days. I learnt from him to throw away a lot of rubbish that I was carrying around with me (which I had picked up during my course of education), and this saved me a lot of time and trouble later on. Of course, it was partly (and no doubt necessarily) a matter of throwing away the baby with the bathwater; and both Huxley and I had to go out subsequently to pick up the baby again. The curious thing is that we picked up different babies.

I am re-reading Sartre's *L'Être et le Néant* with some care to find out the extent of my disagreement with him. Earlier, the book was of some help to me, and was at the same time a hindrance, since I accepted things that had later to be rejected. The basic point of disagreement is that Sartre takes the existence of the subject ('self') for granted, and identifies it with consciousness. But it is stimulating to disagree with him and to try to see exactly where there is disagreement. This exercise has resulted in a number of additions to and insertions in the *Notes*, with the idea of making certain things stand out more clearly. But there is nothing in the way of a major alteration. In the meantime, if you find things in the *Notes* that puzzle you, and you think I might be able to clarify them, then by all means let me know (of course, there are a number of things that are difficult in themselves, and no amount of additional words will simplify them, but there may also be things about which I have been unnecessarily obscure).

**[L. 82]** **15 December 1963**

The Sinhalese gentleman's comment can perhaps be taken as representative of educated interested Buddhist opinion in Ceylon—ready to listen to unfamiliar ideas, but lacking, for the most part, the intellectual equipment to make very much of them. It seems that he has found the discussion of *PS* rather too difficult for him. Granted that the earlier part—paragraphs §§1-7—is, in his words, 'heavy stuff,' I was under the impression that the three final paragraphs—§§8-10—, where the notion of *paramattha sacca* is directly criticized, where fairly straightforward. Is it that my exposition lacks clarity or is the limitation on his side? I think that you had no great difficulty with them.

The students of Maha-Chulalongkorn University [Bangkok] had better be careful how they use the *Notes* as a work of reference. As the Ven. Siridhamma Thera remarked, if people use the *Notes* to help them with their studies they are going to fail their examinations. It is a fatal mistake to overestimate the intelligence of examiners, who do not take it kindly to receive instruction from their victims. The correct answer is usually determined in advance.

I have written to John Blofeld (a lecturer in Mahāyāna Buddhism) to tell him that though I was having a copy of the *Notes* sent to him, I rather thought, knowing his views, that they might not be quite his cup of tea. He wrote back in these terms: 'I am looking forward to receiving your *Notes*. *All* cups of Dhamma tea are welcome to me, the bitter and the sweet, since all combine to make the purest Soma, do they not? ... As you may know, I have for some years been following the Vajrayāna under various Tibetan and other teachers. I have come to feel that, whereas the Vajrayāna, Zen and Theravāda *look* as different as fish, flesh and fowl, they are in essence identical. The highest teaching in each is very, very close—the only difference is that some people (such as myself) need a lot of climbing equipment and others don't. All the gorgeous and glittering methods of the Vajrayāna aim at one thing—perfect mind control with a view to coming face to face with Reality; so you see how little my path differs from yours in essentials.'

But that is just the point—I *don't* see. It is notoriously difficult to talk to Hindus about the Buddhadhamma. Hindus assert that the Buddha was a Hindu (by birth, that is to say, which is the only way to be a Hindu),[a]

**a.** 'Can anybody deny that the Buddha was a Hindu? Can anybody deny that he was the tallest Hindu?'—impassioned Hindu writing in (I think) the *Maha Bodhi Journal*.

and infer from this that whatever he taught must of necessity be a part of Hinduism. The consequence of this conveniently simplified view is that no Hindu will admit that you are telling him anything that he does not already know. And if this is the situation between Hindus and Buddhists, it is a hundred times worse between Mahāyāna Buddhists and Theravādins. Mahāyānists accept the Pali Suttas (at their own valuation) and then claim to go beyond them (rather as Hegelians claimed to have gone beyond Christianity, by mediation in a higher synthesis). The Mahāyānists interpret the Pali Suttas (with which they are usually not very well acquainted) to conform with their own ideas; and the trouble is that there is much in the current orthodox Theravādin interpretation of the Pali Suttas to support the Mahāyānist contention. (An English *bhikkhu* with Theravāda *upasampadā* uses these interpretations to ridicule the Theravādin claims to be different from Mahāyāna; and so long as these interpretations are allowed to be orthodox it is not easy to challenge his argument.)[1]

I think I told you some time ago (in connexion with Huxley and chemical mysticism) that the Mahāyānist view can be summed up in two propositions, the first common to all mystics, and the second supposed to represent the Buddha's solution to the problem raised by the first.

(i) *Behind the ordinary appearance of things there lies Reality*, which it is the task of the Yogi to seek. Existentialist philosophers do not go as far as this: if they admit such a Reality—Jaspers, for example—they qualify it by saying that it is necessarily out of reach. See Preface (m).

(ii) *Reality is the non-existence of things.* In other words, things do not *really* exist, they only appear to do so on account of our ignorance (*avijjā*). (George Borrow[2] tells of a Spanish gypsy in the last century whose grandfather held this view, so it hardly needs a Buddha to declare it. It seems to be closely allied to the Hindu notion of *māyā*—that all is illusion.)

Now the Pali texts say that the Buddha taught *anicca/dukkha/anattā*, and the average Theravādin, monk or layman, seems to take for granted that *aniccatā*, or impermanence, means that things are perpetually changing, that they do not remain the same for two consecutive moments. Failing to make the necessary distinctions (see PAṬICCASAMUPPĀDA (c)), they understand this as implying perpetual flux of everything all the time. This, of course, destroys the principle of self-identity, 'A is A'; for unless something endures unchanged for at least a certain interval of time you cannot even make the assertion 'this is A' since the word 'is' has lost its meaning. Bypassing *dukkha* as something we all know about, they arrive at *anattā* as meaning 'without self-identity'. (This is Mr. Wettimuny's theme,[3] following Dahlke. I do not think he is aware that he is putting himself among the Mahāyānists.) Granted the premise that *anicca* means 'in continuous flux', this conclusion is impeccable. Unfortunately, in doing away with the principle of self-identity, you do away with *things*—including *change*, which is also a *thing*. This means that for the *puthujjana*, who does not see *aniccatā*, *things exist*, and for the *arahat*, who has seen *aniccatā*, *things do not exist.* Thus the Mahāyānist contention is proved.

The difficulty arises when we deal with the *sekha*, who is in between the two; are we to say for him that 'things partly exist and partly do not exist', or that for him 'some things exist and some do not' (in which case we seem to have Eddington and the quantum theory)? The former, no doubt, would be preferable, but what is one to make of *a partly non-existent thing*? And in any case we have the curious state of affairs that there is change (or impermanence) only so long as it is not seen; for in the very instant that it is seen it vanishes. (This is certainly true of *avijjā*—see *NP* §24—but the vanishing of *avijjā*, as *I* understand it, leaves impermanence intact and does not interfere with the three Laws of Thought.) I still don't think the *Notes* are Mr. Blofeld's cup of tea, but I shall be interested to see whether he is able to absorb them into Mahāyāna—if one has a mystical outlook, based on the principle that A is not A, there is nothing that cannot be reconciled with anything else.

I have been writing all this rather at random, and it may perhaps lack coherence, or at least shape. However, since the train of thought still has steam up I shall let it take me where it will. The final sentence of the last paragraph leads me to the reflection that any proposed solution to the problem that disregards the three Laws of Thought[b] is, in the profoundest sense, *frivolous*. I think, perhaps, that you are one of the rather few people who will feel that this must be true, that all thinking in defiance of these Laws is essentially irresponsible.

At this point the rationalist will stand up and say that all his thinking is *already* in conformity with these Laws, and that consequently for him there is no problem to be solved. But the situation is not quite so simple. The present state of scientific thinking (which claims to be rational thinking *par excellence*) shows only too clearly that rationalism can only be maintained at the cost of introducing the most extraordinary absurdities into its premises. In a recent letter I spoke of Eddington's assumption that 'exactly as many things exist as do not exist' and showed that this is good currency in quantum theory; and I now find that I have another example ready to

**b.** Identity—'A is A'; Contradiction—'A is not both B and not B'; Excluded Middle—'A is either B or not B'.

hand. The 'partly non-existent thing' that turned up in the last paragraph also finds its place in quantum theory.

Dirac says: 'The important things in the world appear as the invariants (or more generally the nearly invariants...) of these transformations.' (*PQM*, p. vii) A *thing* as an 'invariant' is quite in order—it is the Law of Identity, 'A is A'. But a 'nearly invariant' is only a quasi-identity, 'A is nearly A'—a '*nearly* invariant' is '*almost* a thing'. Only *things* can be said to *exist* ('to be a thing' is 'to be conceivable', which is 'to be able to exist'),[c] and consequently we can only say of 'almost a thing' that it 'almost exists', which is the same as saying that it is a 'partly non-existent thing'. And Dirac, mark you, is Lucasian Professor of Mathematics in the University of Cambridge. It is reported that a distinguished physicist (I don't know who) recently remarked that no theory that does not look completely crazy stands a chance of being true.[4] The rationalist no doubt does not see any problem to be solved, but this is certainly not because his thinking is in conformity with the Laws of Thought: on the contrary, it is because he successfully turns a blind eye to the fact that his thinking is based on violations of the Laws of Thought. No, the problem certainly is there (for the *puthujjana*, that is to say), and it is brought to light by persistent refusal to disregard the Laws of Thought.

It is the merit of the existentialist philosophers that they do in fact bring the problem to light in this way. What happens is this: the thinker examines and describes his own thinking in an act of reflexion, obstinately refusing to tolerate non-identities, contradictions, and excluded middles; at a certain point he comes up against a contradiction that he cannot resolve and that appears to be inherent in his very act of thinking. This contradiction is the existence of the thinker himself (as *subject*).

You will find this contradiction illustrated in the passage from Camus in NIBBĀNA (a), but it is more concisely presented in the later part of the Mahānidāna Suttanta (D.15/ii,66-8), where the Buddha says that a man who identifies his 'self' with feeling should be asked *which* kind of feeling, pleasant, unpleasant, or neutral, he regards as his 'self'. The man cannot identify

---

**c.** Cf. Parmenides (quoted by Russell in *M&L*, p. 15): 'It needs must be that what can be thought and spoken of is; for it is possible for it to be, and it is not possible for what is nothing [no thing] to be.' This is classed by Russell as 'mystical', which it certainly is not (though Parmenides may have misunderstood himself in the conclusions that he drew from this principle). The point is that the existence of images, and imagination generally, has no place in Russell's philosophy as a logician. It is therefore 'mystical', or, at best, 'psychological'. ('Psychology' is a convenient dumping ground for things for which rationalism has no use but which are too well established to be 'superstition'.)

his 'self' with all three kinds of feeling at once, since only one of the three kinds is present at a time: if he does make this identification, therefore, he must do it with the three different kinds of feeling in *succession*. His 'self', of course, he takes for granted as self-identical—'A is A'—that is to say as the *same* 'self' on each occasion. This he proceeds to identify in turn with the three *different* feelings: B, C, and D. A is therefore both B and C (not to mention D); and C, being different from B, is not B: so A is both B and not B—a violation of the Law of Contradiction. But whether or not it is with feeling that the *puthujjana* is identifying his 'self', he is always identifying it with *something*—and it is a *different* something on each occasion. The *puthujjana* takes his existence for granted—*cogito ergo sum* (which, as Sartre says, is apodictic reflexive evidence of the thinker's existence)—and is in a perpetual state of contradiction.

So we have the following situation. Assuming the validity of the Laws of Thought, the thinker discovers that the whole of his thinking depends upon an irreducible violation of the Laws of Thought, namely the contradictory existence of the thinker. And this itself is a contradiction. If he tolerates this contradiction he denies the validity of the Laws of Thought whose validity he assumed when he established the contradiction in the first place; there is therefore no contradiction for him to tolerate, and consequently he is not denying the Laws of Thought; the contradiction therefore exists and he tolerates it.... Or he may refuse to tolerate the contradiction; but if he does so, it is in the name of the Law of Contradiction that he does so, and refusal to tolerate the contradiction requires him to deny the validity of the Laws of Thought by which the contradiction was originally established; he has therefore no reason to refuse to tolerate the contradiction, which, if the Laws of Thought are invalid, is inoffensive; he therefore does not deny the validity of the Laws of Thought, and the contradiction *is* offensive and he refuses to tolerate it... Or perhaps he neither tolerates the contradiction nor refuses to tolerate it, in which case he violates the Law of Excluded Middle... Most certainly the problem exists!

How is it dealt with? (i) The *rationalist*, by remaining on the level of reason and refusing to look at his premises, asserts the validity of the Laws of Thought, and successfully blinds himself to the standing violation of the Laws of Thought—his own existence. (ii) The *mystic* endorses the standing violation of the Laws of Thought by asserting their invalidity on principle. This obliges him to attribute their apparent validity to blindness or ignorance and to assert a Reality behind appearances that is to be reached by developing a mode of thinking based on the three Laws: 'A is not A'; 'A is both B and not B'; 'A is neither B nor not B'. (iii) The *existentialist* says: 'Contradiction is the truth, which is a contradiction, and therefore the truth. This is the situation, and I don't like it; but I can see no way out of it'. To maintain this equivocal attitude for a long time is exhausting, and existentialists tend to seek relief in either rationalism or mysticism; but since they find it easier to endorse their personal existence than to ignore it they are more inclined to be mystical than rational.

Obviously, of these three attitudes, the first two evade the problem either by arbitrarily denying its existence or by arbitrarily denying the Laws of Thought upon which it depends. Only the third attitude asserts the Laws of Thought and asserts the existence of the problem. Though the *puthujjana* does not see the solution of the problem, he ought at least to see that to *evade* the problem (either by denying its existence or by denying the Laws of Thought on which it depends) is not to *solve* it. He will therefore choose to endure the discomfort of the third attitude until help comes from outside in the form of the Buddha's Teaching, or he himself finds the way out by becoming a Buddha.

I regard addresses in Germany and Austria as having high priority, for the reason that in Germany alone as many as 20,000 people call themselves Buddhists of one kind or another, and also that there is a strong idealist and existentialist philosophical tradition in Germany that may make the *Notes* more easily intelligible than elsewhere. In England, for example, there are few Buddhists—and mostly Zen—, and the prevailing philosophy is rationalist, *à la* Russell; and America is very much worse—hardly any Americans can think at all. After Germany perhaps France. There are few French Buddhists, and what interest there is is mostly in Sanskrit (Mahāyāna) Buddhism—French scholarship pioneered the study of Sanskrit Buddhism, leaving it to the English, who were occupying Ceylon and Burma, to study the Pali texts. But the French have the habit of thinking (though they sometimes overdo it—they proved to themselves by argument that they had lost the war, and then regarded the English as muddleheaded and illogical in deciding to go on with it), and they have fairly recently been initiated into the secrets of existentialism (themselves contributing one pope—Sartre—and one cardinal—Marcel—besides a number of lesser priests and deacons).[5]

You are quite right—I do *not* have in mind a detailed book (a thousand pages?) based on the *Notes*. Unless it is to be simply hack-work, a book like that must force itself on the author: in the first place, the plan of the book must suggest itself, since it is worse than useless to think up an arbitrary plan and try to force the material into it, with inevitable distortions; and in the second place, the bulk of the material must be to hand, and the author must feel himself, like Mrs. Willett, 'heavy with script.' And with me, neither of these two conditions is present. I do not have the necessary weight of reading behind me, nor do I have Sartre's remarkable power of description and lucid development of a theme for pages on end which is quite indispensable for such an undertaking. My talent, such as it is, is for sweating down an idea, not for fattening it up. And as for a plan, I do not have even the ghost of such a thing.

The *Notes*, as it seems to me, are like so many beads inter-connected with numbers of threads, in a kind of three-dimensional network, if you get the idea. Starting from any one bead, you can follow a thread to any of three or four connected beads, and from that bead you can go to any one of a number of others, and so on. Provided all the beads are included, and all the threads indicated (where necessary), it matters not in the least in which order they are presented. Actually, the *NP* is the result of putting together a number of separate notes, but the unity of that essay is due rather to the chain-like unity of the usual detailed *paṭiccasamuppāda* formulation, which imposes a certain order on the discussion. And, really, the loose structure (or absence of any structure) of the *Notes* suits my style and my purpose, and if ever a big book should result from the *Notes* it would still be in the form of notes: I never know what I am going to write about next, and I must always be free to insert something new at any place.

Besides, the Suttas themselves are, in a sense, in the form of notes: this can be seen from the entirely arbitrary way in which they have been collected together in Nikāyas. There is no connexion between one Sutta and the next, and if you change the order it makes not the slightest difference. There is certainly nothing in the way of the development of a theme from the beginning to the end of a Nikāya.

I once asked 'Are the Suttas, as we now have them, complete?' If, by *complete*, is meant 'do they contain all that the Buddha ever said?', the answer is certainly No. If it means 'has anything been lost since the First Council?' (which I think was what I intended by the question), the answer is quite probably that they are complete, that little or nothing has been lost.[6] But all this is quite beside the point. The Suttas are complete *for me* if there is enough to enable me to reach the goal; if not, not. Obviously this is going to be different for each person. One man may need only one Sutta, and then all the rest will be extra. For another man, a lot of Suttas will be required before they are complete *for him*. And for the vast majority the Suttas would not be complete if there were a hundred times as many of them as there are.

On a very much reduced scale the same is true of the *Notes*. The aim is single—to indicate (what for purposes of argument may be called) the proper interpretation of the Suttas. As soon as they have performed that service for any given individual, and not before, they are, for him, complete. Nothing that I add really says anything fresh—it is simply the same thing in different words, and is already implied in the rest of the notes.

**[L. 83]** **17 December 1963**

Disapproval, naturally, is to be expected, particularly in the quarter where it has been expressed. A parallel may be found in the medical profession, where a doctor with an unorthodox but effective remedy meets the greatest opposition from the Medical Association rather than from the patients who have benefited from his unorthodoxy. But we can't make omelettes without breaking eggs.

I could, naturally, soften or omit the passages complained of, but I don't particularly want to. The *Notes* have been written with the purpose of clearing away a mass of dead matter which is choking the Suttas, and some reference to it is necessary. Furthermore, if this is to be effective, shock-treatment is sometimes best: mere hints that all is not quite in order can only too easily be ignored.[a] It is possible that a reader who is not familiar with English idiom might suppose that when I say that the 'rot sets in with the Abhidhamma Piṭaka' (CITTA) I am saying that the Abhidhamma Piṭaka *is rot* (in the colloquial sense of *rubbish*). This, of course, is not my intention, and if it seems likely that many people are going to misunderstand this, the word 'decay' could be substituted without loss of meaning but with loss of strength. The 'vicious' doctrine I cannot help—it *is* vicious—, but I don't suppose that anyone will think that I mean to say that it has taken to drink and debauchery.

I think that you have misunderstood the nature of the objection that is raised to my interpretation of *saṅkhārā*. The traditional interpretation says that *saṅkhārā* in the *paṭiccasamuppāda* formulation are *cetanā* and *not anything else*. The Suttas say that *saṅkhārā* in the *paṭiccasamuppāda* are *kāya-*, *vacī-*, and *citta-saṅkhāra*, and they also define these as the in-and-out-breaths, thinking-and-pondering, and perception and feeling,

**a.** Question: Is this likely to antagonize anyone who might otherwise be sympathetic? Knowing Abhidhamma Piṭaka enthusiasts, I think not. Will it raise organized hostility? Not, I think, unless it is translated. If it does is this necessarily a bad thing? I don't know enough to give a definite answer, but it does not seem to be self-evident.

respectively.[b] The traditional interpretation ignores this definition, and takes these three terms as bodily, verbal, and mental action, respectively; and for this they can find a justification if they are prepared to equate the *cittasaṅkhāra* of the *paṭiccasamuppāda* with the *mano-saṅkhāra* that is sometimes found in the Suttas *but not in the paṭiccasamuppāda context*. For this see *NP* §16.

Furthermore, if you will refer to *NP* §6 you will see that *upon occasion*, the *saṅkhārā* of the *paṭiccasamuppāda do* mean *cetanā*. But though all *cetanā* (intentions) are *saṅkhārā* (determinations), the reverse is not true. And in particular, the in-and-out breaths are called *kāyasaṅkhārā* because (in the terms of the Cūḷavedalla Sutta—M.44/i,301) they are *kāyikā* (bodily) and are *kāyapaṭibaddhā* ('bound up with the body'), and *not* because they are *cetanā*. Similar considerations apply to *vacī-* and *citta-saṅkhārā*. Please refer to the last sentence of *NP* §5. But this argument does not, at this stage, raise the question whether or not the in-and-out breaths are *cetanā*.

[As a matter of fact they *are cetanā*, in the sense that (as you rightly say) breathing is a conscious act (though not necessarily a *deliberate* act, an act of *awareness*), and all consciousness is *intentional* (i.e. involves *volition*, understood, however, in a subtle sense—in the *Notes* the word *volition* is *not* used in this subtle sense, which I call *intention*; but see CETANĀ, fourth paragraph, and NĀMA, second paragraph). While in sleep we breathe, and while in sleep we are conscious; for we can be woken out of sleep by a noise. If we did not in some sense *hear* the noise, we should not awaken, and if we hear it we must be conscious: a noise cannot *provoke* consciousness, it can only *disturb* it.

[In the Suttas, consciousness does not cease until *saññāvedayitanirodha*, 'cessation of perception and feeling', which is above all the *jhānas* and all the *arūpa* attainments. Breathing, on the other hand, stops in the fourth *jhāna*, where there is still consciousness. (This means that, from the point of view of the individual concerned—which is the only point of view that matters—the body ceases in fourth *jhāna* and above. One cannot take one's body with one into the *arūpa* or 'immaterial' attainments.) If you are in any doubt about whether breathing involves intention or volition, put your hand firmly over your nose and mouth so that you are unable to breathe. You will soon discover a growing 'will-to-breathe' that will oblige you to remove your hand before ninety seconds are up. This will is there all the time, but

b. There is no Sutta where it is actually stated that the *kāya-*, *vacī-*, and *cittasaṅkhāra* of the *paṭiccasamuppāda* are the *same kāya-*, *vacī-*, and *citta-saṅkhāra* as those thus defined. But there is no *a priori* reason why they should not be.

it is not normally *noticed* so long as we can breathe freely. If the heart is obstructed, on the other hand, we feel pain, but it cannot be described as a 'will-to-heartbeat'.]

In addition to the foregoing, you may refer to §15 of *NP* and particularly the two sentences starting '*Saṅkhārapaccayā viññāṇaṃ....*' Here the discussion is drawing finer distinctions, and it is most improbable that the Venerable Objector has made anything of it at all. §19 shows that though the breathing is *kāyasaṅkhāra* because it is bound up with the body, it is *saṅkhāra* also as *cetanā* inasmuch as it is *experience* (all experience is intentional), and is thus entitled to a place in the *paṭiccasamuppāda* as *saṅkhāra* on two separate counts.

Confusion is possible if we ask 'As experience, what kind of intention is breathing?'; for the answer is that it is *kāyasañcetanā*, 'body-intention', along with all other intentional bodily actions (such as walking). And, referring again to §16, you will see that *kāyasañcetanā* is *kāyasaṅkhāra*. Thus breathing is twice *kāyasaṅkhāra*. But the word *kāyasaṅkhāra*, 'body-determination', is a grammatical compound that can be resolved in two distinct ways: (i) as 'what determines the body', and (ii) as 'a determination that is bodily'. In the first it is the breaths (as bound up with the body—the body depends on the breathing), and in the second it is any determination (specified by the Sutta of §16 as *intention*) involving the body (breathing, walking, etc.).

*Vacīsaṅkhāra*, 'speech-determination', also has this double sense: in the first it is 'what determines speech', which is thinking-and-pondering; and in the second it is 'a determination (as intention) that is verbal', as (for example) swearing. But thinking-and-pondering is not speech-determination in the second sense: as intentional action (*sañcetanā*) it is obviously *mind*-determination. But, with 'mind-determination', only the English is ambiguous, not the Pali: for the first sense of 'mind-determination' we have *cittasaṅkhāra*, and for the second sense we have *manosaṅkhāra*.

The traditional interpretation takes advantage of this verbal ambiguity—ignoring the *citta/mano* discrepancy—to define *saṅkhārā* in the *paṭiccasamuppāda* as exclusively *cetanā*. (I think, perhaps, if you want to see the distinction clearly, you might take 'thinking-and-pondering' as a test-case. Thinking-and-pondering is said in the Cūḷavedalla Sutta (which gives the *first* sense of *vacīsaṅkhāra*) to be speech-determination, for the following reason: 'First having thought and pondered, then one breaks into speech.' Ask yourself 'Is thinking-and-pondering speech-determination also in the sense of being *verbal action*?'.) Now, it seems, it is *I* who am accused of confusing these two senses (in the reverse direction, of course).

This can only be made by someone who takes for granted the traditional interpretation of *paṭiccasamuppāda*—if the interpretation is not pre-judged, purely verbal considerations as well as those of consistency support the *Notes*.

The discussion, as you see, is rather involved, and there is a temptation to cut the Gordian knot by ignoring these distinctions. Unless one is capable of following the intricacies of the situation, and is actually prepared to do so, a certain amount of good will is necessary if the interpretation of the *Notes* is to be accepted. Unfortunately there seems to be little reason to suppose that the Venerable Objector possesses either the capacity or the good will. But I do not see that any purpose would be served by setting out the argument in greater detail: as I remark in §7, the note is not a polemic, and if the reader is not already dissatisfied with the traditional interpretation no amount of argument will convince him.

The Venerable One who remarked that there are many mistakes in the *Notes* is perfectly correct: there *are* many mistakes in the *Notes*—from the traditional point of view. But if he thinks I am not aware of them he is doing me an injustice.

The question whether it is right to write against books like the Paṭṭhāna seems to be largely rhetorical. I regret that I find it necessary to disagree with the Paṭṭhāna, but since I do I am prepared to state my disagreement in writing. It is, if I may say so without presumption, to the greater glory of the Suttas; but I don't suppose the Venerable One would see it quite in this light.

I am glad to hear that there are some laymen who are finding the *Notes* worth studying. By all means let them send questions about points needing further elucidation. The more sharply the questions can be framed the better it is, not only for me but also for the questioner, who will perhaps find out what it is precisely that he is asking—and may thus discover that he has answered his own question.

Your letter shows only too clearly what I knew all along, namely that the *Notes* will get a more intelligent hearing from laymen than from monks. This *ought* not to be so, but it *is* so. At the very least, criticism from monks should amount to something more than simply pointing out that the *Notes* deviate from the accepted view. Surely, if they have given any thought to the Suttas at all, they must see that the accepted view might perhaps not be altogether infallible—especially in view of the poor results in terms of *ariyapuggalas* produced. Like the one above about the Paṭṭhāna, it is a rhetorical question, or so I fear.

**[L. 84]** **18 December 1963**

Yes, yet another letter from me!

As a concession to the Venerable Objector, I have altered the offending 'rot' to 'decay', which is perhaps less of an irritant. I am sorry that the Ven. Siridhamma Thera had to bear the brunt of the Ven. Objector's displeasure.[1] For my part, I have no wish to irritate anybody at all. On the other hand, if it seems necessary to do so in order that some definite benefit may result elsewhere, then I don't shrink from it. (It is not I who set out to irritate so-and-so, but so-and-so who allows himself to be irritated at what I write; and that is his responsibility.) In any case, I am not prepared to be blackmailed or threatened into silence by pontifical tantrums, though I *am* prepared to be silent if I think no good will come of speaking. The question is, are people *seriously* interested in the *Notes*, or merely ටිකං[2] interested? In any case, we are not obliged to decide immediately, and we can afford to wait until we see if there are further objections to printing. It is depressing to think what a lot of space some people take up in this world. (It seems rather a pity, now, that I was not able to cut the stencils on the Venerable Objector's own typewriter—a very interesting situation might have arisen.)[3]

**[L. 85]** **24 December 1963**

I am sorry that you should have had a slight attack of alarm and despondency after hearing two opinions of *bhikkhus* on the *Notes*. In order that you should know quite clearly 'what the world is coming to' I translate a Sutta from the Aṅguttara (see PAṬICCASAMUPPĀDA).[1] It is quite natural, of course, that you should have doubts from time to time about the validity of the *Notes*, particularly when they are attacked from an 'official' quarter: you are bound to take them largely on trust, and it is always a comfort, when one is feeling a little tired, to be on the side of established opinion. As Kierkegaard says,

> The spirit of dialectical fearlessness is not so easily acquired; and the sense of isolation which remains despite the conviction of right, the sadness of the parting from admired and trustworthy [or *trusted*?] authorities, is the line of demarcation which marks the threshold of its acquirement. (*CUP*, pp. 15-6)

If you are going to champion the *Notes* you must be prepared to feel a little lonely upon occasion.

Possibly you will notice, at times, some doubt and hesitation on my part about the wisdom of publishing the *Notes*. This, you must understand, is entirely concerned with the question of how the *Notes* will be received by other people: about the correctness of the *Notes*, in essentials at least (I cannot guarantee every detail), I have no doubt at all, and there is some heavy artillery in reserve if the situation requires it. I am actually in a double isolation: first, as not knowing of anyone in Ceylon who can confirm the *Notes*, and secondly, as being quite out of touch with people generally. It is on account of the second that I feel hesitant and must seek the advice of others and see what people do actually have to say about the *Notes*.

As you say, specialists in the Abhidhamma books will not like criticism of them. Such specialists are those I referred to a long time ago[2] as 'people with a vested interest in the Dhamma': having acquired a specialized knowledge of some branch of the scriptures as a whole, they depend upon this to maintain them in a position of esteem or material advantage. Dhamma Sunday-school teachers, for example, will not be pleased (they teach the *cittavīthi* to ten-year-olds, which is sheer cruelty to children, apart from anything else).

The elephant season is starting here; they have been trumpeting all day in the middle distance. Perhaps they will come closer tonight.

P.S. The difficulty with the Venerable Objector is that we have to live with him, whereas you don't. We are obliged to pay him respect on account of his seniority, and this is quite as it should be; but it tends to be accepted as a homage to his superior wisdom, which is a debatable inference. The consequence is, however, that if his wisdom is questioned, even by implication, it is immediately interpreted as disrespect.

## [L. 86] 29 December 1963

I expect this letter will be a little dull and prosy since I propose to talk about the *cittavīthi* and the Abhidhamma Piṭaka. My purpose is rather to put you in a position to answer questions that may be raised about the rough treatment that these things receive in the *Notes*.

I have been refreshing my mind about the *cittavīthi* and its origins in the Abhidhamma Piṭaka in order to make sure that CITTA is all in order.

I find, to begin with, that I have given a wrong reference—it should be Chapter XIV, and *not* XXII, of the Visuddhimagga. This is not of much importance, and can easily be corrected; and, anyway, Ch. XXII is the correct reference for the second part of the note. Next, I see that the whole question of the origins of the *cittavīthi* is dealt with in the Ven. Ñāṇamoli Thera's translation, *The Path of Purification*, Ch. IV note 13 (p. 131).[1] The relevant passages from the Vibhaṅga and Paṭṭhāna are given in full, and it can be seen how the Sutta material is there interpreted (or, rather, misinterpreted) for the first time as a temporal 'succession of items each coming to an end before the next appears' (to quote my own words from CITTA). If, therefore, anyone asks why these two particular books are singled out for criticism and on what grounds they are criticized, it is necessary only to point to this footnote in *The Path of Purification*. Turning to Ch. XIV of that book (which chapter contains the principal account of the *cittavīthi*), I find the following footnote (no. 47, p. 515):

> 'For those who do not admit the cognitive series beginning with receiving, just as they do not admit the heart basis [don't worry about this—it has no connexion with the cognitive series], the Pali has been handed down in various places, in the way beginning "For the eye-consciousness-element as receiving (*sampaticchanāya cakkhuviññāṇadhātuyā*)"; for the Pali cannot be contradicted.' (*Paramatthamañjūsa—Visuddhimagga* Sub Commentary) The quotation as it stands is not traced to the *Piṭakas*.

So you see that I am not the first to question the validity of the *cittavīthi*. Apparently there has been, in time past, enough opposition to it to call for official censure of scepticism about it, and quotation of passages from the Pali (i.e. earlier texts) in support of the doctrine. Alas! these would-be authoritative passages are not to be found even in the Abhidhamma Piṭaka. The very fact that it is found necessary to assert the validity of a doctrine (instead of allowing it to speak for itself) is at once enough to arouse suspicions. Compare this passage from Kierkegaard:

> Objective thinking…imparts itself without further ado, and, at the most, takes refuge in assurances respecting its own truth, in recommendations as to its trustworthiness, and in promises that all men will some time accept it—it is so certain. Or perhaps rather so uncertain; for the assurances and the recommendations and the promises, which are presumably for the sake of the others who are asked to accept

> it, may also be for the sake of the teacher, who feels the need of the security and dependability afforded by being in a majority. (*CUP*, pp. 70-1)

How often K. hits the nail on the head! And how quotable he is! So much for the *cittavīthi*.

In my last letter I sent you a translation of Aṅguttara V,viii,9, which contains this passage: '...they, being undeveloped in body, virtue, mind, and understanding, when discussing the advanced teaching and engaging in cross-questioning, falling into a dark teaching will not awaken.' I added a footnote to say that the word *abhidhamma* that occurs in this passage does *not* refer to the Abhidhamma Piṭaka. This needs some further discussion.

In the Ven. Buddhaghosa Thera's Commentary (Atthasālinī) to the first book of the Abhidhamma Piṭaka (Dhammasaṅganī), he gives the traditional account of the origin of the Abhidhamma Piṭaka. This is to the effect that, during the three months of one *vassāna*[2] season, the Buddha stayed in the Tāvatiṃsa heaven (or perhaps Tusita, I forget) teaching *abhidhamma* to the assembled *devatā*. At the end of each day he repeated the day's instruction to the Ven. Sāriputta Thera, who handed it on to the other *bhikkhus*. This instruction was gathered together and now forms the books of the Abhidhamma Piṭaka. According to the tradition, then, the matter contained in the present Abhidhamma Piṭaka was in existence before the Buddha's final extinction at Kusinārа.

In accordance with this tradition, all the other Commentaries of the Ven. Buddhaghosa Thera insist that wherever the word *abhidhamma* occurs in the Suttas it refers to the books of the Abhidhamma Piṭaka. Moreover, the Ven. Buddhaghosa Thera, in the Atthasālinī, utters anathema—perhaps this is too strong, but I don't recall the actual words—against people who doubt that the Abhidhamma Piṭaka is really the Buddha's *ipsissimum verbum*. (As above, with the *cittavīthi*, this circumstance points to a solid body of scepticism about the authenticity of the Abhidhamma Piṭaka, and to the commentator's subconscious uneasiness about the soundness of his position, requiring him to have the majority on his side.)

The word *abhidhamma* occurs in the Suttas, sometimes alone, and sometimes together with the word *abhivinaya*, just as the simple word *dhamma* is sometimes linked with the simple word *vinaya*. This leads at once to the question: If the word *abhidhamma* refers to the Abhidhamma Piṭaka, in distinction from the word *dhamma*, which refers to the *Dhamma* (i.e. Sutta) Piṭaka, are we not entitled to look for an Abhivinaya Piṭaka as well as a Vinaya Piṭaka? But there is no trace of such a thing; and it is quite clear that *abhivinaya* means something like 'advanced discipline', which is part and parcel of the Vinaya Piṭaka. (We can ignore here the possibility that *vinaya*, as well as *abhivinaya*, means something more than just the rules. Literally, it means 'leading out', and as *vineti* it occurs in the Aṅguttara Sutta that I translated for you, where it is rendered as 'to direct'—'they are unable to direct them in higher virtue, higher mind, and higher understanding.')

Similarly, we have no *a priori* reason for supposing that *abhidhamma* means more than 'advanced teaching', understood as the more difficult and essential parts of the Sutta teaching. It is a constant feature of Indian philosophical or religious texts that they are attributed to some ancient and famous teacher in order to give them authority (in the West, on the contrary, the more modern the text the better); and this holds true even of the obviously later Pali books (the Ven. Mahākaccāna Thera is credited with the Nettipakaraṇa and with a grammar, while the Ven. Sāriputta Thera has the Paṭisambhidāmagga and, possibly, the Niddesas attributed to him). It is thus wholly to be expected that attempts should be made to secure the authority of the Abhidhamma Piṭaka (assuming that it is, in fact, a later production) by identifying it with the *abhidhamma* of the Suttas. Add to this the fact that the Atthasālinī and the other commentarial works of the Ven. Buddhaghosa Thera are perhaps nine hundred years later than the Abhidhamma Piṭaka that they set out to defend, and you will see that if we find internal reason for rejecting the books of the Abhidhamma Piṭaka as not authoritative (i.e. if we find that the texts of these books cannot be reconciled with our understanding of the Sutta texts) there is nothing very much to compel us to accept them as the Buddha's own Teaching.

My teacher, the late Ven. Nāyaka Thera,[3] said in private that nobody had ever become *arahat* through listening to the books of the Abhidhamma Piṭaka. He did not, however, say that they were wrong. But if you refer to the passage from the Aṅguttara Sutta that I have quoted above, you will see that a teaching that does *not* lead to awakening (or enlightenment)—that is, if it sets out to do so—can be called a *kaṇha dhamma*, a 'dark teaching'. This prompts the thought that the books of the Abhidhamma Piṭaka originated, not as tradition describes, but as the *kaṇha dhamma* resulting from mistaken *abhidhamma* discussion by monks undeveloped in body, virtue, mind, and understanding.

Be all this as it may, the *Notes* refer to the Abhidhamma Piṭaka only in connexion with two specific things—the *cittavīthi* and the *paṭiccasamuppāda*—and there is no indiscriminate criticism of the Abhidhamma Piṭaka as a whole.

**[L. 87]** **31 December 1963**

The *Notes* seem to have struck Mrs. Quittner[1] with considerable impact, and her immediate reaction is all that could be desired. What disturbs her is the fact that statements are made throughout the *Notes* 'without any reasons' being given for them, on the 'take it or leave it' principle. What the self-respecting reader wants is to have his opinion consulted by the author, who is expected to allow him to make up his own mind about the points at issue, and thus either to agree or to disagree with what is said in the book. If the author does not do this (by failing to give his reasons) he insults the reader (and particularly the feminine reader) by seeming to assume that he (or she) has no opinion worth consulting.

But the one thing I want to avoid is to have readers make up their own mind about the book; for once they have objectively decided whether they agree or disagree with the author's arguments they will shut the book, forget it, and pass on to the next one. No, the *Notes* are designed to be an invitation, a provocation, a challenge, to the reader to come and share the author's point of view; and if the book starts off by democratically assuming that the reader's opinion is as good as the author's, it will simply defeat its own purpose. At all costs the reader must be prevented from fraternizing with the author.

Consider, for example, Mrs. Quittner's complaint that with a few strokes of the author's pen 'we are reduced from three to two baskets and this without giving any reasons for his statement.' (The reference is evidently to note (a) of the Preface.) If I had provided a discussion of my reasons for doubting the authenticity of the Abhidhamma Piṭaka (on the lines, perhaps, of what I said in my last letter to you), at once people would have had something positive to seize hold of, and learned controversy might have started up leading more and more passionately away from the point at issue. As Kierkegaard says,

> In general, all that is needed to make the question simple and easy is the exercise of a certain dietetic circumspection, the renunciation of every learned interpolation or subordinate consideration, which in a trice might degenerate into a century-long parenthesis. (*CUP*, pp. 29-30)

As things are, the reader is informed bluntly (condescendingly?) at the beginning of the *Notes* which canonical books the author proposes to regard as unquestionably correct, so that there will be no room for confusion in the matter. Then, if the reader wants to know the reason for the author's rejection of certain books (the Abhidhamma Piṭaka, for example), he must make the effort to understand the *Notes* and see things as the author sees them. When he has done this, the reason for the rejection of these books will be self-evident.

Mrs. Quittner's 'arrogant, scathing, and condescending' is a clear indication that she has been provoked by the *Notes*, and the fact that she has already read the *NP* no less than five times seems to confirm it. If people are going to take this much interest in the *Notes* they are welcome to use whatever strong language about them as they please. I shall only start worrying when people begin calling them 'insipid, flatulent, and platitudinous.'

Her remark on the difficulties of NĀMA is probably justified. I am well aware that too much is said in too short a space, and that a longer discussion would be desirable. But (i) there is some amplification of what is said here in certain other notes, (ii) to do it justice a whole book would be necessary (as suggested recently by you), and I do not feel inclined to write it, or even capable of doing so, and (iii) there is no harm in letting people make the effort of expanding it (and perhaps correcting it) on their own account—they must not rely wholly on *parato ghoso*, but must exercise themselves also in *yoniso manasikāro*.[2] In any case, there is more said here than is found in the Suttas, so it is already something of a concession to mental laziness (though that applies, I suppose, to the whole book). Time will perhaps make it clearer.

**[L. 88] 1 January 1964**

Thank you for Huxley's article. Generally speaking, a *concept*, an *idea*, and a *thought*, are much the same thing, and can be described as an imaginary picture representing some real state of affairs. But this 'representation' is not simply a photographic reproduction (in the mind) of the real state of affairs in question. In a very simple case, if I now imagine or think of some absent object, the image that I have bears some sort of resemblance to the absent object.

But suppose I want to think about something like 'the British Constitution'. I cannot simply produce an imaginary picture 'looking like' the British Constitution, because the B.C. does not 'look like' anything. What happens is that, over the years, I have built up a complex image, partly visual, partly verbal, and perhaps also with elements from other senses; and this complex image has an internal *structure* that corresponds to that of the B.C., at least in so far as I have correctly understood it. If, in my studies of the British Constitution I have consulted faulty authorities, or omitted part of it, these faults or omissions will be represented in this complex image. Whenever I wish to think about the B.C. (or even whenever anybody mentions it) this complex image comes to my mind, and it is with reference to it that I (for example) answer questions about the B.C. This complex image is a *concept*—it is my concept of the B.C. With luck, it may correspond fairly closely with the original thing, but most probably it is a very misleading representation. (Note that, since the essence of the concept is in the *structure* of the complex image, and not in the individual images that make up the complex image, it is quite possible to have a number of different complex images, but all with the same structure, to represent the real state of affairs in question. Here, the *concept* remains the same, though the *image* is different. Thus, in the world of art, it is possible to express the same idea either in music or in painting.)

Now all conceptual thinking is *abstract*; that is to say, the thought or concept is entirely divorced from reality, it is removed from existence and is (in Kierkegaard's phrase) *sub specie æterni*. *Concrete* thinking, on the other hand, thinks the object *while the object is present*, and this, in the strict sense of the words, is *reflexion* or *mindfulness*. One is mindful of what one is doing, of what one is seeing, while one is actually doing (or seeing) it. This, naturally, is very much more difficult than abstract thinking; but it has a very obvious advantage: if one is thinking (or being mindful) of something while it is actually present, no mistake is possible, and one is directly in touch with reality; but in abstract thinking there is every chance of a mistake, since, as I pointed out above, the concepts with which we think are composite affairs, built up of an arbitrary lot of individual experiences (books, conversations, past observations, and so on).

What Huxley is getting at, then, is simply this. As a result of our education, our books, radios, cinemas, televisions, and so on, we tend to build up artificial *concepts* of what life is, and these concepts are grossly misleading and are no satisfactory guide at all to real life. (How many people, especially in the West, derive all their ideas about love from the cinema or TV—no wonder they run into difficulties when they begin to meet it as it is in reality!) Huxley is advocating a training in mindfulness (or awareness), *satisampajañña*—in thinking about life as it is actually taking place—instead of (or, at least, as well as) the present training in purely abstract thinking. In this way, so he maintains—and of course he is quite right—, people will be better fitted for dealing with life as it really is. Does this answer your question?

**[L. 89]** **3 January 1964**

I cannot say what the Ven. Buddhaghosa Thera's authority is for his statements in the Atthasālinī and elsewhere about the Abhidhamma Piṭaka It was certainly the generally believed tradition at that time that the Buddha himself had taught it to the *devatās*; and I seem to remember that the Chinese pilgrims to India (I forget their dates)[1] were shown the place where the foot of the triple staircase rested down which the Buddha was said to have descended after the Vas season in question.

But though the tradition is certainly earlier than the Ven. Buddhaghosa Thera's time, there is a further complicating element. Each of the early Hīnayāna schools (let alone the Mahāyāna) seems to have had its own particular Abhidhamma Piṭaka, though the Suttas and (for the most part) the Vinaya were held in common (I speak from memory of past readings). In consequence, the question might have arisen (though I don't know that it actually did), *which* of the various Abhidhamma Piṭakas the Buddha taught to the *devatās*. There *may* be earlier books than the present Commentaries reporting the tradition, but I do not know of them. And I do not recall whether the Ven. Buddhaghosa Thera quotes his authority, but I think not. (If you are interested, the Atthasālinī is in English translation as *The Expositor*.)

The Suttas themselves record the earlier part of the Buddha's ministry in some detail, and also the last few months; but there is no connected narrative of his movements and actions in between. But in any case I am not aware that *any* Sutta says that the Buddha taught the Abhidhamma Piṭaka, or even *abhidhamma*, to the *devatās*, or that he spent a Vas season in Tāvatiṃsa. Upon occasion the Buddha did visit various heavens (e.g. Brahmanimantanika Sutta, M.49/i,326) but for the most part, so it seems, the *devatās* came and listened to the Buddha teaching human beings (and attended in great numbers), e.g. Cūḷarāhulovāda Sutta, M.147/iii,278-80; Pāṭika Suttanta, D.24/iii,31-35. There seems to be no reason to suppose that the *devatās* are superior to human beings in *intelligence* (in whatever other way they may be superior). The actual teaching given by the Buddha to Sakka, chief of the Tāvatiṃsa deities, is recorded in the Sakkapañha Suttanta, D.21/ii,263-80; also Cūḷataṇhāsaṅkhaya Sutta, M.37/i,251-56.

**[L. 90]** **4 January 1964**

More about the Abhidhamma Piṭaka. I think I said in my last letter that 'I do not know of *any* Sutta where it is said that the Buddha taught the Abhidhamma Piṭaka, or even *abhidhamma*, to the *devatās*.' The words 'or even *abhidhamma*' should be deleted, since, if *abhidhamma* in the Sutta sense means 'advanced *dhamma*', then the Buddha *did* teach *abhidhamma* to the *devatās*—though not more than to the *bhikkhus*, and not in a Vas season spent in Tāvatiṃsa.[1]

Another point. The Ven. Buddhaghosa Thera and the other Commentators maintain (as I said earlier) that the material contained in the present Abhidhamma Piṭaka was in existence before the Buddha's final extinction. They also maintain, consistently with this opinion, that the Abhidhamma Piṭaka was recited at the First Council (of Rājagaha) after the *Vinaya* and *Sutta Piṭakas*. But in the account of the First Council (which is contained in the Cūḷavagga of the Vinaya Piṭaka, and is certainly authentic), the word *abhidhamma* does not occur at all. The *arahat theras* debated which should be recited first, Dhamma or Vinaya. They concluded that, since there is no practice of the Dhamma without observance of the Vinaya, the Vinaya should have precedence. Accordingly, the Ven. Upāli Thera was questioned about Vinaya, and answered, beginning with an account of the First *Pārājika*. When he had finished, the Ven. Ānanda Thera was questioned about Dhamma, and answered, beginning with a recitation of the Brahmajāla Sutta, which is the first Sutta of the Dīghanikāya. When he had finished, certain other business was disposed of and the Council dispersed. The statement by the Commentators that the Abhidhamma Piṭaka was recited on this occasion is purely gratuitous—one can accept it if one wishes, but there is nothing in the account of the First Council to support it.

One of the books of the Abhidhamma Piṭaka (the Kathā Vatthu) consists of a detailed account of the refutation of a number of heretical views about the Dhamma. This is supposed to have taken place at the Third Council (of Pātaliputta or Patna) during the reign of Asoka. (I forget the authority for this statement but there seems to be no reason to doubt it.)[2] The question has arisen how it was that the text of a debate with members of heretical sects at the time of Asoka had *already* been taught by the Buddha to *devatās* some two-and-a-half centuries earlier. The answer that is given by the Commentators is that the Buddha, foreseeing that such a debate would take place on a future occasion, gave the outline of the correct answers (but not the full text), in advance, to guide the orthodox party when the time came. Once again, one can accept this account, if one wishes. But with whom is the *onus probandi*?

**[L. 91]** **12 January 1964**

I hardly know what to say about the 'prolific writer on Buddhism' and his ideas, but if watching a leopard-dance is a foretaste of the bliss of *nibbāna* there would hardly seem to be anything that isn't. A *dāyaka* persuaded me to write a criticism of his earlier booklet, but my article was not very well received—too scattering, no doubt. If he is so sensitive to criticism ('Why should he criticize my book?'—[subdued laughter]) he is simply asking for trouble by publishing books. There were, if I remember rightly, expressions of joy at his conversion from Christianity, but I feel it would be better for all concerned (perhaps even including himself) if he were now quietly to rejoin the fold.

After reading Mrs. Quittner's letter I decided to give her the opportunity (if she wants it) of communicating direct with me about clarifications of the *Notes*. I do not think she is in the least worried about losing the Abhidhamma Piṭaka, nor do I think she is particularly interested in knowing the reasons for doing so; but what disturbs her is the fact she has not even been *offered* any reasons, good or bad. In my letter to her I have tried to make it clear why I have deliberately refrained from giving reasons (namely, because it is not in accordance with the purpose of the book to put emphasis on objective critical considerations—it is assumed that all this is over and done with before the book starts).

I am glad that you will be having the satisfaction of knowing that one person at least seems to find the book of absorbing interest, and that all the trouble you have taken about producing it has not been entirely wasted.

On the other hand, I fear that, even without the references to the Abhidhamma Piṭaka, *bhikkhus* of the traditional school—the majority, naturally—cannot be expected to like the book if they read it; and it is vain to hope that it is going to win general approval. I do not for a moment imagine that the general atmosphere of Buddhist studies is going to be in the least affected by the *Notes*; but I *do* allow myself to hope that a few individuals (of whom Mrs. Quittner may be one) will have private transformations of their way of thinking as a result of reading them. The question is, how to reach these individuals.

**[L. 92]** **24 January 1964**

C.J. Ducasse is Professor of Philosophy at Brown University. He is an intelligent man, but a rationalist at heart. Reading between the lines of his letter I suspect (as anticipated) that he strongly disapproves of the *Notes*. It is quite true that they are extremely difficult to follow if one is not acquainted with the Pali texts, but Ducasse is a professional philosopher and cannot be quite unaware of the general intention of the *Notes*. In the Preface I make not *one* but *two* assumptions about the reader, and the second one is that he is concerned about his own welfare. But I fancy that Ducasse is *not* concerned about his own welfare (for the rationalist it is an incomprehensible attitude), and, though he excuses himself from understanding the book on the ground that he is not familiar with the texts, the real reason is that he has no *wish* to understand it. If this were not so he would have said something to the effect that he much regretted that his unfamiliarity with the texts had prevented him from understanding as much as he would have liked of such a thought-provoking book, etc., etc. But he is, unfortunately, too polite to say what he really thinks about the *Notes*, which I had hoped that he might.

This is the first expression of opinion (at least by implication) from a university don. I am inclined to think that this will be the normal academic reaction to the *Notes*. Are we perhaps to interpret the silence from Peradeniya[1] as indication that the dons there agree with Ducasse, but don't have the excuse of unfamiliarity with the texts, and so prefer to say nothing rather than admit that they are not really interested? Or am I doing them an injustice? Good will is the first requisite for understanding the *Notes*, and a determined effort may make up for any natural limitation of intelligence.

Mr. Dias writes: 'I was not able to make any headway with the *Notes*. It may be due to the fact that I do not know Pali.' I have written back to assure him that, Pali or not, the *Notes* are difficult. Are you quite sure that there are not some people who regard the *Notes* as a free headache that you have given them?

## [L. 93] 25 January 1964

The reason that I am answering your letter on the back of it is not a hint that I need more paper (far from it!), but to allow you to refresh your memory about your problem.

Please refer to DHAMMA (b) I recently sent you, in the list of amendments, a slight addition to this note. The infinite hierarchy of consciousnesses, one on top of the other, is *always* there, whether we are engaging in reflexion or not. The evidence for this is our consciousness of *motion* or *movement*, which does not require reflexion—we are *immediately* conscious of movement (of a falling leaf, for example)—, but which *does* require a hierarchy of consciousness. Why? Because a movement takes place in *time* (past, present and future), and yet we are conscious of the movement of the falling leaf as a *present* movement. This is perhaps too short an explanation, but it is not very important that you should grasp it.[1] When we wish to reflect (we often do it almost automatically when faced with difficult situations—see my letter to Mr. Dias on 'Awareness')[2] we *make use* of this hierarchy of consciousness by withdrawing our attention from the immediate level to the level above.

The reason why we cannot say 'consciousness is' or 'consciousness of consciousness' is simply that the only thing (or things) that consciousness (*viññāṇa*) can be consciousness *of* is name-and-matter (*nāmarūpa*). Consciousness is the *presence* of the phenomenon, of what is manifested in experience (which is *nāmarūpa*), and we cannot *in the same sense* speak of 'consciousness of consciousness', which would be 'presence of presence'; in other words, the nature of the relation between consciousness and name-and-matter cannot be the same as that between one consciousness and another (the former relation is *internal*, the latter *external*).

What we have in the pre-reflexive hierarchy of consciousness is really a series of layers, not simply of *consciousness* of ascending order, but of *consciousness cum name-and-matter* of ascending order. At *each* level there is *consciousness of a phenomenon*, and the different levels are *superimposed* (this is not to say that the phenomenon at any one level has nothing to do with the one below it [as in a pile of plates]; it has, but this need not concern us at present). The relation between two adjacent layers of consciousness is thus juxtaposition—or rather super-position, since they are of different orders. In reflexion, two of these adjacent layers are combined, and we have complex consciousness instead of simple consciousness, the effect of which is to reveal different *degrees of consciousness*—in other words, different *degrees of presence* of name-and-matter. This does not allow us to say 'consciousness is present' (in which case we should be confusing consciousness with name-and-matter), but it *does* allow us to say 'there is consciousness'. Successive orders of reflexion can be shown verbally as follows:

| | |
|---|---|
| *Immediate experience:* | 'A pain', i.e. 'A pain (is)' *or*<br>'(Consciousness of) a pain'. |
| *First order reflexion*: | 'There is a (an existing) pain' *or*<br>'There is (consciousness of) a pain';<br>and these two are each equivalent to<br>'Awareness of a pain'—but note that awareness (*sampajañña*) is not the same as consciousness (*viññāṇa*). |

*Second order reflexion:* 'There is awareness of a pain'
'Awareness of awareness of a pain'
*Third order reflexion:* 'There is awareness of awareness of a pain'
'Awareness of awareness of awareness of a pain'

And so on. (In your illustration you pass from immediate presence ('Pain is') to reflexive presence ('There is consciousness of pain'). But these two do not correspond. If you say immediately 'Pain is', then reflexively you must say 'There is existing pain'; and only if you say immediately 'Consciousness of pain' can you say reflexively 'There is consciousness of pain'. As you have put it you make it seem as if consciousness only comes in with reflexion.)

I am very far from being in a position to give an opinion of the nature of *viññāṇañcāyatana* and the transition to *ākiñcaññāyatana*,[3] but I feel it might be wiser to regard your conclusions as still to some extent speculative—which raises the question whether I should discourage you from speculation. For my part I have given up thinking about things that are out of my reach, since I have no way of checking my conclusions, and I find this a source of frustration. That the question presents difficulties from the theoretical point of view can be seen from the fact that *ākiñcaññāyatana* is still a *conscious* state—it is the *sattamī viññāṇaṭṭhiti*, or 'seventh station of consciousness' (Mahānidāna Suttanta, D.15/ii,69)—and so long as there is consciousness I don't see how the layers can be removed; indeed, in so far as the transition may be regarded as involving a conceptual abstraction, the layers would seem to be necessary for the abstraction (which is a reflexive act) to be possible. But this, too, is verging on the speculative.

P.S. If you succeed in seeing clearly why reflexion cannot be consciousness of consciousness, I will give you an A.

**[L. 94]** **21 February 1964**

Nalanda, is it not now a centre of Buddhist studies (a kind of Buddhist university)?[1] Perhaps you will know about this. In earlier days, certainly, Nalanda was a very large Buddhist university, with many thousands of students; and some (or at least one) of the early Chinese pilgrims studied there. In the Buddha's day it was a flourishing city (not far from Rājagaha, King Bimbisāra's capital), appearing in several Suttas (see the Brahmajāla Suttanta, Dīgha 1; Kevaddha Sutta, Dīgha 11; Upāli Sutta, Majjhima 56). There is certainly no harm in sending a copy of *Notes* there.

I have just received a letter from London. It is from a man who has been in Ceylon several times, partly on business and partly to practice *bhāvanā*. He was first interested in the Dhamma by a Sinhalese man, and shortly afterwards read my translation of Evola's book, *The Doctrine of Awakening* (which, however, I cannot now recommend to you without considerable reserves).[2] From his accounts, he has actually had a certain amount of success in mental concentration—more than most people who take it up intermittently, though not (as he likes to think) up to the level of *jhāna*. He is, as he himself admits, not a very intellectual type, and I did not at all expect that he would make anything of the *Notes*. But he has been very kindly sending me books from England, so, rather as a matter of courtesy, I included his name in the list of addresses. Since he seems to have a certain liking for *samatha bhāvanā* I have been encouraging him to go on with it—I think it will do him more good than harm, even if he does not quite understand what it is all about, and it is an excellent way of occupying the later years of his life (he is now past sixty, I think). How many people promise themselves to spend their retirement profitably, and then find it is too late to start something new!

**[L. 95]** **9 March 1964**

No, I think it is just your unfamiliarity with Americans that makes you suppose that the letter from Columbia University is a 'translation from another language.' This is quite a good example of what happens when an *educated* American attempts to be *literate*, and I have met much of the same sort of thing during the war in a combined British-American headquarters. The trouble is (so I gather from an article that I read a year or two ago) that American students are no longer required to *write English*; their University studies have become more and more technical and more and more streamlined, with the result that (I quote from the article) young Americans are now leaving their universities with enough technical knowledge to project a man into space, but without the ability to write a grammatical English sentence. Their final examinations (so it seems) are in form of questionnaires to which the candidates are required to answer 'by putting an X in the appropriate space.' American businessmen have taken to employing British secretaries since young American graduates are quite incapable of writing an intelligible memorandum. No doubt this is something of an exaggeration, but, really, what the extract you have sent me actually means is anybody's guess. It is perhaps that Ms. Fowler's admirable dictionary calls 'gobbledegook' (noun, U.S. slang; Pompous official jargon [imit. Of turkey-cock])?

The 'controversial statements which the whole world abounds in' is very puzzling. I should like to think that he wants a copy of the *Notes* to study the 'controversial statements made therein dealing with various opinions that are commonly but uncritically held throughout the whole (Buddhist) world,' but quite probably he means something quite different—perhaps he wishes to say that the *Notes* are yet another example of the controversial (and therefore deplorable?) writings (about the Dhamma) that are now flooding the world. But why should he then want to study them? Or does he simply want to read what the *Notes* have to say about the various controversial matters abounding in the world? Perhaps this is it.

Thank you for your kindly thought about Lin Yutang. I have read the book already, but I don't remember very much about it, except that it left me neither hot nor cold. If you have found it interesting and want my opinion on it, then by all means send it; but I hardly feel that it is worthwhile to do so otherwise (though I shall read it in any case). People who find life worth living are usually confining their attention to *this* particular life; they forget (or do not know) that there has been no beginning to this business of living.[a] This particular life may perhaps be not too bad, but how about when they were a dog, or a hen, or a frog, or a tapeworm? *Alaṃ*—Enough!

Mr. Wijerama[1] has written a very intelligible letter, and I have found something to say in reply; but whether my reply will make things clear is another matter—the question of change and movement is notoriously perplexing and not easily disentangled. But even without entirely clarifying the situation, it is necessary to point out the source of certain current misinterpretations of the Dhamma—in particular, the view that 'since everything is always changing nothing *really* exists, and it is only our ignorance that makes us think that things do exist,' which is quite erroneous but very widespread.[b] If Mr. Wijerama wants further discussion of this or other matters, he has only to write me.

Last month I was visited unexpectedly by a Swiss gentleman who had been recommended to come and see me by a Colombo man. He is Roman

---

**a.** It is always advisable, when taking up a new author, to find out whether he accepts or rejects survival of death. If one knows this, one can make the necessary allowances, and one may perhaps make sense of what would otherwise seem to be rubbish. Camus is a case in point—to find him sympathetic it is necessary to know that he passionately loathes the idea of survival.

**b.** It is a 'controversial statement which the whole world abounds in'.

Catholic, and had been in Ceylon a fortnight (with another fortnight to go), and had just encountered the Buddha's Teaching for the first time. There is no doubt that he had been astonished and profoundly impressed, and he said that his head was still going around in bewilderment. He asked me a number of very pertinent questions, and did not seem to be upset at getting some rather difficult answers. He struck me as being a very intelligent man, and perhaps capable of making use of the Dhamma. I gave him a copy of the *Notes* and he glanced at it saying that there might be some other people (in Switzerland) who would be interested, and asked me if he could show them the book. I said 'by all means,' and he asked if more copies were available, so I told him to write to you. I don't know what he does or who he is. I liked the man, and I hope we hear more of him.

Oddly enough, the night before he came I had a very clear and vivid dream of the Swiss Alps, with one peak (the Dent du Midi—the Southern Tooth—it looks like a jagged row of teeth; I have seen it once or twice from a train) actually named correctly. There is some mention of the Swiss Alps in Balfour's book, which I had been reading about three weeks earlier, and this might be enough to account for the dream, but I think it by no means impossible that it was an instance of precognition.[c]

I was sorry to have to apologize to the gentleman for the fact that the *Notes* contain a lot of Pali, which he would not understand; and I began to think about this later. I finally decided that there would be no harm (you know I am against translations), and perhaps some good, if the *Notes* were provided with a Pali-English Glossary and English translations of all the Pali passages. Accordingly, I set to work to do this, and finished the task last night. It adds about sixteen pages to the *Notes*. I feel that there may be people (such as this gentleman) knowing nothing of the Dhamma, or at least of Pali, who might nevertheless find the *Notes* a better introduction to the Teaching than a popular exposition giving the impression that the Dhamma is really quite a simple matter—indeed, most intelligent people do not *want* anything very simple, since they have understood already that whatever the truth may be it is certainly not a simple affair. The Glossary and Translations will make the book—if it comes to be printed—much more widely accessible than it is at present.

---

**c.** The fact that Kanchenjunga was visible way off to the East does not seem to invalidate the supposition—the geography was remarkably accurate: I was standing to the South on the summit of the Simplon tunnel between Switzerland and Italy, the Dent du Midi was to the North-west, and the Himalayas in the East.

**[L. 96]** **15 March 1964**

The passage on Western philosophy that you quote from Lin Yutang is partly justified, but it must be remarked that it refers only to speculative (or abstract) philosophy, in other words the classical Western philosophies. Existential philosophy, as its name implies, is concerned with *existence*, and Lin Yutang could hardly complain that Kierkegaard, Nietzsche, and Marcel—to name only three—did (or do) not live in accordance with their philosophies (even though he would scarcely agree with them—they do not regard life as a 'poem').[a] Kierkegaard's views on abstract philosophy are quite definite; for example:

> Now if we assume that abstract thought is the highest manifestation of human activity, it follows that philosophy and the philosophers proudly desert existence, leaving the rest of us to face the worst. And something else, too, follows for the abstract thinker himself, namely, that since he is an existing individual he must in one way or another be suffering from absent-mindedness. (*CUP*, p. 267)

(You can refer to some scathing passages from Kierkegaard that I quoted in an earlier letter to you about the essays of Mssrs. Wijesekera, Jayatilleka, and Burtt;[1] and see also the passage in Preface (c).) Certainly, it is futile to look to speculative philosophy for guidance on how to live; and to follow such a philosophy is to be like one of the blind men of the Sutta in the Udāna (vi,4/68-9) who were shown an elephant and told to describe it—one grasps a small fragment of the truth abstracted from the whole, and fondly imagines that one knows all.

On the other hand, a study of such philosophies, in certain circumstances, may not be a waste of time. Shortly before his *parinibbāna*, the Buddha told Māra[2] that he would not pass away before there were disciples who were capable of correctly refuting any outside views that might spring up, and this argues that for those who had themselves reached right view a study of wrong views would be an advantage rather than a disadvantage—that is, when dealing with people who did not accept the Buddha's Teaching. But here, it will be understood, these various specu-

---

**a.** Actually, Kierkegaard would appall Lin Yutang; and this perhaps shows up the weakness of both sides. Though they are agreed in rejecting speculation, Kierkegaard is for self-mortification whereas Chinese philosophy is for self-indulgence (and will not bear too close an intellectual scrutiny).

lative philosophies would be studied against a background of right view, with the effect that they would be fitted into their proper place—just as the king, who could see the whole of the elephant, was able to reconcile the widely divergent descriptions of the blind men and put them in the proper perspective.

It may also not be a disadvantage to have a fairly wide knowledge of various philosophies when one is in the position of having to understand the Suttas when no trustworthy (i.e. non-*puthujjana*) living teacher is available. If one has to find out for oneself what the Texts mean, such a background may—at least for certain people—be a help rather than a hindrance. And, finally, the development of a lucid understanding of these philosophies—of their virtues and their limitations—may become a real pleasure to the mind. (In my present state of health I myself, for example, get most of my pleasure from the smooth working—such as it is—of my intelligence when contemplating the inter-relationships of the various views that come my way. I confess that I should prefer to spend my time practising concentration (*samādhi*), but I can't do it; and so, *faute de mieux*,[3] I enjoy the consolations of philosophy.)

As it happens, I have just received the two volumes of Bradley's *Principles of Logic*. You will see that I refer to Bradley in ANICCA (a), and actually in connexion with the question of identity and difference in the process of change. I have started reading him and find him stimulating and perspicacious (and very sympathetic) in spite of certain limitations—in some respects the *Notes* almost seem to be a continuation of his work.

> It[b] is identical, not because it is simply the same, but because it is the same amid diversity. In the judgment, beside the mere distinction of the terms, we have an opposition in time of A to B. And the subject of which A—B is asserted, being subject to these differences, is thus different in itself, while remaining the same.[c] In this sense every judgment affirms either the identity which persists under difference, or the diversity which is true of one single subject. It would be the business of metaphysics to pursue this discussion into further subtleties. (*PL*, p. 28)

And this is more or less what I have done in *FS*. In any case, you will see

**b.** I.e. the reality to which the adjective A—B is referred.
**c.** This is *ṭhitassa aññathattaṃ* exactly.

that, though one does not reach *nibbāna* through reading Bradley,[d] a study of his views need not be totally irrelevant to an understanding of the Suttas.

So much for philosophy and Lin Yutang[e] except to repeat an anecdote from Plutarch (quoted by Kierkegaard, *CUP*, p. 34). It seems that when a certain Lacedaemonian by the name of Eudamidas saw the aged Xenocrates and his disciples in the Academy, engaged in seeking for the truth, he asked 'Who is this old man?' And when he was told that Xenocrates was a wise man, one of those occupied in the search for virtue, he cried 'But when does he then propose to use it?'.

I can't tell you very much about the Eleatics—the Elastics, if you prefer—, except that (according to Kierkegaard) they held the doctrine that 'everything is and nothing comes into being.' Parmenides, I think, was an Eleatic, and you will see his views on pp. 14-15 of Russell's *M&L*. The doctrine of the Eleatics is the opposite of Heraclitus and his flux: but as Kierkegaard points out, both are speculative views, abstracting from existence where change and unchange are combined (and so back to Bradley!).

As to Achilles and the tortoise, the problem as stated by Russell on p. 88 makes the assumption that all 'places' are the same size. But if Achilles is going faster than the tortoise each 'place' that he goes to must be correspondingly larger (i.e. longer) than the tortoise's 'places'. There is thus no paradox. But there is *also* the assumption that one can be in a 'place' in a 'point-instant' of time—i.e. no time at all. This is really the root of the trouble, both for Zeno and for Russell—they assume that *time* (or *being*, or *existence*) is made up of instants of *no* time, which is a misunderstanding. However many instants of *no* time you add together (or put contiguously) you still get *no* time. So Russell, seeing this, says (p. 82) 'there is no such thing as the next moment,' which means that though his moments are 'in time' they are not 'part of time'. But he does not go on to explain what 'time' is.

The fact is, that one cannot use the word 'be' in connexion with a point-instant of time, and one cannot say that Achilles, or the Arrow, 'is' in a particular place at each 'moment' (understood as a point-instant). (The solution to the problem of time, as I suggest in *FS*, lies in a hierarchy of 'moments', each understood as a 'unit of time', and each with a sub-structure of a plurality of similar moments but of a lesser order.)

---

**d.** A recent Indian philosopher, de Andrade, was an enthusiastic disciple of Bradley's, and refused to consider Russell as a philosopher at all—with some reason.

**e.** Lin Yutang is right in saying that if one pays court to a girl, it is ridiculous not to marry her and have a family; but perhaps the truth that the classical German philosophers were flirting with is not the kind that you can have children by.

But as to the problem of Achilles and the tortoise, all we need to say is that during each *second* of time both Achilles and the tortoise are within the boundaries of a certain extent or strip of ground, but since Achilles is moving faster than the tortoise his successive strips of ground (each occupied for one second) are longer than the tortoise's. So Achilles catches the tortoise. But note that since we decide upon one second of time (or whatever it may actually be) as the *limit to the fineness of our perception*, we are unable to find out what Achilles or the tortoise is doing *within* each second. We know that during any given second Achilles is *occupying* a certain strip of ground (he *is in* that strip), but we are not entitled to say whether he is *moving* or *stationary*. (This does not say what movement is—which needs a more elaborate discussion—, but it does solve Zeno's problem, or at least indicates the solution.)

As a solution to impermanence you suggest that we might forgo 'an impermanent use of what is impermanent'. Impossible! We are making impermanent use of what is impermanent all the time—and this is as true for the *arahat* as it is for the *puthujjana*. So long as there is consciousness at all there is the passage of time, and the passage of time consists in the *use* of things, whether we like it or not. The eating of food, the breathing of breaths, the thinking of thoughts, the dreaming of dreams—all are impermanent use of what is impermanent. Only in *nirodhasamāpatti* does this lapse for any living being.

In the last Sutta of the Majjhima (M.152/iii,298-9) the desperate expedient is suggested of 'not seeing forms with the eye, not hearing sounds with the ear,' but the Buddha ridicules this, saying that this is already achieved by a blind and deaf man. He goes on to indicate *upekkhā*, indifference, as the proper way. The fault does not lie in the impermanence (which is inevitable), but in *attachment to* (and *repulsion from*) the impermanent. Get rid of attachment (and repulsion) and you get rid of the suffering of impermanence. The *arahat* makes impermanent use of the impermanent, but with indifference, and the only suffering he has is bodily pain or discomfort when it arises (and that, too, finally ceases when his body breaks up).

## [L. 97] 25 March 1964

Many thanks for your letter. I am glad to hear that somebody else likes the book, and I am not sorry that it should be 'Les Amis du Bouddhisme'. The French, in general, are not so prone to complacent mental laziness, which (according to Palinurus) 'is the English disease.'

I find reading Bradley a fascinating experience. On every other page I recognize with delighted astonishment a paragraph on some matter that has been occupying my own thoughts and that, often enough, finds a place in the *Notes*. In *FS* (c), for example, I say that 'if anything exists, everything else does' and that 'The images involved in thinking must already in some sense be *given* before they can be thought'; and I find that Bradley says 'everything conceivable has existence in some sense.' (p. 195) Then, in MANO (b) I say 'A universal becomes an *abstraction* only in so far as an attempt is made to think it in isolation from all particular or concrete content'; and Bradley makes a distinction between 'concrete universals' and 'abstract universals'. Again, Bradley remarks 'It takes two to make the same, and the least we can have is some change of event in a self-same thing, or the return to that thing from some suggested difference' (p. 141); and if you will run through the second paragraph of ATTĀ, you will see that it is purely and simply an expansion of Bradley's statement.[1] Sometimes it is almost embarrassing. I read in one place that 'in much imagination we shall find the presence of a discursive element' (p. 76); and turning to MANO, opening sentence, I find I have written 'Much mental activity (imagination) is to some extent reflexive (in a loose sense)' and I later use the expression 'discursive thought' in this very sense.

This looks as if I have simply copied Bradley; and if I were somebody else, with the task of reviewing the *Notes*, I should undoubtedly say that 'the author, quite clearly, owes much to Bradley, from whom he has lifted several passages almost verbatim but without having had the decency to acknowledge his source.' And yet it is not so; apart from my youthful reading (now forgotten) of another work of his, I have no knowledge of his writings, and the authors to whom I am most indebted (Sartre, Eddington, Ross Ashby[2]—whom you do not know of) have almost certainly never read him (Sartre and Bradley, independently, give much the same account of the part played by images in thinking, though their way of expressing it is quite different).

It is satisfactory, of course, to have independent confirmation of certain statements in the *Notes* (the heavy volumes of Bradley can be thrown at an objector with telling effect); but, at the same time, I am given a sobering reminder that nobody has ever thought anything that somebody else has not already thought before him—and this is true even of the Buddhas, who *re*-discover what has already been discovered (nay, *re*-discovered) by their predecessors. On the other hand, this perennial *sameness* of philosophical reflexions can be very stimulating—see this remarkable passage from Dostoievsky's *The Possessed*:

> 'Old philosophical commonplaces, always the same, from the beginning of time' murmured Stavrogin with an air of careless pity. 'Always the same! Always the same from the beginning of time and nothing else!' replied Kirilov, his eyes sparkling, as if his victory were comprised in this idea.[3]

Another consequence is that I can't afford to skip anything, since I have to make sure that I have come out in front of Bradley and not behind him, and that I have not made any blunders that he has avoided (which would make me look very foolish). But so far, at least, so good—he is stimulating, and his sometimes very acute observations (I have now quoted one in the *Notes*) bring things out in a clear light, and even his mistakes (his curiously unjustified assumptions about the nature of time, for example, on which his idealism rests—inherited, no doubt) are illuminating. I am glad to find, in particular, that *FS* is relevant nearly everywhere, and shows the way out of several of his blind alleys.

But also, Bradley is as exciting to read as Russell is dull. Bradley has his hero—Judgement (perhaps you are familiar with him?)—and his heroine—Reality—, and we are made to wonder whether he will succeed in bringing them together (with Inference as go-between) by the end of the book. He gets Judgement into some very tight corners, and we are left in suspense until a later chapter to find out how the hero escapes (if he does). (Looking ahead a few pages, I see that the traditional syllogism is going to come to a sticky end—'A mistake that has lasted two thousand years.' I might almost have written those words myself, though in another connexion.) Part of the fun is trying to anticipate Bradley's solution and to keep a page or two ahead of him; and I felt very satisfied on one occasion when, after reading a paragraph, a scathing comment (Bradley makes them too) occurred to me; I was about to write it in the margin when I noticed that Bradley had already put it as a footnote. You have to get up early if you're going to get the better of him.

The book originally appeared in 1883, but the present edition contains Bradley's own commentary on it written forty years later. It is interesting to see how he sometimes admits to being perplexed, not only by other philosophers, but also by his earlier self. (It might be an encouragement to us when we can't make head or tail of other people's philosophy, or even our own, to remember that it happens even to the best philosophers. Mathematicians are more fortunate: given time, two mathematicians of equal intelligence can always understand each other, since the rules of mathematics are agreed upon beforehand. Not so the rules of philosophy—indeed philosophy really consists in trying to discover what the rules are, if any.) Naturally, there is nothing in Bradley of a *lokuttara* nature, and even the crucial *lokiya* questions about self and the world he does not deal with; but if one is looking for a coherent philosophical background for one's thinking, he can provide things that are quite beyond the powers of modern academical philosophy—not everything, of course, but he is nearly always *relevant* (even when he is mistaken), whereas our present-day realists are monotonously and almost militantly irrelevant. Not surprisingly, they don't like Bradley, and he has suffered an undeserved eclipse. Here is one of them, Miss Stebbing, a female logician (if you please):

> Neither Bradley, nor Bosanquet, nor any of this school of Idealist Logicians, has ever succeeded in making clear what exactly is meant by the principle of identity-in-difference upon which the metaphysical logic of the Idealists is based. Their logic ends in 'shipwreck'... (*MIL*, p. x)

But when are Stebbing and Russell and the rest going to set sail? (I speak of the 'present-day realists', but I believe that, in England anyway, they are no longer in fashion. Their place has been taken by a school of philosophers who seek ultimate truth in modern English usage—if I am to believe Russell. It would seem to follow that what is true when uttered in English is false when uttered in French, since the usages of the two languages are not the same.[a] I hardly think that one could make the Pali texts intelligible to them at all.)

Knowing your sympathy with Lin Yutang's views on European philosophy, it is perhaps rather unkind of me to send you all this. But the fact is that, just at present, this is more or less the only thing I am thinking about. In any case, I shall not ask you to read Bradley, and I shall be quite satisfied if you will contemplate him from a comfortable distance.

### [L. 98] 4 April 1964

It would take more than a few remarks about the sterility of Western philosophy to dry me up. I am fond of the sound of my own voice, but, living

---

**a.** Perhaps it would be more accurate to say that Englishmen have one set of Ultimate Truths, while Frenchmen have quite another set—a conclusion that is sometimes not so ridiculous as it seems.

in solitude, I rarely get the opportunity of hearing it, so I have to make do with the next best thing: if I can't enjoy hearing myself talk, I can at least enjoy reading myself write (if you get the idea). In any case, if I am going to correspond with anybody I assume that he wants my reflections in the original edition, not in a popularized version. If he doesn't love my dog, then he can't love me. (I have rather the same attitude towards the hypothetical readers of the *Notes*: they are given my thought whether they are likely to understand it or not. This may lay the book open to the charge of intellectual immodesty—which I don't deny—but nobody, I think, can justly call it hypocritical. Whether or not everything I say will be of use to the reader is another question, and I am quite ready to admit that some of it may be a positive hindrance. But, rightly or wrongly, I leave that for the reader to decide.)

When I said that the author of the *Notes* seems to have 'lifted passages from Bradley without acknowledgement,' that must be understood as a pardonable exaggeration on the part of a heated (if imaginary) reviewer. In fact, even though I have now quoted Bradley (with acknowledgement), nobody will accuse me of having transcribed him literally in other parts of the book, though people may quite likely (if they are acquainted with Bradley) suppose that I have taken my ideas from him. But, personal vanity apart, this does not matter.

There is nothing very much new to report. Bradley makes a distinction that seems to have a certain (limited) application to the Dhamma. He speaks of the metaphysicians, on the one hand, who speculate on first principles and the ultimate nature of things; and on the other, of

> those who are not prepared for metaphysical enquiry, who feel no call towards thankless hours of fruitless labour, who do not care to risk a waste of their lives on what the world for the most part regards as lunacy, and they themselves but half believe in. (*PL*, p. 340)

(What a cry from Bradley's heart!) This second category contains those who take principles as working hypotheses to explain the facts, without enquiry into the ultimate validity of those principles (this is the normal practice with those who study special subjects—physics, chemistry, biology, psychology, and so on—and who are metaphysicians, if at all, only in their own conceit). In brief: those who look for first principles, and those who take things on trust because they work in practice.

In the Suttas, too, we find something of this distinction between those *sekhā* who are *diṭṭhipattā* ('attained-through-view') and those who are *sad-*

*dhāvimuttā* ('released-through-faith').[a] The former have heard the Buddha's Teaching, reflected on it, and accepted it after considering the ultimate principles on which it is based. The latter have heard the Teaching and reflected on it (as before), but, instead of seeking its first principles, have accepted it because it inspires them with trust and confidence. Both of them have practised the Teaching, and both have attained to *sotāpatti* or beyond, but one puts *paññā* foremost, and the other *saddhā*. But there is also a third kind of *sekha*, the *kāyasakkhi* ('body-witness'), who is quite without any corresponding category in Western philosophy: he is one who puts *samādhi* foremost—he develops mental concentration and gets all the *jhānas*, and needs not so much *paññā* or *saddhā*. In A.III,21/i,118-20, the Buddha is asked which of these three is the best, but he declines to discriminate between them, saying that any one of them may outdistance the other two and arrive first at the final goal.

It is actually on this question of *samādhi* that Eastern thought is at its greatest distance from Western; and the latter can certainly be charged with sterility on this score (and this will include the existentialists). The trouble seems to be this. Western thought has a Christian background (its individual thinkers can almost all be classed as pro- or anti-Christian, and rarely, if ever, as neutral), and, since the practice of meditation is normally connected with religious beliefs (in a wide sense), all states attained through such practices are automatically classed as Christian (or at least as Theist or Deist), and therefore as essentially *mystical*. Now, no philosopher who respects the Laws of Thought can possibly find a place for the mystical in his scheme of things, since mysticism is an act of faith in the principle of non-contradiction (i.e. that the Law of Contradiction does not hold)—in other words, God (who is, one might say, self-contradiction personified, and, being the Ultimate Truth, is therefore no contradiction).[b]

So *samatha* practice (*ānāpānasati*, for example), even were it known in the West (which it is not), would first be misunderstood as mystical, and then, on the strength of this, would be banished from the philosopher's system (except, of course, on Sundays). It was, indeed, the desire for some definite

---

**a.** These *sekhā* are *sotāpanna* and beyond. Before *sotāpatti* (i.e. after reaching the *magga* but not the *phala*)—see CITTA—*sekhā* are *dhammānusārī* or *saddhānusārī*, between whom the same distinction holds.

**b.** Some philosophers take advantage of this situation: they develop their system as far as possible, carefully avoiding self-contradictions; but when they encounter one that they cannot explain, instead of confessing defeat they proudly declare that they have proved the existence of God.

non-mystical form of practice that first turned my thoughts towards the East: Western thinking (of which I really know very little) seemed to me to oscillate between the extremes of mysticism and rationalism, both of which were distasteful to me, and the *yoga* practices—in a general sense—of India offered themselves as a possible solution.

Perhaps you remarked about the first appearance in my letters of the word 'metaphysics'. This word is now rather out of fashion; seemingly for two different reasons. Bradley calls himself a metaphysician, and my dictionary tells me that metaphysics are 'Speculations on the nature of being, truth, and knowledge,' which seems to justify Bradley's claim. But Bradley was an idealist philosopher and was primarily concerned with the relation between 'appearance' on the one hand and 'reality' on the other. And, in fact, metaphysics has rather come to be associated with idealist philosophy, and in particular with the investigation of a 'reality' that, being what lies *behind* appearances, is necessarily hidden from our eyes (except at the present instant). From this philosophy there has been a two-fold reaction. On the one hand, there are the realists (Russell & Co.), who deny the idealist position by the simple expedient of ignoring *consciousness*, thereby conceiving all truths as statistical (which is the position of science). Extreme exponents go so far as to deny philosophy and metaphysics altogether—for example, Wittgenstein (*Tractatus Logico-Philosophicus*, §6.53):

> The right method of philosophy would be this. To say nothing except what can be said, i.e. the propositions of natural science, i.e. something that has nothing to do with philosophy: and then always, when someone else wishes to say something metaphysical, to demonstrate to him that he had given no meaning to certain signs in his proposition. This method would be unsatisfying to the other—he would not have the feeling that we were teaching him philosophy—but it would be the only strictly correct method.

But difficulties are not overcome by leaving them out; and the realists provide no answer to the idealists' questions. Bradley accuses Russell of not facing up to certain problems, and he is right to bring this charge. But the idealist distinction between appearance and reality can be seen to rest on a circular argument; and the existentialists[c] have in fact seen this, though they

c. Beginning perhaps with Nietzsche, who speaks of 'the illusion of hinder-worlds'; whereas Kierkegaard seems to have partly accepted the distinction: he conceded the idealist contention, but regarded it as irrelevant and a temptation—

themselves can provide only compromise solutions, since they are unable to resolve the 'subject/object' duality (which only the Buddha does).

Metaphysics, in consequence, understood as the investigation of a reality—a 'Really Real Reality' as someone has commented—behind appearances, is now discredited; and Sartre, to take an instance, though coming within the dictionary definition of a metaphysician, does not call himself one—indeed, he re-defines metaphysics as dealing with the general question, 'Why should things exist at all?' (*B&N*, p. 297) (The question 'Why are there other people?', for example, would be metaphysical in Sartre's sense. Metaphysics, so understood, lead eventually to the direct intuition 'It is so', beyond which it is impossible to go. One is perhaps tempted to remark that such metaphysics have something in common with feminine reason: 'I love him because I love him.') In view of the prevailing ambiguity of the word, it is probably better to let it sleep. (The word is ambiguous even in its origins. Aristotle wrote his 'Physics', and then *after* his 'Physics' he wrote another chapter or book, which, for want of anything better, he called '*Meta*physics'; but the word has commonly been taken to mean 'what lies *beyond* physics', i.e. a metaphysical world (reality) beyond the physical world of appearance.)

I confess that I don't altogether follow the tangle of names and addresses that you have sent me—would it help matters if we were to suppose that Mr. K. and Mrs. J. are one and the same person? There might be something in Bradley we could use to justify this assumption, should it be necessary. 'Where sameness is asserted difference is presupposed. Where difference is asserted there is a basis of sameness which underlies it.' (*PL*, p. 373) ('Whom Bradley hath joined, let no man put asunder,' as the Anglican Marriage Service almost tells us.) But perhaps you will object that the mere fact of our supposing that Mr. K. and Mrs. J. are one person—even if it is convenient to do so—will not make them one person in actual fact, if they are really two. But we may appeal to Hegel, who maintained that thought and actuality are the same: what I *think*, that actually *is*; and what *is*, that I *think*. So if we care to think that Mr. K. and Mrs. J. are one person, then they are so in

---

The triumphant victory of pure thought, that in it being and thought are one, is something both to laugh at and to weep over, since in the realm of pure thought it is not even possible to distinguish them. That thought had validity was assumed by Greek philosophy without question. By reflecting over the matter one would have to arrive at the same result; but why confuse the validity of thought with reality? A valid thought is a possibility, and every further question as to whether it is real or not should be dismissed as irrelevant. (*CUP*, p. 292)

reality. But alas! here comes 'Gaunt Kierkegaard' (as Palinurus calls him) to tell us that Hegel's view is a 'lunatic postulate' (*CUP*, p. 279) and we are regretfully forced to admit that this is true.[d] However, I have no doubt that you see the situation more clearly than I do, and perhaps you will be able to assure me that no contradiction arises from supposing that Mr. K. and Mrs. J. are, in fact, two distinct people.

I have read Huxley's *Brave New World* twice already, I think, and I have no great desire to read it again. It is, I agree with you, not up to the level of his other books, though I believe it has been his best seller.

> Ride-a-cock gee to Banbury T
> To see a fine bathroom and W. C.

(Perhaps the 'T' puzzles you. I think it comes from the early and celebrated 'Model T' Ford car; and 'Ford', of course, takes the place, in the *Brave New World*, of 'Our Lord'. There is also the *visual* pun between T and †.)

**[L. 99]** **24 April 1964**

The fullest Sutta description of the *kāyasakkhi, diṭṭhipatto*, and *saddhāvimutto* (referred to hereafter as *k*, *d* and *s*) is given in the Kīṭāgiri Sutta, M.70/i,477-78. The *k* is described as an individual who has reached the *arūpa* attainments and dwells therein, and, having seen with understanding, has got rid of some of the *āsavā*. The *d* is an individual who has *not*

---

**d.** It is actually not so entirely lunatic as might seem at first sight. One who has developed *iddhi* powers is able (within limits) to realize (i.e., to make real, to actualize) what he thinks. By applying sufficient concentration to a thought, it can be turned into a reality (there are already indications of this in Prof. J.B. Rhine's experiments with people throwing dice and willing a certain result: statistical investigation shows that the fall of the dice cannot be accounted for by the simple hypothesis of chance.) But not even *iddhi* powers can make Mr. K. and Mrs. J. one single person if they are really two. (You may perhaps recall the discussion on 'possession' of one person's body by another, and of the 'union' of two people's minds, in Balfour's book on Mrs. Willett. In none of these cases do the people actually 'become one'; for if they did they would not separate again. There are satisfactory explanations for the 'feeling of oneness with some other person' that do not require us to suppose that there is any loss of individuality—indeed, a 'feeling of oneness' *presupposes* a duality, otherwise we should all have such a feeling all the time, since we are always one. There is a converse phenomenon sometimes reported, where one person has a feeling of duality—becomes a 'split-personality' in other words—and this *presupposes* a unity.

reached the *arūpa* attainments, but, having seen with understanding, has got rid of some of the *āsavā*, and has thoroughly seen and considered the Teachings of the Tathāgata. The *s* is an individual who has *not* reached the *arūpa* attainments, but, having seen with understanding, has got rid of some of the *āsavā*, and whose *saddhā* in the Tathāgata is thoroughly established and well-rooted. All three are at least *sotāpanna*, but not yet *arahat*; and all three have *some degree* of *samādhi, paññā*, and *saddhā*, but each one emphasizes *one* of these three—the *k* puts *samādhi* first, the *d* puts *paññā* first, and the *s* puts *saddhā* first.

The *Ekāyano ayaṃ bhikkhave maggo sattānaṃ visuddhiyā...* of the Satipaṭṭhāna Sutta (M.10/i,55; D.22/ii,290) is, I regret to say, wrongly translated as 'This, monks, is the only way leading to the purification of beings...'; the proper translation (as pointed out by the late Ven. Ñāṇamoli Thera) is 'This way, monks, leads only to the purification of beings...', but the former translation is preferred by people who write about *satipaṭṭhāna* since it gives an added importance to their subject. Actually, the 'only way' leading to *nibbāna* is the noble eight-factored path (*ariyo aṭṭhaṅgiko maggo*), of which *satipaṭṭhāna* is only *one* of the factors (the seventh).

As regards *samādhi*, the situation is this. As soon as a person reaches the first path (*not* the fruition, which may come much later—see CITTA) he gets the *ariyapuggala*'s right view (*sammādiṭṭhi*), which is his *paññā*. And it is a characteristic of *paññā* that when one has it (as an *ariyapuggala*) one also has *samādhi, viriya, saddhā*, and *sati*.[a]

Now, one who has this *paññā* can, simply by developing his *paññā*, at the same time develop his *samādhi*; and when these have reached sufficient strength (more is required for each successive stage) the attainment of fruition takes place. Although the *development* of *paññā* is, of necessity, *partly* discursive (or intellectual), in the actual attainment of fruition (*sotāpatti*, etc.) the mind becomes steady (since *samādhi* has been automatically developed together with *paññā*, and the two now combine as equal partners—see M.149/iii,289)[1]—and there is direct intuition instead of discursive thinking. So in *all* attainment of fruition there is *samādhi*. But it is also possible for the *ariyapuggala* to develop his *samādhi* separately by means of *ānāpānasati* etc., and this is, in fact, the pleasantest way of advancing (for some people, however, it is difficult, and they have to grind

---

**a.** This fact is not understood by the *puthujjana*, who has no experience of such a phenomenon. Certainly he can get *samādhi* of a kind (by the practice of *ānāpānasati*, for example), but this is not the *sammāsamādhi* of the path (which he does not have). And similarly with *viriya, saddhā*, and *sati*. See BALA.

away at *vipassanā* practice—i.e. development of *paññā*). In this way, a far greater degree of *samādhi* is developed than is actually necessary for the attainment of fruition; and so the *k* has *arūpa* attainments that he does not actually need to reach *nibbāna*.

The minimum strength of *samādhi* that is necessary for fruition is as follows: for *arahattā* and *anāgāmitā*, *jhāna* strength is needed (the first *jhāna* is enough)—see Mahāmāluṅkya Sutta, M.64/i,432-37; for *sakadāgāmitā* and *sotāpatti* full *jhāna* is *not* needed—see A.IX,12/iv,378-82[b]—but it *is* necessary to have the *samādhi nimitta* (which comes long before *jhāna*)—see A.VI,68/iii,422-3.[2] But the *samādhi* can be developed either separately beforehand (as explained above) or together with *paññā*, and presumably in cases where there is attainment simply on listening to the Buddha it is the latter. (I am aware that there has been a controversy about whether *jhāna* is or is not necessary for the attainment of *sotāpatti*, but, as so often in controversies, the disputants have gone to extremes. Those who assert that *jhāna* is necessary believe—rightly or wrongly—that their opponents are maintaining that no *samādhi at all* is necessary. But the fact of the matter is that *some samādhi* is necessary, but not full *jhāna*; and this may or may not, have been developed independently of *paññā*.) I am afraid (as you point out) that this question *is* rather complicated; but I think I have covered the ground. Let me know what is still not clear.

I shall sit on the letter from the French gentleman until I think of something to say to him. It seems that he wants me to publish a journal in French, but (i) my French is by no means equal to the task, and (ii) as the editor of a journal I should have to pass articles for publication that I see to be mistaken (nearly everything that is written these days is), and this I am *not* prepared to do at any price. (Let those who are 'objective' about their Dhamma, and are prepared to see two sides to *every* question—including *nibbāna*—occupy themselves with publishing contradictory articles.)

I have watched the men harvesting their paddy. When they come to a stalk that is still green they do not cut it at once but leave it to ripen. And if they find a stalk that has been cut lying by itself on the ground they bend down and pick it up and carefully put it with its companions where it belongs. In this way they make sure that nothing is lost. Now if only we took as much trouble over our thoughts what a harvest we should have!

---

**b.** This Sutta says that whereas the *anāgāmī* is *samādhismiṃ paripūrakārī*, the *sakadāgāmī* is *na paripūrakārī*. (The former is one who 'fulfils *samādhi*', the latter is one who does not.)

**[L. 100]** **30 April 1964**

Thank you for your letter. Just a quick note, while the postman is here, about the 'S.O.S.' There is no change in my condition whatsoever. The trouble is simply that the Ven. Kheminda Thera asked me how I was, and I was imprudent enough to tell him. Anyway, he gave the letter[1] (unasked by me) to Ananda Pereira, who has sent me a scolding.

As to going to Colombo, I certainly have no intention of doing so until (i) I hear from some reliable doctor that some good might come of it, and (ii) the disturbance that my letter seems to have created has died down. I do not propose to go there simply to listen to a series of lectures (with one thrown in by the Venerable Objector on Abhidhamma for luck!).

**[L. 101]** **1 May 1964**

Since what you so delicately refer to as a 'painful subject' has raised its ugly head again, perhaps this will be a good opportunity for reviewing the situation. To begin with, my condition (physical and mental) is no worse than it has been, and I find myself able to make engagements for a month ahead with comparative equanimity (though further ahead than that will not bear thinking about). But with variations in the state of the weather, and of my guts, so the idea of suicide approaches and recedes; and the situation remains precarious, though not (as I think at the moment) critical.

Now, the reason for the present state of alarm in Colombo is simply this. A week or two ago, the Ven. Kheminda Thera wrote to me saying that he would like to hear how I was, since he had been told that I was not well. So (perhaps injudiciously) I sent him a fairly detailed account of my condition. One reason that led me to do so was the nature of my disorder—satyriasis. If I had kept silent about it, my silence might have been construed (later) as a desire to conceal matters that (in accordance with Vinaya) should be declared. And, having decided to speak of this, I could scarcely leave out all mention of suicide.

It seems that the Ven. Kheminda Thera was much worried about the contents of my letter, and without reference to me (I had not actually asked him to treat it as confidential), he showed it to Ananda Pereira; for a few days ago I had from him a letter of big-brotherly advice, which was quite beside the point and rather difficult to answer. (He says, 'If you chuck it, who knows what sort of a body you will get in your next life?' If this means anything, it means that I am likely to get a *worse* body than my present one.

And this implies that my fifteen years' practice of the Dhamma would leave me worse off than before I started, in which case it follows that the *best* thing for me to do is, precisely, to 'chuck it' as soon as possible before I sink any further. He is thus advocating just the opposite course of action to the one that (presumably) he intends to advocate. I am by no means ungrateful to him for past benefits (which have been generous), but what am I to make of such an equivocal advisor at the present time? And again, he tells me that my body is 'good for many years yet.' I am quite aware of this depressing fact, but it is small comfort to be reminded of it when one is wondering how to get through the next few days. If I were sure that it would not last much longer I might be reconciled to putting up with it; but the thought of another twenty or thirty years makes me reach for the razor.)

I think it is possible that you may be aware that the situation is not quite as simple as it seems, and that bluff common sense is scarcely adequate to deal with it. Both my doctor and yourself, by exercising restraint in the matter of giving advice, have been far more helpful—and I am duly grateful. I know the Ven. Kheminda Thera is not well, so it is quite natural that he should have shifted the burden of a difficult situation on to somebody else's shoulders. I asked neither for advice nor for help, but people are not to be put off by a little thing like that.

As to medical treatment, my doctor has detailed accounts of my disorder. I have several times asked him if the condition can be treated, saying that I am prepared to go to Colombo if it can. But he has at no time suggested that there might be a treatment, even after consulting other doctors. Now, if he, or any other competent doctor who has seen my accounts, is prepared to assure me that there is at least a reasonable chance of improvement after treatment, then I am at least prepared to consider going to Colombo and, if necessary, entering hospital. But what I am *not* prepared to do is to go to Colombo simply on somebody's confident assurance that the trouble *can* be put right. The reason is quite simple: if I accept this assurance and submit to examination and treatment, and then after all the trouble and discomfort involved I find there is no improvement, it is quite possible that I shall be even less inclined to go on living than I am now. As I have said, the situation is precarious but, at the moment, apparently not critical; so before risking a disturbance of the present equilibrium, it would be just as well to find out if there is really any chance of improvement.

Now the question of Colombo. It is clear from Ananda's letter that he thoroughly disapproves my living in solitude: 'I think you are taking life, and yourself, a little too seriously. This talk of suicide also is significant. Maybe you have been alone too much. Solitude is good, but a man needs friends, needs contacts with equals. Otherwise he loses his sense of proportion.' I want to make clear to you my own view of this matter, so I shall discuss it at some length.

When this *kuṭi* was first built, some people from Colombo came and visited me. Soon after, my *dāyaka* came to me in tears and said that he had received a letter from my visitors strongly criticizing him for having built the *kuṭi* in such a remote place. This, of course, was quite unfair, since it was I myself who had chosen the site. But I have found, right from the beginning, that there has been strong resentment by people living in Colombo about my living in solitude. I mentioned this fact once to the late Ven. Ñāṇamoli Thera, and he simply said 'Are you surprised?' It is not that Colombo-dwelling monks feel that I am an example that puts them to shame (since this would not account for the laymen's resentment), but rather that people find it scandalous (though they cannot say so openly) that anyone should take the Buddha's Teaching so seriously as actually to be willing to 'lose his sense of proportion' by living in solitude, and perhaps also to lose his life. People want their Dhamma on easier terms, and they dislike it when they are shown that they must pay a heavier price—and they are frightened, too, when they see something they don't understand: they regard it as morbid, and their one concern (unconscious, no doubt) is to bring things back to healthy, reassuring, normality. So they want to bring me back to Colombo to set their own minds at rest.

And now, of course, when there is the risk of a really public scandal (a suicide), this anxiety is multiplied a hundredfold. But, as I told you before, suicides—with the attainment of *arahattā*, too—were fairly common amongst *bhikkhus* in the Buddha's day. Now, however, things have come to such a pass that, though a suicide for the sake of the Buddha's Teaching would be bad enough, the real scandal would be if it became known that some person or other *still living* had reached one of the stages. People do not, in their heart of hearts, like to think it possible—the shock to their comfortable conventional ideas would be intolerable (I am not thinking here of the village people, who do not, after all, have so many comfortable ideas).

All this, perhaps you will say, may or may not be true; but what has it to do with the advisability or not of my spending some months in Colombo (I mean apart from medical treatment)? It has this to do with it: that I am obliged to ask *why* there is all this insistence on my staying in Colombo—do people say I should because it would really be to my benefit? or for the sake of their own peace of mind?

One thing is quite likely: if I were to stay in Colombo, there would be less risk of my deciding on suicide (at least while I was there). In this matter, Ananda's instinct is not mistaken—if I have contacts and company, the thought of suicide recedes—; and it might be concluded that, in this way, both I should be benefited, and other people's minds would be set at rest. But the trouble is this: the more I get into company, and the closer I get to Colombo, the more insistent become my lustful thoughts. I stated this quite clearly in my letter to the Ven. Kheminda Thera, saying that even at the Hermitage I have little peace from such thoughts, and that it is only here, where I am quite cut off from all disturbing contacts and I do sometimes manage to concentrate my mind (as in the last few days, oddly enough), that I have periods of freedom in which I can, to some extent at least, practise the Dhamma.

But Ananda has chosen to ignore this part of my letter completely, no doubt because it is inconvenient. The fact is, then, that thoughts of suicide can be reduced at the cost of increasing lustful thoughts (and I know from experience that even *before* this trouble when I had simply the intestinal disorder, *most* of my time in Colombo was devoted to lustful thoughts—what it would be like now, I hesitate to think). In other words, *as the risk of suicide decreases so the risk of disrobing increases*. I wish to emphasize this point, since as things are at present this consideration must take first place. And whatever anybody else may think about it, if I *have* to choose between the two evils, I choose suicide rather than disrobing.

The fact that suicide would create a scandal and that disrobing would not, cannot under any circumstances whatsoever be made a reason (in my case, at least) for preferring the latter course. So, if I fear disrobing more than I fear suicide, then I fear Colombo more than I fear Būndala. (I make no mention of the misery of living in Colombo even at the best of times.) Possibly this obstinacy will meet with your disapproval, possibly not; but at least I want you to know that I shall not easily be dislodged from this position. (I do not think that you will press the matter, but you may meet people who are more determined upon it, and you will be able to make my position—whether it is right or wrong—clear to them.) So much for that.

I was a little puzzled about your S.O.S. I do not see that an alarm could arise until I had actually killed myself or else botched the job and was in need of medical attention. If ever I do again decide on suicide I shall certainly not tell anyone *in advance*—they would only come and interfere with the business. If I was actually contemplating it I should never have mentioned it in my letter to the Ven. Kheminda Thera.

What am I to make of a young village boy who brings me *dāna*, worships me respectfully, and then, as he leaves, says 'Cheerio!'? Is there any suitable reply to this?

**[L. 102]** **6 May 1964**

Joyce's *Dubliners* was, I think, his first book, followed by *A Portrait of the Artist as a Young Man*, then *Ulysses*, and finally the astonishing *Finnegan's Wake*. *Dubliners* is much amired for its literary merit, but it can hardly, as far as I can remember, be described as 'exciting'. It throws light on the *Portrait*, and the *Portrait* throws light on *Ulysses*. But don't judge *Ulysses* by *Dubliners*; it is a battleship to a rowing-boat. I shall be glad to read *Dubliners* again.

I wrote a slightly astringent reply to Ananda,[1] and he has sent me a graceful recantation, admitting that he was tired and rather short of sleep when he wrote his earlier letter. I have sent off a reply to his reply, apologizing for anything excessive that I may have said; so I think we are all friends again. Though I do not see much likelihood of improvement, I do not want to give the impression that I am obstinately and neurotically refusing all offers of help. I don't at all want to go to Colombo, but if people are going to be upset if I refuse, then I am willing to agree (on the understanding, naturally, that I return here when treatment is finished).

*Point Counter Point* I have been through several times, but I should be quite happy to go through it once more. Perhaps you may be amused to hear how I first encountered the book. When I was eighteen, after leaving school but before going up to Cambridge, I went to Italy for six months to learn Italian and to 'broaden my mind', as they say. I went first to Florence, where I was a paying guest in a family. Two or three times a week I had tuition in Italian from a young Italian doctor in the city, and there were also two young ladies (about twenty-five, perhaps) who (separately) wanted me to give them practice in English conversation. (Whether they had designs on me, I really don't know—I was far too innocent. Dear me, yes! I blush to think of it.) Anyway, I remember the first session I had with one of the young ladies. I walked to her house in the hot sunshine and was admitted to her cool shady drawing-room. She motioned me to a seat beside her, and then explained that she had just bought *Point Counter Point* but had found it too difficult for her. Would I give her some help with it? She produced the book, and opened it in front of me at page one... Now, if you will look at page one, the first paragraph,[2] you will see that, from a linguistic point of view, the passage offers considerable difficulties to a would-be translator with only three months' Italian at his command. It is not at all easy to put into Italian. But, far worse than that, the subject matter is hardly the sort of thing that an eighteen-year-old English schoolboy is accustomed to discuss with strange young ladies (indeed, with *any* young ladies at all). But I was committed, and I took the plunge. I explained that there was a *worm*; and I explained that the worm was *growing*... but *where* was the worm growing? That was the difficulty—the young lady wanted to know where the worm was growing, and I did not know the Italian word for the place where the worm was growing. What on earth was I to do—draw a picture? or point to the spot? I forget how I eventually explained the situation, but to my astonishment the young lady was not in the least embarrassed when I had made matters clear.... Yes, my six months in Italy certainly 'broadened my mind'.

I don't in the least object to the young boy saying 'Cheerio!'—he is very proud of his English, and probably has no idea at all of the meaning of the word. But it seemed so remarkably incongruous. There was another Sinhala I used to know with some strange English—he would refer to a group of monks as 'a click (clique) of *biskus* (*bhikkhus*)'.

On the subject of friends and suicide, here is Camus in rather a bitter mood (it got him the Nobel Prize, all the same):

> Friendship is less simple. It is long and hard to obtain, but when one has it there's no getting rid of it; one simply has to cope with it. Don't think for a minute that your friends will telephone you every evening, as they ought to, in order to find out if this doesn't happen to be the evening when you are deciding to commit suicide, or simply whether you don't need company, whether you are not in a mood to go out. No, don't worry; they'll ring up the evening you are not alone, when life is beautiful. As for suicide, they would be more likely to push you to it, by virtue of what you owe to yourself, according to them. May heaven protect us, *cher monsieur*, from being set on a pedestal by our friends! Those whose duty is to love us—I mean relatives and connections (what an expression!)—are another matter. They find the right word, all right, and it hits the bull's eye; they telephone as if shooting a rifle. And they know how to aim. Oh, the Bizaines! (*The Fall*, pp. 31-32)

An English gentleman has written to me, saying: 'that it will give me much pleasure to be present for the opening ceremony on 22nd May at 3 p.m. I look forward greatly to meeting you.' I have replied[3] that 'positively the only thing to be opened at my *kuṭi* is the door, and that can be opened without any ceremony at all.' I have suggested that there may be something more important than this to be opened on 22nd May, but that it will be in some other place, and that would be pity if he came here by mistake and missed the ceremony in question. I rather fancy it is something to do with the Kiri Vehera at Kataragama. No doubt he will come and see me either before or after.

**[L. 103]** **19 May 1964**

Thank you for sending *Dubliners*, which I ought to have acknowledged before. I had completely forgotten the contents of the book, but I find there is nothing really to add to what I said in my last letter. Though the actual content is slight, the writing is masterly, and one is left with a feeling of despair that life should be so completely futile. Life *is* like this, and there is nothing else to be expected from it. The final pages of the last story ('The Dead') are a little sentimental, and we have the impression that Joyce is saying that life is worth living provided only we have some romantic episode in our past. But I find this a blemish; and in *Ulysses* Joyce is quite merciless—there is no loophole at all for hope.

The German student's letter can, I think, be taken as a sign that people in Germany are at least prepared to read the *Notes*, whether or not they agree with them; and this is more than can be said for the English (Mrs. Quittner seems to be a startling exception). The copy of *Mind* (the principal English philosophical review) shows quite clearly that the *Notes* will be of no interest whatsoever to current professional English philosophy. This is all rather as I had anticipated.

I am not a great reader of poetry—I prefer ideas to images—but the books that I have been recently sent on mystical Christian poets and Mahāyāna Buddhism are of interest as entirely confirming the view that I have expressed in the *Notes* (Preface (m)). Though I am not an artist, I occupy the corresponding position as a *producer* of culture—in this case of, shall we say, Buddhist thought—as opposed to that of a *diffusionist* of culture; and it is true to say of me—quoting Palinurus quoting Flaubert—that 'a man who has set himself up as an artist [for which read *bhikkhu*] no longer has the right to live like other people'. This statement is closely paralleled in the Suttas: 'One who has gone forth should frequently reflect that he must behave differently (*scil.* from householders).' (A.X,48/v,87-8) The pure culture-diffusionist is obliged to regard all culture as good *per se*; but the solitary artist (or monk) will discriminate ruthlessly. There is no-one I abhor more than the man who says 'all religions are the same'.

I was glad to hear that you managed to write something about *Point Counter Point*—the fact that it turned out to be nonsense is of no significance at all. It is absolutely essential, if one is going to learn anything in this life that is worth learning, not to be afraid to make a fool of oneself. The real fool is the man who has never discovered his foolishness—or rather, the man who is *afraid* of discovering his foolishness.

**[L. 104]** **24 July 1964**

I am glad to get a letter from you again after this interval and I shall be happy to take up our correspondence again. It has been very considerate of you not to have written before this and, indeed, I have really been feeling little inclined to answer letters. Ever since I left Colombo (and also while I was there) I have been getting a slight daily fever. This slight rise in temperature is quite enough to rule out any kind of intelligent thinking. Besides, as I foresaw quite well, my stay in Colombo provided plenty of stimulation for my already over-stimulated sensual appetite, and the effect has been taking some time to wear off. It is quite plain that if I were to have a prolonged stay in a town it would take little to induce me to disrobe.

But even if (as anticipated) my stay in Colombo brought about no improvement in my health (except for the cure of *aluhaṃ*,[1] which covered half my body), it was not, I think, altogether a waste of time. In the first place, people who might otherwise have been worrying both themselves and me will now be satisfied that, medically speaking, there does not appear to be anything very much that can be done to improve my condition. This, at least, clears the air a little. And in the second place, I decided to speak openly to the Ven. Kheminda Thera about a certain matter (which, I think, did not come as a surprise to you).[2]

It was not originally my intention to speak about this matter at all, but I found myself more and more at cross-purposes with various people, and the increasing strain of trying to provide a plausible account of my behaviour without mentioning the most important item eventually persuaded me that I was perhaps not justified in perpetuating false situations in this way. Whether my decision was right I am not sure (it is not the sort of thing about which one can consult someone else), but I feel that my position is much simplified since this rather awkward cat is out of the bag and is semi-public property for which I am no longer solely responsible. This seems to make living rather easier for me (though, of course, it also makes it easier to die). But what the effect of the announcement (which was actually intended for the Ven. Kheminda Thera's ears only) on other people will be—whether of benefit to them or not, I mean—I really don't know.

It is fortunate, in any case, that the *Notes* have already made their appearance since (i) they provide something more solid than a mere assertion for anyone who wants to make up his mind about the author, and (ii) they are perhaps sufficiently forbidding—and unpalatable—to protect their author from becoming a popular figure (it is, to my mind, of the greatest importance that no occasion should be given for complacency about the traditional interpretation of the Suttas—people must *not* be encouraged to think that they can reach attainment by following the Commentaries).

Now, as to the two Suttas you mention, the first goes like this:

> —What, lord, is the benefit, what is the advantage, of skilful virtue?
> —Non-remorse, Ānanda, is the benefit, is the advantage, of skilful virtue.
> Gladness ............................................ of non-remorse.
> Joy ..................................................... of gladness.
> Calm .................................................. of joy.
> Pleasure .............................................. of calm.
> Concentration ...................................... of pleasure.
> Knowing-and-seeing in accordance with reality of concentration.
> Disgust and dispassion............................ of knowing-and-seeing in accordance with reality.
> Knowing-and-seeing of release ................ of disgust and dispassion.
> Thus it is, Ānanda, that skilful virtue gradually leads to the summit. (A.X,1/v,1-2)

Strictly speaking, this Sutta refers only to the *sekha* and not to the *puthujjana*, since the latter needs more than just good *sīla* to take him to release. It is the *sekha* who has the *ariyakanta sīla* that leads to *(sammā-)samādhi*. But, *samādhi* becomes *sammāsamādhi* when one gains the *magga*. Of course even the *puthujjana* needs to have good *sīla* and be free from remorse if he hopes to make progress in his non-*ariya samādhi*.

The second Sutta (A.X,61/v,113-16) runs like this:

> An earliest point of nescience, monks, is not manifest: 'Before this, nescience was not; then afterwards it came into being'. Even if that is said thus, monks, nevertheless it is manifest: 'With this as condition, nescience'. I say, monks, that nescience, too, is with sustenance, not without sustenance. And what is the sustenance of nescience? The

> five constraints (hindrances).[3] I say, monks, that the five constraints, too, are with sustenance, not without sustenance. And what is the sustenance of the five constraints? The three bad behaviours[4].... Non-restraint of the faculties.... Non-mindfulness-and-non-awareness.... Improper attention.... Absence of faith.... Not hearing the Good Teaching (*saddhamma*).... Not frequenting Good Men (*sappurisa*, i.e. *ariyapuggala*).

Then later you have:

> I say, monks, that science-and-release, too, is with sustenance, not without sustenance. And what is the sustenance of science-and-release? The seven awakening-factors[5].... The four stations of mindfulness.... The three good behaviours.... Restraint of the faculties.... Mindfulness-and-awareness.... Proper attention.... Faith.... Hearing the Good Teaching.... Frequenting Good Men.

No doubt you can fill in the rest for yourself.

I am, very slowly, re-typing the *Notes*, correcting mistakes (I found I had misunderstood the Commentary in one place—a lamentable exhibition of carelessness!) and making additions.

**[L. 105] 6 August 1964**

*Sati*, in a loose sense, can certainly be translated as 'memory'; but memory is normally memory of the *past*, whereas in the eight-factored path *sati* is more particularly concerned with the *present*. In so far as one can speak of memory of the present, this translation will do, but memory of the present—i.e. calling to mind the present—is less confusingly translated as 'mindfulness'. In MANO (a) you will find two Sutta passages illustrating these two meanings of *sati*: in the first passage *sati* is 'memory', and in the second it is 'mindfulness'.

About the 'over-stimulation', I certainly agree that there is nothing abnormal about it in the sense that it is something unnatural—indeed, as a layman I should have been very glad of this degree of 'virility', but it is hardly likely that I should have been able to decide to become a monk. It is abnormal only in this, that it is something to which I am quite unaccustomed. I have had it (in this strength, I mean) for only two years, and its onset was quite abrupt. It is like having a daily dose of cantharides! You are quite right in saying that it is more obtrusive in one who has been practising *sati* than in one who lives unmindfully, and that is because the unmindful person does not find it a nuisance and may positively welcome it. But when the task is to get rid of it then it becomes burdensome. It does not disgust me (I have never found sex disgusting), but it *is* a most unwelcome affliction.

I have been sent Huxley's last novel—*Island*. It is a most unsatisfactory book. Since Huxley had visited Ceylon shortly before writing the book, and since the inhabitants of the Island are Buddhists, it has been thought that the Island is Ceylon. But this is clearly a mistake. The Island is undoubtedly Bali (Huxley calls it Pala), both from its geographical and political environment, and the women wear nothing above the waist (which is—or was—the case in Ceylon, I believe, only with Rodiyas).[1] Besides, the people are Mahāyāna Buddhists (Tantric to boot) with a strong admixture of Shiva worship. The book is a kind of *Brave New World* turned inside out—it describes a Utopia of which he approves. It is based almost entirely on *maithuna* and mescaline (one of the characters quotes a Tantric Buddhist saying that Buddhahood is in the *yoni*—a very convenient doctrine!), which in combination (so it seems) are capable of producing the Earthly Paradise. The awkward fact of rebirth is eliminated with the statement that the Buddha discouraged speculation on such questions (whereas, in fact, the Buddha said quite bluntly throughout the Suttas that there *is* rebirth: the speculation that the Buddha discouraged was whether the Tathāgata [or *arahat*] exists after death, which is quite another question).[a] And precisely, the worst feature of the book is the persistent misinterpretation (or even perversion) of the Buddha's Teaching.

It is probable that Huxley picked up a certain amount of information on the Dhamma while he was in Ceylon but, being antipathetic to Theravāda (this is evident in his earlier books), he has not scrupled to interpret his information to suit his own ideas. We find, for example, that according to Freudian doctrine Mucalinda Nāgarāja (Udāna 11/10) is a phallic symbol, being a serpent. So 'meditating under the Mucalinda tree' means sexual intercourse. And this in complete defiance of the verses at the end of the Sutta:

| | |
|---|---|
| *Sukhā virāgatā loke* | Dispassion for worldly pleasure, |
| *kāmānaṃ samatikkamo* | getting beyond sensuality, |
| *Asmimānassa yo vinayo* | putting away the conceit 'I am', |
| *etaṃ va paramaṃ sukhaṃ.* | —this indeed is the highest pleasure.[2] |

a. To ask these questions is to assume that *before* death at least the *arahat does* exist. But even in this very life there is, strictly, no *arahat* to be found.

In short, the book is a complete misrepresentation of the Buddha's Teaching in a popular form that is likely to be widely read. Huxley, of course, is sincere in his views and no doubt means well; but that does not make the book any the less unfortunate.

**[L. 106]** **15 August 1964**

I am sending you, under separate (registered) cover, a package of Sister Vajirā's letters to me, written between the beginning of November 1961 and the end of January 1962.[1] I think you will find them of interest, but for obvious reasons they should be treated as confidential. Without, for the present, commenting on the letters themselves, I shall fill in the background for you.

Up to 1961 I do not recall having met Sister Vajirā on more than one occasion, and then for hardly more than a minute. Before then, in 1956, I think, I wrote an article, 'Sketch for a Proof of Rebirth',[2] which was printed in the *Buddha Jayanti*. Sister Vajirā read the article and wrote to me saying that she was much impressed by it, and asking whether she could translate it. I gave my consent, but owing (partly) to a misunderstanding I was not satisfied with her translation and it was never published. We exchanged a few slightly acrimonious letters (neither of us being inclined to mince our words), and the matter was closed. After that, she sent me once or twice some articles she had written, asking me to comment on them. Being busy with my own affairs, I discouraged her from this habit and generally froze her off.

About July 1961 Sister Vajirā wrote to ask whether she could visit me to discuss Dhamma. I agreed, and she came one afternoon for about two hours. Thereafter we had a brief exchange of letters on vegetarianism (which she practised) and also to discuss an English translation of the Dhammapada that she was making. (I have not kept those letters.) Then I sent her my typescript of the *NP* and *PS*, which I had just finished writing. Sister Vajirā replied with a letter dated 12th November 1961, which is the first of the set I am sending you. She came again to the Hermitage on the 18th November and spent the whole day discussing Dhamma. I did not see her again after that.

At the beginning of the correspondence I did not expect anything very much to come of it but, having the time to spare, I was prepared to go on with it until it seemed pointless to continue. As it progressed, however, I found that she was giving attention to what I was saying, and I decided to keep it alive even though she seemed inclined to let it die. Towards the end (after her letter of 6th January 1962) I began to think it possible that something might happen, without however really expecting that it would. Anyway, I wrote my letter of the 10th January (of which you will find a rough draft)[3] with the thought, 'If this doesn't do it, nothing will'. Even so, her letter of the 21st came as a surprise, and I was delighted. (This letter alone was enough to convince me, and the next one, of the 23rd, came only as confirmation, though it was nonetheless welcome for all that!)

Things were now happening much too fast for me to keep up with them. (It seemed—and seems—to me that she went through in about five days what took me three months and a half—though of course our circumstances were different—and I was quite unprepared for her subsequent behaviour, though she gave me notice of it at the end of the letter of the 23rd.) Evidently what happened was that with the sudden release of the central tension all her compensating tensions found themselves out of work and began aimlessly expending themselves this way and that, and some time was required before she found a new position of stable equilibrium. In any case I wrote to Mrs. Salgado (who seemed much worried) to say that I thought that Sister Vajirā's condition was not serious and that she would soon recover. I also wrote and asked the Ven. Siridhamma for a report, and he replied (as I *hoped* he would) that although she had recovered she 'seemed to be a changed person.'[4]

I was not at all pleased when she was bundled out of the country and back to Germany before I was able, as the doctors say, to 'follow up the case'. But later reports seem to confirm that she has remained 'a changed person'. The fact that she now seems to have lost interest in the Dhamma and no longer associates with her former Buddhist friends is a good sign, not a bad one—when one has got what one wants, one stops making a fuss about it and sits down quietly. (In my own case, I had previously been maintaining a continuous correspondence with the Ven. Ñāṇamoli Thera about the Dhamma, and then afterwards I stopped it entirely, finding it pointless. There was no longer anything for me to discuss *with* him, since the former relationship of parity between us regarding the Dhamma had suddenly come to an end. I could only have renewed the correspondence if he had been made aware—which he was not—of our new relationship.) Anyway, even though I have only Sister Vajirā's letters to go on, I do not see any reason to doubt her statement (23rd January 1962) that she has ceased to be a *puthujjana*. Perhaps I should add that though she seems to have had a fairly strong emotional attitude towards me (as 'representing the *arahat*'), this has not been mutual. At no time have I found myself emotionally interested in her in any way, though, naturally enough, from the point of view of Dhamma I regard her with a friendly eye.

**[L. 107]** **24 August 1964**

It is interesting to read your reactions to the letters I sent you. Sister Vajirā is an extremely passionate and self-willed person, with strong emotions, and, apparently, something of a visionary. In other words, she is totally different, temperamentally, from either of us (though in different ways). Besides, she is a woman. You will see, in her letters, how she alternates between moods—one could almost say *attacks*—of emotional periods and of admirable clear-headedness. During the former her letters tend to become incoherent, and she *assumes* that her reader is in a similar state and can fill in all the gaps. But, quite clearly, she is perfectly *at home* in her emotions, in a way that you and I find difficult to understand: emotion, for her, is quite normal, as it is for nearly all women. And it must not be forgotten that she was living more or less alone with her thoughts, and solitude always has the effect of magnifying and intensifying one's inner life. I do not at all think that Sister Vajirā's emotional manifestations are (or were—since they are now past history) anything to be alarmed at, and far less a sign of mental disorder. Certainly, she does not find them alarming, and even gives due notice to other people in case *they* do.

One thing must be kept in mind when reading her letters: for about a dozen years she had had the idea that the Buddha taught that *nothing really exists*, and she had been developing this mistaken notion in solitude. But, being a mistake, it leads nowhere except to a state of exasperation and nervous tension (there is someone else, known to both of us, who is doing the same thing, and he is certainly not achieving inward calm). Furthermore, she was convinced (her teacher was evidently partly responsible)[1] that she had already reached the first *magga* (though not the *phala*); and this was the cause of her impatience, bad temper, and extreme conceit.[a] I was quite aware of her discourteous attitude and even bad manners, but I said nothing at that time since I did not want to prejudice the outcome of our correspondence by pulling her up over a matter of secondary importance. We Europeans are much more accustomed to casual manners, and (perhaps wrongly) stand less on our dignity in this matter than Easterners. (The act of *vandanā*, for me, still keeps a faint air of artificiality—we are not brought up with it.) And now, as I think, there is no longer any need to check her.

---

**a.** This explains, for example, the letter beginning 'Dear Bhikkhu'—it is quite evident that she knows better, since all her later letters (I think this was an early one) are perfectly respectful. And the Ven. Kassapa Thera once complained that she had come into his room and taken a chair without so much as 'By your leave'.

About the burning of my letters, I rather think that you must have misread what she says. You quote a passage[2] that you (quite rightly) describe as a 'song of victory',[b] but then go on to say that this idea was completely changed for you by the incident of the burning of the letters. From this I gather that you take the burning of the letters to have taken place *after* her would-be 'victory'. But I think this is a mistake. She herself says that it was *after* she had burnt my letters that she 'got the result'. The letter in question gives the result first (it was, after all, the important thing) and then goes on to apologize for having burnt the letters in a fit of passion.[3]

Nothing is done in this world, either good or bad, without passion. 'Mental stability' too often means lack of passion. But passion must be disciplined and used intelligently and some people need a teacher to do this for them. 'By means of craving, craving must be abandoned' say the Suttas (A.IV,159/ii,445-46). That, in any case, was how I read it. She had (so I gathered) been wrestling with the meaning of my letters and getting nowhere, until finally, in a fit of exasperation, she had decided that they were all wrong and had consigned them (and me too, by implication) to the flames. It was only then that she grasped the meaning of what I had written—hence her later remorse. From her point of view it was indeed a 'dangerous act'[4] since she had not yet understood them when she destroyed them. But (I am inclined to think) some such act of despair was perhaps necessary to release an accumulation of tension before the meaning of the letters could occur to her. Attainment does not come at the moment when we are making a conscious effort to attain, because at that time we have *uddhacca-kukkucca*, 'distraction and worry', but rather at the unexpected moment when we relax after an apparently fruitless effort.

For my part I am satisfied (judging solely from the letters) that, however strange her behaviour may have seemed to her well-wishers in Colombo, there was nothing in it to contradict my opinion. What you speak of as the 'breaking point' was (as I see it) no more than the entry into a particularly strong (and pleasurable) emotional state consequent upon the realization (which, at the beginning especially, can be breath-taking) that 'nothing matters any more.' I don't suppose she was within a hundred miles of telling the people who were caring for her what the reason was for her condition. Certainly, her last letter,[5] for all its emotional colouring, gives no sugges-

**b.** I am unable to see that it could have been written by a *puthujjana*, even if he were trying to deceive. It would never occur to him to add the part about 'losing a dimension of thought'. One must actually have had the experience to know how exactly this describes it.

tion that she is in any way unhappy or distressed, or even that she has any doubts about her new state. And you will observe that I am quietly but firmly dismissed at the end of the letter. Whatever else happened, one thing is certain—she no longer finds herself in any way dependent upon me. A psycho-analyst, at least, would be gratified with that result!

About *paṭiccasamuppāda*. I do not see that it is possible for anyone to reconcile my view of *paṭiccasamuppāda* with the three-life view. If anyone says that they are both correct, then I would suggest that he has failed to understand what I have written—though, as I freely admit, that may be because I have failed to make myself clear. As to Sister Vajirā's statements, I think you will find that one was written 'before' and one 'after'. This distinction, actually, is crucial; and Sister Vajirā's change of view is significant.

P.S. The word 'sister' (*bhaginī*) seems to be used in the Suttas as a quite general term or form of address for women, particularly by *bhikkhus*. In my letters to her I addressed Sister Vajirā as 'Dear Upāsikā'. I do not see that there is any objection to the word 'sister' as used for *dasa-sil upāsikā*. Laymen used to address *bhikkhunīs* as *ayye*, which means 'lady', but an *upāsikā* is not a *bhikkhunī*. In the Suttas, *bhikkhus* used to address *bhikkhunīs* as *bhaginī*.

**[L. 108] 30 August 1964**

You said that, in your view, the incident of the burning of the letters was the act of an unstable mind. To this I replied that nothing is done in the world, either good or bad, without passion; and I said that 'mental stability', too often, is simply lack of passion. As it happens, I was reading yesterday one of Huxley's earlier books of essays (*Proper Studies*, 1927) and I came across a passage that discusses this very point. Perhaps it will make my own statement clearer. Here it is:

> The man who will lightly sacrifice a long-formed mental habit is exceptional. The vast majority of human beings dislike and even actually dread all notions with which they are not familiar. Trotter, in his admirable *Instincts of the Herd in Peace and War*, has called them the 'stable-minded,' and has set over against them a minority of 'unstable-minded people,' fond of innovation for its own sake.... The tendency of the stable-minded man... will always be to find that 'whatever is, is right.' Less subject to the habits of thought formed in youth, the unstable-minded naturally take pleasure in all that is

> new and revolutionary. It is to the unstable-minded that we owe progress in all its forms, as well as all forms of destructive revolution. The stable-minded, by their reluctance to accept change, give to the social structure its durable solidity. There are many more stable- than unstable-minded people in the world (if the proportions were changed we should live in a chaos); and at all but very exceptional moments they possess power and wealth more than proportionate to their numbers. Hence it comes about that at their first appearance innovators have generally been persecuted and always derided as fools and madmen. A heretic, according to the admirable definition of Bossuet, is one who 'emits a singular opinion'—that is to say, an opinion of his own, as opposed to one that has been sanctified by general acceptance. That he is a scoundrel goes without saying. He is also an imbecile—a 'dog' and a 'devil,' in the words of St. Paul, who utters 'profane and vain babblings.' No heretic (and the orthodoxy from which he departs need not necessarily be a religious orthodoxy; it may be philosophic, ethical, artistic, economic), no emitter of singular opinions, is ever reasonable in the eyes of the stable-minded majority. For the reasonable is the familiar, is that which the stable-minded are in the habit of thinking at the moment when the heretic utters his singular opinion. To use the intelligence in any other than the habitual way is not to use the intelligence; it is to be irrational, to rave like a madman. (pp. 71-2)

Amongst people of Buddhist countries it is, I think, not properly understood (quite naturally) that, generally speaking, Europeans who become Buddhists belong necessarily to the 'unstable-minded' and not to the 'stable-minded'. The Buddha's Teaching is quite alien to the European tradition, and a European who adopts it is a rebel. A 'stable-minded' European is a Christian (or at least he accepts the Christian tradition: *religion* for him—whether he accepts it or not—, *means* Christianity; and a *Buddhist* European is not even 'religious'—he is simply a lunatic).

But in a Buddhist country, naturally, to be a Buddhist is to be 'stable-minded', since one is, as it were, 'born a Buddhist'. And 'born-Buddhists' find it difficult to understand the unstable-minded European Buddhist, who treats the Buddha's Teaching as a wonderful new discovery and then proposes, seriously, to practise it.[a] The stable-minded traditional Buddhist

**a.** It often happens, of course, that he has got it upside-down and inside-out; but at least he has enthusiasm (at any rate to begin with).

cannot make out what the unstable-minded European Buddhist is making such a fuss about.[b]

I am not, naturally, speaking in praise of odd behaviour for its own sake (the Buddha always took into account the prejudices and superstitions of the mass of laymen, and legislated as far as possible to avoid scandal), but I do say that it is wrong to regard odd behaviour as bad simply because it is odd. I myself am in a very ambiguous situation: here, in Buddhist Ceylon, I find that I am regarded as a most respectable person—complete strangers show me deference, and uncover their head as they pass—; but my relatives in England, and no doubt most of my former friends too, think that I am a freak and a case for the psychiatrist, and if they were to take off their hat when they saw me that could only be to humour my madness. Actually, however respectable and stable-minded I may appear (if we choose to ignore a deplorable tendency to suicide), I do not feel in the least respectable (I don't care tuppence for the durable solidity of the social structure) and I certainly count myself amongst the 'unstable-minded' (which does not mean, of course, that I am mentally fickle). But although the passage from Huxley is quite good, I really mean something rather more subtle than the mere expression of unorthodox opinions.

**[L. 109] 31 August 1964**

As to that Sutta you mention (A.IV,159/ii,144-7): a *bhikkhunī* sends for the Ven. Ānanda Thera, being infatuated with him and hoping perhaps for sexual intercourse. The Ven. Ānanda understands the situation and gives her a suitable Dhamma-talk. He tells her (i) that this body is a product of food and that, depending on food, food is to be given up (a *bhikkhu*'s body is made of food, but he must go on taking food to keep alive and practise the Dhamma if he wishes to give up food in the future by not being reborn); (ii) that this body is a product of craving and that, depending on craving, craving is to be given up (a *bhikkhu*, having been born on account of craving in his previous life, hears that so-and-so has become an *arahat* and, craving that for himself, sets to work to get it; and in course of time he succeeds, his success being, precisely, the giving up of all craving); (iii) the same with *māna* or conceit (the *bhikkhu*, hearing that so-and-so has become an *arahat*,

b. And so it is not in the least astonishing that Sister Vajirā's supporters are scandalized when she 'goes off her head' for a fortnight with joy (which is my view of what happened).

thinks 'I'm as good as he is, and if he can do it, so can I,' and sets to work; and in due course, prompted by conceit, he puts an end to conceit); (iv) that this body is a product of copulation, and that the Buddha has said that (for monks) copulation is absolutely not to be practised. In (ii), the *bhikkhu* craves for *arahat*ship since he thinks in terms of 'I' or 'self' ('When shall *I* attain that?'), and all such thoughts contain *bhavataṇhā*, though of course here there is no *sensual* craving (*kāmataṇhā*). But anyone who thinks 'When shall *I* become an *arahat*?' is *ipso facto* failing to understand what it means to be an *arahat* (since being an *arahat* means *not* thinking in terms of 'I'). So, on account of his craving for *arahat*ship, he sets out to get it. But, since he does not understand what *arahat*ship is, he does not know what it is that he is seeking; and when, in due course, he *does* come to know what it is he is seeking, he has *ipso facto* found it (or at least the first installment of it). It is by making use of *bhavataṇhā* that he gives up *bhavataṇhā* (and *a fortiori* all other kinds of *taṇhā*). I think that Sister Vajirā, in her last letter but one, says that she had not known what it was that she had been fighting against, but that she now saw that the solution had been staring her in the face all the time without her being able to see it. This describes the situation very well. It is *because* of *bhavataṇhā* that, *with the Buddha's help*, we make an attempt to recognize *bhavataṇhā* and succeed in doing so, thereby bringing *bhavataṇhā* to an end.

I fully agree with you that the curtain came down on the drama too suddenly. I was hoping for a further letter but was disappointed, and all I could do was to ask the Ven. Siridhamma Thera to keep me informed (though, naturally, I did not tell him why I was interested). But the Ven. Siridhamma tends to write his letters as if they were telegrams, and I did not get much detail. And when she was packed off to Germany there was no further chance of meeting her and filling in the gaps. But if in fact she really did cease to be a *puthujjana* as she claims (and I see no reason to doubt it), then we are perhaps fortunate in having as much as we do have in the way of a written record of an actual attainment of the *magga* (and probably also of the *phala*) as it took place. An account written afterwards from memory would not have the dramatic force of these letters which are so striking.

**[L. 110] 29 September 1964**

I quite realized that you used the words 'unstable mind' only in connexion with a certain incident (and in any case under a misapprehension), and my reason for pursuing the matter was simply that I happened to come across the passage in Huxley—certainly not in any criticism of your use of the words.

You are quite right to doubt the value of the 'stable-mindedness' of the irresponsible politicians (though I sometimes wonder whether politicians can really be regarded as having a mind at all), and it has to be emphasized (as I think Huxley does) that unstable-mindedness is just as likely to do evil as it is to do good. Obviously it will depend on one's situation as well as on one's character whether it is a good thing or a bad thing to be unstable-minded. If you are a follower of the Buddha and unstable-mindedness leads you to become a Christian or a Muslim, then it is clearly better to be stable-minded; but if it leads you to abandon the home life and become a *bhikkhu*, then your unstable-mindedness is good. Here, as almost everywhere else, it is necessary to discriminate.

The episode of the Ven. Ānanda Thera and the love charms is not in the Suttas, but I think I recall reading it myself somewhere in the Commentaries.[1] But we do find in the Suttas several instances of the Ven. Ānanda Thera's championing (though that word is too strong) the cause of women (it was on his initiative—as you will remember—that the Buddha was persuaded to allow women to become *bhikkhunīs*).[2] It was perhaps this tendency to speak up on behalf of women that led commentators and later writers (including some Europeans) to describe the Ven. Ānanda Thera as a rather simple and weak-minded person (Prof. Rhys Davids uses the word 'child-like'), which in point of fact he most certainly was *not*. But he came in for some criticism at the First Council, even though he was then *arahat*. (This is to be found in the Vinaya Cūḷavagga towards the end.)[3]

Generally speaking, it is the first business of anyone who gets ordained to learn Pali and find out what the Dhamma is all about, and not to rely on faulty European translations; but perhaps Ven. S.[4] will be spending his time better practising *samatha* (which can be done without a knowledge of Pali) than doing nothing. On the other hand he should really still be living with his teacher and getting instruction from him. But his teacher seems to be otherwise occupied. Anyway *I* do not propose to become his teacher, though I am prepared to help him if he asks for help.

## [L. 111] 3 November 1964

Many thanks for the press cuttings. The offer of the Nobel Prize to Sartre is not really very surprising, nor is his refusal of it. He has been a considerable influence in European intellectual circles (outside Britain) for almost twenty years, and his books have been widely read. He is probably now fairly affluent, and can afford to do without the prize-money, and he still gets the credit (whether he likes it or not) of having been offered the prize—and additional credit for having refused it! None the less, his reasons for refusing the award are sound and set a good example for others.

The height of absurdity in the matter of official distinctions is the award of titles to distinguished *bhikkhus* by the Burmese Government—quite oblivious of the fact that if a *bhikkhu* accepts an official distinction he shows himself *ipso facto* to be a bad *bhikkhu*. And perhaps the topmost pinnacle of this height of absurdity is the 'official recognition' by the said Government, not many years ago, of the claim of a certain *bhikkhu* (which, for all I know, may have been justified) to be an *arahat*. (The Catholic Church, of course, has to do this sort of thing. Since there is no attainment—*samāpatti*—in Christianity, nobody can claim to be a saint. The Church—the Vatican, that is—simply waits until the likely candidates have been safely dead for a number of years and then pronounces officially that they were saints when they were living. Since the Church is infallible—if you are a believer—, all this is quite in order. But if you do *not* happen to be a believer it is all a huge joke.)

Babbler's statement that Sartre is 'the founder and leader of existentialism' is very inaccurate—existentialism, as a distinct philosophy, is universally agreed to have started with Kierkegaard (1813-1855), and there have been other existentialist philosophers—notably Heidegger—before Sartre. But what Babbler calls 'the fundamental tenet', though not recognized as such by existentialists, is more or less correct (and you will have noted that, so stated, it is not repugnant to the Buddha's Teaching—we can agree that 'man is what he makes of himself').

November, with its rains, is rather a bad month for me, and my thoughts tend to darken like the skies. Since, as you will understand, I no longer have any compelling reason to go on living—and what a relief it is too!—I have to look around, in difficult periods, for makeshift reasons for carrying on; and my principal resort is preoccupation with the *Notes*. I correct them, add to them, polish them, re-type them, and then consider various ways and means of having them published—and all this is not so much because I am really concerned about them (though I will not pretend that I am totally disinterested) as because it is a way of getting through my day.

**[L. 112]** **23 November 1964**

I have just run through Mr. Bandy's[1] comments on the *Notes*, and it seems at first glance that the principal objection he is raising is against my interpretation of *paṭiccasamuppāda* as not describing a process in time. As a matter of fact, you are already familiar with this objection, since in an earlier letter you told me of someone who maintained that the three-life interpretation was compatible with the views expressed in the *Notes*. At the same time you remarked that Sister Vajirā had earlier preferred a 'temporal' interpretation of the *paṭiccasamuppāda* but had later changed her mind. I replied, first, that I did not see that my interpretation was compatible with the three-life interpretation (and certainly Mr. Bandy does not find it so!), and secondly, that Sister Vajirā's change of view took place when (as it seems) she ceased to be a *puthujjana*.[a] If I can work up the energy to reply to him, it will be more concerned with discussion of different general points of view than with answering the particular points he raises (which largely depend on the difference in our points of view).

He remarks in his letter, 'Another big fault is the Ven. Author...nearly always tries to discover his ideas in the Canon instead of *deducing* from the passages what *they* teach.' This criticism is unavoidable. From *his* point of view it will seem justified. The thing is, that I have a source of information (my own experience) that he does not know about; and when I say that a certain thing *is* so, without giving Sutta backing (though I always try to give supporting references where I can), he will naturally get the impression that I am imposing arbitrary views (much the same sort of thing happened with Mrs. Quittner when she described the *Notes* as 'arrogant'). Unless the *Notes* are read with the idea that the author *may* have something to say that the reader does not already know about, they will remain incomprehensible. (In the Suttas, the Buddha says that one listening to the Dhamma who is *randhagavesī*, 'looking for faults',[2] will not be able to grasp it. Note, again, Sister Vajirā's change of attitude in the course of her letters, and her eventual admission that she had formerly been 'conceited'.)

I enclose a press cutting about Sartre.[3] The view that he is expounding here ('A writer has to take sides...') finds no justification at all in his philosophy. If, therefore, he holds this view, he does so simply because he finds

---

**a.** This actually is not irrelevant here, since Mr. Bandy is one of the group of Buddhists to which Sister Vajirā formerly belonged, and there is much in common between his present views and Sister Vajirā's former views: both, presumably, derive from the same source.

it emotionally satisfactory. This view, of course, is quite familiar to us—it is the Socialist argument we sometimes hear, that since one cannot practise the Dhamma if one is starving, therefore food comes first; and therefore food is more important than the Dhamma; and therefore it is more important to produce food than it is to behave well; and therefore any kind of violence or deceit is justified if it helps to increase food production.

As Sartre puts it, it seems plausible—it is better to feed the poor than to entertain the rich. But when we look at it more closely we see that certain difficulties arise. To begin with, it assumes (as all socialists, Sartre included, do assume) that this life is the only one, that we did not exist before we were born, and shall not exist after we die. On this assumption it is fairly easy to divide mankind into two groups: the rich oppressors, and the poor oppressed, and the choice which to support seems easy. But if this is not the only life, how can we be sure that a man who is now poor and oppressed is not suffering the unpleasant effects of having been a rich oppressor in his past life? And, if we take the principle to its logical conclusion, should we not choose to be on the side of the 'oppressed' inhabitants of the hells, suffering retribution for their evil ways, and to condemn the fortunate ones in the heavens, a privileged class enjoying the reward of virtue, as the 'idle rich'? And then this view ignores the fact that our destiny at death depends on how we behave in this life. If bad behaviour in this life leads to poverty and hunger in the next, can we be sure that bread is more important than books? What use is it providing the hungry with bread if you don't tell them the difference between right and wrong? Is metaphysics so unimportant if it leads men—rich and poor, no matter—to adopt right view and to behave accordingly?

Of course, the very fact that Sartre's philosophy does not have anything to say about the hungry and oppressed is a blemish on his philosophy; and it might be argued that Sartre is therefore better occupied standing up for the hungry and oppressed than in propagating his metaphysical views; but that still does not justify the principle. And, in the last analysis, the Buddha's Teaching is for a privileged class—those who are fortunate enough to have the intelligence to grasp it (the Dhamma is *paccattaṃ veditabbo viññūhi* (M.38/i,265)—'to be known by the wise, each for himself'), and they are most certainly not the majority! But Sartre's attitude is symptomatic of a general inadequacy in modern European thought—the growing view that the majority must be right, that truth is to be decided by appeal to the ballot-box. (I read somewhere that, in one of the Western Communist countries, it was decided by a show of hands that angels do not exist.)

**[L. 113]** **29 November 1964**

A few days ago I received from you a letter containing Mr. Bandy's comments on the *Notes on Dhamma*. I have been through it with some care (though unfortunately I do not read Sanskrit), and it is obvious that he has taken considerable trouble about preparing them. He clearly has a considerable wealth of learning at his command, and seems to be quite familiar with the Pali texts, from which he quotes freely. At the same time, however, it is evident to me that the differences between his point of view and mine go too deep to be removed simply by a discussion of the various points he has raised. In order to explain my meaning I should have to make use of arguments that he would probably feel inclined to dispute, and the difficulties would thus merely be shifted from one place to another. But I have the impression that he is well satisfied that his position is the right one, and I do not think it would serve any useful purpose for me to call it in question.

In his letter he remarks that I explain too inductively, that I tend to look for my ideas in the Canon instead of *deducing* from the passages what *they* mean. This criticism, however, supposes that we are, in fact, able to approach the Canon with a perfectly virgin mind, equipped only with a knowledge of Pali and a sound training in logic. But this is precisely what we cannot do. Each of us, at every moment, has the whole of his past behind him; and it is in the light of his past (or his background or his presuppositions) that he interprets what is now presented to him and gives it its meaning. Without such a background nothing would ever appear to us with any meaning at all—a spoken or written word would remain a pure presentation, a bare sound or mark without significance. But, unfortunately, each of us has a different past; and, in consequence, each of us approaches the Canon with a set of presuppositions that is different in various ways from everybody else's. And the further consequence is that each of us understands the Canon in a different sense. We try to discover our personal ideas in the Canon because there is nothing else we can do. It is the only way we have, in the first place, of *understanding* the Canon. Later, of course, our understanding of the Canon comes to modify our ideas; and thus, by a circular process, our later understanding of the Canon is better than, or at least different from, our earlier understanding, and there is the possibility of eventually arriving at the right understanding of the *ariyapuggala*. Certainly we can, to some extent, deduce from the Canon its meaning; but unless we first introduced our own ideas we should never find that the Canon had any meaning to be deduced.

For each person, then, the Canon means something different according to his different background. And this applies not only to our understanding of particular passages, but also to what we understand by the Buddhadhamma as a whole.

(i) We may all agree that certain passages were spoken by the Buddha himself and that they represent the true Teaching. But when we come to ask one another what we understand by these passages and by the words they contain we often find a profound disagreement that is by no means settled simply by reference to other Sutta passages. (He and I are evidently agreed—to take a case in point—that the Sīvaka Sutta[1] represents the Teaching of the Buddha. But whereas I understand it as indicating that only one out of eight kinds of feeling is *kammavipāka*, he brings forward an argument to justify its interpretation in a quite contrary sense—that *all* eight kinds are *kammavipāka*. And though I entirely disagree with his interpretation, I very much doubt whether I should be able to produce a Sutta passage to convince him of—as I see it—his mistake. And this for the simple reason that he will inevitably interpret whatever passage I may produce according to *his* ideas. We may agree on the text, but we shall disagree on the interpretation.)

(ii) Since everybody already has his own ideas (vague or precise) of what constitutes happiness, he will naturally look to the Buddha (that is, if he has placed his *saddhā* in the Buddha) to supply that happiness, and he will interpret the Dhamma as a whole in just that sense. Later, of course, he may find that the Dhamma cannot be taken in the sense that he wishes, and he will then either change his ideas or else abandon the Dhamma for some other teaching. But, in any case, there is no reason at all for supposing that two people (unless they have both ceased to be *puthujjana*) will be agreed on what it is, precisely, that the Buddha teaches. (So, in the present case, I do not find that Mr. Bandy's view of the Dhamma—so far as I can grasp it—has any very great resemblance to mine; and that difference evidently reflects the difference in our respective backgrounds against which we interpret the Dhamma. He may (perhaps) say that he reads and understands the Suttas without any reference to a background, and (if so) I have no wish to argue the point; but I know that, for my part, I never come without a background (in a sense I *am* my background) when I consider the texts, even though that background is now very different from what it was when I first looked at a Sutta. And if he disagrees with what I am saying, that disagreement will itself be reflected in the way each of us understands the nature of the Dhamma.)

Probably he is not much concerned to understand the mode of thinking that refuses a horizontal (or temporal) interpretation of *paṭiccasamuppāda* and requires instead a vertical (or simultaneous) view; but if it should so happen that he is interested, then he could read—if his studies leave him time—either Heidegger's *Sein und Zeit* or Sartre's *L'Être et le Néant*. It must be made clear, however, that these works are in no way a substitute for the Canon and, further, that the philosophies of these thinkers, when considered in detail, are open to criticism in several respects. It is their *manner* of thinking that is instructive. (In this connexion, Mr. Bandy might note that by the term 'reflexion' I mean *paccavekkhana*, not *pariyatti*.)[2]

**[L. 114]** **30 November 1964**

After some hesitation I have decided to reply to Mr. Bandy's letter. But since it is evident that he is more concerned to maintain his own position (in a sense, the *Notes* seem to have drawn blood, touching him at several weak points) than to understand the *Notes*, it seems important that I should keep a certain distance and not come to blows with him; and so I have addressed my reply[1] to you—all my remarks are addressed to the Court.

It is obvious that he has a good knowledge of the Suttas (of which he is perhaps rather proud), and a very poor understanding of the Dhamma. A reply, therefore, that is going to be of any benefit to him (and not simply make the situation worse) needs rather careful wording: it is necessary to convey to him that he is very far from understanding the Dhamma, without actually telling him so in so many words. Whether or not my reply (which avoids his tactical sallies by the strategical manoeuvre of suggesting a profound difference in point of view—which is true—making any discussion of details futile at the present stage) achieves this aim, I really can't say—how does it strike you? Have I said anything that will merely irritate him without shaking his complacency?

The myth that was growing up about me here—that my presence was the cause of the good rains that have been enjoyed since I came here—is now being rudely shattered. There has been a shortage of rain in this district, and what little there has been has very carefully (almost by design) avoided Būndala. Perhaps the drought has come in order to demonstrate to the villagers that *post hoc ergo propter hoc* is a fallacy—or does this supposition itself fall into the same fallacy?

**[L. 115]** **14 December 1964**

I have been busy these last two or three weeks with rather lengthy correspondence. First there was Mr. Bandy to deal with. Then I wrote a letter, just as long, to Mr. Brady on the question of God.[1] He spent a week in a Hindu ashram at Rishikesh (in the Himalayas). He was originally a Catholic, but gave it up at the age of twenty, but he is one of those people who rather naturally incline towards a mystical view, and he rather likes the idea of God, without altogether being satisfied of his existence. So he finds the Hindu teachings much more sympathetic than the cold Teaching of the Buddha. And it seems likely that the Swamis at Rishikesh have been saying that all religions are One, and that the Buddha, being a Hindu, taught a form of Hinduism. So I set out to correct these ideas. He tells me that he reads my letters repeatedly, so he is worth the trouble of a little effort on my part.

*Those Barren Leaves* is (or was) probably the one of Huxley's novels that I read more than any other. This perhaps due to the Italian setting, with which I am familiar; but also to the aniromantic attitude of Francis Chelifer, a character from whom I learned a great deal (and much less painfully than by finding out for myself). But perhaps you will find the book less striking than some of the others (*Point Counter Point* for example).

**[L. 116]** **30 December 1964**

I am glad to see that you have found some passages of interest in *Those Barren Leaves*. I myself started thinking about the unpleasant business of dying, perhaps three or four years ago. Up to then, like most people, I had not given it much thought. But I was struck by the statements of two doctors on the subject. The first said that if we overeat we tend to die earlier than if we take less; and that since death is more painful when one is still young (because the body has stronger resistance) than when one is old and decrepit, it is advisable to eat less and live as long as possible. The other doctor was commenting (in a medical journal) on a proposal to institute voluntary euthanasia for people who had reached the age of sixty. He was in favour of the proposal because, he said, as a doctor he was well aware of the horrible diseases that are liable to attack us in the seventh and eighth decades of our lives. So there you are; if you die young you probably have a difficult death because your body is strong and if you keep alive into old age you run the risk of dying unpleasantly from some frightful affliction. And, after that, I was struck by the obsessive thought of death that runs right through Dr. Axel Munthe's book, *The Story of San Michele*. In the Suttas, whenever the Buddha speaks of severe pain, it is always 'pain like that of dying'.

The question of the 'lovely young temptation' is, of course, the difficult one. But one has to make up one's mind about it if one is to live as a recluse. The Buddha is reported to have said (though I have never come across the passage) that if there were another thing such as sex (*kāma*)—i.e. if there were two such things—then it would not be possible to live the *brahmacariya* and put an end to suffering.

Although the Suttas give several ways of dealing with the 'lovely young temptation' when she comes toddling down the road, there is one (a kind of pincer movement) that I have sometimes found very useful. It is based on the episode of the Buddha and the Ven. Nanda Thera (which you can read at Udāna iii,2/20-4). When the 'lovely young temptation' comes in sight, you say to yourself: 'Well, if I really must have sex, and cannot do without it altogether, the best plan is to restrain myself now and thereby to gain merit that, in my next life, will bring me much bigger and better sex than I can get here.' By the time you have considered this aspect of the question, the temptation has perhaps gone past and is out of sight round the next corner, and it is now too late to do anything about it. But you still have this unsatisfactory desire for sex. In order to get rid of this, you set to work to see that sex *never* lasts; that, in the long run, the misery involved outweighs the pleasure; and that final peace can only be obtained when all thought of sex has vanished. This procedure is often quite enough to put the question out of one's mind—until, of course, the next temptation comes along balancing her haunches! But, each time, there is a little progress, and it gradually becomes easier to keep one's peace of mind, even when a temptation actually appears.

Mr. Brady has contacted L'Alliance Française (the French British Council, if you will allow me to be Irish), and has obtained for me a number of French books on loan (nearly all on existentialism). One of these is Camus's long novel *La Peste* ('The Plague'). This has a character who declares 'The only concrete problem that I know of today is whether it is possible to be a saint without God.' In the Christian tradition, of course, one is good, one becomes a saint, in order to please God or to fulfil his will. But when (as is largely the case in Europe today) people no longer believe in the existence of God, is there any reason (apart from the police) for continuing to behave well or for aspiring to sainthood? This character in *La Peste* has seen human suffering, and has seen that much of this suffering is due to the cruelty or thoughtlessness of human beings themselves; and the question that he asks himself is whether a belief in God is necessary before one can live a good life, or whether a concern for other people's welfare is enough, and whether this will give a man final peace.

Actually, in one of the Suttas, the Buddha more or less answers this question by saying (in effect) that *so long as one believes in God it is not possible to become a saint*. And the reason is quite simple: if God exists, he is responsible—since he created us—for all our actions, good or bad; and so, if I believe in God, I shall not myself feel responsible for my actions, and so I shall have no motive for behaving well rather than badly. (The question of God's responsibility for evil is one that perpetually torments Christian theologians, and they have never found an adequate answer.)

One of the conclusions that this character of Camus's arrives at is that if one is going to live well, one can never afford to be distracted. In other words, one must always be mindful. And one of the striking things in the book is the contrast between the deaths of the ordinary victims of the plague, who are indeed no more than, in Huxley's expression, 'moaning animals', tossing about on their beds 'with no more thoughts, but only pain and vomiting and stupor,'—between these and the death of this one character who aspires to sainthood and practises mindfulness. Like the others, he dies of plague; but the whole time he is dying (according to Camus's description) he gives the impression of being intelligent and retaining his lucidity right up to the last. He *knows* that he is dying, and he is determined to have 'a good death'. Naturally, this is only a death in a novel, and we can't take it as necessarily true of real life (did Camus, I wonder, ever see a man trying to die mindfully?); but I myself am rather of the opinion that, if one is *really* determined to make an effort, a great deal can be done towards remaining intelligent at the time of one's death. But I do not suppose that it is very easy unless one has already made a long habit of mindfulness.

**[L. 117]** **10 January 1965**

If you have your own copy of the Ven. Ñāṇamoli Thera's *Ānāpānasati* there is a mistake in translation that should be corrected. On page 8, last paragraph but one, instead of

> I say that this, *bhikkhus*, is a certain body among the bodies, namely respiration-mindfulness

which is nonsense, since mindfulness is not a body or part of one, read

> I say that this, *bhikkhus*, is a certain body among the bodies, namely the in-and-out-breath.

The translator (evidently through carelessness) has read *assāsapassāsa* as *ānāpānasati*.

The visitors I spoke of in my postcard came and talked and took photographs and notes for several hours on the afternoon of the 8th. The older one is Robin Maugham, a nephew of the celebrated Somerset Maugham. He is a novelist (third-rate, I suspect) and a writer of travel books. Although they both seemed interested in the Dhamma, I rather think that their principal reason for visiting me was to obtain material for their writings. I had a slightly uncomfortable feeling of being exploited; but, unfortunately, once I start talking, I like going on, without proper regard for the possible repercussions later on. So probably, in perhaps a year's time, there will be a new travel book with a chapter (complete with photographs) devoted to yours truly, and the romantic life he is leading in the jungle.[1]

Whether or not this would (or will) be a bad thing or not, I really can't say. I thoroughly dislike the idea myself, but people are already so much misinformed about the Dhamma in the West (particularly in England) that—if Robin Maugham gives a reasonably accurate account of his visit—it is possible that some good might come of it. Not to me, of course, since it will be a source of disturbance; but that no longer matters so very much. If only he doesn't go and give the impression that I am seeking publicity by building me up into a kind of character in a novel! But it is so difficult to know what to say and what not to say to the people who come and see me.

Maugham was at Eton and Cambridge (he went down the year before I went up) and was in the Middle East during the war; so, since we have much the same sort of background, we were quite at ease with one another. His friend, a much younger man, but no less charming, gave a rupee to one of the villagers because of his poverty-stricken appearance. Unfortunately, the man in question is the second-wealthiest person in the village, owning a tractor, a house, and about twenty-five thousand rupees in cash. They roared with laughter when I told them, and I still find myself chuckling when I think about it. Delicious irony!

I have long since stopped trying to understand how the *sīl-poya*[2] is arrived at. Presumably it is worked out by astrologers rather than by astronomers, which means to say that it probably has little connexion with the dates of the astronomical phases of the moon. Actually, the interval between one (astronomical) full moon and the next is by no means constant: I calculated (from the Government calendar) that the longest interval is 29 days, 19 hours, 29 minutes, as against the shortest, which is 29 days, 6 hours, 52 minutes. The effect of this is that the full moon may fall one or two days either earlier or later than what it would if the interval were regular (the average is 29 days, 11 hours, 18 minutes). But I do not think that the astrologers (or the makers of Sinhala almanacs) pay much attention to the *Nautical Almanack* issued by the Admiralty and probably use their own traditional method of calculation. On the other hand, our Vinaya Uposatha days do not seem to have any connexion with the *sīl-poya*. I have known our *Saṅgha-poya* to fall two days *before* the *sīl-poya*, and, on another occasion, to fall one day *after* the *sīl-poya*.

But the principle upon which our *Saṅgha-poya* days are calculated is quite clear. The year is divided up into three seasons each of four lunar months (with an extra month intercalated about once in three years). These four lunar months are subdivided into eight periods each of fifteen days, with the exception of the third and the seventh, which are only fourteen days, so:

| | | | | | | | |
|---|---|---|---|---|---|---|---|
| ● (1) | ○ (2) | ● (3) | ○ (4) | ● (5) | ○ (6) | ● (7) | ○ (8) |
| 15 | 15 | 14 | 15 | 15 | 15 | 14 | 15. |

(● = new moon, ○ = full moon)

Obviously, this system pays no attention at all to the astronomical dates of the phases of the moon; except that, at the end of the year, the various differences have more or less cancelled out (in this system, the average interval between full moons is 29 days, 12 hours). Actually, this system certainly goes back to Kautilya (I discovered it in his celebrated treatise on government), and Kautilya is thought to have been Chandragupta's grandfather.[3] So in all probability this is the self-same system that was in use in the Buddha's day. Perhaps the *sīl-poya* days on the government calendar have simply been calculated by the Government printer. Who knows?

P.S. There is an additional complication to all this, *viz.* that the day of the *sīl-poya* (as also the *Saṅgha-poya*) goes from dawn (4:24 a.m.) to dawn, whereas the astronomical day is from midnight to midnight. Thus, if the moon is full at 2 a.m., it falls on a different day according to which system is used.

**[L. 118]** **21 January 1965**

From Herr B.'s letter you will see that he is honest enough to admit that he does not understand the meaning of the *paṭiccasamuppāda* formula, which he rightly describes as 'difficult.' At the same time he has observed that *kāya-, vacī-*, and *citta-saṅkhāra* cannot be identified with *kāya-, vacī-*, and *mano-sañcetanā*, and he consequently approves what I have written about these terms in the *Notes*. You may remember that this was one of the points about which I wrote to you at some length (about December 1963). Anyway, here is independent confirmation (if you need it) that my view that these two sets of terms must be kept distinct (they are confused in the Visuddhimagga) is not without foundation. Herr B. is right to want to make clear the distinction between *citta, mano*, and *viññāṇa*, but his ideas about *citta* are a little mixed up. (Actually, these words, and especially *citta*, have variable meanings according to their context—like 'mind' and 'consciousness' in English, and the task Herr B. has set himself—to write a thesis on these three terms—is more difficult than he supposes.)

The word *saṃsāra* comes from *sam* plus *sarati*; *sarati* means 'to go, flow, run, move', etc. and *sam* is an intensifying prefix. *Saṃsarati* therefore means literally 'to go on, to flow on, to run on, or to move on'; and there is nothing in the word *saṃsāra* itself to justify its translation as 'cycle or round of rebirths'. And also, as you say, we do not traverse the same existence twice. Actually, this book, *Mindfulness of Breathing*, is an early translation of the Ven. Ñāṇamoli Thera's (possibly he might not have approved its being reprinted),[1] and his later translation of *saṃsāra* is simply 'roundabout'. Though there is no etymological justification for such a rendering, it perhaps conveys something of the endless repetition of 'birth, ageing, and death', and then back to 'birth' again. We do not, certainly, repeat any *given* birth, ageing or death; but we *do* repeat the cycle of birth, ageing and death. No doubt the translation of *saṃsāra* as 'cycle of rebirths' has been encouraged by the (erroneous) view that the *paṭiccasamuppāda* formulation represents a cycle of three successive existences—indeed, the twelve terms of the *paṭiccasamuppāda* are sometimes represented in the form of a circle (see, for example, the Ven. Piyadassi Thera's booklet 'Dependent Origination', *Wheel* 15). As far as I remember, I used to translate *saṃsāra* as 'the course' or 'the coursing on' (on referring to my new glossary in the *Notes*, I see that I have written: *saṃsāra*—running on [from existence to existence]).

We are very short of rain in this district, and no cultivation has been possible in this season. I have enough water for drinking and sponging down of the body, but I shall have to do without proper baths.

**[L. 119]** **12 February 1965**

*Ulysses* should keep you quiet for a bit. One of the middle chapters may puzzle you a little (a little more than the others, I mean)—it starts in archaic English in the style of Sir Thomas Malory (*Morte d'Arthur*) and gradually proceeds, imitating the style of progressively more and more modern English writers (as the company gets more and more drunk), until it finishes up in the style of an American hot-gospeller. Some of the people in *Dubliners* appear again in *Ulysses*.

**[L. 120]** **28 February 1965**

I am sorry to hear that you are having difficulty with *Ulysses*, but you can console yourself with the thought that very few people indeed manage to make very much of it, particularly on a first reading. And, of course, it is ten times more difficult for anyone who has not been brought up in the English—or at least European—literary tradition. It is, in spite—or perhaps because—of its difficulties, one of the most important books (from the literary, or artistic, point of view at least) to appear in this century. Only yesterday, reading Sartre, I came across a footnote where he acknowledges his indebtedness to Joyce for his 'interior monologue' style (and there is a short story by Sartre[1] which seems to be almost directly copied from the last chapter of *Ulysses*).

I have no doubt that you found *Lady Chatterley* rather easier to cope with; but though both books are obscene (though not pornographic), the purpose or treatment of the obscenity in the two cases is widely different. Lawrence is propaganda; Joyce is art. Lawrence is out to exalt sex (or at least to be open and honest about it—but for him it is almost a religion); Joyce only talks about sex because it is part of life, and he is out to represent life—to hold a mirror up to the average sensual Western man, in which he can recognize his image. Joyce has had a great influence on me (in earlier days), but Lawrence none at all (and, of course, there is nothing fundamentally *new* in *Lady Chatterley*). Perhaps you will recall Rampion and his wife in Huxley's *Point Counter Point*? This is a portrait of Lawrence, with whom Huxley was once closely associated. Lawrence was himself the son of a coal miner, and he married a titled woman (a German Baroness). So you can see that, in some respects, the story of Mellors and Lady Chatterley is parallel to Lawrence's own life-story.

**[L. 121]** **7 April 1965**

I am glad to hear that you have managed to make something of *Ulysses* after all. Your reaction to the book (a feeling of sadness) is appropriate and shows that you have not misread it; but surely the sympathy you feel for the ageing Molly Bloom should be extended to Mr. Bloom himself (and, in a lesser degree, to most of the other characters)? Bloom has lost his first-born son, Rudi, and this had affected his relations with his wife: he himself says somewhere that he is now less happy than he used to be in earlier days.

Actually, when I first read the book, it was not so much the ageing of the characters that affected me as the ultimate meaninglessness and futility of all their actions and aspirations. They are busy, all of them, seeking their immediate satisfactions and avoiding their immediate discomforts; and everything that they do—whether it is making money, making music, making love, or simply making water—is quite pointless—in terms, that is to say, of an ultimate purpose or meaning in life.

At the time I read it—when I was about twenty—I had already suspected (from my reading of Huxley and others) that there *is* no point in life, but this was still all rather abstract and theoretical. But *Ulysses* gets down to details, and I found I recognized myself, *mutatis mutandis*, in the futile occupations that fill the days of Joyce's characters. And so I came to understand that all our actions, from the most deliberate to the most thoughtless, and without exception, are determined by present pleasure and present pain. Even what we pompously call our 'duty' is included in this law—if we do our duty, that is only because we should feel uncomfortable if we neglected it, and we seek to avoid discomfort. Even the wise man, who renounces a present pleasure for the sake of a greater pleasure in the future, obeys this law—he enjoys the present pleasure of knowing (or believing) that he is providing for his future pleasure, whereas the foolish man, preferring the present pleasure to his future pleasure, is perpetually gnawed with apprehension about his future. And when I had understood this, the Buddha's statement,

> *Pubbe cāhaṃ bhikkhave etarahi ca dukkhañ c'eva paññāpemi dukkhassa ca nirodhaṃ*
>
> Both now and formerly, monks, it is just suffering that I make known and the ceasing of suffering

(M.22/i,140), came to seem (when eventually I heard it) the most obvious thing in the world—'What else' I exclaimed 'could the Buddha possibly teach?'

Had I delayed my return here for a few more days I should have missed a rare experience these times in Ceylon (though perhaps still common enough in India)—a fine foul corpse. After my early *dāna* this morning one of the villagers came to tell me that a man had been killed in the jungle by an elephant on Monday (5th) and that now, two days later (7th), his body had been found—should I like to go and see it? So, together with Ven. S., I went.

The body was lying in the jungle about a mile and a half from here, and about three hundred yards from the metalled road. The corpse was covered with *kajans* when we got there, but one arm, rather swollen, was exposed. On it, evidently at the site of a wound, was a heap of small maggots. The *kajans* were removed, but the head was covered with a blood-stained cloth. Taking a stick, I raised the cloth and pushed it back. The head, which was partly crushed, was seething with maggots, much larger than those on the arm. The face, what could be seen of it under the maggots, was quite unrecognizable, and the jawbone was protruding to one side. There was no hair on the head, and the maggots appeared to be crawling on the skull. The Visuddhimagga (Ch. VI) describes this kind of corpse as follows:

> There is a *worm-infested* corpse when at the end of two or three days a mass of maggots oozes out from the corpse's nine orifices,[a] and the mass lies there like a heap of paddy or boiled rice as big as the body, whether the body is that of a dog, a jackal, a human being, an ox, a buffalo, an elephant, a horse, a python, or what you will. It can be brought to mind with respect to any one of these as 'Repulsiveness of the worm-infested, repulsiveness of the worm-infested'. ...Here the learning sign (*uggaha-nimitta*) appears as though moving; but the counterpart sign (*paṭibhāga-nimitta*) appears quiet, like a ball of boiled rice. (p. 198)

In fact, I was astonished to find that I had no feeling of horror at seeing the maggoty corpse, and very little disgust (except when I got the stink, which inclined me to vomit), and I was particularly struck by the aptness of the Visuddhimagga's description—it (i.e. the head) did look exactly like a heap of paddy. I have no difficulty at all in understanding why the *nimitta* (which, however, I made no attempt to develop) should be 'like a ball of boiled rice'. Though the impression afterwards was not very lasting, I found that I did

**a.** Surely they are deposited on the corpse by flies and blue bottles?

not eat my noon *dāna* with my usual relish (Ven. S. told me that he had altogether lost his appetite). But my concentration (*samādhi-bhāvanā*) was quite good for the rest of the day.

There is still no rain here, but this bright weather suits me well.

**[L. 122] 1 May 1965**

I am sorry to hear about your renal colic. I believe it can be extremely painful—so much so that morphia is inadequate and the victim has to be given chloroform. Having once been threatened with something like this, I have taken good care to drink plenty of liquid, enough to keep my urine more or less colourless.

Yes, it is a dangerous thing indeed to possess a body. So long as we have it we are at the mercy of violent and prolonged sufferings of one kind or another. You now have direct experience of the fact that the possession of a genito-urinary tract is very much of a mixed blessing. Suppose you had to pay for the pleasures in bed that you can get from it with a monthly attack of renal colic—would you think it a price worth paying? And yet the majority of women don't seem to be put off their pleasures by the prospect of childbirth, which, I believe, is no less painful than renal colic. Perhaps if the pleasure and the pain came together we might think twice before indulging ourselves. It is no wonder that the Buddha said 'One who lays down this body and takes hold of another body, he I say is blameworthy.' (M.144/iii,266 & KAMMA (b)).

I have just been given the English translation of Heidegger's *Sein und Zeit* (*Being and Time*). About five hundred pages. It should keep me occupied for some time.

**[L. 123] 29 May 1965**

I am glad to hear that you have recovered your health and are no longer standing uncomfortably undecided with one foot in the bath and one on the bath mat. To have one ailment is bad enough; to have two is worse; but when they require contrary treatment it can be infuriating. For the past month I have been busy with Heidegger, and it will still take me two or three weeks to reach the end. But he is really first class: once I can discover through his rather difficult language (which translation does not make any easier) what he is actually saying then I find him beautifully perspicacious.

Sartre has criticized him in many places (though he is very greatly indebted to him), but I now find that nearly always Heidegger is in the right (naturally, within the limits of the *puthujjana*'s field).

In a general way, if I had to name any single Western philosopher who could profitably be read as affording a way of approach to the Buddha's Teaching, I would choose Heidegger (but not in his later writings—only *Being and Time*). I do not mean that the Buddha's Teaching is a continuation or development of Heidegger's; by no means; but rather that Heidegger clears the ground for all those misconceptions that *can* be cleared away—indeed *must* be cleared away, if they are present—before a start can be made on the Suttas.

Of course, I now find it not so excessively difficult going because I have already spent much time over Sartre and have read two separate summaries of the book, and probably I tend to under-estimate the difficulties that it presents to a reader approaching it with no knowledge at all of what it is about. And also, it may well be that I tend to over-emphasize the importance of a philosophical approach to the Suttas; but I do think that, if one is not able to get a living teacher who can give the necessary guidance and orientation, a consideration of some of these existentialist thinkers can be helpful. Even Bradley (you may remember how much I was enjoying his *Principles of Logic* a year ago) can give certain indications, at least of a negative kind. But there must always come a time when one asks oneself, 'These philosophers are all very well, but they don't get me out. What is it, precisely, that the Buddha sees and that these thinkers fail to see? Where is it that they go wrong?'

The situation about the printing of the enlarged edition of the *Notes* is simply that we are more or less back where we started—that is to say, that both typescript copies are now here with me and that there is no proposal on foot to have it printed. This is not due to any lack enthusiasm, or at least interest, on anyone's part, but rather to the nature of the book itself. It can never be a popular book (it is far too difficult and—in a sense—too specialized) and is of no interest to scholars; so it is most unlikely that any publisher will take it unless it is financed from outside. (It is hardly necessary for me to be telling you this.) Anyway, here is a summary of the steps taken so far.

(i) There was my doctor's proposal to have the book printed privately. This perhaps remains a possibility. But, as the doctor himself remarked—and I fully agree with him—, it is unlikely that more than a hundred copies would be sold in Ceylon; and there would be all the labour and difficulty and expense of getting rid of the remaining 900 copies abroad.

(ii) An English friend has shown the cyclostyled version to Allen and Unwin, who have said that studies on Buddhism are not selling in England and that they themselves have stopped publishing them, and also that they know of no other English publisher who might publish the book. This is dictated by purely financial considerations, and is regardless of any intrinsic merit the book may possess.

(iii) He has also written to an acquaintance in England about approaching some other publisher—possibly Kegan Paul, who do publish both philosophical books and Buddhist books—, and this might be done. But it is unlikely that it would be accepted without outside financial backing. (In the case of philosophical books, which necessarily have a limited appeal, the financial support is usually provided by the university to which the author is attached.)

(iv) He also gave it to the representative of an American firm to find out whether any American publisher might consider it (they seem to have a lot of money to spare and are publishing all sorts of books on this and that). The American gave it to a professor at a Buddhist university who knows the situation in the States, for an opinion whether an American university press might be interested. The expert's opinion was that the work is too high-flown for the interested layman, and not sufficiently scholarly to interest the serious scholar, and that a university press would not be interested. With this opinion I entirely concur—though I am unlikely to agree with the said expert when he suggests 'a major re-writing...which would conform with modern standards of scholarship.' (Has he not even read the Preface? Or does he not understand plain English? Anyway, this is beside the point.) The American, in his letter, says 'I recognize that Rev. Ñāṇavīra Thera's manuscript is in the nature of a philosophical speculation and by its very character would not satisfy the average Buddhist scholar. Since this is the chief group which might have interest in a book of this type, however, the likelihood of a university press taking it on is almost nil unless it was financed from outside.' Actually, I have a slight feeling of relief that the book is not to be published in America. Personally, if there is any choice in the matter, I would prefer Kegan Paul in London.

Yes, the Ven. Siridhamma Thera is quite right, and so are you. It *is* a personal book. But then, what other kind of book is worth writing? Palinurus, as you may remember, says—perhaps pushing matters to extremes—'None but the truths which have been extracted under mental torture appeal to us'; and any good novel is drawn from the author's own experience. (This, however, is not always to the author's advantage, since a good many writers seek for experiences in order to write about them. If you want to write a good book about life in a brothel or about addiction to opium, the best way to set about it is to go and live in a brothel or become an opium-addict. As Kierkegaard says somewhere,[1] there are many artists who sell their souls to the devil in order to produce a first-rate work of art.)

At the other extreme, it is possible to regard the Suttas as the product of the Buddha's 'personal' experience. The Buddha is *dhammabhūta*, 'become Dhamma', and the Suttas are an account of Dhamma. In the Suttas, however (unlike in a novel, where the emphasis is in the other direction, upon the particular), the Buddha expresses, for the most part, what is *universal* in his experience—i.e. what can be experienced by anyone who makes the appropriate effort in the appropriate conditions. So it is that the Buddha says 'He who sees the Dhamma sees me' (and this, I take it, is what Sister Vajirā meant when she wrote, 'I saw the Buddha as *paṭiccasamuppāda*').

A few days ago Ananda Pereira wrote to me and asked if I could throw any light on the relation (if any) between humour and Buddhism. 'Obviously there is *dukkha*' he says 'and its cause is *taṇhā*. The picture is ever so given and one feels one should be deadly serious. But, one cannot be.... Why, besides being meaningless and often tragic, is life also funny? I do not think it is ignorance—or only ignorance—of life's true nature that makes one laugh. On the contrary, I have found that consistently solemn people are invariably stupid and lacking in sympathy. They see less, not more than the laughers.' In reply to this I sent back (not entirely without malice aforethought) between five and six thousand words, heavily weighted with quotations from Kierkegaard and Heidegger. If you would be interested to read this mass of words, Mr. Ananda Pereira might lend it to you (though perhaps it is more Mr. Pereira's sort of question than your—I don't mean to say that you are solemn, but simply that you react to the grimness of the world in not quite the same way, rather more sensitively, perhaps, in certain respects, and more concerned with the tragic than with the comic (two sides of the same coin, however)).

During the last three or four weeks a visitor and I had some long Dhamma discussions, mostly about the meaning of the word *saṅkhāra*—which, as you will have gathered from the *Notes*, I regard as perhaps the most important word of all to understand correctly (see SAṄKHĀRA—and particularly the reference to King Mahāsudassana).

9

# Letter to Mr. Gerriet Bandy[1]

**[L. 124]** **8 December 1964**

I recently received from Mr. Samaratunga your carefully prepared comments on my *Notes on Dhamma*. I read them with great interest and sent a reply to Mr. Samaratunga. I now hear from him that he has sent it on to you, so no doubt it will reach you in due course. Unfortunately, I find that I have made a slip that needs correcting. In my discussion of *viññāṇaṃ anidassanaṃ anantaṃ sabbatopahaṃ*, I said (as I remember) that 'the *arahat*'s consciousness neither indicates nor originates a "self" or "subject".' This should be: 'neither indicates a "self" or a "subject" nor originates *from* a "self" or "subject".' Actually, the meaning of *anidassanaṃ* and *sabbato-apahaṃ* is the same: it is simply that, since there is no more *Ahan ti vā Maman ti vā Asmi ti vā*[2] with the *arahat*, consciousness is no longer 'mine'. And *anantaṃ* may be taken in the same sense—for the *arahat* consciousness is no longer limited by being 'my' consciousness (a determination is always a limiting, being a negation; and consciousness is now, in this respect, *asaṅkhata* or non-determined). In the Asaṅkhata Saṃy. (S.xliii/iv,359-73) you will see that *asaṅkhata, anidassana*, and *nibbāna* are all synonyms, and are all defined as *rāgakkhaya dosakkhaya mohakkhaya*, which, in the *Itivuttaka* (v,5: 38) is said to be *saupādisesā nibbānadhātu*.[3]

Edward Conze's translation as 'invisible infinite consciousness which shines everywhere' is quite wild (no doubt he has taken it without considering the Pali at all), and one is tempted to ask how consciousness can be 'invisible' if it 'shines everywhere'. But what, precisely, it is that Mahāyānists understand by *nibbāna* is very difficult to make out.

# 10

# Letters to Ven. Kheminda Thera

**[L. 125]** **(undated)**

Dear Bhante,[1]

I was very pleased to get a letter from you, but I confess I was much distressed when I came to read it. I had heard reports that your operation had been successful after all, but now it seems that this cannot altogether be taken for granted. If sympathy could cure, you would at once be recovered; but, as it is, if your surgeon can't help, and you can't help, then I very much fear that I can't help either. Someone[2] once said 'the important thing is not to get cured, but to live with one's ills'; and so it is. Cure may be out of reach, but we do something difficult when we endure patiently.

As to myself, if I am to say anything I shall have to say rather a lot. But since you specifically ask me, and I have the time, paper, and ink to spare, I shall try to give you some account of my condition.

You know of course that since my early amœbiasis my guts have continued to give me trouble. This, however, had not become worse, and I was able to make some progress in spite of it. But in 1960 and 1962 I had fresh infections, and my condition deteriorated. In particular there was increased wind, constipation, and general intestinal discomfort, together with lassitude and debility, especially in bad weather. All these things I am long since accustomed to, and I mention them only to give you the background to what follows.

In June 1962, then, I found myself once more with live amœbiasis (blood and mucus and the rest), and so I wrote to Dr. de Silva, who kindly sent me a box of pills to take. After two or three days I began experiencing a violent erotic stimulation, as if I had taken a very strong aphrodisiac. If I lay down on the bed I at once started to enter upon an orgasm that could only be checked by a prodigious effort of attention to the breath, or else by standing up. Even after stopping the course of treatment this persisted, so I decided to go to the Hermitage for Vas, to be within reach of Colombo for treatment if necessary. Dr. de Silva sent me some medicines, saying that he thought I would return to normal in due course. At the end of three months the intensity of the stimulation was certainly much less, but it was still very far from normal; and it did not seem to be improving any further.

This state of affairs, of course, was hardly satisfactory; and I decided, since there seemed to be no further promise of improvement, that the best course would be to rid myself of this body (I had already had vague thoughts of such a thing when my stomach was particularly bad). Accordingly, shortly after I returned here, I attempted suicide, but, as no doubt you will observe, without success (lack of experience, no doubt: it is not as easy as one might think to reach the point of making the attempt in earnest, and even then there remains the practical difficulty of actually killing oneself: sleeping tablets, if one has them, are all very well, but then one does not die mindfully). I wrote and told Dr. de Silva of the attempt, and said that unless there was some likelihood of getting a substantial improvement in my condition it was quite possible that I should make a further attempt. Dr. de Silva did not offer me any assurance that effective treatment was available, but after consultation with a specialist, sent me a tranquillising drug which, in fact, does give relief for a week or ten days, but thereafter loses its effectiveness and cannot again be used for about two months.

By now (February 1963) the weather had improved, and I succeeded in achieving a certain degree of concentration (with *ānāpānasati*); which, as I found, temporarily removed the affliction. Indeed, if only I did not have the chronic intestinal disorder to contend with, I have no doubt but that I could altogether overcome this nuisance; but, as it is, even if I get three or four days' reasonable concentration, it is immediately brought to an end by my guts or by a change in the weather (to which I am now very sensitive) and I find myself once more lying on the bed feeling good for nothing and invaded by lustful thoughts that I have neither the inclination nor the energy to resist.

From the very start, naturally, I have been much exercised about the Vinaya situation; and I took good care to study the relevant passages in the first *saṅghādisesa*[3] (which, fortunately, Miss Horner has left in Pali, so I am not dependent upon her fanciful translations). I was determined not to fall into a *saṅghādisesa āpatti*, and, in fact, I am not aware that I have done so; and for this reason I have not thought it necessary to come to Colombo to discuss the situation. (I may say that, except with my late venerable teacher, who always gave a definite answer 'yes' or 'no', I have more often than not found myself in greater doubt after discussion of Vinaya questions in Colombo than before; and in the present critical situation I cannot afford to have the ambiguous answer 'No, but...', which only increases worry. I do not want to add to my present difficulties by being made to feel morally obliged to undertake a *vinayakamma* that is not necessary.)

The situation is, in fact, precarious. Perhaps I shall be asked, 'Have you never heard of *indriyasaṃvara*?' Certainly I have; but at this point I have to confess my weakness. If it is a question of restraining my faculties (especially the mind) for a limited period, a week or a month say, then no doubt I can make the effort and do it; but this is not the question here. I have to decide how much restraint I can manage to practise *as a normal rule*, and then to consider on that basis the best course to follow. And I find, in fact, that with the persistent erotic stimulation and the persistent intestinal discomfort (a very demoralizing combination) I can manage only so much and no more.

What, then, should I do? (I don't think a day passes on which I do not consider this question.)

In the first place, there is (for obvious reasons) a frequent and pressing invitation to disrobe; but, on the one hand, I did not seek this nervous disorder, and I do not, in my calmer moments, see why it should be allowed to have its own way; and, on the other hand, as I understand the Dhamma and Vinaya, the only valid reason for disrobing is the fear of being *pārājika* if one does not. Now, I do not see at present that I am likely to become *pārājika*, and probably not even *saṅghādisesa* (though in this matter I may not always have avoided *dukkaṭa*); so disrobing does not commend itself at all.

In the second place, at the other extreme, there is suicide. Though I do not say this is good, I will say that, under the circumstances and in the long run, it is better than disrobing. See, for example, the Ven. Sappadāsa Thera's *gāthā* (Thag.407).[4] (This, of course, is not the layman's view, and Mr. Samaratunga, when I told him the state of affairs, urged me to disrobe rather than kill myself; but then I pointed out that, whereas it is known that monks have become *arahats* in the act of suicide, it is nowhere recorded that anyone has ever become *arahat* in the act of disrobing.)

In the third place, there is the possibility of continuing as I am. But the question here is whether I am doing myself more harm than good in doing so; and this is an extremely difficult question to answer. On the one hand, I am certainly practising more restraint than I should be as a layman in similar circumstances; but, on the other hand, I should really prefer not to be accepting alms in my present state of mind. (Actually, I should be only too happy just quietly to starve to death; but I don't suppose I should be allowed to do it undisturbed.)

In addition to these theoretical considerations about what I had best do under the circumstances, there are practical ones about what I am going to do. As it is, I find myself in a state of delicate equilibrium: even a slight increase of my present burdens (fresh sickness, for example) might well tip the scale in favour of suicide (the thought is constantly with me, though it remains at arm's length), or the presence of some *subhanimitta* (a chance encounter, perhaps, or change to more worldly surroundings) might easily tip it the other way towards a return to lay life.

Possibly you will be wondering whether I am well advised to go on living here alone as I am doing. The answer seems to be quite simple: here I am as well insulated as I could possibly be against disturbing influences (few visitors, no newspapers, no gossip), and I do find it possible to gain some respite by *samatha* practice or by reflective thinking. Even at the Hermitage this is not possible—the climate is not good, and there are visitors, newspapers, and people to talk to—and I find myself occupied most of the time with *kāmavitakka*. And if it is like this at the Hermitage, how much more so would it not be in Colombo! I have so far avoided all visits to Colombo since the trouble started. (As it happens, I have just now been offered a three-month's holiday in England to improve my health, and I am afraid to accept for this very reason—I might quite well decide not to return to Ceylon. But, also, there are other reasons for not accepting; for example, since I cannot manage bread or potatoes what should I eat in England?)

Perhaps, after all this, you may be thinking that I live in a state of depression and gloom. This is not so. I do not say that I am complacent about my situation or that I do not find it difficult. But I am not a person of moods, and also I am aware that it is necessary to accept limitations imposed on one with good grace. I recognize that—unless my bodily condition improves, which is most unlikely—I cannot hope to make any further progress in this life: now is the time to draw a line under the account and add it up, and then see whether it shows profit or loss. And I have to say that, while the sum might have been greater, I have no reason for dissatisfaction. I have done what I did not expect to do, and so I am content. Certainly, the age of forty-four is rather early to close the account, but when I left England at the time of the first Berlin crisis I told myself that if I managed to practise the Dhamma for even one year I should count myself fortunate.

And what, then, of the future—now that I can no longer hope to make progress, what have I to look forward to? At present I find that more or less my only concern is with the *Notes*; I spend much of my time revising them and adding to them to prepare them for eventual printing. This means that I do a lot of thinking and a certain amount of reading (when I can get the books), and this in itself also helps to keep my trouble at a distance. But publication of the *Notes* (which I *think* is desirable, in spite of the fact that they may be unpopular) is, after all, a purely temporal (*kālika*) aim, and I can only regard it as a device for killing time until I am rid of this disordered body. But this throws me back to the crucial question, whether or not I should do better to abbreviate the process, and instead of killing time, simply to kill the body.

And so the matter rests—in the air.

**[L. 126]** **(undated)[1]**

I was sorry to hear, the other day, that your condition is apparently getting no better and that you are having to endure increasing pain. It is rather unwillingly that I am writing this to bother you again with my own affairs. Actually, you already know how I am situated, and this letter will not really tell you anything that you might not already be expecting. If I write at some length, then, it is more for the sake of other people who, finding it difficult to understand my position, may be puzzled or worried about what I am proposing to do.

As you know, the satyriasis with which I am afflicted (and which is no better) presents me with a constant temptation to disrobe, and, when it becomes acute, the only means I have of resisting it is by contemplating suicide. To some extent, however, these alternatives (disrobe/suicide) are kept at arm's length when I find myself with something to say or write about Dhamma; and since last June I have been busy enlarging and retyping my *Notes on Dhamma*. But in due course this came to an end, and I found myself with nothing further to say.

In consequence of this—and since my amœbiasis more than doesn't permit *samatha* practice—my situation once again became acute and, in fact, I again made an attempt to end my life. (After the Ven. Ñāṇamoli Thera's death I came into possession of a few objects that had belonged to him. Amongst these was a small glass ampoule containing a liquid that, for various reasons, I thought was very probably a solution of potassium cyanide—which, as you know, is an extremely quick and efficient poison. I was glad to have this, but I did not want to break the ampoule until I actually intended to use the contents. And when eventually, having made all the necessary arrangements, I did come to break it I found that the contents, whatever they were, were certainly not cyanide, which has a very characteristic smell. So I was most reluctantly obliged to go on living. These repeated attempts at suicide are instructive—I am rapidly becoming an expert—and they certainly provide good practice in preparing for death; but it is always a painful business to face this life again once one has decided that one has no further interest in it.)

This second unsuccessful attempt leaves me at present without any particular desire to go on living, but without any very comfortable way of dying. (I have my razor, of course, but it is not so easy to make up one's mind to cut one's throat.) But what is significant about the whole episode is that it tends to confirm what I had already long suspected, that is to say, that sooner or later I shall either disrobe or else make a successful attempt at suicide. For a few weeks, a few months perhaps, possibly longer, I might manage to keep my balance between these two alternatives; but if it is to be a question of years (and I see no prospect of an early natural death), then it is extremely unlikely that I shall do it—and the reason (as you know[2]) is quite simply that I no longer have any very strong motive for making the necessary effort. Even if I fail in keeping a balance and fall to one side or the other (and, obviously, in my case suicide is the lesser evil), it will not make any difference to the ultimate outcome, and so I am not ultimately *interested* in keeping my balance.

At this point, no doubt, people will come forward with constructive suggestions how I should employ my time so as not to fall into either temptation. But this is not so easy. The good doctor, for example, who has the best of intentions, has asked me to 'forget my troubles and busy myself with some research work into the Dhamma'. But the advice to 'forget my troubles', however excellent it may be from the medical point of view, is directly opposed to *satisampajañña*; and further, once one has acquired the habit of mindfulness—and it is quite soon acquired in solitude—then one simply 'forgets how to forget', and one is incapable of following the advice even if one wants to. This idea of 'research work into the Dhamma', as far as I am concerned at least, has ceased to have any meaning for me—what possible interest can I have in that? Is this not putting me back into the kindergarten? No—with the best will in the world I cannot disengage myself from my existence and make believe that my troubles don't exist.

11

# Letters to Ananda Perera

**[L. 127]** **29 April 1964**

Dear Ananda,[1]

It is extremely good of you to have taken all this trouble about writing to me on this tiresome affair. Though I did not actually anticipate that the Ven. Kheminda Thera would show my letter[2] to you in particular, I did not ask him to keep it private, since I do not think it is fair to burden people with confidences that they have not sought.

I had better explain why I wrote about this matter to the Ven. Kheminda Thera. He had earlier written to me telling of his condition, and then saying that he would like to know how I was, since he had heard that I was not well. I could, of course, have replied in general terms without committing myself in this way; and this would have spared the Ven. Kheminda Thera his present worry, and things would have gone on peacefully as before. But there was another consideration.

As you may know, sexual matters are not things the Vinaya takes light-heartedly (however much a *bhikkhu* may feel inclined to do so), and if I had kept silent about my condition, that silence might have been taken by others (and perhaps also by myself) as a desire to conceal matters that should be declared, and I might thus have found myself in a false position *vis-à-vis* my fellow *bhikkhus*. I did not feel justified in being silent when asked about my condition by the Ven. Kheminda Thera. (The point here is that I was, and am, anxious to be in conformity with the Vinaya; and it is *this* that causes me concern, not sex as such. As far as sex goes I have few inhibitions, and I certainly do not regard it with the horrified fascination that some people seem to. I do not have a 'thing' about sex.) But, having decided to speak about my satyriasis, I could not, without begetting future misunderstandings, say nothing about suicide. Besides, since it was (and is) a possibility, I felt it was better to let the Ven. Kheminda Thera know in advance, so that in the actual event it would not come as so much of a shock.

Naturally, since the Ven. Kheminda Thera has only known about this affair for a few days, he may be a little upset; but I have lived with it for nearly two years (and also discussed it in considerable detail with my doctor and with Mr. Samaratunga), and I cannot now be expected to get worked up about it.

It is unfortunate, really, that you have become involved in this business to the extent of seeking to help me; and this for the reason that I am actually, as a *bhikkhu*, not in a position to give you the whole picture, and unless you have this I am afraid that discussion between us, however well intended, will be at cross purposes. You, on your side, will remain convinced that I am in a state of anxiety, and any denial that I may make will only go to confirm your opinion. On my side, I shall never be able to convey to you that the key to the situation (that is, to an understanding of it) is not that I am *worried* but that I am *tired*, and further, that I am not even worried about being tired. Whatever you may say, however right in itself, is almost certain to be regarded by me as irrelevant. But if you press me to make this clearer, there is nothing that I can say to you. You may be sure, however, that I am not likely to have overlooked any considerations that might be urged against my contemplated action.

You assure me that my condition *can* be put right, and I should be only too glad to believe you. But the fact is that I have several times pressed my doctor to tell me if a treatment for this disorder is available, and I have told him that I am prepared to come to Colombo to take it. But he has never given me the slightest reason to believe that there is any such treatment. If a doctor is willing to assure me that a cure or a partial cure is possible, I am prepared to consider coming to Colombo. But not otherwise. The simple reason is that it is much more wearing to set out in hopes of recovery and then, after all the trouble and discomfort of investigation and treatment, to be disappointed, than it is to accept the assurance that one's condition is probably incurable and then to try to live with it. (In this connexion, I am a little astonished that you so confidently predict a cure—do you not perhaps see that if, at the end, there is no cure, one's mental state is liable to be much worse after than before? Here, possibly, my doctor has given better advice by refraining from giving any.)

You tell me, too, that a man needs friends and contact with equals. Assuming this is so (which remains to be proved), whom would you suggest? Besides, in my letter I said that it is precisely in solitude that my condition gives me some peace, whereas in company it is worse. In spite of the fact that my living in solitude is a source of irritation to people generally, I can by no means disregard this fact in considering what I should do. Admittedly, if I follow your advice and go into company I am less likely to kill myself, but also I am more likely eventually to disrobe, and whatever the public feeling may be, the former is (for me) by far the lesser evil. So if I want to play safe, I must remain in solitude, even if I risk forfeiting my sense of proportion.

It is quite true that lepers and the like are in a worse bodily condition than myself, and if they go on living, no doubt it is because they still find a use for their body; but that, after all, is their decision. The point at issue, surely, is whether one can still use one's body for the purpose that one has decided upon. (I know that this is not the only consideration, but I do not see that a leper displays any particular virtue in not committing suicide.)

As for exercise, I have not taken any simply for its own sake since I left school, and I do not propose to start now. The importance of exercise is one of those great myths of the Twentieth Century that make living in it such hell. If nobody took any exercise unless he actually wanted to go somewhere everybody would be a lot happier.

In any case, please tell the Ven. Kheminda Thera that the situation is at least not worse than it has been; and also to consider the survival value of Nietzsche's dictum 'The thought of suicide gets one through many a bad night.' And say, also, that I am sorry to have worried him. Perhaps it would have been better if I had kept quiet after all.

P.S. I expect that your letter cost you as much trouble to write as this one has me, so please do not think me unappreciative. If you find one or two sharp edges in this letter they are not meant unkindly, but can perhaps be taken as an indication that you may have picked up this affair by the wrong end.

**[L. 128]** **4 May 1964**

Your second letter arrived this afternoon. Though you say 'Don't bother to reply,' it would be very churlish of me not to do so. In so far as anyone acknowledges a mistaken judgement, it is only a fool who refuses to accept it. And on my part I would ask you to forgive me anything I may have said that I should not have said. This sort of affair easily sends people's temperatures up, including my own when I get their first reactions. It is then a question of returning to normal as quickly as possible in order to discuss whatever needs discussing.

Certainly, I can't be *sure* in any absolute sense that there is no remedy for the satyriasis. But it does not seem to me that the growth of a tumour or the enlargement of the prostate would adequately account for the actual symptoms as they occurred. Now, I do know that damage to the nervous system is (notoriously) difficult to cure by direct treatment, and that the usual remedy (if it is a remedy) is simply *time*. (You may remember, many years ago, my right leg went numb through sitting in *padmāsana* on a hard floor. This—so the doctor told me—was due to damage to the sciatic nerve, and I was given vitamin B, in some quantity. The leg has partly recovered, but my toes remain paralysed.)

And the situation is not improved by the fact that the disorder and its ramifications are not very easy to discuss with other people. Besides, I know also from past experience that I suffer from (or enjoy—whichever is the right term) erotic thoughts *more* in Colombo than anywhere else, and on that account alone I am reluctant to go there. So, although I am very much disinclined to come to Colombo, and do not propose to take any initiative myself in this matter, if there is anyone who feels strongly enough about it, and is himself prepared to take the necessary steps to get me to Colombo, arrange for examination, for treatment, and so on, then I am prepared, passively as it were, and without enthusiasm, to fall in with his arrangements. I say this, because I don't want to give the outward impression that I am sitting here brooding over my miseries and neurotically refusing all efforts to help.

On the other hand, I propose to be obstinate about continuing here. People in Colombo frequently advise me to stay there and not to go back to my solitude; but, particularly in the present circumstances, this is a misunderstanding of my needs. You will see that there are two sides to this question, since you have presented them both, one after the other, in your two letters.

I think I should add that even a completely successful treatment of the satyriasis does not get me out of the wood. It is the persisting digestive disorder that is the root of the trouble, and the satyriasis is simply the last straw that broke the camel's back (or nearly did).

I have been wondering about the rights and wrongs of telling people about myself in this way. The three or four people I have told were alarmed and upset when I first spoke of it, but now seem to be rather unwillingly reconciled to the prospect. Should I perhaps have done better to keep silent (as I could have done, being the sort of person I am) instead of disturbing their peace of mind? The Anglo-Saxon tradition, of course (which has a certain prevalence in this country), is in favour of the strong silent man. But it seems to me that, without going to the other extreme of the French, who dramatize themselves on every possible occasion, it should be possible to speak of such a 'painful subject' in, shall we say, a normal tone of voice. In the first place, it may actually ease the tensions and postpone a decision (Fabian tactics are the thing—putting off a definite engagement with the enemy from day to day); and in the second place, if the worst does come to the worst people are partly prepared for it, and they have some understanding, at least, of what has happened. And in any case, if one is prepared to bring it out into the daylight, it is hardly likely that one has shirked the issues.

Please convey my respectful salutations and kindly thoughts to the Ven. Kheminda Thera.

**[L. 129][1]** **18 May 1965**

Thank you for your letter. The popular interpretation of *uccāsayana-mahāsayanā* seems rather odd. Surely laymen, even when observing the Eight Precepts,[2] are not expected to be *more* austere than monks? I should have thought that chairs and beds that are ordinarily allowable for monks (and we are not prohibited from sitting on chairs with our feet lower than our bottoms) would *a fortiori* be allowable for laymen. But no doubt this interpretation has a long and venerable tradition.

Yes, this existence of ours is no laughing matter, and yet we laugh. And the great laughers are not those who least see the grimness. Perhaps, then, laughter is something less simple than the sigh of pure innocent bliss. When do we laugh most spontaneously, with the least affectation? Is it not, possibly, when we have been threatened by some horrible menace and have just escaped by the skin of our teeth? The experience is familiar enough, and we may well take it as a starting point. It seems to suggest that laughter is in some way connected with fear. We are threatened; we fear; the threat passes; we laugh. Let us pursue this idea.

A few weeks ago, at the Hermitage, an unwanted young dog was dumped on the island from the mainland. I watched it, lying on its belly in front of one of the long-resident old curs there, whining and laughing (baring its teeth as dogs do when they are pleased) for all it was worth. Why? Because it actually was pleased? Because it was delighted to meet a new acquaintance? Far from it. There was every probability that it was extremely nervous and apprehensive about its reception by the other dogs, and was doing its utmost to placate them. But why should it laugh? In order, simply, to show the others and to persuade itself that *no danger was threatening*. Its laughter was a mode of conduct, a kind of charm, to keep danger at a distance. Since we laugh when danger passes, danger passes when we laugh—or that, at least, is the idea. The ingratiating grin that some people wear on their face (perhaps we all do at times) is simply to prove to themselves that they are *not nervous*—when, of course, they are shaking in their boots. So far, so good.

But why do we laugh at jokes? Let us ask, rather, why we tell one another jokes. Might it not be so that we can enjoy the pleasure of escaping from *imaginary* dangers? Most of our jokes, surely, are about somebody else's misfortune, are they not? So-and-so (a real or fictitious person, but in any case not ourselves) has some unfortunate—usually humiliating or ridiculous—experience, an experience that *might* have happened to us but *actually* happened to somebody else; and the relief we feel that the discomfort was *his*, not *ours*, takes the form of laughter. (Compassion, of course, may inhibit laughter; but some of our jokes are pretty heartless.)

We laugh, then, when fear passes; we laugh as a charm to make fear pass; and we entertain imaginary fears to make ourselves laugh. But do we not sometimes laugh when fear is not involved at all? Kierkegaard, much of whose principal philosophical work is concerned with humour,[a] says this:

> The comical is present in every stage of life (only that the relative positions are different), for whenever there is life there is contradiction, and whenever there is contradiction, the comical is present. The tragic and the comic are the same, in so far as both are based on contradiction; but *the tragic is the suffering contradiction, the comical, the painless contradiction*. (*CUP*, p. 459)

He gives some examples; here is one:

> It is for this reason that an intoxicated man can produce so comical an impression, because he expresses a contradiction in his movements. The eye requires steadiness of gait; the more there still remains some sort of reason to require it, the more comical the contradiction (a completely intoxicated man is therefore less comical). Now if a purposeful man for example, comes by, and the intoxicated individual, his attention drawn to him, gathers himself together and tries to steady

**a.** *Concluding Unscientific Postscript*—the book itself bristles with wit, much of it still fresh after a hundred years. It is the only serious discussion of the comic that I know of, and I owe much to it. There is a theological background for which due allowance must be made, but some of K.'s studies on the Christianity of his day apply with full force to modern Buddhism.

> his gait, then the comical becomes more evident; because the contradiction is clearer. He succeeds for a couple of steps, until the spirit of contradiction again runs away with him. If he succeeds entirely while passing the purposeful man, the first contradiction becomes another: that we know him to be intoxicated, and that this is, nevertheless, not apparent. In one case we laugh at him while he sways, because the eye requires steadiness of him; in the second case we laugh at him because he holds himself steady when our knowledge of his condition requires that we should see him sway. So it also produces a comic effect when a sober man engages in sympathetic and confidential conversation with one whom he does not know is intoxicated, while the observer knows of the condition. The contradiction lies in the mutuality presupposed by the conversation, that it is not there, and that the sober man has not noticed its absence. (*CUP*, p. 461)

According to Kierkegaard, then, we laugh when we apprehend a contradiction; there is not a word about fear. But might it not be that a contradiction is something to be feared—that it is, in some way, a *threat*?

Heidegger tells us that we normally exist in a state of 'fallenness'. By this he means that most men hide from themselves by identifying themselves with the anonymous 'one' or 'they' or 'the Others' and people in general.

> We have shown earlier how in the environment which lies closest to us, the public 'environment' already is ready-to-hand and is also a matter of concern *[mitbesorgt]*. In utilizing public means of transport and in making use of information services such as the newspaper, every Other is like the next. This being-with-one-another dissolves one's own Dasein completely into the kind of Being of 'the Others', in such a way, indeed, that the Others as distinguishable and explicit vanish more and more. In this inconspicuousness and unascertainability, the real dictatorship of the "they" is unfolded. We take pleasure and enjoy ourselves as *they [man]* take pleasure; we read, see, and judge about literature and art as *they* see and judge; likewise we shrink back from the 'great mass' as *they* shrink back; we find 'shocking' what *they* find shocking. The 'they', which is nothing definite, and which all are, though not as the sum, prescribes the kind of Being of everydayness. (*B&T*, p. 164)

This kind of existence Heidegger calls 'inauthenticity'; and it is what Sartre calls 'serious-mindedness—which, as we all know reigns over the world'

(*B&N*, p. 626). It is the inauthentic, the serious-minded, the solemn, who are your non-laughers. Or rather, they *do* laugh—but only at what the 'they' have decided is funny. (Look at a copy of *Punch* of a hundred, or even fifty, years ago; you will see how completely the fashion in humour has changed. The 'sick joke' was quite unthinkable in Victoria's day—'one' simply did not laugh at that sort of thing, it was 'not done'.) The inauthentic, absorbed by the world 'like ink by a blotter' (*B&N*, p. 626),[b] accept their views and values ready made, and go about their daily business doing whatever 'is done'. And this includes their relaxations. To be 'serious-minded' is to go to see comic films and laugh at whomever 'one laughs at', and see tragedies and have one's emotions purged by the currently approved emotional purgative—the latest version, perhaps, of *Romeo and Juliet*.

That, as you know, is to be 'well-adjusted'. But if one should happen *not* to laugh at whatever 'one laughs at', or should find *Romeo and Juliet* emotionally constipating, then one is accused, paradoxically enough, of 'not being serious'. Variations, of course, are permitted; Bach or the Beatles, both are recognized; and one is not *obliged* to laugh at Bob Hope or Kingsley Amis.

Now if we agree with Kierkegaard that both comedy and tragedy are ways of apprehending contradictions, and if we also consider how much importance people attach to these things, we shall perhaps at least suspect that contradiction is a factor to be reckoned with in everyday life. But all this is on the inauthentic level, and to get more light on the question we must consider what Heidegger means by 'authenticity'.

Our existence, says Heidegger, is '*care*': we are concerned, positively or negatively, for ourselves and for others. This care can be described but it cannot be accounted for—it is primordial and we just have to accept it as it is. (Compare here the Buddha's statement [A.X,62/v,116] that there is no first point to *bhavataṇhā*, 'craving for being'. The difference is that whereas Heidegger sees no way of getting rid of it, the Buddha *does* see the way and has followed it.) Care, says Heidegger, can be 'lived' in either of two modes: authentic or inauthentic. The authentic man faces himself reflexively and sees himself in his existential solitude—he sees that he is alone in the world—; whereas the inauthentic man takes refuge from this disquieting reflexion of himself in the anonymous security of people-in-general, of the 'they'. The inauthentic man is fleeing from authenticity—from *angst*, that is to say,

---

**b.** Cf. the Khajjaniya Sutta (Khandha Saṃy.—S.xx.79/iii,87-8) where it is said that we are normally 'devoured' by matter, feeling, perception, determinations, and consciousness.

or 'anxiety'; for anxiety is the state of the authentic man (remember that Heidegger is describing the *puthujjana*, and he sees no way out of anxiety, which, for him, is the mark of the lucid man facing up to himself).

But the normally smooth surface of the public world of the 'they' sometimes shows cracks, and the inauthentic man is pierced by pangs of anxiety, recalling him for a moment or two to the state of authenticity. Chiefest amongst these is the apprehension of the possibility of death, which the inauthentic man suddenly realizes is *his* possibility (death, of course, is *certain*: but this simply means that *at any moment it is possible*). He is torn from his complacent anonymity and brought up against the hard fact that he is an *individual*, that he himself is totally responsible for everything that he does, and that he is sure to die. The hitherto friendly and sheltering world suddenly becomes indifferent to him and meaningless in its totality. But this shattering experience is usually fleeting, and the habitually inauthentic man returns quickly enough to his anonymity.

At this point let us see what the Suttas have to say about *angst* or anxiety (*paritassanā*). In the Alagaddūpama Sutta (M.22/i,136-7; & cf. NIBBĀNA (c)) a monk asks the Buddha, 'Can there be anxiety, lord, about objective absence?' The Buddha says that there can be such anxiety, and describes a man grieving about the way his possessions slip away from him. Then the monk asks, 'Can there be anxiety, lord, about subjective absence?', and again the Buddha says that there can. In this case we have a *sassatavādin*,[3] holding himself and the world to be eternal, who hears about extinction (*nibbāna*) and apprehends it as annihilation. These two aspects, objective and subjective, are combined in the Uddesavibhaṅga Sutta (M.138/iii,227-8), a passage from which I translate as follows:

> And how, friends, is there anxiety at not holding? Here, friends, an uninstructed commoner, unseeing of the nobles, ignorant of the noble Teaching, undisciplined in the noble Teaching, unseeing of good men, ignorant of the good men's Teaching, undisciplined in the good men's Teaching, regards matter (feeling, perception, determinations, consciousness) as self, or self as endowed with matter (... consciousness), or matter (... consciousness) as belonging to self, or self as in matter (... consciousness). That matter (... consciousness) of his changes and becomes otherwise; as that matter (... consciousness) changes and becomes otherwise, so his consciousness follows around (keeps track of) that change of matter (... consciousness); anxious ideas that arise born of following around that change of matter (... consciousness) seize upon his mind and become established; with that mental

seizure, he is perturbed and disquieted and concerned, and from not holding he is anxious. Thus, friends, there is anxiety at not holding.

This, you will see, fairly well confirms Heidegger's view of anxiety; and the more so when he makes the distinction that, whereas fear is shrinking in the face of something, anxiety is shrinking in the face of—nothing. Precisely. We experience anxiety when we find that the solid foundation upon which our precious and familiar self rests—upon which it *must* rest—*is not there*. Anxiety is shrinking in the face of a contradiction—or rather, not *a* contradiction, but *the* contradiction. *This* is the contradiction that we fear; *this* is the contradiction that threatens us in our innermost being—the agonizing possibility that, after all, we have *no* being, and that we *are not*. And *now* we can see why all the seemingly little contradictions at which we laugh (or weep) in our everyday life are really veiled threats, sources of danger. These are the little cracks and fissures in our complacent serious-minded existence, and the reason why we laugh at them is to keep them at a distance, to charm them, to exorcise them, to neutralize them—just as the young dog at the Hermitage laughed at the older one to ward off danger.

Anxiety—shrinking before nothing—is the father of all particular fears—shrinking before this or that. (Heidegger emphasizes that the prior condition to all fear is anxiety. We *can* fear only because we are fleeing from anxiety.) And the contradiction between our *eternal* self and its *temporal* foundation is the father of all particular contradictions between this and that. Whether we laugh because we have just crawled out unscathed from a car smash, or wear a sheepish grin when the boss summons us to his office, or split our sides when we hear how Jones had his wife seduced by Smith, or smile when we see a benevolent tourist giving a few cents out of compassion to an ill-dressed but extremely wealthy *mudhalali*—it can all be traced back to our inherent desire to fly from anxiety, from the agonized recognition that our very being is perpetually in question. And when we laugh at a comedy or weep at a tragedy what we are really doing is busying ourselves repairing all the little crevices that have appeared in our familiar world in the course of the day or the week, which, if neglected, might become wider and deeper, and eventually bring our world crashing down in ruins about us. Of course, we don't actually admit to ourselves that this is what we are doing; and the reason is that inauthentic existence is a *degraded* mode of existence, where the true nature of things is concealed—or rather, *where we conceal the true nature of things from ourselves*. Obviously, the more serious-minded one is, the less one will be willing to admit the existence of these cracks and crevices in the surface of the world, and consequently one will take good care not to look too closely—and, of course, since laughter is already a tacit admission of the existence of such things, one will regard all kinds of levity as positively immoral.

Without leaving the sphere of the *puthujjana*, let us turn to the habitually authentic man—one who is anxious, and lucid in his anxiety, who keeps perpetually before him (though without being able to resolve it) the essential contradiction in human existence. Here Kierkegaard has quite a lot to say. (His expressions, 'the subjective existing thinker', 'doubly reflected consciousness', 'the ethicist', are more or less equivalent to Heidegger's 'authentic existence'.)

> That the subjective existing thinker is as positive as he is negative, can also be expressed by saying that he is as sensitive to the comic as to the pathetic. As men ordinarily live, the comic and the pathetic are divided, so that one person has the one and another person has the other, one person a little more of the one, another, a little less. But for anyone who exists in a double reflection, the proportions are equal: as much of the pathetic, so much also of the comic. The equality in the relationship provides a mutual security, each guaranteeing the soundness of the other. The pathos which is not secured by the presence of the comic is illusion; the comic spirit that is not made secure by the presence of pathos is immature. Only one who himself produces this will understand it, otherwise not. (*CUP*, p. 81)

Once one has accepted anxiety as one's normal and proper state, then one faces the contradiction, and this, *granted* the anxiety, neither as plain tragic nor as plain comic, but as tragi-comic. This, of course, can be put in several ways (you can do it yourself). This is perhaps as good as any: it is tragic that we should take as meaningful a world that is actually meaningless, but comic that the world we take as meaningful should actually be meaningless. Kierkegaard puts it this way:

> Existence itself, the act of existing, is a striving, and is both pathetic and comic in the same degree. It is pathetic because the striving is infinite; that is, it is directed toward the infinite, being an actualization of infinitude, a transformation which involves the highest pathos. It is comic, because such a striving involves a self-contradiction. Viewed pathetically, a single second has infinite value; viewed comically, ten thousand years are but a trifle, like yesterday when it is gone. And yet, the time in which the existing individual lives, consists of just

> such parts. If one were to say simply and directly that ten thousand years are but a trifle, many a fool would give his assent, and find it wisdom; but he forgets the other, that a second has infinite value. When it is asserted that a second has infinite value, one or another will possibly hesitate to yield his assent, and find it easier to understand that ten thousand years have an infinite value. And yet, the one is quite as hard to understand as the other, provided merely we take time to understand what there is to be understood; or else are in another manner so infinitely seized by the thought that there is no time to waste, not a second, that a second really acquires infinite value. (*CUP*, pp. 84-5)

What he is getting at is that man is a discrepant combination of the *infinite*, God,[c] and the *finite*, the world. Man, as he looks at himself, sees himself as pathetic ('pathos' in the sense of 'passion', as in 'so-and-so is passionately interested in his work') or as comic, according as he looks towards the Eternal or towards the world.

Without endorsing Kierkegaard's theistic bias, we can see the main point of all this. The tragi-comedy of the human (*puthujjana*'s) situation as apprehended by the authentic man in his lucid anxiety is the source of all tragedy and comedy on the purely everyday level. And, whereas the inauthentic man laughs or weeps without knowing why he does so—in other words, *irresponsibly*—, the authentic man, when he laughs or weeps, does so *responsibly*. The authentic man, when he laughs at something (it will very often be at the serious-minded man, who is both *very* comic and *very* tragic), will always have the other side of the picture present to mind, as the shadow of his comic apprehension. (And when he weeps, the comic aspect of the situation will be there outlined on the background.) He laughs (and weeps) *with understanding*, and this gives his humour a depth and an ambiguity that escapes the inauthentic man.

In consequence of this, the authentic man is able to use his humour as a screen for his more *authentic* seriousness—seriousness, that is to say, about the human—or rather, the *existential*—paradox (he is looking for the solution and concluding, again and again, that the solution is that there is no solution; and this is the limit of the *puthujjana*'s field of vision.) See, for a literary expression of the *puthujjana*'s ultimate frustration, the pas-

c. Not, of course, the bearded old gent who is angry every day, but rather as Eternity, or perhaps the Eternal Law (which is rather what I understand him to mean by the term 'Idea'—something akin to '*dhammatā*', though in a theistic sense).

sage from Camus that I have quoted with translation in NIBBĀNA (a). Thus Kierkegaard:

> In order not to be distracted by the finite, by all the relatives in the world, the ethicist places the comical between himself and the world, thereby insuring himself against becoming comical through a naive misunderstanding of his ethical passion. An immediate enthusiast assails the world's ears with his twaddle early and late, always on his feet and arrayed in buskins, he plagues people with his enthusiasm, and he does not notice that what he says does not inspire them, unless they begin to beat him. He is well informed, and the orders are to effect a complete transformation—of the world; but there he has heard wrong, for the orders are to effect a complete transformation of himself. If such an enthusiast happens to be contemporary with an ironist, the latter will know how to utilize him profitably as comic material. The ethicist is, on the other hand, ironical enough to perceive that what interests him absolutely does not interest the others absolutely; this discrepancy he apprehends, and sets the comical between himself and them, in order to be able to hold fast to the ethical in himself with still greater inwardness. Now the comedy begins. The judgement of men on such an individual will always be: for him there is nothing that is important. And why not? Because for him the ethical is absolutely important, differing in this from men in general, for whom so many things are important, aye, nearly everything, but nothing absolutely important. (*CUP*, pp. 450-51)

This sort of thing allows the authentic man to indulge in a kind of humour that horrifies and outrages the inauthentic. So an authentic man, dying and in a state of lucid anxiety, aware that he is dying, might protect himself from his oh-so-well-meaning inauthentic visitors (who are fully determined to hide, not only from the dying man but also from themselves, their awful suspicion that there is such a thing as death) by maliciously asking them if they propose coming to his funeral—and pressing for an answer.

It is obvious enough that there can be no progress in the Dhamma for the inauthentic man. The inauthentic man does not even see the problem—all his effort is devoted to hiding from it. The Buddha's Teaching is not for the serious-minded. Before we deal with the problem we must see it, and that means becoming authentic. But, now, when we consider your original question about the relation of humour to the Buddhadhamma, a certain distinction must be made. There is a cardinal difference between the solution to the problem offered by the Buddha and that (or those) offered by other teachings; and this is perhaps best illustrated in the case of Kierkegaard himself.

Kierkegaard sees that the problem—the essential existential contradiction, *attā hi attano n'atthi*, (his) very self is not (his) self's[d] (Dhp. 62)—is in the form of a paradox (or, as Marcel would say, a mystery—'a problem that encroaches on its own data'). And this is quite right as far as it goes. But he does not see how to resolve it. Further, he concludes (as I have suggested above) that, in this temporal life at least, the solution is that there is no solution. This itself is a reduplication of the original paradox, and only seems to make the problem more acute, to work up the tension, to drive man further back into himself. And, not content with this, he seizes upon the essential Christian paradox—that God became man, that the Eternal became temporal—, which he himself calls 'absurd', and thus postulates a solution which is, as it were, a raising of the original paradox to the third power. A kind of paradox cubed, as one might say—$(\text{paradox})^3$.

But as we have seen, the original paradox is tragi-comical; it contains within its structure, that is to say, a humorous aspect. And when the paradox is intensified, so is the humorous—and a joke raised to the third power is a very tortuous joke indeed. What I am getting at is this: that in every teaching where the paradox is not resolved (and *a fortiori* where it is intensified), *humour is an essential structural feature*. You see this in Kierkegaard where he speaks of 'the comic expression for worship'. But perhaps the most striking case is Zen. Zen is above all the cult of the paradox. ('Burn the scriptures!', 'Chop up the Buddha image for firewood!', 'Go listen to the sound of one hand clapping!'), and the old Zen masters are professional religious jokers, sometimes with an appalling sense of humour. And all very gay too—but it is *not* the Buddha's Teaching. The Buddha alone teaches the resolution of the original paradox, not by wrapping it up in bigger paradoxes, but by *unwrapping* it—but for my discussion of this, see *Notes*, Preface, particularly note (m).

If humour is, as I have suggested, in some way a reaction to fear, then so long as there remains a trace of the contradiction, of the existential paradox, so long will there remain a trace of humour. But since, essentially, the Buddha's Teaching is the cessation of fear (or more strictly of anxiety, the condition of fear), so it leads to the subsidence of humour. Not, indeed, that the *arahat* is humourless in the sense of being serious-minded; far from it; no—it is simply that the *need* he formerly felt for humour has now ceased.

---

**d.** More freely: He himself is not his own.

And so we find in the Suttas (A.III,105/i,261) that whereas excessive laughter 'showing the teeth' is called childishness, a smile when one is rightly pleased is not out of place. Perhaps you may like to see here a distinction between inauthentic and authentic humour.

You ask also about play; but I can't tell you very much about this, I'm afraid. Sartre observes that in play—or at least in sport—we set ourselves the task of overcoming obstacles or obeying rules that we arbitrarily impose upon ourselves; and he suggests that this is a kind of anti-serious-mindedness. When we are serious-minded we accept the rules and values imposed upon us by the world, by the 'they'; and when we have fulfilled these obligations we feel the satisfaction of having 'done our duty'. In sport it is we who impose the obligations upon ourselves, which enables us to enjoy the satisfaction of fulfilling them, without any of the disadvantages that go along with having to do what 'they' expect us to do (for example, we can stop when we are tired—but you just try doing that when you are in the army!). In sport, we *play* at being *serious*; and this rather suggests that play (sport), like plays (the theatre), is really a way of making repairs in a world that threatens to come apart at the seams. So there probably is some fairly close connexion between play and humour. Certainly, we often laugh when we are at play, but I don't think this applies to such obviously serious-minded activities as Test Matches.

Rather an unhumorous letter on humour, I'm afraid, and rather quickly thrown together.

**[L. 130]** **24 May 1965**

Reflecting on what I wrote a few days ago about humour (which in any case was perhaps rather speculative and can hardly have done much more than scratch the surface), it occurs to me that I might have brought out certain aspects of what I had to say rather more clearly—in particular the actual relationship between laughter and fear. I think I merely said that laughter is 'in some way a reaction to fear.' But this can be defined more precisely. To be 'authentic' is to face the existential paradox, the essential contradiction, in a state of lucid anxiety, whereas to be 'inauthentic' is to take refuge from this anxiety in the serious-mindedness of the anonymous 'they'. But the contradiction is tragi-comic; and this (I suggested) is the source of all tragedy and comedy in the everyday world. It follows from this that the inauthentic man, in hiding in his serious-mindedness from the anxiety of contradiction, is actually hiding from the two aspects of existence, the comic and the tragic. From time to time he finds his complacent unseeing seriousness threatened with a contradiction of one kind or another and he *fears.* (The fearful is contradictory, and the contradictory is fearful.)

Pain, of course, is painful whether it is felt by the *puthujjana* or the *arahat*; but the *arahat*, though he may avoid it if he can, does not *fear* pain; so the fear of the inauthentic man in the face of physical danger is not simply the thought 'there may be pain'. No—he *fears* for his physical *existence.* And this is the tragic aspect of the contradiction showing itself. And when the threat passes, the contradiction shows its other face and he laughs. But he does not laugh because he *sees* the comic aspect (that may happen later), his laughter *is* the comic aspect (just as his fear *is* the tragic aspect): in other words, he is not *reacting to* a contradictory situation, he is *living* it. Tragedy and comedy, fear and laughter: the two sides of a contradiction.

But he may be faced with other contradictions to which, because they are less urgent, he *is* able to react. He half-grasps the contradiction *as* a contradiction, and then, *according to the way he is oriented* in life, either laughs or weeps: if he finds the tragic aspect threatening he will laugh (to emphasize the comic and keep the tragic at a distance), and if he finds the comic aspect threatening he will weep. (A passionate woman, who finds life empty and meaningless when she is not emotionally engaged [in love, or perhaps hate], and fearing the comic as destructive of her passion, may weep at the very contradiction that provokes laughter in a man who has, perhaps, discovered the ghastly boredom of being loved without loving in return and who regards the comic as his best defence against entanglements.) Laughter, then, is not so much *reaction* to fear as its *counterpart.*

Another question is that of the *sekha* and anxiety. Granted that he is now fairly confidently authentic, by nature does he still experience anxiety? To some extent, yes; but he has that faculty in himself by means of which, when anxiety arises, he is able to extinguish it. He knows of another escape from anxiety than flight into inauthenticity. He is already leaving behind him both laughter and tears. Here is a passage from Khandha Saṃy.—S. xx.43/iii,43:[1]

> Having seen, monks, the impermanence, changeability, absence of lust for and ceasing of matter (feeling, perception, determinations, consciousness), and that matter (...consciousness) was formerly as it is now, thus seeing with right understanding as it actually is that all matter (...consciousness) is impermanent, unpleasurable, of a nature to change, then whatever is the arising of sorrow, lamentation, pain, grief, and despair, those are eliminated. These being eliminated, there

is no anxiety. Not having anxiety he dwells at ease. Dwelling at ease, this monk is called 'extinguished to that extent'.

**[L. 131]** **2 June 1965**

Certainly, I quite agree that we often, and perhaps mostly, laugh when no fear is present. But then (though I may not have made myself clear) I did not really want to maintain that fear *is* always present—indeed, I would say, precisely, that we laugh when fear is *absent*. Whenever we laugh—I think you may agree—there is always some contradiction or absurdity lurking in the situation, though this is not usually *explicit*: we laugh in a carefree way, then we may pause and ask ourselves 'Now, why did I laugh then?', and finally we see (if we have some reflexive or introspective facility—a child has none) that what we laughed at was some incongruity—or more precisely, that our laughter was our mode of apprehending that incongruity. What I had in mind, when I associated laughter with fear, was rather this: that every contradiction is essentially a threat (in one way or another) to my existence (i.e. it shakes my complacency); and that fear and laughter are the two alternative modes in which we apprehend a threat. When the threat is advancing and may reach us, we *fear*; when the threat is receding or at a safe distance, we *laugh. We laugh when there is no need to fear.*

Children, as you rightly observe, laugh and laugh; and this—as I see it—is often because the child lives in a world where there are grown-up people, and the function of grown-up people—in a child's eyes—is to keep threats at a distance. The child is *protected* from threats; he knows that they will not reach him, that there is nothing to fear, and so he laughs. The sea can be a dangerous thing; but if it is calm, or there is a grown-up about the place, the child can splash about and *play* with this danger because it is merely potential. He pits his puny strength against the vast might of the ocean; and this is a contradiction (or incongruity), which he can apprehend (or *exist*—to use the verb in a particular sense ['to exist an experience']) in one of two ways, fear or laughter. If the ocean has the upper hand, he fears, but if he is getting the best of it (he plunges into the sea and emerges unharmed, he splashes, he kicks it, and the sea does not resent it) then he laughs: his laughter shows that 'there is nothing to fear', that fear is *absent*. But it does *not* show that fear is non-existent; merely that it is not there *today*.

You ask, rhetorically, if superiority feelings, 'self' feelings, are not at the root of all guilt complexes. Certainly they are. But with guilt goes anxiety (we are superior—or we just 'are'—, and we are unable to justify our superiority, our existence, and so we are anxious. Pride goes before a fall—and this is true right back as far as *asmimāna*, the conceit 'I am'). And anxiety is anxiety before the essential contradiction, which, in your example (i.e. when we are white—and superior—and find we can't share the mirth of blacks laughing at the colour bar), shows its un-funny aspect. So, as you say, our feeling of superiority inhibits laughter. But it does not necessarily follow that when we lose the superiority we shall laugh along with everybody else. A practised yogin, certainly, particularly if he has been doing *karuṇā*, is not in the least superior; but it may well be that, by his practice, he has put fear so far from him that he has lost the urge to laugh.

How far our investigation of humour tends to destroy it in the act of investigating it (like atomic physicists when they 'observe' an electron), depends principally upon the method used. If we adopt the scientific attitude of 'complete objectivity'—actually an impossibility—then we kill it dead, for there is nobody left to laugh. This leads to the idea that jokes are funny in themselves—that they have an intrinsic quality of funniness that can be analysed and written about in a deadly serious manner.

The other way is to watch ourselves as we laugh, in a reflexive effort, and then to *describe* the experience. This is the phenomenological (or existential) method of 'going direct to the things themselves'. Of course, this needs practice; and also it *does* modify the original humour (for example, it tends to bring into view the tacit pathetic background, which is normally hidden when we laugh in the immediate, or inauthentic, mode). Nevertheless, the humour, though modified, is still there, and something useful *can* be said about it—though what is said will be very unlike what is said by the serious-minded university professor who writes his two scholarly volumes. Kierkegaard is insistent upon the principle, *Quidquid cognoscitur, per modum cognoscentis cognoscitur*, 'Whatever is known is known in the mode of the knower'; and he would say that a serious-minded person is inherently incapable of knowing anything of humour. If we are going to find out what is funny in this or that joke, we must allow ourselves to be amused by it and, while still amused, *describe* our amusement.

Yes, the existentialist idiom is difficult, until you get the feel of it. The difficulty arises from the phenomenological method that I have just been talking about. The scientist (or scholar) becomes 'objective', puts himself right out of the picture (Kierkegaard is at his best when he describes this 'absent-minded' operation), and concerns himself only with *abstract facts*; the existentialist remains 'subjective' (not in the derogatory sense of being irresponsible), keeps himself in the picture, and describes *concrete things* (that is, things in relation to himself as he experiences them). This radical difference in method, naturally enough, is reflected in the kind of language used by the scientist on the one hand and the existentialist on the other—or rather, in the difference in the way they make use of language. I was struck, when I first read Sartre, by the strange sort of resemblance between certain of his expressions and some of the things said in the Suttas. Sartre, for example, has this:

> ...we defined the senses and the sense-organs in general as our being-in-the-world in so far as we have to be it in the form of being-in-the-midst-of-the-world. (*B&N*, p. 325)

In the Suttas (e.g. Saḷāyatana Saṃy.—S.xxxv.116/iv,95) we find:

> The eye (ear, nose, tongue, body, mind) is that in the world by which one is a perceiver and conceiver of the world.

Now whatever the respective meanings of these two utterances[a] it is quite clear that despite the two thousand five hundred years that separate them, Sartre's sentence is closer in *manner* of expression (as well as in content) to the Sutta passage than it is to anything produced by a contemporary neurophysiologist supposedly dealing with precisely the same subject—our sense organs and perception of the world. This remarkable similarity does not oblige us to conclude that Sartre has reached enlightenment, but simply that if we want to understand the Suttas the phenomenological approach is more promising than the objective scientific approach (which, as we all know, reigns over the world).

Although the existentialist philosophers may seem close to the Buddha's Teaching, I don't think it necessarily follows that they would accept it were they to study it. Some might, some might not. But what often happens is that after years of hard thinking, they come to feel that they have found the solution (even if the solution is that there is none), and they lie back resting on their reputation, or launch themselves into other activities (Marcel has become a Catholic, Sartre is politically active); and so they may feel disinclined to re-open an inquiry that they have already closed to their satisfaction (or dissatisfaction, as the case may be). Besides, it is not so easy to induce them to take up a study of the Dhamma. It is worse than useless

**a.** Where the Sutta says 'the eye is that in the world...', Sartre says that we (as our sense-organs) are 'amidst-the-world'; and where the Sutta says 'one is a perceiver and conceiver of the world', Sartre speaks of 'our being-in-the-world'.

to give them a copy of *Buddhism in a Nutshell*[1] or a life subscription to the BPS, which make the Buddha's Teaching easy...by leaving out the difficulties. And even translations of the Suttas are not always adequate, and anyway, they don't practise *samatha bhāvanā*.[2]

I don't want to be dogmatic about the value of a familiarity with the existential doctrines; that is, for an understanding of the Dhamma. Of course, if one has a living teacher who has himself attained (and ideally, of course, the Buddha himself), then the essence of the Teaching can sometimes be conveyed in a few words. But if, as will be the case today, one has no such teacher, then one has to work out for oneself (and *against* the accepted Commentarial tradition) what the Suttas are getting at. And here, an acquaintance with some of these doctrines can be—and, in my case, has been—very useful. But the danger is, that one may adhere to one or other of these philosophers and fail to go beyond to the Buddha. This, certainly, is a very real risk—but the question is, is it a justifiable risk? It is better, anyway, to cling to Heidegger than it is to cling to Bertrand Russell.

It seems to me that, whether or not the Kumbhakāra Jātaka is reporting the truth, it does a disservice in representing enlightenment as something attainable without hard work. It is *too* simple if we can attain *just* by seeing a ravished mango tree; and we turn away from the Jātakas with the disgruntled thought: 'It happened to them, so why doesn't it happen to me? Some people have all the luck'. No, in my view, the emphasis should be on the hard work—if not in the life when one actually attains, then in a previous life (or being).[3]

You say, 'Questions that strike a Sartre or a Kierkegaard as obvious, urgent, and baffling may not have even occurred to Bāhiya Dārucīriya'. I am not so sure. I agree that a number of 'uneducated' people appear, in the Suttas, to have reached extinction. But I am not so sure that I would call them 'simple'. You suggest that Bāhiya may not have been a very complex person and that a previous 'Sartre' phrase may not have been essential for him. Again I don't want to be dogmatic, but it seems to me that your portrait of him is oversimplified. For one thing, I regret to say, you have made something easy...by leaving out the difficulty. Your quotation of the brief instruction that the Buddha gave Bāhiya is quite in order as far as it goes; but—inadvertently, no doubt—you have only given part of it. Here is the passage in full (Udāna 10/8 and cf. Saḷāyatana Saṃy.—S.xxxv.95/iv,73):

> Then, Bāhiya, you should train thus: 'In the seen there shall be just the seen; in the heard there shall be just the heard; in the sensed there shall be just the sensed; in the cognized there shall be just the cog-

> nized'—thus, Bāhiya, should you train yourself. When, Bāhiya, for you, in the seen there shall be just the seen...cognized, then, Bāhiya, you (will) not (be) that by which (*tvaṃ na tena*); when, Bāhiya, you (shall) not (be) that by which, then, Bāhiya, you (shall) not (be) in that place (*tvaṃ na tattha*); when, Bāhiya, you (shall) not (be) in that place, then, Bāhiya, you (will) neither (be) here nor yonder nor between the two: just this is the end of suffering.

This is a highly condensed statement, and for him simple. It is quite as tough a passage as anything you will find in Sartre. And, in fact, it is clearly enough connected with the passage that I have already quoted alongside a passage from Sartre: 'The eye (etc.) is that *in the world by which* one is a perceiver and conceiver of the world'.

Let us now try, with the help of Heidegger's indications,[4] to tie up these two Sutta passages.

(i) To begin with, 'I—here' is I as identical with my senses; 'here', therefore refers to my sense organs (eye, ear, nose, tongue, body, and also mind). The counterpart of 'here' is 'yonder', which refers to the various things in the world as sense-objects. 'Between the two' will then refer (though Heidegger makes no mention of this) to consciousness, contact, feeling, and so on, as being dependent upon sense organ and sense object—*cakkhuñca paṭicca rūpe ca uppajjati cakkhuviññāṇaṃ, tinnaṃ saṅgati phasso, phassapaccayā vedanā*, etc. (Saḷāyatana Saṃy.—S.xxxv.107/iv,87).[5]

(ii) In the second place Heidegger says that 'here' and 'yonder' are possible only in a 'there'; in other words, that sense-organs and sense-objects, which are 'amidst-the-world', in Sartre's phrase, are possible only if there *is* a world for them to be 'amidst'. 'There', then, refers to the world. So the 'here' and 'yonder' of the Bāhiya Sutta correspond in the other Sutta to the 'eye (and so on)' as 'that in the world...'.

(iii) But Heidegger goes on to say that there is a 'there' only if there is an entity that has made a disclosure of spatiality as the being of the 'there'; and that being-there's existential spatiality is grounded in being-in-the-world. This simply means that, in the very act of *being*, I disclose a spatial world: my being is always in the form of a spatial being-there. (In spite of the Hindus and Hegel, there is no such thing as 'pure being'. All being is limited and particularized—if I *am* at all, I am in a spatial world.) In brief, there is only a 'there', a spatial world (for senses and objects to be 'amidst'), if *I am there*. Only so long as *I am there* shall I be 'in the form of being-amidst-the-world'—i.e. as sense-organs ('here') surrounded by sense-objects ('yonder').

(iv) But on what does this 'I am there' depend? 'I am there' means 'I am in the world'; and I am 'in the world' in the form of senses (as eye...mind). And Heidegger tells us that the 'here' (i.e. the senses) is always understood in relation to a 'yonder' ready-to-hand, i.e. something that is *for* some purpose (of mine). I, as my senses, 'am towards' this 'yonder'; I am 'a being that is de-severant, directional, and concernful'. I won't trouble you with details here, but what Heidegger means by this is *more or less* what the Venerable Ānanda Thera means when he said that 'The eye (and so on) is that...by which one is a perceiver and a conceiver of the world'. In other words, not only am I *in the world*, but I am *also*, as my senses, that *by which* there is a world in which I am. 'I am there' *because* 'I am that by which there is an I-am-there'; and consequently, when 'I shall not be that by which', then 'I shall not be there'. And when 'I shall not be there', then 'I shall neither be here nor yonder nor between the two'.

(v) And *when* shall we 'not be that by which'? This, Heidegger is not able to tell us. But the Buddha tells us: it is when, for us, in the seen there shall be just the seen, and so with the heard, the sensed, and the cognized. And when in the seen is there just the seen? When the seen is no longer seen as 'mine' (*etaṃ mama*) or as 'I' (*eso'ham asmi*) or as 'my self' (*eso me attā*): in brief, when there is no longer, in connexion with the senses, the conceit 'I am', *by which* 'I am a conceiver of the world'. Do you get my point?

So, although it would certainly be going too far to suggest that Bāhiya had already undergone a course of existentialist philosophy, the fact remains that he was capable of understanding at once a statement that says more, and says it more briefly, than the nearest comparable statement either in Heidegger or Sartre. You say, 'Question that strike Sartre or a Kierkegaard as obvious, urgent and baffling many not have ever occurred to Bāhiya Dārucīrya.' I am not so sure. Bāhiya, I allow, may not have been a cultured or sophisticated man-of-the-world; but I see him as a very subtle thinker. Authenticity may be the answer, as you suggest; but an authentic man is not a *simple* person—he is *self-transparent* if you like, which is quite another matter.

My health—thank you for asking after it—remains poor to middlin', and I manage to do almost no *bhāvanā* at all; at best a certain amount of *dhammavitakka*.

12

# Letters to Mr. Robert K. Brady

**[L. 132]** **18 March 1964**

Dear Sir,[1]
I should be most grateful if you could let me know the address of the English philosophical journal 'Mind'. Can you also tell me if the 'Hibbert Journal' is still alive and, if so, what its address is?

**[L. 133]** **23 April 1964**

Many thanks for your letter of the 21st, just received. It is very good of you indeed, not only to have sent the addresses, but also to have been so thoughtful as to make the suggestion about an occasional loan of 'books with a philosophical background.' As things are, your suggestion is really rather welcome. Although a preoccupation with books should not be our prime concern, I am much handicapped by chronic sickness and find that some reading and a little writing do help out over difficult periods. And, as you will be aware, we are more or less entirely dependent on the kindness of others in such matters as the provision of books.

As I expect you are aware, a copy of my *Notes on Dhamma* was sent to your library a few months ago (and duly acknowledged). But I quite recognize that it is not everybody's cup of tea—Buddhists, at least in Buddhist countries, have long since given up thinking, and thinkers have not yet begun to learn Pali. For the benefit of the thinkers, any future edition will be provided with English translations, but the problem is not solved so easily of getting the Buddhists to think.

**[L. 134]** **6 May 1964**

Thank you for your letter of the 1st, in which you inform me that you hope to be seeing me on the 22nd in connexion with some books. In view of our past correspondence, this is quite intelligible to me. But you speak also of an 'Opening ceremony' which, I must confess, mystifies me. There is positively nothing to be opened at my *kuṭi* except the door, and that can be opened without any ceremony at all.

I have no doubt that there is something much more important than this to be Opened on the 22nd, but in some other place. Since there seems to be some slight confusion, I thought it better to let you know, so that you do not miss the ceremony in question by coming to the wrong place.

**[L. 135] 10 May 1964**

I received a copy of the 'Hibbert Journal' and also one of 'Mind', some two or three weeks back, and found them both illuminating—I mean on the present atmosphere of religious and philosophical thinking in England.

**[L. 136] 26 May 1964**

Just a few words to express my appreciation of all the trouble you have taken in coming to visit me and in concerning yourself about my welfare—particularly intellectual. The books that you brought me are all of interest to me in one way or another, and not the least the Zaehner (in spite of the fact that I find him partly unreadable).

The book on time confirms my suspicion that the whole subject is in a state of chaos, and I am glad to think that my own contribution (in the *Notes*), if it is mistaken, at least errs in good company. I see that the question of time has occupied not a few ecclesiastics in the Middle Ages, and their findings have been as intelligent as anything that is produced today. (The particular question of the 'variability of qualities'—i.e., that a quality can vary in intensity while remaining unchanged in kind—is one to which I myself have given some attention, and I find that it has already been considered by Duns Scotus.) St. Augustine—a man of parts in more senses than one—has made some very acute remarks. (Are his *Confessions* available?)

The book is, in part, a combination of the philosophical naivety so typical of the dedicated scientists[a] and a kind of ultra-sophistication (also typical of

---

**a.** How can he pass such a statement as this: '…the newborn is not conscious and only gradually becomes so in the first five or ten months of life'?

scientists) that does not shrink from a more-than-Hegelian dialectic.[b] The effect of this alternation is far from displeasing, but it convinces me that my world must be very different from that of the scientist (I used to be a mathematician in a small way, but with the pure mathematician's dislike of any practical applications).

Huxley has certainly set the cat amongst the pigeons with his implied suggestion that the Holy Ghost may, after all, turn out to be no more than a rather obscure chemical compound—it puts the other two members of the Trinity in a strange light. No wonder the learned rescue-corps (Kierkegaard's expression) has to rush in to defend! However, in this particular controversy I am merely a spectator: I am more interested in Zaehner's references[1] to Pali Buddhism. He does not say much (and he admits he does not know much) about Theravāda texts, but what he does say is wrong in two respects.

(i) In the first place, he more or less identifies the *anattā* ('not-self') doctrine with Advaita Vedānta, and he does this with more than a suspicion that neither Buddhists nor even the Buddha himself would allow this.[c] Though this identification is quite gratuitous,[d] there is some excuse for it in view of certain books published in Europe which hold this view (Horner and Coomaraswamy in England, and Georg Grimm in Germany). No doubt you will gather from the *Notes* that I certainly do not hold the view that the object of the exercise is to get rid of my temporal 'self' in order to attain the permanent 'Self' behind it. But, this is not the place to pursue this question.

(ii) In the second place, Zaehner appears to assume that all experience attained in the practice of meditation (I use the word here in the widest sense) is of the mescalin/manic-depressive type, or at least that one has to pass through this state to reach the 'Beatific Vision'. Now, whatever the case may be with the Christian mystics, or with the Mahometan Sufis, or with the Hindus—or even with Mahāyāna and Zen Buddhists—about none of

---

**b.** No doubt you are aware that scientific research has established the existence of an 'Absolute Zero of Temperature'—about -273.4°C—but did you know that some scientists now think that there may be things even colder than that? Heat is envisaged as the movement of particles, and Absolute Zero is the state where all these particles are at rest. A temperature *below* Absolute Zero seems to take us through the looking-glass.

**c.** '... the Buddha saw something that did not change, over against *prakriti* he saw *purusha* though he would not have formulated it thus.' And again, 'Moreover the Hindus, overwhelmingly, and the Buddhists when they are off their guard, speak of this eternal being as the "self"...' (p. 126).

**d.** There is one text (at least) that directly opposes the idea that *nibbāna* (extinction) is *attā* (self).

whom am I well informed (and, still less, practised in their disciplines), I can quite definitely assert that (to speak only of the practice of concentration—*samādhi*) the effect of practice according to the Theravāda tradition (details in the Visuddhimagga—*Path of Purification*) is quite different from anything Zaehner has described.

I myself have practised fairly continuously for one year, and then (after amœbiasis had crippled my capacity for practice) spasmodically for about fourteen years, and I am quite familiar with the low-level results of this practice. There is a gradual and increasing experience of calm and tranquillity as the object of meditation (in my case, the in- and out-breaths) becomes clearer and more definite, and at the same time distracting thoughts about other matters become less. (If one *does* turn one's attention to such matters, they are seen much more clearly and steadily than at normal times.) As one proceeds, one's capacity for practice increases, and one may be able to continue (with interruptions for meals, etc.) for many hours;[e] and also one positively dislikes any outside interruption, and necessary breaks are most unwelcome.

In all this there is, right from the start, no sign at all of elation and depression (or expansion and contraction—Zaehner, pp. 85*ff.*), and no experience of 'one-ness' (with nature, with Self, with God, or with anything else). There is nothing one could possibly call 'ecstatic' about it—it is pleasurable, and the more so the more one does it, but that is all. To begin with, certainly, one may be attacked either by sleepiness or by mental agitation (i.e. about other matters), but with persistence, and particularly when the object of meditation begins to appear clearly, these things no longer arise; but sleepiness is not depression and mental distraction is not manic exultation.

About the higher states (called *jhānas*), I am, unfortunately, unable to give you any personal account, since I have never reached them (though my motive in coming to Ceylon in the first place was to obtain them); but I am perfectly satisfied that they are attainable (given good health, persistence, and so on). In any case, in the descriptions of these attainments in the Suttas there is, once again, nothing that corresponds to what Zaehner describes; and, in particular, these practices *alone* do not lead to 'liberation' in the highest sense—*nibbāna*—though Zaehner seems to assume that they do (pp. 155-6). Moreover, it is by no means necessary to reach the highest stages of concentration in order to attain *nibbāna*—first *jhāna* (minimum) is sufficient.

---

**e.** In the Suttas, the Buddha and others continue for a week at a time[2] 'without changing their sitting position', and this is, to me, perfectly credible.

I have wearied you with all this only because it seems possible that, in denying that there was anything 'mystical' about the Buddhism of the Pali Texts, I might have given you the impression that there was (in my opinion, at least) no *practice of meditation*. This, however, would be a mistake. In denying that Pali Buddhism was mystical, all I intended to convey was that (i) the practice of meditation (or, more specifically, concentration—*samādhi*) that it teaches cannot in any way be described as *mystical* (though certainly its effects are, to begin with, *unusual* [because few people practise], and eventually, *supernormal* [they can lead to mastery of *iddhi* powers: levitation, clairvoyance, memory of past lives, and so on]); and (ii) that eventual liberation—*nibbāna*, extinction—is not a mystical union with the Deity, nor even absorption in a Higher Self (both of which cover up and intensify the fundamental ambiguity of the subject ['I', 'myself', etc.]), but rather the attainment of the clear understanding and comprehension (*paññā, aññā*) about the nature of this ambiguity (which, when combined with suitable *samādhi* actually causes—or, rather, allows—the ambiguity to subside once for all).

Our actual discussion on the Dhamma was, I am afraid, rather indecisive. There are many world-views against which as a background the Buddha's Teaching is wholly incomprehensible—indeed, the Buddha himself, upon occasion, when asked about his Teaching, would answer, 'It is hard for you, having (as you do) other teachers, other persuasions, other views, to understand these matters' (e.g. M.72/i,487). Zaehner's *Weltanschauung*, for example, is hopeless—and doubly so, since he is both a Roman Catholic and a University Professor, making him either hostile or indifferent (or both) to the Buddha. (Is there not, incidentally, something rather *louche*[3] about being at one and the same time a Catholic and a professor of comparative religion? Kierkegaard would have something to say about this. Perhaps he is objective on week-days and subjective on Sundays. But I know that I could never endure such a situation.) Anyway, I hope your visit was not entirely time wasted.

## [L. 137] 16 July 1964

It was a disappointment to me, too, not to see you last Sunday, not merely because I should have been interested to meet some intelligent twenty-year-old Britons (how many light-years away from them am I?), but rather because I find you a very pleasant person to talk to, and though I feel no need of a confidant (I have kept my own counsel all my life, and indeed now find that I have no alternative) it is an unaccustomed luxury for me to be able to talk about myself (sometimes perhaps indirectly) with little feeling of constraint.

In my letter to you about Zaehner and, more particularly, in letting you see Sister Vajirā's correspondence, I hoped to be able to convey to you that the Buddha's Teaching is very far from being understood in the West. Zaehner's misapprehension about the nature of our concentration (*samādhi*) is quite understandable, and one need only do some personal practice (mindfulness of one's breathing, for example) to see his mistake. But the Sister Vajirā correspondence is another matter: though I do not know your latest reactions on rereading the letters, it seemed to me that your first reaction was one of bewilderment. And this is quite in order—it *is* a matter for bewilderment, and if you had produced some facile interpretation I should have felt that it was a mistake to show you the letters. Their significance for you personally is, I think, that loss of faith in the Christian Myth[a] is no reason for despair. (I could, of course, say this more emphatically, but you might not then accept it.)

About the books that I have borrowed from you I am still bothered by a daily temperature of 99° or so, and in spite of (I think) William James' remark that spiritual truths, for aught we know, might flourish much better at, say, a temperature of 103° than at normal blood heat, I find that even one degree's rise in temperature makes the reading of plain philosophy an almost impossible undertaking. So I have not made much headway in this department, though I can perhaps expect my temperature to settle by and by.

As for the novels and drama, there is really a great deal to say, and at another time, I might take pleasure in saying it. But for the present I shall only remark that Huxley's 'Buddhism' in *Island* is in almost complete contradiction, point for point, with what the Buddha actually taught. In particular, there is absolutely no justification at all to be found in the Suttas for the idea that the way to salvation is through sex (however mystically conceived). The Buddha is quite explicit on this point—without giving up attachment (let alone sex) there is no putting an end to suffering. The view that 'there is no harm in sensuality' (M.45/i,305) fills the charnel grounds (i.e. it leads to repeated birth and death). Durrell's attitude is better: for the artist, love is justified as providing the raw material of suffering out of which

---

**a.** How far you have lost it, I am not sure; it remains implicit, anyway, in the Western cultural tradition—even Jimmy Porter in *Look Back in Anger* accepts the church bells as valid for the 'next world'.

the artist produces his masterpiece. But the question still remains 'What is there to justify the artist?'

Certainly, one might reply that the artist is justified by the existence of suffering, of the limitations of the human condition; but the Buddha removes suffering, and the artist's position is undermined. Laclos[1] is really the only consistent one, since he offers no justification at all.

P.S. Huxley speaks of the pain of bereavement as right and proper, for if we did not feel it we should be less than human beings. How, then, can he approve the Buddha's Teaching, which leads to the end of suffering—to the end, that is, of 'sorrow, lamentation, pain, grief, and despair'? Just as the *arahat* has no need of art, so he is incapable of grief; it is all one and the same thing. But Huxley wants the Buddha without the *arahat*—impossible!

**[L. 138]** **26 July 1964**

Part of me is thoroughly jealous of Jimmy Porter's generous fury—how satisfying to get one's own back so articulately on the wearisome hypocrisy of those who appoint themselves our elders and betters! (I have all my life been miserably tongue-tied at just those moments when a vigorous protest seemed what was most needed. But I have never been able to believe in my own anger, and the only thing I can do is to turn my back on the whole affair and walk away.) Part of me, I say, is green with envy of Jimmy Porter's extraordinary vitality—his anger is justified (so I almost feel) by his existence. But has Jimmy Porter ever asked himself whether his existence is justified?

The other part of me sees that my existence is purely gratuitous and that, without any logical inconsistency at all, I could perfectly well not be. My presence in the world and therefore *a fortiori* also my anger (or my lack of it) are *de trop*. So long as I exist there will be occasion for anger (or for restraint); but why exist? The immediate answer, of course, is that we can't help it. We *do* exist, and that's an end of the matter: let us rage furiously together or turn our backs in silence, *au choix*; it is all the same in the end (that is, if there were an end). But no—there *is* a way out, there *is* a way to put a stop to existence, if only we have the courage to let go of our cherished humanity.

And so, too, the question of sex (about which, as you know, I feel rather strongly these days). How much I wish I could enter into the fun of the game with Durrell's unquestioning enthusiasm! What a fascinating experience to have been a sculptor of one of those incredible erotic groups on the outside of the Indian temples (why not on the outside of our English cathedrals to take the place of the figures destroyed by the Puritans?)—to recapture and perpetuate publicly in stone, by day, the intimate and fleeting carnal extasies of the night! But suppose one sees also the other side of the picture, what then? I don't mean death (whose presence, in any case, may only sharpen one's living desire) but the understanding that love (all brands) must be without significance (however passionately we may wish to believe otherwise) if life is pointless. The Buddha, at any rate, tells us that the only purpose of existence is to put an end to it. And how do we put an end to it?

*Hitvā icchañ ca lobhañ ca,*
*yattha satto puthujjano,*
*cakkhumā paṭipajjeyya*
*tareyya narakaṃ imaṃ.*

Forsaking desire and lust
where the commoner is stuck
Let the man with eyes proceed
and get across this hell.

(Sn. 706/137) And there is no way of compromise, in spite of Huxley and the mystics. Huxley wants the best of both worlds, *maithuna* and mescalin; and where the Hindus say, not altogether without reason, that the self is in the *yoni*, Huxley quotes a Tantric Buddhist text to the effect that Buddhahood is in the *yoni*, which is mere wishful thinking—how quickly we should all become Buddhas! And the mystics, what little I have read of them, seem to describe their union with the Divine in terms of copulation.

Augustine certainly knows that chambering and wantonness must be given up if any sort of mental calm is to be obtained, but the poor fellow sadly deceived himself when he imagined that, once given up, these things would never be with him again for all eternity. No doubt they were given up for his lifetime, and perhaps for some time after (where is he now?), but the root of sex is not dug up finally until the *third* stage of attainment on the Path to Awakening. Both the *sotāpanna* (stream-attainer, whose future human births are limited in number) and the *sakadāgāmī* (once-returner [*scil.* to human existence]) have, or may have, sexual appetite (and corresponding performance; for there is no question of impotence), and it is only the *anāgāmī* (non-returner) who is free of sensual cravings. Augustine, then, though temporarily victorious over the Bed, still had the root of desire within him, and his mystical experience was only possible because of this.

No one who had attained any of the stages on the Buddha's Path could think of regarding sex or its mystical sublimations as something of value.

I am enclosing two passages, from Grenier and from Tennent, that might be of interest. You will see that Tennent seems to confirm Grenier's main contention, that the idea of a (beginningless) transmigration is no less acceptable to the natural understanding of the average ignorant Oriental than the idea of a single unique existence is to that of the average ignorant Occidental. But Tennent, who is using a more powerful microscope, sees that the idea of cessation of existence through extinction of desire is not such a popular notion, such a *croyance biologique*, as Grenier perhaps likes to think. We may suspect that Grenier has less firmly grasped than Tennent that there is a radical distinction between the Hindu and the Buddhist teachings of *nirvāṇa*. (The situation is complicated by the fact that the Mahāyāna Buddhists adopt, without due acknowledgement, the Hindu notion of *māyā*—that all is illusory, that nothing *really* exists—and in consequence that their ideas of *nirvāṇa* are closer to the Hindu concept than to the Teaching of the Pali Suttas. The French, through historical accident, are more familiar with Mahāyāna than with Theravāda.)

Of course, Tennent himself has not said the last word on the subject (though as far as it goes his account is surprisingly accurate—how often do we not find that hostile evangelizing Christians take more trouble to understand what the Buddha taught than disinterested scholars!), and if we turn on Tennent a still more powerful microscope we shall see that 'the nature of Nirwana' is not quite so obvious from his account as he assumes. But here I must refer you to NA CA SO of my *Notes on Dhamma*.

I wonder if you are put off by the rather didactic tone of my letters? I should prefer, really, to be wholly a pupil amongst other pupils—or better still, not at school in any capacity at all. But if there is something to be said that someone else has perhaps not heard before, and wants to hear, then in the nature of things there must be a speaker as well as a listener. I only hope that didacticism has not invaded my ordinary conversation—living alone one gets out of the habit of conversing with people.

### ABSOLUTE AND CHOICE[1]

Are we entitled to reject the testimony of Hindu thought? On whose behalf? Are these not, for millions of minds, truths of common sense as stable as the so-called universal principles of the Greco-Europeans? Do not Hindus and Chinese, for instance, when religious common sense is involved, have postulates inverse to ours? We have the fear of death. Lucretius asserts that all religions originate from this fear, that in any case the aim of all of them is the healing of it. But we see that entire peoples in the Orient start from the opposite idea and look for an opposite aim: the universe follows an eternal change (while the Europeans are particularly sensitive to its permanence) and a future life, far from being desirable in any specific form, is the most dreadful thing in the world. It is necessary to observe that these are not only philosophical theories reserved for an elite, nor even just religious dogmas imposed by education or by the clergy, but common popular concepts, beliefs, which are, so to say, biological. An illiterate Hindu, an illiterate Chinese Buddhist, believes in transmigration with the same spontaneity as an *illiterate* French or German believes in a unique and personal life. Where the Occidental fears the cessation of life, the Oriental fears the continuation of survival. Thus one understands that 'salvation' is sought in opposite directions; by Europeans in the 'eternal life' and by Indians in the extinction of desire and consequently of all life.

### 'BUDDHIST DOCTRINE OF THE TRANSMIGRATION OF SOULS AND NATURE OF NIRWANA'[2]

The general mass of the Buddhists in Ceylon are not orthodox in their view of transmigration, as they believe that the same soul migrates into different bodies. But this is contrary to the teaching of Buddhu, and of this the learned priests are fully aware; but they do not attempt to correct the error, regarding the subject as too difficult to be understood by the unlearned. His doctrine is that of *a series of existences*, which he illustrates by the metaphors of a tree and a lamp. A tree produces fruit, from which fruit another tree is produced, and so the series continues. The last tree is not the identical tree with the first, but it is a result, so that if the first tree had not been, the last tree could not have existed. Man is the tree, his conduct is the fruit, the vivifying energy of the fruit is desire. While this continues, the series will proceed: the good or evil actions performed give the quality of the fruit, so that the existence springing from these actions will be happy or miserable as the quality of the fruit affects the tree produced from it. According to this doctrine the present body and soul of man never had a previous existence, but a previously existing being under the influence of desire performed virtuous or vicious actions, and in consequence of these upon the death of that individual a new body and soul is produced. The metaphor of the *lamp* is similar. One lamp is lighted from another; the two lamps are distinct, but the one could not have been lighted had not the other existed. The nature of Nirwana, or cessation of being, is obvious from this. It is not the *destruction* of an existent being, but the *cessation of his existence*. It is not an absorption into a superior being, as the Brahmans teach; it is not a retreat into a place of eternal repose, free from further transmigration; it is not a violent destruction of being, but a complete and final cessation of existence.

**[L. 139] 27 July 1964**

Postscript to my yesterday's letter. I have just found in Camus (*La Chute*, pp. 113-14)[1] exactly what I wanted to say about Durrell.

> You are wrong, *cher*, the boat is going at full speed. But the Zuyderzee is a dead sea, or almost. With its flat shores, lost in the fog, there's no knowing where it begins or ends. So we are steaming along without any landmark; we can't gauge our speed. We are making progress and yet nothing is changing. It's not navigation but dreaming.
>
> In the Greek archipelago I had the contrary feeling. Constantly new islands would appear on the horizon. Their treeless backbone marked the limit of the sky and their rocky shore contrasted sharply with the sea. No confusion possible; in the sharp light everything was a landmark. And from one island to another, ceaselessly on our little boat, which was nevertheless dawdling, I felt as if we were scudding along, night and day, on the crest of the short, cool waves in a race full of spray and laughter. Since then, Greece itself drifts somewhere within me, on the edge of my memory, tirelessly.... Hold on, I too am drifting; I am becoming lyrical! Stop me, *mon cher*, I beg you.
>
> By the way, do you know Greece? No? So much the better. What should we do there, I ask you? there it requires pure hearts. Do you know that there friends walk along the street in pairs holding hands? Yes, the women stay at home and you often see a middle-aged, respectable man, sporting moustaches, gravely striding along the pavements, his fingers locked in those of his friend. In the Orient likewise, at times? I don't say no. But tell me, would you take my hand in the

> streets of Paris? Oh, I'm joking. *We* have a sense of decorum; scum gives us a stilted manner. Before appearing in the Greek islands, we should have to wash at length. There the air is chaste, the sea and sensual enjoyment transparent. And we...

No, decidedly, I do not have Durrell's *coeur pur*.

**[L. 140]** **2 August 1964**

This letter gives me an opportunity to add something to what I said earlier. In my letter of the 26th I think I remarked that Mahāyāna Buddhism had taken over the Hindu idea of *māyā* without even proper acknowledgement. But this statement is obviously too simple, and is perhaps unjustified (since I do not know that the Mahāyānists did not think up the idea for themselves). It almost sounds as if there were no real difference between the two teachings; whereas, in fact, distinctions must be made. At the same time it is true to say that the Mahāyāna concept of *nirvāṇa* is separated by an abyss from the *nibbāna* of the Pali Suttas.

The question hinges on the scandal of the world's relativity, or variety, (which stubbornly resists all our efforts to reduce it to a single Whole)—'The primitive hostility of the world rises up to face us across millennia.' (*Le Mythe*, p. 28; *The Myth*, p. 11) Three quotations will perhaps illustrate this. Here, first, is Jean Grenier on the Hindu *māyā*:

> The world may be the product of a sort of dream, not the dream of a spirit but the dream of a power inherent in the world. That would be the case of this illusion that the Vedantists call *Māyā*. ... For Indians *Māyā* is *Shakti*, which is to say a power from (and of) Brahma, through which the latter takes a perceptible appearance.... The Vedic hypothesis of *Māyā*, a hypothesis that would better be called a postulate, because of its generality and indemonstrability, consists in supposing that the world is the product of a cosmic illusion, a modification of Brahma. This modification would be apparent only, like the rope one thinks to be a snake but which nevertheless remains a rope. The absolute would not be more easily reached through it than the desert through the mirage. (pp. 53-5)

Secondly, here is a passage from the Prajñāpāramitā on the Mahāyānist *avidyā*:

> Objects exist only insofar as they do not exist in reality. Insofar as they do not exist they are called *avidyā*, which means 'non-knowledge'. Common and ignorant people are attached to these things because they do not receive guidance (teaching) on this subject. They picture to themselves all these objects as existing, whereas in reality no one (nothing) exists.[1]

Finally, a verse from the Pali Suttas:

> *Saṅkapparāgo purisassa kāmo*
> *Na te kāmā yāni citrāni loke*
> *Saṅkapparāgo purisassa kāmo*
> *Tiṭṭhanti citrāni tath'eva loke*
> *Ath'ettha dhīrā vinayanti chandaṃ.* (A.VI,63/iii,411)
>
> Thought and lust are a man's sensuality,
> Not the various things in the world;
> Thought and lust are a man's sensuality,
> The various things just stand there in the world;
> But the wise get rid of desire therein.

For the Hindu, then, the variety of the world is *illusion*, and for the Mahāyānist it is *ignorance*; and in both cases the aim is to overcome the world, either by union with Brahma or by attainment of knowledge. Unlike the Hindus and the Mahāyānists, the Pali Suttas teach that the variety of the world is neither illusion (*māyā*) nor delusion (*avidyā*) but perfectly real. The attainment of *nibbāna* is certainly cessation of *avijjā*, but this leaves the variety of the world intact, except that *affectively* the variety is now uniformly indifferent. *Avidyā*, clearly enough, does not mean to the Mahāyānist what *avijjā* does in the Pali Suttas. You will have noticed, I expect, that Sister Vajirā was holding more or less the Mahāyānist view that nothing really exists, and that relief came when she was induced to abandon this idea.

I do hope that all this stuff I am sending you does not make you feel under any obligation to reply to it. That is not the idea at all—it is simply for you to read or not as you will, nothing more. The trouble is that when I get some coherent thoughts (or that seem so to me at least) I have to do something with them or else they get in the way; and the easiest thing is to write them down and post them to somebody. You will remember that Stephen Daedalus got rid of an aphorism by telegraphing it to Buck Mulligan at his pub. Tolstoy's toenails.

**[L. 141]** **20 September 1964**

Your question about the propriety of sending good wishes ('Is not wishing desire, and so to be shunned?') can be answered, though not in one word. There is desire and desire, and there is also desire to end desire. There is desire that involves self-assertion (love, hate) and desire that does not (the *arahat*'s desire to eat when hungry, for example), and the former can be either self-perpetuating (unrestrained passion) or self-destructive (restrained passion). Self-destructive desire is bad in so far as it is passionate, and therefore good in so far as, translated into action, it brings itself to an end. (By 'translated into action' I mean that the desire for restraint does not remain abstractly in evidence only when one is not giving way to passion, but is concretely operative when there is actually occasion for it, when one is actually in a rage. To begin with, of course, it is not easy to bring them together, but with practice desire for restraint arises at the same time as the passion, and the combination is self-destructive. The Suttas say clearly that craving is to be eliminated by means of craving [A.IV,159/ii,145-46]; and you yourself are already quite well aware that nothing can be done in this world, either good or bad, without passion—and the achievement of dispassion is no exception. But passion must be intelligently directed.) Since an *arahat* is capable of desiring the welfare of others, good wishes are evidently not essentially connected with self-assertion, and so are quite *comme il faut*.

I had actually written you a long letter, mostly about Toynbee and Graves, but decided that it was intolerably prosy and not worth sending. My mind, of late, has been rather turbid—ideas are there, but will not crystallize out—perhaps as a result of reading *The White Goddess*. I found myself in much the same sort of fantastic wonderland as when reading Dirac's *Principles of Quantum Mechanics* a few years ago: in both I encountered a wholly compelling argument from wholly unacceptable premises.

I have been busy re-typing my *Notes on Dhamma* for printing. There are a few additions—notably a Pali-English Glossary and Translations of quoted Sutta passages, which will make the book accessible to those who don't know Pali. But will anyone care to publish it? I don't think anyone would describe the *Notes* as a 'popular' work: in the first place because it is specialized and assumes in the reader some acquaintance (or at least a willingness to become acquainted) with the Suttas on the one hand and with modern philosophical ideas on the other; and in the second place because it is openly hostile to the disengaged critical attitude of the scholar, and so is hardly likely to be popular amongst the pundits, at least if they are no more than that. (In my own way, I am just as much 'engaged' as Graves is in his; and I am at one with him in his scathing remarks in the *Goddess* about scholars, having also myself had experience of the conspiracy of silence with which they habitually greet the unfamiliar or the unorthodox. No doubt you will recall Samuel Butler with his professors at the Colleges of Unreason:

> It seemed to be counted the perfection of scholarship and good breeding among them not to have—much less to express—an opinion on any subject on which it might prove later that they had been mistaken. [*Erewhon*, Ch. 22]

'The scholars' says Graves [p. 21] 'can be counted upon to refrain from any comment whatsoever.')[a]

So then, assuming that there are people in England (there are, certainly, a few in Germany and perhaps France), neither stuffy scholars nor yet silly sheep, who might read the *Notes*, what is needed is a publisher who is prepared to accept a work that is both unpopular (learned) and unpopular (unorthodox). My first thought was the Oxford University Press, who certainly publish learned books, and occasionally on Buddhism. In view of the proposal to have a Chair of the Buddhist Studies at the Oxford perhaps the O.U.P. might be interested (how close is the connexion between the O.U.P. and the University?). But is the *Notes* respectable enough? I have sprinkled it with references to reputable philosophers, but I can't be sure

---

**a.** The real trouble is not the mere difference of opinion, as between one scholar and another, but the fact that Graves (like myself) refuses to treat his subject as *dead*. A scholar only feels secure if he is sure that the subject of his study is not one day going to get up and look him between the eyes; and nothing could be in worse taste than a suggestion that anything more is required of him than a chaste rational disinterestedness. Both the Buddha and the White Goddess, it is felt, have been safely dead these two thousand years and more, and the professors of these subjects congratulate themselves on having chosen such admirably extinct fields of study. (Quite the last thing that a professor of Buddhism would dream of doing is to profess Buddhism—*that* is left to mere amateurs like myself.) But what happens? Here comes Graves and myself shouting out one, that you cannot know the Goddess unless you worship her—and in the flesh, to boot (or, should I say, to buskin?)—, and, the other, that you cannot understand the Buddha unless you practise his teaching—in the jungle, preferably, and barefoot. If I have my way, these comfortable scholars will have to exchange the fleshpots of Oxford for the almsbowl of India; and if Graves has his, their dutiful wives will become Bassarids, dancing naked with Dionysian fury on Boar's Hill, and tearing the Vice-Chancellor to pieces and devouring him raw at the summer solstice. And that would never do, would it?

that the cloven hoof is not still showing through this disguise. (Take Zaehner, for example. He has his own ideas about Pali Buddhism, holding, in spite of the Pali Buddhists, that it can be included under the general heading of 'Mysticism'. Is he, or is he not, one of those who, according to Samuel Butler, 'devote themselves to the avoidance of every opinion with which they are not perfectly familiar, and regard their own brains as a sort of sanctuary, to which, if an opinion has once resorted, none other is to attack it'? Would he or his colleagues approve of publishing the *Notes*?)

But perhaps it would be a waste of time to try and get such a book published in England—it is, as Graves said about his *White Goddess*, 'a very difficult book, as well as a very queer one, to be avoided by anyone with a distracted, tired, or rigidly scientific mind.' (p. 9) Besides, I have never heard the book criticized, and it may be, for all I know, a bad book (I mean as regards form and style and so on: I myself am prepared to answer for the content—except, perhaps, for the last part, which is my own speculative effort, and for which I can cite neither chapter nor verse in support). I am certainly more than half inclined to make no effort to get it published, particularly if it is going to encounter difficulties. (I think I told you earlier that both the P.T.S. and the Buddhist Society have been sent copies of the cyclostyled edition of the *Notes* and have 'refrained from any comment whatsoever.' It is hardly likely, though for different reasons, that they will have approved of the book.)

I hope that your leave is passing pleasantly for you—that is, I do not hope that it is passing, but that it is pleasant in its passing: whether I hope or do not hope, it will pass, alas! like all good things, save one. But that one thing—again alas!—is not to be had simply by wishing.

> *Jātijarāmaraṇadhammānam āvuso sattānaṃ evaṃ icchā uppajjati: Aho vata mayaṃ na jātijarāmaraṇadhammā assāma, na ca vata no jātijarāmaraṇaṃ āgaccheyyā ti. Na kho pan'etaṃ icchāya pattabbaṃ; idaṃ pi yaṃ p'icchaṃ na labbhati, taṃ pi dukkhaṃ.* (D.22/ii,307)
>
> In creatures subject to birth, ageing, and death, friends, there arises such a wish as 'O that we were not subject to birth, ageing, and death! O that birth, ageing, and death might not come nigh us!' But that is not to be attained by wishing; and in this, too, not to get what one wishes is to suffer.

With all best wishes, including this (that is, if you would wish it for yourself).[1]

P.S. Now that you are in Europe, I am tempted to wonder whether Camus' *La Peste* [*The Plague*] is still in print. One of the characters in it remarks:

> *Peut-on être saint sans Dieu, c'est le seul problème concret que je connaisse aujourd'hui.*
>
> Is it possible to be a saint without a God, that is the only concrete problem I know at the present time.

We may, no doubt, take this as the *cri de coeur*[2] of a Europe that has lost its faith; and I think perhaps that the Buddha might give the unexpected reply '*Ce n'est que sans Dieu qu'on peut être un saint*'.[3] But the book is not of any importance to me, and I should prefer that you did not go out of your way if there is the slightest difficulty.

**[L. 142]** **2 November 1964**

It is extremely good of you to think of taking this trouble about the *Notes on Dhamma*. I am glad to discover (quite apart from the question of publication) that you considered the *Notes* were (or might be) of sufficient interest to take the book with you on your leave. (Actually, I did not send it to you with any specific idea that it should be put in the library, but simply in the hope that it might find at least one interested reader—which perhaps it has done. But what have you made of it? There is the difficulty about Pali, and a lot of background knowledge is taken for granted; and, besides, I tend rather to condense my thought. One reader, who knows Pali, read the first Note five times before grasping the argument. Is this excessive?). On comparing the cyclostyled version with my latest typescript, I find that as well as the addition of a Glossary and Translations the actual text has grown by about 8000 words, mostly on general philosophical points, and that the whole book is now 47,000 words. It is decidedly more substantial now. The increase in the text, I may say, has been due in part to books on loan from you. I am always glad to find possible points of contact between the Suttas and Western philosophy, since a first reading of the texts—particularly in the light of the traditional interpretation—seems to suggest that there are none. But this is perhaps due in some measure to the particularly futile stuff turned out of recent times in British philosophy—I am thinking of the logical positivists and the linguistic analysts—which really has singularly little connexion with the business of existing as a human being. (The English, I think, in general don't like to inquire too closely into the question of existence—even in present fiction it seems to be taken for granted, the emphasis being always towards 'a quickened sympathy in personal relations.'[a] But perhaps my reading is too limited.) In any case, by way of contrast to the atmosphere of current British philosophy[b] here is the opening passage of Jean Grenier's book *Absolu et Choix* (p. 3):

> *We do not belong to the world*: that is the first thought which sets philosophy in motion. Not *belonging* to the world and yet in the world, living, happy to live, acting, happy to act. It is not that the world seems bad to us, but that it seems *alien*. Pessimism is not necessarily the starting point of philosophical reflection, and it is not always when considering evil, old age, and death that we start asking ourselves the questions which are most important for us. It is a more general feeling, a feeling of estrangement. Pursued to its very end, this feeling sometimes becomes not only the source but also the goal of philosophy: *to exist*.

Grenier goes on to say:

> The philosophical state is a state of breaking with the world, in contrast to the state of communion where live the child, and the man who innocently enjoys his senses.

But is the philosopher, then, guilty? You will remember that Joseph K. in Kafka's *Trial* wakes up one fine morning to find that a serious charge has been brought against him. He is charged with guilt. But what is he said to be guilty of? That we are not told—or rather, since Joseph K. himself makes no effort to find out but devotes his energies to defending himself, we gather that he is guilty of *guilt*. And what does this mean? Simply that he has come to *know* that he *exists* ('innocence' is also spelt 'ignorance'), and

---

**a.** Not necessarily a bad thing—sensibility is not taught in English schools, and we could do with more of it (how often have I not, abroad, felt hot with shame at my own boorishness!). But sensibility is not the answer—witness Chamfort: '*Quand on a été bien tourmenté, bien fatigué par sa propre sensibilité on s'aperśoit qu'il faut vivre au jour le jour, oublier beaucoup, enfin* éponger la vie *ā mesure qu'elle s'écoule.*'[1]

**b.** And also by way of comment on Toynbee's view that the Buddha's going forth from home into the homelessness was a direct consequence of the widespread social unrest of his time—which Toynbee has *deduced* from the Buddha's going into homelessness (or literally, exile) and then used to account for it.

that he finds himself faced with the pressing need to justify his existence.

In the end he fails; but he comes to recognize that his existence is unjustifiable and accepts his sentence with equanimity (actually, in recognizing his guilt, he condemns himself to die to immediacy in the world—he is *dépaysé*, an exile). So then, the philosopher *is* guilty, guilty of self-knowledge, of ravishing himself (Adam's fall comes with his knowledge of good and evil, when he knows his wife Eve—and you may recall Durrell's Clea wanting to be rid of her 'blasted virginity', to become a mature artist).

But, this being the case, is not the acquisition of 'knowledge' a pure loss, being a fall from innocence into guilt? That will depend. Kierkegaard speaks of the *acquired* virgin purity of ethical passion, compared with which the purity of childhood is but an amiable joke; and knowledge of his crime of existing can put this within the philosopher's reach (that is, if he will persist—but see the *Notes*, KAMMA). Kierkegaard is harder on the artist, remarking that it is a commoner practice than is generally supposed to sell one's soul to the devil for the sake of producing masterpieces (Marlowe knew all about that!). But the artist, though guilty of self-knowledge, is still something of a juvenile delinquent.

**[L. 143]** **19 November 1964**

The English publisher's attitude[1] is, of course, quite normal. A publishing house, like any other association of businessmen, exists for the mutual benefit of its members, not for the purpose of edifying people; and we cannot expect that an exception will be made to the general principle of Business First. Even if he should personally like the book, he cannot accept it if its publication will not be to the material advantage of his colleagues. It is unfortunate, no doubt, that I should have hit upon such a dated subject as Buddhism to write about. But what would you? It seems that I must have got on the wrong boat some fifteen or twenty years ago and have been exploring a backwater ever since and now I find myself unable to write about anything more progressive. It is true, of course, that I have recently become unexpectedly well equipped (my health is just the same, thank you for your kind wishes) to make investigations in quite a different field of activity, still fashionable; but the subject seems to have been adequately covered—that appears to be the right word[a]—by people before me, and I

**a.** There are others, e.g. (a supposed *Daily Mirror* headline):
UNDERGRADS PROBE SEX SENSATION.

do not feel I really have the talent to write another Kāma Sūtra. (It is quite possible, you know, that people might be more profoundly shocked by the *Notes* than by the Kāma Sūtra. The Kāma Sūtra—which I have never read—suggests only that we should abandon morality; the *Notes* suggest that we should abandon humanity.)

Certainly, people have to make money to live; and just because I have been fortunate enough never to have been in need of it (least of all, perhaps, now that I don't have any) there is no occasion for me to give myself airs. But, beyond a certain point, devotion to money becomes scandalous ('Money is lovely, like roses'), and we finish up with the dying Rimbaud: '*Que je suis malheureux, que je suis donc malheureux...et j'ai de l'argent sur moi*[b] *que je ne puis même passurveiller!*'[2]

Ven. S. who has just came here tells me—it is his *leitmotiv*—that nobody in Europe now thinks of anything but money, and some firms (notably the pharmaceuticals) make so much of it that they don't know what to do with it all. He himself has had a letter from his people urging him to return, on the grounds that he will never make money by being a Buddhist monk. (Evidently they are not very well informed about the present state of the monkhood in Ceylon.)

The late Ven. Soma Thera aspired to poetry; here is a translation of his from the Sanskrit (the second line might be improved, but the last two make their effect):

In him who ever and again
Reflects on death's hard hand of pain
The drive for gross material gain
Grows limp as hide soaked through with rain.

The Ven. Soma was a man of moods and enthusiasms. On one occasion, quoting a Sutta passage as his authority, he violently denounced all book-learning. Here is the Ven. Ñāṇamoli Thera's comment:

Lowly stoic Epicteatise
Never wrote a single treatise:
The utterances of the man
Were taken down by Arrian.
Imperial Mark Aureliorse,
His bibliophobia was worse:

**b.** Eight kilos of gold!

He wrote a book himself instead
When 'Throw away your books!' he said.

I have added a couple of pages to NIBBĀNA. The Suttas define *nibbāna* as 'destruction of lust, hate and delusion.' But the Visuddhimagga qualifies this by saying that it is 'not merely destruction,' which introduces chaos. If *nibbāna* is not merely destruction of lust, hate and delusion, then it must be something else besides. But what? Why, practically anything you like to imagine. It is, if you so wish, destruction of lust, hate and delusion *and* ten thousand a year and a seductive mistress. But perhaps you may care to look at the whole new typescript now that the translations have been appended and the text enlarged.

**[L. 144]** **3 December 1964**

Clearly you are one of those people who manage to feel and perhaps to recreate the atmosphere and associations belonging to buildings and places, and so, when you visit these places, you are able almost to take yourself back in time in a bodily way. Whatever little capacity I had in this direction (I used to enjoy travelling and visiting places) was blighted by my years in the wartime Army where, having abused my brain all day (I was in Intelligence—of which, as Huxley has pointed out, there are three kinds: human, animal, and military), I only sought (with indifferent success—my education was against me) to abuse my body all the night. Anyway, it simplified my world and brought out the issues clearly.

But now, even though there are the places of significance for the Buddhist in India, and the Buddha himself spoke in praise of visiting them (the Birthplace, the place of Enlightenment—strictly this is a mistranslation, it should be Awakening—, of the First Sermon, of the Final Passing Away), I have never felt either the need or inclination to visit them.

How irritating the Buddha's Teaching must sometimes appear! Here you are, having been to an *ashram* and learned or realized the Great Truth that 'reality is consciousness—not consciousness OF, not knowledge, but consciousness,'—and now here am I with the distressing duty of having to inform you that the Buddha says (I simplify slightly) 'Without matter, without feeling, without perception, without determinations (intention, volition), that there should be consciousness—such a thing is not possible.' (cf. Khandha Saṃy.—S.xxii.51/iii,53) (An exception is made for the highest spheres of consciousness, where matter is transcended by a process of successive abstraction, but all the other items are still present.) I am sorry about it, but there it is—but then I am not obliging you to accept the Suttas.[a] (Hindus have the habit of saying that all religions are One, with particular reference to the Buddha's Teaching. Since the Buddha was a Hindu, they say, his Teaching must be Hinduism. Besides, they say he was the eighth avatar of Vishnu. Buddhists, on the other hand, do *not* say that all religions are One—thus demonstrating at least one difference from Hinduism.)

Perhaps this very point will throw light on my preference (within due limits) for the existentialist philosophers: Husserl maintained, and Sartre confirms, that all consciousness is consciousness *of* something, e.g.

> Consciousness is consciousness *of* something. This means that transcendence is the constitutive structure of consciousness; that is, that consciousness is born *supported* by a being which is not itself. (*B&N*, p. lxi)

And from this, again, you will see why I am essentially anti-mystical. And this explains why, from the Western point-of-view I am not a religious person. There seems to be a paradox in the fact that my tastes—literary and other—are more secular and less spiritual than yours.

I have just received a lengthy and detailed criticism from a German law student who clearly has just as good an acquaintance with the texts as I have—even better, perhaps, since he quotes grammar at me (in Latin, too!)—and it is obvious that he has not understood one word of it. It is quite clear that the *Notes* can never be a popular work (except by mistake), but it is perhaps more difficult than you or I quite realize. Possibly it might be of interest to professional or semi-professional philosophers, but, to judge from *Mind*,[1] there don't seem to be any in England. Perhaps we should do better to discuss the matter personally before taking any further step. Why should the book be published at all? I don't quite know.

P.S. You say in your letter that it is hard to understand the Buddha's teaching in view of the flux of all sense-objects. Quite so—but contrary to common opinion the Buddha did *not* teach that there is a *flux*. I have enlarged on this in the new version of the *Notes*, and an alternative view is given in *FS*.

---

**a.** I don't in the least doubt that you were benefitted by your visit to the *ashram*; and it may be that (in a manner of speaking) this is the Truth for you. But the question is, ultimately, how far it takes you. And the Buddha says that it does not take you (or anyone) to extinction. But perhaps that is not what you wanted.

**[L. 145]** **8 December 1964**

You speak of 'feeling the incarnating of God in ourselves so that we realize that we are of the very stuff of God,' and then you go on to say 'Oh, I know how you will react to any such statement....' Well, how do I react? I say that to take what we call 'experience of God' as evidence of the existence of God is a mistake. But there are mistakes and mistakes, and it is perhaps worth looking a little more closely.

Observe, to begin with, that I do not *deny* that we may have 'experience of God'. It is a fashionable blunder (as I remark in the *Notes*) to hail modern science as vindicating the Buddha's Teaching. The assumption is, that the Buddha solved the whole question of transcendence (self) or Transcendence (God) by anticipating the impersonal attitude of the scientist. But this is rubbish, and it simply makes the Dhamma a kind of logical positivism and myself a kind of Bertrand Russell in Robes. No—numinous experience is just as real as sex or romantic love or aesthetic experience; and the question that must be answered is whether these things are to be taken at their face value as evidence of some kind of transcendent reality or whether the eternity they point to is a delusion.

Certainly in sexual love we do seem to experience eternity; and this is often taken as religiously significant (by the Hindus, for example, with their Shivalingam, not to mention their temple eroticism). But what a derisory eternity it is that lasts for a few seconds or minutes and then leaves us wondering what all the fuss was about! As the rude rhyme puts it bluntly:

> Cold as the hair on a polar bear's bum,
> Cold as the love of a man when he's come.

As an advertisement for eternity, sex is a joke. In romantic love, true, we manage to live in a kind of eternity for months and perhaps years: every love-affair lasts forever—while it lasts. But, all the same, when Jouhandeau (quoted by Palinurus in *The Unquiet Grave*) asks '*Quand l'univers considére avec indifférence l'être que nous aimons, qui est dans la vérité?*',[1] we have to answer '*l'univers*'. Our past loves can be absolutely dead, even when we meet the loved one again (Darley and Justine in *Clea*, for example), and it is usually only in favour of the present beloved (if any) that we dissent from the universe's verdict. And so with aesthetic enjoyment. The transcendental sense of Mozart's G Minor Quintet, his Adagio and Fugue, the late Beethoven, Bartok's quartets, Stravinsky's Octet for Wind Instruments, so evident to me before I joined the army—where was it when I got back home after the war?

When we come to more specifically numinous experience the situation is more delicate. In its grosser forms, certainly—awe in a cathedral, panic fear in a thunderstorm—it can come and go, and we oscillate between eternity and transience; and even if transience can be eternal, eternity cannot possibly be transient. Palinurus is doubtful and suggests a compromise:

> Man exudes a sense of reverence like a secretion. He smears it over everything, and so renders places like Stonehenge or the lake of Nemi (Diana's mirror) particularly sacred,—yet the one can become a petrol-station, and the other be drained by a megalomaniac; no grove is too holy to be cut down. When we are tired or ill, our capacity for reverence, like our capacity for seeing the difficulty of things, increases till it becomes a kind of compulsion-neurosis or superstition; therefore it would seem that the mythoclasts are always right,—until we know what these mother-haters, these savagers of the breast, will worship in their turn. Lenin, the father figure mummified, replaces the Byzantine Christ. Reverence and destruction alternate; therefore the wise two-faced man will reverence destructively, like Alaric or Akbar, and, like Gibbon, Renan, Gide, reverently destroy. (p. 87)

But a more subtle approach is possible. For Karl Jaspers the world has a three-fold aspect. There is 'being-there', 'being-oneself', and 'being-in-itself'. The first is everything that can be an object for me, thoughts as well as things. The second is personal existence, or *myself*. This transcends the first, and can be apprehended, though not wholly, in an act of self-reflexion. The third transcends the second as the second transcends the first, and is Transcendental Being. This is the ultimate sense or meaning of the other two, but it can never be directly apprehended. All we can do is to approach it. And Jaspers here develops his doctrine of 'ciphers': a cipher (which is quite unintelligible to abstract reason) is an experience that is apprehended as incomplete—but only as pointing to a reality that is 'present but hidden'.

Although Jaspers distinguishes various kinds of ciphers, the important point is that *anything* can be read as a cipher if we care to make the effort of 'existential contemplation'. Since anything can indicate Transcendental Being, there is at least the theoretical possibility that one might pass the whole of one's life reading one's every experience as a cipher, and in such a case we should perpetually be approaching Eternity. This attitude is less easy to dismiss, and Jaspers has taken care to tie up all the loose ends with an ultimate cipher. Although we can perpetually approach Being, we can never actually reach it, and this inevitable failure and frustration of our efforts may be a temptation to despair. This temptation to despair, says Jaspers, should spur us on to 'assume' the cipher of frustration. 'The non-being which appears in the frustration of all our efforts to achieve a direct understanding of Being is now seen to be an indirect revelation of the presence of Transcendence.' (I quote from Grimsley's book, p. 188.) But it must be emphasized that the assumption of this cipher is an act of faith in Transcendence and without such faith we can never make the necessary jump—indeed, they are really one and the same thing.

So, then, Jaspers leads us to the point where everything indicates Transcendence and nothing reveals it, and thence to despair; and despair is an invitation to jump to the conclusion that Transcendence (or Eternity, or God) exists. But different attitudes are possible in the face of this invitation. The theists, of course, accept the invitation with many thanks. Jaspers himself is inclined to accept it in spite of the difficulties involved. Lessing declined the invitation, perhaps regretfully ('*Das, das ist der garstige breite Graben, über den ich nicht kommen kann, so oft und ernstlich ich auch den Sprung versucht habe.*')[2] Sartre explains away the invitation, too easily dismissing what is a real problem. Camus accepts the invitation to Transcendence in a contrary sense—as evidence of the non-existence of God. For him it is a matter of '*la protestation lucide de l'homme jeté sur une terre dont la splendeur et la lumière lui parlent sans relâche d'un dieu qui n'existe pas*'.[3]

And what, then, about the Buddha's Teaching—how does it tell us to deal with the question whether or not God exists? The first thing is to refuse to be bullied into giving a categorical answer, yes or no, to such a treacherous question. The second thing is to see that the answer to this question will depend on the answer to a more immediate question: 'Do I myself exist? Is my self in fact eternal, or is it something that perishes with the body?' And it is here that the difficulties begin. The Buddha says that the world is divided, for the most part, between the Yeas and the Nays, between the eternalists and the annihilationists, and that they are forever at each other's throats. But these are two extremes, and the Buddha's Teaching goes in between.

So long as we have experience of our selves, the question 'Does my self exist?' will thrust itself upon us: if we answer in the affirmative we shall tend to affirm the existence of God, and if we answer in the negative we shall deny the existence of God. But what if we have ceased to have experience of ourselves? (I do not mean reflexive experience as such, but experience of our selves as an ego or a person. This is a hard distinction to see, but I must refer you to the *Notes* for further discussion.) If this were to happen—and it is the specific aim of the Buddha's Teaching (and of no other teaching) to arrange for it to happen—then not only should we stop questioning about our existence and the existence of God, but the whole of Jaspers' system, and with it the doctrine of ciphers, would collapse.[a] And what room, then, for despair? 'For the *arahat*' (I quote from the *Notes*) 'all sense of personality or selfhood has subsided, and with it has gone all possibility of numinous experience; and *a fortiori* the mystical intuition of a trans-personal Spirit or Absolute Self—of a Purpose or an Essence or a Oneness or what have you—can no longer arise.'

**[L. 146] 25 December 1964**

The philosophical works with me will be enough to occupy me for the time being. Actually, with a well-written bit of philosophy I probably take as much time to read it as I suppose you do with a good volume of poetry. And also, the satisfaction that philosophy can provide (when the philosopher has a valid thought—i.e., a thought that one has oneself thought, or might have thought—and succeeds in communicating) is surely not less than what an experienced reader of poetry derives from a good poet, even if the atmosphere is not quite the same. For example, the passage from the Grenier on being *dépaysé* (which you yourself recognize as part of your own experience) can be read repeatedly, each time with the same, or increased, resonance. And an opening passage such as this (from

**a.** Jaspers' scheme, as I said before, consists of the world of objects (thoughts and things), which is 'being-there', and, transcending that, the world of self, which is 'being-oneself', and, transcending that, the world of Being, which is 'being-in-itself'. You will see that when, as is the case with the *arahat*, all transcendence (in this sense) has ceased, all that is left is the world of objects (so long, at least, as the *arahat* continues to live). For the Buddha, in other words, reality—in the sense of what is left after ignorance (*avijjā*) has been removed—consists, precisely, of thoughts and things. This is diametrically opposed to the Hindu teaching of *māyā*, which holds that the world of thoughts and things is what is unreal or illusory and that the task is to transcend this and attain the ultimate reality of pure Being (or pure objectless Consciousness). See, on this question, an earlier letter of mine (containing a Pali verse starting *Saṅkapparāgo purisassa kāmo*). Does this make it clearer why the empirical world is more real and substantial in the Buddha's Teaching than in the Hindu? The Buddha says (approximately) that the self is illusory and the empirical world is real, whereas with the Vedantists it is the other way round.

Heidegger), despite—or perhaps because of—its apparent simplicity, at once reveals endless unsuspected perspectives to the mind, and, for me at least, is extraordinarily stimulating:

> Why, in a general way, is there something rather than nothing? That is the question. And probably it is not just any question. Why is there something rather than nothing? It is, manifestly, the first of all questions...[a]

And notice the subtle nuance of the word 'probably'—'probably it is not just any question'—which leaves us the tantalizing possibility, the bare possibility, that there *may* be other questions—as yet unsuspected—that take precedence over this one.

This last paragraph is rather by way of apologizing for having returned the four volumes of Yeats quite so quickly. I have a feeling that you would like me to like Yeats, and I feel a little guilty that I am unable to do very much about it. In earlier days, perhaps, I might have convinced myself that I *ought* to like him, and with persistence I might even have to some extent succeeded. But now it is too late. He is pleasing, certainly; but if one is no more than *pleased* by a poet, then it is quite obvious that one is incapable of reading poetry.

Graham Greene, I allow, is a first-class writer—at least he would be if he were a little less convinced of the infallibility of Catholic dogma. If one believes in this dogma (as he evidently does), no doubt all the tensions and anguishes that his characters go through will seem valid enough; but if one does not happen to share these beliefs, one comes away from his books with the feeling that he is making things unnecessarily difficult for everybody. He is quite right to insist that more is at stake in our worldly affairs than meets the eye—I know this myself, and I am satisfied that I have (from the Suttas) some idea of what is at stake (beyond this life, I mean)—; but it weakens one's case, not strengthens it, to be dogmatic about it, no matter whether that dogma is right or wrong. There is more eschatological dogma in one of Graham Greene's novels than there is in my *Notes on Dhamma.*

Isherwood is very entertaining, and his inconsequential mole attitude to life contrasts astonishingly with Rosamond Lehmann's feminine view. Do they *always* take us seriously? I suppose so. Michael Ayrton's diaphragms are magnificent; so is the head at high velocity.

---

**a.** It is probably a bogus question.

**[L. 147]** **1 January 1965**

A pleasant surprise to get your letter! But how hard it is to communicate! Kierkegaard held that direct communication was impossible, and said (with Dostoievsky) that the surest way of being silent is to talk. I have been reading your letter and trying to grasp its meaning (the words and sentences, of course, are quite clear)—trying, in other words, to get the feel of it, to seize upon its Archimidean point. Instead of saying very much myself by way of reply (though I shall say something), I thought rather of sending you a few translations from the Suttas about food,[1] ranging, as you may think, from the warmly human to the coldly inhuman, from the simple to the abstruse (and yet the warmest [2] and the coldest [4] are from the same Sutta!). Perhaps you do not know that the Buddha has summed up the entire Dhamma in the single phrase: *Sabbe sattā āhāraṭṭhitikā*, All creatures are stayed (supported, maintained) by food (D.33/iii,211, etc.).

Your reference to the autonomous mood in the Irish grammar can perhaps be turned to account, particularly since you yourself go on to suggest that a linguistic approach to the deeper questions of life might be rewarding. There is, in fact, a Sutta in which all the five aggregates (the factors present in all experience) are defined in this very way.

> Matter is what *matters*;[a] feeling is what *feels*; perception is what *perceives*; determinations (or intentions) are what *determine* (or *intend*); consciousness is what *cognizes*. (*Khandha Saṃy.*—S.xxii.79/iii,86-7)

(Refer, later, to *Notes on Dhamma*, VIÑÑĀṆA & SAÑÑĀ.)

The ordinary person (the *puthujjana* or 'commoner') thinks, '*I* feel; *I* perceive; *I* determine; *I* cognize', and he takes this 'I' to refer to some kind of timeless and changeless ego or 'self'. But the *arahat* has completely got rid of the ego-illusion (the conceit or concept 'I am'), and, when he reflects, thinks quite simply, '*Feeling* feels; *perception* perceives; *determinations* determine; *consciousness* cognizes'. Perhaps this may help you to see how it is that when desire (craving) ceases altogether 'the various things just stand there in the world'. Obviously they cannot 'just stand there in the world' unless they are felt, perceived, determined and cognized (Berkeley's *esse est percipi*[2] is, in principle, quite correct); but for the living *arahat* the

---

**a.** I.e. is afflicted or breaks up—the phrase *ruppatī ti rūpaṃ* is untranslatable into English.

question '*Who* feels, perceives, determines, cognizes, the various things?' no longer arises—the various things are felt by feeling, perceived by perception, determined by determinations, and cognized by consciousness; in other words, they are 'there in the world' *autonomously* (actually they always were, but the *puthujjana* does not see this since he takes himself for granted). With the breaking up of the *arahat*'s body (his death) all this ceases. (For other people, of course, these things continue unless and until they in their turn, having become *arahats*, arrive at the end of their final existence.)

A further point. When an *arahat* is *talking* to people he will normally follow linguistic usage and speak of 'I' and 'me' and 'mine' and so on; but he no longer (mis)understands these words as does the *puthujjana* (see Additional Texts 91).

It would be unfair on my part to allow myself to suggest, even by implication, that the Buddha's Teaching is easier to understand than it is; and still more unfair to lead you to suppose that I consider myself capable of benefiting you in any decisive manner. All I can do is to plant a few signposts in your way, in the hope, perhaps, of giving a certain orientation to your thinking that might stand you in good stead later on.

Thank you kindly for your offer of theatre tickets, but our rules rule out visits to theatres, however much we might like to attend a performance.

P.S. A few weeks ago you queried about whether *Notes on Dhamma* had reached Mr. Van Zeyst and Mr. L., since they had not acknowledged receipt. But the reason for their silence is almost certainly something quite different. The *Notes* are almost exclusively concerned with elucidation of the matters referred to by the Buddha in the last of the translated passages (No. 4). Neither Mr. Van Zeyst nor Mr. L. (though not quite for the same reason) has the slightest idea of what the Buddha is talking about in such passages as these; and for them, consequently, the *Notes* are more of an embarrassment than anything else. In the same way, the professors at Peradeniya who are supposed to know something about the Dhamma, have kept silent.) Do you know that in Prof. Jayatilleke's book, *The Buddhist Theory of Knowledge* (which you have kindly sent me) the words '*sotāpanna*' (stream-enterer) and '*arahat*' are not to be found in the index? Nor have I met with them in the text. This is simply *Hamlet* without the Prince of Denmark.

**[L. 148]** **22 January 1965**

Two Englishmen—Robin Maugham and his friend[1]—visited me. I rather fear that they are proposing to write me up and present me in print and picture to the British Public—let us hope not too grotesquely. I dislike this sort of thing; but also I dislike being disagreeable to people—and, besides, I am fond of talking. The British Public wants romance—and I am *not* a romantic figure, and have no desire to be portrayed as one. 'The World Well Lost for Love' is something the public can understand, and they can perhaps also understand 'The World Well Lost for Love of God'; but what they can *not* understand is 'The World Well Lost' *tout court*.

**[L. 149]** **7 February 1965**

How clever of you not to have come for me today! We have just had—between six and seven this evening—our heaviest rain for twelve months, an unexpected thunderstorm; and I have filled my cisterns and taken a much-needed bath. How irritating if I had left here a few hours before the rain, leaving the cisterns with an aching void in them! We needed this, even if only to save the cattle and the wild animals. Actually, your letter arrived yesterday, just in time to stop me from making needless preparation for departure. So your postponement has been fortunate, and no trouble at all.

Thank you for the *Hibbert Journals*—in general suffocatingly parochial, but one or two things of interest. I shall not attempt to reply in detail to your letter (it will be easier to discuss it when we meet), but it seems worthwhile sending you a passage from Jean Grenier (*Absolu et Choix*, pp. 69-71) on the very question that you raise about a personal God as against an impersonal (neuter) Brahman. Here is the passage:

> Consider the metaphysicians of the Vedanta. The view that before the Absolute *everything is indifferent* has not prevented them from acting *as if the Absolute were not indifferent* before anything whatsoever. In the speculative sphere this is the transition from the apophantic theology *[théologie apophantique]* to the prophetic theology: and so Śaṅkara, while avoiding any definition of the Absolute, designating it only by negations (*neti, neti*), yet admits that one can refer to it using 'indirect expressions' (*lakṣana*), which 'aim at making known those things of which our mind, being finite, has no direct measure, because they are, at least, in a certain respect, infinite, and as such escape all

generic commonality.'[a] This indirect expression approximates *analogy*. Thus one can in some measure know the Absolute. And in his commentary on the 'No, no…' which defines this Absolute according to the Bṛhad-Āraṇyaka Upaniṣad, Rāmānuja claims that this formula means 'Not thus, not thus', and that this 'No' does not deny that the Brahman is endowed with distinctive attributes, but only that it is not circumscribed by the attributes mentioned earlier.[b] For Rāmānuja, who admits 'the natural variety of Being and beings', minds and bodies exist as modes of the absolute substance. His monism is thus quite attenuated compared to that of Śaṅkara, since he allows both positive *attributes* and *modes* of the Absolute. Even Śaṅkara distinguishes between the unconditioned Brahman and the conditioned Brahman, between the impersonal Absolute and the personal God. How is that possible? It is because Brahman is transpersonal rather than impersonal, and the *atman* that serves it as a means of access is rather a self than a non-I, as Lacomte perceptively notes.[c] We know how the cult of the personal God (Iśvara) triumphed more and more in India thanks to this transition, and also the piety accompanying every cult devoted to a god, whereas the importance of knowledge concerning the divinity declined. More and more, the Absolute approaches the individual.

The Absolute is named, it is God, it has negative and even positive attributes; finally it can even enter into relations with the world, whether it be the supreme goal towards which the latter tends, or its Providence, or its Creator. The last stage is attained when God takes on a human form: the Incarnation actualizes the fusion between what is essentially composite and what is essentially one.

The philosophers have proceeded in the same way, and each time they wanted to take hold of the real, their most abstract metaphysics evolved into a specific ethics. The cosmic thesis is thus *practically* untenable. Once granted, this truth raises the question of the suitable point at which to stop in the slide from the Absolute to the individual. Now, everyone selects his own stopping-point, and that is the whole history of theologies and philosophies. For speculation, in its beginnings, almost everything is a matter of indifference; at the extreme limit of the practical almost nothing is. This transition is inevitable.

---

**a.** Lacomte, *L'Absolu selon le Vedanta*, p. 80.
**b.** *Ibid.* p. 299
**c.** *Ibid.* p. 217

We seem to gather from this that God as an utterly impersonal Absolute is no more than a metaphysical postulate, and in practice quite unthinkable (i.e., thinkable—to be a little Irish—only on paper). The concept of an impersonal God, in other words, in so far as it is actually conceivable, is always, ultimately, an extension of, or an abstraction from, the concept of a personal God; and thus *beyond* only in the sense that Būndala is beyond Hambantota. Utter impersonality, certainly, is attainable—it is the *arahat*—but one would scarcely think of calling him God (an equivocal concept, anyway; unless—to recall Bradley's comment on Herbert Spencer—it is merely the name we give to something when we don't know what the devil else to call it). And the reason is clear: the *arahat*, though no longer in any way *personal*, continues (until death) to be *individual*—he walks and talks, that is to say, just like any ordinary man (at least to the vulgar eye and ear), and whatever God might be, he (or it) is necessarily something manifestly extra-ordinary.

You say that personality is not (as it now seems to you) the highest value conceivable. I agree—*provided* you will let me at once qualify this statement by saying that it is a grotesque understatement: personality is the *lowest* value conceivable, the root of all evil. Of all reprehensible things (says the Buddha) wrong view—and *sakkāyadiṭṭhi*, 'personality-view', is the foundation of all other (ethically) wrong views—is the most reprehensible. But I think I hear you muttering, 'That is not what I meant. That is not it at all.'

## [L. 150] **2 April 1965**

The Claudel[1] appears to be a masterpiece. It is very cleverly written, with an astonishing atmosphere; and I have had to read it rather warily—it is full of emotional pitfalls and (as I told you) my visceral reaction is liable to be almost physically painful. But Claudel's presuppositions are wholly repugnant to me: I can by no means accept the view that a man's love for a woman (or hers for him) is of ethical value—that is, that it can lead him to salvation, which, however we may look at it, must surely be defined as eternal peace of heart. And this is precisely what love is *not*—and least of all when (as in Claudel) the woman insists upon keeping herself and the man on the rack. *C'est magnifique, mais ce n'est pas la paix.*[2]

If you have the time you might find the Beauvoir worth reading. It is her autobiography, in considerable detail, up to the time she met Sartre (when they were both completing their degrees in philosophy). I was interested enough to read it straight through in a couple of days. How unfeminine (I do not say masculine) is she? I think she is a woman, but she is also a philosopher (but does she do much more than interpret Sartre?), and I do not manage to reconcile the two. But perhaps she is more successful than I am. Would one want (or have wanted—she is fifty-seven, and must be something of a battle-axe) to sleep with her? And would she want it? She wants equal rights for men and women, but how does that work out in bed?

If you have not read it before, Diderot's *Le Neveu de Rameau* (the second *Satire*) is really something of a must, and it is not very long.

I am returning on Monday and shall be there until further notice. The Hermitage, though pleasant enough, gives me neither companionable conversation nor yet the advantages of solitude. But I have been exercising my Italian with a certain Sig. S., who (so I gather) was advised to contact me on account of my 'excellent French.' His arrival, as it happened, was satisfyingly dramatic. He appeared just as I had sat down in a circle of young German monks to discuss certain Dhamma points. He presented me with a letter of introduction that informed me of his identity, and I found myself, to my own astonishment no less than to his (and, I resume, to everybody else's), embarked on a conversation in the purest Tuscan (on his side, anyway—he comes from Florence). But he is rather a *jeune homme rangé* and, apart from telling me that Italian Teddy boys are called *pappagalli*, has left me very much where I was before.

Any news of the *Notes*? If it seems unlikely that anyone is going to publish them, you can return the typescript to me when you have finished with it.

**[L. 151]** **8 May 1965**

> *Deux êtres séparés* [says Simone de Beauvoir] *placés en des situations différentes, s'affrontant dans leur liberté et cherchant l'un à travers l'autre la justification de l'existence,*[a] *vivront toujours une aventure pleine de risques et de promesses.*[1]

Perhaps you will agree with her. I don't altogether disagree myself;[b] but, as

**a.** Cf. Sartre: *Au lieu que, avant d'être aimés...*[2]

**b.** I have to admit, though, that under the pressure of unrelieved satyriasis I rather like the idea of having the girls tied up ready for me—perhaps this will explain certain

you know, I don't regard this question as the important one to decide—in the last analysis it is irrelevant; *la justification de l'existence* is to be found neither *l'un à travers l'autre* nor anywhere else, *except* in bringing it to an end. Anyway, in the teeth of what is evidently the latest enlightened opinion—that chastity is the wickedest of the perversions[c]—the question remains for me purely academic.

I have just been presented with the English translation of Heidegger's *Sein und Zeit* (*Being and Time*). I have long had in mind, vaguely, a reading of Heidegger as 'one of the things I must do before I die'; but hitherto, not knowing German, it has been an unfulfilled ambition. Now, however, I have already made a start on it, but if my ambition is to be fulfilled I must read another three hundred fifty rather tough pages before I swallow the cyanide or reach for the razor.

Actually, it's extremely stimulating. Up to now my knowledge of Heidegger has been derived from short summaries and other writers' comments, and particularly through the refractive medium of Sartre's philosophy, and I am beginning to see that he (H) is a better thinker than I had been led to believe. I accepted Sartre's criticisms of him in good faith,[d] and in several places where I couldn't quite make out what Sartre was talking about I gave him (S) the benefit of the doubt—if Sartre was obscure, that was because I had failed to understand, not because Sartre was mistaken. But now I find that Sartre's criticisms and obscurities arise from (in my view) seriously wrong ideas—where Sartre differs from Heidegger, and it is where he differs from Heidegger that he is obscure, Heidegger is in the right. Anyway, apart from his formidable array of technical terms in 'the Awful German Language'—and not improved by translation—Heidegger is beautifully perspicuous—hardly a philosophical opacity anywhere. But I think I should hardly have found this so had I not first sweated over Sartre. And Sartre still gives you a great deal that you don't get from Heidegger.

I am sending you a book with the snappy little title, *A Study of the Psychological Aspects of Mrs Willett's Mediumship, and of the Statements of the Communicators concerning Process* by Gerald William Earl of Balfour,

---

ambiguities in my attitude towards *le deuxième sexe*: a satyr is much too hard pressed to have time to be a feminist.

**c.** Is not the Pill the eucharist of the New Morality?

**d.** In one place (*B&N*, p. 249) Sartre refers to Heidegger's views as '*une sorte de psychologisme empiriocriticiste*'. I don't quite know what this means, but it sounds to me like pretty severe philosophical abuse—almost as bad, when applied to a philosopher, as insinuating that his parents weren't properly married.

P.C., LL.D. The book contains an account of some extremely high quality 'communications' purporting to come from the deceased members of the Society for Psychical Research (Henry Sidgwick, F.W.H. Myers, E. Gurney, S. H. Butcher, A. W. Verrall, William James) and addressed to Oliver Lodge and Gerald Balfour (the author). The book does not discuss the question of survival at all but accepts for the nonce the 'communications' at their face value—i.e. as actually coming from the (late) individuals that they claim to come from—and then, with this assumption, proceeds to discuss how the messages were transmitted and the actual contents of the messages—but the contents of the messages are themselves actually a discussion of how they were transmitted.

Anyway, I found the book of remarkable interest from several points of view; and I thought that you might like to see it. I know that some people find such books (i.e. on mediumistic communications) extremely distasteful, and I shall not press it upon you. In any case it is not to be regarded as an attempt to 'prove re-birth' to you (re-birth, anyway, cannot be *proved* as one 'proves Pythagoras'; whether one accepts—or rejects, as the case may be—the account of some event as 'evidence' for re-birth depends upon one's temperament and one's presuppositions): I merely remark that since, as you know, I accept re-birth as a matter of course, I found no antecedent obstacle opposing my taking part (by way of marginal comments) in the Myers-Gurney-Balfour controversy about the divisibility of the self. But, whether you read the book or not, would it be too much if I were to ask you if you could possibly get the book bound for me? I think it is worth preserving, and it will not last long with only paper cover.

P.S. I see Iris Murdoch has written (1953) a book on Sartre—*Sartre, Romantic Rationalist*, a general survey of his work as a whole. This is simply for the record. (Incidentally, I rather wonder whether the moral of *A Severed Head* does not lie somewhere in the direction of Simone de Beauvoir's ideal. I am thinking particularly of the last scene: having got all the inauthentic characters out of the way—and especially Palmer Anderson, who is obviously a first class shit, inauthentic as hell—Murdoch brings together the only couple who are genuinely concerned to seek justification each in the other, and not without a struggle. Or is this altogether too simple?)

P.P.S. (11 May 1965) My expected visitor (a retired English psychiatrist) has not yet come, so I am tempted to add something. Here is Camus on Heidegger; perhaps it says more about Camus than Heidegger—and also something about me, since I trouble to quote it.

Heidegger considers the human condition coldly and announces that existence is humiliated. The only reality is "anxiety" in the whole chain of being. To the man lost in the world and its diversions this anxiety is a brief, fleeting fear. But if that fear becomes conscious of itself, it becomes anguish, the perpetual climate of the lucid man "in whom existence is concentrated." This professor of philosophy writes without trembling and in the most abstract language in the world that "the finite and limited character of human existence is more primordial than man himself." His interest in Kant extends only to recognizing the restricted character of his "pure Reason." This is to conclude at the end of his analyses that "the world can no longer offer anything to the man filled with anguish." This anxiety seems to him so much more important than all the categories in the world that he thinks and talks only of it. He enumerates its aspects: boredom when the ordinary man strives to quash it in him and benumb it; terror when the mind contemplates death. He too does not separate consciousness from the absurd. The consciousness of death is the call of anxiety and "existence then delivers itself its own summons through the intermediary of consciousness." It is the very voice of anguish and it adjures existence "to return from its loss in the anonymous They." For him, too, one must not sleep, but must keep alert until the consummation. He stands in this absurd world and points out its ephemeral character. He seeks his way amid these ruins. (*Myth*, p. 18)

**[L. 152] 18 May 1965**

The professor, to judge by an article of his that appeared a few years ago, seems to exclude philosophy altogether from Buddhism, and strongly protests against all talk of such things as *nibbāna*, *kamma*, *saṃsāra*, and *magga*. After this there does not seem to be much left.

I enclose a trifle that I wrote in 1957 (to the Ven. Ñāṇamoli) and have just come across.[1] Perhaps it will slightly amuse you, perhaps not. Anyway, now that everybody is dialogging (a combination of 'dialogue' plus 'log-rolling') with everyone else, here is my contribution.

AN UNCERTAIN ENCOUNTER

Were I to meet Professor Heisenberg (a very remote possibility) I imagine the conversation might run something like this.

*Professor Heisenberg* (pontifically): Ignorance is now included amongst the Laws of Science. The behaviour of an electron, for example, involves the Principle of Uncertainty.
*Myself* (incredulously): What? You surely don't mean *objectively*?
*Prof. H.* (a little surprised): Why not? An electron, we discover, is, by nature, uncertain. That is perfectly objective.
*Myself* (with heavy sarcasm): An electron really is uncertain! I suppose you are going to tell me that you can read an electron's mind.
*Prof. H.* (quite unmoved): Of course. How else should we know that it was uncertain?
*Myself* (completely taken aback): Read an electron's mind? How?
*Prof. H.* (expansively): Perfectly simple. The mind, as we all know, is the nervous system; and, as the latest and most scientific authorities assure us, we can always discover the state of the nervous system by observation and study of behaviour patterns. All we have to do, then, is to observe an electron and deduce from its behaviour how its nervous system is; and we have discovered, in fact, that it is indeterminate. We are thus able to say that an electron cannot make up its mind.
*Myself* (fascinated): Yes! Yes! Of course!
*Prof. H.* (with finality): So you see, an electron *is* uncertain, just as we may observe that Schmidt *is* phlegmatic or that Braun *is* choleric or that you, my dear friend, *are*, if I may be permitted to say so, a little psychopathic. And what could be more objective than that?

23 August 1957

**[L. 153]** **20 May 1965**

Thank you for the return of the typescript of the *Notes*. I cannot say that I am much astonished by the opinion that the book would not be attractive to the University publishers. I am faintly amused by the 'expert's' complete failure to perceive what kind of book it is. How can he read my preface and *then* go on to suggest a 'major re-writing in conformity with modern standards of scholarship'? Yes, I know—these people *are* like that. But they do shake one's faith in human nature, don't they? I suppose it's too late to thank for the trouble he has taken—and also for *not* being quite dead from the neck up? Thank to you anyway.

**[L. 154]** **26 June 1965**

Many thanks for your letter. I can't say I am much astonished by Mr. Van Zeyst's reaction, since I already know of his views (as I told you); but I am sorry in a way not to have his criticisms in detail. I suppose they would be on the usual lines—that I am going against the traditional commentaries (but why else should I write the book?). I heard of another adverse comment a few days ago. Ven. S. asked one of the important *paṇḍita mahātheras* of I forget which of the Sinhalese universities whether he had read the *Notes*. Yes, he had read them, but the author had evidently understood nothing of the Dhamma. Why? Because his explanation was not in accordance with the *abhidhamma* method. But on what particular point, for example, was the book wrong? That, it seemed, was not worth discussing. I don't appear to be in much danger of becoming a popular hero—not amongst the Buddhists, anyway.

*Nindanti tuṇhim āsīnaṃ,*
*nindanti bahubhāniṇaṃ*
*mitabhāṇinam pi nindanti*
*n'atthi loke anindito.* (Dh. 227)

You're blamed if you sit quiet,
you're blamed if you say a lot,
you're blamed if you say a little;
there's no one in the world that's not blamed.

On the other hand,

*Na cāhu na ca bhavissati*
*na c'etarahi vijjati,*
*ekantaṃ nindito poso*
*ekantaṃ vā pasaṃsito.* (Dh. 228)

There never was, there will not be,
nor is there now,
a man that's wholly blamed
or wholly praised.

And so I get a few kisses amongst the kicks. A Dr. James W. Gair of Cornell University, Ithaca, New York, is presently (as they say) at Peradeniya doing research on the Sinhalese language. Pursuing his researches in Būndala the other day,[1] he was dragged by the village boys to my *kuṭi* where he introduced himself. He is faintly Anglican (so he told me) and has no particular interest in the Dhamma; but we got talking and I showed him the *Notes.* When he came to the last part, *FS* (the noughts and crosses), he started reading and said, much to my astonishment, 'Ah! This is familiar—we have something like it in Linguistics. Yes, "o o is *one*, and o x is *two*," I follow that. I'm going to have fun reading this.' 'I had fun writing it' I replied. And so we parted on the best of terms. Wasn't that nice?

I see what you mean about the Balfour's book on Mrs. Willett, and in fact I did not want to press it on you because I rather thought you might feel that way about it. Our temperaments are too different—which, of course, you very well understand when you disapprove my preference for ideas over images. It is not easy for me to think mythically—in terms, that is to say, of myths (in the good sense)—and I always tend to ask myself 'Is it true as a matter of fact? Is such a thing actually possible?' whereas for you, as I understand you, the question is 'Is it a valid myth?' And so by a commodious vicus of recirculation, we come back to Balfour and *Willett.*[2] For me the question that this book raises (whether or not it provides the answer) is obviously 'Are these communications actually what they purport to be? Is rebirth (or personal survival of death) true *as a matter of fact*?' And, of course, this question is perfectly intelligible to me.

But to you, I rather imagine, this question is *not* intelligible: it is not the sort of question that can be raised at all—or at least, it *ought* not to be raised. Re-birth, survival, yes, by all means, but as a metaphor for something else, perhaps for everything else (the continuation of the human race, of one's seed in one's progeny, of one's fame in the successive editions of one's books, of the traditions and culture of a people; the re-birth of the year at the winter solstice, of the foliage of a tree each spring, and of the tree itself in the germinating of its seeds—your list will be far better than mine can ever hope to be).

Perhaps you will say (or am I misrepresenting you?) that the truths of religion *are* mythical truths, that they are *not* matters of fact; and if you do say this, I shall not contradict you. But then I shall have to say, with infinite regret, that if it is a religion you are after (in the sense of a 'valid myth'), then I have nothing to offer you, because the Dhamma is not a religion.[a]

---

**a.** I don't mean to say that the truths of Buddhism are necessarily matter-of-fact truths in an objective scientific sense: the Four Noble Truths are not even, properly speaking, propositions at all. (Cf. Heidegger's idea of 'truth' as the self-disclosure of a thing for what it really is.)

In other words, before we can even begin to discuss the Dhamma we have to agree whether or not the question 'Is there re-birth?' can be raised at all, and if so in what sense. It is simply a matter of first securing our lines of communication. But I am not suggesting that you will want to do this. (What makes the situation all the more difficult is the popular and mistaken idea that the Buddha's Teaching 'explains re-birth'.)

So you think perhaps that I have my knife into Christianity—or even into God? But really it's not true. After all, Christianity never did me very much harm, and I soon forgot it. I was brought up to be (I suppose) 'a Christian and a Gentleman', and I found it much easier to unlearn being a Christian—but then I was not a Catholic (thank God!). Actually, I rather find myself at a loss when a question of God is raised: I feel that I am expected to say something (even if it is only goodbye), and I don't find anything to say. There is no shortage of epitaphs on God, and if I felt the need of one I could say, with Stendhal (*la seule excuse de Dieu, c'est qu'il n'existe pas*[3]) that God, if he existed, would have a lot to answer for; but even to feel the need to excuse him on the ground of his non-existence, the question of his existence would first have to raise itself. And for me the question does not raise itself. As to the author of the *Jeu d'esprit*—well, they might start a *Buddhist Digest* on the lines of the *Readers' Digest* (isn't there already a *Catholic Digest*?), and then he could be the editor.

P.S. I once heard it said that 'a gentleman is a man who makes it easy for a woman to be a lady.' I suppose the corollary is that 'a lady is a woman who makes it difficult for a gentleman to be a man.'

## [L. 155] 2 July 1965

Many thanks indeed for having the Balfour's book on Mrs. Willett bound for me. It has been done very adequately, and the book should last for a long time (though I expect you will be thinking that the sooner such abominable superstitions perish the better for all concerned).

About your query—the 'Q.E.D.'[1] at the end gives it rather a rhetorical air, and it looks as if it might have been aimed at me as a sockdologer. Let me see if there is anything left for me to say.

> Query: If all things are adjudged as characterized by *dukkha*, who does the judging? And with reference to what criterion or norm? *A subject* (immortal soul) with reference to an objective *sukha*, no? Q.E.D.

You ask 'Who does the judging?' This question takes for granted that judging is done 'by somebody'. But this is by no means a foregone conclusion: we are quite able to give an account of judgement (or knowing) without finding ourselves obliged to set it up as 'a relation between subject and object'. According to Bradley (and Heidegger, who however is not conveniently quotable, would not entirely dissent), judgement is

> the more or less conscious enlargement of an object, not in fact but as truth. The object is thus not altered in existence but qualified in idea.... For the object, merely as perceived, is not, as such, qualified as true. (*PL*, p. 626)

For Bradley, all inference is an ideal self-development of a real object, and judgement is an implicit inference. (See also SAÑÑĀ, last paragraph.) In my own understanding of the matter, I see knowledge as essentially an *act of reflexion*, in which the 'thing' to be known presents itself (is presented) *explicitly* as standing out against a background (or in a context) that was already there implicitly. In reflexion, a (limited) totality is given, consisting of a centre and a periphery—a particular cow appears surrounded by a number of cattle, and there is the judgement, 'The cow is in the herd'. Certainly, there is an *intention* to judge, and this consists in the deliberate withdrawal of attention from the immediate level of experience to the reflexive (cf. DHAMMA (b)); but the question is not whether judgement is an intentional action (which it is), but whether there can be intention (even reflexive intention) without a subject ('I', 'myself') who intends. This, however, is not so much a matter of argument as something that has to be seen for oneself (cf. CETANĀ (f)).

Of course, since knowledge is very commonly (Heidegger adds 'and superficially') defined in terms of 'a relation between subject and object', the question of the subject cannot simply be brushed aside—no smoke without fire—and we have to see (at least briefly) why it is so defined. Both Heidegger and Sartre follow Kant in saying that, properly speaking, there is no knowledge other than intuitive; and I agree. But what is intuition? From a *puthujjana*'s point of view, it can be described as immediate contact between subject and object, between 'self' and the 'world' (for how this comes about, I must refer you to PHASSA). This, however, is not yet knowledge, for which a reflexive reduplication is needed; but when there is this reflexive reduplication we then have intuitive knowledge, which is (still for the *puthujjana*) immediate contact between *knowing* subject and *known* object. With the *arahat*, however, all question of subjectivity has subsided, and we are left simply with (the presence of) the *known thing*. (It is *present*, but no longer present 'to somebody'.) So much for judgement in general.

But now you say, 'If all things are characterized by *dukkha*....' This needs careful qualification. In the first place, the universal *dukkha* you refer to here is obviously not the *dukkha* of rheumatism or a toothache, which is by no means universal. It is, rather, the *saṅkhāra-dukkha* (the unpleasure or suffering connected with determinations) of this Sutta passage:

> There are, monk, three feelings stated by me: *sukha* feeling, *dukkha* feeling, neither-*dukkha*-nor-*sukha* feeling. These three feelings have been stated by me. But this, monk, has been stated by me: whatever is felt, that counts as *dukkha*. But that, monk, was said by me with reference just to the impermanence of determinations.... (*Vedanā Saṃy.*—S.xxxvi.11/iv,216)

But what is this *dukkha* that is bound up with impermanence? It is the *implicit* taking as pleasantly-permanent (perhaps 'eternal' would be better) of what actually is impermanent. And things are implicitly taken as pleasantly-permanent (or eternal) when they are taken (in one way or another) as 'I' or 'mine' (since, as you rightly imply, ideas of subjectivity are associated with ideas of immortality). And the *puthujjana* takes *all* things in this way. So, for the *puthujjana*, all things are *(saṅkhāra-)dukkha*. How then—and this seems to be the crux of your argument—how then does the *puthujjana* see or know (or adjudge) that 'all things are *dukkha*' unless there is some *background* (or criterion or norm) of non-*dukkha* (i.e. of *sukha*) *against which* all things stand out as *dukkha*? The answer is quite simple: he does *not* see or know (or adjudge) that 'all things are *dukkha*'. The *puthujjana* has *no* criterion or norm for making any such judgement, and so he does not make it.

The *puthujjana*'s experience is *(saṅkhāra-)dukkha* from top to bottom, and the consequence is that he has no way of knowing *dukkha* for himself; for however much he 'steps back' from himself in a reflexive effort he still takes *dukkha* with him. (I have discussed this question in terms of *avijjā* ('nescience') in *NP* §§23 & 25, where I show that *avijjā*, which is *dukkhe aññāṇaṃ* ('non-knowledge of *dukkha*'), has a hierarchical structure and breeds only itself.) The whole point is that the *puthujjana*'s non-knowledge of *dukkha is* the *dukkha* that he has non-knowledge of;[a] and this *dukkha*

---

**a.** In one Sutta (M.44/i,303) it is said that neither-*dukkha*-nor-*sukha* feeling (i.e. in itself neutral) is *dukkha* when not known and *sukha* when known.

that is at the same time non-knowledge of *dukkha* is the *puthujjana*'s (mistaken) acceptance of what seems to be a 'self' or 'subject' or 'ego' at its face value (as *nicca/sukha/attā*, 'permanent/pleasant/self').

And how, then, does knowledge of *dukkha* come about? How it is with a Buddha I can't say (though it seems from the Suttas to be a matter of prodigiously intelligent trial-by-error over a long period); but in others it comes about by their hearing (as *puthujjanas*) the Buddha's Teaching, which goes *against* their whole way of thinking. They accept out of trust (*saddhā*) this teaching of *anicca/dukkha/anattā*; and it is *this* that, being accepted, becomes the criterion or norm with reference to which they eventually come to see for themselves that all things are *dukkha*—for the *puthujjana*. But in seeing this they cease to be *puthujjanas* and, to the extent that they cease to be *puthujjanas*,[b] to *that* extent *(saṅkhāra-)dukkha* ceases, and to *that* extent also they have in all their experience a 'built-in' criterion or norm by reference to which they make further progress. (The *sekha*—no longer a *puthujjana* but not yet an *arahat*—has a kind of 'double vision', one part unregenerate, the other regenerate.) As soon as one becomes a *sotāpanna* one is possessed of *aparapaccayā ñāṇaṃ*, or 'knowledge that does not depend upon anyone else': this knowledge is also said to be 'not shared by *puthujjanas*', and the man who has it has (except for accelerating his progress) no further need to hear the Teaching—in a sense he *is* (in part) that Teaching.

So far, then, from its being a Subject (immortal soul) that judges 'all things are *dukkha*' with reference to an objective *sukha*, it is only with subsidence of (ideas of) subjectivity that there appears an (objective) *sukha* with reference to which the judgement 'all things are *dukkha* (for the commoner)' becomes possible at all.

Does this sort you out?

**b.** Strictly, only those are *puthujjanas* who are wholly *puthujjanas*, who have nothing of the *arahat* at all in them. But on ceasing to be a *puthujjana* one is not at once an *arahat*; and we can perhaps describe the intermediate (three) stages as partly one and partly the other: thus the *sotāpanna* would be three-quarters *puthujjana* and one-quarter *arahat*.

# 13
# Letters to Sister Vajirā

**[L. 156]** **21 November 1961**

Dear Upāsikā,[1]
Your argument as I understand it assumes that the *anāgāmī* is liable to *phassa*, and concludes that, since all *phassa* is *sa-āsava sa-upādāna* therefore the *anāgāmī* has *upādāna*. I shall do my best to do as you ask and refute you.

1. I shall take your second question first. 'Is there *phassa* apart from being *sa-āsava sa-upādāna*?' The answer is: no, there is not.

2. 'Is the *anāgāmī* liable to *phassa* or not?' It is evident that your argument depends upon an affirmative answer to this question, and that this, in turn, depends upon the absurdities of a negative answer—i.e. that the *anāgāmī* is *not* liable to *phassa*, which can be truly said only of the *arahat*. It follows from this that your argument is dependent upon the assumption that the question is one that can be answered categorically—if the answer 'no' is absurd, then the answer 'yes' must be correct.

In the Aṅguttara (III,67/i,197; IV,42/ii,46) the Buddha speaks of four kinds of questions: those that can be answered categorically, those that require a discriminating answer, those that require a counter question, and those that must be put aside. Perhaps the question, 'Is the *anāgāmī* liable to *phassa* or not?' cannot be answered categorically and is one that must be set aside.

We know that the *puthujjana* is liable to *phassa*, and that the *arahat* is not. But your question asks about the *anāgāmī*, who is neither *puthujjana* nor *arahat*. It is quite true that if I deny that the *anāgāmī* is liable to *phassa* I confound him with the *arahat*; but it is no less true that if I allow that he is liable to *phassa* I fail to distinguish him from the *puthujjana*. Thus the question cannot be answered.

To this it can be objected that since both *puthujjana* and *anāgāmī* are liable to re-birth, that since neither of them has reached the goal and become *arahat*, in this respect at least, they are indistinguishable, and consequently that the question can in fact be answered affirmatively. It will be noticed, however, that we are now no longer debating whether or not the *anāgāmī* is liable to *phassa*, but whether or not your question 'Is the *anāgāmī* liable to *phassa*?' is answerable. And whether we decide that it is answerable or not depends upon whether we regard the *paṭiccasamuppāda* formulation as a Universal Law (which will include the *sekha*) or as a pedagogical device (which treats the *sekha* as irrelevant). In this way we establish that your argument does not in any way invalidate my view of *paṭiccasamuppāda*; at most it represents a rival point of view; and we are free to choose between them.

3. Can we go further and show that the 'Universal Law' point of view, with its positive assertion that the *anāgāmī* has *upādāna*, may be at variance with the Suttas? Consider this passage: *Evam eva kho...pahīyetha; api ca te evam assa, dīgharattaṃ vata bho ahaṃ iminā cittena nikato vañcito paladdho; ahaṃ hi rūpaṃ yeva upādiyamāno upādiyiṃ...* .[2] We know (M.44/i,299) that *yo...pañcas'upādānakkhandhesu chandarāgo*[3] is *upādāna*; and *cakkhuppāda* is the arising of the *dhammacakkhu* of the *sotāpanna*: *yaṃ kiñci samudayadhammaṃ sabbaṃ taṃ nirodhadhammanti.*[4] If, then, we adopt the 'Universal Law' point of view and press the question 'Does the *anāgāmī* have *upādāna*?' we meet with the answer that *upādāna* (including, presumably, *kām'upādāna*) is put aside even by the *sotāpanna*; and from this we arrive at the inconvenient conclusion that the *sotāpanna* is an *arahat*. If, on the other hand, we adopt the 'pedagogical device' point of view, we regard the question 'Does the *sotāpanna*, does the *anāgāmī*, have *upādāna*?' as *ṭhapaniya*, and we refrain from asking it; and in this way these difficulties do not arise. When a *puthujjana* obtains the *dhammacakkhu* he there and then ceases to be a *puthujjana* and (in due course) becomes *arahat*.

4. Is *sammādiṭṭhi* to be reckoned as *diṭṭhupādāna*? If the foregoing discussion is accepted this question will not arise; for we are no longer called upon to decide whether or not the *diṭṭhisampanna* (*sotāpanna*) or *anāgāmī* possesses *upādāna*. If not, the following remarks may be relevant.

Though I do not know of any Sutta where *diṭṭhupādāna* is specified in detail, reference to Majjhima 11/i,66 shows that whereas *samaṇabrāhmaṇā* other than the Buddha may be capable of teaching *pariññā* of the first three *upādāna*, it is only the Buddha who can teach *pariññā* of *attavādupādāna*. But if *diṭṭhupādāna* includes *sammādiṭṭhi* then it is beyond the scope of outside *samaṇabrāhmaṇā* to teach *pariññā* of *diṭṭhupādāna*, since *sammādiṭṭhi* is found only within the Buddha's Teaching. From this one might conclude that *sammādiṭṭhi* is not to be reckoned as *diṭṭhupādāna*.

5. *Saupādisesā*. Majjhima 10/i,63 and other Suttas say *sati vā upādisese anāgāmitā.*[5] This, obviously, refers to the *anāgāmī*. But *Itivuttaka* 44/38

speaks of *saupādisesā nibbānadhātu* and *anupādisesā nibbānadhātu*. It is clear enough that *upādisesā* cannot refer to the same thing in these two different contexts; for in the first the *upādisesā* of the *anāgāmī* is what distinguishes him from the *arahat* (i.e. some impurity) and in the second *upādisesā* is what distinguishes the 'living' *arahat* from the 'dead' *arahat*. (N.B. It is, strictly, no less improper to apply the word 'life' to an *arahat* than it is the word 'death'.) It is perhaps tempting to look for some significant connexion between the word *upādisesā* and the word *upādāna*, and to attempt to explain these contexts in terms of *upādāna* (possibly also with reference to the phrases *catunnaṃ mahābhūtānaṃ upādāya rūpaṃ*[6] and *taṇhupādiṇṇa kāye*[7] of Majjhima 28/i,185); but as the Ven. Ñāṇamoli Thera pointed out to me the words *saupādisesā* and *anupādisesā* occur in Majjhima 105/ii,257&259, where they can hardly mean more than 'with something remaining' and 'without something remaining' or 'with/without residue'. This seems to indicate that we are not entitled to deduce from *sati vā upādisese anāgāmitā* that the *anāgāmī* is *sa-upādāna*—all that it implies is that the *anāgāmī* still has something (i.e. some infection) left that the *arahat* does not.[8]

**[L. 157]** **(undated[1])**

I do not say that *rūpa* is appearance. I say, rather, that *rūpa* is what appears. *Rūpa, on its own*, cannot appear (and therefore does not exist): in order to appear (or to exist) *rūpa* requires *nāma*; that is to say, it requires feeling and perception. Similarly, *rūpa*, on its own, is not *significant*; for a thing is significant, has an intention, only when it appears *from a certain point of view*; and without *nāma* (and *viññāṇa*) *rūpa* is without a point of view (or orientation). Thus *cetanā* (intention) is *nāma* (see M.9/i,53, where *nāma* is defined as *vedanā saññā cetanā phassa manasikāra* [attention = point of view; my present point of view is what I am at present attending to]).[2] Without *nāma* we cannot *speak* of *rūpa*: there is no *adhivacana*. But without *rūpa* there is nothing to speak *of*: there is no *paṭigha*.

Though *purpose* is a form of intention, it is rather a crude and obvious form (though useful as a starting-point)—there is intention of a much more subtle nature (which, however, we need not discuss here). The varieties of intention are infinite. I agree, of course, that there is no purpose in existence, as such. There is no reason why I or anything else should exist. But *when* something exists it is always (negatively) related to other things, i.e. it is significant.

**[L. 158]** **27 December 1961**

I have indicated the points of difference between us on this question of the *ariyapuggalā*, and I do not have any doubt that I am right. But if you can give me a Sutta text that clearly shows that I am mistaken I shall not be greatly worried. It is not within my powers to check for myself that all four (or eight) stages are necessarily gone through by all who eventually attain *arahattā*, nor can I know for myself that there are just four (or eight) stages, no more and no less. And whether or not a *sotāpanna* is or is not to be called *kāyasakkhi, diṭṭhipatto*, or *saddhāvimutto* is, after all, a question of terminology rather than anything else. For all these matters I rely on the Buddha (or the Suttas), since I cannot know them for myself; and if it is pointed out to me that I have misunderstood the Suttas, I am prepared to reconsider my views on this matter. Nothing of any great importance depends upon a person's knowing about the various kinds of *ariyasāvakā*: what *is* of importance is that he should become one of them—the rest will follow as a matter of course.

By way of contrast, I remember that a few years ago (at the Hermitage) the question arose whether or not *viññāṇa* is included in *nāma*, and at that time I said in public that if anyone were to show me a Sutta where *viññāṇa* definitely was included in *nāma* I should be extremely upset. (Fortunately nobody did.) The reason for my statement was that as a result of an examination of my own experience (guided also by certain outside philosophers) I had come to the conclusion that it was quite wrong to include *viññāṇa* in *nāma*; this was (and is) a matter wherein I could (by reflexive experience) know for myself what was right and what was wrong; and a Sutta in direct contradiction to my own experience would have been most disturbing.

Perhaps you will see from this distinction that I have made (between what I *can* know for myself at the present time and what I can *not* know) why it is that I am unable to make any useful comment on your 'tidy chart' of *rūpa*. Nearly all of it is quite beyond my present experience and nothing I could say would be anything more valuable than a discussion of certain words. And the same applies, generally, to any argument based upon etymology and Sutta usage. At best I can only indicate Suttas to complete or to correct your scheme. (Thus, I can say that you may find the answer to your question 'Where do the four *jhānas* belong?' in A.IV,123 & 124.)

**[L. 159]** **10 January 1962**

1. It is going too far to say that, to me, the *sekha* is essentially *arahat*, and that, rigorously, I exclude him from *paṭiccasamuppāda anuloma*. Where *paṭiccasamuppāda* is concerned, we are dealing with the difference between the *puthujjana* and the *arahat*, and the question of the *sekha* simply *does not arise*. He is in between. The *sekha*, like the two-faced Roman god Janus (whose month this is), is looking both ways, to the past and to the future. The past is *anuloma*, and the future is *paṭiloma*, and if it is too late to include the *sekha* in *anuloma* it is too early to include him in *paṭiloma*. Or if you wish he is something of both.

2. There is no 'but' and 'when' about the *arahat*'s being *paṭiccasamuppāda paṭiloma*—he is *paṭiccasamuppāda paṭiloma* entirely, and in no way *anuloma*. *Anuloma* is *avijjāpaccayā*, and *paṭiloma* is *avijjānirodha*, and there is not the smallest trace of *avijjā* where the *arahat* is concerned. It is not possible to put 'him' back to *anuloma*, since, with cessation of *avijjā*, there is cessation of 'him' (*attavāda, asmimāna*)—*diṭṭh'eva dhamme saccato thetato Tathāgato anupalabbhamāne* (S.xliv/iv,384).[1] There is certainly no 'outside the *paṭiccasamuppāda* context' as far as persons are concerned, since *paṭiloma* is cessation of the person. Thus it is only if we think of the *arahat therī* Sonā as a *person*, as *somebody* (*sakkāya*), that she seems to be putting herself back to *anuloma* when she says: *pañcakkhandhā pariññātā tiṭṭhanti chinnamūlakā* (Thig.106).[2]

You suggest that when I describe the *arahat* I do so in terms other than negative to *pañc'upādānakkhandhā*; but when I describe him 'as such' I do not say he is *saupādāna*, any more than Sonā Therī when she describes herself 'as such'. But the fact is that no one, not even the Buddha, can describe an *arahat* in such a way as to be intelligible to a *puthujjana*; and the reason is, as you point out, that the whole of the *puthujjana*'s experience is *saupādāna*, including his experience of the *anupādāna arahat* (whether he sees him, thinks about him, visualizes or imagines him, or hears him described). Your account of the difficulties that you encounter when you consider the *arahat* and his robe, *as far as it goes*, is quite correct. (I say 'as far as it goes' since *to you* the *arahat*'s robe is to be worn '*by him*', whereas *to him* it is to-be-worn, not '*by me*' but '*on this body*'.)

For a *puthujjana* even the terms *khīṇāsava, akataññū*, and so on, *to the extent that they are intelligible to him*, are all *saupādāna*. In other words, it is impossible for a *puthujjana* to 'see' (= understand) an *arahat*—as soon as he does 'see' him he ceases to be a *puthujjana*. But this does not in the least mean that a *puthujjana* should not *try* to understand an *arahat*—he might succeed and then he would cease to be a *puthujjana*.

3. (i) *Āneñja* (*na iñjatī ti āneñjaṃ*), which literally means 'not shaking', seems to have two quite distinct connotations in the Suttas. In the first place it refers either (as in A.IV,190/ii,184) to the four *arūpa* attainments or more strictly (as in M.106) to the fourth *jhāna* and *ākāsānañcāyatana* and *viññāṇañcāyatana*—note that the second and third *āneñjasappāya* refer to *both* these last two; and these are attainable by the *puthujjana*, the *sekha*, and the *arahat* alike, provided, of course, that they make the effort. See, for example, A.IV,172 (which should be a continuation of 171/ii,159), where certain *devā*, having been *nevasaññānāsaññāyatanūpagā* are liable to return to this world (which cannot happen to an *ariyasāvaka* in the same position). And see A.III,114/i,267 for the same of the first three of the *arūpa devā*. In the second place it refers to *arahattā*. *Anejo anupādāno sato bhikkhu paribbaje* (Sn.751). In both cases there is 'not shaking', but in two different senses. There is nothing mysterious about this; it is merely a question of Sutta usage.

(ii) As regards the passage you quoted from Majjhima 106/ii,264, I understand it in this way. When a *puthujjana* attains *nevasaññānāsaññāyatana* that is clearly enough *saupādāna*, that is, *sakkāya*. When a *sekha* attains this, he *sees* that it is *saupādāna*, that it is *sakkāya*. Now the condition for *upādāna* is *avijjā*, that is to say, *not seeing*—not seeing *upādāna* as *upādāna*. But the *sekha*, unlike the *puthujjana*, *does* see this, so his *upādāna* is *seen* and is also, therefore, *an-upādāna*. (As I have said before, all one can say of the *sekha* is *mā upādiyi*.) Similar remarks apply to the frequent passages in the Suttas where the *sekha* sees or considers or is urged to consider the *pañc'upādānakkhandhā* as *anicca* and so on. The *puthujjana* cannot see *pañc'upādānakkhandhā* as *anicca* or anything else, since he does not *see* them at all.

4. About *saḷāyatana* and *phassa*. Within limits I follow your argument (except that I have no experience of the *dibbacakkhu* and cannot therefore usefully comment upon it), but I note that you seem to regard the *cakkhundriya* as '*subject*'. The question remains, 'What do you mean by "subject"?'

In visual experience (considered alone) the eye does not appear (*na pātubhavati*) at all, either as *cakkhundriya* or as *maṃsacakkhu*, since vision itself is not visible, and the eye does not see itself. Since visual experience alone neither reveals *cakkhundriya* nor *maṃsacakkhu* there is (or should be) no justification for calling either of them *subject*. When other faculties (or a looking glass) are used the *maṃsacakkhu* appears (*pātubhavati*), but it appears as a phenomenon (to avoid using the word 'object' for the moment) amongst other phenomena, and, as such, has no claim to be called *subject*.

In neither case is there any subject to be found. This being so, when these two experiences, visual and the other, occur together (as is usual), although there is the *constriction* you speak of (I would rather call it a *superposition*) there is no reason whatsoever for any 'discrepancy between subject and object'; for we have not found any subject. And in the *arahat* (do I disconcert you?) no discrepancy is, in fact, experienced, and no *dukkha*. It is only in the *puthujjana*, for whom an apparent *self* is manifest, and who necessarily divides things into *subject* and *object*, that the discrepancy you speak of can arise. But it seems to me that perhaps you do not find the approach by way of the *saḷāyatana* as congenial to you as the approach by way of *pañcakkhandhā*, and I shall not pursue the question any further.

5. In my early days in Ceylon I myself was something of a 'tidy-chart' maker, and I hoped and believed that it was possible to include all that the Suttas said in a single system—preferably portrayed diagrammatically on one very large sheet of paper. In those innocent days—which however did not last very long—I believed that the Commentaries knew what they were talking about. And I had the idea that everything that happened to me was *vipāka* and everything that I did about it (my reaction, that is, to the *vipāka*) was fresh *kamma*, which in turn produced fresh *vipāka*, and so on *ad inf.* And this is as tidy as anyone could wish.

Then I came across the Sutta that I transcribe below. This, as you will see, was enough to shatter my illusions, and it came as a bit of a shock (though also as a bit of a relief). In due course after asking people about it and getting no satisfactory explanation, I decided that my 'tidy idea' could be true only in a general sense, and that, in any case, it could not possibly be of any vital importance in the essential part of the Dhamma. Since then I have stopped thinking about it. Here is the Sutta (Vedanā Saṃy.—S.xxxvi.21/iv,229-31):[3]

> Once the Auspicious One was staying near Rājagaha, at the Squirrel's feeding-ground in the Bamboo Grove.
>
> Now at that time the Wanderer Sīvaka of the top knot approached the Auspicious One. Having approached, he exchanged courtesies and, having done so, sat down at one side. Sitting at one side the Wanderer Sīvaka of the top knot said this to the Auspicious One:
>
> —There are some recluses and divines, Master Gotama, of such a belief, of such a view: 'Whatever this individual experiences, be it pleasant, unpleasant, or neutral, all that is due to former actions.' Herein what does Master Gotama say?
>
> —Some feelings, Sīvaka, arise here (1) *with bile as their source.* That can be known by oneself, Sīvaka, how some feelings arise here

with bile as their source; and that is reckoned by the world as truth, Sīvaka, how some feelings arise here with bile as their source. Therein, Sīvaka, the recluses and divines who are of such a belief, of such a view: 'Whatever this individual experiences, be it pleasant, unpleasant, or neutral, all that is due to former actions', they both go beyond what is known by themselves and go beyond what is reckoned as truth in the world. Therefore I say that these recluses and divines are in the wrong.

Some feelings, Sīvaka, arise here (2) *with phlegm as their source*....

Some feelings, Sīvaka, arise here (3) *with wind as their source*....

Some feelings, Sīvaka, arise here (4) *due to confluence of humours*....

Some feelings, Sīvaka, arise here (5) *born from seasonal change*....

Some feelings, Sīvaka, arise here (6) *born from improper care*....

Some feelings, Sīvaka, arise here (7) *due to exertion*....

Some feelings, Sīvaka, arise here (8) *born from the ripening of action*.... Therefore I say that these recluses and divines are in the wrong.

6. Let us return to §2. Your letter encourages me to think that, in a way, you understand your own failure to understand the *arahat*. And it is because I thought this also before that I felt it was worthwhile to speak of the 'sterility of making tidy charts'. The making of tidy charts (even if they are accurate, which is rarely the case—a chart of the Dhamma tends to distort it just as a map-maker distorts the curved surface that he represents on a flat sheet), the making of tidy charts, I say, is sterile because it is essentially *takka*, and the Dhamma is *atakkāvacara*. To make tidy charts, though not in itself reprehensible, does not lead to understanding. But it is useless to say such a thing to a convinced tidy-chart-maker—such as a commentator, who is satisfied that the Dhamma is understood when it is charted.

In your case, however, though you do tend to make tidy charts (it is an attitude of mind), there is also another aspect. You seem to be well aware that there is a discrepancy in your present position in that you are disconcerted when the *arahat* is described 'as such', and you are perhaps prepared to allow my statement that this is due to failure to see that things can be significant without being 'mine', that they can be teleological without being appropriated. And I think, also, that you are aware that *this*, in fact, is the central problem and that all else (including the tidy charts) is secondary and unimportant. This attitude is not sterile; and from the first it has been my principal concern, directly or indirectly, to encourage it and make it stand out decisively. As you have noted I have consistently underlined this matter (in whatever terms it has been stated) and rejected any possibility of arriving at a compromise solution. It is because you have been prepared to listen to this one thing that I have continued the correspondence. The other things we have discussed, except in so far as they have a bearing in this, are of little importance. But it is one thing for me to insist on this matter and quite another for you to see it. Even *bhikkhus* who heard the Dhamma from the Buddha's own mouth had sometimes to go away and work it out for themselves. *Tassa me Bhagavā...so kho ahan...paṭiladdho* (Bojjhaṅga Saṃy.—S.xlvi.30/v,89-90).[4]

*Afternote*: You say that, as far as you see it, the *arahat*'s experience functions automatically. By this I presume that you mean it functions without any *self* or *agent* or *master* to direct it. But I do not say otherwise. All that I would add is that this automatically functioning experience has a complex teleological structure.

The *puthujjana*'s experience, however, is still more complex, since there is also *avijjā*, and there is thus appropriation as well as teleology. *But this, too, functions automatically, without any self or agent to direct it.* On account of the appropriation, however, it *appears* to be directed by a *self*, *agent*, or *master*. *Avijjā* functions automatically, but conceals this fact from itself. *Avijjā* is an automatically functioning blindness to its automatic functioning. Removal of the blindness removes the appropriation but not the teleology.

As for exercise.... The importance of existence is one of those great myths of the 20th century that make living in it such hell. If nobody took any exercise unless he actually wanted to go somewhere everybody would be a lot happier.

**[L. 160][1]** **29 January 1962**

Thank you for your letter of the 25th. You have, I fear, returned to your habit of writing in riddles, which makes it extremely difficult for a person like me to follow you. I do not see why an *arahat* should be hidden amongst the *kāyasakkhi*, *diṭṭhipatto*, and *saddhāvimutto*—all these three have something further to do, as you may see from the Kītāgiri Sutta (M.70), and this cannot be said of any *arahat*. I did not comment on this since I agreed that the reading '*arahī vā*' (which is not in the P.T.S. edition, even as a v.l.) was wrong. I still think it is.

It may seem to you that the wind-element obeys me, but to me it appears otherwise. The wind element comes and *lodges* in my intestines for a large part of each day and causes a persistent discomfort that nearly prevents me from doing any *ānāpānasati* at all. This has been going on for the last ten years, and at present seems to be getting worse (it is largely for this reason that I have spent so much time thinking about the Dhamma rather then practising *jhāna*, which was my prime reason for coming to Ceylon; but things having turned out in the way they have, I can have no reason for complaint). As a means of communication I prefer the post to the wind-element—though it is no doubt slower it is less liable to deliver a corrupt text. It may be that you have seen in me the *arahat* or that the wind-element has told you that I actually am *arahat*; but the plain fact is that I am *not arahat* and, partly on account of obstruction by the wind-element, I have no great hopes of becoming one in this lifetime. I am a long way from *arahattā*, I have far to go before reaching that. What exactly I am is a matter of no great importance, and for reasons of Vinaya, which have to be complied with, discussion of this matter is not advisable. It is obvious enough that you, with your present understanding, may arrive at certain general conclusions about what I am or am not; but that is neither here no there. In any case I must ask you, as far as possible, to keep these conclusions to yourself—it will be a considerable embarrassment to me to be talked about, and it will not serve any useful purpose.

You ask if I think that anyone ever understood me. As far as one person may understand another I have both understood, and been understood by, other people. But there are always limitations in this; however long one has known another person he can still behave in unexpected ways. No person, in the normal way, ever *completely* understands another. There are certain things about me that have been better understood by men and certain things that have been better understood by women, but nobody has ever completely understood me. At present it is a matter of complete indifference to me whether anybody understands me, or thinks he understands me,—*as an individual*, that is to say. On the other hand, it is possible that a certain person may understand and see the *Buddha's* Teaching, and it may happen that another person may come to see this Teaching from this first person; but when this happens it cannot properly be said that the second person understands the first person in the sense discussed above—what can properly be said is that both understand the Teaching. And anyone else who understands the Teaching (no matter by what means) comes to join the first two; they all understand one another in so far as they all understand the same thing; but as far as understanding one another as individuals goes, they may be complete strangers. No doubt you will follow this. If so, I would ask you not to confuse the two things. To me, you, as an individual, are nearly a stranger; I am not interested in you *as an individual* except in so far as it is necessary for the purpose of communicating the Dhamma. When this has been done (and, as far as I can judge, it *has* been done), you become of interest to me *as one who understands the Dhamma*, but not otherwise. Conversely, I very much doubt whether you understand very much about me *as an individual*, however it may be in the other sense. I am aware, because you have told me, that you are an emotional person and that you depend much upon personal relationships with others. Knowing this fact, I made use of it in our recent correspondence—communication of the Dhamma was made on a personal basis (you would never have accepted it on an intellectual basis); and the bonfire of my letters was the logical conclusion (though I did not actually anticipate this). You have built up a certain picture me, a certain idea of me, *as an individual* (to you, as *puthujjana*, I represented the *arahat*), and since this was necessary to you I did not interfere with it. But now that it is no longer necessary to you (if you have seen the Dhamma you are quite independent of anyone else), I take the liberty of saying that there is no reason whatsoever for supposing that your idea of me has any essential connexion with what I am in reality. I lay some emphasis on this matter since you seem to suggest in your letter that it is necessary to understand me as an individual in order to understand the Dhamma (you say that now many will have a better chance of understanding me; which almost sounds as if you propose to set about *interpreting* me to other people—is this what you mean?). [In this connexion I find your reference to the double hierarchy as 'tension in itself' most obscure. And in what way does the entry of the new phenomenon—yourself—affect it? The double hierarchy as a picture of the fundamental structure of negatives and as an instrument of thought was valid and remains valid—indeed it enables me to give myself a more precise idea of the nature of the fundamental appropriation of things (when there is *avijjā*) then any that I have actually set down on paper. It is one of the things that has *not* been self-destructive).]

It may seem to you, perhaps, that I am being unnecessarily hard on you, especially at the present moment with your newly won *dhammapīti*. In my last letter I told you that I was delighted; and it remains true. I *am* delighted at your success—you have won a great victory over yourself, a victory that cannot be taken away. (I am a very cautious person, and I keep saying to myself 'I *hope* there is no mistake, I *hope* she really does see'. But from [? illeg.] your letter I *think* there is no mistake). But I must say also this: that if you want to make progress (and progress has to be made), you cannot afford to indulge in emotional states. I said that you are rapidly becoming a tower of strength; but it will not be 'rapidly' without a good deal of *nekkhammasaṅkappa*. Do you not see the *dukkha* of emotions? Why torment yourself with myths of your own creation? Practise *samatha*, and let the myths die of neglect.

With best wishes,

Ñāṇavīra

# 14
# A Letter to the Coroner

**[L. 161]** **5 July 1965, 2:45 p.m.**

To the coroner, Hambantota:

Owing to chronic (and apparently incurable) ill-health, I have decided to put an end to my life. I have been contemplating such action for some considerable time; indeed, I made an unsuccessful attempt at suicide in November 1962; since then the situation has deteriorated rather than improved. The responsibility for this action is purely mine, and no other person whatsoever is involved.

Ñāṇavīra

# C

# WRITINGS

[EDITORIAL NOTE: The draft of an article was found among the Ven. Ñāṇavīra's effects. The date is unknown.]

# The Foundation of Ethics

The ethical paradox—What should I do?—is beyond the province of the natural sciences; for the natural sciences, based as they are upon the principle of public knowledge, are inherently incapable of comprehending the idea of personal choice. What about the sciences of man—history, anthropology, sociology—can they help us? These certainly tell us how man has behaved in the past, and how in fact he now behaves. And when we ask them whether man *ought* to behave in the way he has and does, they are able to point to the manifest consequences in this world of man's various kinds of behaviour, and if we press them further to indicate which of these consequences are good and which bad, they can often tell us which have been most generally approved by man and which disapproved.

But if we ask them whether the majority of mankind has been *right* in approving what in fact it has approved and in disapproving what it has disapproved, they are silent. The answer of course is simply that if I, personally, approve what the majority of mankind has approved I shall say that the majority is right, but if I disapprove I shall say that it is wrong. But the scientific method eliminates the individual on principle, and for the humanist sciences man is essentially a collective or social phenomenon. For them, in consequence, I as an individual do not exist at all; at best I am conceded a part-share in the general consensus of opinion. The individual's view as an absolute ethical choice is systematically swallowed up in the view of mankind as a whole; and if the ethical question is raised at all, the sciences of man can only reply that the opinion of the majority represents the ultimate truth (a view that the defeated candidates in any election, who are themselves always in the majority, know to be false).

Furthermore, the only consequences of man's behaviour that these sciences are in a position to consider are the social consequences; what effects an individual's behaviour has upon himself or upon some other individual is not a comprehensible question. This means that a person seeking ethical enlightenment from the sciences of man is likely to conclude that only social values are moral values, and that a man can do as he pleases in private. It is hardly necessary to remark that with the growth of these sciences this view has already become extremely fashionable, and no great wonder: it puffs up the politician into an arbiter and legislator of morals—a function hitherto restricted to Divine Personages or their Representatives—and it allows the private citizen to enjoy his personal pleasures with a clear conscience. Eventually, we meet with political systems that have been raised to the status of religions. It is evident that the question of ethics, of the personal choice, does not come within the competence of the sciences either of nature or of man to answer.

It may happen, of course, that a man who clearly understands this may nevertheless decide that the service of man is the highest good. But if we press him to say why he has decided that concern with human society is the aim and purpose of his life, he will perhaps explain since he himself is a human being his personal happiness is bound up with human societies, and in promoting the welfare of mankind in general he is advancing his own welfare.

We may or may not agree with him, but that is not the point. The point is that, in the last analysis, a man chooses what he does choose in order to obtain happiness, whether it is the immediate satisfaction of an urgent desire or a remote future happiness bought perhaps with present acceptance of suffering. This means that the questions 'What is the purpose of existence?' and 'How is happiness to be obtained?' are synonymous; for they are both the ethical question, 'What should I do?' But there is happiness and happiness, and the intelligent man will prefer the permanent to the temporary.

The question, then, is 'How is permanent happiness, if such a thing exists, to be obtained?' This question in the West, with its Christian tradition, has always been associated with that of the existence of God, conceived as the ultimate source of all values, union with whom (or the admittance to whose presence) constitutes eternal happiness. The traditional Western Ethic is thus 'Obey the Laws of God'. But with the decline of Christianity before the triumphal progress of science God was pronounced dead and the question of the possibility of permanent happiness was thrown open. '*Has existence then any significance at all?*...the question,' Nietzsche declared, 'that will require a couple of centuries even to be completely heard in all its profundity.'

# Suttas & Sartre

1. Just so, monks, for a monk engaged in higher mentality there are coarse defilements: bad body-conduct, bad speech-conduct, bad mind-conduct. A conscientious and able monk puts them away, drives them out, gets rid of them, brings them to naught. When these are put away and got rid of, then for a monk engaged in higher mentality there are medium defilements: sensual thoughts, angry thoughts, cruel thoughts. A conscientious and able monk puts them away, drives them out, gets rid of them, brings these to naught. When these are put away and got rid of, then for a monk engaged in higher mentality there are fine defilements: thoughts of birth, thoughts of country, thoughts connected with reputation. A conscientious and able monk puts them away, drives them out, gets rid of them, brings them to naught. When these are put away and got rid of, then there remain thoughts about the Nature of Things. There is concentration that is neither peaceful nor exalted nor tranquil nor arrived at unification, that is together with determinations,[a] constrained, obstructed, confined. There comes a time, monks, when that mind is internally steadied, settled, unified, and concentrated. There is concentration that is peaceful, exalted, tranquil, and arrived at unification, that is without determinations, unconstrained, unobstructed, unconfined.

(A.III,100/i,254-5)

2. His mind being thus concentrated, purified, cleansed, unblemished, with defilements gone, supple, workable, steady, and unshakeable, he directs it and turns it to the knowledge of recollection of former abodes. He recalls manifold former abodes: that is to say, one birth, two births, three births, four births, five births, ten births, twenty births, thirty births, forty births,

---

**a.** §1. In mental concentration there is progressive subsidence of speech-determination (second *jhāna*), body-determination (fourth *jhāna*), and mind-determination (attainment of cessation of perception and feeling). Majjhima 44. See footnote §21.

fifty births, one hundred births, one thousand births, one hundred thousand births, manifold involutions of aeons; manifold evolutions of aeons, manifold involutions-and-evolutions of aeons: 'There, thus was my name, thus was may clan, thus my appearance (colour), thus my food, thus the pleasure and unpleasure experienced, thus the ending of my life; having fallen away thence, I re-arose here'. Thus he recalls manifold former abodes together with their features and indications.

Just as, Mahārāja, a man might go from his own village to another village, and from that village might go to yet another village, and from that village might come back to his own village; and it might occur to him, 'Indeed, I went from my own village to that village, and there I stood thus, I sat thus, I spoke thus, I was silent thus; and from that village I went to that other village, and there too I stood thus, I sat thus, I spoke thus, I was silent thus; and then I came back to my own village'—just so, Mahārāja, a monk, his mind being thus concentrated, purified, cleansed, unblemished, with defilements gone, supple, workable, steady, and unshakeable, directs it and turns it to the knowledge of recollection of former abodes.[a]

His mind being thus concentrated, purified, cleansed, unblemished, with defilements gone, supple, workable, steady, and unshakeable, he directs it and turns it to the knowledge of falling away and re-arising of creatures. With a purified divine eye, surpassing that of man, he sees creatures falling away and re-arising; he understands the going of creatures according to their actions, debased and exalted, of good colour and of bad colour, well-destined and ill-destined: 'These folk, indeed, are creatures possessed of bad body-conduct, of bad speech-conduct, of bad-mind-conduct, they are revilers of the noble ones, holders of wrong views and performers of actions in accordance with wrong views. They, on the breaking up of the body, after death, have re-arisen in perdition, the ill destiny, the realms of misery, hell. But these folk, indeed, are creatures possessed of good body-conduct, of good speech-conduct, of good mind-conduct, they are non-revilers of the noble ones, holders of right views, and performers of actions in accordance with right views. They, on the breaking up of the body, after death, have re-arisen in the good destiny, in the heavenly world'. Thus with a purified divine eye, surpassing that of man, he sees creatures falling away and re-arising; he understands the going of creatures according to their actions,

**a.** §2. 'For finally the foetus *was* me; it represents the factual limit of my memory but not the theoretical limit of my past. There is a metaphysical problem concerning birth in that I can be anxious to know how *I* happen to have been born from that particular embryo; and this problem is perhaps insoluble.' *B&N*, p. 139.

debased and exalted, of good colour and of bad colour, well-destined and ill-destined.

Just as, Mahārāja, there might be a terrace in the middle of a square, and a man with eyes might stand there and see people entering and leaving houses and wandering about the roads and streets and sitting in the middle of the square; and it might occur to him, 'These people are entering and leaving houses, these are wandering about the roads and streets, these are sitting in the middle of the square'—just so, Mahārāja, a monk, his mind being thus concentrated, purified, cleansed, unblemished, with defilements gone, supple, workable, steady, and unshakeable, he directs it and turns it to the knowledge of falling away and re-arising of creatures.

(D.2/i,81-3)

3. Beginningless, monks, is this running on of existence; a starting point of creatures who are coursing and running on constrained by nescience and attached by craving is not manifest.

How do you conceive this, monks: which is more, the blood that has flowed and streamed from your severed heads in this long stretch of coursing and running on, or the water in the four great oceans?

—According, Lord, to our comprehension of the Teaching (*dhamma*) set forth by the Auspicious One, the blood that has flowed and streamed from our severed heads in this long coursing and running on is indeed more than the water in the four great oceans.

—Well said, well said, monks: well have you thus comprehended the Teaching set forth by me. The blood that has flowed and streamed from your severed heads in this long coursing and running on is indeed more than the water in the four great oceans. A long time, monks, has the blood flowed and streamed from your severed heads when you were oxen: more than the water in the four great oceans. ...when you were buffaloes ... sheep ... goats ... deer ... chickens ... pigs ... when you were taken as village robbers ... when you were taken as highway robbers ... when you were taken as adulterers.... Why is this? Beginningless, monks, is this running on of existence: a starting point of creatures who are coursing and running on constrained by nescience and attached by craving is not manifest. For so long, monks, have you enjoyed (*éprouvé*) suffering (*dukkha*), agony, and misfortune, and swelled the charnel grounds: long enough, monks, for disgust for all determinations, for the fading out of lust for them, for release from them.

(S.xv.13/ii,187-9)

4. Beginningless, monks, is this running on: a first point of creatures coursing and running on hindered by nescience and attached by craving is not evident. It is not easy, monks, to find that creature who has not formerly been your mother in this long stretch ... your father ... your brother, sister, son, daughter.... Why is this? Beginningless, monks, is this running on: a first point of creatures coursing and running on hindered by nescience and attached by craving is not evident. For so long, monks, have you enjoyed suffering, agony, and misfortune, and swelled the charnel grounds: long enough, monks, for disgust for all determinations, for the fading out of lust for them, for release from them.

(S.xv.14-19/ii,189-90)

5. It is through non-discernment and non-penetration of four noble truths that there has been this long stretch of coursing and running on, both for me and for you. Of which four?

It is through non-discernment and non-penetration of the noble truth of suffering (*dukkha*) that there has been this long stretch of coursing and running on, both for me and for you. It is through non-discernment and non-penetration of the noble truth of the arising of suffering ... the noble truth of the ceasing of suffering ... the noble truth of the way that leads to ceasing of suffering that there has been this long stretch of coursing and running on, both for me and for you.

When, monks, this noble truth of suffering is discerned and penetrated, when this noble truth of arising of suffering is discerned and penetrated, when this noble truth of ceasing of suffering is discerned and penetrated, when this noble truth of the way that leads to ceasing of suffering is discerned and penetrated, craving for being is cut off, what leads to being is exhausted, there is then no more being.

(D.16/ii,90)

6. This indeed, monks, is the noble truth of suffering. Birth is suffering, ageing is suffering, sickness is suffering, death is suffering, union with what is disliked is suffering, separation from what is liked is suffering, not to get what one wants, that too is suffering; in brief, the five holding aggregates[a] are suffering. This indeed, monks, is the noble truth of arising

---

**a.** §3. The five holding aggregates: matter (or substance), feeling, perception, determinations, consciousness.

of suffering. This craving leading to more being, conjoined with desire and lust, taking delight here and there, that is to say: sensual craving, craving for being, craving for non-being. This indeed, monks, is the noble truth of ceasing of suffering. The entire fading out and cessation, the giving up, the relinquishment of that same craving, release from it, its abandonment. This indeed, monks, is the noble truth of the way that leads to ceasing of suffering. This noble eightfold path, that is to say, right view, right thought, right speech, right action, right livelihood, right effort, right mindfulness, right concentration.

(S.lvi.11/v,421-2)

7. The noble truth of suffering is to be known absolutely. The noble truth of arising of suffering is to be abandoned. The noble truth of ceasing of suffering is to be realized. The noble truth of the way that leads to ceasing of suffering is to be developed.

(S.lvi.29/v,436)

8. Because of six elements,[a] monks, there is descent of the embryo; when there is descent there is name-&-matter; with name-&-matter as condition, six bases; with six bases as condition, contact; with contact as condition, feeling; to one who feels, monks, I make known 'This is suffering', I make known 'This is arising of suffering', I make known 'This is ceasing of suffering', I make known 'This is the way that leads to ceasing of suffering'. And which, monks, is the noble truth of suffering? Birth is suffering, ageing is suffering, sickness is suffering, death is suffering, sorrow, lamentation, pain (*dukkha*), grief, and despair are suffering; not to get what one wants, that too is suffering; in brief, the five holding aggregates are suffering. This, monks, is called the noble truth of suffering.

And which, monks, is the noble truth of arising of suffering? With nescience as condition, determinations; with determinations as condition, consciousness; with consciousness as condition, name-&-matter; with name-&-matter as condition, six bases; with six bases as condition, contact; with contact as condition, feeling; with feeling as condition, craving; with craving as condition, holding; with holding as condition, being; with being as condition, birth; with birth as condition, ageing-&-death, sorrow, lamentation, pain, grief, and despair, come into being; thus is the arising of this whole

a. §4. Six elements: earth, water, fire, air, space, consciousness.

mass of unpleasure (suffering). This, monks, is called the noble truth of arising of suffering.

And which, monks, is the noble truth of ceasing of suffering? With entire fading out and cessation of nescience, ceasing of determinations; with cessation of determinations, ceasing of consciousness; with cessation of consciousness, ceasing of name-&-matter; with cessation of name-&-matter, ceasing of six bases; with cessation of six bases, ceasing of contact; with cessation of contact, ceasing of feeling; with cessation of feeling, ceasing of craving; with cessation of craving, ceasing of holding; with cessation of holding, ceasing of being; with cessation of being, ceasing of birth; with cessation of birth, ageing-&-death, sorrow, lamentation, pain, grief, and despair, cease; thus is the ceasing of this whole mass of unpleasure (suffering). This, monks, is called the noble truth of ceasing of suffering.

And which, monks, is the noble truth of the way that leads to ceasing of suffering? This noble eightfold path, that is to say, right view, right thought, right speech, right action, right livelihood, right effort, right mindfulness, right concentration. This, monks, is called the noble truth of the way that leads to ceasing of suffering.

(A.III,61/i,176-7)

**9.** And which, monks, is ageing-&-death? The decay, the ageing, the brokenness, the greying, the wrinkledness, the dwindling of life, the decrepitude of the faculties of creatures of various orders: this is called ageing. The falling away, the breaking up, the disappearance, the death, the coming of the time, the breaking up of the aggregates, the laying down of the corpse of creatures of various orders: this is called death. This is ageing and this is death. This, monks, is called ageing-&-death.

And which, monks, is birth? The birth, the coming to birth, the descent, the appearance, the becoming manifest of the aggregates, the obtaining of the bases, of creatures of various orders: This, monks, is called birth.

And which, monks, is being? There are, monks, these three beings: sensual being, material being, immaterial being. This, monks, is called being.[a]

And which, monks, is holding? There are, monks, these four holdings: sensual holding, holding to view, holding to virtue and duty, holding to belief in self. This, monks, is called holding.[b]

---

**a.** §5. Being: *être*.

**b.** §6. Holding: *maniere d'être*. 'The desire of being is always realized as the desire of a mode of being.' *B&N*, p. 567.

And which, monks, is craving? There are, monks, these six bodies of craving: craving for visible form, craving for sounds craving for smells, craving for tastes, craving for touches, craving for images/ideas (*dhammā*). This, monks, is called craving.[a]

And which, monks, is feeling? There are, monks, these six bodies of feeling: feeling born of eye-contact, feeling born of ear-contact, feeling born of nose-contact, feeling born of tongue-contact, feeling born of body-contact, feeling born of mind-contact. This, monks, is called feeling.[b]

And which, monks, is contact? There are, monks, these six bodies of contact: eye-contact, ear-contact, nose-contact, tongue-contact, body-contact, mind-contact. This, monks, is called contact.[c]

And which, monks, are the six bases? The eye-base, the ear-base, the nose-base, the tongue-base, the body-base, the mind-base. These, monks, are called the six bases.[d]

And which, monks, is name-&-matter? Feeling, perception, intention, contact, attention: this is called name. The four great entities and matter held (i.e. taken up by craving) from the four great entities: this is called matter. Thus, this is name and this is matter. This, monks, is called name-&-matter.[e]

And which, monks, is consciousness? There are, monks, these six bodies of consciousness: eye-consciousness, ear-consciousness, nose-consciousness, tongue-consciousness, body-consciousness, mind-consciousness. This, monks, is called consciousness.[f]

And which, monks, are determinations? There are, monks, three determinations; body-determination, speech-determination, mind-determination. These, monks, are called determinations.[g]

---

**a.** §7. Craving: *manque d'être*. 'Freedom is precisely the being which makes itself a lack of being. But since desire, as we have established, is identical with lack of being, freedom can arise only as being which makes itself a desire of being...' *B&N*, p. 567.

**b.** §8. Feeling: *appectivité*. 'It is this original relation which subsequently allows the empirical establishment of particular lacks as lacks *suffered* or endured.' *B&N*, p. 199.

**c.** §9. Contact: *liberté en situation*.

**d.** §10. The six bases: *le corps pour soi*.

**e.** §11. Name-&-matter: *signification-et-existent-brut/l'objet transcendant/l'être-en-soi/la chose-ustensile/ceci*. 'There is an unchangeable element in the past... and an element which is eminently variable. But since, on the other hand, the meaning of the past fact penetrates it through and through... it is finally impossible for me to distinguish the unchangeable brute existence from the variable meaning which it includes.' *B&N*, p. 497-8.

**f.** §12. Consciousness: *conscience/l'être-pour-soi*, etc.

**g.** §13. Determinations: *néatisation*.

And which, monks, is nescience? Non-knowledge of suffering, non-knowledge of arising of suffering, non-knowledge of ceasing of suffering, non-knowledge of the way that leads to ceasing of suffering. This, monks, is called nescience.[a]

(S.xii.2/ii,2-4)

10. An earliest point of nescience, monks, is not manifest: 'Before this, nescience was not; then afterwards it came into being'. Even if that is said thus, monks, nevertheless it is manifest: 'With this as condition, nescience'. I say, monks, that nescience, too, is with sustenance, not without sustenance.[b]

(A.X,61/v,113)

11. An earliest point of craving-for-being, monks, is not manifest: 'Before this, craving-for-being was not; then afterwards it came into being'. Even if that is said thus, monks, nevertheless it is manifest: 'With this as condition, craving-for-being'. I say, monks, that craving-for-being, too, is with sustenance, not without sustenance. And what is the sustenance of craving-for-being? 'Nescience' would be the reply.[c]

(A.X,62/v,116)

12. Thus I heard. Once the Auspicious One was dwelling among the Kurus: the name of the Kurus' town was Kammasadamma. Then the Venerable Ānanda, approaching the Auspicious One, paying the Auspicious One homage and sitting down at one side, said this to the Auspicious One.—

---

**a.** §14. Nescience can perhaps be regarded as the tacit assumption (*Project*) that there is permanence, failing which there can be no *néatisation*. See footnote §31. 'The first potentiality of the object as the correlate of the engagement, an ontological structure of the negation, is permanence...' *B&N*, p. 193

**b.** §15. 'There cannot be "nothingness of consciousness" *before* consciousness.' *B&N*, p. lv. Cf. *NP* §§24 & 25. 'Consequently it is impossible at any particular moment when we consider a For-itself, to apprehend it as not-yet-having a Past.' *B&N*, p. 138. '... there can be no consciousness without a past.' *B&N*, p. 138.

**c.** §16. 'Fundamentally man is the desire to be, and the existence of this desire is not to be established by an empirical induction; it is the result of an *a priori* description of the being of the for-itself, since desire is a lack and since the for-itself is the being which is to itself its own lack of being.' *B&N*, p. 565.

Wonderful it is, Lord, marvellous it is, Lord, how deep is this dependent arising and how deep, Lord, it seems. But to me it appears quite plain.

—Say not so, Ānanda, say not so, Ānanda. This dependent arising is deep and deep, Ānanda, it seems. It is, Ānanda, through non-discernment and non-penetration of this Teaching that this generation is as a matted skein, a tangled thread, a heap of grass, and has not overcome perdition, the ill destiny, the realm of misery, the course. Being asked, Ānanda, 'Is there that with which as condition, there is ageing-&-death?', 'There is' would be the reply. If it were asked, 'With what as condition, ageing-&-death?', 'With birth as condition, ageing-&-death' would be the reply. Being asked, Ānanda, 'Is there that with which as condition, there is birth … being … holding … craving … feeling … contact … six bases … name-&-matter … consciousness?', 'There is' would be the reply. If it were asked, 'With what as condition, consciousness?', 'With name-&-matter as condition, consciousness' would be the reply.[a] Thus, Ānanda, with name-&-matter as condition, consciousness; with consciousness as condition, name-&-matter; with name-&-matter as condition, contact … feeling … craving … holding … being … birth; with birth as condition, ageing-&-death, sorrow, lamentation, pain, grief, and despair, come into being; thus is the arising of this whole mass of unpleasure (suffering).

'With birth as condition, ageing-&-death'. Thus it was said; how it is, Ānanda, that with birth as condition, ageing-&-death, should be seen in this manner. Were there, Ānanda, no birth at all in any way whatsoever of anything anywhere, that is to say, of deities as deities, of fairies as fairies, of spirits as spirits, of entities as entities, of men as men, of animals as animals, of birds as birds, of reptiles as reptiles,—were there no birth, Ānanda, of any of these creatures as such—, were birth altogether absent, with cessation of birth, would ageing-&-death be manifest?

—No indeed, Lord.

—Therefore, Ānanda, just this is the reason, this is the occasion, this is the arising, this is the condition of ageing-&-death, that is to say, birth.

'With being as condition, birth'. Thus it was said; how it is Ānanda, that with being as condition, birth, should be seen in this manner. Were there, Ānanda, no being at all in any way whatsoever of anything anywhere, that is to say, sensual being, material being, or immaterial being, were being altogether absent, with cessation of being, would birth be manifest?

---

**a.** §17. 'The for-itself arises as the nihilation of the in-itself and this nihilation is defined as the project towards the in-itself. Between the nihilated in-itself and the projected in-itself the for-itself is nothingness.' *B&N*, p. 565.

—No indeed, Lord.

—Therefore, Ānanda, just this is the reason, this is the occasion, this is the arising, this is the condition of birth, that is to say, being.

'With holding as condition, being'. Thus it was said; how it is, Ānanda, that with holding as condition, being, should be seen in this manner. Were there, Ānanda, no holding at all in any way whatsoever of anything anywhere, that is to say, sensual holding, holding to view, holding to virtue and duty, holding to belief in self, were holding altogether absent, with cessation of holding, would being be manifest?

—No indeed, Lord.

—Therefore, Ānanda, just this is the reason, this is the occasion, this is the arising, this is the condition of being, that is to say, holding.

'With craving as condition, holding'. Thus it was said; how it is, Ānanda, that with craving as condition, holding, should be seen in this manner. Were there, Ānanda, no craving at all in any way whatsoever of anything anywhere, that is to say, craving for visible forms, craving for sounds, craving for smells, craving for tastes, craving for touches, craving for images/ideas, were craving altogether absent, with cessation of craving, would holding be manifest?

—No indeed, Lord.

—Therefore, Ānanda, just this is the reason, this is the occasion, this is the arising, this is the condition of holding, that is to say, craving.

'With feeling as condition, craving'. Thus it was said; how it is, Ānanda, that with feeling as condition, craving, should be seen in this manner. Were there, Ānanda, no feeling at all in any way whatsoever of anything anywhere, that is to say, feeling born of eye-contact, feeling born of ear-contact, feeling born of nose-contact, feeling born of tongue-contact, feeling born of body-contact, feeling born of mind-contact, were feeling altogether absent, with cessation of feeling would craving be manifest?

—No indeed, Lord.

—Therefore, Ānanda, just this is the reason, this is the occasion, this is the arising, this is the condition of craving, that is to say, feeling.

But, Ānanda, dependent upon this feeling, craving; dependent upon craving, seeking, dependent upon seeking, gain; dependent upon gain, anticipation; dependent upon anticipation, desire-&-lust; dependent upon desire-&-lust, attachment; dependent upon attachment, possession; dependent upon possession, jealousy; dependent upon jealousy, guarding; dependent upon guarding, taking up of clubs and knives, fights, disputes, quarrels, contention, slander, lying, and various evil unprofitable things come to be.

'Because of guarding, taking up of clubs and knives, fights, disputes, quarrels, contention, slander, lying, and various evil unprofitable things come to be'. Thus it was said; how it is, Ānanda, that with guarding, taking up of clubs and knives, fights, disputes, quarrels, contention, slander, lying, and various evil unprofitable things come to be should be seen in this manner. Were there no guarding at all in any way whatsoever of anything anywhere, guarding being altogether absent, with cessation of guarding, would taking up of clubs and knives, fights, disputes, quarrels, contention, slander, lying, and various evil unprofitable things come to be?

—No indeed, Lord.

—Therefore, Ānanda, just this is the reason, this is the occasion, this is the arising, this is the condition of taking up of clubs and knives, fights, disputes, quarrels, contention, slander, lying, and various evil unprofitable things, that is to say, guarding.

'Dependent upon jealousy, guarding'. Thus it was said; how it is, Ānanda, that with jealousy, guarding, should be seen in this manner. Were there, Ānanda, no jealousy at all in any way whatsoever of anything anywhere, would guarding be manifest?

—No indeed, Lord.

—Therefore, Ānanda, just this is the reason, this is the occasion, this is the arising, this is the condition of guarding, that is to say, jealousy.

'Dependent upon possession ... attachment ... desire-&-lust ... anticipation ... gain ... seeking ... craving, seeking'. Thus it was said; how it is, Ānanda, that with craving as condition, seeking, should be seen in this manner. Were there, Ānanda, no craving at all in any way whatsoever of anything anywhere, that is to say, craving for visible forms, craving for sounds, craving for smells, craving for tastes, craving for touches, craving for images/ideas, were craving altogether absent, with cessation of craving, would seeking be manifest?

—No indeed, Lord.

—Therefore, Ānanda, just this is the reason, this is the occasion, this is the arising, this is the condition of seeking, that is to say, craving,

Thus, Ānanda, these two things, as a dyad, have a meeting place in feeling.

'With contact as condition, feeling'. Thus it was said: how it is, Ānanda, that with contact as condition" feeling, should be seen in this manner. Were there, Ānanda, no contact at all in any way whatsoever of anything anywhere, that is to say, eye-contact, ear-contact, nose-contact, tongue-contact, body-contact, mind-contact, were contact altogether absent, with cessation of contact, would feeling be manifest?

—No indeed, Lord.

—Therefore, Ānanda, just this is the reason, this is the occasion, this is the arising, this is the condition of feeling, that is to say, contact.

'With name-&-matter as condition, contact'. Thus it was said; how it is, Ānanda, that with name-&-matter as condition, contact, should be seen in this manner. Those tokens, Ānanda, those marks, those signs, those indications by which the name-body is described,—they being absent, would designation-contact be manifest in the matter-body?

—No indeed, Lord.[a]

—Those tokens, Ānanda, those marks, those signs, those indications by which the matter-body is described,—they being absent, would resistance-contact be manifest in the name-body?

—No indeed, Lord.[b]

—Those tokens, Ānanda, those marks, those signs, those indications by which the name-body and the matter-body are described,—they being absent, would either designation-contact or resistance-contact be manifest?

—No indeed, Lord.

—Those tokens, Ānanda, those marks, those signs, those indications by which name-&-matter is described,—they being absent, would contact be manifest?

—No indeed, Lord.

—Therefore, Ānanda, just this is the reason, this is the occasion, this is the arising, this is the condition of contact, that is to say name-&-matter.

'With consciousness as condition, name-&-matter'. Thus it was said; how it is, Ānanda, that with consciousness as condition, name-&-matter, should

---

**a.** §18. 'It is by its very surpassing of the given towards its end that freedom causes the given to exist as *this* given here (previously there was neither *this* nor *that* nor *here*) and the given thus *designated* is not formed in any way whatsoever; it is a brute existence, assumed in order to be surpassed.' *B&N*, p. 508.

The fact that designation-contact affects matter—i.e. adaptation of the body or senses, appearance of a/the future state of the world, defining the present state, but whose presumed effects (always 'magical') are manifest objectively as bodily disturbances after emotion, for example, or as bodily movement or as psychokinetic phenomena etc.—would seem to account for the various supernormal accomplishments (*iḍḍhi*) obtainable by the practice of mental concentration (D.2), and also for obtaining a fresh body after death. This text and 27 appear to require that ideas (*dhammā*)—'What are cognized by the mind'—be regarded as 'matter' (or *existence brut*) along with visible forms, sounds, smells, tastes, and touches. In other words, ideas are images. See footnote §33.

**b.** §19. 'The In-itself is what the For-itself was *before*.' *B&N*, p. 139. '...since the for-itself is the being which always lays claim to an "after" there is no place for death in the being which is for-itself.' *B&N*, p. 540. See 17.

be seen in this manner. If, Ānanda, consciousness were not to descend into the mother's womb, would name-&-matter be consolidated in the mother's womb?[a]

—No indeed, Lord.

—If, Ānanda, having descended into the mother's womb, consciousness were to turn aside, would name-&-matter be delivered into this situation?

—No indeed, Lord.

—If, Ānanda, consciousness were cut off from one still young, from a boy or a girl, would name-&-matter come to increase, growth, and fullness?

—No indeed, Lord.

—Therefore, Ānanda, just this is the reason, this is the occasion, this is the arising, this is the condition of name-&-matter, that is to say, consciousness.

'With name-&-matter as condition, consciousness'. Thus it was said; how it is, Ānanda, that with name-&-matter as condition, consciousness, should be seen in this manner. If, Ānanda, consciousness were not to obtain a stay in name-&-matter, would future arising and coming-into-being of birth, ageing, death, and unpleasure (suffering), be manifest?[b]

—No indeed, Lord.

—Therefore, Ānanda, just this is the reason, this is the occasion, this is the arising, this is the condition of consciousness, that is to say, name-&-matter.

Thus far, Ānanda, may one be born or age or die or fall or arise, thus far is there a way of designation, thus far is there a way of language, thus far is there a way of description, thus far is there a sphere of understanding, thus far the round proceeds as manifestation in a situation,—so far, that is to say, as there is name-&-matter together with consciousness.[c]

How far, Ānanda, does one consider self? One considers self, Ānanda, in regard to feeling: 'My self is feeling. My self is not in fact feeling, my

---

**a.** §20. 'Thus at the end of this account sensation and action are rejoined and become one.' *B&N*, p. 325.

**b.** §21. 'The result is that the psychic form contains two coexisting contradictory modalities of being, since it is *already made* and appears in the cohesive unity of an organism and since at the same time it can exist only through a succession of "nows", each one of which tends to be isolated in an in-itself.' *B&N*, pp. 165-6.

**c.** §22. This double 'movement', name → matter, matter → name, calls to mind the 'feedback' characteristic of end-seeking machines. Cf. also *B&N*, pp. 126-7. Cf. also *NP* §19, NĀMA, PHASSA (a), SAṄKHĀRA.

self is devoid of feeling.[a] My self is not in fact feeling but neither is my self devoid of feeling, my self feels, it is the nature of my self to feel'.[b]

Herein, Ānanda, to one who says 'My self is feeling' this would be the reply: 'There are, friend, these three feelings, pleasant feeling, unpleasant feeling, neither-unpleasant-nor-pleasant feeling: which of these three feelings do you consider to be self?' Whenever, Ānanda, one feels a pleasant feeling, at that time one neither feels an unpleasant feeling, nor does one feel neither-unpleasant-nor-pleasant feeling; at that time one feels only a pleasant feeling. Whenever, Ānanda, one feels an unpleasant feeling, at that time one neither feels a pleasant feeling nor does one feel neither-unpleasant-nor-pleasant feeling. Whenever, Ānanda, one feels neither-unpleasant-nor-pleasant feeling, at that time one neither feels a pleasant feeling, nor does one feel an unpleasant feeling.

A pleasant feeling, Ānanda, is impermanent, determined, dependently arisen, it has the nature of exhaustion, of dissolution, of fading out, of cessation. An unpleasant feeling, Ānanda, is impermanent, determined, dependently arisen, it has the nature of exhaustion, of dissolution, of fading out, of cessation. A neither-unpleasant-nor-pleasant feeling, Ānanda, is impermanent, determined, dependently arisen. It has the nature of exhaustion, of dissolution, of fading out, of cessation.

In one to whom it occurs, when feeling a pleasant (unpleasant, neither-unpleasant-nor-pleasant) feeling, 'This is my self', it will also occur, when that same pleasant (unpleasant, neither-unpleasant-nor-pleasant) feeling ceases, 'My self has dissolved'.

Thus, one who says 'My self is feeling' is considering self to be something that is here and now impermanent, a mixture of pleasure and unpleasure, and that has the nature of rising and falling. Therefore, Ānanda, it will not do to consider 'My self is feeling'.

Herein, Ānanda, to one who says 'My self indeed is not feeling; my self is devoid of feeling', this would be the reply: 'But where, friend, there is no feeling at all, would there be any saying "I am"?'

—No indeed, Lord.

—Therefore, Ānanda, it will not do to consider 'My self indeed is not feeling, my self is devoid of feeling'.

Herein, Ānanda, to one who says 'My self, indeed, is not feeling, nor yet

**a.** §23. 'It is precisely my *being-for-others*, this being which is divided between two negations with opposed origins and opposite meanings.' *B&N*, p. 286.

**b.** §24. 'Pleasure is the being of self-consciousness and this self-consciousness is the law of being of pleasure.' *B&N*, p. 286

is my self devoid of feeling; my self feels; to feel is the nature of my self', this would be the reply: 'Were all feeling, friend, in every way whatsoever to cease without remainder, were feeling altogether absent, with cessation of feeling would there be any saying "It is this that I am"?'

—No indeed, Lord.

—Therefore, Ānanda, it will not do to consider 'My self, indeed, is not feeling, nor yet is my self devoid of feeling; my self feels; to feel is the nature of my self'.

When, Ānanda, a monk does not consider self to be feeling, nor considers self to be void of feeling, nor considers 'My self feels, to feel is the nature of my self', he, not so considering, holds to nothing in the world; not holding, he is not anxious; not being anxious, he individually becomes extinct; 'Birth is exhausted, the life of purity is fulfilled, what was to be done is done, there is no more of this existence to come', so he understands.

For one, Ānanda, to say of a monk whose mind is thus released that his view is 'After death the Tathāgata is (the Tathāgata is not; the Tathāgata both is and is not; the Tathāgata neither is nor is not)'—that would not be proper. Why is this? In however far, Ānanda, there is designation, in however far there is mode of designation, in however far there is expression, in however far there is mode of expression, in however far the is description, in however far there is mode of description, in however far there is understanding, in however far there is the sphere of understanding, in however far there is the round, in however far there is the coursing on—it is by directly knowing this that a monk is released. To say of a monk released by directly knowing this, that he does not know, that he does not see, that his views are thus—that would not be proper.

(D.15/ii,55-68)

**13.** This consciousness turns back from name-&-matter; it does not go further; thus far one may be born or age or die or fall away or arise; that is to say, with name-&-matter as condition, consciousness. With consciousness as condition, name-&-matter. With name-&-matter as condition six bases... thus is the arising of this whole mass of unpleasure (suffering).[a]

(S.xii.65/ii,104)

**a.** §25. '... it is the very nature of consciousness to exist "in a circle".' *B&N*, p. liii, Cf. also *NP* §17.

**14.**—What the Venerable Sāriputta said just now we comprehend thus: Not, friend Koṭṭhita, 'Name-&-matter is made by oneself'. Not, friend Koṭṭhita, 'Name-&-matter is made by another'. Not, friend Koṭṭhita, 'Name-&-matter is made both by oneself and by another'. Not, friend Koṭṭhita, 'Name-&-matter is made neither by oneself nor by another but arises by chance'; but with consciousness as condition, name-&-matter.

But also what the Venerable Sāriputta said just now we comprehend thus: Not, friend Koṭṭhita, 'Consciousness is made by oneself'. Not, friend Koṭṭhita, 'Consciousness is made by another'. Not, friend Koṭṭhita, 'Consciousness is made both by oneself and by another'. Not, friend Koṭṭhita, 'Consciousness is made neither by oneself nor by another but arises by chance'; but with name-&-matter as condition, consciousness.

How, friend Sāriputta, should the meaning of these sayings be seen?

—Then, friend, I shall give you a simile; for through a simile some intelligent men comprehend the meaning of a saying. Suppose, friend, there were two bundles of reeds standing leaning against each other; just so, friend, with name-&-matter as condition, consciousness; with consciousness as condition, name-&-matter; with name-&-matter as condition, six bases... thus is the arising of this whole mass of unpleasure (suffering).

(S.xii.67/ii,114)

**15.** What, monks, one intends and what one projects and what one tends to, that is the support for the standing of consciousness; when there is increase of consciousness supported thereby, there is descent of name-&-matter; with name-&-matter as condition, six bases... this whole mass of unpleasure (suffering).

(S.xii.39/ii,66)

**16.** What, monks, one intends and what one projects and what one tends to, that is the support for the standing of consciousness; when there is increase of consciousness supported thereby, there is inclination; when there is inclination there is coming and going; when there is coming and going there is falling away and arising; when there is falling away and arising, further birth, ageing-&-death... this whole mass of unpleasure (suffering).[a]

(S.xii.40/ii,67)

**a.** §26. 'The project of being or desire of being or drive towards being ... in fact ... is not distinguished from the being of the for-itself.' *B&N*, pp. 564-5.

17. By means of matter, monks, consciousness will stand; supported by matter, established in matter, pursuing delight, it will come to increase, growth, and fullness. Supported by feeling… Supported by perception… Supported by determinations, established in determinations, pursuing delight, it will come to increase, growth, and fullness.

That anyone should (truly) say 'Apart from matter, apart from feeling, apart from perception, apart from determinations, I shall show the coming or the going or the falling away or the arising or the increase or the growth or the fullness of consciousness'—that is not possible.[a]

(S.xxii.53/iii,53)

18. Action, monks, I say is intention; intending one does action by body, by speech, by mind.[b]

(A.VI,63/iii,415)

19. And which, monks, is matter? …And which, monks, is feeling? …And which, monks, is perception? There are, monks, these six bodies of perception: perception of visible forms, perception of sounds, perception of smells, perception of tastes, perception of tangibles, perception of images/ideas. This, monks, is called perception. And which, monks, are determinations? … And which, monks, is consciousness?

(S.xxii.56/iii,59-61)

20. And what, monks, do you say is matter?… And what, monks, do you say is feeling?… And what, monks, do you say is perception?… And what, monks, do you say are determinations? 'They determine the determined': that, monks, is why they are called 'determinations'. And what is the determined that they determine? Matter as matter is the determined that they determine, feeling as feeling is the determined that they determine, perception as perception is the determined that they determine, determinations as determinations are the determined that they determine, consciousness as

---

**a.** §27. Thus it seems that the first four aggregates—matter, feeling, perception, determinations—are equivalent to name-&-matter, though the Suttas never say so specifically—a fact that is unusually significant. See 12.

**b.** §28. 'Besides, if the act is not pure *movement*, it must be defined by an *intention*.' *B&N*, p. 477. Cf. *NP* §4.

consciousness is the determined that they determine. 'They determine the determined': that indeed, monks, is why they are called 'determinations'. And what, monks, do you say is consciousness?...[a]

(S.xxii.79/iii,87)

**21.** Matter, monks, is impermanent, feeling is impermanent, perception is impermanent, determinations are impermanent, consciousness is impermanent; matter, monks, is not-self, feeling is not-self, perception is not-self, determinations are not-self, consciousness is not-self; all determinations are impermanent, all things are not-self. (*dhammā*: ideas [of things] → [ideas of] things)

(M.44/i,301)

**22.** That, friend, which is feeling, that which is perception, that which is consciousness,—these things are associated, not dissociated, and it is not possible to show the distinction between these things having separated them one from another. For what, friend, one feels that one perceives, what one perceives that one cognizes,—that is why these things are associated, not dissociated, and it is not possible to show the distinction between these things having separated them one from another.

(M.43/i,293)

**23.** A stupid/intelligent man, monks, constrained by nescience and attached by craving, has thus acquired this body. So there is just this body and name-&-matter externally: in that way there is a dyad. Dependent upon this dyad, contact—just six bases, contacted by which, or by one of which, the stupid/intelligent man experiences pleasure and unpleasure.[b]

(S.xii.19/ii,24)

---

**a.** §29. Note that in this passage the description of matter, feeling, perception, and consciousness are not as in 9 and 19: 'Matter' is afflicted by heat, cold, hunger, thirst, insects, etc.; 'feeling' is pleasant, unpleasant, and neither-pleasant-nor-unpleasant; 'perception' is of blue, yellow, red, etc.; 'consciousness' is of sour, bitter, etc. Cf. *NP* §14.

**b.** §30. 'All that there is of *intention* in my actual consciousness is directed toward the outside, toward the table; all my judgments or practical activities, all my present inclinations transcend themselves; they aim at the table and are absorbed in it.' *B&N*, pp. li-lii. 'What the world makes known to me is only "worldly".' *B&N*, p. 200. 'It is the instrumental-things which in their original appearance indicate our body to us.

**24.** 'Not by going, monks, do I say that the end of the world is to be known or seen or reached; but neither, monks, do I say that without reaching the end of the world there is a making an end of suffering.' The expanded meaning, friends, of this brief indication and outline of the Auspicious One's, whose expanded meaning he did not explain, I comprehend thus.

That by which, friend, in the world, one is a perceiver and conceiver of the world, that, in the Noble discipline, is called the world. And by what, friends, in the world, is one a perceiver and conceiver of the world? By the eye (ear, nose, tongue, body, mind), friends, in the world, is one a perceiver and conceiver of the world. That by which, friends, one is a perceiver and conceiver of the world, that, in the Noble discipline, is called the world.[a]

(S.xxxv.116/iv,95)

**25.** 'With entire fading out and cessation, friend, of the six contact-bases, there is something else'—saying thus, one diversifies non-diversification. 'With entire fading out and cessation, friend, of the six contact-bases, there is not something else ... there both is and is not something else ... there neither is nor is not something else'—saying thus, one diversifies non-diversification. So long, friend, as the six contact-bases continue, so long diversification continues; so long as diversification continues, so long the six contact-bases continue. With entire fading out and cessation of the six contact-bases, ceasing and subsidence of diversification.[b]

(A.IV,174/ii,161-2)

---

The body is not a secret between things and ourselves; it manifests only the individuality and the contingency in our original relation to instrumental-things.' *B&N*, p. 325. 'It would be useless to look there (in the body for-me) for traces of a physiological organ, of an anatomical and spatial constitution. Either it is the centre of reference indicated emptily by the instrumental-objects of the world or else it is the contingency which the for-itself exists. More exactly, these two modes of being are complementary.' *B&N*, p. 339. Cf. NĀMA.

**a.** §31. 'Thus it is the upsurge of the for-itself in the world by which the same stroke causes the world to exist as the totality of things and causes senses to exist as the objective mode in which the qualities of things are presented.' *B&N*, p. 319. 'In this sense we defined the senses and the sense organs in general as our being-in-the-world in so far as we have to be it in the form of being-in-the-midst-of-the-world.' *B&N*, p. 325. Cf. MANO.

**b.** §32. 'It is through human reality that multiplicity comes into the world...' *B&N*, p. 137.

**26.** Dependent upon eye and forms, eye-consciousness arises; the coming together of the three is contact; with contact as condition, feeling... this whole mass of unpleasure (suffering). This is the arising of the world. Dependent upon ear and sounds... Dependent upon nose and smells.... Dependent upon tongue and tastes... Dependent upon mind and images/ideas... the arising of the world.[a]

(S.xxxv.107/iv,87)

**27.** There are, friend, these five faculties with various provinces and various pastures, and they do not enjoy (*éprouver*) one another's pasture and province; that is to say, eye-faculty, ear-faculty, nose-faculty, tongue-faculty, body-faculty. These five faculties with various provinces and pastures, that do not enjoy one another's pasture and province, mind is the association, mind enjoys their pasture and province.[b]

(M.43/i,295)

---

**a.** §33. 'If the situation is neither subjective nor objective, this is because it does not constitute a *knowledge* nor even an affective comprehension of the state of the world by a subject. The situation is a *relation of being* between a for-itself and the in-itself which the for-itself nihilates. The situation is the whole subject (he is *nothing but* his situation) and it is also the whole "thing"...' *B&N*, p. 549. 'Six internal/external (subjective/objective) bases' are sometimes spoken of (e.g. D.22/ii,292-304). The external bases—visible forms, sounds, smells, tastes, touches, images/ideas—are *existence brut* and appear to correspond to the 'matter' of name-&-matter or rather, the 'matter' of name-&-matter is (at any level) the discrepancy between the external bases and the internal bases as (bodily) adaptation ('...the glass-drunk-from haunts the full glass as its possible and constitutes it as a glass to be drunk from' *B&N*, p. 104). The internal bases—eye, ear, nose, tongue, body, mind—have name-&-matter as condition; and they may perhaps be thought of as a field (in the mathematical sense) defined by name-&-matter (cf. 'The "this" always appears on a ground; that is, on the undifferentiated totality of being inasmuch as the For-itself is the radical and syncretic negation of it.' *B&N*, p. 182). But since every name-&-matter, every *ceci*, that is to say, is itself a project to change a *ceci* of lower order ('But at the same time that freedom is a surpassing of *this given*, it chooses itself as *this* surpassing of the given. Freedom is not just any kind of surpassing of any kind of given. By assuming the brute given and by conferring meaning on it, freedom has suddenly chosen itself; its end is exactly *to change this given*, just as the given appears as this given in the light of the end chosen.' *B&N*, p. 508), every field (of whatever order) is a field of field-changes. It is perhaps significant that there is a Sutta passage (A.IV,171/ii,158) where 'field (*khetta*) and 'ground' (*vatthu*) are synonyms for 'base'(*āyatana*).

**b.** §34. 'In fact the lemon is extended throughout its qualities and each of its qualities is extended throughout each of the others.' *B&N*, p. 186. '...it is this total

**28.** What is impermanent is suffering; what is suffering is not-self.

(S.xxxv.4/iv,3)

**29.** All determinations are impermanent. All determinations are unpleasurable (suffering). All things are not-self.[a]

(Dhp.277-9/xx,5-7)

**30.** There are, monks, these three determined-characteristics of what is determined. Which are the three? Arising (appearance) is manifest; disappearance is manifest; change while standing is manifest. These, monks, are the three determined-characteristics of what is determined.

There are, monks, these three undetermined-characteristics of what is undetermined. Which are the three? Arising (appearance) is not manifest; disappearance is not manifest; change while standing is not manifest. These, monks, are the three undetermined-characteristics of what is undetermined.[b]

(A.III,47/i,152)

**31.** Attention to the foul should be developed to put away lust; amity should be developed to put away anger; mindfulness of breathing should be devel-

---

inter-penetration which we call the *this*.' *B&N*, p. 186. The word 'faculty' (*indriya*) aprears to be used when the senses are spoken of without reference to the situation, and may refer either to one's own senses (as here) or to the sense *d'autrui*, sometimes in the same passage. The word 'six bases' (*saḷāyatanā*) is never, it seems, used of other' senses.

**a.** §35. 'The revelation of the table as table requires a permanence *of* table which comes to it from the future and which is not a purely established *given*, but a potentiality.' *B&N*, p. 193. 'The being of human reality is suffering because it rises in being as perpetually haunted by a totality which it is without being able to be it; precisely because it could not attain the in-itself without losing itself as for-itself.' *B&N*, p. 90. Why is this *of necessity* a condition for suffering? 'The possible is *that which* a For-itself lacks in order to be itself or, if you prefer, the appearance of what I am—at a distance.' *B&N*, p. 125. 'The eternity which man is seeking is not the infinity of duration, of that vain pursuit after the self for which I am myself responsible; man seeks a repose in self, the atemporality of the absolute coincidence with himself.' *B&N*, p. 141-2. Cf. *NP* §12 *et seq*.

**b.** §36. 'The "thing" exists straightway as a "form"; that is, a whole which is not affected by any of the superficial parasitic variations which we can see on it. Each *this* is revealed with a law of being which determines its threshold, its level of change where it will cease to be what it is in order simply not to be.' *B&N*, pp. 205-6.

oped for the cutting off of thoughts; perception of impermanence should be developed to remove the conceit 'I am'. In one who perceives impermanence, Meghiya, perception of not-self becomes steady (*santhāti*); one who perceives not-self reaches removal of the conceit 'I am' and extinction (*nibbāna*) here and now.

(Ud.31/37)

**32.** But when 'I am' is not done away with, then there is descent of the five faculties: of the eye-faculty, of the ear-faculty, of the nose-faculty, of the tongue-faculty, of the body-faculty. There is mind, monks, there are images/ideas, there is the nescience element. To the uninstructed commoner, monks, contacted by feeling born of nescience-contact, it occurs '(I) am', it occurs 'It is this that I am', it occurs 'I shall be', it occurs 'I shall not be'....[a]

(S.xxii.47/iii,46)

**33.** Suppose, friends, there was a fragrant lotus, blue or red or white. Were one to say 'The fragrance belongs to the petals or the colour or the filaments', would one be speaking rightly?

—No indeed, friend.

—But how, friends, would one be speaking rightly?

—'The fragrance belongs to the flower', thus indeed, friend, would one be speaking rightly.

—Just so, friends, I do not say 'I am matter (feeling, perception, determinations, consciousness)', nor do I say 'I am other than matter (feeling, perception, determinations, consciousness)'. And yet, friends, with regard to the five holding aggregates, 'I am' occurs to me, but I do not consider 'This am I'. Although, friends, the five lower fetters may be put away in a noble disciple, yet there is still a remnant for him, regarding the five holding aggregates, of the desire 'I am', of the aroma 'I am', that is not removed. At a later time he dwells contemplating arising and dissolution of the five holding aggregates: 'Thus matter (feeling, perception, determinations, consciousness), thus arising of matter (...consciousness), thus passing away of matter (...consciousness). For him, contemplating arising and dissolution of these five holding aggregates, the remnant regarding the five holding aggregates, of the desire

**a.** §37. 'In order for value to become the object of a thesis, the for-itself which it haunts must also appear before the regard of reflection.' *B&N*, p. 95. Cf. DHAMMA [b].

'I am', of the aroma 'I am', that was not removed, comes to be removed.[a]

(S.xxii.89/iii,130-1)

**34.** At present, indeed, I am devoured by matter (...consciousness); in the past too I was devoured by matter (...consciousness), just as I am at present devoured by presently arisen matter (...consciousness); and indeed, if I were to delight in future matter (...consciousness), in the future too I should be devoured by matter (...consciousness), just as I am at present devoured by presently arisen matter (...consciousness).[b]

(S.xxii.79/iii,87-8)

**35.** Matter (...consciousness), monks, is not-self. For if, monks, matter (... consciousness) were self, then matter (...consciousness) would not lead to affliction, and one would obtain of matter (...consciousness) 'Let my matter be thus, let my matter not be thus'. As indeed, monks, matter (... consciousness) is not-self, so matter (...consciousness) leads to affliction, and it is not obtained of matter (...consciousness) 'Let my matter be thus, let my matter not be thus'.[c]

(S.xxii.59/iii,66)

**36.** Might there be anxiety about subjective absence, lord?

—There might be, monk, the Auspicious One said. Here, monk, someone holds this view: 'The world is self; and when I have departed I shall be permanent, enduring, eternal, not having the nature of change; and like this shall I remain for ever and ever'. He listens to the Tathāgata or his disciple setting forth the Teaching for the destroying of all tendencies to views, assertions, obsessions, and insistencies, for the calming of all determinations, for the relinquishing of all foundations, for the destroy-

**a.** §38. 'Pure reflection is never anything but a quasi-knowledge....' *B&N*, p. 162. '...everywhere and in whatever manner it affects itself, the for-itself is condemned to be-for-itself. In fact, it is here that pure reflection is discovered.' *B&N*, p. 160.

**b.** §39. 'My attitude ... is ... a pure mode ... of causing myself to be drunk in by things as ink is by a blotter...' *B&N*, p. 259.

**c.** §40. '...a being which would be its own foundation could not suffer the slightest discrepancy between what it is and what it conceives, for it would produce itself in conformance with its comprehension of being and could conceive only of what it is.' *B&N*, p. 80. Cf. *PS* §6, DHAMMA.

ing of craving, for fading out, for ceasing, for extinction. It occurs to him 'I shall surely be annihilated! I shall surely perish! I shall surely be no more!' He sorrows, is distressed, and laments, and, beating his breast and bewailing, he falls into confusion. Thus indeed, monks, there is anxiety about subjective absence.[a]

(M.22/i,136-7)

**37.** There is, monks, a non-born, non-become, non-made, non-determined; for if, monks, there were not that non-born, non-become, non-made, non-determined, an escape here from the born, become, made, determined, would not be manifest.

(Ud.viii,3/80)

**38.** There is, monks, that base where there is neither earth nor water nor fire nor air nor the base of endless space nor the base of endless consciousness nor the base of nothingness nor the base of neither-perception-nor-non-perception nor this world nor another world, neither sun nor moon; there, monks, I say that there is neither coming nor going nor standing nor falling away nor arising; that is without establishment, without procedure, without basis; that is just the ending of unpleasure (suffering).

(Ud.viii,1/80)

**39.** Since herein for you (i.e., as, within, or without any or all of the five aggregates), friend Yamaka, here and now the Tathāgata actually and in truth is not to be found, is that explanation of yours proper: 'As I comprehend the Teaching set forth by the Tathāgata, at the breaking up of the body of

---

**a.** §41. 'Yet at each moment I apprehend this initial choice as contingent and unjustifiable; at each moment therefore I am on the site suddenly to consider it objectively and consequently to surpass it and to make-it-past by causing the liberating *instant* to arise. Hence my anguish, the fear which I have of being suddenly exorcized (i.e., of becoming radically other); but hence also the frequent upsurge of "conversions" which cause me totally to metamorphose my original project.' *B&N*, p. 475. Cf. SAÑÑĀ.

a monk whose cankers are destroyed, he is annihilated, he perishes, after death he is not'?[a]

(S.xxii.85/iii,112)

**a.** §42. 'It is impossible to conceive of a consciousness which would not exist in these three dimensions.' *B&N*, p. 137. It is clear from the Suttas that extinction is attained in this very lifetime and that this does not entail immediate death. The question might be asked how it is that an *arahat* (the Buddha himself, for example) while he still lives can walk and talk and eat and drink, even though consciousness (*Pour-soi*) has ceased. But since a living *arahat* cannot actually and in truth be said to exist, except by another who is not himself an *arahat*, it seems hardly reasonable to look to ontology for an answer. The question, however, is invalid, since it assumes the *arahat*'s existence: where name-&-matter and consciousness have ceased, what conceivable mode of designation, expression, or description can there be? In 37 and 38 the Buddha asserts that release is possible. I see no way of showing that assertion to be false, but without individually attaining release, I see no way of showing it to be true. Cf. *PS* §4.

# Glossary

This Glossary contains all Pali, Sanskrit (Sk) and Sinhalese (Sn) words occurring in the 'Letters' and 'Editorial Notes' other than those found only in phrases for which translation is provided. *Notes on Dhamma* is provided with its own 'Glossary'. Those words which are to be found in both glossaries are preceded in this listing by an asterisk. Some words are defined more fully in the 'Glossary' of the *Notes*. Both Glossaries are arranged according to the Pali alphabet:

a, ā, i, ī, u, ū, e, o, k, kh, g, gh, ṅ, c, ch, j, jh, ñ, ṭ, ṭh, ḍ, ḍh, ṇ, t, th, d, dh, n, p, ph, b, bh, m, y, r, l, ḷ, v, s, h, ṃ

*akataññū*—ungratefulness.
* *akusala*—unskilful, bad.
*aññā*—the *arahat*'s knowledge. (N.B. Another word, *añña*, meaning 'other, another', is to be found in *Notes*.)
*aṭṭhaṅgika*—eight-factored.
* *atakkāvacara*—unattainable by reasoning.
* *attavāda*—belief in self.
*attavādupādāna*—holding to the belief in self.
* *attā*—self.
*atman* (Sk)—self.
* *adhivacana*—designation.
*an-* —without (prefix).
*anattasaññā*—perception of not-self.
* *anattā*—not-self.
*anantaṃ*—endless.
*anāgāmitā*—non-returning.
* *anāgāmī*—non-returner.
* *anicca*—impermanent.
* *aniccatā*—impermanence.
*aniccasaññā*—perception of impermanence.
* *anidassana*—non-indicative.
*anupādāna*—without holding.
* *anuloma*—with the grain.
* *aparapaccaya*—not dependent on others.
*abhāvita*—undeveloped.
*abhidhamma*—higher (or extended) Teaching.
*abhivinaya*—higher (or extended) discipline.
* *arahat*—worthy one.
* *arahattā*—worthiness.

* *ariya*—noble.
*ariyakanta*—pleasing to the nobles.
*ariyacakkhu*—noble eye.
*ariyapuggala*—noble individual.
* *ariyasāvaka*—noble disciple.
* *arūpa*—immaterial.
*ayye*—lady.
*alaṃ*—enough.
*aluhaṃ* (Sn)—ash-skin.
* *avijjā*—nescience.
*avidyā* (Sk)—ignorance.
* *asaṅkhata*—non-determined.
*asubha*—foul.
*asubhasaññā*—perception of the foul.
*asekha*—non-trainee (i.e. one who has finished his training, = *arahat*).
* *asmimāna*—the conceit 'I am'.
* *assāsapassāsā*—in-&-out-breaths.
*ashram* (Sk)—a Hindu centre of retreat.
*ākāsānañcāyatana*—the base of infinite space.
* *ākiñcaññāyatana*—the base of nothingness.
*ācariya*—teacher.
*ānāpānasati*—mindfulness of breathing.
* *āneñja*—imperturbability.
*āneñjūpaga*—arrived at imperturbability.
*āpatti*—offence.
* *āyatana*—base.
* *āsava* – canker.
*ida(p)paccayatā*—dependence on this.
*iddhi*—accomplishment; power (usu. supernormal).
*indriyasaṃvara*—restraint of the faculties.
*issaranimmāna*—creator God.
*uccāsayana-mahāsayanā*—high and large resting places.
*ucchedavāda*—belief in annihilation.
*uddhacca-kukkucca*—distraction and worry.
*upaga*—reaching to.
*upajjhāya*—preceptor.
*upasampadā*—ordination (into the status of *bhikkhu*).
* *upādāna*—holding.
*upādiyi*—held.
*upādisesa*—residue.
*upāsaka*—male lay-follower.
*upāsikā*—female lay-follower.
* *upek(k)hā*—indifference.
*uppāda*—arising.
*ekaggatā*—one-pointedness.
*kajan* (Sn)—woven coconut fronds.
*kaṇha*—dark.
* *kamma*—action.
*kammavipāka*—action-&-result.
*karuṇā*—compassion.
*kāma*—sensuality.
*kām'upādāna*—holding to sensuality.
*kāmesu micchācārinī*—transgressor in lusts.
* *kāya*—body.
*kāyasakkhi*—body-witness.
* *kāyika*—bodily.
*kālika*—temporal.
*kuṭi*—cottage.
*kuṭṭhi*—leper.
* *kusala*—skilful, good.

* *khandha*—aggregate.
*khīṇāsava*—destruction of the cankers.
*gāthā*—verses.
*ghoso*—utterance.
*cakkhundriya*—eye-faculty.
*cakkhuppāda*—arising of the eye (of knowledge).
* *citta*—mind.
* *cittavīthi*—cognitive series.
*citt'ekaggatā*—one-pointedness of mind.
* *cetanā*—intention.
*chandarāga*—desire-and-lust.
*chinna*—cut.
* *jhāna*—meditation.
* *ñāṇa*—knowledge.
*ñāṇadassana*—knowing-&-seeing.
*ṭhapaniya*—to be set aside.
*ṭhitassa aññathattaṃ*—change while standing.
*ṭhiti*—station.
* *takka*—reasoning.
* *taṇhā*—craving.
* *Tathāgata*—(epithet of) the Buddha.
*thera*—(male) elder.
*therī*—(female) elder.
*dasa-sīl* (Sn)—ten precepts.
*dassana*—seeing.
*dāna*—gift, esp. of a meal.
*dāyaka*—(male) giver.
* *diṭṭhi*—view.
*diṭṭhipatta*—attained through view.
* *diṭṭhisampanna*—attained to (right) view.
*diṭṭhupādāna*—holding to views.
*dibbacakkhu*—divine eye.
*dukkaṭa*—wrong-doing (a category of minor offences in the *bhikkhu*'s disciplinary rules).
* *dukkha*—suffering.
*dukkhasaññā*—perception of suffering.
*deva* (pl. *devā*)—deity.
*devatā*—deity.
*devaloka*—heavenly world.
* *dosa*—hate.
*dosakkhaya*—destruction of hate.
* *dhamma*—thing, Teaching, etc.
*dhammacakkhu*—eye of the *dhamma*.
*dhammatā*—nature (*dhamma*-ness).
* *dhammanvaya*—inferability of the *dhamma*.
*dhammapīti*—delight on teaching.
*dhammabhūta*—become Dhamma.
* *dhammānusārī*—teaching-follower.
* *dhātu*—element.
*na*—not.
* *nāma*—name.
* *nāmarūpa*—name-&-matter.
*nicca*—permanent.
* *nibbāna*—extinction.
*nimitta*—sign, object.
* *nirodha*—cessation.
*nirodhasamāpatti*—attainment of cessation.
*nirvāṇa* (Sk)—extinction.
*nissaya*—support.
*nīvaraṇa*—hindrance.
*nekkhammasaṅkappa*—thought

of renunciation.
*neti* (Sk)—not this.
*nevasaññānāsaññāyatana*—the base of neither-perception-nor-non-perception.
* *paccaya*—condition.
*paccavekkhana*—reflexion.
* *pañcakkhandhā*—five aggregates.
* *pañc'upādānakkhandhā*—five holding aggregates.
* *paññā*—understanding.
* *paṭigha*—resistance.
*paṭicca-saṃ*—dependent-together.
* *paṭiccasamuppāda*—dependent arising.
*paṭibaddha*—bound up with.
* *paṭiloma*—against the grain.
*paṭissati*—mindfulness.
*paṇḍita*—learned.
*padmāsana*—lotus position (sitting cross-legged).
*parato*—other.
* *paramattha*—highest.
*pariññā*—absolute knowledge.
*pariññeyya*—to be known absolutely.
* *paritassanā*—anxiety.
*parinibbāna*—full extinction.
*paripūrakārī*—fulfills.
*paribbājaka*—wanderer.
*pariyatti*—texts; book-learning.
*pahātabba*—to be abandoned.
*pātubhavati*—to appear.
*pārājika*—defeat.
*pirivena* (Sn)—temple school; university for monks.
* *puggala*—individual.
* *puthujjana*—commoner.
*purusa* (Sk)—person.
*poya* (Sn)—lunar day (half-moons, new moon, full moon).
*polonga* (Sn)—viper.
*prakriti* (Sk)—nature.
* *phassa*—contact.

*baliṃ*—offerings.
*bāhira*—outside.
*bujjhissanti*—will awaken.
*Buddharūpa*—an image of the Buddha (the earliest are some centuries after the Buddha).
*bodhi*—awakening, enlightenment.
*bodhipakkhiya*—on the side of awakening.
*brahmacariya*—the life of purity (i.e. celibacy).
*brahmacārī*—one living a pure life.

*Bhagavā*—Auspicious One.
*bhaginī*—sister.
*bhante*—sir (monastic address, junior to senior; seniors address juniors, and equals to equals, as *āvuso*).
*bhavaṅga*—life-continuum.
*bhavataṇhā*—craving for existence.
*bhāvanā*—development.
*bhāvetabba*—to be developed.
* *bhikkhu*—monk. *passim*
* *bhikkhunī*—nun.
*bhūta*—become.

*maithuna* (Sk)—sex.
* *magga*—path.
*maggaṅga*—factor of the path.
* *manasikāra*—attention.
* *mano*—mind.
*manoviññāṇa*—mind-

consciousness.
*maraṇasati*—mindfulness of death.
*mahāthera*—great elder.
*maṃsacakkhu*—fleshly eye.
*mā*—don't; shouldn't.
*māna*—conceit.
*māyā*—illusion.
* *micchādiṭṭhi*—wrong view.
*mudhalali* (Sn)—merchant.
*mūla*—root.
*mettā*—friendliness.
* *moha*—delusion.
*mohakkhaya*—destruction of delusion.
*yoga*—yoke; discipline.
*yogin*—one in (meditative) discipline.
*yoni*—vagina.
*yoniso*—proper.
*randhagavesī*—looking for faults.
* *rāga*—lust.
*rāgakkhaya*—destruction of lust.
*rilawa* (Sn)—macaque.
* *rūpa*—matter.
*lokiya*—worldly.
* *lokuttara*—beyond the world.
*vandanā*—worship.
*wandura* (Sn)—langur.
*vaya*—disappearance.
*vassāna*—rain, rainy season.
* *viññāṇa*—consciousness.
*viññāṇañcāyatana*—base of endless consciousness.
*vinaya*—discipline, 'leading out'.
*vinayakamma*—disciplinary act.
*vineti*—(to) direct.
*vipassanā*—insight.
* *vipāka*—result.
* *viriya*—energy.
* *vedanā*—feeling.
*vedallakathā*—cross-questioning.
* *sa-* —with (prefix).
*saupādāna*—with holding.
*sakadāgāmitā*—once-returning.
*sakadāgāmī*—once-returner.
*Sakka*—chief of the gods.
* *sakkāya*—person; personality.
* *saṅkhāra*—determination.
* *saṅgha*—Order (of monks).
*saṅghādisesa*—an offence requiring a meeting of the Order.
* *sacca*—truth.
*sacchikātabba*—to be realized.
* *sañcetanā*—intention.
* *saññā*—perception.
* *saññāvedayitanirodha*—cessation of perception and feeling.
* *sati*—mindfulness.
*satindriya*—faculty of mindfulness.
*satipaṭṭhānā*—foundations of mindfulness.
*satibala*—the power of mindfulness.
*satisampajañña*—mindfulness-&-awareness.
*satisambojjhaṅga*—the awakening factor of mindfulness.
*satta-bojjhaṅgā*—seven awakening factors.
*sattamī*—seventh.
*saddhamma*—Good Teaching.
* *saddhā*—faith, confidence.
* *saddhānusārī*—faith-follower.
*saddhāvimutta*—released

through faith.
*sandosa*—rot, decay.
*sappāya*—beneficial.
*sappurisa*—Good Man.
*sabba*—all, every.
*samaṇabrāhmaṇā*—recluses and divines.
*samatha*—calmness; mental concentration.
* *samādhi*—concentration.
*samāpatti*—attainment.
* *samudaya*—arising.
* *sampajañña*—awareness.
*sambuddha*—awakened.
*sammā*—full; right.
*sammādiṭṭhi*—right view.
*sammāsati*—right mindfulness.
*sammāsamādhi*—right concentration.
* *saḷāyatana*—six bases.
*sassatavāda*—eternalist belief.
*saha*—with.
*saṃvara*—restraint.
* *saṃsāra*—running on (from existence to existence).
*Sāsana*—advice; usu. used today in the sense of 'the Buddha's Dispensation'.
*sītabhūta*—become cold.
*sīl* (Sn) = *sīla*.
*sīla*—virtue, (right) conduct.
*sīlabbata*—rites and rituals; conduct and customs.
* *sukha*—pleasure.
*subhanimitta*—lovely object.
* *sekha*—one in training.
*senāsana*—resting place.
* *sotāpatti*—attaining of the stream.
* *sotāpanna*—stream-attainer.
*shivalingam* (Sk)—the phallus of Shiva (a stone found in many Hindu temples).
*hitānukampā*—beneficial compassion.

# Editorial Notes

**[L. 1]**

1. [editors' translation]

HOMAGE TO THE AUSPICIOUS ONE, WORTHY, FULLY AWAKENED

—At one time the monk Ñāṇavīra was staying in a forest hut near Būndala village. It was during that time, as he was walking up and down in the first watch of the night, that the monk Ñāṇavīra made his mind quite pure of constraining things, and kept thinking and pondering and reflexively observing the Dhamma as he had heard and learnt it. Then, while the monk Ñāṇavīra was thus engaged in thinking and pondering and reflexively observing the Dhamma as he had heard and learnt it, the clear and stainless Eye of the Dhamma arose in him: 'Whatever has the nature of arising, all that has the nature of ceasing.'

Having been a teaching-follower for a month, he became one attained to right view.[1]

(27.6.59)

> There is, Kassapa, a path, there is a way by following which one will come to know and see for oneself: 'Indeed, the recluse Gotama speaks at the proper time, speaks on what is, speaks on the purpose, speaks on Dhamma, speaks on Vinaya.' [D.8/i,165]

> 'I have gone beyond the writhings of view.
> With the path gained I have arrived at assurance.
> Knowledge has arisen in me and I am no longer to be guided by another.'
> —[Knowing this,] let him fare lonely as the rhinoceros!
> [Suttanipāta 3,21—verse 55]

(See also the second note to L. 104)

---

1. The teaching-follower (*dhammānusārī*) is one who, having attained the path (*magga*), puts Dhamma-investigation foremost. Upon reaching the fruit (*phala*) he becomes one attained to (right) view (*diṭṭhipatta*). See L. 98, 99, Glossary.

[L. 2]

1. **legal circles:** to which Mr. Dias belonged. He later became Ceylon's High Commissioner to India and Permanent Secretary to the Ministry of Defense & External Affairs.
2. **third precept:** see second editorial note to L. 129.

[L. 3]

1. **repeat these words:** Cf. A.VII,60/iv,94-98.

[L. 6]

1. **Jīvaka Sutta:** M.55/i,369.

[L. 9]

1. **Mrs. Irene R. Quittner** (1909-1984) was a prominent figure among British Buddhists. A few details that led to this correspondence are given in L. 87 and L. 91.
2. **P.T.S.:** The Pali Text Society (c/o CPI Antony Rowe Ltd, Unit 4, Pegasus Way, Bowerhill Industrial Estate, Melksham, Wilts, SN12 6TR, England; www.palitext.com) has published all the Sutta and Vinaya texts in both the original Pali (roman-script) and in translation, as well as a Pali-English dictionary and other scholarly aids.
3. **Book of the Fives:**

   > Monks, endowed with five things one is unable, even when hearing the true Teaching, to get down to sure practice, the correct way in skilful things. Which five? He disparages the talk; he disparages the talker; he disparages himself; he hears the Teaching with a distracted mind lacking one-pointedness; he pays improper attention. (A.V,xvi,1)

   The next two Suttas differ from this Sutta by substituting, in xvi,2, 'he has a poor understanding, is dull or witless' and 'he conceives as directly known what has not been directly known' for the last two terms and, in xvi,3, also substituting 'he hears the Teaching with contempt, obsessed with contempt,' 'he hears the Teaching with a censorious mind, looking for faults,' and 'regarding the one who expounds the Teaching his mind is upset and has become (non-receptive) like barren ground' for the first three terms.
4. ***l'orgueil européen*:** 'The prodigious history evoked here is the history of European pride.' (*The Rebel*, p. 16)

5. **Three baskets:** The Pali Canon is known, collectively, as the Tipiṭaka, the Three Baskets, since it consists of three major sections: the Vinaya Piṭaka (Basket of Discipline), Sutta Piṭaka (Basket of Discourses), and Abhidhamma Piṭaka (Basket of Further Truth). Readers of the *Notes* can hardly be unaware that the Ven. Ñāṇavīra Thera rejected the Abhidhamma Piṭaka as a scholastic invention not representing the Buddha's Teaching.
6. ***parinibbāna*:** 'full extinction' can refer to the breaking up of the body of any *arahat*, but in this case it is used with specific reference to the Buddha.

[L. 10]

1. **Ven. Dewalapola Siridhamma Thera** (1919-2008) is brother of Hon. Lionel Samaratunga (recipient of L. 46-L. 123). He was a lawyer and served as a junior to a well known criminal lawyer. He resided for long years at the Mrs. F. R. Senanayake Forest Hermitage Udawattekelle, Kandy. During the World War II he resided at the Island Hermitage, Dodanduwa, and lastly at Vajirārāma. Generally he admired Ven. Ñāṇavīra Thera's intelligence and called him 'a deep thinker' and 'highly intelligent man,' however he warned that 'Ven. Ñāṇavīra gives his own interpretation of the Dhamma [which] differ[s] from traditional explanations. They will provoke thought, but have to be read critically and with all reserves.' (Letter to Mrs. Irene R. Quittner, 23 November 1963).
2. ***Path of Purification*, p. 676, note 48:**

> The Dependent Origination, or Structure of Conditions, appears as a flexible formula with the intention of describing the ordinary human situation of a man in his world (or indeed any conscious event where ignorance and craving have not entirely ceased). … each member has to be examined as to its nature in order to determine what its relations to the others are…. A purely cause-and-effect chain would not represent the pattern of a situation that is always complex, always subjective-objective, static-dynamic, positive-negative, and so on. Again, there is no evidence of any historical development in the various forms given *within the limits of the Sutta Piṭaka* (leaving aside the Paṭisambhidāmagga), and historical treatment within that particular limit is likely to mislead, if it is hypothesis with no foundation.
>
> In this work … the Dependent Origination is considered from only one standpoint, namely, as applicable to a period embracing

a minimum of three lives. But this is not the only application. With suitable modifications it is also used in the Vibhaṅga to describe the structure of the Complex in each one of the 89 single type-consciousnesses laid down in the Dhammasaṅgani; and Bhadantācariya Buddhaghosa says 'This Structure of Conditions is present not only in (a continuity period consisting of) multiple consciousness but also in each consciousness singly as well' (VbhA 199-200). Also the Paṭisambhidāmagga gives five expositions, four describing dependent origination in one life, the fifth being made to present a special inductive generalization to extend what is observable in this life (the fact that consciousness is always preceded by consciousness...i.e. that it always has a past and is inconceivable without one) back beyond birth, and (since craving and ignorance ensure its expected continuance) on after death. There are, besides, various other, differing, applications indicated by the variant forms given in the Suttas themselves.

3. ***Imasmiṃ sati idaṃ hoti:*** 'When there is this this is'—see A NOTE ON PAṬICCASAMUPPĀDA.
4. **'Nobody can say...':** See A.VII,55/iv,83:

   > Monks, the Tathāgata is one whose Teaching is well-proclaimed. Herein, monks, I see no sign that any recluse or divine or Evil One or Divinity or anyone else in the world should rightly reprove me: "In this way you are one whose Teaching is not well-proclaimed." And, monks, seeing no such sign, I dwell attained to security, attained to fearlessness, attained to confidence.

5. **strange bedfellows:** see L. 11.
6. **Dahlke...:** The Ven. Ñāṇatiloka Mahāthera (1878-1957), a prolific Buddhist scholar, was a follower of the traditional Commentarial view. Paul Dahlke was a more independent-minded German writer and lay-leader.
7. **BPS Wheel:** The Buddhist Publication Society (P.O.Box 61, Kandy, Sri Lanka; *www.bps.lk*) publishes Buddhist tracts in two series—the *Wheel* and the *Bodhi Leaf*—as well as occasional books on Buddhism. For the most part their publications used to represent the strictly traditional Commentarial view which the Ven. Ñāṇavīra was concerned to undermine. Therefore he often used their publications as a foil for explicating his own views.

[L. 11]

1. **The Middle Way:** the organ of the London Buddhist Society.
2. **Audiberti:** the secret blackness of milk. (Jacques Audiberti—1899-1965—was a French poet, playwright, and novelist noted for his extravagance of language.)
3. **Colombo:** Ven. Ñāṇavīra was staying at Siri Vajirārāmaya (or Vajirārāma) Temple. This is a well known Sri Lankan Buddhist temple due to the renowned resident monks. The temple in the heart of Colombo was founded in 1901 by Venerable Pelene Siri Vajirañaṇa Mahā Nāyaka Thera. It has been declared a Sacred Site by the State on 6 September 2009. More on *www.vajirarama.lk*.

[L. 12]

1. **Entamide:** also known as Diloxanide. It is an anti-protozoal drug used in the treatment of *Entamœba histolytica* and some other protozoal infections.

[L. 14]

1. **The Cūḷamāluṅkya Sutta** is posited on the following event: A monk named Māluṅkyāputta demands of the Buddha the answers to a series of speculative questions. The Buddha replies that he does not teach such matters, and offers the simile of a man grievously wounded who, rather than submit to medical treatment, demands to know, instead, the history of the dart that wounded him, its manufacture, the materials it is made of, and so on. That man, the Buddha says, would die of his wounds before his questions were answered. So too, the Buddha warns Māluṅkyāputta, a person will die still bound up with suffering unless he ceases his quest for answers to speculative questions and devotes himself instead to ridding himself of attachment, the condition for suffering.

> *Therefore, Māluṅkyāputta, bear in mind that which has not been explicated by me as not explicated; and bear in mind that which has been explicated by me as explicated.* And what, Māluṅkyāputta, has not been explicated by me? I have not explicated whether the world is eternal or non-eternal; whether the world is finite or infinite; whether the self and the body are one; whether the self and the body are separate; whether the Tathāgata [i.e., the Buddha] exists or does not exist after death; whether the Tathāgata both exists and does not exist after death; nor have I explicated whether the Tathāgata neither exists nor does not exist after death.

And why, Māluṅkyāputta, have I not explicated these? Because, Māluṅkyāputta, these are not useful, are not part of the divine life, do not lead to disenchantment, to dispassion, to ceasing, to calm, to direct knowledge, to awakening, to extinction; that is why they are not explicated by me. And what, Māluṅkyāputta, is explicated by me? This is suffering...

2. **monkey:** A *wandura* (wanduroo) is a black-faced silver-furred langur that sits about three feet high, feeds on leaves and fruit, and is very shy. A *rilawa* is a smaller pink-faced auburn-haired macaque that will eat anything it can find or steal. The latter is both more amusing and more troublesome than the quiet *wandura*.

**[L. 15]**

1. **one or two passages:** Here and elsewhere in his letters the Ven. Ñāṇavīra prepared his own translations from the French. Where published translations now exist they have been substituted. The Ven. Ñāṇavīra translated most of the Introduction, pp. 3-11, of Sartre's *Esquisse d'une Théorie des Émotions*. Since an English translation is now available we give below only the Ven. Ñāṇavīra's nine interpolated comments, preceded by our bracketed indication of the topic alluded to.
2. This passage is to be found in the Preface to *Notes*. (This letter was written before *Notes on Dhamma* was compiled.)
3. Following the extracts from *CUP*, the Ven. Ñāṇavīra concluded his compilation with the complete text of Edmund Husserl's article 'Phenomenology', which appeared in Vol. 17 of the 1955 edition of *Encyclopædia Britannica*. (Several passages from this article are to be found in CETANĀ.) He remarked: 'The article is well worth reading. But it is highly condensed and written in a Germanized English: it is thus not very easy to understand, particularly if one is new to the subject.' Within his own copy of the article (not the copy sent to Dr. de Silva) the Ven. Ñāṇavīra interpolated two comments:

   (i) [in Section II, §4, after 'being for us':] See PHASSA [d] & ATTĀ, §3.
   (ii) [in Section II, §7, after 'bare subjectivity of consciousness':] *Viññāṇaṃ attato samanupassati* (M.138/iii,227-8) 'he regards consciousness as self'.

**[L. 16]**

1. **Hermitage:** The Island Hermitage, Dodanduwa, Sri Lanka, was a centre

for Western Buddhists. The Ven. Ñāṇavīra spent some of his early years there and returned in later years for visits. The Hermitage was founded in 1911 by the German-born monk, the Ven. Ñāṇatiloka Mahāthera (cf. L. 10, editorial note 6).

[L. 17]

1. **E.S.P.:** Extrasensory perception, apparent power to perceive things that are not present to the sense.
2. **phenomena:** A similar view has been reported in Soviet research on E.S.P.. See Sheila Ostrander *et al.*, *Psychic Discoveries Behind the Iron Curtain* (New York: Bantam, 1971), especially pp. 306-7. *The Mind Unshaken* is by John Walters.

[L. 18]

1. **Jefferson:** Prof. Jefferson's article is the one quoted anonymously at PHASSA (e). The postcard referred to in the next sentence was not found.
2. **inseparable:** See M.43/i,293, SAÑÑĀ and Additional Texts 92.

[L. 19]

1. **Beverley Nichols:** Nichols' output is copious. We have not discovered which book discusses opium addiction. However, in his later book, *Father Figure* (London: Heinemann, 1972), Nichols not only refers again (on page 160) to the Oxford Group's Principle of Absolute Unselfishness (cf. L. 14) but also discusses the instant cure of his father from lifelong alcoholism, albeit not by 'faith in God,' but rather through 'loss of faith in inheritance.'
2. **black is white:** Cf. Bhayabherava Sutta—M.4/i,21:
   There are, divine, some recluses and divines who perceive day when it is night and who perceive night when it is day. Those recluses and divines dwell confused, I say. I, divine, perceive night just as night; I perceive day just as day…
3. **Dr. Helmut Klar** was prominent in German Buddhist circles.
4. **coloured squares:** This sounds similar to the Lüscher Color Test, used by clinicians. A paperback book, *The Lüscher Color Test*, published in the '70s, discusses this approach and includes a set of coloured cards and detailed (but not always clear) instructions on interpretations of the results. In our experience self-interpretation is far more difficult and complicated than the book claims.

[L. 20]

1. **amœbiasis:** His doctor, Dr. Sunil Wickramasuriya (1926-1999; worked in Tangalla and Ambalantota at that time), discovered after Ven. Ñāṇavīra's death (1965) that he was wrongly diagnosed and he probably had colitis, i.e. small perforations to the colon.
2. **Albert Schweitzer** (1875-1965) received the 1952 Nobel Peace Prize in 1953 for his philosophy of 'Reverence for Life', but most famously in founding and sustaining the Albert Schweitzer Hospital in Lambaréné. Schweitzer's quest was to discover a universal ethical philosophy, anchored in a universal reality, and make it directly available to all of humanity.
3. **actual note**: The note appears in *The Dhammapada, Pali Text and Translation with Stories in Brief and Notes* by Nārada Thera (Chapter 12: Atta Vagga, The Self).

[L. 21]

1. **a cutting:**

Daily Telegraph and Morning Post, Thursday, March 15, 1962

MAN IS THE ONLY ANIMAL ABLE TO THINK AND FEEL

Sirs—In *The Facts of Insect Life*, Dr. Anthony Michaelis raises the problem of the relation of life and consciousness, i.e., awareness of individuals of their existence.

Insects are automata reacting mechanically to stimulation of a cybernetic nervous system. They act by instinct. Instincts are chains of reactions to stimuli so linked that reaction to the first stimulus causes the organism to receive the second, the second the third, and so on until the goal is reached. The sequence of actions resulting is intelligent in the sense that it is directed to an end.

Dr. Michaelis assumes the activities of mammals are not so explicable and 'vertebrates like the rat are conscious.'

Consider a hunting cat. The first stimulus to its cybernetic brain is an empty stomach causing it to prowl to and fro. The next the rustling noises of its prey in the herbage as the animal accidentally comes within range. Its sonar direction finders swing the head to the direction of the sound, bringing the eyes to bear. Their registration of movement causes the pounce and capture. Grasping claws draw blood, smell provokes the bite, taste then plays its part and the prey is consumed.

The process is repeated till a full stomach coupled with depletion of the brain's fuel brings things to a halt. The animal curls up and sleeps.

Since conscious intelligence is not involved, instinct chains can be set in action by anything applying the appropriate stimulus at any point. Cats hunt rustling leaves blown by the wind or the glimpsed tips of their tails as avidly as real prey. In mammals the instinct-provoking object must apply the correct stimuli in the correct order to five perceptors: sound, sight, touch, smell, and taste. In nature this means instinct is in practice infallible.

Our own acts fall into three classes: (1) reflexes which do not reach consciousness; (2) reflexes of which we are conscious but which could equally well be the result of unconscious instinct; and (3) acts impossible to produce without the use of conscious intelligence and will.

The majority fall into classes 1 and 2 and these we share with the animals. Class 3 activities are found only in Man. The inference? Man alone is conscious; Man alone thinks and feels.

Yours faithfully,

J.J. Coghlan Hull

**[L. 23]**

1. In response to the problem of amœbiasis (L. 20) the Ven. Ñāṇavīra had taken a course of medicine, Entamide, which resulted in a sudden and unexpected stimulation of the nervous system ('effects for which I am no doubt partly to blame—no smoke without fire'). A number of letters not reproduced here detail the (mostly unsuccessful) efforts to find a counter-medication.

**[L. 24]**

1. **placebo**: There are reports on 'placebo effect', that our beliefs and expectations about treatments can have a dramatic effect on our health. Doctor and writer Ben Goldacre presented on BBC Radio 4, that the studies suggest that the placebo effect can have a significant impact on the course of a wide range of illnesses, including depression, irritable bowel syndrome and angina. For example, research shows that the colour of an inert sugar-pill and even the branding on the box, can alter a pill's effect.

**[L.25]**

1. *Panminerva Medica* is a medical journal published in Turin.

[L.27]

1. **simply by wishing:** See L. 141.
2. **School is hell:** The school would have been either St Edmund's School, Hindhead, or Wellington College. At Cambridge he attended Magdalene College.
3. **marry:** Had he chosen to disrobe the Ven. Ñāṇavīra might not have to marry a rich widow nor to take up with a 'woman of easy virtue', because his family was quite well-to-do.
4. **setting oneself alight:** This letter was written a half-year before the self-immolations of the Vietnamese monk. See L. 60.
5. **Camus:** *Myth*, pp. 4*f*.
6. **Nietzsche:** 'The thought of suicide is a powerful comfort: it helps one through many a dreadful night.' *Beyond Good and Evil*, p. 91.

[L. 28]

1. **others as 'they':** Among various loose papers found after the Ven. Ñāṇavīra's death was a copy of a quotation from Schopenhauer's *The Wisdom of Life*:

> It is only the highest intellectual power, what we may call genius, that attains to this degree of intensity, making all time and existence its theme, and striving to express its peculiar conception of the world, whether it contemplates life as the subject of poetry or of philosophy. Hence undisturbed occupation with himself, his own thoughts and works, is a matter of urgent necessity to such a man; solitude is welcome, leisure is the highest good, and everything else is unnecessary, nay, even burdensome.
>
> This is the only type of man of whom it can be said that his centre of gravity is entirely in himself; which explains why it is that people of this sort—and they are very rare—, no matter how excellent their character may be, do not show that warm and unlimited interest in friends, family, and the community in general, of which others are so often capable; for if they have only themselves they are not inconsolable for the loss of everything else. This gives an isolation to their character, which is all the more effective since other people never really quite satisfy them, as being, on the whole, of a different nature: more, since this difference is constantly forcing itself upon their notice, they get accustomed to move about amongst mankind as alien beings, and in thinking of humanity in general, they say *they* instead of *we*.

[L. 29]

1. **the Ven. Ñāṇamoli Thera:** It was Ven. Ñāṇamoli who (then Osbert Moore) accompanied Ven. Ñāṇavīra (then Harold Musson) to Ceylon in 1949, at which time they both took ordination, receiving the *upasampadā* in 1950. They carried on a prodigious correspondence from about 1954 (when Ven. Ñāṇavīra left the Island Hermitage) until shortly before L. 1, at which time the correspondence was discontinued by Ven. Ñāṇavīra [see L. 106, §6]. The letters are published in *StP*. Ven. Ñāṇamoli (who is remembered for his translations of the Majjhimanikāya, the Visuddhimagga, and other Pali texts) died of a heart attack in 1960. (The view which Ven. Ñāṇavīra expresses here seems to reflect the nearly universal finding of forest monks who briefly visit any urban area.)
2. **Sir Sydney Smith** (d. 1969) was the author of *Mostly Murder*.
3. **footnote a:** A loose undated note found among the Ven. Ñāṇavīra's papers, not part of his letters but apparently written after this letter, included a more complex version of the diagram. The top line was labelled 'multiplies into COMPATIBLES'; the bottom line was labelled 'divides into COMPATIBLES'; and the diagonal line between OBJECTIVITY and REFLEXION was extended in both directions. To the upper left it was extended to the label 'Statistics'; to the lower right to the label 'Ontology'.
4. **decreased interest in living:** Here as in so many places throughout these letters the Ven. Ñāṇavīra is making a veiled reference to his own attainment (L. 1) of *sotāpatti*.
5. **Kataragama:** In Sinhalese mythology Kataragama (Hindi: Skandha) is the chief deity of the island. His residence is a mountain not far from Būndala and he is believed to be particularly useful as a support to students in their examination. (The Chestov quote is from p. 25 of *Myth*.)
6. **footnote d:** The translation on pp. 5-6 of *Repetition* is somewhat different from this, which the Ven. Ñāṇavīra has taken from the Translator's Introduction (pp. xxii-xxxiii) to Kierkegaard's *Philosophical Fragments*.

[L. 31]

1. **Wilkins Micawber,** in Dickens' *David Copperfield*, was a projector of bubble schemes, sure to lead to a fortune but always ending in grief. Though indigent, he never despaired, always 'waiting for something to turn up' while on the brink of disaster.

[L. 34]

1. ***CUP*, pp. 81 and 84:** These passages are quoted in full at L. 129.
2. **the eternal:** So the Ven. Ñāṇavīra's letter; but the published translation reads 'Idea' rather than 'eternal' throughout this passage.

[L. 35]

1. **phenobarbitone:** nowadays known as phenobarbital. It is an organic compound having powerful soporific effect (a barbiturate). It has sedative and hypnotic properties.

[L. 36]

1. **no agitation:**

   > When mindfulness-of-breathing/mindfulness-of-breathing-concentration is developed and made much of, there is neither vacillation nor agitation of the body nor vacillation nor agitation of the mind. (Ānāpāna Saṃy.—S.liv.7/v,316)

2. **all breathing ceases:** D.34/iii,266; Vedanā Saṃy.—S.xxxvi.11/iv,217; A.IX,31/iv,409.

[L. 37]

1. **farewell letters:** from that period (1963) none were discovered.

[L. 38]

1. **another attempt:** The sequence begins with L. 52.

[L. 40]

1. **Medical Mirror:** The quotation is found in issue 6 of 1963, as part of a translated extract from a talk (in German) by Prof. Dr. Thure von Uexküll given at a symposium on 'Fear and Hope in Our Times.'
2. **Sartre:** 'Americans do not enjoy the process of thinking. When they do concentrate, it is in order to escape all thought.' *Troubled Sleep*, p. 29.
3. **quoting Camus:** This passage paraphrases sections of *The Rebel*, pp. 57-67.
4. **Nietzsche:** From *6ET*, p. 30.
5. **Connolly:** *The Unquiet Grave*, p. 79.
6. **What should I do?:** See an article *The Foundation of Ethics*, p. 499
7. **Nietzsche:** The quote is found at *The Rebel*, pp. 68-9.

[L. 41]

1. **Grotius** is also credited with founding international law. According to Gibbon's account it was George of Cappodocia who was slain (in 361 A.D.), whereas Athanasius died of old age in 373.

[L. 42]

1. **your book:** *Buddhism and its Relation to Religion and Science*. See Mr. Wettimuny's two subsequent books, listed in 'Acknowledgments'.

[L. 43]

1. ***anupādāya...*:** 'freed in mind by not holding to the cankers.'
2. ***pañcakkhandhā...*:** 'The five aggregates, being completely known, stand with the root cut off.'
3. ***upādāna*:** On the same theme see also L. 156 #5.
4. **self-identity:** See ATTĀ.

[L. 44]

1. **Phenomenology:** See CETANĀ.
2. **Khandha Saṃy.:** 'Arising (appearance) is manifest; disappearance is manifest; change while standing is manifest.' See ANICCA.
3. **a difficult distinction:** As his letters to the Ven. Ñāṇamoli Thera (*StP*, EL. 99) make clear, this distinction was the Ven. Ñāṇavīra Thera's last major insight prior to his attainment of *sotāpatti*. Although certainly this particular perception need not be pivotal for all who achieve the Path, that it was so for him is one reason for the strong emphasis the author lays on this point in the *Notes* as well as in various letters.
4. **Oppenheimer's dictum:**

> If we ask, for instance, whether the position of the electron remains the same, we must say 'no'; if we ask whether the electron's position changes with time, we must say 'no'; if we ask whether the electron is at rest, we must say 'no'; if we ask whether it is in motion, we must say 'no'. The Buddha has given such answers when interrogated as to the conditions of a man's self after death; but they are not familiar answers for the tradition of seventeenth and eighteenth-century science. (*Science and the Common Understanding*, pp. 42-3, quoted on pp. 49-50 of Mr. Wettimuny's book.)

[L. 45]

1. *Tassa...*: '...the clear and stainless Eye of the Dhamma arose in him: "Whatever has the nature of arising, all that has the nature of ceasing."' (at e.g. Sacca Saṃy.—S.lvi.11/v,423) See L. 1.
2. **not to be rushed:** Mr. Wettimuny abandoned his plans for a second edition. His two subsequent books were both dedicated to the Ven. Ñāṇavīra Thera.

[L. 46]

1. **Honourable Lionel Samaratunga** was the district judge of Balapitiya. He came to know Ven. Ñāṇavīra Thera through his brother Ven. Siridhamma Thera.
2. **without exception:** It might be useful to mention that the *Notes* also discuss some wrong views that have arisen *independent* of the traditional interpretation.
3. In 2009 Path Press Publications published a new edition of Ven. Ñāṇavīra's *Notes on Dhamma* based on a carbon copy of the final manuscript. This carbon copy was also more than that, by its inclusion of directly typed, neatly pasted-in paragraphs reflecting the author's final decision on certain segments of the notes; numerous hand corrections and additions in black ink; instructions for layout and typesetting; and a few remarks, mostly reminders to himself in pencil. This new and final edition of *Notes on Dhamma* reflects the original manuscript as close as possible, and brings the book to the interested reader, for the first time in almost fifty years, the way Ven. Ñāṇavīra Thera intended it to be. See also 'Note to the second edition' on p. IX.

[L. 49]

1. **call themselves Buddhists:** In fact, all three authors have called themselves Buddhists.
2. **Cūlahatthipadopama Sutta:** The introductory section includes the following passage:

> 'How does Master Vacchāyana conceive the monk Gotama's ability of understanding? He is wise, is he not?'
>
> 'Sir, who am I to know the monk Gotama's ability of understanding? One would surely have to be his equal to know the monk Gotama's ability of understanding.'
>
> 'Master Vacchāyana praises the monk Gotama with high praise indeed.'

'Sir, who am I to praise the monk Gotama? The monk Gotama is praised by the praised—as best among gods and men.' (Translation by the Ven. Ñāṇamoli.)

[L. 51]

1. **passionate chess:** There is a similar instance of the idea of a 'passionate chess' occurring in George Elliot's novel *Felix Holt, The Radical.*
2. **Sartre's waiter:** For the passage on the waiter, see *B&N*, pp. 59-60 (Methuen, 1969) or pp. 82-83 (Routledge, 2003).
3. **Letter to Mr. Dias:** L. 2.
4. ***viññāṇa* and *nāmarūpa*:** Cf. 'Thus it seems that the first four aggregates—matter, feeling, perception, determinations—are equivalent to name-&-matter, though the Suttas never say so specifically—a fact that is unusually significant.' ('Suttas and Sartre', p. 519, note §27)
5. **D.15/ii,64:** See *NoD*, 'Additional Texts', §86 (D.ii,2).

[L. 52]

1. ***dukkaṭa*:** In the Vinaya, or monastic Code, offences are grouped according to seriousness, the most serious being *pārājika*, involving expulsion from the Order (cf. L. 63) and *saṅghādisesa*, involving confession and temporary suspension of certain privileges. *Dukkaṭa* (lit. 'wrongly done') is the least offence except for *dubhāsita* ('wrongly said'). However there is a view among a few Vinaya scholars that suicide is not even *dukkaṭa* offence.

[L. 53]

1. **Kierkegaard:** *CUP*, p. 317, quoted in *6ET*, p. 13.
2. **Judge:** The point seems to have interested the Ven. Ñāṇavīra greatly. He had already made lengthy remarks on the subject to Dr. de Silva (see editorial notes, L. 15, vii, [h]) and he makes the point again at L. 60, footnote *e*.

[L. 54]

1. **not in a position:** Again, the reference is to the author's attainment of *sotāpatti* (L. 1), for it is an offence requiring confession to announce such an attainment to another who is not himself a *bhikkhu* (if, that is, the claim is true: if it is made knowing it to be false the offence is that of *pārājika*—see editorial note for L. 52).

2. **suicide:** Ven. Channa Thera: M.144/iii,263-66 and Saḷāyatana Saṃy.—S.xxxv.87/iv,55-60; Ven. Godhika Thera: Māra Saṃy.—S.iv.23/i,121-22; Ven. Vakkali Thera: Khandha Saṃy.—S.xxii.87/iii,119-24.

**[L. 55]**

1. **BPS booklet:** 'Pathways of Buddhist Thought' (*Wheel* 52/53).
2. **ambiguous:** In their correspondence, lasting from 1954 to 1960, the Ven. Ñāṇamoli repeatedly returned to the theme of the ambiguity of experience. See *StP*, Part A.

**[L. 57]**

1. ***satisampajañña*:** On the same theme see also *NoD*, *NP* (a), *NP* §25, and L. 2.
2. **human births:** Let alone human births, the Suttas seem to indicate that a *sotāpanna* cannot take an eighth birth of any sort, even in the *devaloka*. See A.III,86/i,233.
3. **Mirror of the Dhamma:**

> Those who comprehend clearly the Noble Truths, well taught by Him of wisdom deep, do not, however exceeding heedless they may be, undergo an eighth birth. Verily, in the Sangha is this precious jewel—by this truth may there be happiness!

4. **statistical evidence:** This remark would have had particular significance for Mr. Samaratunga, inasmuch as his own brother, Ven. Siridhamma Thera, created a stir in Colombo a decade earlier when, after having completed his own university studies, he thought it worthwhile to become a *bhikkhu* and did so.

**[L. 59]**

1. **late in the Majjhima:** M.143/iii,258-63.

**[L. 60]**

1. **The Ven. Ñāṇāloka Mahāthera** was the second abbot of the Island Hermitage, from 1957 (when the founder, the Ven. Ñāṇatiloka Mahāthera, died) until his own death in 1976. The Ven. Ñāṇavīra's *kuṭi* was constructed on the same pattern as many of the *kuṭis* at the Hermitage: a ten foot by fifteen foot room with an attached and covered ambulatory, thirty feet by three, for walking meditation. Construction was of brick and tile.

2. **Barbara:** A mnemonic term designating the first mood of the first syllogistic figure, in which both premisses and the conclusion are universal affirmatives.
3. **my letter:** L. 18.
4. **'to one who feels':** See 'Suttas and Sartre' §8.
5. **'witness for the faith':** In a 'Commonplace Book' (see *StP*, Part B) the author kept in his early years as a monk is the entry:

   Q. Why the Buddha rather than Jesus?
   A. Jesus wept.

6. **committed to the flames:** See L. 106-108, 156-160.

[L. 61]

1. **Pali Suttas:** Cf. L. 92. [N.B. British 'cyclostyle' will be familiar to American readers as 'mimeograph'.]

[L. 62]

1. **Huxley's book:** *Doors of Perception and Heaven and Hell.*
2. **week at a time:** See e.g. Thig.44:

   For seven days I sat in one cross-legged posture enveloped by happiness; then on the eighth I stretched forth my feet, having sundered the mass of darkness.

3. **become cold:** e.g. Brahma Saṃy.—S.vi.3/i,141; Brāhmaṇa Saṃy.—S.vii.15/i,178; A.X,29/v,65; Sn. 542, 642, etc.

[L. 63]

1. **Prof. Jefferson's article:** See L. 18.

[L. 64]

1. The first edition did indeed consist of 250 copies.

[L. 65]

1. Nevertheless, in both the original edition and in the final typescript the author's name was typed, not signed.

[L. 66]

1. During the war Musson served primarily in Algiers, in varying capacities

including work in the Prisoner of War Interrogation Section. For nearly the whole of 1945 he was in hospital, first in North Africa and then in Sorento, for reasons unknown. At the time of his release, in 1946, he held the rank of Temporary Captain. On his Release Certificate he was noted as a holder of the Military Cross. He queried this: 'I am not aware of having won the MC nor of ever having been in the position of being able to do so.' The entry was found to be an error.

**[L. 67]**

1, **'I am wrong':** Cf. M.70/i,480:

> Monks, a faithful disciple, having scrutinized the Teacher's advice, proceeds in accordance with this: 'The Auspicious One is the teacher, I am the disciple. The Auspicious One knows. I do not know.'

**[L. 68]**

1. **Arjuna, Krishna:** See *Bhagavad-Gita*, the best-known of Hindu texts.
2. **Younghusband:**

> He was silent on the Nature of God not from any inadequacy of appreciation, but from excess of reverence. (From Younghusband's introduction to Woodward's *Some Sayings of the Buddha*)

**[L. 69]**

1. **Housman:**

> And how am I to face the odds
> Of man's bedevilments and God's?
> I, a stranger and afraid
> In a world I never made.
> —*Last Poems*, XII

2. **Balfour; Gurney:** On page 269 of the book the Ven. Ñāṇavīra noted, in the margin:

> All the muddle of this chapter comes of the *puthujjana*'s failure to distinguish *personality* from *individuality*. Personality as 'self' is indivisible. Individuality is as divisible as you please; that is, *within the individual*. The word *individual* does not exclude

*internal* divisions; it simply means that you cannot treat these internal divisions as a *collection* of individuals. 'Individual' is opposed to 'class'.

And on page 308 there is the marginal note:

> From a *puthujjana*'s point of view, Balfour's objections are valid—'self' cannot be divided into separate 'selves'... This paradox cannot be resolved in the sphere of the puthujjana. If Gurney is right, that is only because he has, in fact, failed to appreciate Balfour's dilemma...

[L. 72]

1. **Penguin books** is a publisher founded in 1935. Penguin revolutionized publishing in the 1930s through its high quality two and a half pence paperbacks, sold through high street stores.
2. **Françoise Sagan** was a French playwright, novelist, and screenwriter. She was best known for works with strong romantic themes involving wealthy and disillusioned bourgeois characters.

[L. 74]

1. **Russell:** The book being discussed is *An Inquiry Into Meaning and Truth*.
2. **Society for Psychical Research**: Today the organization is based at 49 Marloes Road, Kensington, London, with a library and office open to members, and with large archival holdings in Cambridge, England. It publishes the peer reviewed quarterly *Journal of the Society for Psychical Research*, the irregular *Proceedings* and the magazine *Paranormal Review*.

[L. 75]

1. **innocence:** In an early letter (29 June 1958) to the Ven. Ñāṇamoli the author remarked:

> *Avijjā* is a primary structure of being, and it approximates to innocence, not to bad faith, which is a reflexive structure, far less fundamental. Is it not odd that, existentially, *avijjā* would be translated alternatively by "guilt"—Kafka, Kierkegaard—and "innocence"—Camus, Sartre? Innocence and guilt, both are nescience.

[L. 76]

1. **the papers:** This letter as well as the previous one were written from the Island Hermitage, where a daily newspaper would have been available.

[L. 77]

1. **NA CA SO:** The book was sent out with an accompanying note requesting reactions to the book so that necessary revisions could be made in a proposed printed (and not cyclostyled) edition.

[L. 78]

1. **concerned to propagate:** For the most part publications of the Buddhist Publication Society used to represent the strictly traditional Commentarial view which the Ven. Ñāṇavīra was undermining.

[L. 80]

1. **137:** A fraction very close to 1/137 is known to physicists as the 'fine structure constant'. It and its factors are involved in considerations of the weak nuclear and electromagnetic forces and as such it is an important constant for quantum physicists in describing basic electron-electron scattering. See also *StP*, Part A ('Letters to Ven. Ñāṇamoli').

[L. 81]

1. **Huxley's death:** Both, President Kennedy and Huxley, died on the same day, 22 November 1963.

[L. 82]

1. **An English *bhikkhu*:** It is likely to be Bhikshu Saṅgharashita (ordained in the same year as Ven. Ñāṇavīra). Ven. Ñāṇavīra was reading his article 'The Meaning of Orthodoxy in Buddhism: A Protest' (published in *Presence du Bouddhisme*, 1959). Ven. Ñāṇavīra noted in this article:

   > Broadly speaking, the doctrine of *anattā* denies that in the absolute sense there exists in any object, whether transcendental or mundane, an eternal unchanging principle of individuality or selfhood. Logically it amounts to a repudiation of the ultimate validity of the principle of self identity.

2. **George Borrow** (1803-81) travelled in Spain as an agent for the Bible Society. He wrote *The Bible in Spain* as well as several novels, all published in the Everyman series.

3. **Mr. Wettimuny:** L. 42-45. Mr. Wettimuny, of course, subsequently relinquished this view.
4. **I don't know who:** As long ago as 1927 the British biologist, J.B S. Haldane, said that '... my suspicion is that the universe is not only queerer than we suppose, but queerer than we *can* suppose.' But the Ven. Ñāṇavīra may have had someone else in mind.
5. **French existentialism:** The Ven. Ñāṇavīra seems not to have read Merleau-Ponty, whose reputation as an existentialist philosopher has grown enormously in the last few decades. The author's assessment of European Buddhism was valid for the 1960s: some 40 years on there is a considerably stronger Theravādin tradition in England, and roots have been established in America.
6. **Are the Suttas complete?:** For a brief account of the origins of the Pali Suttas and of their probable development as far as the Third Council see *Beginnings: The Pali Suttas* (BPS *Wheel* 313/315, 1984) or *Beginnings, Collected Essays of S. Bodhesako* (BPS, 2008).

[L. 84]

1. **offending 'rot' to 'decay':** Ven. Siridhamma Thera writes (on 30 December 1963) to Mrs. Irene Quittner (recipient of L. 9-11):

> Certain Mahā Theras, who are also *Abhidhamma* scholars, were much perturbed by the reference to *citta-vīthi* as 'a vicious doctrine' and also by the statement: 'The rot first seems to set in with Vibhaṅga and Paṭṭhāna of the *Abhidhamma Piṭaka*'. They also do not like his going against the traditional teachings in *Visuddhimagga* and so forth. In order to avoid confusion in future (because the expression the 'rot sets in' has been misunderstood) Ven. Ñāṇavīra has changed it to 'the decay sets in', which though weaker, has exactly the same meaning. He says he is not a person to be silenced by pontifical thunderings if he thinks it is necessary to speak; on the other hand, he is prepared to be silent if he does not think that any good will come of speaking. His attitude is: 'Let the Truth be proclaimed though the heavens should fall.'

2. නිකං: The Sinhalese word *nikang* means both 'simply', 'for no reason' ('I simply came to see') and 'nothing' ('there is nothing in the pot'; 'something for nothing'). Many times, as in this letter, the meanings of *nikang* are combined to convey a slightly derogatory connotation.

3. **typewriter:** The stencils were cut on a typewriter belonging to the Ven. Kheminda Thera who, later, was the recipient of L. 1, 125, and 126.

[L. 85]

1. **a Sutta from the Aṅguttara:** Pañcaka Nipāta, Yodhājīva Vagga, 9/iii, 105-08:

> 1. There are, monks, these five future fearful things, not arisen at present but which will arise in the future; you should be on watch for them, and being on watch for them you should strive to eliminate them. What are the five?
>
> 2. There will be, monks, monks in time to come who will be undeveloped in body,[2] virtue, mind,[3] and understanding. They, being undeveloped in body, virtue, mind, and understanding, will give ordination to others and will be unable to direct them in higher virtue, higher mind, higher understanding; and these, too, will be undeveloped in body, virtue, mind, and understanding. And they, being undeveloped in body, virtue, mind, and understanding, will give ordination to others and will be unable to direct them in higher virtue, higher mind, higher understanding; and these, too, will be undeveloped in body, virtue, mind, and understanding. Thus, monks, with the decay of the Teaching there will be decay of the discipline[4] and with decay of the discipline there will be decay of the Teaching.
>
> This, monks, is the first future fearful thing, not arisen at present...
>
> 3. Again, monks, there will be monks in time to come who will be undeveloped in body, virtue, mind, and understanding. They, being undeveloped in body, virtue, mind, and understanding, will give support[5] to others and will be unable to direct them in higher virtue, higher mind, higher understanding; and these, too, will be undeveloped in body, virtue, mind, and understanding. And they, being undeveloped in body, virtue, mind, and understanding, will

---

2. *Abhāvitakāya.* This does not mean lacking in physical training, but not being able to remain unmoved in the face of pleasurable feelings.

3. *Abhāvitacitta.* Not being able to remain unmoved in the face of painful feelings. It also means unpractised in mental concentration, *samādhi.* The two things go hand in hand.

4. *Dhammasandosā vinayasandoso. Sandosa* = decay or rot—'the rot sets in'.

5. 'Support' is *nissaya.* Para. 2 deals with the *upajjhāya* or 'preceptor', and para. 3 with the *ācariya* or 'teacher'.

give support to others and will be unable to direct them in higher virtue, higher mind, higher understanding; and these, too, will be undeveloped in body, virtue, mind, and understanding. Thus, monks, with the decay of the Teaching there will be decay of the discipline, and with decay of the discipline there will be decay of the Teaching.

This, monks, is the second future fearful thing, not arisen at present...

4. Again, monks, there will be monks in time to come who will be undeveloped in body, virtue, mind, and understanding. They, being undeveloped in body, virtue, mind, and understanding, when discussing the advanced teaching[6] and engaging in cross questioning,[7] falling into a dark teaching[8] will not awaken.[9] Thus, monks, with the decay of the Teaching there will be decay of the discipline, and with decay of the discipline there will be decay of the Teaching.

This, monks, is the third future fearful thing, not arisen at present...

5. Again, monks, there will be monks in time to come who will be undeveloped in body, virtue, mind, and understanding. They, being undeveloped in body, virtue, mind, and understanding, when those discourses uttered by the Tathāgata are preached, profound, profound in meaning, beyond the world, concerned with voidness—they will not listen to them, they will not give ear to them, they will not present a comprehending mind to them, and they will not consider those teachings worth grasping and learning; but when those discourses made by poets are preached, poetic, elegantly tuned, elegantly phrased, alien,[10] uttered by disciples—to them they will present a comprehending mind, and those teachings they will consider worth grasping and learning. Thus, monks, with the decay of the Teaching there will be decay of the discipline, and with decay of the discipline there will be decay of the Teaching.

---

6. *Abhidhamma*. This does *not* mean the Abhidhamma Piṭaka, but simply the essential Dhamma.

7. *Vedallakathā*. When one monk asks questions on the Dhamma and another gives the answers.

8. *Kaṇha dhamma*, in contrast to the 'bright teaching' that does lead to awakening.

9. *Na bujjhissanti*. Will not reach *bodhi* or enlightenment.

10. *Bāhiraka*. Outside (the Dhamma). This refers to the *puthujjana*.

This, monks, is the fourth future fearful thing, not arisen at present…

6. Again, monks, there will be monks in time to come who will be undeveloped in body, virtue, mind, and understanding. They, being undeveloped in body, virtue, mind, and understanding, the elder monks[11] will become luxurious and lax, and, falling from former ways[12] and laying aside the task of solitude, they will not make the effort to attain what they have not attained, to reach what they have not reached, to realize what they have not realized. And those who come after will follow their example and will become luxurious and lax, and, falling from former ways and laying aside the task of solitude, they too will not make the effort to attain what they have not attained, to reach what they have not reached, to realize what they have not realized. Thus, monks, with the decay of the Teaching there will be decay of the discipline, and with decay of the discipline there will be decay of the Teaching.

This, monks, is the fifth future fearful thing, not arisen at present…

7. These, monks, are the five future fearful things, not arisen at present but which will arise in the future; you should be on watch for them, and being on watch for them you should strive to eliminate them.

2. **long time ago:** L. 46.

**[L. 86]**

1. ***Path of Purification*, p. 131, note 13:** This long note begins:

> *Bhavaṅga* (life-continuum, lit. Constituent of becoming) and *javana* (impulsion) are first mentioned in this work at Ch. I §57 (see n. 16); this is the second mention. The 'cognitive series (*citta-vīthi*)' so extensively used here is unknown as such in the Piṭakas…

2. ***Vassāna* (Sinh: *Vas*):** Rains. The rainy season, following the four months of the hot season and preceding four months of cold, lasts (in the Ganges Valley area) from July to November. During three of these four months

11. *Therā bhikkhū.*

12. 'Falling from former ways' is wrong: *okkamane pubbaṅgamā* means 'going first in falling', i.e. taking the initiative in low practices.

monks are expected to live in one place and not wander about; and thus the Vas is sometimes regarded as a period of retreat.

3. **Ven. Nāyaka Thera:** Venerable Pälānē Siri Vajirañāṇa Mahā Nāyaka Thera was Founder of Vajirārāma (or Vajiraramaya) Temple in Colombo and also Upajjhāya of Venerables Ñāṇavīra and Ñāṇamoli.

[L. 87]

1. **Mrs. Quittner:** Section 3, L. 9-11.
2. ***parato ghoso; yoniso manasikāro*:** See the opening quotation to *Notes on Dhamma*.

[L. 89]

1. **Chinese pilgrims:** Fa Hien (Fa Hsien) travelled from 399 to 413 A.D. Translations of his report are available as *A Record of Buddhist Kingdoms* (London: Oxford University Press, 1886, tr. James Legge) and as *A Record of the Buddhist Countries* (Peking: The Chinese Buddhist Association, 1957, tr. unidentified). The account by Hiuen Tsiang (Yuan Chwang) of his travels has been translated by Samuel Beal in *Buddhist Records of the Western World* (London: Kegan Paul, Trench, Trübner & Co., n.d.). Hiuen, who was in India between 629 and 645 A.D., was primarily concerned with differences in points of Vinaya practice: he returned to China with hundred of texts.

[L. 90]

1. ***abhidhamma*:** Although various disciples are sometimes said to discuss *abhidhamma* and *abhivinaya* amongst themselves, in fact the Suttas nowhere describe the Buddha himself as teaching either *abhidhamma* or *abhivinaya* to either humans or deities. This suggests that perhaps the prefix *abhi-* might best be taken in this instance not as 'higher' or 'advanced' but as 'extended', and to understand that the monks sometimes discussed *dhamma* and *vinaya* in their own terminology rather than in the terminology used by the Buddha. See in particular A.VI,60/ iii,392f.
2. **Third Council:** Traditional views on the Kathā Vatthu are set forth at Mahāvaṃsa v,278 and Dīpavaṃsa vii,41, 56-8. Source material on the Third Council is also to be found in the Samantapāsādikā (i,57ff) and Papañca Sūdanī (vv. 240ff).

[L. 92]

1. **Peradeniya:** The University of Peradeniya, near Kandy, is the centre of Buddhist scholarship in Sri Lanka.

[L. 93]

1. Apparently the author was not acquainted with Edmund Husserl's *Vorlesungen zur Phänomenologie des inneren Zeitbewusstseins*, originally written as lectures from 1904 to 1920 and compiled and published by Martin Heidegger in 1928. An English translation by James S. Churchill, *The Phenomenology of Internal Time-Consciousness*, was published in 1963 (the year of this letter) by Indiana University Press. Husserl had developed a similar idea concerning the present movement of time.
2. **Letter to Mr. Dias:** L. 2.
3. ***ākiñcaññāyatana*:** Beyond the four *jhāna* states are the four higher attainments or perceptions, the perceptions of the limitlessness of space, of the limitlessness of consciousness, of the sphere of nothingness, and of the sphere of neither-perception-nor-non-perception. It is the second and third of these to which the author refers.

[L. 94]

1. **Nalanda:** Yes, it has been re-established as a university for monks, foreign as well as Indian. In 2006 some nations announced a proposed plan to restore and revive the ancient site as Nalanda International University.
2. ***Doctrine of Awakening*:** During World War II the author (then known as Captain Harold Musson) served as an interrogator with intelligence in North Africa and Italy. He came across Evola's book and, in order to brush up his Italian, translated it. It was in fact his first contact with the Buddha's Teaching, aside from a distant look when, from 1927 to 1929, his father serving in Rangoon, Port Blair, and Maymyo, the sight of monks would have become familiar to young Musson. But there is no evidence that as a boy he came to know anything of the Teaching. His translation of Evola's book was published by Luzac in 1951, and republished in 1997.

[L. 95]

1. **Mr. Wijerama:** Section 5, L. 12-14.

[L. 96]

1. **earlier letter:** L. 49.
2. **Māra** = The Evil One, a non-human being.
3. ***faute de mieux*:** for want of anything better.

[L. 97]

1. **Bradley quote:** The quotation was subsequently incorporated into *Notes*, ATTĀ (b).
2. **Ross Ashby** is a prolific and intelligent writer on cybernetics, and the Ven. Ñāṇavīra Thera seems to have found his views to be thought-provoking, even if largely unacceptable. Some time prior to 1957 the Ven. Ñāṇavīra Thera had read Ross Ashby's *Design for a Brain* (London: Chapman and Hall, 1952), and he may also have read *Introduction to Cybernetics* (London: Chapman and Hall, 1957).
3. **Dostoievsky:** See L. 29.

[L. 99]

1. **Mahāsaḷāyatanika Sutta:** The Buddha discusses a man who knows and sees the eye, forms, eye-consciousness, eye-contact, and the pleasurable, painful, and neutral feelings that arise dependent upon eye-contact, as they really are (and *mutatis mutandis* for the other senses).

> That view as to what really is is his right view. That attitude as to what really is is his right attitude. That effort as to what really is is his right effort. That mindfulness as to what really is is his right mindfulness. That concentration as to what really is is his right concentration. And his bodily actions, his verbal actions, and his livelihood have already been well purified earlier. So this noble eightfold path comes to development and fulfillment in him. When he develops this noble eightfold path, the four foundations of mindfulness come to development and fulfillment in him. And the four right endeavours... the four bases of potency... the five faculties... the five powers... the seven factors of awakening come to development and fulfillment in him.
>
> These two things—peace and insight—are yoked harmoniously in him. By comprehension he fully understands those things that should be fully understood by comprehension. By abandoning he fully understands those things that should be fully understood by abandoning. By developing he fully understands those things that should be fully understood by developing. By realizing he fully understands those things that should be fully understood by realizing. And what, monks, should be fully understood by comprehension?...

2. **A.VI,68:**

> 'One not delighting in solitude could grasp the sign of the mind (*cittassa nimittaṃ*)': such a state is not to be found. 'One not grasping the sign of the mind could be fulfilled in right view': such a state is not to be found. 'One not having fulfilled right view could be fulfilled in right concentration': such a state is not to be found. 'One not having fulfilled right concentration could abandon the fetters': such a state is not to be found. 'One not having abandoned the fetters could realize extinction': such a state is not to be found.

**[L. 100]**

1. **the letter:** One letter (labelled here L. 125) and one undated rough draft of a letter (L. 126) have survived.

**[L. 102]**

1. **Ananda:** Part 11, L. 127-128.
2. **the first paragraph:** The correct reference is to the seventh paragraph.
3. **opening ceremony:** See Part 12, to Mr. Robert K. Brady, L. 134.

**[L. 104]**

1. ***aluhaṃ*:** Ash-skin, skin with ash-colored spots: a dry scaly mildly-itching disease, widespread in the drier areas of Sri Lanka.
2. **a certain matter:** During his stay in Colombo the author handed over L. 1 to the Ven. Kheminda Thera. The envelope of L. 1 was inscribed: 'In the event of my death, this envelope should be delivered to, and opened by, the senior *bhikkhu* of the Island Hermitage, Dodanduwa. Ñāṇavīra Bhikkhu, 20th September 1960.' Apparently the letter had been kept at Būndala until 1964, when it was handed over already opened and its contents were then discussed. This discussion became known to others, and thus the author's attainment of *sotāpatti* came to be known (and accepted and denied and debated) even before his death.
3. **The five constraints** (*nīvaraṇa*) are desire-and-lust, ill-will, sloth-and-torpor, distraction-and-worry, and doubt.
4. **The three bad behaviours:** i.e. by body, speech, and mind.
5. **The seven awakening-factors** (*satta-bojjhaṅgā*) are: mindfulness, investigation of phenomena, energy, gladness, tranquillity, concentration, and indifference (equanimity).

[L. 105]

1. **Rodiyas:** Caste is not as important among Sinhalese as it is among Indians, but it exists. The Rodiyas are outcaste.
2. **Udāna 11:** Alternatively this verse might be rendered:

> Pleasurable is dispassion in the world,
> The getting beyond sensuality.
> But the putting away of the conceit 'I am'
> —this is the highest pleasure.

[L. 106]

1. The letters have been published as *The Letters of Sister Vajirā*, Path Press Publications, 2010.
2. **'Proof of Rebirth':** This 15,000-word essay was reprinted several times in abridged form. The typescript found among the author's papers contains a number of pencilled comments indicating later disagreement with his earlier views. It has been published in *StP*.
3. **rough draft:** See L. 159.
4. **replied:** The replies from Ven. Siridhamma Thera and Mr. and Mrs. Salgado. They are published is *The Letters of Sister Vajirā*, pp.83-7.

[L. 107]

1. **her teacher:** Paul Debes, one of the prominent lay Theravada teachers in Germany at that time.
2. **a passage:** All her letters together with Ven. Ñāṇavīra's reply are published in *The Letters of Sister Vajirā*. The letter being discussed begins:

> I feel that I owe a few lines to you, even though I am hardly able to give an adequate account of what happened; I am still rather benumbed.
>
> Your notes on *viññāṇa nāmarūpa* have led me away from the abyss into which I have been staring for more than twelve years. (As if I did not know what I was asking from you! At the last moment you gave them to me; when I had almost abandoned all hope!) I had been addicted to a fallacious notion of the Teaching, which I held to be its clue, while, in reality, it was diametrically opposed to it. In accordance with my nature, however, I was given to it in such a way that, even though conscious that I was hanging between earth and sky, neither able to step forward nor backward, I could not surrender myself earlier than this, and, of course,

after tremendous struggle. You must have seen what this notion consisted in, especially from my notes on *saññā*, though you did not directly name it, nor did I (or, rather, I somewhat concealed it)—I would have fallen if we had done so. Even now, *I* shall not do so, in order not to fall from delusion into delusion. It concerns the reality of things;[13] I am not really interested in *kamma* and *vipāka*—those only served me to support my misconception, and well indeed! Even my latest argument on the *Arahat* consciously aimed at the same thing. I do not think you saw it—and that was good.

Your dispassionate description of *nāmarūpa* and *viññāṇa* has made me realize that I was unable to remove the tint of passion from things—while at the same time denying their existence (or more concisely, *because* of doing so). I do not know how I stood that position for such a long time. I do not know either by what miraculous skill you have guided me to a safe place where at last I can breathe freely.

It should scarcely be necessary to say that the question of *pañcakkhandhā* was not just one among others, but was *the* question. Your interpretation of *cetanā* as intention *and* significance, which to me were just the *antipodes*, was such a nuisance that only your last letter compelled me to enter into the matter at all; I had so far just pushed it aside. The connection *cetanā/saṅkhāra* had entirely escaped my consciousness.... I had never any difficulty to follow your argument '*omnis determinatio...*', provided, of course, I took it as pertaining to *saṅkhārā*, and not to *cetanā*. I can see the matter clearly now, though not, of course, all its implications. In that way, the subject is removed from experience, and the *pañcakkhandhā* can function apart from *upādāna*. Thus the question is settled. I have lost a dimension of thought, at least to the degree to grasp this matter, i.e. my own *upādāna*... (*The Letters of Sister Vajirā*, pp. 71-2)

3. **a fit of passion:** Later in the same letter Sister Vajirā wrote:

You have seen that I took your repeated references to the *puthujjana* in connection with me as a challenge—though I once denied it proudly. In your last letter you have put that challenge masterly;

---

13. The last six words were underlined by Ven. Ñāṇavīra.

I could not possibly not take it up—and this time seriously.... In fact, I was always passing from one thing to the other—through the depths of my being. In connection with this, I have to confess something that will hardly come out from my pen. I must, however, at once say that, while doing it, I denied only myself—not you; there was no disrespect in doing it towards you. I had recognized your letter as precious, so I have written already, but, nevertheless, the next day, at night, I burnt it—along with all the rest. Even your precious notes. (That appeared, however, quite different at that moment—a temptation of Māra, who seemed to whisper that were there teleological experience, without a self, and free from all *dukkha*, it could be a fine thing as such!) I cannot even ask your pardon, for I did not offend you. I was constantly trying to find my own image in you by reading the letters; you know that I am passionate, and, accordingly I acted, that is all. And I got the results as soon as I had done it. So the highest purpose of all your *hitānukampā* has been achieved, and, moreover, I have a good memory, and know almost every word that you have written....

Can the *puthujjana* really make such a quest as mine has been, even though, as yet, negatively, his own, so as never even for a second to depart from it, as, in fact, I did? Whatever it may be, I am no longer worried about it, now that I have got rid of a great deal of delusion.... (pp. 72-3)

4. **a dangerous act:** Two days later Sister Vajirā wrote:

That I burnt your letters and notes was the most dangerous act that I ever committed. I did it as a *puthujjana*. I was indeed *bāhira*; I had no grain of *saddhā*; I did not know what *saddhā* is. I realize now, where I most urgently need them, that I cannot remember the most essential parts, for the simple reason that those were the most obscure to me. I know that you will forgive me; it is hardly possible to offend you, though I am fully conscious that you gave your innermost to me. From the following you will see that I am also worth to be forgiven.

Yesterday, when I once more tried to see *pañcakkhandhā* guided by your notes, I suddenly came across the thorn that had been sticking me uninterruptedly since '49. And I discovered—*dukkha*. The conceit on which I had built my *Ariyasāvaka*hood was this thorn, which, somehow, I had received along with the 'Dhamma'.

But I know now that the *puthujjana* can take upon himself any *dukkha*—even for the 'Dhamma'—because he does not know anything else. My conceit, however, did not stand out decisively (I hardly ever thought about it, except during certain periods, where circumstances were very trying) until now; and the moment I realized what it really *means* to be *puthujjana*, I ceased to be one.[14]

...I won a victory over myself; and when I awoke this morning I had found refuge in the Dhamma, and I realized everything (or a great many things) that we had been discussing. At least, Bhante, I did not conceal myself; I was proud, conceited, and, most of all, deluded, but I was straight. My strongest weapon was humility—though I can see now also how you look upon it; *anatimānī*[15] is somewhat different; only an *Ariyasāvaka* possesses it, I think. I fought a fight knowing not for what—and you have helped me most wonderfully.

I begin now to discover the Dhamma. I can just stay in one place and see everything passing before my eyes that I knew without knowing. It is an entirely new landscape. I had concerned myself much with the most essential problems—and yet the meaning was hidden from me. ...I do not know, but perhaps you do, why your notes on *viññāṇa* etc. are opening out what I could not find in the texts. I mistook it all. What your notes essentially reveal to me is to allow things to be (present), whilst the Suttas seemed to say that I must deny them. Once I had found justification of *cetanā* = *saṅkhārā* (as already indicated), I laid hold of your notes in the way that I do things—either/or. I wrestled with them to the utmost, always in turns with emotional states. ...I find that my position was most curious (but, of course, there is nothing particular in it, as I now understand)[16]—I had no time to investigate into the nature of the *pañcakkhandhā*, because, radically, I

---

**14.** In the margin of the letter the Ven. Ñāṇavīra had written: 'This claim can be accepted.'

**15.** Non-arrogance: Sister Vajirā may have had in mind the first verse of the well-known *Mettā Sutta* (Discourse on Friendliness), Sn. 143: 'One skilled as to the goal, having entered upon the way of peace, should do this: he should be capable, straight, upright, of good speech, gentle, non-arrogant.' The phrase 'I fought a fight knowing not for what' was underlined by the Ven. Ñāṇavīra, as were, in the next paragraph, the eleven words beginning 'that I knew without'.

**16.** The parenthetical phrase was underlined by the Ven. Ñāṇavīra.

negated everything as soon as I became aware of it. My blindness really was total. I brought myself into immense tension, and, in fact, it is strain that I also now experience to an extreme degree, especially while writing this (but I feel that I should do so). I can also understand something about *akālika* now. I had no idea that things can stand in relation to each other other than temporally (do I use the word now correctly? I think so). I meant it was a most sublime idea that *rūpa* should be *saññā*; it is crude indeed. I discovered the real meaning of *anicca* in connection with *viññāṇa*, and many other things.

It is hard for me to imagine that you do not know everything already, but, remembering that you are not a visionary (unnecessary to say that I know you are indefinitely much more), I must give you at least some evidence now itself, for I do really not know what will happen the next moment (I may not be able to keep full control over myself—as I appear to others) ....[17] In deepest veneration, V. (pp. 74-6)

## 5. her last letter:

...I have seen the Buddha as Paṭiccasamuppāda,[18] and I heard the Mūlapariyāya Sutta intoned—but I was tossing about in pains seeing it as *saṅkhārā*. I could never have found *Nibbāna*—with your face veiled. This you must have felt. I began to see the *Paññāvimutta Arahat* in you before you had attained it[19]—seeing at the same time that there was no *āsava* in a P. A. ...Everything was evident in our discussion—even the question of *upadhi*—which was probably the only thing that I had rightly grasped. It will still take me time to relax; I am simply passing from one emotional state into the other[20]—but now, at last, I have found you.

---

17. The parenthetical phrase was underlined by the Ven. Ñāṇavīra. In the margin he wrote: 'Advance notice.' At the end of the letter he wrote: '*Sammattaniyāmaṃ okkanti*?' (= 'entry into surety of correctness': see A.VI,86 & 98/iii,435 & 441).

18. This phrase was underlined by the Ven. Ñāṇavīra, who wrote in the margin: '*Yo paṭiccasamuppādaṃ passati so dhammaṃ passati. Yo dhammaṃ passati so maṃ passati.*' (= 'He who sees dependent arising sees the Teaching. He who sees the Teaching sees me'. The first sentence is ascribed to the Buddha by the Ven. Sāriputta at M.28/i,190-191. The second sentence is spoken by the Buddha at Khandha Saṃy.—S.xxii.87/iii,120.)

19. In the margin: Who said?

20. In the margin: Evidently.

Do you know that the wind-element obeys you? It is to me the sweetest comfort. This also I knew; it is your most sublime *ānāpānasati* that surrenders it. You need not write to me (or, of course, as you please).

I could tell you many more things, but it is not so important.

In deepest veneration,[21] V. (pp. 78-79)

[L. 110]

1. **love charms:** The story is not found even in the Commentaries: it occurs first, apparently, in the Sanskrit Divyāvadāna, of the Sarvāstivādin school. A partial version is also found in the Śūrangama Sūtra.
2. ***bhikkhunīs*:** Vin. ii,253: A.VII,51/iv,274-79.
3. **towards the end:** Kh. XI: Vin. ii,289.
4. **Ven. S.:** The reference is to a newly-ordained (*sāmaṇera*) Western monk who had just settled into a *kuṭi* about one-half mile from the Ven. Ñāṇavīra and who remained there for several years before disrobing and returning home. To informally give help is one thing; to become a teacher is (in terms of Vinaya) a formal undertaking of responsibility. It is this responsibility that the Ven. Ñāṇavīra declines.

[L. 112]

1. **Mr. Bandy.:** Recipient of L. 124. Gerriet Bandy (1941-1968) became involved with the Arya Maitryea Mandala through the buddhist circle of Wiesbaden. On 12 December 1966 he became a AAM-candidate under the name of Guhyasiddhi. A year later he was accepted as member of the AMM order as Nagabodhi-Siddhapada. Soon after he entered the Frankfurt hospital where he died of cancer.

2. **looking for faults:** See editorial note 3 to L. 9.
3. **a press cutting:** It is from the *London Sunday Times* of 24 May 1964:

BREAD BEFORE BOOKS

JEAN-PAUL SARTRE who, at 58, has just published the first volume of his autobiography has been explaining what he means by the confession in the book, 'I no longer know what to do with my life.'

For most of the period during which he became famous he has,

---

21. The phrase 'You need not write to me' is underlined by the Ven. Ñāṇavīra, who wrote, at the end of the letter: 'Letting off steam.' This was the final letter by Sister Vajirā. At the end of the collection the Ven. Ñāṇavīra wrote: 'Exit unwanted *ariyasāvikā*.'

he says, been in a state of 'neurosis' and 'folly.' This was bound up with the idea that, as a writer, he was engaged in a 'sacred' activity and only in the last decade has he awoken from this. Now he is finding the cerebral imaginative world of the literary man receding before the grimness of the real world.

'I've suddenly discovered that the exploitation of men by men and undernourishment relegate luxuries like metaphysical ills to the background. Hunger is a real evil. I've been getting through a long apprenticeship to reality. I've seen children die of hunger.

'What does literature mean to a hungry world? Literature like morality needs to be universal. A writer has to take sides with the majority, with the hungry—otherwise he is just serving a privileged class. Do you think you could read Robbe-Grillet in an underdeveloped country?'

[L. 113]

1. **Sīvaka Sutta:** The text is at L. 159. A reference is to be found in *NP* §3.
2. There follows a postscript to this letter which has been omitted here because it consists of a long quotation from Sartre—*B&N*, p. 477—and passages added to the *Notes* after the book was first published (which additions have all been included in the present edition of *Notes*), including a comment on *viññāṇaṃ anidassanaṃ* (non-indicative consciousness: cf. *NP* §22) which resulted in the following letter to Mr. Bandy himself, L. 124.

[L. 114]

1. **my reply:** L. 124.

[L. 115]

1. **the question of God:** L. 145.

[L. 117]

1. **Maugham:** See L. 148. The younger one was Peter Maddock, who was eighteen at the time. He was the photographer. The visit resulted in an article in *The People* (of London) dated 26 September 1965 (below), which was reprinted in greater (but not more accurate) detail as a chapter of Maugham's book, *Search for Nirvana* (London: W. H. Allen, 1975). Unfortunately, the visit also resulted in a novel, *The Second Window* (London: William Heinemann, 1968) and, *papañcaratino*, a radio play, 'A Question of Retreat'. The English monk of the novel and play bears no resemblance to the man who emerges from these letters.

## I SOLVE THE STRANGE RIDDLE OF THE BUDDHIST MONK FROM ALDERSHOT

SOMERSET MAUGHAM, world-famous novelist now 91 and living in seclusion in his Riviera villa, sent his nephew Robin Maugham on a strange mission earlier this year. 'An author must seek out his stories all over the world,' he said. 'You should go to Ceylon. Find that rich Englishman who is living in a jungle hut there as a Buddhist monk.' Robin Maugham did that. And he brought back this fascinating story—complete with a surprise ending.

HAROLD EDWARD MUSSON—the British Army officer turned Buddhist priest whom I had travelled seven thousand miles to find in the jungle of southern Ceylon—sat back against the wooden bedstead in his hut and stared at me pensively.

'What made you decide to become a Buddhist?' I asked him. He was shy and reticent. He had not spoken with anyone for years. And yet he had an urge to communicate.

'I suppose my first recollection of Buddhism was when I joined my father in Burma,' he said. 'He was commanding a battalion out there. I'd seen statues of Buddha, and I was told the Buddha was a man who sat under a tree and was enlightened.'

Musson smiled, almost apologetically.

'Then and there,' he said, 'I decided: "this is what I want to do."'

Musson, born in 1920 in Aldershot barracks, went to Wellington College and Cambridge University. In the war he served as an officer in Field Security in North Africa and Italy. 'I came back to England at the end of the war and settled in London,' he told me. 'I had private means so I didn't have to work. I tried to get as much pleasure out of life as I could. But somehow I wasn't happy. I felt that it was all pretty futile. Then one evening in a bar in London I ran into an old Army friend called Moore. We began talking about our common interest in Buddhism. Gradually we came to the conclusion—both of us—that the lives we were leading were utterly pointless. And by the end of the evening we'd decided that to abandon our Western lives and go to Ceylon to become Buddhist monks.

### NEARLY DIED

'We settled our affairs in England as best we could and left for Ceylon. That was in November 1948. And in April 1949 we were ordained Buddhist monks.'

Musson gently brushed away a fly that had settled on his bare shoulder.

'A year later Moore, seven years older than I, died of coronary thrombosis. And I nearly died of typhoid.'

Outside the sun was beginning to set. Monkeys were chattering in the trees and the jungle birds were screeching.

I shifted uncomfortably on my mat and continued to take notes as he spoke of the religion to which he had devoted his life.

'Whatever deliberate action you do brings its result in a future life,' he said. 'Thus, if you kill—or cause to be killed—an animal, that will have its results. This is why a Buddhist will not kill any living creature.'

I felt that by now I knew him well enough to argue a bit with him. 'How do you reconcile that belief with eating meat?' I asked.

'Provided that one has no part in the killing of it one can eat meat,' he replied. 'So a monk can accept meat brought to him as alms if he doesn't see or hear it being killed—or suspect it has been killed specially for him.'

I thought that Musson's argument was false, and I was about to say so, when suddenly he smiled and said: 'I have something to show you.'

He picked up a glass jam-jar with a screw top. Inside it was a large tarantula. The bite of this poisonous spider can kill a man.

'Where did you find it?' I asked.

Musson smiled gently. 'I found him crawling up my leg last night.'

'But why didn't you kill it?'

'Because a Buddhist does not believe in taking the life of any living creature,' he said. 'I told you that just now—though I could see that you didn't believe me.'

'So now what will you do with him?'

Musson smiled at me. By way of answer, he motioned to me to follow him away from his little hut a few yards into the undergrowth. Carefully he unscrewed the top of the jam-jar, removed the tarantula, and let it fall to the earth.

'He won't be able to harm anyone here,' he said.

A Buddhist monk may not kill—not even a deadly tarantula spider like the one Edward Musson found crawling on his leg. Instead, he trapped it in a jam-jar—and then freed it, out of harm's way, in the jungle.

'Aren't you lonely, with no other living person for miles around?' I asked him when we had settled down in his hut again.

'When I first came here,' the hermit replied, 'it took me some time to get used to the sounds of the jungle. But after a bit you find you simply don't *want* other people. You become self-contained.'

'How do you eat?' I asked him. 'How do you keep going?'

I knew that a Buddhist monk's religion forbids him to sow or reap or provide for himself in any way. He must exist only on what is freely given to him.

'Someone from the local village generally brings me tea—either very early in the morning or late in the afternoon,' the hermit told me. 'And before noon they bring me alms in the form of a gruel of rice and a little fruit.' He gave me his wonderfully gentle smile.

### BEGGING-BOWL

'The villagers are very good about it,' he said. 'But sometimes they forget. And they don't bring me any food before noon. So then I don't have anything to eat all day[22] for we are not allowed to eat anything after mid-day. But the following morning I'll take my begging-bowl into the village, and I'll be given food.

'You see, I have no money,' Musson told me. 'If I ever have to go to Colombo—to see a doctor, for instance—I take my begging-bowl and stand by a bus-stop. People will come up to me and will try to put food into my bowl. But I will cover up the bowl with my hands. Then they will ask me: "What is it you require, Venerable Sir?" And I will reply, "A bus-ticket." I won't say, "The money for a bus-ticket," because a Buddhist priest must not handle money. The reason for this is that with money you can buy women. And this rule of the Lord Buddha is intended to put temptation out of a monk's way.'

The hermit stroked the side of his face with his bony hand.

'A Buddhist monk's bank balance is his bowl,' he said. 'Even his clothes are given to him. If no one gives him his robe, then he must go and scavenge on dust-heaps to find rags. And then he must stitch the rags together to make himself a robe.'

I decided to ask the question I had been longing to ask since I first met him. I took a deep breath.

'When you look back at the life you led in England,' I said, 'when you think of the wealth and comfort you enjoyed, when you remember your friends—don't you have any regret?'

The hermit gazed at me in silence. 'No,' he said after a while. 'I can't say

**22.** No attempt is made to correct Maugham's many mis-statements, but on this point an exception must be made. In a letter to the Ven. Ñāṇamoli (4 August 1958, when he had been resident at Būndala for about sixteen months) the Ven. Ñāṇavīra commented that out of more than twelve hundred breakfasts/noon meals/afternoon beverages, the villagers had failed in only two afternoon beverages, 'that is, over 99.8% regularity'. Maugham's article, then, is more than a little unjust in its implications. Cf. *StP*, EL. 76.

I have any regrets at all…besides, the one advantage of these surroundings is that you don't put yourself in the way of temptation.

'I now find the thought of sex is abhorrent. And I can find pleasure in living here because I enjoy the process of concentration. The whole point of Buddhism,' he said, 'is to bring to an end this farcical existence. Nothing is permanent,' he said. 'So the wise man, when he sees that there is nothing he can hold for ever, chooses to opt out. He decides to get out of the race.'

From my uncomfortable position on the straw mat on the hard floor with my legs tucked beneath me I glanced up at the hermit. He looked tired and ill. The light was fading. It was time for me to go. I began to move, but the hermit moved his hands in a gesture to stop me.

'You'll go now,' he said. 'And we may never meet again. But I don't want you to misunderstand me.'

'NO SACRIFICE'

He paused, and his gentle, sad eyes rested on me. 'If you write about me,' he said, 'I don't want you to make me out a saint. It's no sacrifice to give up everything for the sake of doing exactly what you want to do.'

He leaned back on his bed and was silent. Our meeting was at an end. I got up stiffly from the roll of matting.

'Goodbye,' he said.

I joined my hands and raised them above my head. I bowed to him in the ritual act of obeisance. He stood watching me in silence. His face was expressionless. In the dim light I moved away down the little path through the jungle that joined the track that led to the village—and thence back to civilization. Behind me I left the hermit—the Venerable Nanavira Thera from the Island Hermitage, or Harold Edward Musson from Aldershot—alone to face the long night.

My uncle Somerset Maugham's instinct had been right. He was indeed a most unusual man….

But there is an even more unusual post-script to this story.

A short while ago I received a cable from Nalin Fernando, the Ceylonese journalist who had helped me to find Musson's secret hut. The cable read: 'MUSSON SUICIDED MONDAY INHALED ETHER NALIN.'

Strangely enough, during our second meeting I had asked Musson about suicide.

'If an ordinary person commits suicide,' he said, 'it is wrong. But if a monk who has "attained liberation" kills himself, then it is only a minor offence in our philosophy because he is only anticipating the next stage in the chain of rebirth.'

I wonder if Musson did not kill himself because he was suddenly overwhelmed by the realisation that he had turned his back on the world in vain.
Perhaps in a long night of despair he realised that all his years of meditation and suffering had been completely useless.
No one will ever know.

NEXT WEEK: The amazing predictions of the man who says he knows the royal family's future.
© Robin Maugham, 1965

2. ***Sīl-poya*** is the day, based on the lunar week, on which laypeople observe special restraints (see, e.g., L. 129, first paragraph). New moon day and, even more so, full moon day, are regarded as particularly auspicious for undertaking such observances. See A.VIII,41/iv,248-51. *Saṅgha-poya* (= *Uposatha*, Observance day) is the (more or less) fortnightly day on which *bhikkhus* convene for confession of faults, recitation of the Pāṭimokkha (Code of Discipline), and business of the Order.
3. **Asoka's grandfather**: Kautilya (Chanakya) was the *éminence gris* behind the Mauryan throne. Our considerable knowledge of Mauryan India comes largely from the account of Megasthenes, the Greek ambassador to the Court of Chandragupta at Pātaliputta. Although his account has not survived in the original, copius extracts are to be found in later writers, especially Strabo.

**[L. 118]**

1. **Mindfulness of Breathing**, by Bhikkhu Ñāṇamoli, was first published by Mr. Weerasinghe in 1952. It was re-issued by the BPS in 1964, with the help of Irene Quittner. The first publication was cyclostyled. The book was reprinted in 1998 by the BPS.

**[L. 120]**

1. **Sartre:** It is called 'Intimacy', and it has been published in a collection of short stories.

**[L. 123]**

1. ***CUP*, p. 349:**

> Aesthetically it would be in order for a man to sell his soul to the devil, to use a strong expression which recalls what is perhaps

still done more often than is ordinarily supposed—but also to produce miracles of art. Ethically it would perhaps be the highest pathos to renounce the glittering artistic career without saying a single word.

[L. 124]

1. **Mr. Bandy:** See editorial note to L. 112.
2. ***Ahan ti vā...:*** '"I" or "mine" or "am"'.
3. ***saupādisesā nibbānadhātu:*** Cf. L. 43.

[L. 125]

1. **Ven. Kheminda Thera** was an active Buddhist missionary and author. In 1934 he and his close friend Ven. Soma Thera, with the help of a Japanese scholar N.R.M. Ehara, translated the Chinese translation of the Vimuttimagga into English, which was published as the *Path of Freedom.* During Word War II he and Ven. Soma Thera stayed at the Island Hermitage, and later in Vajirārāma, Colombo. Despite suffering from a painful illness he was afflicted with since 1963 he participated in missions to India and Germany and continued with writing and translating. One of his work was *Path, Fruit and Nibbāna.*
2. **Someone:** Abbé Galiani, to Mme. D'Epinay.
3. ***saṅghādisesa:*** See editorial note to L. 52.
4. **Ven. Sappadāsa Thera's gāthā:** See L. 54.

[L. 126]

1. This draft was obviously written after revision of *Notes* had been completed, or nearly so: perhaps as late as 1965. It was therefore not involved in the 'stir' revolving around L. 100. It is included here inasmuch as it is addressed to the same recipient, and deals with the same topic, as L. 125.
2. **the reason:** See editorial note 2 to L. 104.

[L. 127]

1. **Ananda Pereira** was the son of Dr. Cassius Pereira from Colombo (who later became the Ven. Bhikkhu Kassapa—see L. 29), and was himself a well-known supporter of the Saṅgha and of individual monks. His generosity was cut short by an early death in 1967.
2. **my letter:** See editorial notes, L. 125.

[L. 129]

1. This and the following two letters were all destroyed by their recipient.

They are presented here as editorial reconstructions from a somewhat confused handwritten copy of the earlier letters and from earlier drafts found among the author's papers.

2. **Eight Precepts:** 1. I undertake the training precept to not kill. 2. ...to not steal. 3. ...to not be incelibate. 4. ...to not lie. 5. ...to not take intoxicants and liquors that cause carelessness. 6. ...to not take food out of (the proper) time (not between noon and dawn). 7. ...to not attend shows, fairs, dancing, singing, and music, and to not use adornments of garlands, perfumes, and cosmetics. 8. I undertake the training precept to not use a high or wide (i.e. luxurious) resting place. It is this last precept that is under discussion here.

   Laypeople traditionally observe, at least in theory, the first five precepts (number three modified to prohibit only 'wrongful sensual indulgence') at all times. Some of the laity will, for certain periods of time and particularly on new- and full-moon days, undertake the Eight Precepts, usually while in attendance at a temple.

3. **The *sassatavādin***, who holds that he and the world are eternal, and the *ucchedavādin*, who holds that he and the world cease to exist, are annihilated, at his death, are two holders of wrong views discussed in the Brahmajāla Suttanta, Dīgha 1. See L. 145.

**[L. 130]**

1. The draft contains the Sutta reference but not the text, which is translated by the editors.

**[L. 131]**

1. ***Buddhism in a Nutshell*** was written by Ven. Nārada Mahā Thera and first appeared in 1933. Since then several editions were published for free distribution.
2. ***Samatha bhāvanā*** (development of calmness) is the counterpart of *vipassanā bhāvanā* (development of insight), with which the West is somewhat more familiar. The two together, along with development of faith (*saddhā*) and conduct (*sīla*) are four parts of the Dhamma that are compared (A.IX,4/iv,360) to the four feet of the quadruped.
3. **Kumbhakāra Jātaka:** (408: book VII, no. 13). King Karandu is said to have become a *paccekabuddha*—a silent, or non-teaching, Buddha—by contemplating the difference between a tree ravaged for its fruit (and thus like the lay life) and a beautiful but fruitless tree, unplundered (compared to the monk's life).

'A mango in a forest did I see
Full-grown, and dark, fruitful exceedingly:
And for its fruit men did the mango break,
'Twas this inclined my heart the bowl to take.'
(from the translation by H.T. Francis and R.A. Neil [Cambridge University Press, 1897, reprinted Pali Text Society 1969], iii, 228)

4. **Heidegger:** Apparently a portion of the letter immediately preceding this paragraph is missing. The context suggests that the missing portion may have involved discussion of *B&T*, pp. 169-72, particularly the passage on page 171:

> The entity which is essentially constituted by Being-in-the-world *is* itself in every case its 'there'. According to the familiar signification of the word, the 'there' points to a 'here' and a 'yonder'. The 'here' of an 'I—here' is always understood in relation to a 'yonder' ready-to-hand, in the sense of a Being towards this 'yonder'—a Being which is de-severant, directional, and concernful. Dasein's existential spatiality, which thus determines its 'location', is itself grounded in Being-in-the-world. The "yonder" belongs definitely to something encountered within-the-*world*. 'Here' and 'yonder' are possible only in a 'there'—that is to say, only if there is an entity which has made a disclosure of spatiality as the Being of the 'there'. This entity carries in its ownmost Being the character of not being closed off. In the expression 'there' we have in view this essential disclosedness. By reason of this disclosedness, this entity (Dasein), together with the Being-there of the world, is 'there' for itself.

5. ***cakkhuñca...*:** 'Dependent upon eye and visible forms, eye-consciousness arises; the coming together of these three is contact. With contact as condition, feeling,' etc.

[L. 132]

1. **Dear Sir:** This first letter was addressed to the British Council Library. All subsequent letters were addressed to Mr. Brady who, from 1958 to 1968, was the Colombo Representative of the Library.

   Mr. Brady was born in 1912 in Scotland. Degree in Philosophy (M.A.) at Edinburgh University. After a short time he was teaching in England and in Malta, and he joined the British Council in 1936 until his retirement in 1968. Then he did a degree in Theology at Cambridge University and worked in Egypt-Alexandria as an Anglican priest for seven years. He died in 1979.

[L. 136]

1. **Zaehner:** *Mysticism: Sacred and Profane.* London: Oxford University Press, 1957.
2. **week at a time:** See editorial note 2 to L. 63.
3. ***louche*:** suspect.

[L. 137]

1. **Laclos:** *Les Liaisons Dangereuses*, by Choderlos de Laclos.

[L. 138]

1. **Grenier:** p. 23. All translations from Grenier are by the editors.
2. **Tennent:** p. 241. Tennent, Colonial Secretary during the mid-Nineteenth Century, was influential as an administrator who held decidedly anti-Buddhist views.

[L. 139]

1. ***La Chute*:** The text is taken from pp. 72-3 of the Penguin edition of *The Fall.*

[L. 140]

1. **Prajñāpāramitā:** The Ven. Ñāṇavīra's letter contains a French translation of this passage, apparently taken from an essay, 'Le Bouddhisme d'après les Textes pālis', by Solange Bernard-Thierry on p. 608 of *Présence du Bouddhisme*, the Feb.-June 1959 issue of the journal *France-Asie*, published in Saigon. The quotation would seem to be from one of the more recent strata of the Prajñāpāramitā Sūtra, not identified by Ms. Bernard-Thierry. English translation is by the editors. (The aphorism at the end of this letter is from Joyce's *Ulysses*.)

[L. 141]

1. The author's usual closing salutation was 'With best wishes'. See L. 27.
2. ***cri de coeur*:** 'cry of heart'; an impassioned outcry, as of entreaty or protest.
3. ***Ce n'est...*:** 'It is only God that can not be a saint.'

[L. 142]

1. **Chamfort:**

> 'When one has been sufficiently tormented, sufficiently wearied by one's own sensibility, one finds out that it is necessary to live from day to day, forget a lot, in brief, *suck up life* as it flows by' (quoted in French on p. 46 of *The Unquiet Grave*).

[L. 143]

1. **English publisher:** Mr. Brady had taken the typescript of *Notes* with him when he went on home leave. L. 141 to 143 were addressed to England. The typescript remained in England for about six months (see L. 153) making the rounds of the publishers. (It was on Mr. Brady's return to the East, it seems, that he stopped off at an *ashram* in India, discussed in L. 144.)
2. **Rimbaud:**

> 'How wretched I am, oh! how wretched I am... and I've got money on me that I can't even watch!'

[L. 144]

1. **Mind:** a leading British journal of philosophy. It is one of Oxford Journals which is a division of Oxford University Press.

[L. 145]

1. **Jouhandeau:**

> 'When the universe considers with indifference the being whom we love, who is in truth?'

2. **Lessing:** Gotthild Ephraim Lessing (1729-1781), German critic and dramatist. 'That, that is the hideous wide gulf, across which I can never get, no matter how earnestly and often I have tried to make the jump.' The passage is quoted (in German) at *CUP*, p. 90.
3. **Camus:**

> 'the lucid protestation of men cast into a land whose splendour and light speak ceaselessly to them of a non-existent God.' *Selected Essays*... 'The Desert', p. 93 (originally published in *Noces* [Charlot, 1939]).

[L. 147]
**1. Translations on Food:**

1. All creatures are stayed by food. (A.X,27/v,50)

2. With the coming together of three things, monks, there is descent into the womb. If mother and father come together, but the mother is not in season and the one to be tied[23] is not present, then so far there is not descent into the womb. If the mother and father come together and the mother is in season, but the one to be tied is not present, then still there is not descent into the womb. But when, monks, mother and father come together and the mother is in season and the one to be tied is present—then, with this coming together of three things, there is descent into the womb. Then, monks, for nine or ten months the mother carries him about in the womb in her belly with great trouble, a heavy burden. Then, monks, at the end of nine or ten months the mother gives him birth with great trouble, a heavy burden. Then after he is born she nourishes him with her own blood; for in the discipline of the noble ones, monks, the mother's milk is blood. (M.38/i,265-66)

3. Thus I heard. Once the Auspicious One was living at Sāvatthi in Jeta's Grove, in Anāthapiṇḍika's Park. There the Auspicious One addressed the monks.
—Monks!
—Lord! those monks assented to the Auspicious One. The Auspicious One said this.
—There are, monks, these four foods staying creatures that have become[24] or assisting those seeking to be. Which are the four? Solid food, coarse or fine; secondly contact; thirdly mental intention; fourthly consciousness. These, monks, are the four foods staying creatures that have become or assisting those seeking to be.

And how, monks, should solid food be regarded? Suppose, monks, a man and his wife taking few provisions set out on a desert track; and they have a beloved only son. And when they are in the desert the few provisions of that man and wife are consumed and run out; and they still have the rest of the desert to cross. And then, monks,

23. I.e. the being to be reborn.
24. 'Become' both here and below (in 4) is equivalent to 'come into being'.

that man and wife think 'Our few provisions are consumed and have run out, and there is the rest of the desert to cross: what if we were to kill this darling and beloved only son of ours, prepare dried and cured meat, and eating our son's flesh we were in this way to cross the rest of the desert? Let not all three perish.' Then, monks, that man and wife kill that darling and beloved only son, prepare dried and cured meat, and eating their son's flesh in this way they cross the rest of the desert. And as they eat their son's flesh they beat their breast 'Where is our only son! Where is our only son!' What think you, monks, would they be taking food for sport? Would they be taking food for pleasure? Would they be taking food for adornment? Would they be taking food for embellishment?

—No indeed, lord.

—Would they not be taking food, monks, just for crossing the desert?

—Yes, lord.

—It is in just this way, monks, that I say solid food should be regarded. When solid food is comprehended, monks, the lust of the five strands of sensuality[25] is comprehended: when the lust of the five strands of sensuality is comprehended, there is no attachment attached by which a noble disciple should again return to this world.

And how, monks, should contact-food be regarded? Suppose, monks, there is a flayed cow: if she stands against a wall she is devoured by the animals living on the wall; if she stands against a tree she is devoured by the animals on the tree; if she stands in the water she is devoured by the animals living in the water; if she stands in the open she is devoured by the animals living in the open. Wherever, monks, that flayed cow may stand she is devoured by the animals living in that place. It is in just this way, monks, that I say contact-food should be regarded.

When contact-food is comprehended, monks, the three feelings[26] are comprehended; when the three feelings are comprehended, there is nothing further, I say, for the noble disciple to do.

And how, monks, should mental-intention-food be regarded? Suppose, monks, there is a charcoal-pit deeper than a man's height, and full of clear glowing charcoal; and there comes a

25. Pleasing sights, sounds, smells, tastes, and touches.
26. Pleasant, unpleasant, and neutral.

man who likes life and dislikes death, who likes pleasure and dislikes pain; and two powerful men seize his two arms and drag him towards that charcoal-pit: then, monks, that man's intention would be directed elsewhere, his desire would be directed elsewhere, his aspiration would be directed elsewhere. Why is that? That man, monks, thinks 'If I fall into this charcoal-pit I shall thereby meet with death or with pains like those of dying'. It is in just this way, monks, that I say mental-intention-food should be regarded.

When mental-intention-food is comprehended, monks, the three cravings[27] are comprehended; when the three cravings are comprehended, there is nothing further, I say, for the noble disciple to do.

And how, monks, should consciousness-food be regarded? Suppose, monks, a guilty thief is caught and brought before the king: 'This, sire, is a guilty thief: sentence him to what punishment you please'. The king says 'Go, my friend, and wound this fellow a hundred times this morning with a spear'. And they wound him a hundred times in the morning with a spear. Then at midday the king says 'My friend, how is that fellow?' 'Sire, he is still alive.' The king says 'Go, my friend, and wound that fellow a hundred times now at midday with a spear'. And they wound him a hundred times at midday with a spear. Then at nightfall the king says 'My friend, how is that fellow?' 'Sire, he is still alive.' The king says 'Go, my friend, and wound that fellow a hundred times now at nightfall with a spear'. And they wound him a hundred times at nightfall with a spear. What do you think, monks, would this man being wounded three hundred times during the day with a spear thereby experience pain and grief?

—Even, lord, being wounded once with a spear he would thereby experience pain and grief. How much more three hundred times!

—It is in just this way, monks, that I say consciousness-food should be regarded. When consciousness-food is comprehended, monks, name-&-matter is comprehended; when name-&-matter is comprehended, there is nothing further, I say, for the noble disciple to do.

So said the Auspicious One. Those monks were gladdened and delighted in the Auspicious One's words. (Nidāna Saṃy.—63/ ii,97-100)

**27.** Being, un-being, sensuality.

4. Monks, do you see 'this has become'?
—Yes, lord.
—Monks, do you see 'coming-to-be with this food'?
—Yes, lord.
—Monks, do you see 'with cessation of this food, what has become is subject to cessation'?
—Yes, lord.
—In one who is doubtful, monks, 'What if this has not become?', there arises uncertainty.
—Yes, lord.
—In one who is doubtful, monks, 'What if there is not coming-to-be with this food?', there arises uncertainty.
—Yes, lord.
—In one who is doubtful, monks, 'What if with cessation of this food, what has become is not subject to cessation?', there arises uncertainty.
—Yes, lord.
—By one who sees with right understanding as it really is, monks, 'This has become', uncertainty is abandoned.
—Yes, lord.
—By one who sees with right understanding as it really is, monks, 'Coming-to-be with this food', uncertainty is abandoned.
—Yes, lord.
—By one who sees with right understanding as it really is, monks, 'With cessation of this food, what has become is subject to cessation', uncertainty is abandoned.
—Yes, lord.
—'This has come to be': herein, monks, are you free from uncertainty?
—Yes, lord.
—'Coming-to-be with this food': herein, monks, are you free from uncertainty?
—Yes, lord.
—'With cessation of this food, what has become is subject to cessation': herein, monks, are you free from uncertainty?
—Yes, lord.
—'This has come to be' is well seen with right understanding as it really is?
—Yes, lord.
—'Coming-to-be with this food' is well seen with right understanding as it really is?

—Yes, lord.
—'With cessation of this food, what has become is subject to cessation' is well seen with right understanding as it really is?
—Yes, lord.
—If, monks, you were to cling to this cleansed and purified view, if you were to treasure it, adhere to it, or cherish it, would you then, monks, be comprehending the teaching of the parable of the raft[28] as something for crossing over with, not for holding on to?
—No indeed, lord.
—If, monks, you were not to cling to this cleansed and purified view, if you were not to treasure it, adhere to it, or cherish it, would you then, monks, be comprehending the teaching of the parable of the raft as something for crossing over with, not for holding on to?
—Yes, lord.
—There are, monks, these four foods staying creatures that have become or assisting those seeking to be. Which are the four? Solid food, coarse or fine; secondly contact; thirdly mental intention; fourthly consciousness. And these four foods: what is their occasion, what is their arising, what is their provenance, what is their origin? These four foods: craving is their occasion, craving is their arising, craving is their provenance, craving is their origin.

And this craving...? ...feeling is its origin.
And this feeling...? ...contact is its origin.
And this contact...? ...the six bases are its origin.
And these six bases...? ...name-&-matter is their origin.
And this name-&-matter...? ...consciousness is its origin.
And this consciousness...? ...determinations are its origin.

And these determinations: what is their occasion, what is their arising, what is their provenance, what is their origin? These determinations: nescience[29] is their occasion, nescience is their arising, nescience is their provenance, nescience is their origin.

Thus, monks, with nescience as condition, determinations; with determinations as condition, consciousness; with consciousness as condition, name-&-matter; with name-&-matter as condition, the six bases; with the six bases as condition, contact; with contact as condition, feeling; with feeling as condition, craving; with craving

28. See M.22 for the parable of the raft.
29. Or 'ignorance'—*avijjā*.

as condition, holding; with holding as condition, being; with being as condition, birth; with birth as condition, ageing-&-death, sorrow, lamentation, pain, grief, and despair, come to be: thus is the arising of this whole mass of suffering. (M.38/i,260-263)

2. ***esse est percipi*:** To be is to be perceived.

[L. 148]

1. **Robin Maugham:** See L. 117, and also the editorial note 1.

[L. 149]

1. **'not what I meant':** 'That is not what I meant at all. That is not it, at all.'—The Love Song of J. Alfred Prufrock (*Selected Poems*, p. 12). This is not the Ven. Ñāṇavīra's only allusion to T.S. Eliot: in the first paragraph of the Preface to the *Notes*, the phrase 'Human kind cannot bear very much reality' is taken from a line of Thomas à Becket in Eliot's verse play, *Murder in the Cathedral.*

[L. 150]

1. **Claudel:** *Le Soulier de Satin.*
2. ***C'est magnifique...*:** 'It's magnificent, but it's not peace': the allusion is to a French comment ('It's magnificent, but it's not war') on the charge of the Light Brigade at Balaclava.

[L. 151]

1. **de Beauvoir:** 'Two separate beings, placed in different situations, facing each other in their freedom and seeking, one through the other, the justification of existence, will always live an adventure full of risks and promises.'
2. **Sartre:** The Ven. Ñāṇavīra quoted the passage (in French) in full. For the English translation, see L. 76.

[L. 152]

1. **just come across:** Evidently, the Ven. Ñāṇavīra had been going through his papers. After his death, seven weeks later, those papers were found to be neatly stored away. Some were noted as having been written before 1960; on a few pages he noted sections which were no longer acceptable to him. Doubtlessly any papers he did not wish to be made public were destroyed during those final preparations for death. The imaginary encounter of the Author with Heisenberg is also published in *StP,* EL. 35, p. 46.

[L. 154]

1. **researches:** They resulted in a grammar, *Colloquial Sinhalese*, published by his university. Dr. James W. Gair also compiled *A New Course in Reading Pāli: Entering the Word of the Buddha*, with Prof. W.S. Karunatillake in the 1998.
2. **recirculation:** The previous sentences were afterthoughts which, squeezed along the margins, took their reader on an excursion around all four edges of the paper and back to where they began. The 'commodius vicus' etc. alludes, of course, to the opening lines of Joyce's *Finnegans Wake*. Many (but not all) of the passages in the Letters which appear as footnotes were originally afterthoughts, though not usually so well-travelled.
3. ***la seule…***: 'the only excuse for God is that he does not exist.' (*The Rebel*, p. 58)

[L. 155]

1. **Q.E.D.:** It is abbreviation of '*quod erat demonstrandum*'. It used to denote the end of a proof of some proposition.

[L. 156]

1. **Sister Vajirā (Hannelore Wolf,** 1928-1991**)** was disciple of Paul Debes, one of the prominent lay Theravada teachers at that time. At that time she worked as a private teacher. In June 1954 the Sinhalese monk Ven. Nārada Mahā Thera visited Hamburg and Hannelore took the opportunity to request to go to Ceylon and become a nun. She took on the 10 training rules and was ordained as Sister Vajirā by Ven. Nārada on the full moon of July in 1955 at the Vihāra Mahā Devi Hermitage at Biyagāma near Colombo, where other Buddhist nuns (*dasa sil mata* or *dasa sila upāsikā*) lived. To provide her with greater quietude, supporters built a bungalow for her in the palm-tree forest of the monastery garden. However, she suffered internal lack and noticed that she could not possibly meditate all day long and became physically ill. Taking on scholastic work offered itself as a way out of her frustration. Having learned English quickly, she then started intensive Pali studies and soon started to translate texts and carried on correspondence about Dhamma topics with various people. One of the *dāyakas* of the monastery offered her healthier conditions and arranged for a bungalow to be built, into which she moved in 1959.

   Around autumn of 1961 Ven. Ñāṇavīra Thera, who lived 40 km from her in a *kuṭi*, had sent her a text he had written, *A Note on*

*Paṭiccasamuppāda*. Thereupon an intensive exchange of letters followed. The early letters show a woman who, in her own thinking and discussion with Ven. Ñāṇavīra, earnestly searches a way to approach the essence of the Buddha's Teaching by repeated trial-and-error. This search finally yielded its fruit when she attained *sotāpatti* in late January 1962. But the rapidity and intensity of the change of her views caused a kind of nervous breakdown and she disrobed, returning to Germany in 22 February 1962. After recovering from her breakdown she started to work for a textile machine factory in Hamburg. She still held Ven. Ñāṇavīra in high esteem. She died on 7 December 1991 in Maschen.

See also the P.S. to L. 100. This Section has been edited from rough drafts of letters to Sister Vajirā, the final copies having been burnt by their recipient. See L. 99-101. On the verso of one page of Sister Vajirā's letters to him the Ven. Ñāṇavīra had drafted a paragraph, apparently in response to her request for additional notes (in the same letter which she began 'That I burnt your letters and notes was the most dangerous act that I ever committed'—see editorial note 3 to L. 100). This fragmentary reply is reproduced, reduced from foolscap, on pp. 489-490. 'The last sentence of para II' seems to refer to the second paragraph of L. 149 (which predates Sister Vajirā's request by about ten days) and which itself seems to refer to PHASSA (d). It will be noticed that most of the draft reproduced here is, in the event, an early version of the third paragraph of ATTĀ. In fact, a considerable part of the Shorter Notes in *Notes on Dhamma* seems to be material reworked from those letters to Sister Vajirā which 'perished in the great flames'.

All her letters, together with Ven. Ñāṇavīra's replies, are published in *The Letters of Sister Vajirā*.

2. ***Evam eva kho...*:** Also quoted in *PS* §4:

> 'Just so, Māgandiya, if I were to set you forth the teaching, "this is that good health, this is that extinction", you might know good health, you might see extinction; with the arising of the eye, that in the five holding aggregates which is desire-&-lust would be eliminated for you; moreover it would occur to you, "For a long time, indeed, have I been cheated and deceived and defrauded by this mind (or heart—citta): I was holding just matter, holding just feeling, holding just perception, holding just determinations, holding just consciousness".'

See *NoD*, PARAMATTHA SACCA §4.

3. *Yo pañcas'...*: Quoted also in *PS* §3: 'that...in the five holding aggregates which is desire-&-lust.'
4. *Yaṃ kiñci...*: 'Whatever has the nature of arising, all that has the nature of ceasing.' See also L. 1 and L. 45.
5. *sati vā*: 'Or, if there is a remainder, non-returning.'
6. *catunnaṃ...*: 'matter held from the four great entities.' See also 'Additional Texts' §78.
7. *taṇhupādiṇṇa...*: 'the body, taken up by craving.'
8. *upādāna*: On the same theme see also L. 43.

[L. 157]

1. **(undated):** But apparently in response to a letter dated 20.xi.1961.
2. **M.9/i,53:** See 'Additional Texts' §78.

[L. 159]

1. **S. iv,384:** Also quoted in *PS* §4 (a): 'since here and now the Tathāgata actually and in truth is not to be found...'
2. **Thig. 106:** See L. 43 and editorial note thereto.
3. **Sīvaka Sutta:** The draft did not include a translation of this Sutta, which is provided here by the editors. See L. 114 and note.
4. *Tassa me...*: It is likely that the letter sent to Sister Vajirā contained a more extensive extract from this discourse, wherein Ven. Udāyi tells the Buddha that his strong reverence for the Buddha has done much for him. 'The Auspicious One taught Dhamma to me: "This is matter, this is the arising of matter, this is the ceasing of matter...".' Ven. Udāyi relates how he then went into solitude and, reflecting on the fluctuations and vicissitudes of the five aggregates, he came to realize as it really is suffering, suffering's arising, suffering's ceasing, and the path leading to the ceasing of suffering. 'Then, lord, I fully understood Dhamma and attained the Path.' Having become *sotāpanna*, Ven. Udāyi then understood the way which would lead him to extinction.

[L. 160]

1. The letter, not included in the first edition of *Clearing the Path* (1987, Path Press), was found in Sri Lanka. It concludes the correspondence between Ven. Ñāṇavīra Thera and Sister Vajirā.

# Comparative index of letter numbers

Many critical works which discuss *Clearing the Path* refer to letter numbers in the standard *Clearing the Path* edition published in 1987. The following table shows correspondence between letters in the new 2010 edition.

| '10 | '87 |
|---|---|
| 1 | 1 |
| 2 | 2 |
| 3 | – |
| 4 | – |
| 5 | – |
| 6 | – |
| 7 | – |
| 8 | – |
| 9 | 3 |
| 10 | 4 |
| 11 | 5 |
| 12 | 6 |
| 13 | 7 |
| 14 | 8 |
| 15 | 9 |
| 16 | 10 |
| 17 | 11 |
| 18 | 12 |
| 19 | 13 |
| 20 | 14 |
| 21 | 15 |
| 22 | 16 |
| 23 | 17 |
| 24 | – |
| 25 | 18 |
| 26 | 19 |
| 27 | 20 |
| 28 | 21 |
| 29 | 22 |
| 30 | 23 |
| 31 | 24 |
| 32 | 25 |
| 33 | 26 |
| 34 | 27 |
| 35 | 28 |
| 36 | 29 |
| 37 | 30 |
| 38 | 31 |
| 39 | 32 |
| 40 | 33 |
| 41 | 34 |
| 42 | 35 |
| 43 | 36 |
| 44 | 37 |
| 45 | 38 |
| 46 | 39 |
| 47 | 40 |
| 48 | 41 |
| 49 | 42 |
| 50 | 43 |
| 51 | 44 |
| 52 | 45 |
| 53 | 46 |
| 54 | 47 |
| 55 | 48 |
| 56 | 49 |
| 57 | 50 |
| 58 | 51 |
| 59 | 52 |
| 60 | 53 |
| 61 | 54 |
| 62 | 55 |
| 63 | 56 |
| 64 | 57 |
| 65 | 58 |
| 66 | 59 |
| 67 | 60 |
| 68 | 61 |
| 69 | 62 |
| 70 | 63 |
| 71 | 64 |
| 72 | 65 |
| 73 | 66 |
| 74 | 67 |
| 75 | 68 |
| 76 | 69 |
| 77 | 70 |
| 78 | 71 |
| 79 | 72 |
| 80 | 73 |
| 81 | 74 |
| 82 | 75 |
| 83 | 76 |
| 84 | 77 |
| 85 | 78 |
| 86 | 79 |
| 87 | 80 |
| 88 | 81 |
| 89 | 82 |
| 90 | 83 |
| 91 | 84 |
| 92 | 85 |
| 93 | 86 |
| 94 | 87 |
| 95 | 88 |
| 96 | 89 |
| 97 | 90 |
| 98 | 91 |
| 99 | 92 |
| 100 | 93 |
| 101 | 94 |
| 102 | 95 |
| 103 | 96 |
| 104 | 97 |
| 105 | 98 |
| 106 | 99 |
| 107 | 100 |
| 108 | 101 |
| 109 | 102 |
| 110 | 103 |
| 111 | 104 |
| 112 | 105 |
| 113 | 107 |
| 114 | 106 |
| 115 | 108 |
| 116 | 109 |
| 117 | 110 |
| 118 | 111 |
| 119 | 112 |
| 120 | 113 |
| 121 | 114 |
| 122 | 115 |
| 123 | 116 |
| 124 | 107A |
| 125 | 93A |
| 126 | 93B |
| 127 | 117 |
| 128 | 118 |
| 129 | 119 |
| 130 | 120 |
| 131 | 121 |
| 132 | 122 |
| 133 | 123 |
| 134 | 124 |
| 135 | 125 |
| 136 | 126 |
| 137 | 127 |
| 138 | 128 |
| 139 | 129 |
| 140 | 130 |
| 141 | 131 |
| 142 | 132 |
| 143 | 133 |
| 144 | 134 |
| 145 | 135 |
| 146 | 136 |
| 147 | 137 |
| 148 | 138 |
| 149 | 139 |
| 150 | 140 |
| 151 | 141 |
| 152 | 142 |
| 153 | 143 |
| 154 | 144 |
| 155 | 145 |
| 156 | 146 |
| 157 | 147 |
| 158 | 148 |
| 159 | 149 |
| 160 | – |
| 161 | 150 |

# Chronological order of the letters

| *Letter* | *Receiver* | *Date* |
|---|---|---|
| 1 | ‘to be opened in the event of my death’ | 27 June 1959 |
| 3 | to Mr. and Mrs. Perera | 16 October 1960 |
| 4 | to Mr. and Mrs. Perera | 12 March 1961 |
| 5 | to Mr. and Mrs. Perera | 2 August 1961 |
| 15 | to Dr. M. R. de Silva | 5 September 1961 |
| 6 | to Mr. and Mrs. Perera | 26 October 1961 |
| 156 | to Sister Vajirā | 21 November 1961 |
| 157 | to Sister Vajirā | (undated) |
| 16 | to Dr. M. R. de Silva | 10 December 1961 |
| 158 | to Sister Vajirā | 27 December 1961 |
| 159 | to Sister Vajirā | 10 January 1962 |
| 17 | to Dr. M. R. de Silva | 13 January 1962 |
| 160 | to Sister Vajirā | 29 January 1962 |
| 18 | to Dr. M. R. de Silva | 26 March 1962 |
| 2 | to Mr. N. Q. Dias | 27 March 1962 |
| 42 | to Mr. R. G. de S. Wettimuny | 12 May 1962 |
| 19 | to Dr. M. R. de Silva | 25 May 1962 |
| 20 | to Dr. M. R. de Silva | 6 June 1962 |
| 21 | to Dr. M. R. de Silva | 19 June 1962 |
| 22 | to Dr. M. R. de Silva | 20 June 1962 |
| 43 | to Mr. R. G. de S. Wettimuny | 29 June 1962 |
| 23 | to Dr. M. R. de Silva | 6 July 1962 |
| 44 | to Mr. R. G. de S. Wettimuny | 8 July 1962 |
| 24 | to Dr. M. R. de Silva | Vassa 1962 |
| 25 | to Dr. M. R. de Silva | 12 July 1962 |
| 45 | to Mr. R. G. de S. Wettimuny | 18 July 1962 |
| 7 | to Mr. and Mrs. Perera | 19 July 1962 |
| 26 | to Dr. M. R. de Silva | 11 December 1962 |
| 27 | to Dr. M. R. de Silva | 21 December 1962 |
| 28 | to Dr. M. R. de Silva | 4 January 1963 |

| | | |
|---|---|---|
| 29 | to Dr. M. R. de Silva | 15 January 1963 |
| 30 | to Dr. M. R. de Silva | 22 January 1963 |
| 31 | to Dr. M. R. de Silva | 28 January 1963 |
| 32 | to Dr. M. R. de Silva | 9 February 1963 |
| 33 | to Dr. M. R. de Silva | 1 March 1963 |
| 46 | to the Hon. Lionel Samaratunga | 3 March 1963 |
| 34 | to Dr. M. R. de Silva | 7 March 1963 |
| 47 | to the Hon. Lionel Samaratunga | 8 March 1963 |
| 48 | to the Hon. Lionel Samaratunga | 9 March 1963 |
| 49 | to the Hon. Lionel Samaratunga | 22 March 1963 |
| 50 | to the Hon. Lionel Samaratunga | 1 April 1963 |
| 51 | to the Hon. Lionel Samaratunga | 11 April 1963 |
| 35 | to Dr. M. R. de Silva | 16 April 1963 |
| 36 | to Dr. M. R. de Silva | 22 April 1963 |
| 37 | to Dr. M. R. de Silva | 25 April 1963 |
| 52 | to the Hon. Lionel Samaratunga | 28 April 1963 |
| 53 | to the Hon. Lionel Samaratunga | 2 May 1963 |
| 54 | to the Hon. Lionel Samaratunga | 4 May 1963 |
| 55 | to the Hon. Lionel Samaratunga | 15 May 1963 |
| 56 | to the Hon. Lionel Samaratunga | 16 May 1963 |
| 57 | to the Hon. Lionel Samaratunga | 19 May 1963 |
| 58 | to the Hon. Lionel Samaratunga | 29 May 1963 |
| 38 | to Dr. M. R. de Silva | 9 June 1963 |
| 59 | to the Hon. Lionel Samaratunga | 11 June 1963 |
| 60 | to the Hon. Lionel Samaratunga | 22 June 1963 |
| 61 | to the Hon. Lionel Samaratunga | 27 June 1963 |
| 62 | to the Hon. Lionel Samaratunga | 3 July 1963 |
| 63 | to the Hon. Lionel Samaratunga | 6 July 1963 |
| 64 | to the Hon. Lionel Samaratunga | 10 July 1963 |
| 65 | to the Hon. Lionel Samaratunga | 13 July 1963 |
| 66 | to the Hon. Lionel Samaratunga | 23 July 1963 |
| 67 | to the Hon. Lionel Samaratunga | 2 August 1963 |
| 68 | to the Hon. Lionel Samaratunga | 20 August 1963 |
| 69 | to the Hon. Lionel Samaratunga | 25 August 1963 |
| 70 | to the Hon. Lionel Samaratunga | 2 September 1963 |
| 71 | to the Hon. Lionel Samaratunga | 7 September 1963 |
| 72 | to the Hon. Lionel Samaratunga | 12 September 1963 |
| 73 | to the Hon. Lionel Samaratunga | 21 September 1963 |
| 74 | to the Hon. Lionel Samaratunga | 28 September 1963 |
| 75 | to the Hon. Lionel Samaratunga | 3 November 1963 |

| | | |
|---|---|---|
| 76 | to the Hon. Lionel Samaratunga | 6 November 1963 |
| 77 | to the Hon. Lionel Samaratunga | 14 November 1963 |
| 78 | to the Hon. Lionel Samaratunga | 18 November 1963 |
| 39 | to Dr. M. R. de Silva | 23 November 1963 |
| 79 | to the Hon. Lionel Samaratunga | 24 November 1963 |
| 80 | to the Hon. Lionel Samaratunga | 30 November 1963 |
| 81 | to the Hon. Lionel Samaratunga | 8 December 1963 |
| 82 | to the Hon. Lionel Samaratunga | 15 December 1963 |
| 83 | to the Hon. Lionel Samaratunga | 17 December 1963 |
| 84 | to the Hon. Lionel Samaratunga | 18 December 1963 |
| 85 | to the Hon. Lionel Samaratunga | 24 December 1963 |
| 86 | to the Hon. Lionel Samaratunga | 29 December 1963 |
| 87 | to the Hon. Lionel Samaratunga | 31 December 1963 |
| 88 | to the Hon. Lionel Samaratunga | 1 January 1964 |
| 89 | to the Hon. Lionel Samaratunga | 3 January 1964 |
| 90 | to the Hon. Lionel Samaratunga | 4 January 1964 |
| 9 | to Mrs. Irene Quittner | 11 January 1964 |
| 91 | to the Hon. Lionel Samaratunga | 12 January 1964 |
| 92 | to the Hon. Lionel Samaratunga | 24 January 1964 |
| 93 | to the Hon. Lionel Samaratunga | 25 January 1964 |
| 40 | to Dr. M. R. de Silva | 13 February 1964 |
| 94 | to the Hon. Lionel Samaratunga | 21 February 1964 |
| 12 | to Mr. Wijerama | 4 March 1964 |
| 95 | to the Hon. Lionel Samaratunga | 9 March 1964 |
| 96 | to the Hon. Lionel Samaratunga | 15 March 1964 |
| 132 | to Mr. Robert K. Brady | 18 March 1964 |
| 13 | to Mr. Wijerama | 20 March 1964 |
| 97 | to the Hon. Lionel Samaratunga | 25 March 1964 |
| 98 | to the Hon. Lionel Samaratunga | 4 April 1964 |
| 10 | to Mrs. Irene Quittner | 12 April 1964 |
| 125 | to Ven. Kheminda Thera | (undated) |
| 126 | to Ven. Kheminda Thera | (undated) |
| 133 | to Mr. Robert K. Brady | 23 April 1964 |
| 99 | to the Hon. Lionel Samaratunga | 24 April 1964 |
| 127 | to Ananda Perera | 29 April 1964 |
| 100 | to the Hon. Lionel Samaratunga | 30 April 1964 |
| 101 | to the Hon. Lionel Samaratunga | 1 May 1964 |
| 14 | to Mr. Wijerama | 2 May 1964 |
| 128 | to Ananda Perera | 4 May 1964 |
| 134 | to Mr. Robert K. Brady | 6 May 1964 |

| | | |
|---|---|---|
| 102 | to the Hon. Lionel Samaratunga | 6 May 1964 |
| 135 | to Mr. Robert K. Brady | 10 May 1964 |
| 103 | to the Hon. Lionel Samaratunga | 19 May 1964 |
| 136 | to Mr. Robert K. Brady | 26 May 1964 |
| 11 | to Mrs. Irene Quittner | 14 July 1964 |
| 137 | to Mr. Robert K. Brady | 16 July 1964 |
| 104 | to the Hon. Lionel Samaratunga | 24 July 1964 |
| 138 | to Mr. Robert K. Brady | 26 July 1964 |
| 139 | to Mr. Robert K. Brady | 27 July 1964 |
| 140 | to Mr. Robert K. Brady | 2 August 1964 |
| 105 | to the Hon. Lionel Samaratunga | 6 August 1964 |
| 106 | to the Hon. Lionel Samaratunga | 15 August 1964 |
| 41 | to Dr. M. R. de Silva | 19 August 1964 |
| 107 | to the Hon. Lionel Samaratunga | 24 August 1964 |
| 108 | to the Hon. Lionel Samaratunga | 30 August 1964 |
| 109 | to the Hon. Lionel Samaratunga | 31 August 1964 |
| 141 | to Mr. Robert K. Brady | 20 September 1964 |
| 110 | to the Hon. Lionel Samaratunga | 29 September 1964 |
| 142 | to Mr. Robert K. Brady | 2 November 1964 |
| 111 | to the Hon. Lionel Samaratunga | 3 November 1964 |
| 143 | to Mr. Robert K. Brady | 19 November 1964 |
| 112 | to the Hon. Lionel Samaratunga | 23 November 1964 |
| 113 | to the Hon. Lionel Samaratunga | 29 November 1964 |
| 114 | to the Hon. Lionel Samaratunga | 30 November 1964 |
| 144 | to Mr. Robert K. Brady | 3 December 1964 |
| 124 | to Mr. Bandy | 8 December 1964 |
| 145 | to Mr. Robert K. Brady | 8 December 1964 |
| 115 | to the Hon. Lionel Samaratunga | 14 December 1964 |
| 146 | to Mr. Robert K. Brady | 25 December 1964 |
| 116 | to the Hon. Lionel Samaratunga | 30 December 1964 |
| 147 | to Mr. Robert K. Brady | 1 January 1965 |
| 117 | to the Hon. Lionel Samaratunga | 10 January 1965 |
| 118 | to the Hon. Lionel Samaratunga | 21 January 1965 |
| 148 | to Mr. Robert K. Brady | 22 January 1965 |
| 8 | to Mr. and Mrs. Perera | 23 January 1965 |
| 149 | to Mr. Robert K. Brady | 7 February 1965 |
| 119 | to the Hon. Lionel Samaratunga | 12 February 1965 |
| 120 | to the Hon. Lionel Samaratunga | 28 February 1965 |
| 150 | to Mr. Robert K. Brady | 2 April 1965 |
| 121 | to the Hon. Lionel Samaratunga | 7 April 1965 |

| | | |
|---|---|---|
| 122 | to the Hon. Lionel Samaratunga | 1 May 1965 |
| 151 | to Mr. Robert K. Brady | 8 May 1965 |
| 129 | to Ananda Perera | 18 May 1965 |
| 152 | to Mr. Robert K. Brady | 18 May 1965 |
| 153 | to Mr. Robert K. Brady | 20 May 1965 |
| 130 | to Ananda Perera | 24 May 1965 |
| 123 | to the Hon. Lionel Samaratunga | 29 May 1965 |
| 131 | to Ananda Perera | 2 June 1965 |
| 154 | to Mr. Robert K. Brady | 26 June 1965 |
| 155 | to Mr. Robert K. Brady | 2 July 1965 |
| 161 | to the coroner | 5 July 1965 |

INDEX I

# Names and subjects

Numbers following entries refer to the page number. This index is arranged in the order of the English alphabet. Diacritical marks are not considered in this order. Book titles are generally listed only as sub-headings under their respective authors.

**B**

INDEX II

# Suttas

Suttas quoted in this book are listed below by page number. This listing includes material quoted in *Notes on Dhamma*. The arrangement is according to the traditional ordering of the texts: Vinaya Piṭaka, Dīgha Nikāya, Majjhima Nikāya, Saṃyutta Nikāya, Aṅguttara Nikāya, Khuddaka Nikāya (Suttanipāta, Dhammapada, Udāna, Itivuttaka, Theratherīgāthā). Volume and page number of the P.T.S. edition is given in brackets.

**Khuddaka Nikāya**

APPENDIX

# Ñāṇavīra Thera's Life and Work

Ven. Ñāṇavīra Thera was born Harold Edward Musson on January 5, 1920, in a military barracks in Aldershot, England, to father, Edward Lionel Musson (a captain in the 1st Manchester Regiment stationed in the Salamanca Barracks in Aldershot), and mother, Laura Emily, née Mateer.

The setting of his youth was Alton, and his schooling was at Wellington College. He enrolled in Magdalene College, Cambridge, in 1938, and spent one summer (probably the same year) studying Italian in Perugia, Italy. In June, 1939, he sat for Mathematics, and in 1940, for Modern Languages (in which he earned a 'Class One'). In 1939, immediately after the outbreak of war, he enlisted in the Territorial Royal Artillery, and in July, 1941, was commissioned 2nd Lieutenant in the Intelligence Corps, for which his knowledge of modern languages was doubtless an asset (he was an interrogator). In October, 1942, he was promoted to Lieutenant, and in April, 1944, to Temporary Captain. His overseas service with the British Eighth Army, from 1943 to 1946, was primarily in Italy. A family acquaintance spoke of him, however, as having 'completely resented warfare,' and in a letter written in 1964 in Ceylon may be found the sardonic comments that he had much enjoyed travel before the wartime army, and that he agreed with the classification of intelligence into three classes: 'human, animal, and military'. He received a B.A. degree in Modern and Medieval Languages from Cambridge University for six terms of university study together with three terms allowed for military service.

Little can be surmised concerning Musson's initial interest in Buddhism. In his university days James Joyce's novel, *Ulysses*, had exerted a powerful influence on him, because (according to a letter dated February 28, 1965) Joyce had held up a mirror to the 'average sensual Western man' and had shown that 'nothing matters'. He wrote of himself (May 19, 1964) as having always preferred ideas to images. The first public indication of his involvement with Buddhist thought was his translation of an Italian book, written in 1943 by J. Evola, and published in English by Luzac (London) in 1951 under the title, *The Doctrine of Awakening—A Study on the Buddhist As-*

*cesis*. Apparently he had chanced upon the Italian work during his wartime assignment in Italy. (In a letter written much later, in 1964, Ven. Ñāṇavīra expressed 'considerable reserves' about the soundness of the book.)

After the war Musson found himself, according to his own account, in no special need of money (November 19, 1964) yet highly dissatisfied with his life. In 1948, he ran into a onetime fellow-officer and a friend, Osbert Moore, who felt similarly dissatisfied. Osbert Moore was born on June 25, 1905, in England and graduated Exeter College, Oxford. His interest in Buddhism was roused by reading Evola's book, later translated into English by his friend Musson, during his time as an army staff-officer in Italy. After the war Moore held the post of Assistant Head of the BBC Italian section at Bush House. In 1948 both Musson and Moore decided to settle their few affairs in England, put the Western milieu behind them, and go to Ceylon to become Buddhist monks. In 1949 they received Novice Ordination at the Island Hermitage, Dodanduwa (from Ven. Ñāṇatiloka), and in 1950 they received Higher Ordination as bhikkhus at the Vajirārāma monastery, Colombo. Osbert Moore was given the monastic name of Ñāṇamoli, and Harold Musson that of Ñāṇavīra. Both returned soon to the Island Hermitage (an island monastery situated in a lagoon of southwest Ceylon), where Ven. Ñāṇamoli spent almost his entire monastic life of 11 years, until his sudden death, on March 8, 1960, due to heart failure (*coronary thrombosis*). He is remembered for his outstanding scholarly work in translating from the Pali into lucid English some of the most difficult texts of Theravāda Buddhism.

Ven. Ñāṇavīra was more solitary than Ven. Ñāṇamoli and moved from the Island Hermitage to a remote section of southeast Ceylon, where he lived alone for the rest of his life in a one-room, brick-and-plaster *kuṭi* (hut) with a tile roof, about a mile from the village of Bundala on the edge of a large game-reserve. It was an uncomfortable, all-day bus ride to the capital city Colombo, where he had to repair at times for medical treatment. The change of lifestyle for Ven. Ñāṇavīra in Ceylon was physically difficult, and not long after arriving in the country he contracted a severe case of amœbiasis,[1] which continued to plague him for the next fifteen years. The tropical climate and the local food must have been taxing for the physi-

1. However, as we learn later from his doctor, it is likely that Bhante might have been wrongly diagnosed and probably had colitis, i.e. small perforations to the colon. If that is true then we can assume that Ven. Ñāṇavīra was not getting the proper medication and treatment. Whatever the cause, it was this illness that prevented him from having a comfortable life, not to speak of attaining *jhānas*.

cally ailing Westerner; bhikkhus accept food which is offered to them by laypeople and this custom often leaves them with few options concerning their diet.

On July 5, 1965, Ven. Ñāṇavīra Thera died, by his own hand and deliberate decision. In his correspondence with others he wrote extensively and carefully on the question of suicide, which arose for him because of the severity of the amoebiasis and other health problems, stating in one letter that the illness, combined with the effects of the prescribed medication, 'leave me with little hope of making any further progress in the Buddhasāsana in this life'. Suicide is, of course, a highly controversial subject, and a careful reading of Ven. Ñāṇavīra's analysis of the dangers and limited justification of its employment is necessary to elucidate his views. (These letters are published in *Clearing the Path*.)

COLOPHON
Typeset at Path Press Publications
in Stempel Garamond SouthAsia (MacCampus)
using Adobe InDesign CS4 on Mac OSX
Printed by Wilco, Amersfoort
Bound by Abbringh, Groningen

PRINTED AND BOUND IN THE NETHERLANDS